PIETER BRUEGEL

PIETER BRUEGEL

Philippe and Françoise Roberts-Jones

Harry N. Abrams, Inc., Publishers

Editor, English-language edition: Elaine M. Stainton
Design Coordinator, English-language edition: Ellen Nygaard Ford
Typesetting, English-language edition: Tina Thompson
Translated from the French by Translate-A-Book, Oxford, England

Library of Congress Cataloging-in-Publication Data

Roberts-Jones, Philippe.
  [Pierre Bruegel l'Ancien. English]
  Pieter Bruegel / Philippe and Françoise Roberts-Jones.
    p. cm.
  ISBN 0-8109-3531-7
  1. Bruegel, Pieter, ca. 1525–1569—Criticism and interpretation.
  I. Roberts-Jones, Françoise. II. Title.
  ND673.B73 R62513 2002
  759.9493—dc21

                                         2002005148

Jacket front: Pieter Bruegel, *The Harvest,* 1565 (detail).
The Metropolitan Museum of Art, Rogers Fund, 1922. (19.164).
Photograph © 1998 The Metropolitan Museum of Art

Printed and bound in Italy
10 9 8 7 6 5 4 3 2 1

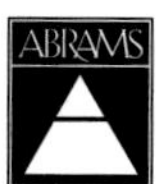

Harry N. Abrams, Inc.
100 Fifth Avenue
New York, N.Y. 10011
www.abramsbooks.com

Abrams is a subsidiary of

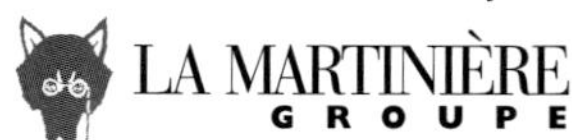

CONTENTS

PREFACE

Pieter Bruegel stands at the crossroads of medieval mystery and Renaissance humanism. He was a true cosmopolitan, a man open to exchanges between North and South at a time of political, religious, and philosophical unrest. All works of art are merely a potentiality, existing only by virtue of whether they are discussed, now as in the past. To fix art in a particular period reduces it to a mere illustration of its period and place. But when a work remains significant and lasts in time, it becomes part of the distillation of the creativity of all humanity, even though, across the span of four centuries, people will see it from many different points of view.

With Bruegel, the underlying idea and the actual work are integral—from *The Fall of the Rebel Angels* to *The Magpie on the Gallows* to the *Seasons*—and the genius responsible for this extraordinary unity is one of the greatest. But Bruegel's output is not limited to the forty or so paintings that survive. It also includes magnificent drawings—variously put at between 150 and 160 examples—and some superb engravings. Although only one of these is by Bruegel's own hand, they are perfect replicas of his work, as his surviving preparatory drawings demonstrate. *Bruegel inventor* therefore looms very large in the museum of the imagination, for his mind was as important as his hand. Some eighty prints, engraved by Pieter van der Heyden, Philipp Galle, and Frans Huys, and edited by Hieronymus Cock, bear witness to his visual intelligence, and they stand apart from the more interpretative prints made as reproductions of his work, published, for the most part, after the artist's death. Bruegel's body of work is therefore a multifaceted one; reflecting his powerful vision, sensitivity, and intelligence, it presents a rich harvest of images and ideas.

The authors of this book have turned to many sources in collecting material for this book, although, given the abundance of what has been published, they make no claim to being comprehensive. Those who offered references, advice, and help are mentioned in the bibliography—efficiently compiled by Bénédicte Schifflers—and in the notes to the text. Better to mention no one than to forget someone. We are immensely grateful to our publisher, whose encouragement supported the efforts of Jean-François Barrielle, Claire Rouyer, Martine Mène, and Frédéric Mazuy, in listening to, helping, and stimulating each other both as colleagues and as friends. In all of our work, our primary concern was the brilliance of the artist.

Philippe Roberts-Jones
Françoise Roberts-Jones

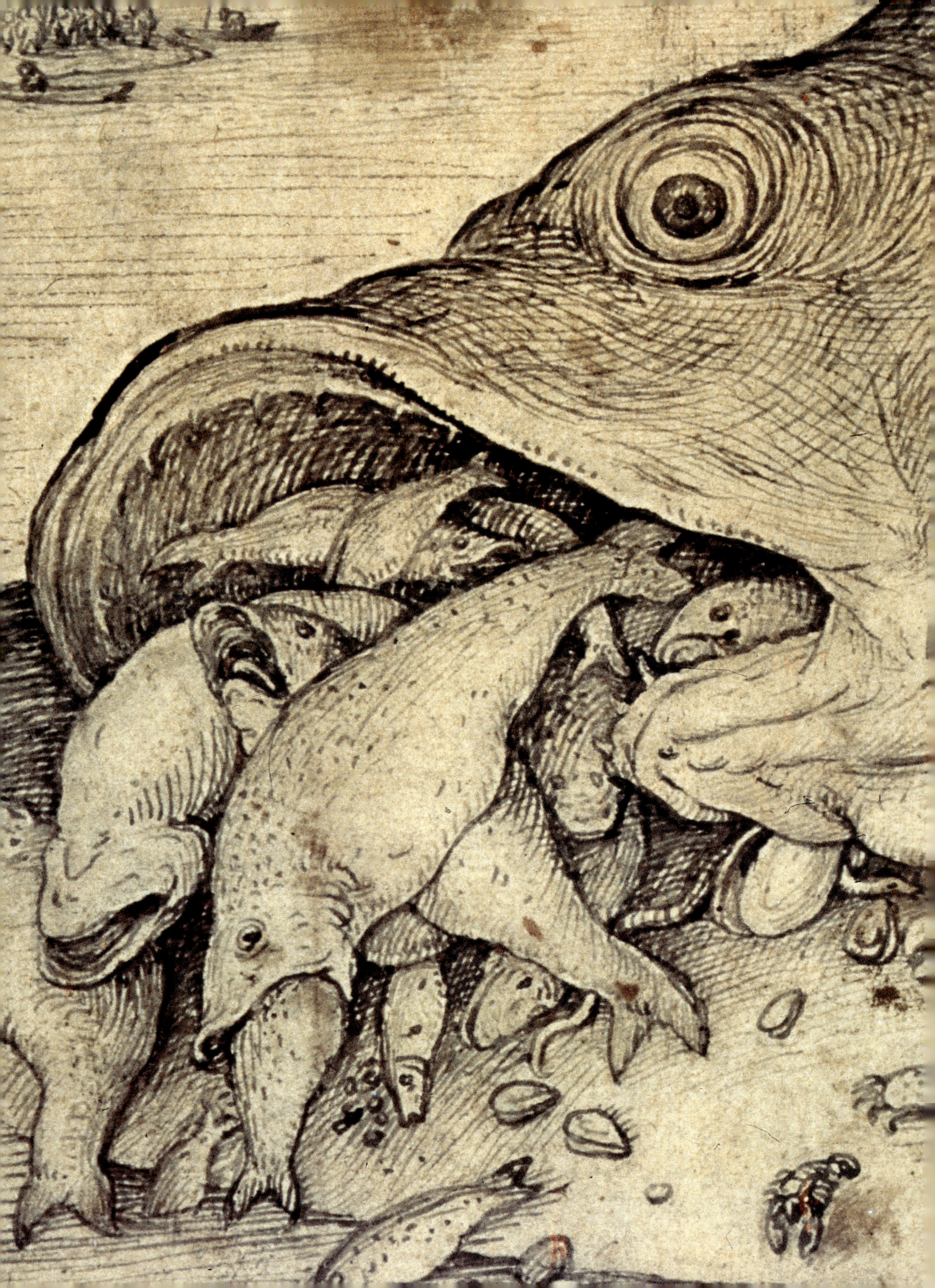

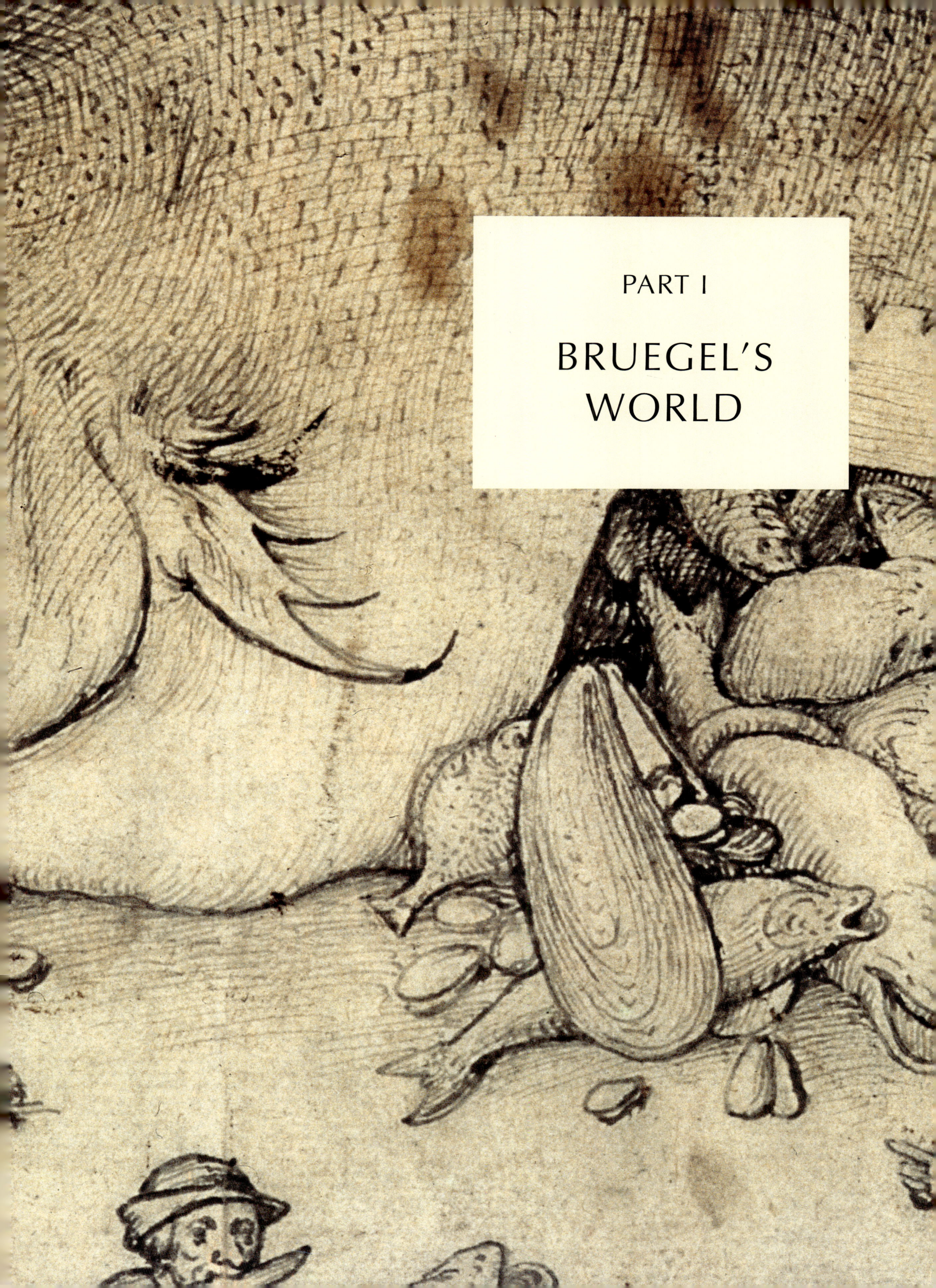

PART I

BRUEGEL'S
WORLD

In 1569, probably on 5 September (although some sources give 9 September or 13 December) the painter Pieter Bruegel (fig. 1) died in Brussels.[1] He was buried in the right aisle of the church of Notre-Dame-de-la-Chapelle, in the heart of the city (fig. 2).

The year of his death was engraved in Latin on the gravestone—*Obiit ille anno MDLXIX* —which bears, also in Latin, the inscription: "To Pieter Bruegel, flawless painter of most elegant skill, whom Nature herself, mother of all things, could well praise, whom the most experienced artists admire, and whose rivals imitate in vain. Also to Mayken Coucke [*sic*], his wife. Jan Brueghel devoutly caused [this stone] to be erected for his most excellent parents. The first died in the year 1569, the second in 1578. David Teniers the Younger, one of the heirs, restored this monument in 1676."[2] Later, the monument was further adorned with a painting by Peter Paul Rubens, *Christ Handing the Keys to St Peter,*[3] for the great master of the northern Baroque style was not only a friend of Jan Bruegel (sometimes called "Velvet Bruegel"), but also an admirer of his father, Pieter Bruegel the Elder, some of whose works he possessed. The epitaph, beyond its expression of Jan's devotion to his parents, also suggests the qualities that Pieter was thought to exemplify as an artist at the time: diligence, enthusiasm, wit, and an immense creative gift. It makes no mention of the types, subjects, or styles that later historians of art would note in his work, which range from simple rusticity to social comment. The epitaph also bears witness to the reverence of those who succeeded him, both directly and by association, by blood and by art—the dynasty of Bruegels whose branches were to stretch down through several generations.[4]

While Bruegel's place in posterity is assured, the details of his biography are uncertain. The lack of specific records prevents us from knowing the dates of his

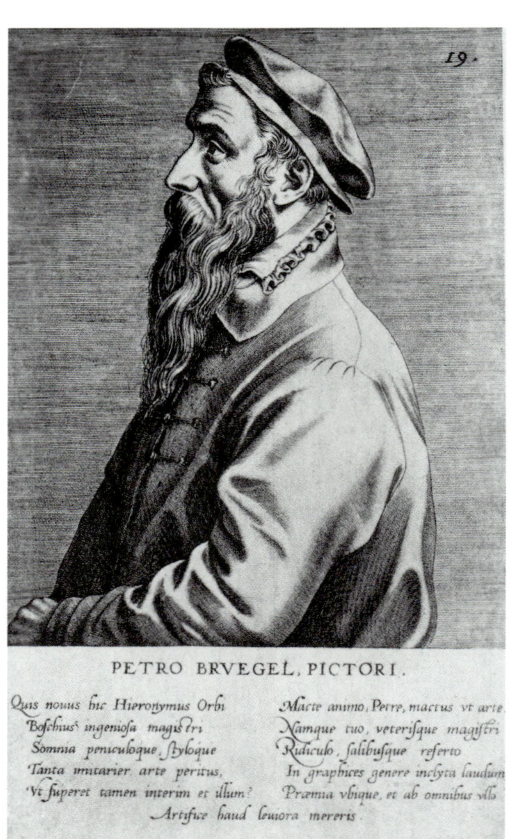

1. *Pieter Bruegel*, from Dominicus Lampsonius, *Effigies of the Famous Painters of the Netherlands*, Antwerp, 1572, plate 19. Brussels, Bibliothèque royale Albert I, print room

2. Map of Brussels with the La Chapelle district marked, in Braun and Hogenberg, *Civitates Orbis Terrarum*, Brussels, 1572. Colored engraving. Paris, Bibliothèque nationale de France, map department

PREVIOUS PAGES:
Pieter Bruegel, *The Big Fish Eat the Little Fish* (detail), 1556. Pen and wash, grey and black ink, 8½ x 12⅛ in. (21.6 x 30.7 cm). Vienna, Graphische Sammlung Albertina

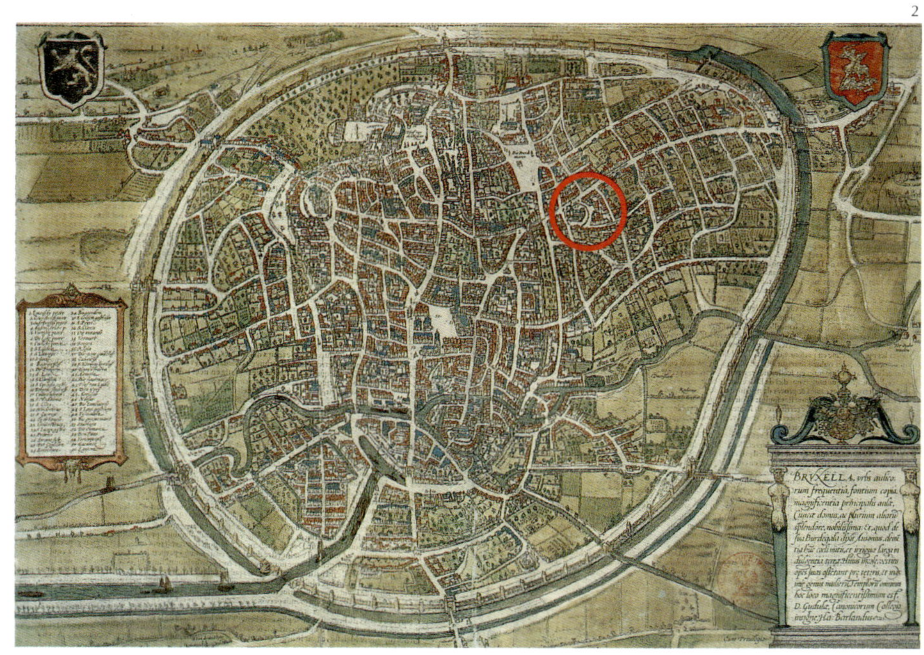

death or of his funeral. Just a few reliable documents (fewer than 10) and the dates inscribed on his paintings allow the course of his life to be sketched out. His burial would have been attended by his wife, Mayken Coecke, daughter of the painter Pieter Coecke van Aelst (fig. 3); perhaps his two sons, Pieter, who was five years old, and Jan, who was barely one; and his mother-in-law, Mayken Verhulst, the second wife of Pieter Coecke, and a painter herself. Also present would have been neighbors, friends, and probably a few notables too, since at about this time Bruegel had received an official commission to commemorate the opening in 1561 of the Willebroeck canal linking Brussels and Antwerp, the cities that had been the two poles of Bruegel's life.

BRUSSELS IN 1569

At the time of Pieter Bruegel's death, Brussels was an important city. Lying in a wide flood plain crossed by a narrow river, the Senne, it was already a large settlement from the early thirteenth century, a town surrounded by walls and rugged countryside. Two centuries later Philip the Good, duke of Burgundy, established his court there, and from the middle of the fifteenth century, Brussels was virtually the capital of Burgundy. Trade grew constantly: Links forged around 1270 with England and the Rhineland favored, among other things, the development of an internationally famous textile industry.

In 1531 Mary of Hungary, chosen by her brother Charles V, Holy Roman Emperor, to rule the Netherlands, established herself in Brussels, in the Coudenberg palace. Following this, the presence of her court, the city's administrative importance, and visits by foreign ambassadors and merchants made Brussels a European center where the fine arts flourished. As Lodovico Guicciardini, the Florentine ambassador to Brussels at the time, wrote: "Finally, in the city of Brussels, for a long time now, the Court has habitually resided, with all its Magistrates and special Advisers…so that it may rightfully be called a Royal City, also as it is populous, rich, and powerful."[5]

In the fifteenth century Rogier de le Pasture, known as Rogier van der Weyden, who came from Tournai, had painted for the city of Brussels a series of panels on the theme of justice, which were sadly destroyed during the bombardment by Marshal Villeroy in 1695. As the city's official painter from 1436, Rogier in a sense founded the Brussels school of painting. A century later, Rogier was succeeded in his position as most eminent artist of the school by Bernard van Orley, court painter to Margaret of Austria, whose portrait he painted in Mechelen in 1518. Later, in the service of Mary of Hungary, Bernard painted cartoons for the stained-glass windows that were installed in the transept of the cathedral of St. Michael in 1537–38, thus creating what the art historian Germain Bazin would later call "one of the masterpieces of princely art in Europe in the sixteenth century."[6] At the same time, the craft of lace-making was also developing, a trade that was to achieve lasting fame.

Brussels in 1569 was a thriving city then, both in commerce and in culture; an international city, and a prosperous bourgeois one, as well. Rue Haute—which, despite its name, lies lower than the ducal palace—was one of its main arteries, and there Bruegel is thought to have lived from about 1563 onward. This theory is based on a document from the archives that says that a house in this street,

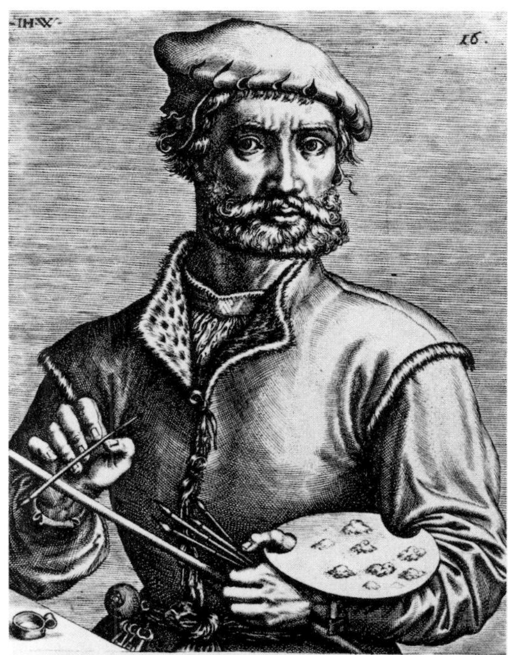

3. *Pieter Coecke*, in Dominicus Lampsonius, *Effigies of the Famous Painters of the Netherlands*, Antwerp, 1572, plate 16. Brussels, Bibliothèque royale Albert I, print room

probably no. 132, belonged to David Teniers III, Bruegel's great-grandson, who had inherited it from his mother, Anne, the daughter of Pieter's son, Jan Brueghel.[7]

4. Karel van Mander, *Het Schilder-Boeck*, Brussels, 1604, fol. 233 recto. Paris, Bibliothèque nationale de France, print department

OBSCURE ORIGINS

While there are some uncertainties surrounding Bruegel's death, we can only speculate about where and when he was born. There are no written records. His first biographer was the painter Karel van Mander, author of the celebrated *Het Schilder-Boeck* ("The Book of Painters") of 1604 (fig. 4)—a collection of artists' biographies modeled after Vasari's *Lives of the Painters*—in which he wrote, thirty-five years after Pieter Bruegel's death, that the artist had been born in "an obscure village in Brabant" near Breda, "whose name he took" and which he spells "Brueghel."[8]

On the face of it this information seems helpful, but it is vague enough to raise some doubts. While there is a village of that name in northern Brabant, some 50 kilometers (31 miles) from the town of Breda (now in the Netherlands), there is another village now in the Belgian province of Limburg, called Brogel. Divided into two settlements of unequal size, Grote and Kleine Brogel, this village lies near the town of Brée, which, in the sixteenth century, could be Latinized as Breda. As the likely site of Pieter Bruegel's birth, each of these two places has its champions, usually motivated by regional pride. However, in Bruegel's time the second village, Brogel, lay within the principality of Liège. It seems unlikely that Van Mander would have confused a village in that principality with one in Brabant. The first village is therefore the more likely candidate.

During Bruegel's lifetime, Guicciardini referred to the artist as "Pieter Bruegel of Breda,"[9] as did Vasari, in the second edition of his *Lives*, published in 1568. Furthermore, in Vasari's chapter entitled *Di diversi artifici fiamminghi* (On Several Flemish Artists), the biographer also describes him as "Pietro Brueghel d'Anversa, maestro eccellente" (Pieter Bruegel of Antwerp, an excellent master).[10] In other words, within the space of a few pages, Vasari first gives the painter's place of origin ("Breda"), then locates him by the site of his activity as a painter: For, although by the time Vasari's second edition was published Bruegel had moved on to Brussels, he had begun his career and made his reputation in Antwerp.

A MASTER OF THE GUILD: 1551

The first firm date that we have for Bruegel's life relates to Antwerp: the enrollment of "Peeter Brueghels schilder" as a master in the guild of St Luke in 1551 (fig. 5). There were thirty-six masters enrolled that year, including twenty-four painters— some who would become famous, including Martin van Cleve and Bruegel himself, and others who are now almost forgotten—but also a copper engraver, Giorgio Ghisi, from Mantua, who worked with the celebrated Antwerp print publisher Hieronymus Cock, for whom Bruegel, too, was to work.[11]

If we assume that a master was enrolled some time between the ages of 20 and 25, this would mean that Pieter Bruegel was born between 1525 and 1530. Some writers have tried to be more precise, but without offering any proof of their thinking.[12] One detail relating to the guild is worth noting. The final "s" in "Peeter Brueghels" can be interpreted in two ways: It could denote a place of origin, or it could be a genitive form of a person's father's name. Many examples are known from the period of names used in the latter sense, as patronymics, without reference to a particular locality, and this interpretation is favored by several specialists.[13]

EDUCATION

From Bruegel's birth to his acceptance into the guild as a master, we know very little of the man and his life as an artist. According to Van Mander, Bruegel "learned art under Pieter Coecke van Aelst."[14] Pieter Coecke, who was born in 1502, was made a master in Antwerp in 1527, and died in Brussels in 1550, was "ordinary painter to Charles V" according to his epitaph.[15] His characteristic style, which was distinctly Italianate, would seem to be far removed from that of Pieter Bruegel, and this disparity has lead several distinguished art historians, among them Max J. Friedländer and Charles de Tolnay,[16] to doubt Van Mander's statement that Pieter Coecke was Pieter Bruegel's teacher. However, the Antwerp humanist Franciscus Sweertius, who published Pieter Coecke's epitaph, noted in his introduction of 1628, that "He had a disciple, the painter Pieter Brueghel, to whom he gave his daughter in marriage."[17] The marriage did not take place until thirteen years after Coecke's death, but Van Mander explains that Bruegel had "often carried her in his arms when she was a child."[18] But apart from these connections, there are also parallels between the two men in the context of art at that time and in the subjects they painted. It should be noted, too, that no surviving work of Bruegel's can be dated with certainty before 1552, which makes it difficult to form an opinion on his early work.

Other documents referring to a court case that was opened in Mechelen in 1608 (fig. 6) indicate that in 1551–52 Bruegel and the painter Peeter Baltens worked together on an altarpiece for the town's guild of glove-makers, which had been commissioned by Claude Dorisi, whose workshop was celebrated and wealthy. The documents, published in 1964 by Adolf Monballieu,[19] reveal that Baltens apparently painted the central panel and Bruegel the side panels which, on the outside, depicted St. Gommaire and St. Rombaut in grisaille. This joint work was not the only contact between the two artists.

After studying under Pieter Coecke, Bruegel "moved on to work with Hieronymus Cock" according to Van Mander, who made no mention of the Mechelen episode.[20] This new stage in the artist's life has been established beyond doubt. Hieronymus Cock was the son of Jan Wellens de Cock—a Mannerist painter who was also close in style to Hieronymus Bosch—and brother of the landscape painter Matthijs Cock. He had been a master at the Antwerp guild from 1546 and an engraver—and, according to Guicciardini, was the "inventor and publisher (by means of printing) of the works of Hierosme Boys, and other well known painters; and for this reason his art has merit and deserves to be remembered."[21]

These references carry considerable weight, for Hieronymus Cock (fig. 7), after making a journey to Italy from which he brought back views of Rome, opened a printing press that was to become celebrated under the name of At the

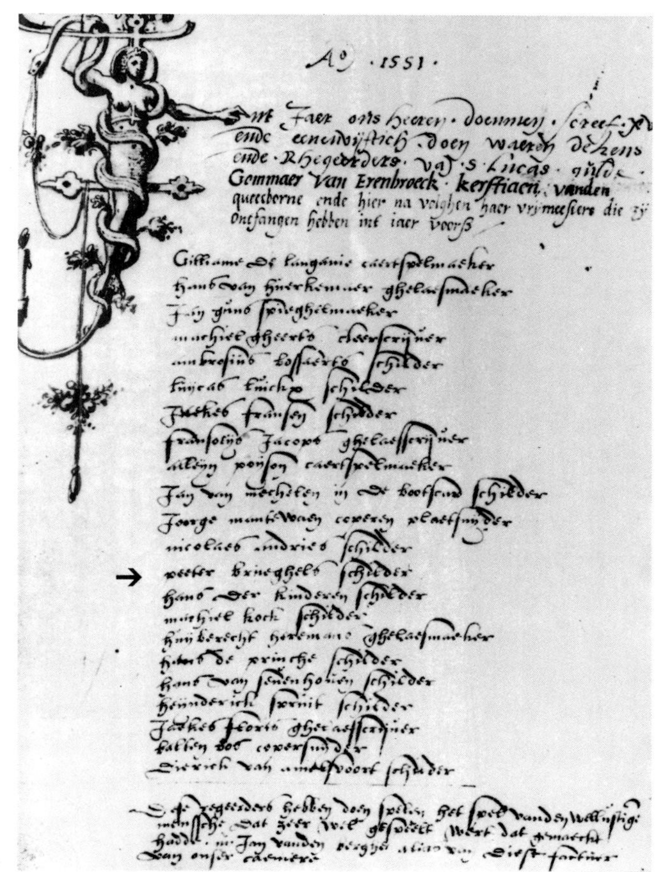

5. *Register of the Guild of St Luke in Antwerp,* for the year 1551. Antwerp, Archief Nationaal Hoger Instituut en Koninklijke Academie voor Schone Kunsten

6. The first mention of Bruegel's name, relating to the years 1550–51, *Archives of the Town of Mechelen,* DD 51 no. 32, document 9, 1608. Mechelen, Stadsarchief

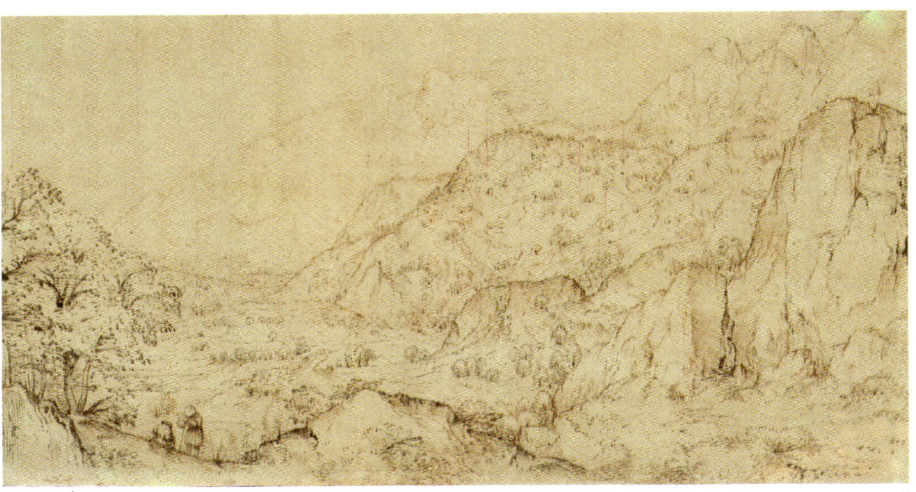

8

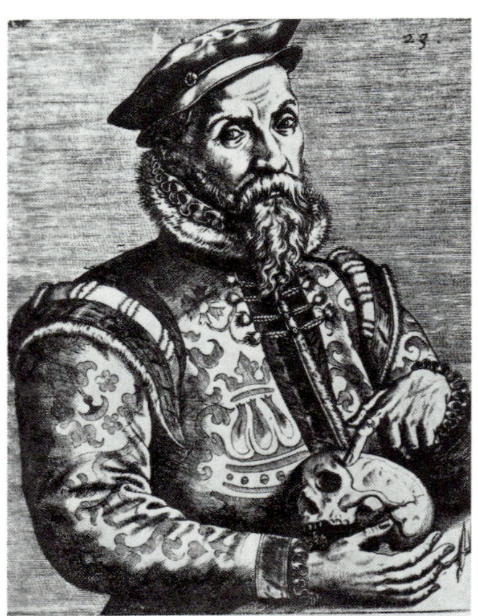

HIERONYMO COCO ANVERPIAN.
PICTORI.

Fallor? an effigiem vultus, Hieronyme, primum
Hanc auxit pictor post tua fata tui?
Nescio quid certè torpens & languidum in illa
Non prorsum indoctis innuit hoc oculis.
Clariùs, heu, sed enim loquitur caluaria cunctis,
Indice commonstrat quam tua læua manus:
Hi præière Cocum artifices · quos deinde secutus
Vos ijsdem comites ille , sibíque vocat.

7

7. *Hieronymus Cock*, in Dominicus
Lampsonius, *Effigies of the Famous Painters
of the Netherlands*, Antwerp, 1572,
plate 23. Brussels, Bibliothèque royale
Albert I, print room

8. Pieter Bruegel, *Mountain Landscape:
The Martinswand, near Zirl*, ca. 1554–55.
Pen and brown ink, 7⅞ x 15⅜ in.
(20 x 39.2 cm). Berlin, Staatliche Museen,
Kupferstichkabinett

FACING PAGE:
9. Pieter Bruegel, *View of the Ripa Grande*,
ca. 1552–53. Pen and two shades of brown
ink, 8³⁄₁₆ x 11⅛ in. (20.8 x 28.3 cm).
Chatsworth, The Duke of Devonshire
and the Chatsworth Settlement Trustees

10. Pieter Bruegel, *Mountain Landscape
with Italian Cloister*, 1552. Pen and brown
ink with later retouching, 7⁵⁄₁₆ x 12⅞ in.
(18.6 x 32.7 cm). Berlin, Staatliche Museen,
Kupferstichkabinett

Sign of the Four Winds (In de Vier Winden). This firm was to publish, in 1555–
56, Pieter Bruegel's *Great Landscapes* series, the first fruit of a long partnership
that would continue even after the artist's death with the plates *Spring* and
Summer, published in 1570.

Before the appearance of Bruegel's signed and published works, it may be—
and it is plausible, as Van Mander suggests—that Cock and Bruegel spent time
together and that Cock contributed to the final stages of Bruegel's training.
According to Louis Lebeer, an historian of engraving, the printer "needed to
ensure that he got the best-known, or most promising, artists of the time to work
for him." Lebeer adds that these artists had "opportunities to work which, as well
as offering financial gain, could greatly enhance their reputations."[22]

THE ITALIAN JOURNEY

Perhaps it was to enhance his reputation, as Lebeer's words suggest, that Bruegel
conceived the idea of traveling to Italy. Such extended journeys, which a few
Netherlandish artists—Rogier van der Weyden, for example—had undertaken in
the previous century, became common in the sixteenth century. Between 1508 and
1598 a number of artists from the Antwerp guild, from Jan Gossart to Peter Paul
Rubens, made this very pilgrimage. Indeed, the earliest signed and dated work that
we have from Bruegel's hand is a drawing of a mountain landscape with an Italian
cloister, bearing the date 1552 (fig. 10). Not only did Bruegel's journey yield
sketches and notes which he later used to make finished drawings and prints, but
also—and perhaps most importantly—it trained his eye and gave him a feeling for
space. Later, memories of his trip were to enliven many of his paintings too.

Bruegel stopped in many places on his journey, and scholars have been able to
trace his itinerary from the drawings and engravings he produced later. Although
it is not known whether he traveled from France to Italy via Switzerland, or by
sea,[23] many places he drew can be identified, from the Rhône valley to Reggio
Calabria, from the Ripa Grande in Rome (fig. 9) to the Martinswand, near Zirl,
in the Tyrol (fig. 8), and the Waltersspurg in the Upper Rhine (fig. 11), as well as
other places in the Alps, which left a deep impression on the artist. The Lake of
Geneva, the mountains of Savoy, and the castle at Aigle[24] appear in the engravings.

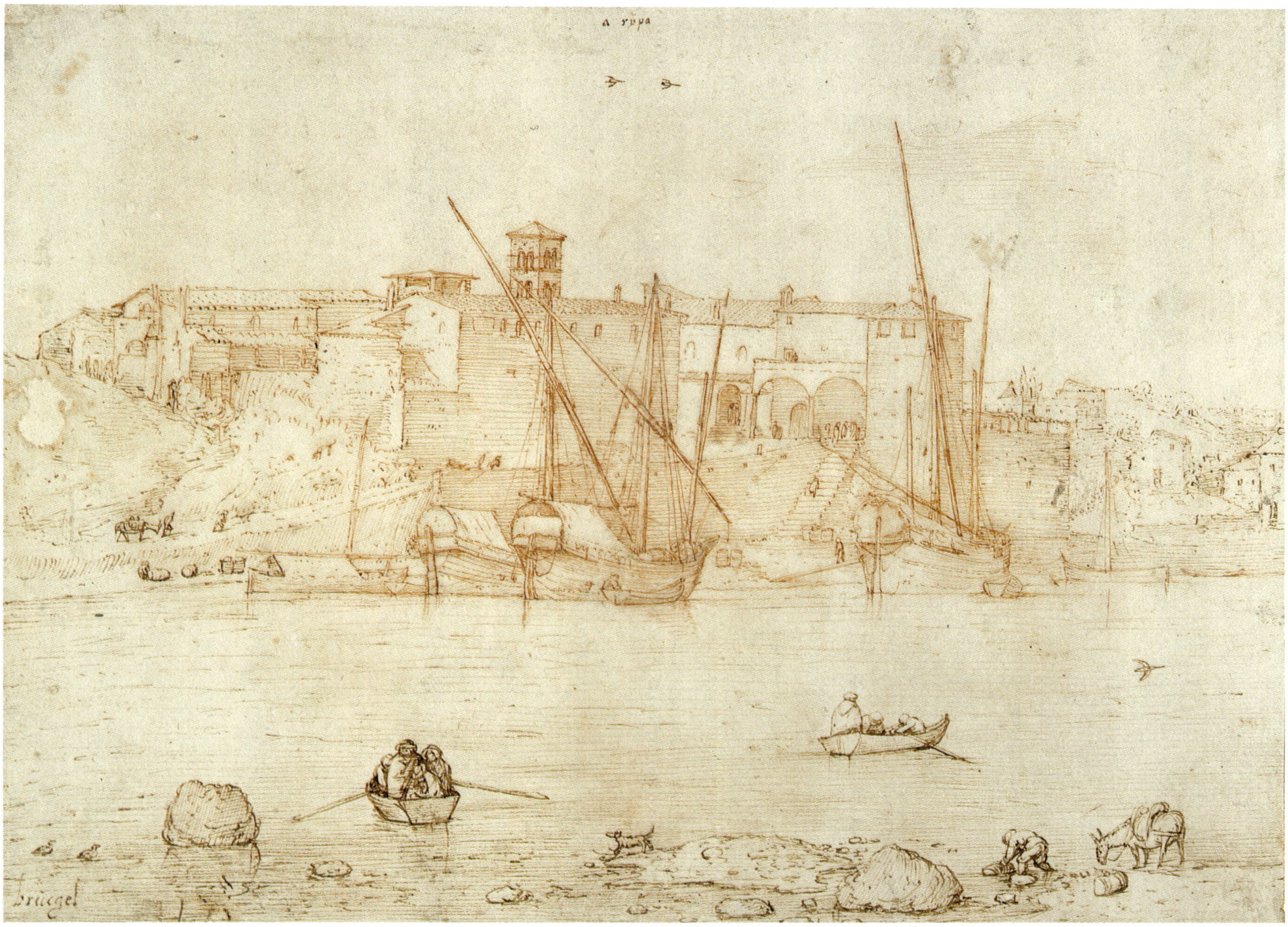

9

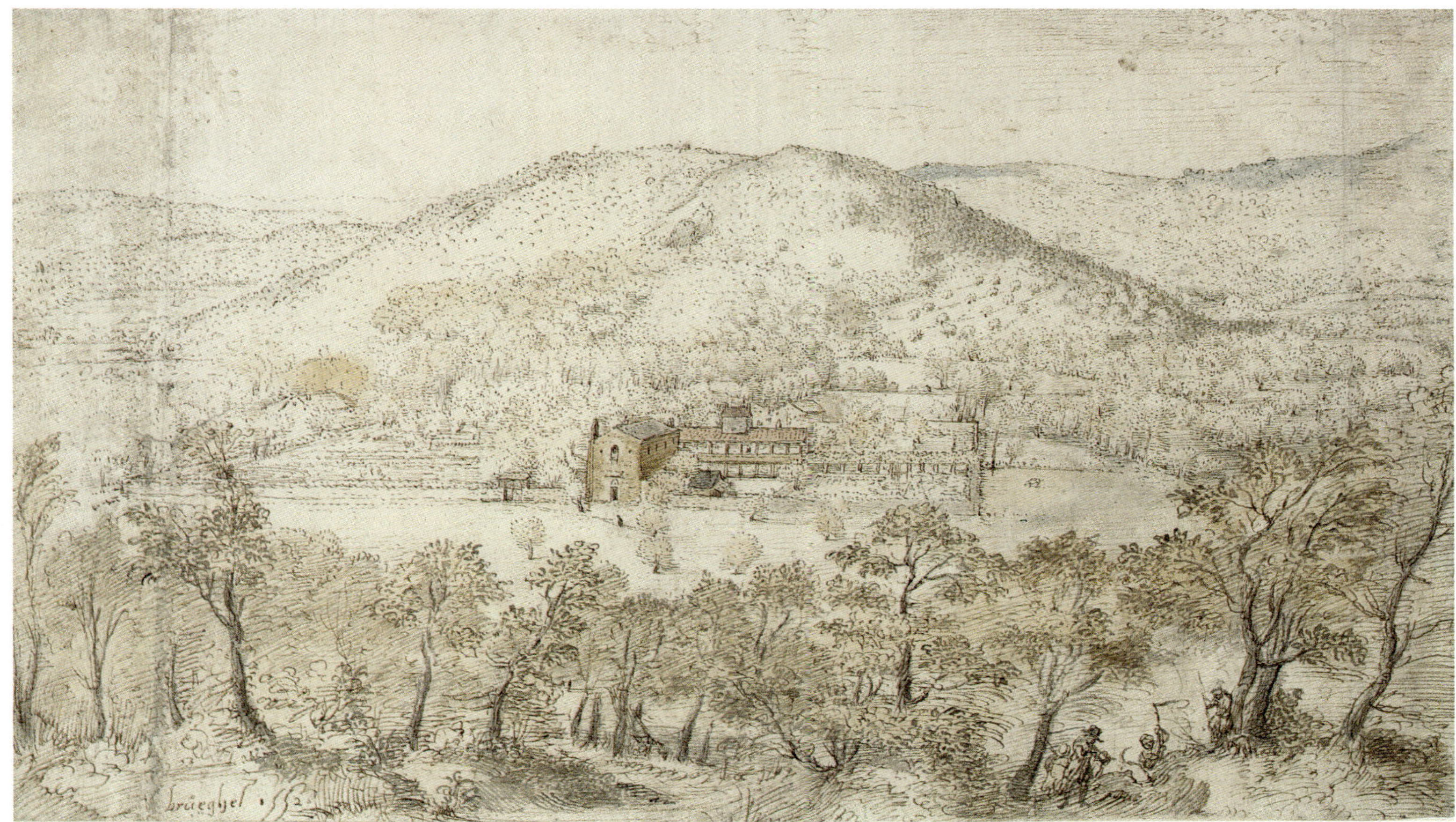

10

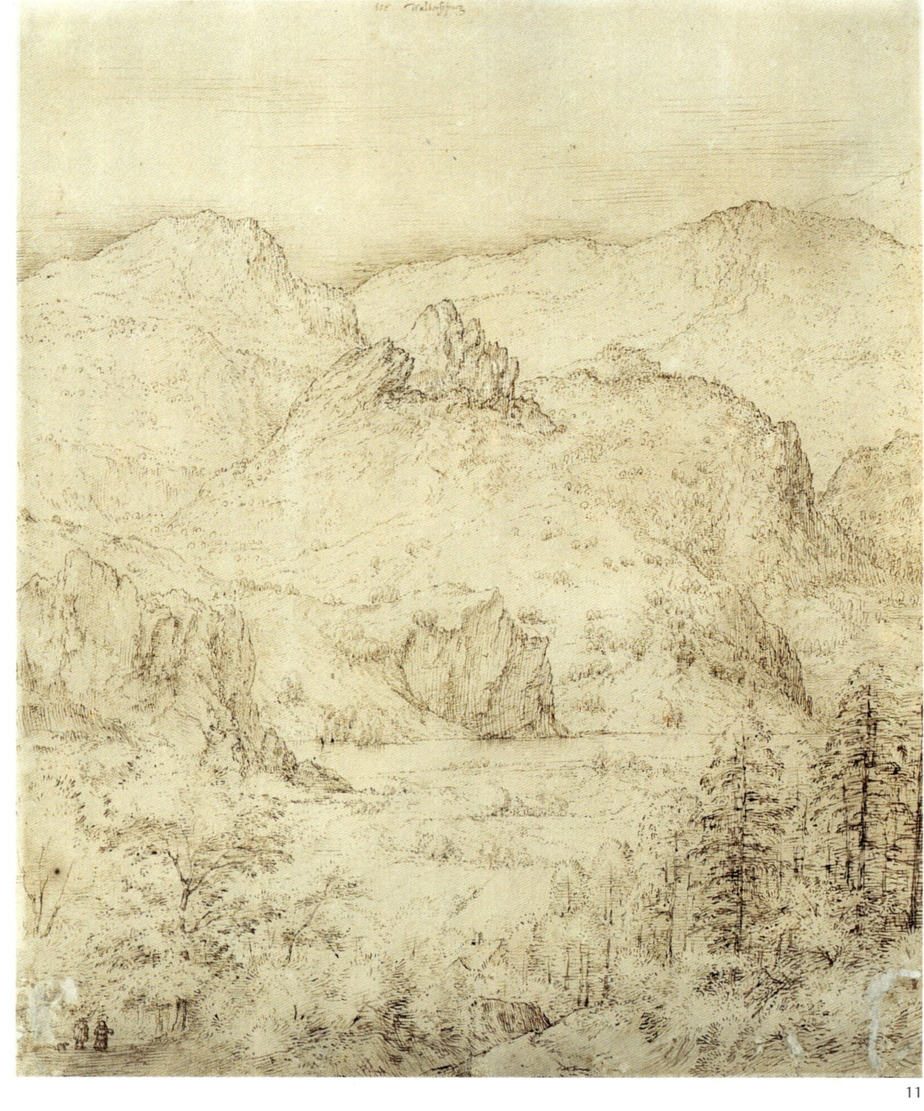

11

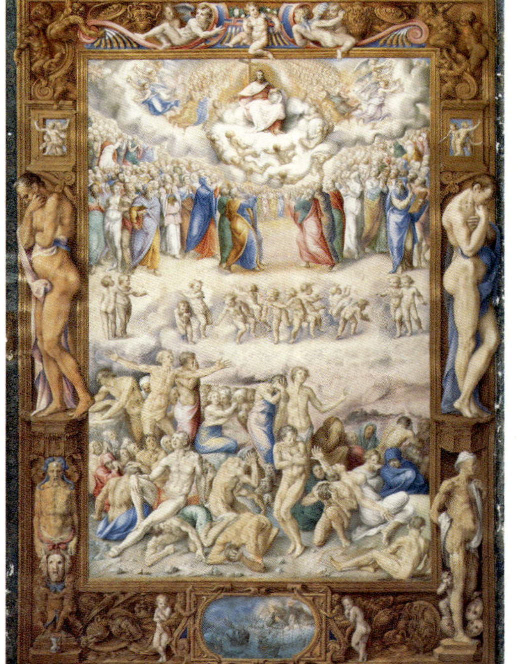

12

11. Pieter Bruegel, *"Waltersspurg" Mountain Landscape*, ca. 1554–55. Pen and brown ink, 12½ x 10⅜ in. (31.7 x 26.3 cm). Brunswick, Maine, Bowdoin College Museum of Art

12. Giulio Clovio, *The Last Judgment, Townley Lectionary*, ca. 1553–60, fol. 23. Illumination on parchment, 19⅜ x 12¹³⁄₁₆ in. (49.2 x 32.5 cm). New York Public Library

An engraving of 1561 by Frans Huys depicts a naval battle in the Strait of Messina (fig. 319), while two etchings published by Georges Hoefnagel after drawings by Bruegel (fig. 326) bear the legend "Romae Aº 1553."

Other documents yield more information. In 1577 the inventory of Giulio Clovio, an Italian miniaturist well known at the time (fig. 12), mentions four works by Bruegel in his possession: a *Tower of Babel*, on ivory; a *View of Lyon*, in distemper; a tree; and a miniature, half of which was Clovio's own work, the rest being by "Pietro Brugole."[25] It is known that Clovio, who had left Rome in 1551, returned there two years later. Another inventory, that of the Antwerp collector, Jan-Baptist Borrekens, this one dating from 1668, cites a "fragment of a canvas painted in Rome by Brueghel."[26] Finally, Peter Paul Rubens's inventory mentions a painting depicting "the Mont Saint-Godard, by Brueghel the Elder."[27]

ANTWERP: AT THE SIGN OF THE FOUR WINDS

The precise date of Bruegel's return to Antwerp is unknown. Since it is generally accepted that the series of twelve *Great Landscapes* was published by Hieronymus Cock between 1555 and 1558, Bruegel must clearly have begun work before the

16

earlier of these dates. Indeed, a preparatory sketch, *Alpine Landscape Crossed by a Deep Valley* (fig. 13), bears the date 1555. What is certain is that the series marks the beginning of a period during which Bruegel produced a large number of drawings for engravings for Cock's Antwerp publishing firm, At the Sign of the Four Winds.

In the mid-1550s, Antwerp was a center where artistic, intellectual, commercial, and financial influences combined to produce a ferment of activity. From the beginning of the century, the city, which is situated on the Scheldt River, had begun to replace Bruges as the principal Flemish seaport. As the channels of the Zwin River at Bruges gradually silted up, the more accessible estuary of the Scheldt became a major trade artery. The result was that around the turn of the sixteenth century English shipping companies established berths and warehouses in Antwerp, as did the great German traders such as the Hochstetter, Fugger, Welser, and Tucher families. The Italian trading families such as the Spinola and Grimaldi from Genoa, and the Frescobaldi from Florence all did business there, as did Spaniards, Portuguese, and traders from the Hanseatic ports. Exotic products of all kinds, minerals, industrial and manufactured goods—not forgetting, as Guicciardini emphasizes, "the good wine of Madeira"[28] —all passed through this city, whose population of more than 100,000 persons made it, in Bruegel's time, the largest in western Europe, after Paris, London, Venice, and Naples (fig. 14).

13. Pieter Bruegel, *Alpine Landscape Crossed by a Deep Valley*, 1555. Pen and brown ink, 11 1/2 x 16 7/8 in. (29.3 x 43 cm). Paris, Louvre, graphic arts department

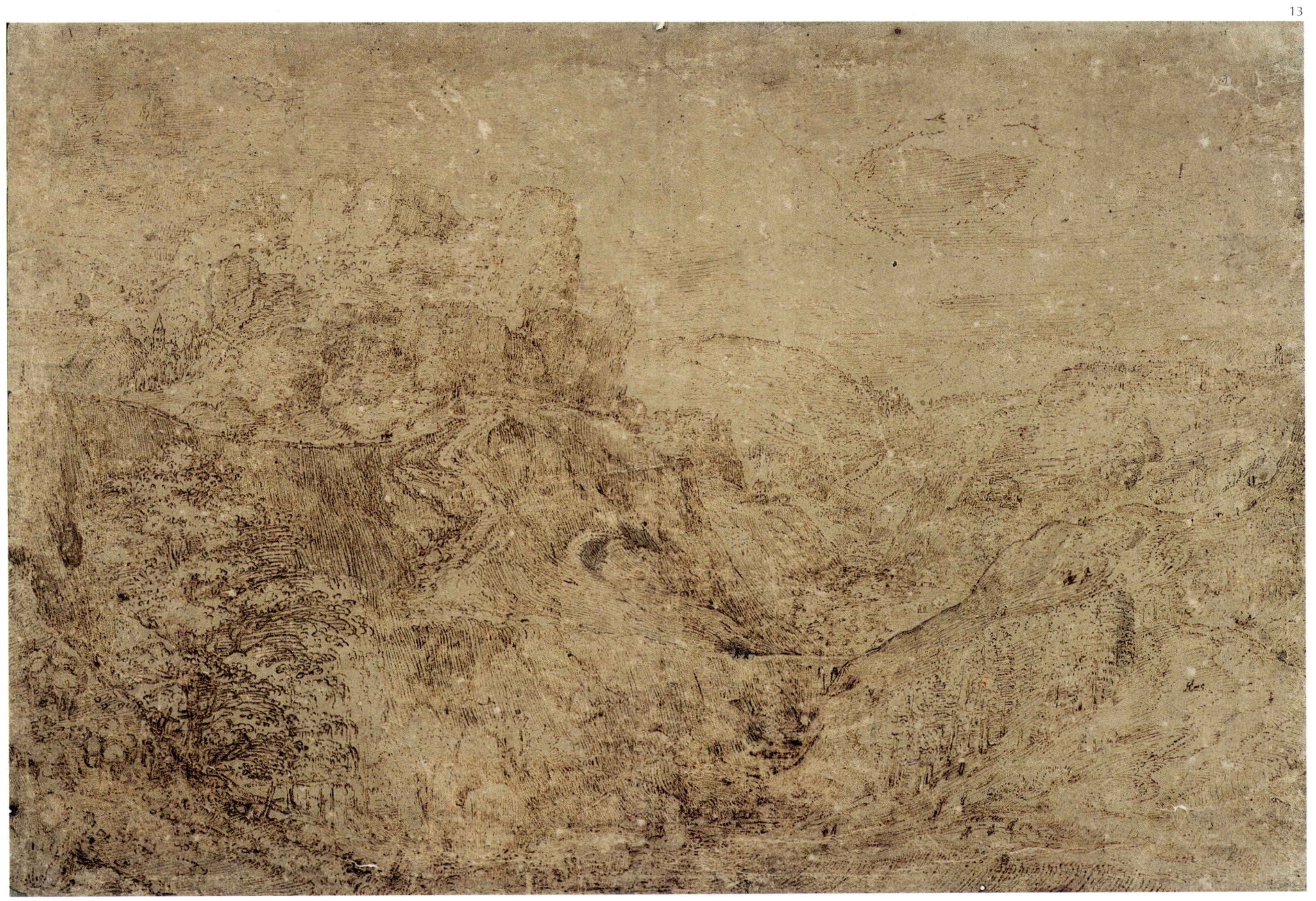

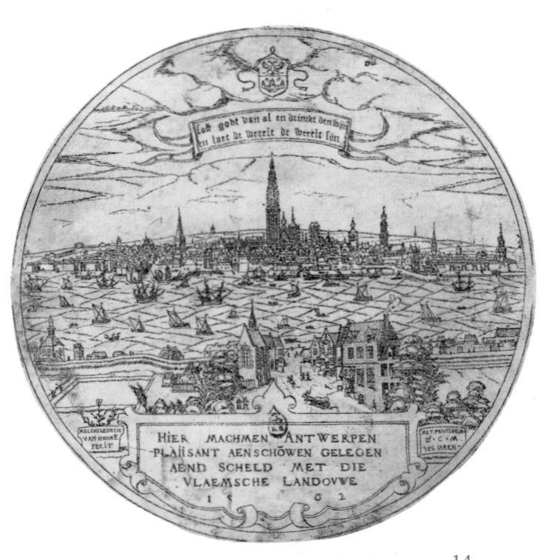

14

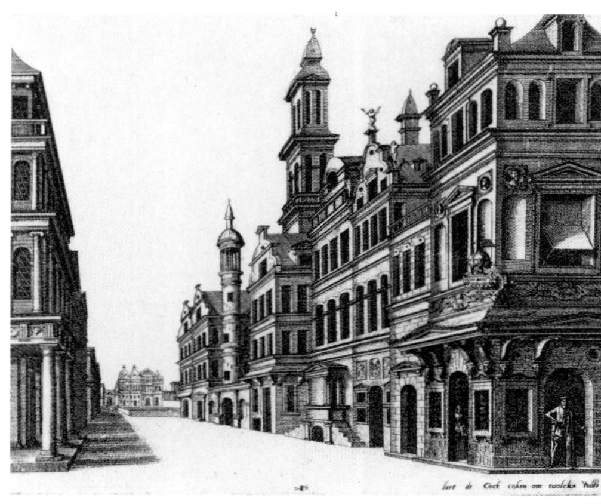

15

14. Melchisedech van Horen, *View of Antwerp*, 1562. Engraving. Paris, Bibliothèque nationale de France, print department

15. Lucas and/or Johannes van Duetecum, *Street View*, after Hans Vredeman de Vries. *Scenographiae sive Perspectivae*, Brussels, 1560, plate 1. Brussels, Bibliothèque royale Albert I, print room

FACING PAGE:
16. Pieter Bruegel, *The Big Fish Eat the Little Fish*, 1556. Brush and pen, grey and black ink, 8½ x 12⅛ in. (21.6 x 30.7 cm). Vienna, Graphische Sammlung Albertina

17. Pieter van der Heyden, *The Big Fish Eat the Little Fish*, after Pieter Bruegel, 1557. Engraving, 9 x 11⅝ in. (22.9 x 29.6 cm)

The New Stock Exchange built in 1531, a lively place if ever there was one, was not reserved exclusively for financial transactions but also contained, from 1550 onward, a "Schilderpand"—a gallery where works of art were exhibited and sold. The premises of At the Four Winds were close by, at the corner of two streets, as can be seen in a drawing by Hans Vredeman de Vries dating from about 1557, which, although the buildings it depicts are more imaginary than real, also shows Hieronymus Cock standing on his threshold. The engraving was published by Cock himself, as the frontispiece of de Vries's *Scenographiae* series of 1560 (fig. 15), which was dedicated to Antoine Perrenot de Granvelle, one of the ministers of Philip II of Spain and a future cardinal.

Cock's print editions, with which Bruegel was closely associated, enjoyed an international renown comparable to that enjoyed, in the sphere of books, by the publications of Christophe Plantin, a native of Tours who settled in Antwerp in 1549 and established a press there, At the Sign of the Golden Compasses (Au Compas d'Or). At the Sign of the Four Winds, an environment filled with the spirit of Erasmus and enlivened by the presence of the geographer Ortelius, the botanist Dodoneus, and the cartographer Mercator, was a meeting place, a seat of intellectual inquiry and of humanism, and indeed, a focal point of the Flemish Renaissance.

Bruegel's drawing, *The Big Fish Eat the Little Fish* (fig. 16), which dates from 1556, was reproduced as an engraving the following year by Pieter van der Heyden (fig. 17). Interestingly, the plate falsely attributes the original design to Hieronymus Bosch. Was this done simply for commercial reasons, Bosch's name being better known than Bruegel's? Or was the artist perhaps trying to distance himself from the political allusions of the picture? The question is inevitable, although, it should be noted, the proverb was a common saying in the Netherlands at the time.

The image is unquestionably by Bruegel, as the original drawing of the composition clearly proves, but its spirit and its vocabulary are indeed borrowed from the work of Hieronymus Bosch. These same qualities can be seen in other drawings by the artist and engravings made after them, for example *The Temptation of St Anthony* (fig. 89) and *The Ass at School* (figs. 81 and 82). This vision of the world according to Bosch—full of humor and satire, observation and invention, morality and daring—was further expressed by Four Winds' publication of another series by Bruegel, the *Deadly Sins*, also engraved by Pieter van der Heyden. Bruegel's preparatory drawings show his knowledge of Bosch's painterly vocabulary, and, at the same time, his mastery of the fantastic world that he was to bring to life, not as a follower of Bosch, but as a creator of new images that resonate on many levels (figs. 93–100).

Bruegel's contact with Hieronymus Cock, who was already publishing engravings based on drawings by Bosch, and the success that these images enjoyed, help explain this new direction in Bruegel's work, which gave shape to the first of the paintings for which he is so famous today: *Flemish Proverbs* (fig. 223) and *The Battle of Carnival and Lent* of 1559 (fig. 125). Both of these are large compositions in oil on oak panel—skillfully orchestrated, detailed scenes filled with large numbers of figures. The painter signed these "Bruegel"—no longer "Brueghel," suppressing the "h" he had used until then—and the dated paintings he produced thereafter can be seen as landmarks in his career.

18

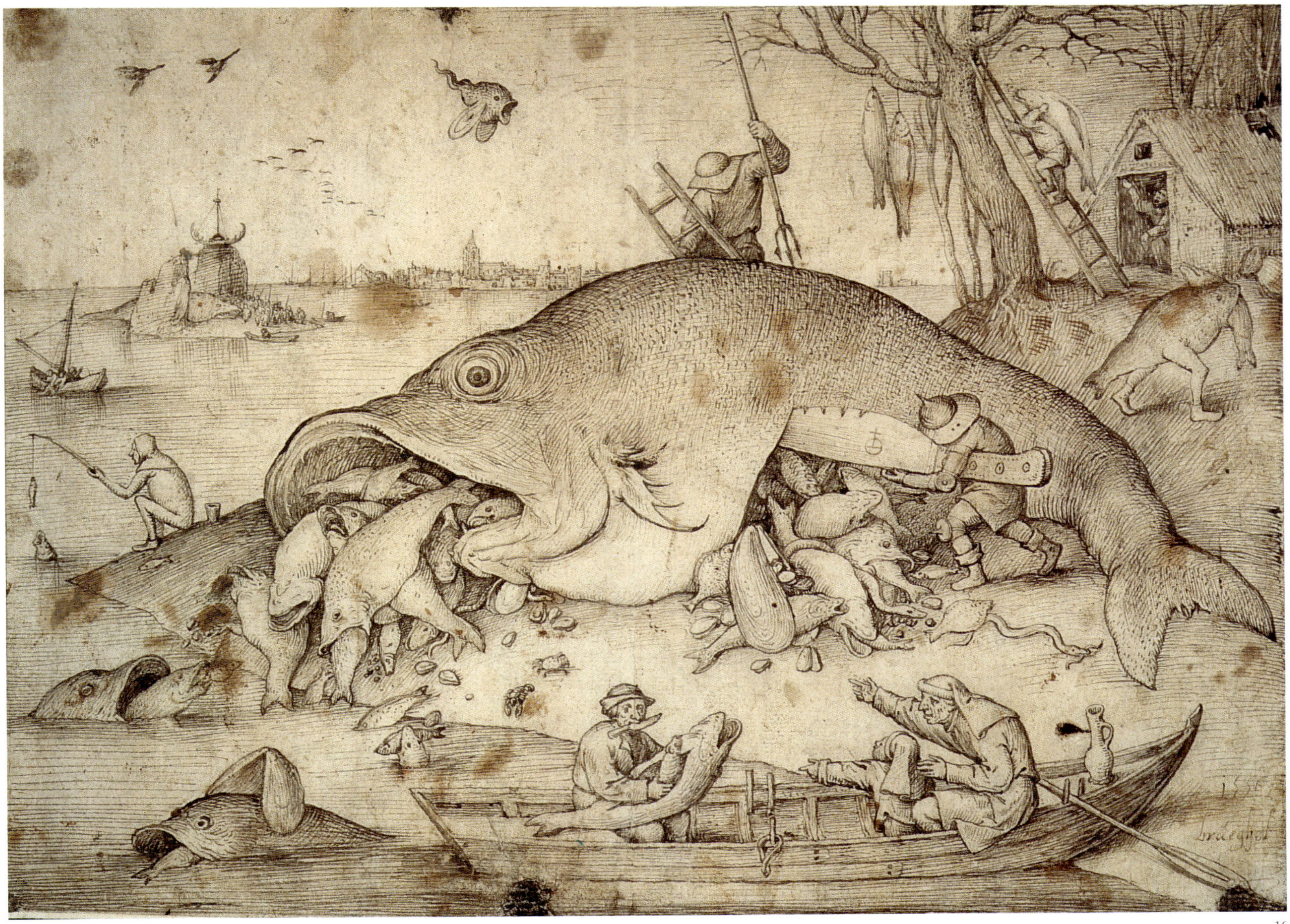

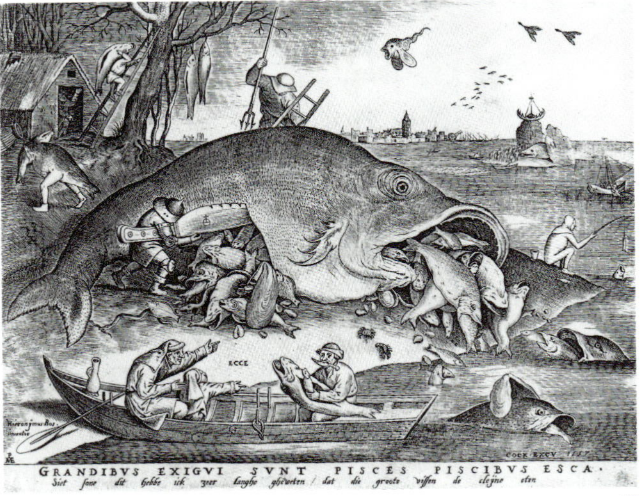

16

One important document from the archives bears the date 1561. It is a letter written on 16 June of that year to the geographer Abraham Ortelius by a colleague in Bologna, Scipio Fabius, who asks for news of his friend the eminent painter "Petrus Bruochl," whom he links to "Martinus Vulpes," that is, to Martin de Vos.[29] This letter, which refers to contacts Bruegel made in Italy, has led to suggestions that the two Flemish painters might have traveled to Italy together, or met while there.

MARRIAGE IN BRUSSELS

One of the few surviving pieces of evidence about Bruegel's life is the mention of his marriage in 1563 in the marriage register of the church of Notre-Dame-de-la-Chapelle in Brussels (fig. 20): "Peeter brùgel Mayken cocks soluit" (the "s" in "cocks" means "daughter of"). As Van Mander wrote later, "Finally, when the widow of Pieter Coecke came to live in Brussels, he [Bruegel] began to court his daughter whom, as I have already said, he had often carried in his arms, and married her."[30] The biographer's use of the word "finally" suggests a conclusion,

17

the ending of some phase or episode in the painter's life. "While he was still residing in Antwerp," Van Mander also wrote "he was living with a servant or young girl whom he would certainly have married, were it not for his dislike of her habit of lying (since she was niggardly with the truth)." A happy outcome, then. "But the mother," adds the narrator "placed the condition on it [the marriage] that Bruegel leave Antwerp to move to Brussels, in order to separate himself from his former relationship and forget it."

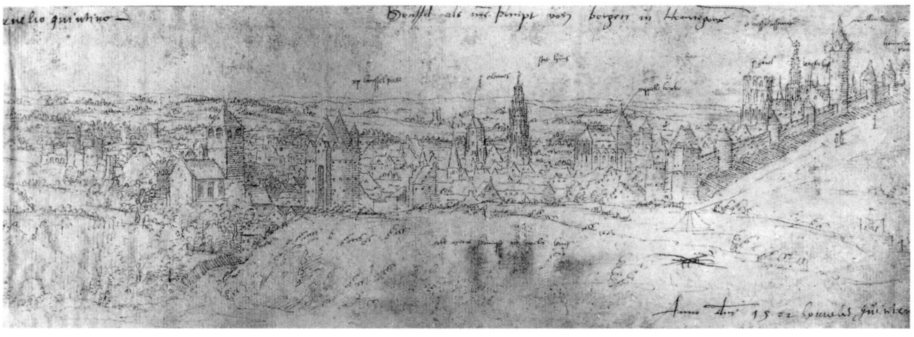

19

This anecdote—which appears bland alongside the magnitude of Bruegel's works, yet is nevertheless intensely human—is perfectly believable. Although Van Mander, writing in 1604, often gives incomplete or summary information, when it has been possible to check the accuracy of his information, it has almost invariably proved to be correct. Under the circumstances, the reason given for the painter's move to Brussels appears more plausible than a supposed flight from Antwerp for political or religious reasons—as was the case with Plantin, who briefly left the city in 1562.[31] Indeed, Brussels—the center of political power—would have been an odd place for a dissident to seek refuge.

The marriage was prolific in more ways than one. At the end of 1564 or the beginning of 1565 Pieter Bruegel the Younger (sometimes known as "Hell Bruegel"), was born. At the same time, the artist produced a growing number of works, and in these attained his artistic maturity. Already in 1559–60 his vision had become less Bosch-like in his print series, the *Virtues* (figs. 214–21), whose drawing style, though still as dense and detailed as ever, concentrates more on the real than on the fantastic. The last known painting from the Antwerp period, the *Two Monkeys* of 1562 (fig. 213) shows, against the background of a view of the city, a simple image that is extremely powerful despite its small size.

In Brussels, the painter cast his eyes more widely than ever before, whether focusing on subjects such as the Tower of Babel, the Adoration of the Magi, or the parable of the Blind leading the Blind, developing the themes of Christ carrying the Cross or the conversion of St Paul, broadening his philosophical conception of society—as in *The Misanthrope* and *The Bird-Nester* (figs. 267 and 209)—restoring the breath of nature and sense of time to the synthesizing scenes of the *Seasons* (figs. 173–75 and 186–67), pondering on the joys and sufferings of mankind—or conveying everyday reality by timeless paintings such as *Winter Landscape with Skaters and Bird Trap* (fig. 54) or *The Magpie on the Gallows* (fig. 360). This great variety of works included many masterpieces in which Bruegel's genius asserted its lofty, human vision, and the forcefulness of its language. However, aside from these masterly qualities and the works that resulted from them, little information is

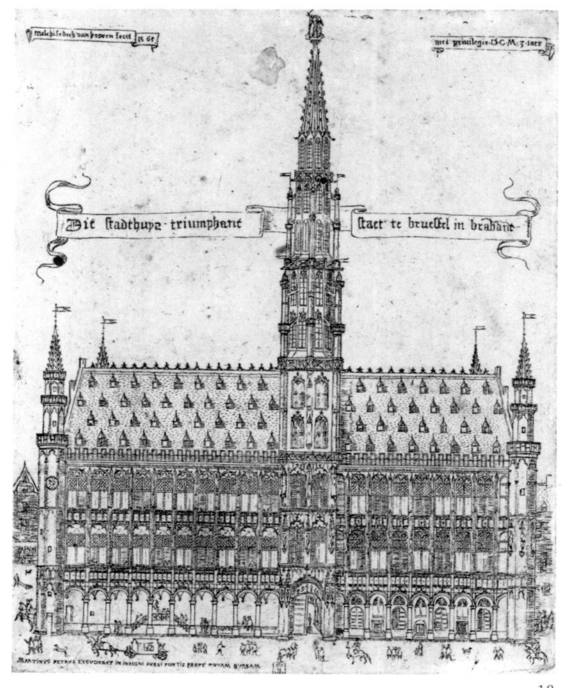

18

20

18. Melchisedech van Hooren, *Brussels Town Hall*, 1565. Engraving. Brussels, Bibliothèque royale Albert I, print room

19. Cornelis Metsys, *View of Brussels from the South*, 1522. Pen and brown ink. Berlin, Staatliche Museen, Kupferstichkabinett.

20. Notation of the marriage of Pieter Bruegel and Mayken Coecke, *Marriage Register*, 1563, fol. 5. Brussels, City Archives, Church of Notre-Dame-de-la-Chapelle

available about the artist. In 1565, in a letter to Ortelius, the Bolognese Scipio Fabius asks to be remembered to "Petrus Brouchel."[32] Documents in the Antwerp city archives (fig. 22) reveal that the following year Nicolas Jongelinck, an associate of Cardinal Granvelle and brother of Jacques Jongelinck, sculptor to Philip II, pledged as security on behalf of a friend his collection of paintings which included "sixteen pieces by Brueghel; among them is *The Tower of Babel*, a *Christ Carrying the Cross*, [and] the twelve *Months*."[33]

In 1567 Guicciardini, it is known, mentions "Pieter Brueghel from Breda, imitator of the skill and imagination of Hierosme Boys"; and the following year comes another landmark: a mention in Vasari's new edition of the *Lives*. Also in 1568 the painter's wife gave birth to another son, Jan, who would become celebrated under the name "Velvet Brueghel." There was also a daughter, Marie, remarked on by only a few biographers.[34]

In 1569 Bruegel died—and the eulogies began. As early as 1572 Dominicus Lampsonius praised "this new Hieronymus Bosch … who could imitate, with brush or crayon, the inspired dreams of his master with such skill that sometimes he even surpasses him."[35] The humorous or facetious nature of Bruegel's work

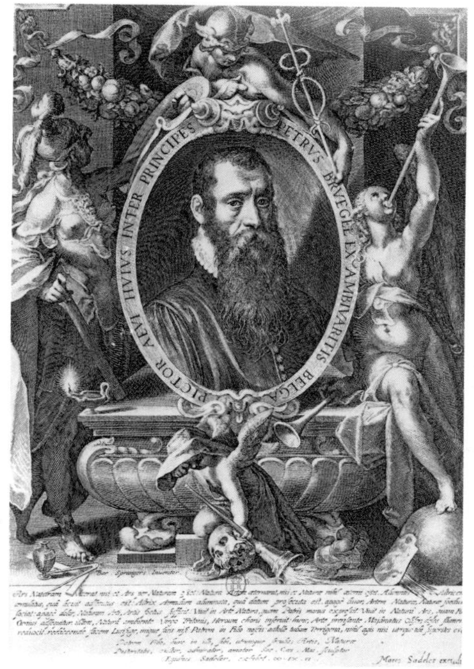

21. Aegidius Sadeler, *Allegorical Portrait of Pieter Bruegel,* after Bartholomeus Spranger, 1606. Engraving. Paris, Bibliothèque nationale de France, print department

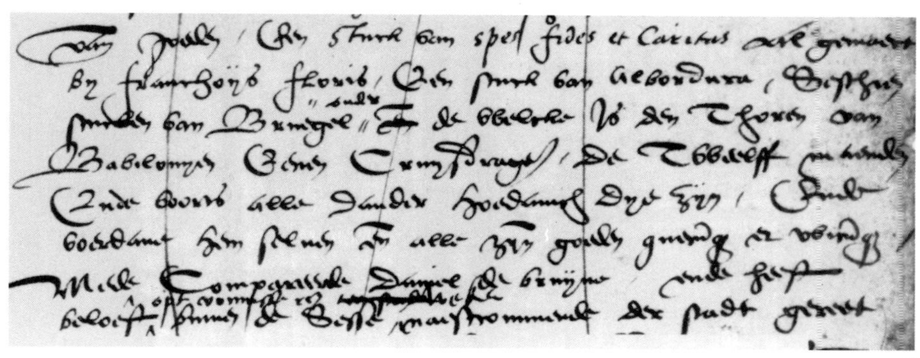

22. Document recording Nicolas Jongelinck's pledge of his paintings as security, 21 February 1566. Antwerp, Stadsarchief

aroused interest, as it would later that of Van Mander at the beginning of the seventeenth century. However, in about 1573 Abraham Ortelius, in his *Album Amicorum* (fig. 23) rightly dissociated Bruegel from this Boschian or earthy image recognizing in him "not the best of painters but 'the character of a painter '… In all his works there is always something to understand beyond what is depicted."[36]

The market value of Bruegel's works began to increase, as a letter to Cardinal Granvelle from the provost Morillon in December 1572 confirms. On being asked by Granvelle to "retrieve Bruegel's works," which had disappeared from the palace of Mechelen after it had been sacked by the Duke of Alva's forces, the provost informs him of the high price these command since "they are more in demand since his death."[37] This was hardly surprising. As Van Mander confirms, "Some of his better works are now in the possession of the Emperor."[38] Posthumous portraits of the artist were also published, one engraved by Theodor Galle in 1572 and another by Aegidius Sadeler in 1606, after Bartholomeus Spranger, bearing the inscription: "Petrus Bruegel ex ambivaritis Belga pictor aevi hujus inter principes." "Ambivaritis" here denotes an inhabitant of the marquisate of Antwerp, which included Breda and the surrounding district[39]—thus confirming the theory that Brueghel was born in Brabant.

And so among tributes, portraits, and a strong demand for his works, fame took possession of the painter of whose life only the faintest outline remained.

23. Abraham Ortelius, *Album Amicorum,* ca. 1573, fol. 13, verso. Cambridge University, Pembroke College

HISTORICAL BACKGROUND

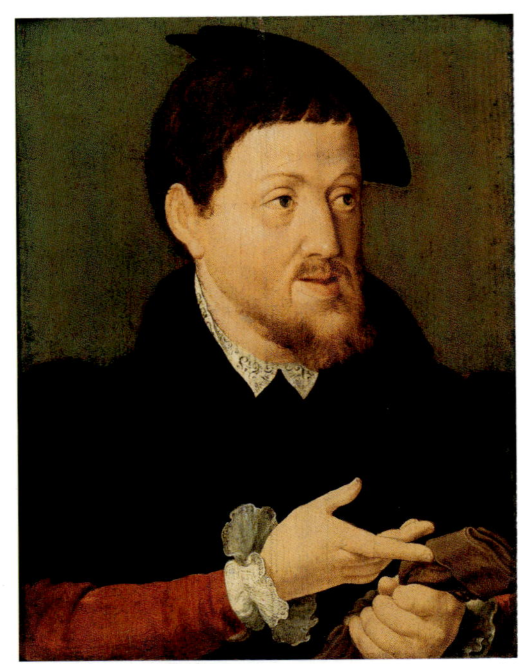

BURGUNDY AND THE NETHERLANDS

In the fifteenth century, during the lives of the Burgundian dukes Philip the Bold (1342–1404), John the Fearless (1371–1419), and Philip the Good (1396–1467), the lands known as the Old Netherlands became part of the Duchy of Burgundy. This gathering of power was carried out judiciously, taking account of the region's existing institutions. Philip the Good's son Charles the Bold (1433–1477) expanded this domain, clashing with Louis XI of France, and established his seat of power at Mechelen before he died at the siege of Nancy in 1477. Charles's daughter and heiress, Mary of Burgundy (1457–1482), found herself in a precarious situation. At home, some provinces were trying to loosen their ties to the duchy and reestablish certain ancient privileges; abroad, Louis XI was a threat. Maximilian of Austria (1459–1519), her young husband, resisted the French pressure with the help of the city of Namur, the Flemish militias, and, after Mary's death, by the support of the southern provinces from Hainaut to Namur and Luxembourg.

At the end of the fifteenth century, with peace finally secured, Maximilian, now the Holy Roman Emperor, ceded the Burgundian lands to his son Philip the Handsome (1478–1506). The young prince married Joanna of Castille (1479–1555, who was to become known as Joanna the Mad), daughter of Ferdinand V and Isabella of Castile—thus bringing Spain into the picture. With the death of Isabella, Joanna and Philip made a claim to the throne of Castile. One of their children, born in Ghent in 1500, was named Charles: the future Charles V of the Holy Roman Empire (fig. 24). Thus began the century that Bruegel was to enrich with his art, a century that was to be illuminated—or set alight—by great achievements, works of art, wars, and feuds.

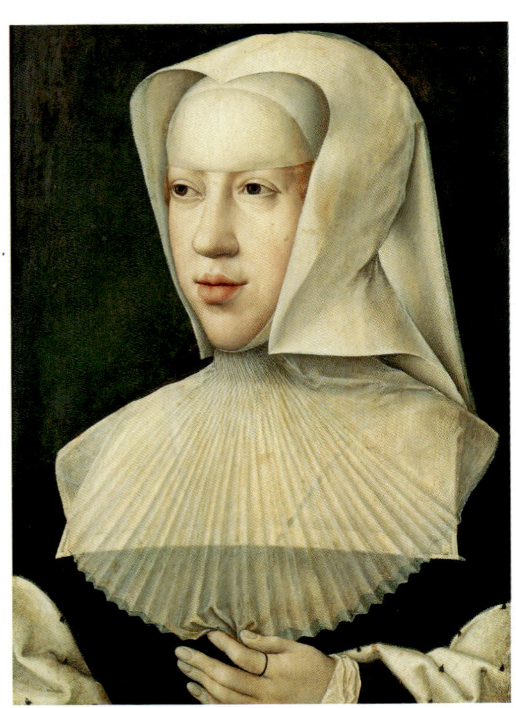

24. Jan Cornelisz Vermeyen, *Portrait of Charles V*, ca. 1530. Oil on panel. Brussels, Musées Royaux des Beaux-Arts de Belgique

25. After Bernard van Orley, *Portrait of Margaret of Austria*, ca. 1520. Oil on panel. Brussels, Musées Royaux des Beaux-Arts de Belgique

POLITICS, ECONOMICS, AND RELIGION UNDER CHARLES V

Although he was to be thoroughly educated by two tutors, Adrien Florizonne, provost of St Peter's in Leuven (the future Pope Adrian V) and Guillaume de Croy, lord of Chièvres, Charles was only five years old and thus far too young to rule the Netherlands in 1506 when his father, Phillip, died. The boy's grandfather, the emperor Maximilian, named one of his own daughters, Margaret of Austria (1480–1530; fig. 25)— the heir's aunt—as regent. Margaret continued in this office even after Charles was crowned king of Spain in 1516, and when, upon Maximilian's death in 1519, he became Holy Roman Emperor. When Margaret died in 1530, Charles appointed his sister, Mary of Hungary, as the new regent. The regent's government was supported by three councils: the State Council, which dealt with politics and foreign relations; the Private Council, in charge of justice; and the Finance Council. Although he did not want to concern himself with day-to-day affairs in the Netherlands, Charles was determined to consolidate his power there by uniting the seventeen provinces— the duchies of Brabant, Limburg, Luxembourg, and Gelderland, the counties of Flanders, Artois, Hainaut, Holland, Zeeland, and Zutphen, the marquisates of Namur and Antwerp, and the domains of Tournai, Utrecht, Overijssel, Friesland, and Groningen—into a single political unit. His will was codified in the Pragmatic

Sanction of 1549, which established the Netherlands as an indivisible whole. The region, as depicted by cartographers of the day, was known as Leo Belgicus, because its shape resembled that of a powerful feline (fig. 28).

However, Charles V had other problems to solve, beasts to tame, and battles to fight. He was at war with France, and the conflict was fierce, from the battle of

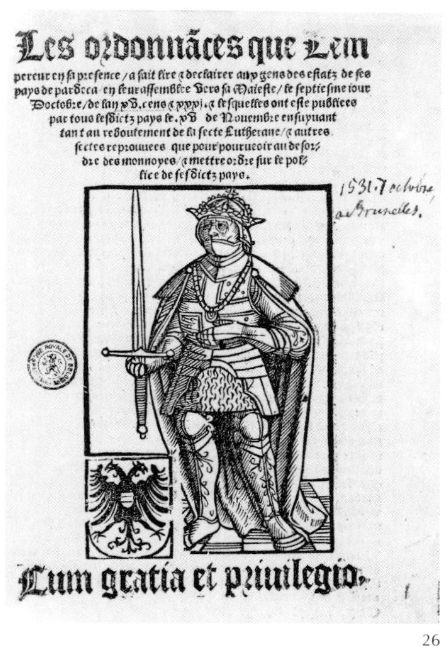

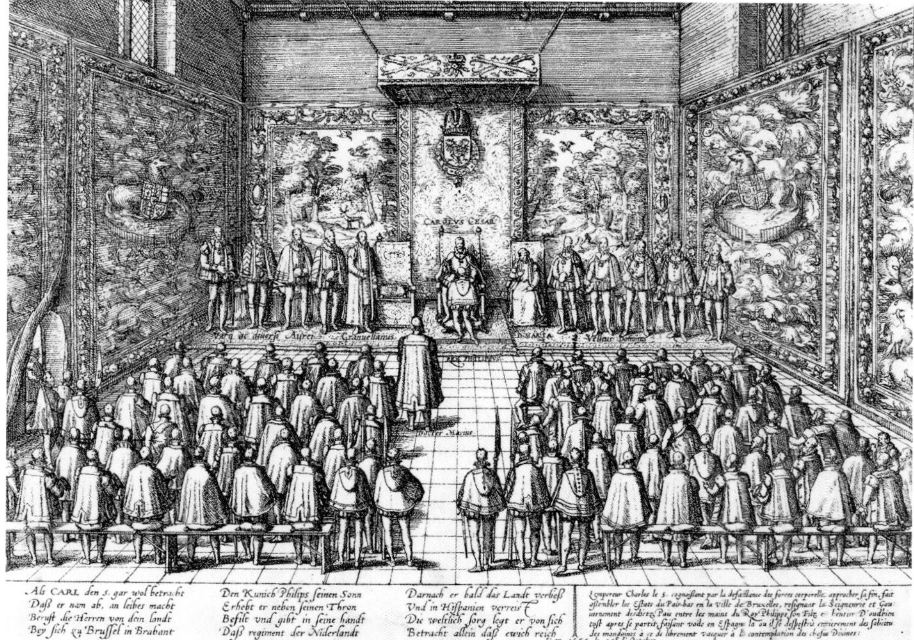

Pavia in 1525, where Francis I of France was taken prisoner, to the Treaty of Cambrai in 1529, which was concluded by Louise of Angoulême, the mother of the French king, and Margaret of Austria, and therefore known as the "Ladies' Peace." The war was prolonged, and there were two further wars during the reign of Charles V, which pitted the great powers of the day against each other, changed national boundaries, strained government coffers, and sparked off unrest in the Netherlands that the authorities were forced to repress—among other places, in Ghent.

Religious conflicts were to rage throughout the century. In 1517 the theologian Martin Luther (1483–1546) started to organize the Protestant reformation of the church in Germany, and shortly thereafter Ulrich Zwingli (1484–1531) began to lead a similar movement in Switzerland. In 1527, soldiers in the army of Charles V, many of whom were mercenaries and also adherents to the new Protestant movement, sacked Rome. Only two years later, Suleiman the Magnificent, sultan of Turkey, laid siege to Vienna; Charles responded in 1535 by capturing Tunis, which had been seized by the Turks the previous year. During the 1530s, John Calvin, another Protestant theologian, established a theocratic state in Geneva; in England, Henry VIII created the independent Anglican church; and in Germany, a group of Anabaptists seized the town of Münster, only to be massacred a year later by a Catholic army led by the local bishop. In France, from 1545 onward, persecution of Protestants sparked off the Wars of Religion, which precipitated the massacre of many thousands of Protestants by Catholics on St. Bartholomew's Day (August 22) in 1572. The Wars of Religion were finally ended in 1598 by Henry IV's Edict of Nantes, which granted Protestants a limited measure of religious freedom.

To try to restore some order to religious affairs in Europe, in 1545 Pope Paul III convened the Council of Trent, the aim of which was to reform the Catholic church and to defend it against the Protestant movement. The council set in motion the program that we know as the Counter-Reformation. In the same

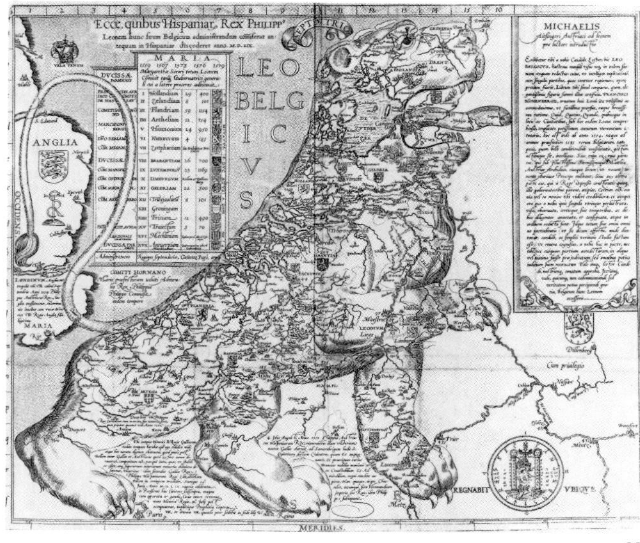

26. *Printed Leaflet against Heresy,* issued by Charles V, 7 October 1531. Brussels, Bibliothèque royale Albert I, special collection

27. Frans Hogenberg, *The Abdication of Charles V at Brussels in 1555.* Etching. Brussels, Bibliothèque royale Albert I, print room

28. Frans Hogenberg, *Leo Belgicus: The Seventeen Provinces of the Netherlands,* 1559. Etching. Brussels, Bibliothèque royale Albert I, special collection

spirit, Ignatius Loyola founded the Society of Jesus in 1540, a missionary order intended to propagate the Catholic faith.

Charles V was a formidable enemy of Protestantism. As early as 1521, with the Edict of Worms, he declared war on Lutheranism; by 1529 he was threatening heretics with execution in a series of printed leaflets (fig. 26), and in 1547 he defeated an army of the German Protestant princes at Mühlberg. In 1555, however, he granted freedom of worship in the Treaty of Augsburg. On 25 October of the same year, in the great state hall of the palace of Coudenberg in Brussels, he ended his reign, abdicating in favor of his son Philip II (fig. 27) and his younger brother, Ferdinand. Philip, the son of Charles and Isabella of Portugal, inherited the crown of Spain and the Netherlands, while Ferdinand received the imperial title and the crown of Austria.

After the economic boom in Antwerp that had marked the beginning of Charles V's reign, and made the city the main financial center of the time, a slowdown set in towards the middle of the century—brought on by, among other things, the transfer of the city's spice market to Lisbon, and by the financial burden of warfare. Bankruptcies occurred around 1558, as they did also in France and Spain. Guicciardini reports that soon afterwards a wave of speculation took hold of the city[40] In 1566, a series of iconoclastic riots dealt the city a terrible blow, and prosperity began to shift elsewhere: to the England of Elizabeth I, to the Hanseatic towns, and to Amsterdam. At the end of the century, the Dutch blockade of the Scheldt river worsened matters and hastened Antwerp's decline.

PHILIP II AND THE COUNCIL OF TROUBLES

Charles V's religious and secular absolutism—which had been more or less accepted despite revolts and hardships, since, as a native of Ghent, Charles was seen as a "natural" prince—was reinforced by his son, Philip II, who applied it harshly. This was resented however—all the more so because Philip II (fig. 30) left the Netherlands for Spain, naming as regent Margaret of Parma, the illegitimate daughter of Charles V and a woman from Audenarde. He also granted wide powers to his minister Granvelle (fig. 29), who in 1561 was elevated to archbishop of Mechelen and made a cardinal. Granvelle was the head of a secret triumvirate, the Consulta, whose other members were the jurist Viglius van Aytta and the Count of Berlaymont, president of the Finance Council. When the State Council discovered this, it was deeply resentful.

Abroad, France was once again on the offensive; Henry II invaded Artois. Lamoral, count of Egmont, first defeated the French near St. Quentin in 1557, and then again at Gravelines in 1558. The Treaty of Cateau-Cambrésis ended the war in 1559. Domestically, however, the situation was deteriorating. The Inquisition, with the strong backing of Philip II, declared war on heretics, particularly Anabaptists, and Calvinists. To make matters worse, religious tensions were compounded by social problems and a growing hostility to the presence of Spanish troops who, being poorly paid, not surprisingly behaved badly.

There were increasing confrontations between the Consulta, who faithfully followed the king's orders, and the local nobility, led by Egmont, Philip, count of Hoorn, and William of Orange-Nassau, known to history as William the Silent. Faced with this growing defiance, Margaret of Parma asked the king to remove Granvelle. Her request was granted, and the cardinal left the Netherlands in

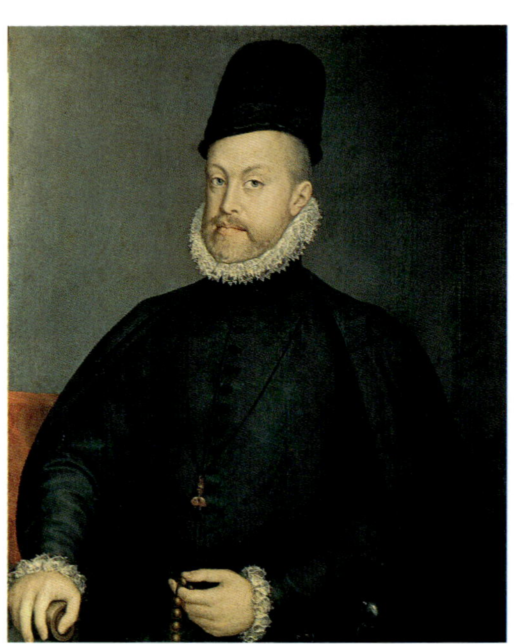

29. Lambert Suavius, *Portrait of Antoine Perrenot de Granvelle*, 1556. Burin engraving. Brussels, Bibliothèque royale Albert I, print room

30. Sofonisba Anguissola, *Portrait of Philip II*, ca. 1575. Oil on canvas. Madrid, Prado

1564. The nobles, for their part, closed ranks and, on the suggestion of the burgomaster of Antwerp, Philips Marnix van Sint Aldegonde drafted a petition, the Compromise of Breda, demanding an end to the persecution of heretics and the suppression of the Inquisition, as well as respect for the country's traditional rights and privileges. The petition won the backing of both Catholics and Calvinists, and several hundred supporters rallied to the cause. At the suggestion of William of Orange, the Compromise was solemnly presented to Margaret of Parma in the form of a Request on 5 April 1566 by a group of 200–300 horsemen from several provinces. One of the regent's courtiers, seeing that she was visibly alarmed, is said to have exclaimed: "What, madam, do you fear these beggars?" The word "beggar" was therefore adopted by the petitioners as a mark of distinction, and at the banquet that followed the meeting with Margaret, the delegation's leader, Hendrik van Brederode, cried: "Long live the Beggars!"[41] Margaret of Parma was obliged to pass the Request that she had received on to the king. Meanwhile, unrest continued. On 19 August iconoclastic riots broke out in Antwerp, where the cathedral and other churches were looted. These were followed by riots in Ghent, Ypres, Zeeland, and Friesland. However, the rebels, divided by their own violence, soon splintered into factions, and the revolt was put down. Nevertheless, Philip II decided to reassert his authority and to defeat heresy. In August 1567 he sent the Duke of Alva to the Netherlands with an elite force of 17,000 men, who entered Brussels on 22 August (fig. 31). Three days later, Margaret resigned her regency and returned to Italy.

The Spanish set up a special court, the Council of Troubles, popularly known as the Council of Blood. A string of trials and executions followed (fig. 32) and heavy taxes were levied. The Beggars' resistance was led by William of Orange, and in October 1573, the Duke of Alva was forced to abandon the siege of Alkmaar. The provinces of Holland and Zeeland were lost to Spanish control, and Alva was relieved of his command.

Other military leaders were to serve under the king at the end of the century: Luis de Zuniga y Requesens, Don Juan of Austria, and Alessandro Farnese, who clashed repeatedly with the Beggars. In 1576 the Spanish sacked Antwerp, killing 6,000 people, an incident still remembered as "The Spanish Fury," and Ghent joined the revolt. The Pacification of Ghent, which was signed that same year, was an alliance of the provinces of the Netherlands aimed at driving the Spanish from the country. In 1584, however, William the Silent was assassinated, and the following year Antwerp was retaken by Alessandro Farnese. However, these last two developments were not enough to restore Spain's control over all of its former territory. Weakened by the defeat of the Armada at the hands of the English in August 1588, as well as by his military campaigns in France, in May 1598 Philip II ceded the Netherlands to his daughter, the Archduchess Isabella, and to his future son-in-law, Archduke Albert of Austria, along with the task of reconquering them. However, the seventeen provinces were to remain partitioned. After Ostend was retaken, the archdukes signed a truce with United Provinces of the north that was to last twelve years, from 1609 to 1621.

Forty years after Brueghel's death, a new era was dawning: the century of Rubens.

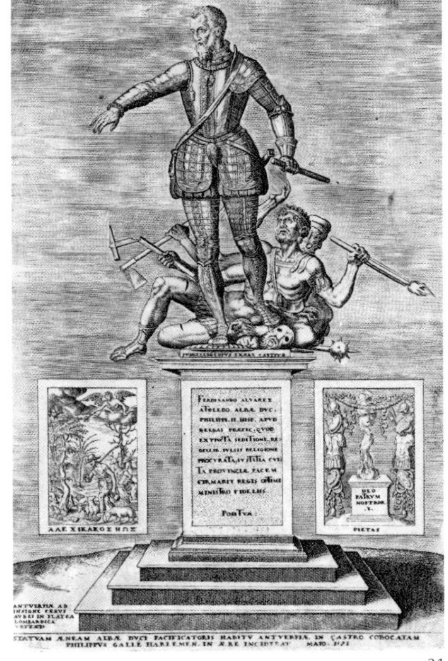

31

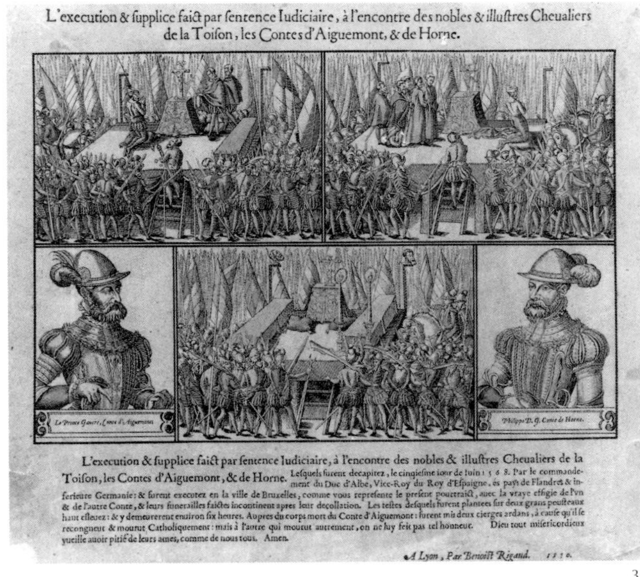

32

31. Philipp Galle, *Statue in Honor of the Duke of Alva Erected in 1571 in the Citadel of Antwerp*. Engraving. Brussels, Bibliothèque royale Albert I, print room

32. Benoist Roigaud, *Execution of the Counts of Egmont and Hoorn in 1568*. 1570. Engraving. Gasbeek, castle

THE CULTURAL CLIMATE

Politics and economics determined the cultural environment. From the fifteenth century onward the Burgundian states were flowering, especially in the realm of the arts. In painting there were Jan van Eyck, Robert Campin (the Master of Flémalle), Rogier van der Weyden, Petrus Christus, Dirck Bouts, and Hugo van der Goes, who between them spanned the schools of Bruges, Tournai, Brussels, Ghent, and Leuven. The Burgundian Library in Brussels during the reign of Philip the Good had one of the richest collections of illuminated manuscripts in the western world. From 1425 onward the university at Leuven gave Brabant one of the intellectual centers of Christendom. Tapestries from the large towns such as Arras, Audenarde, Tournai, and Brussels, as well as carved altarpieces from Brabant and Antwerp, were exported all over Europe.

The momentum continued in the sixteenth century. Raphael's large-scale cartoons depicting the Acts of the Apostles, which were destined to be woven into tapestries for the Sistine Chapel, were executed by Pieter van Aelst in Brussels between 1517 and 1519, to the order of Pope Leo X. Tapestries woven after cartoons by Bernard van Orley—such as the *Story of Jacob*, the *Battle of Pavia*, and *Maximilian Hunting*—adorned many walls in the western world. And the theme of the Eucharist, made into stained-glass windows, illuminated the collegiate church of St. Michael and St. Gudule in Brussels. Humanism, which tended to ignore national borders, also favored the development of music, an art in which the Netherlands already had a tradition begun by Johannes Ockeghem and Josquin Desprès, and which saw remarkable growth in the sixteenth century. Tylman Susato, originally from Cologne, was a music publisher and composer in Antwerp whose works included the *Hoboecken dans*, a work based on stylized folk music. It could well be to this piece that the circle of peasants in Bruegel's *Kermis at Hoboken* (fig. 34) are dancing. Adrien Willaert, from Bruges, became choir master at St. Mark's, Venice, in 1527. As for the great Orlande de Lassus from Mons (fig. 33), Susato published his first songs in 1555—the starting point of a body of work "that was to make him … the most successful of composers."[42] Such was the renown of musicians from the Netherlands that Philip II, despite the conflicts at the time, asked Margaret of Parma to send some to him.[43]

Sculpture, too, enjoyed real prestige. Jacques Dubroeucq, also originally from Mons, made the Renaissance rood-screen for St. Waudru in Mons, and the reclining figure of Boussu (fig. 35). He is a typical example of the versatile artists of the time, for he was also an architect (who notably designed Mary of Hungary's palaces at Binche and Mariemont), engineer, decorator, and urban planner. He was awarded the title of "master artist to the emperor" in 1555. One of his pupils was Jean de Boulogne—Giambologna—who was to achieve greatness in Florence

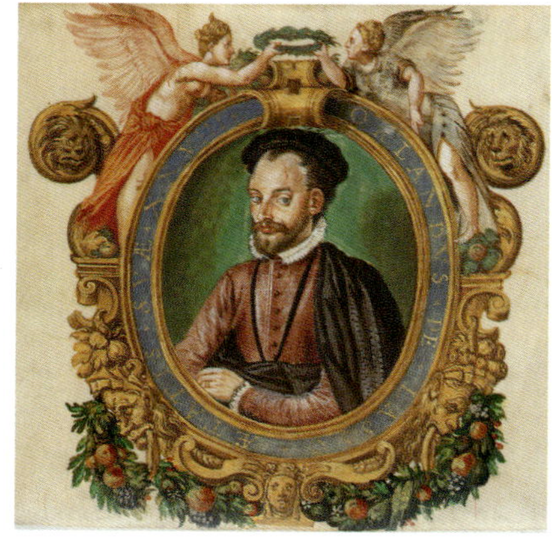

33

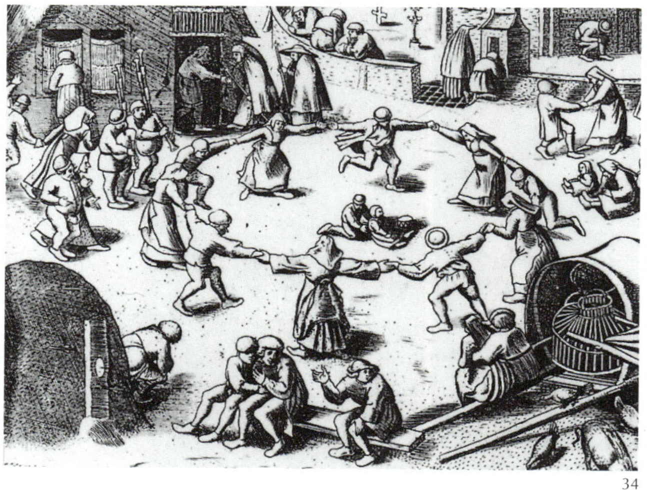

34

33. Hans Muelich, *Portrait of Orlande de Lassus at the Age of Twenty-Eight*, Codex 18744, 1558–60, fol. 35. Gouache. Vienna, Österreichische Nationalbibliotek, Musikabteilung

34. Frans Hogenberg, *Kermis at Hoboken* (detail), after Pieter Bruegel, ca. 1559. Engraving. Brussels, Bibliothèque royale Albert I, print room

35. Jacques Dubroeucq, *Reclining Figure of Jean de Hennin-Liétard, Count of Boussu*, ca. 1551–62. Alabaster. Boussu-lez-Mons, cultural center

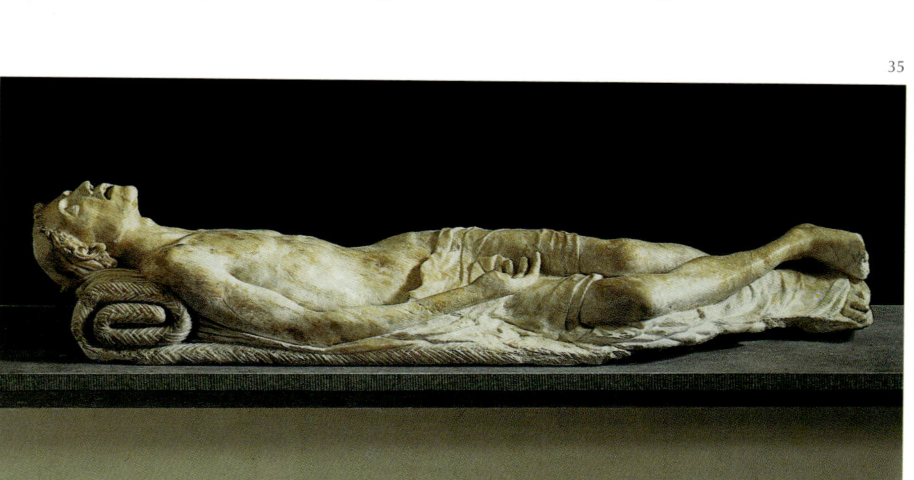

35

under the Medici. Cornelis Floris de Vriendt, who built the mausoleum of Christian III of Denmark, and brother of the painter Frans Floris, supervised the building of Antwerp town hall, described at the time as a "very magnificent building [which] can be counted among the wonders of the world."[44]

In the realm of intellectual life, the ideas of Erasmus were spread as he traveled from Rotterdam to Basel, via Paris, England, Italy, and Brussels, and as he attempted to reconcile ancient and Christian thought. Erasmus was equally at home writing satire: His *In Praise of Folly* was published in 1511 and dedicated to his friend Thomas More, whose *Utopia* was published in 1516 in Leuven by Thierry Martens, who was also the publisher of the works of the Spanish humanist Juan Luis Vives. The following year, also in Leuven, the celebrated College of the Three Languages was founded, where a scholar could study Hebrew, Latin, and Greek. Editions of Sebastian Brant's famous 1494 allegory *Ship of Fools* were translated from the German into Flemish and other languages from 1500. The first half of the sixteenth century also saw the publication of Anna Bijns's poems, *Refreinen*, and of Rabelais's earthy fantasy *Gargantua*. Bruegel can hardly have been oblivious to all these developments.

In 1549 Christophe Plantin set up his printing workshop, At the Sign of the Golden Compasses, in Antwerp (fig. 38). Famous both as a publisher and an illustrator, Plantin opened channels of communication between classical and popular culture, publishing both in Latin and in the vernacular languages

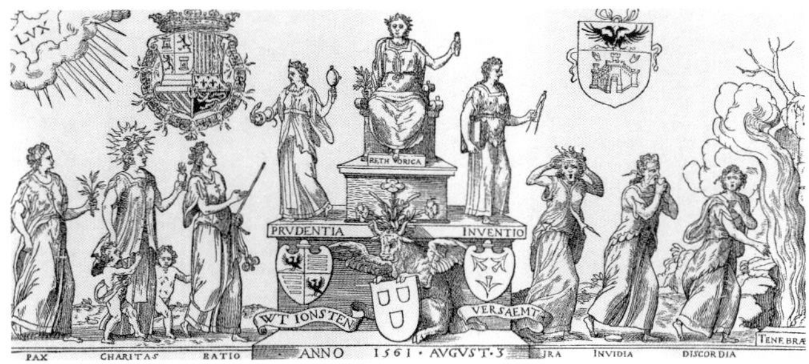

36

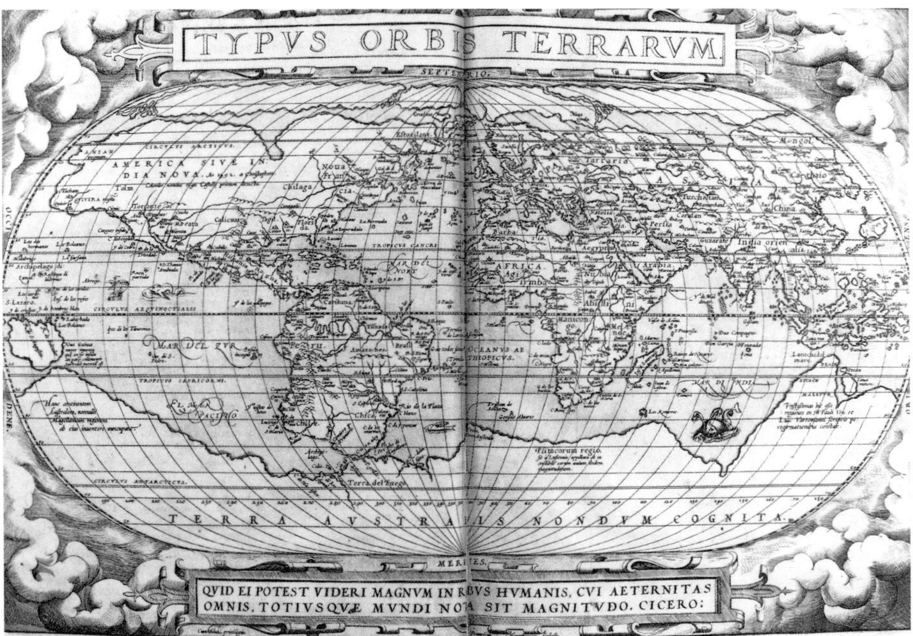

37

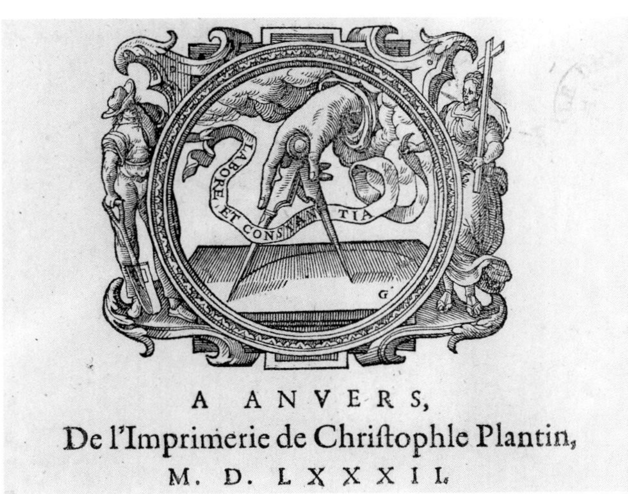

38

French and Flemish. He produced sacred works, grammars, Erasmus's *Adages*, Ronsard's *Roman de Renart*, and many others—a total of some 1,500 works. In the field of science Plantin published the work of the anatomist Vesalius and the botanist Dodoneus. His greatest achievements were the *Theatrum Orbis Terrarum* by Ortelius (who had joined the Antwerp guild as a map illuminator in 1547), published in 1570 to outstanding acclaim, and the Polyglot Bible, in Greek, Latin, Hebrew, Syriac, and Chaldean, published in 1572 and 1573.

Ortelius and cartography were evidence of an opening up to the outside world during a century of discoveries. Cortez had completed his conquest of Mexico in 1527, and Pizarro, Almagro, and Valdivia that of Peru in 1541. The work of Mercator, Copernicus, and Sebastian Munster saw the light during the same decade.

36. *Invitation from the "De Violieren" Chamber of Rhetoric to the "Landjuweel" to an event held in Antwerp in 1561.* Woodcut. Antwerp, Museum Plantin-Moretus

37. Frans Hogenberg, *Theatrum Orbis Terrarum,* map of the world by Abraham Ortelius, 1570. Engraving. Antwerp, Museum Plantin-Moretus

38. Plantin's typographical mark printed on the title page of Guicciardini's *Description of All of the Netherlands,* 1582

Chambers of rhetoric—that is, literary societies—played an important role in the spread of ideas. In Antwerp the celebrated "De Violieren" (The Wallflower) allied itself, from 1480 onwards, with the St Luke painters' guild (fig. 39). Rhetoricians—who came from many social classes but especially from among the skilled craftsmen and traders—put on plays and held poetry readings either in private or in public.[45] Bruegel shows an example of these in *Temperance* (1560). The link between drama and painting was therefore strong, as Bruegel again demonstrates, a year later, in *The Kermis of St George* (fig. 296). The chambers of rhetoric would periodically come together at literary competitions called "Landjuwelen" (jewels of the land), which featured processions and festivities; one of the most famous in this period was held in Antwerp in 1561 (fig. 36).

39. Medal of the guild of St Luke. Recto: *Winged Ox Holding the Arms of the Guild;* Verso: *The Art of Painting, Between Architecture and Sculpture.* Copper. Antwerp, Museum Vleeshuis

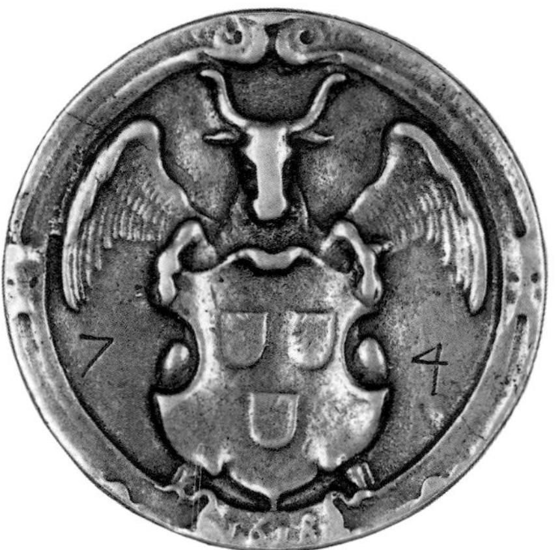
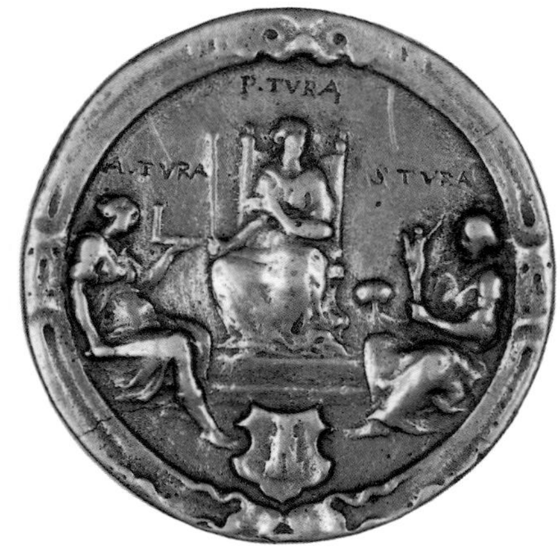

39

PAINTING IN CONTEXT

As well as the subjects offered by folk tradition, painters in the Netherlands could also draw on a great range of images from illuminated manuscripts. The best work of this type at the beginning of the sixteenth century was by Simon Bening and Gerard Horenbout, in the *Grimani Breviary* or the *Hours of Notre-Dame of Hennessy*. However, the technique of illumination, which had been a major art form during the fourteenth and fifteenth centuries, in the sixteenth began to decline in popularity and gave way to engraving. The engravings of Martin Schongauer, Albrecht Dürer (who visited Brussels and Antwerp in 1520–21), the Beham brothers, Lucas van Leyden, and others, became a vehicle for new forms and ideas. The works of Dürer—his own genius aside—exemplified the Italian formal vocabulary that he had learned from Jacopo de' Barbari, Andrea Mantegna, and Giovanni Bellini. Already at the end of the fifteenth century themes inspired by the history and mythology of the ancient world, such as the *Judgment of Paris,* were being disseminated by engravings. The plates of Marcantonio Raimondi, for example, carried the style of Raphael north to the Netherlands. The art of engraving found a home at the Four Winds, the famous workshop Hieronymus Cock set up in 1548.

While Hieronymus Bosch and his brilliant creations dominated Dutch painting at the turn of the century, the spirit of the Italian Renaissance began to permeate all categories of painting—portraits, landscapes, mythological, religious, and genre scenes—and this continued until the dawn of the succeeding century, with Martin de Vos, Paul Bril, and the young Rubens. The later Bruges school of Isenbrant and Benson, pupils of Gerard David, was already imbued with the new spirit. Humanism and mannerism came to the fore in the art of Quentin Metsys, Jan Gossart, and

Bernard van Orley. Italian art also influenced the work of Pieter Coecke, Jan Vermeyen (who accompanied Charles V to Tunis), and Lambert Lombard, born in Liège, who was a great admirer of classical antiquity. Later came Jan Metsys, the son of Quentin, whose female figures were inspired by Italian painting and perhaps by the School of Fontainebleau, as well as by the work of Michiel van Coxcie, nicknamed "the Flemish Raphael," and Frans Floris, Bruegel's exact contemporary. With this new interest in Italian art, a journey to Italy came to be regarded as essential to an artist's training, and gave rise to the term "Fiamminghi" ("Flemings") used in Italy to denote these artists from the Netherlands.

As we have noted, according to Karel van Mander, Pieter Coecke was Bruegel's teacher. While Coecke's direct influence on his pupil may be debatable, it is certainly present in Bruegel's choice of such subjects as the conversion of St. Paul, Christ carrying the Cross, John the Baptist preaching, the Triumph of Death, the seven deadly sins, or the story of Daedalus, as well as his composition of various works—for example *The Manners and Customs of the Turks* (fig. 40)— and certain details in his paintings. Coecke also played a decisive role in the spread of humanism through his editions and translations of the architectural treatises of Vitruvius and Serlio. These writers had an obvious influence on painters of architectural subjects such as Hans Vredeman de Vries, notably in his *Scenographiae*, published by Hieronymus Cock in 1560.

Before landscape painting blossomed to its fullest extent in the work of Bruegel, it underwent its own evolution in the paintings of Joachim Patinir, Cornelis Metsys, Jan van Amstel, Lucas Gassel, Matthijs Cock, and Herri met de Bles. Religious themes were often embedded in what appeared to be predominantly secular compositions, and this more genre-like approach characterized the treatment of subjects that developed in Antwerp from 1530 onward in the works of Jan van Hemessen, Pieter Aertsen (both natives of northern provinces), and Aertsen's nephew, Joachim Beuckelaer. Among these various tendencies, Bruegel went his own way. After his death, Michiel van Coxcie, official painter under Philip II, was to produce religious works; Hans Bol and Gillis van Valckenborch would concentrate on landscape painting; while the portraitists Frans Pourbus, Adrien Thomasz Key, and Antonis Mor enjoyed international careers painting likenesses of the great men and women of their day.[46]

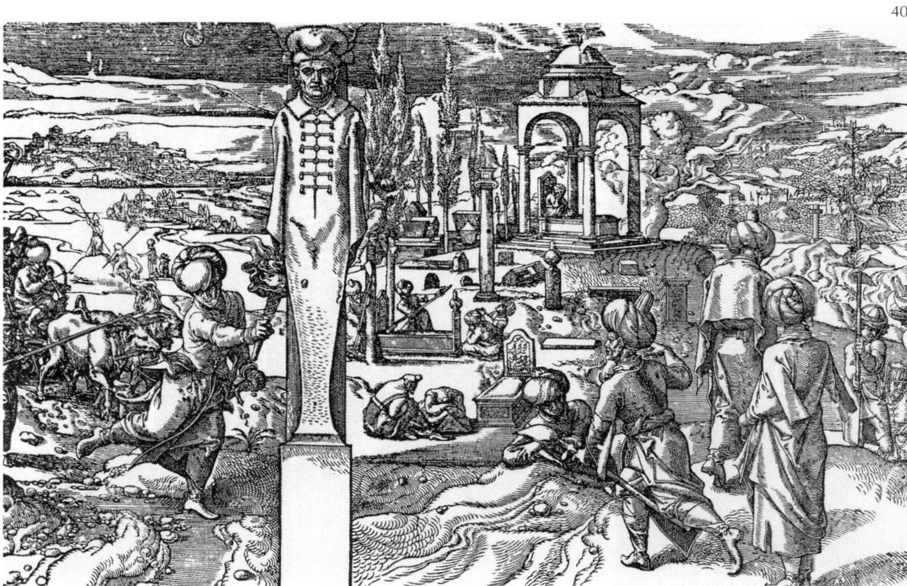

40. Pieter Coecke van Aelst, *The Manners and Customs of the Turks* (detail). Woodcut published in 1553, after drawings made the same year. Brussels, Bibliothèque royale Albert I, print room

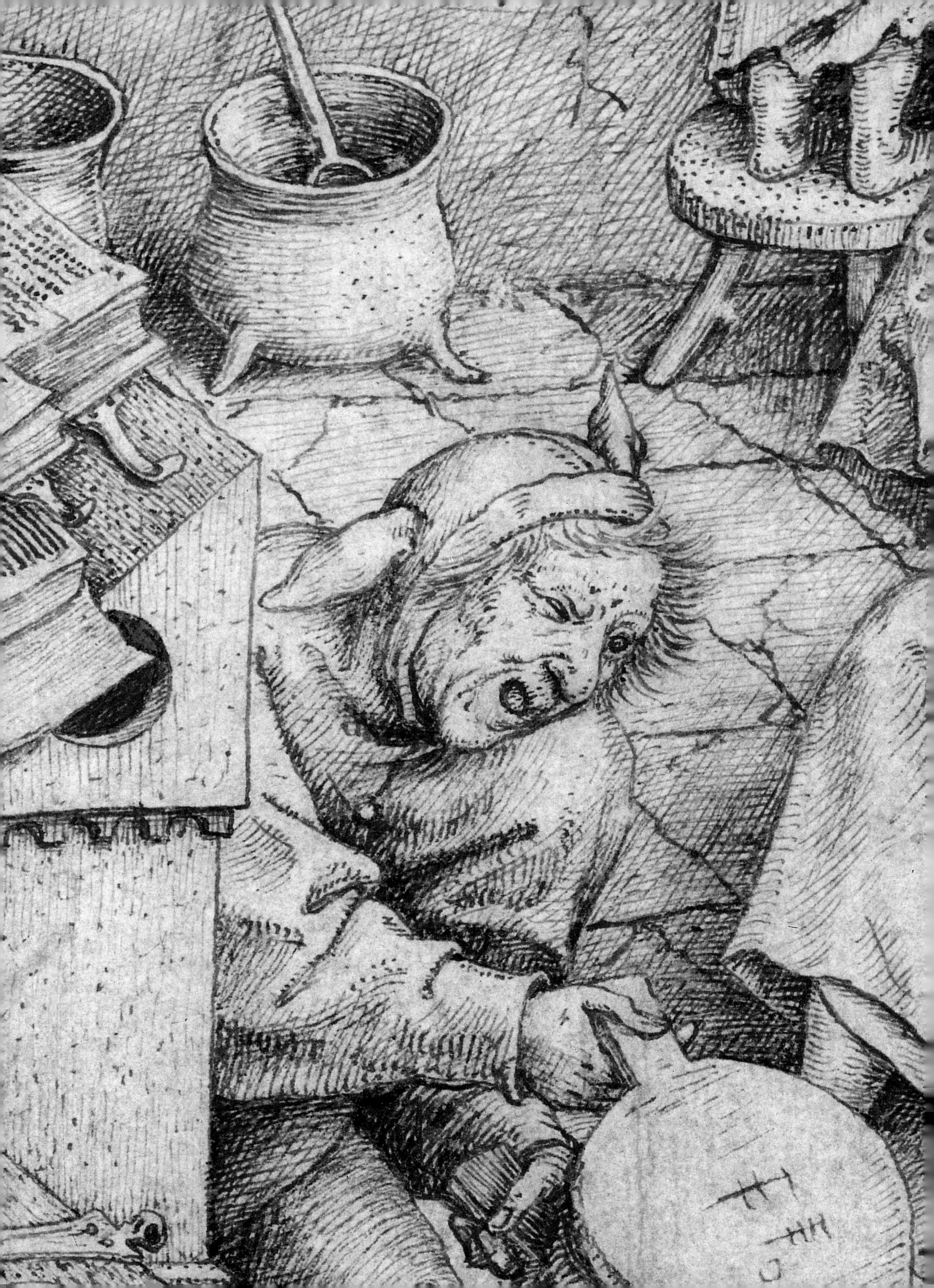

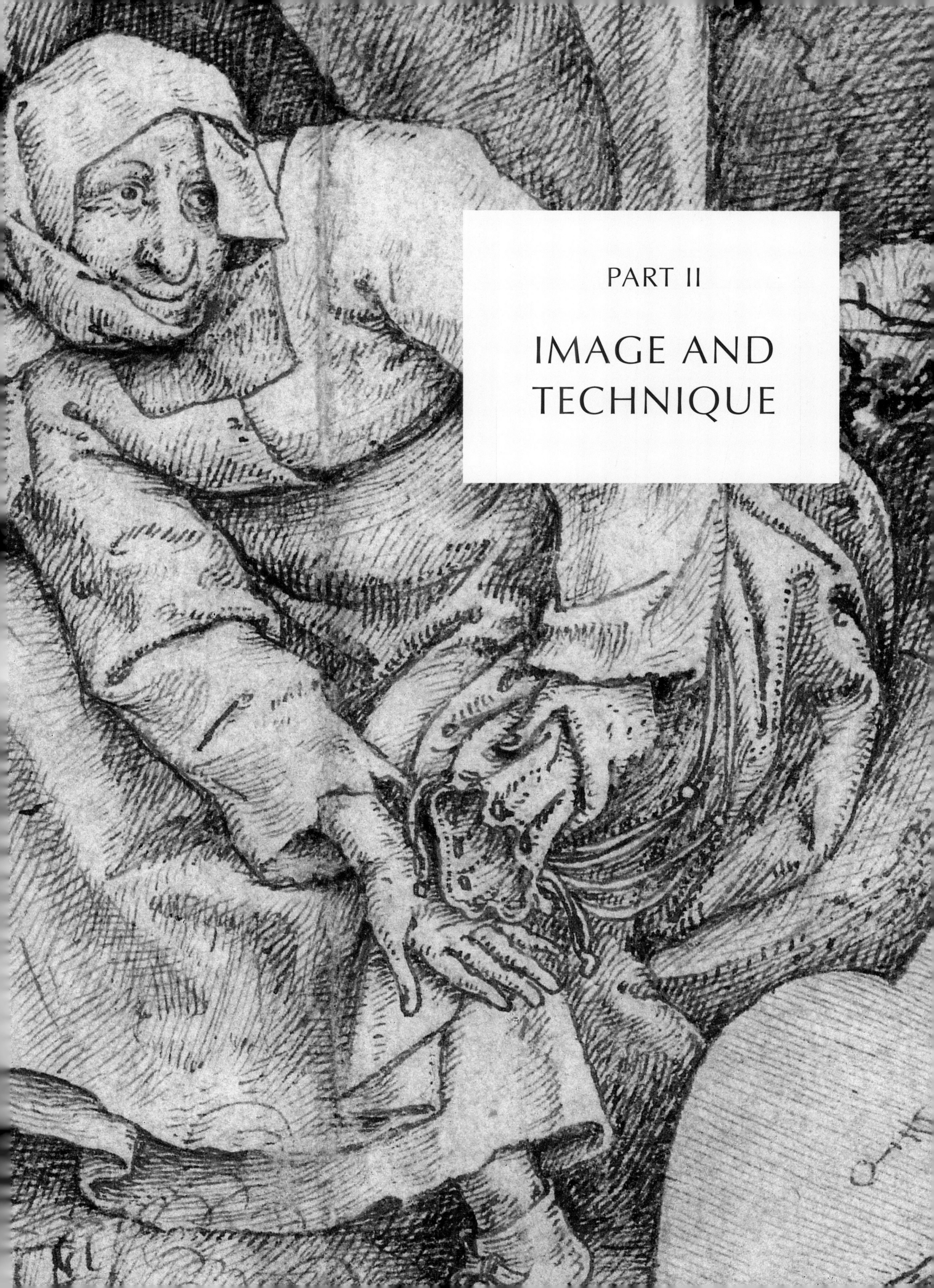

PART II

IMAGE AND TECHNIQUE

THE BRUEGEL IMAGE

Is there a characteristic Bruegel image? It would be truer to say that there are many, for the diversity and richness of Bruegel's work has been the subject of many studies, allusions, and interpretations. As a result the Bruegel image has been beset by preconceptions and used to demonstrate a number of theories. It has been pressed into service, commented upon, even travestied. But of course, as with any artistic creation, neither the works nor the artist who produced them came out of nowhere. The man himself—his origin, qualities, and faults, as well as the time, place, and social circumstances in which he lived—all played their part, as did talent, skill, professional contacts, and luck. Add genius to the mix and the result is dazzling, but also complex and very difficult to summarize.

If we look at a great work of art—Jan van Eyck's *Adoration of the Mystic Lamb* altarpiece in Ghent, Hugo van der Goes's *Adoration of the Shepherds*, Albrecht Dürer's *Melancholia,* Raphael's *School of Athens*, or Michelangelo's *Last Judgment*— we are aware, beyond our purely subjective response to these works, that we are in the presence of a masterly creation. What do the faith, happiness, intelligence, or strength of these artists matter? The image is there in front of us—whether expressive or mysterious—in all its brilliant intensity. The same can be said of many paintings of the succeeding centuries, of works by Rubens, Rembrandt, Velasquez, Watteau, Goya, Turner, Manet, and Cézanne, and equally of Picasso, Seurat, and Klee. We can appreciate the worlds these artists have created more or less completely, depending on our knowledge and taste. But beyond that, what should we consider? Subject, form, color, the approach to representation, expression, invention? Should we see Rubens primarily as the painter of the ceiling at the Banqueting House at Whitehall, or the master of the brilliant oil sketch? Should we remember Goya for his *Nude Maja,* or for his *Disasters of War*? Is Picasso most significant for his blue period, rose period, his cubist paintings, or *Guernica*? There are many styles and approaches that a single view of an artist's work can combine, that an artist can capture, and that the passage of time can blur, emphasizing some things and forgetting others, or can rediscover in a new light.

Then there is Bruegel, with his images created in a distant time that is nonetheless close to our own in its questioning humanism, its curiosity about the past, its openness to the wider world, its ideological struggles, its absolutism, and its commercialism. In the midst of that time, Bruegel thought for himself and remained independent, perhaps because he rejected conventional ideas and ways of thinking imposed by others. But, of course, Bruegel's images do not represent a complete break from the past—they are merely different. Although most appear not to have been painted in response to aristocratic commissions, since he worked for a print publisher many of them must have been painted in response to the demands of customers. And, as always, when the direction in which one should move is not completely clear or rigorously laid out, the risks of moving along it are hard to spot. Bruegel had great freedom because he worked in an age of change.

Bruegel's surviving body of work is small, consisting of about forty paintings, a similar number of drawings, and twice that number of engravings, plus works

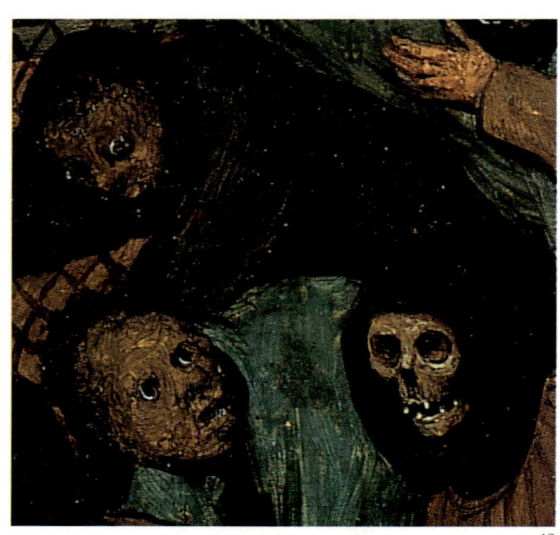

41. Pieter Bruegel, *Haymaking* (detail), 1565.
Oil on panel, 44¾ x 62¼ in. (114 x 158 cm).
Prague, Národní Galerie

42. Pieter Bruegel, *The Triumph of Death* (detail),
ca. 1562. Oil on panel, 46 x 63¾ in. (117 x 162 cm).
Madrid, Prado

PRECEDING PAGES
Pieter Bruegel, *The Alchemist* (detail), 1558.
Pen and brown ink, 12⅛ x 17⅞ in. (30.8 x 45.3 cm).
Berlin, Staatliche Museen, Kupferstichkabinett

whose authorship is debatable and others that are known to us through copies. Yet this limited oeuvre contains enormous variety: images of nature in its many moods, of people and human behavior, fantastic visions, religious subjects, allegories, proverbial themes, esoteric images, genre scenes, and social realism. All are facets of his work, but they often overlap.

COMPLEX WORKS, MULTIPLE READINGS

Bruegel's works can be read on several levels, for they always contain some interfering element—a door left ajar, a window that can be opened, a shadow to probe. Their scope is widened not only by the complexity of their content but by the artist's obvious desire to capture the world and convey the life within it. Bruegel makes himself known through his images alone: he left no written statements about them, and no explanation; nothing comes across from his works as a whole to indicate for certain whether he had a political, social, or philosophical message. Such ideas are certainly there, but he takes no discernible stand on any subject. In any case, why should an artist's works simply be reduced to the expression of a set of beliefs? Bruegel's century was one in which opinions clashed and humanism came under scrutiny. Because he lived in an age of violent disagreement, and because there were many conflicts of viewpoint during his lifetime, many have endeavored to find in Bruegel the illustrator of one line of argument or another— hence the prejudices with which he has been tarnished and the influences that supposedly left an impression on him. But according to Van Mander, Bruegel simply "took pleasure in watching peasants eat, drink, dance, jump, woo each other, and otherwise enjoy themselves."[1] And Guicciardini described him, while he was still alive, as "the second Hieronymus Bosch."[2]

Posterity has long been unjust in remembering chiefly the works that cast him in the role of a joker, conjuring up visions of country festivals, popular entertainments, bloated faces, and vulgar incidents. If this image is based on subjects such as *The Wedding Banquet* (fig. 300) or *The Peasants' Dance* (fig. 307), it applies only to the painting's outer skin; and if it seeks justification in some detail or other, it wrongly draws a generalization from just a single element. This leaves the image truncated; a work of art—which is neither a slogan nor a stereotype—cannot be reduced to a label. Bruegel the Joker, in isolation, does not exist. While there are satirical aspects to his work, they are mixed with many other qualities that are much more intrinsically human and universal.

Bruegel's breadth of resonance can irritate anyone drawn to simplistic explanations. The result has been misguided shortcuts and reductive formulae to satisfy critics who are intellectually in a hurry. Such thinking, however, can reduce the achievements of even the greatest artists to the lowest common denominator. Bruegel belongs to that race of giants who disturb us, who can keep us awake at night. When we reduce his art to his peasant pictures, his country revels, and his proverb-pieces, we can see him as merely anecdotal, or even comical. This particular misinterpretation is so ingrained in the thinking of our time, that many people cannot tell the masterpiece from the copy, and in their minds merge, in one simpleminded view, Bruegel, his sons, and all of his imitators. But if this is our understanding of Pieter Bruegel, how then do we think about *The Triumph of*

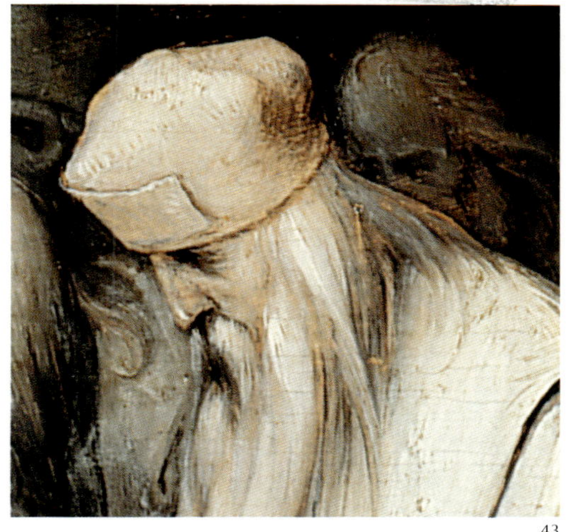

43. Pieter Bruegel, *Christ and the Woman Taken in Adultery* (detail), 1565. Oil on panel, 9$\frac{1}{2}$ x 13$\frac{1}{2}$ in. (24.1 x 34.3 cm). London, Courtauld Institute of Art, Count Antoine Seilern Collection

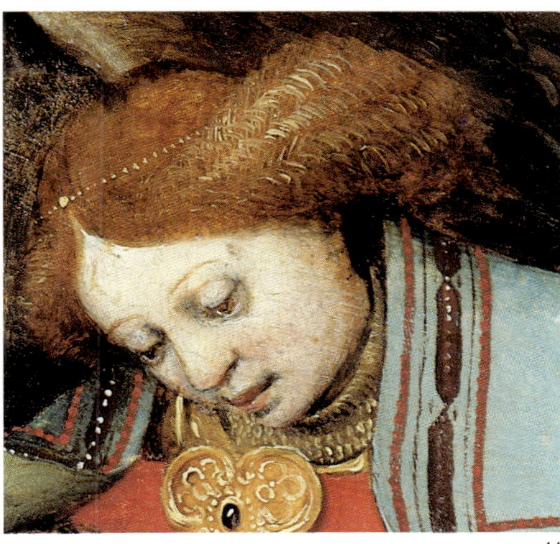

44. Pieter Bruegel, *The Fall of the Rebel Angels* (detail), 1562. Oil on panel, 46$\frac{5}{8}$ x 64 in. (118.5 x 162.5 cm). Brussels, Musées royaux des Beaux-Arts de Belgique

Death (fig. 109), *Christ Carrying the Cross* (fig. 51), or *The Blind Leading the Blind* (fig. 69)? Where is Bruegel the Joker in these paintings?

Even during the artist's lifetime the disturbing visions and timeless truths of Bruegel's art, presented as they were, were brushed aside in favor of seeing in his work a simple, everyday realism. Barely three years after the painter's death, Lampsonius paid tribute above all to his depiction of "jokes."[3] One is tempted to believe that people must always turn away when a relentlessly truthful mirror is held up to their faces, preferring instead to take pleasure in their own vision of themselves. This urge to prettify has often brushed aside a worrying image to make way for a reassuring one, an attitude of mind that has been reinforced often down the centuries. Now that a number of distinguished art historians—Georges Hulin de Loo, Gustav Glück, and Fritz Grossmann, to name only three—have restored to our understanding some of the harder truths of Bruegel's art and revealed many of his hidden meanings, can we see Bruegel once more as he was? Probably not. Bruegel's works are a universe so manifold, so rich, and so complex, that they will always be open to new interpretation.

THE LIMITS OF INTERPRETATION

Let us, for simplicity's sake, divide the analysts of Bruegel's work into two categories. The first are those who, concerned with total objectivity, argue that his sole sources of inspiration were illustrations in breviaries and calendars, prints, and country proverbs. The second group are those who use his images to construct theories about his work that range from seeing it as a series of political or religious statements to an exposition of esoteric symbols. Even though all of these theorists manage to support their claims, the first group are excessively cautious, and the second, too reckless. One must ask: Is it even possible to place Bruegel within a given stylistic category? Should we call him "Gothic" because he painted the Virgin, St. John, and the Holy Women in the tradition of his fifteenth-century Flemish forebears? Can we call him a "Mannerist" because the figures in his painting of the Adoration of the Magi are elongated?

Should he be seen—as a contingent from Guicciardini on have insisted—as a follower of Hieronymus Bosch, because he used elements of Bosch's vocabulary in *Dulle Griet* (fig. 101) and *The Fall of the Rebel Angels* (fig. 114)? Or should we call him a "realist," giving the greatest weight to everyday aspects of his work, placing him in the company of Pieter Aertsen and the other sixteenth-century Flemish genre-painters, and giving credence to the legend of the peasant-loving Bruegel that has been circulating since the time of Van Mander?

All of these questions, propositions, and extrapolations could just as well be used to support the idea of Bruegel as a Catholic or heretic, a humanist philosopher, or a pessimistic moralizer. But such a diversity of ideas is inherent in the breadth of genius, and in the fact that the sixteenth century in northern Europe was a highly complex period that cannot easily be summed up. For it was complex indeed, from its earliest years for Dürer, as it was, some decades later, for Shakespeare. The multitude of possible interpretations makes Bruegel all the more important today, in an equally protean and contradictory age.

To glorify Bruegel for having combined, in a single painting, a hundred proverbs or children's games is to reduce him to a mere inventor of parlor games.

But his genius lies in his juxtaposition of lifelike details while concealing the virtuosity of his work. It consists of creating a three-dimensional universe by gathering together a multiplicity of incidents and figures, a teeming world encompassed by laws of composition that cannot be explained merely by manual dexterity and a recourse to the tradition of Flemish painting.

Bruegel's density of content also reflects the breadth of the subjects, which attract the eye with their feeling for life and emotion, from the brightly colored *Wedding Feast* (fig. 300) to the sober grisaille of *The Death of the Virgin* (fig. 152), from the heavy stillness of *Harvest* (fig. 175), to the expressive tumult of *The Gloomy Day* (fig. 187). This very richness of incident, created in response to the stimuli of the visible world, allowed the artist to attain a superb equilibrium, bringing together a tradition whose every resource he knew intimately with the spirit of his own time.

Bruegel was a philosopher, too; he knew that all extremes oppose each other in vain. In *The Battle Between Carnival and Lent* (fig. 125), he depicts such an absurd conflict, around which are scattered fragments of the real world, mixed with shreds of dream and fantasy. He knew the consequences of foolishness and excess; he fixes the leg of Icarus forever into the oblivion of the ocean—and in human memory—and he carelessly envelops the top of an unfinished Tower of Babel in a fold in the clouds.

Although Bruegel described things that he saw in his own time, he also gave his viewers a number of glimpses into the future. His carnival figures foreshadow the ghoulish clowns of James Ensor, just as the skies and water of his landscapes seem to speak the language of expressionism. *The Triumph of Death* (fig 109) is a terrifying vision, a prescient image of the concentration camps and genocidal wars of the twentieth century. And *The Blind Leading the Blind* (fig. 69) seems to foretell the capture of movement on camera.

Bruegel's figures cannot be reduced to a type. They are individuals distinctly marked by life, by the society around them, and by their own inner worlds. We do not see generalized faces so much as particular personalities, from the satisfied bride in *The Wedding Feast* (fig. 300) to the dreamer in *The Land of Cockaigne* (fig. 269). We do not see a single gesture so much as complex movement, from the dramatic march of *Dulle Griet* (fig. 101) to the noble reserve of St. Joseph. And yet, the painter's creative generosity is not diluted by being cast so widely. On the contrary, Bruegel's art conveys expressions and moods through his paintings' three-dimensional creations, no two of which are alike. Each is complete in its richness and power. And in each work we can discern, within its fundamental rhythms, aspects of nature that are ceaselessly renewed, along with the range of feelings that can animate an individual or take hold of a crowd.

Destiny does not rule supreme, nor does the despair of the human condition. Even when tragedy is at its height, even as the mounted figure of Death, in *The Triumph of Death* (fig. 109), drives before him an army of skeletons, a pair of lovers remains alive, exchanging glances, defying destruction, and leaving a door open to the future. Conversely, when the rhythm of events, people, or indeed the *Seasons* is a peaceful one, as in *The Return of the Herd* (fig. 174)—when all seems to be following its regular course, a grating note appears: it is only a detail, but the distant gallows reminds us of another reality (fig. 183). Bruegel always seems to be aware of the other side of the story; and he warns us, gives us hope.

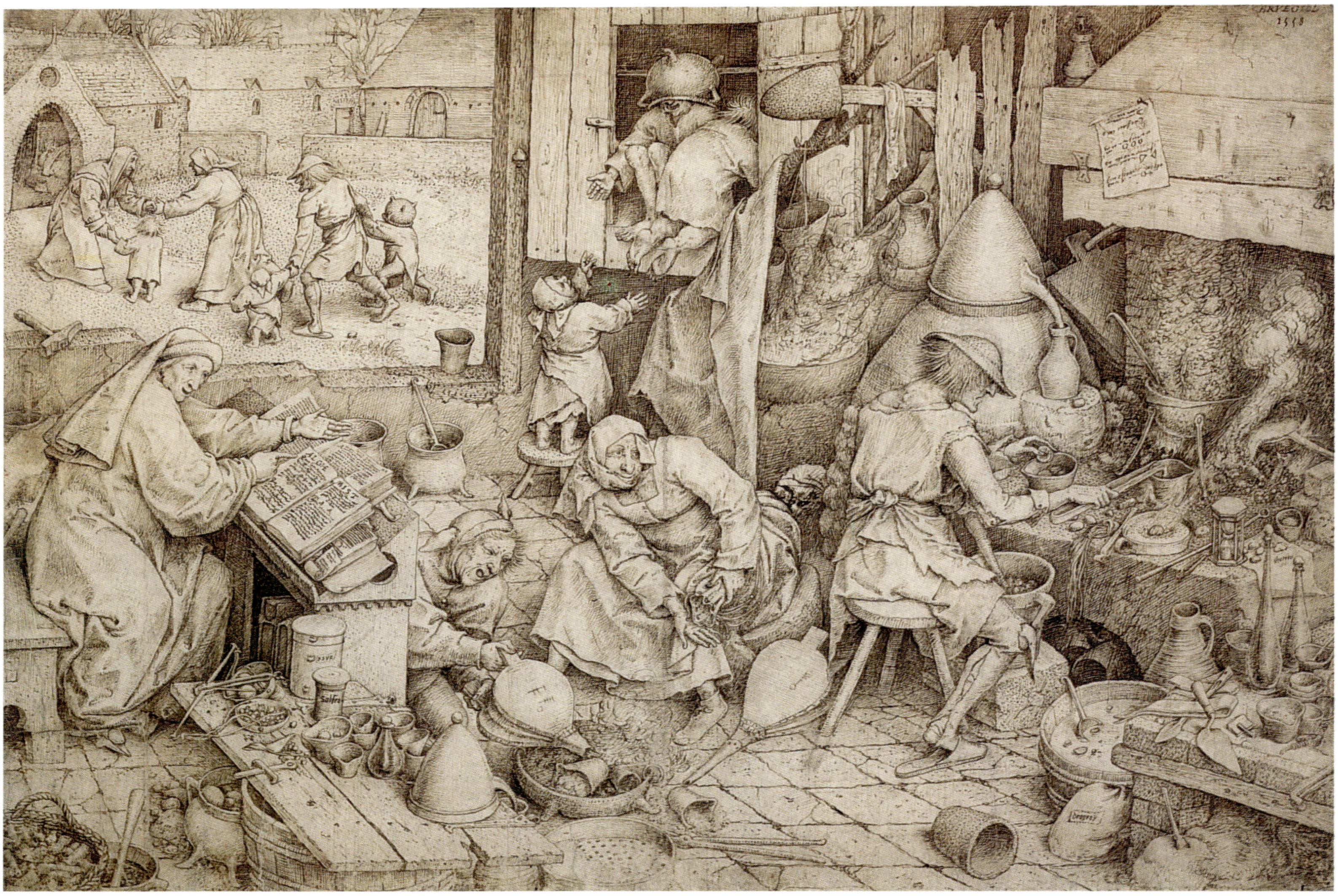

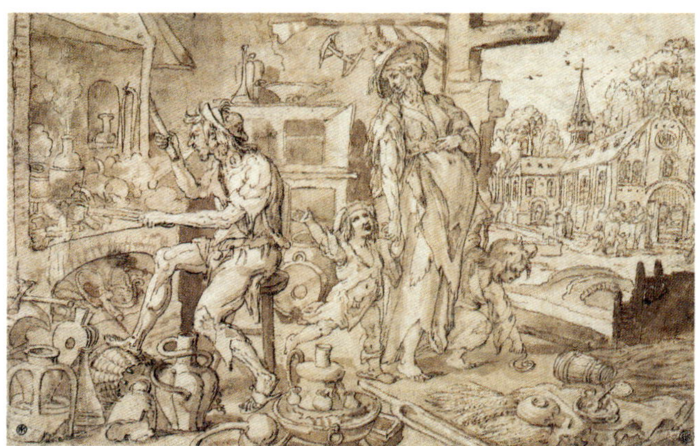

45. Pieter Bruegel, *The Alchemist*, 1558. Pen and brown ink, 12⅛ x 17⅞ in. (30.8 x 45.3 cm). Berlin, Staatliche Museen, Kupferstichkabinett

46. Martin de Vos, *The Alchemist*, ca. 1570. Pen, brown ink, brown wash, and traces of black chalk, 7¼ x 11⅛ in. (18.3 x 28.4 cm). Paris, École nationale supérieure des beaux-arts

As a painter Bruegel constructs his works carefully. If his idea leads him into a blind alley, as in the *Two Monkeys* (fig. 213), which are chained, the image does not confine itself to the sad reality it depicts, but opens up to something else—literally, in this case: The sense of the two monkeys' yearning for freedom is answered by a luminous, open sky. When the composition is panoramic and expansive, suggesting that there is room for the whole world to breath, as in *The Census at Bethlehem* (fig. 200), our gaze is eventually drawn to a concentrated mob of people who seem ready to explode into violence. Bruegel was already looking carefully at what people in the nineteenth century called the "human comedy" and what people in the twentieth called the "human condition." To understand the lessons he drew from it, we need to look long and hard at his paintings, for nothing is accidental, or superfluous. Every element has its place, like a word in a sentence; and if a particular detail holds our attention, it is all the better to lead the eye along its journey.

THE LESSONS OF *THE ALCHEMIST*

Bruegel's complexity can be distracting and provocative. This is true of *The Alchemist* (fig. 45) of 1558, a drawing that was to be made into an engraving, which intrigues us and raises questions in our minds. The subject attracted great interest at the time, in the same way that other sciences or occult practices such as magic and witchcraft did. Bruegel shows us an alchemist in his laboratory, busy at his furnace, while his wife tries in vain to extract some means of subsistence from his flat purse. The last coin this family has seems to be the one her husband is about to throw into the crucible, in his mad belief that he will be able to transmute base metal into gold. Two of the couple's children rummage in a cupboard, and a third, standing on a stool, cries and gesticulates impatiently, while all around is a confusion of instruments, converters, flasks, pots, bags, and bellows.

Through a window we can see in the background a later episode in the story of the alchemist: he and his destitute family finding refuge in a building that the engraving labels "hospital." The conclusion appears simple enough. Folly leads to ruin. Bruegel, however, introduces other elements into the composition: a hunched figure almost in the center of the drawing, wearing a fool's cap, busying himself with a bellows; and on the left, a man seated at a desk covered with open books, pointing to one on which we can read the words "Alghe mist"—Dutch for "All failed," and, of course, a pun on "alchemist." With his other hand, the scholar points to the alchemist, who is busily sealing his fate. Should we see a contrast between these two characters, one wise, the other foolish? The engraving, further-more, bears a Latin caption that we can read; however, it was added by the publisher, not the artist. The physical details of this work suggest that Bruegel had real—perhaps intimate—knowledge of his theme. Is the image simply a joke, or was it produced by someone who knew destitution well, who was not denouncing alchemy itself but merely the bad practice in alchemy? Did the artist show other currents of thought, or evince an interest in the philosopher's stone and its sym-bolism?[4] This apparently unambiguous work contains contradictory ideas—each of which may find echoes, suggestions, even firm statements, to support it among the customs, literature, or art of the time. Commentary that peels away the layers of this work and examines its period context is worthy of our attention—but does it bring us closer to Bruegel or is it simply a distraction? Did not the artist above all succeed in making an indelible image of a problem of his time? Even more important, does he not use that problem to teach a universal, human truth? That would seem to be the understanding of Martin de Vos in his own drawing *The Alchemist* (fig. 46), which was inspired by Bruegel's version.[5]

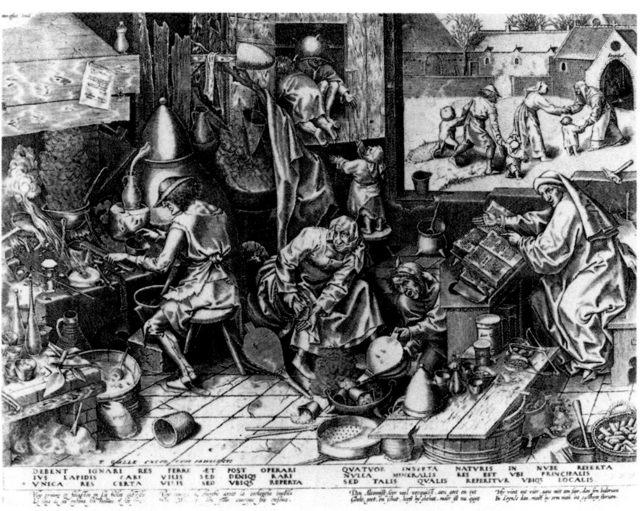

47. Philipp Galle, *The Alchemist*, after Pieter Bruegel, ca. 1558. Third state, signed by Theodor Galle. Engraving, 13 1/2 x 17 5/8 in. (34.2 x 44.9 cm). Brussels, Bibliothèque royale Albert I, print room

THE PERMANENCE OF *CHRIST CARRYING THE CROSS*

Another work by Bruegel shows the discrepancy between what happens by chance and the search for a deep emotion: *Christ Carrying the Cross* (1564), whose depiction and modeling are laden with resonances (fig. 51). In this case, the subject may be simple, but the composition is no less complex. Here the artist's approach is not new—it can already be seen in works by Herri met de Bles (fig. 48) and Jan van Amstel (fig. 49), though those works lack the liveliness and vast sweep of Bruegel's painting.

What strikes us first is the panoramic landscape, dotted with myriad details and swarming with people. There are two lighter areas to the right and left, be-tween which the painting's action flows. The sky, on the other hand, ranges in tone from brilliant luminosity to a dark mass of clouds—from morning to evening; at the right a tree flourishes alongside the spare shape of a wheel of torture, juxtaposing life and death. To the left is a sunlit town (did Bruegel live there?), and to the right a bare, open space.

Each of these details communicates a feeling of permanence, and of passing time, which the painter reinforces with further elements. In the right foreground are a group of lamenting figures; Gothic in spirit, they seem to have stepped out of a fifteenth-century painting. Why this anachronism? Is it the influence of another artist? That seems unlikely. Is it a quotation? Isn't the group outside the main story, which is taking place far behind it, outside the everyday, as if it were a painting within a painting?

The figure of Christ is not immediately apparent. Yet he is at the very center of the composition, at the intersection of two diagonals that can be traced between the painting's corners. He falls, halting the procession, which is moving from left to right (in the opposite direction to that in de Bles's painting). This astonishing cortège, which lies across several planes and follows several paths, is broken at intervals by secondary events, such as the arrest of Simon of Cyrene, which have the effect of prolonging the central action and thus accentuating the sensation of time passing.

Speaking of this work, the poet and critic Emile Verhaeren remarked at a conference in Paris in 1913: "The main action is swamped by a thousand others; it is not unity but multiplicity that characterizes Bruegel's art. He strikes not one blow but a hundred—first to seize our attention and then to jolt our sensibility."[6] A quarter of a century later André Lhote, a painter and an outstanding interpreter of art, remarked in his *Treatise on Landscape Painting*: "You can move a photographic mask, of any format, over the surface of this extraordinary painting (though what work of Bruegel's isn't?) and what appears within it *will always be a perfect composition*. This is because each element forms, with its neighbor, a proper composition, based on a system of compensating angles (right, acute, and obtuse), curves (more or less tight) and dimensions that all differ from one another. Nothing is more ordered, more baffling to analyze, or more inexhaustible than this apparent scattering. But this unparalleled skill is disguised by good humor; it is not aggressive like that of the great virtuosi of decorative composition such as Botticelli. The ordinary viewer does not notice hidden strength, as Cézanne, after Bruegel, was to discover."[7]

The colors contribute to the feeling of unity and passing time: light or dark patches echo each other across the composition, but also create a feeling of movement through the reds and blacks of the figures' clothes. The soldiers who accompany or guide this walk to Calvary wear red tunics, which suggest the "roode rocx" worn by the mercenaries of the Spanish crown at the time. How close these garments are to the uniforms of those soldiers, however, is debated.[8] Is this work intended as a commentary on events of its own time, denouncing the Spanish oppressor? Does it take sides?

Artists have often set scenes from the past in their own present, representing them to suit the tastes of their day. In Van Amstel's work of several decades earlier, the soldiers' standard is emblazoned with the coat of arms of Charles V.[9] In the nineteenth century, to pick an example closer to the present, James Ensor showed Jesus accompanied by a "civic guard" wearing the uniform of the time.[10] Is such commentary the heart of the painting's meaning? Or are the red tunics a happy

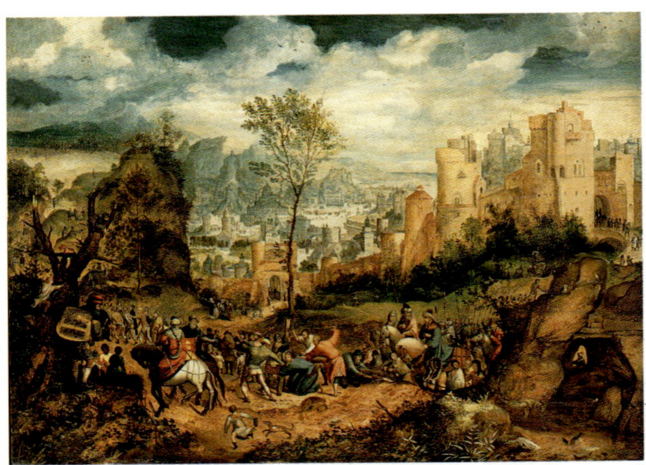

48. Herri met de Bles, *The Road to Calvary*, after 1536. Oil on panel, 32¼ x 45 in. (82.2 x 114.3 cm). Princeton, Princeton University, The Art Museum

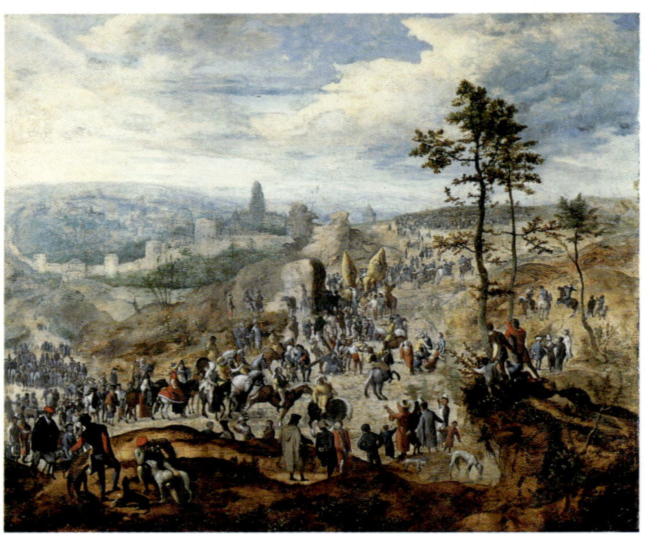

49. Jan van Amstel, *The Road to Calvary*, ca. 1530–35. Oil on panel, 27½ x 33 in. (70 x 84 cm). Paris, Louvre

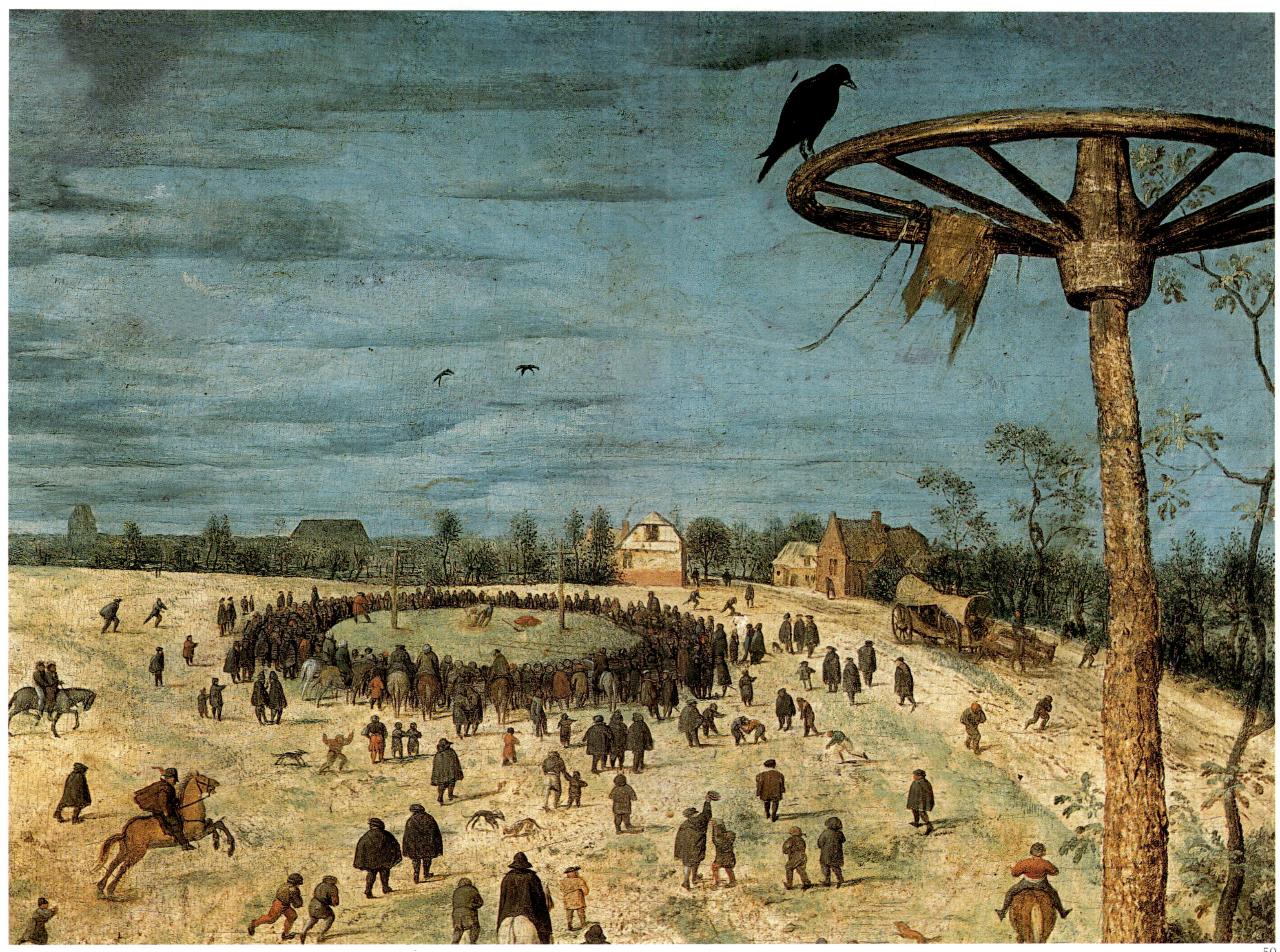

50. Pieter Bruegel, *Christ Carrying the Cross* (detail), 1564. Oil on panel, 48¾ x 66⅞ in. (124 x 170 cm). Vienna, Kunsthistorisches Museum

coincidence, meeting exactly the painter's desire and the picture's compositional demands, marking its passage of time with a vermilion trace, like a trail of blood across the painting? Here the interlocking meanings serve the needs of art—and vice versa.

However, this dense work contains many other elements, large and small, that can be highlighted or interpreted. A windmill, oddly perched on a rocky pinnacle, dominates the scene like a raised finger pointing at the sky. What does it mean, what might it symbolize? Is the pinnacle an obstacle that must be climbed before one can achieve the nourishment of ground flour? In compositional terms, the crag is almost essential; it is the axis around which the entire picture pivots—yet it has about it a touch that is almost whimsical. Today, we might see in it the prototype of a wind-powered generator, or of a Buddhist prayer wheel. Since there are already anachronisms in this work, one is tempted to interject a few from the present day, seeing that the picture seems so alive. Other explanations for the windmill have been suggested; for example, a sixteenth-century saying that "he turns with every wind."[11] The four winds would have been familiar to Bruegel the engraver; but this windmill does not move—it faces the lowering storm clouds like some heavenly clock.

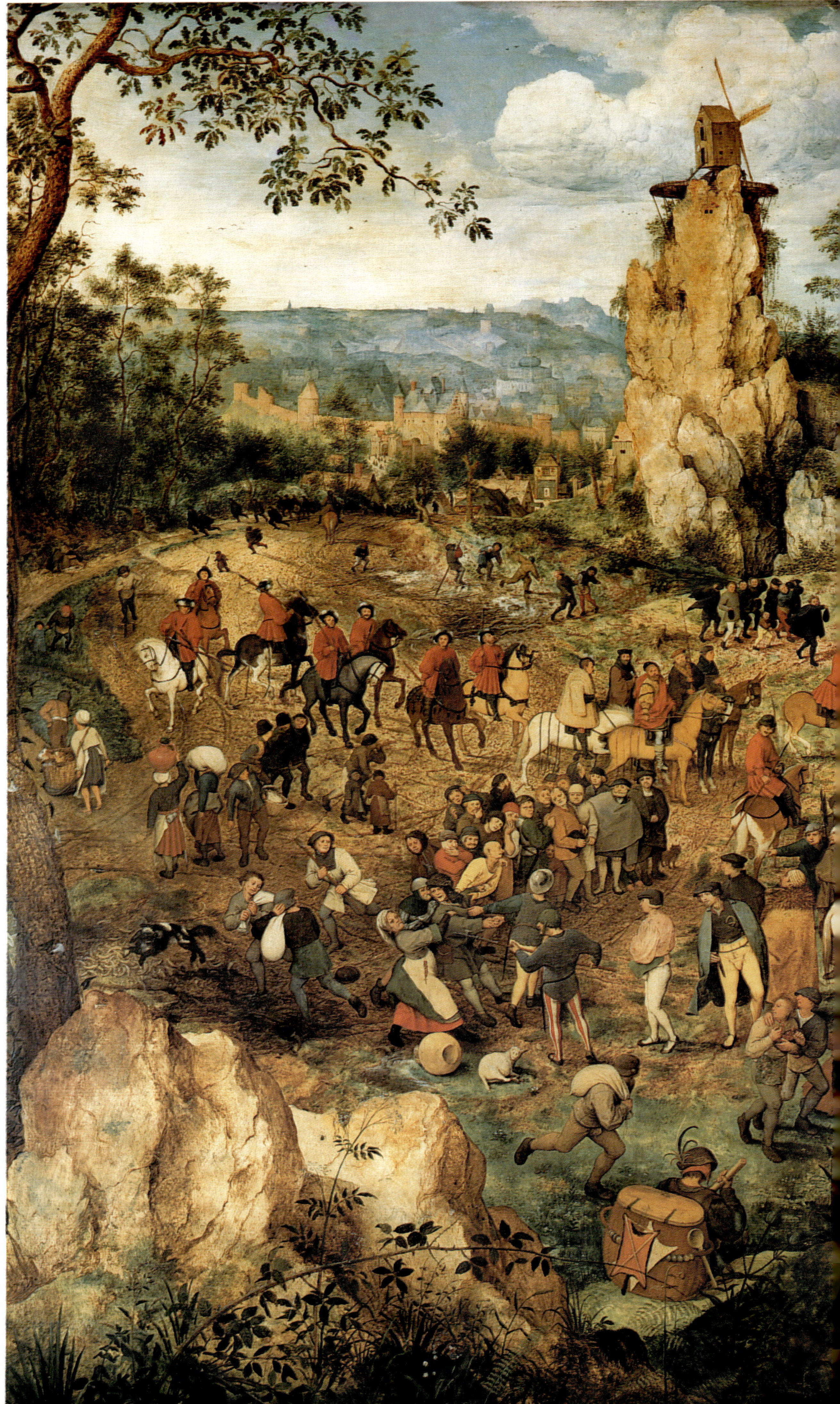

51–53. Pieter Bruegel, *Christ
Carrying the Cross*, 1564,
whole work and details. Oil on panel,
48³/₄ x 66⁷/₈ in. (124 x 170 cm).
Vienna, Kunsthistorisches Museum

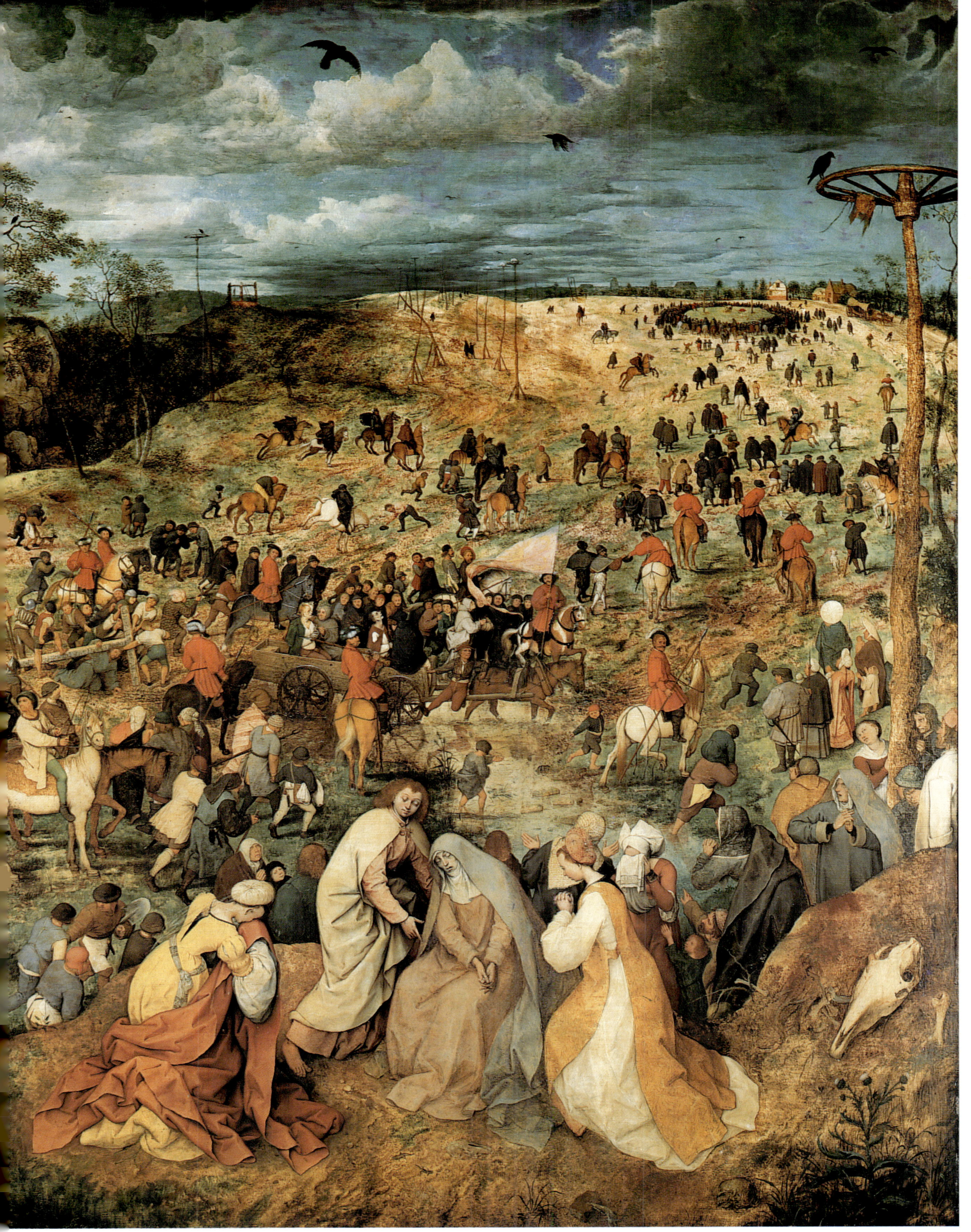

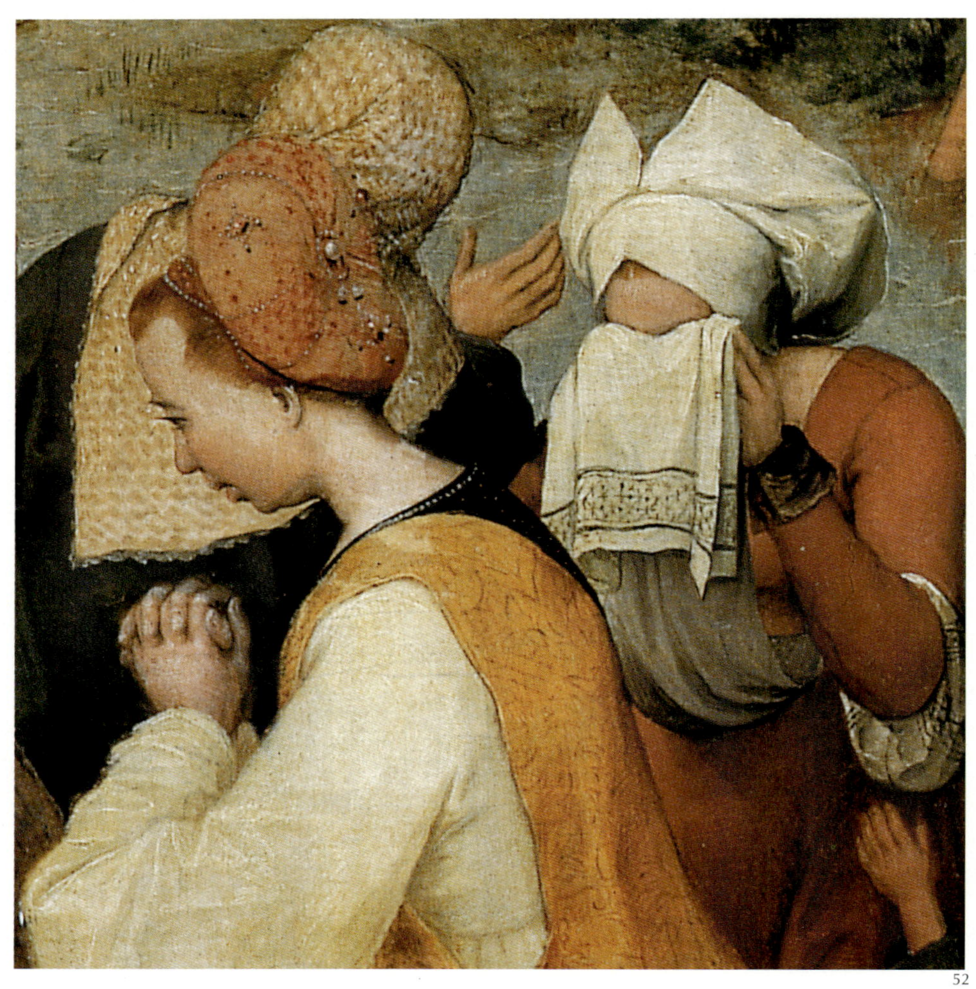

52

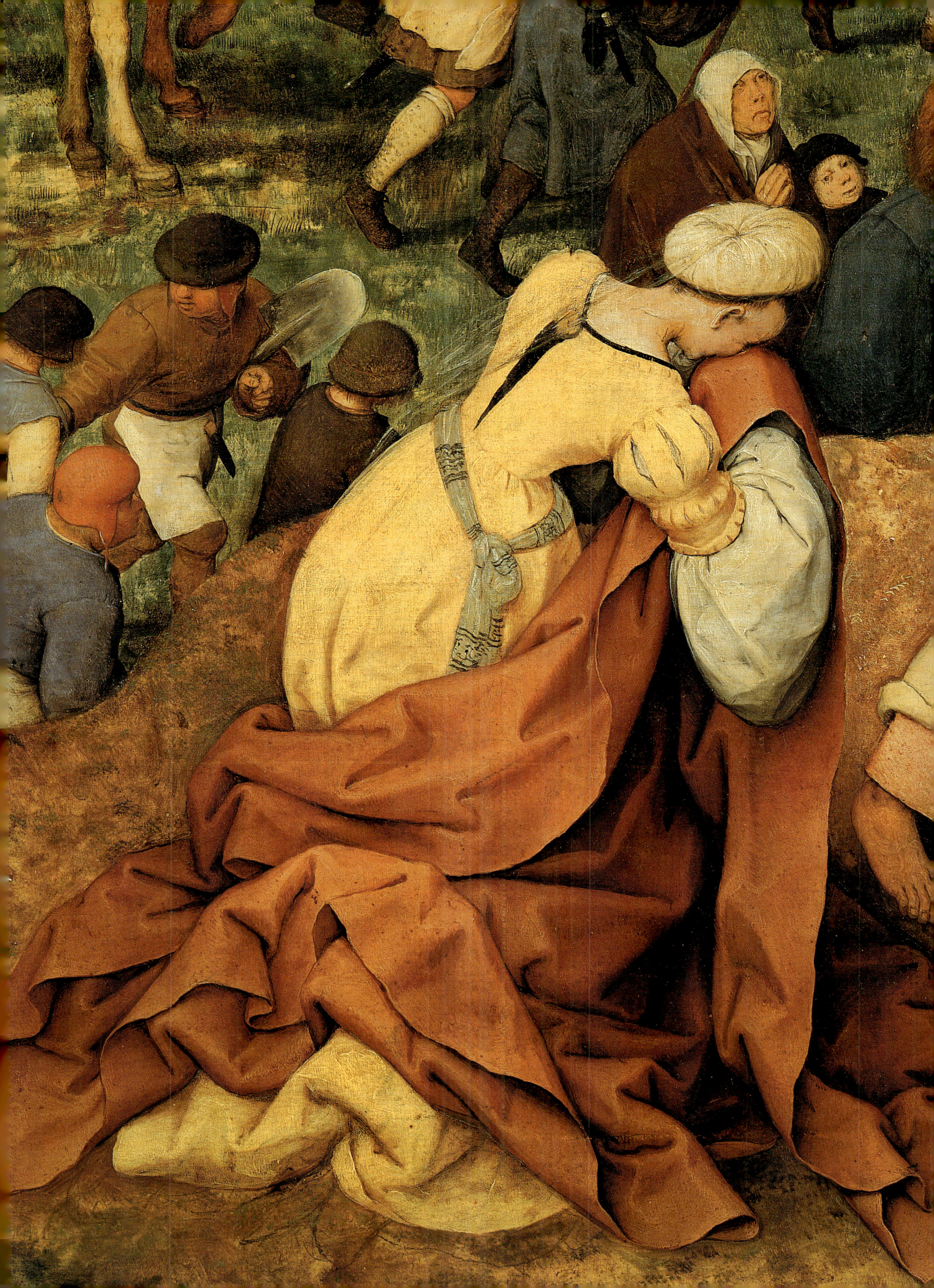

In the foreground, immediately in line with the rock pinnacle, sits a strange character with his back to us, observing the scene. His heavy bag suggests he is a peddler, a haberdasher who, besides selling needles and thread, peddles the ideas of the Reformation.[12] If this man gazes toward Christ, while at the same time the Virgin, who often represents the embodiment of the Catholic church, turns her back on the martyrdom of her son, was Bruegel intending this as a heretical statement? If so, why then does he make a mockery of a similar figure in the engraving *Haberdasher Robbed by Monkeys* (fig. 242), which Hieronymus Cock published in 1562? Simply because this is a comic subject for a popular engraving? Perhaps.

It is hard to see any consistency here, or any conclusive aim. The allusion to problems of the time, ideas, and events is clear. The characters in *Christ Carrying the Cross* are the painter's contemporaries; transformed into gaping onlookers, they follow the walk to Calvary, and if they take their hats off, it is not out of respect to Christ but to the authorities who are passing by on horseback. Some figures are indeed filled with grief and emotion. Behind the group containing the Virgin, four women are horrified by the scene they are watching, or, at least, have caught sight of (fig. 52). Weeping, they form part of the group of mourners in the foreground, and their presence seems to weaken the anti-Catholic message seemingly suggested by the picture. Close to these women, at the painting's very edge, at the foot of the pole carrying its sinister wheel, are also two men who contrast sharply with the onlookers. One communicates his despair and rage by screwing up his face and clenching his fist, while the other, his hands together, watches the unfolding drama more calmly. These two individuals could by themselves represent the impact of this event, the rage of the artist and the faith of the believer. Some writers believe that the second man is a self-portrait.[13] The painting thus contains a rich, and ambiguous, accretion of readings.

Such is this great landscape, filled with people, shapes, colors, and lines running from left to right, that we can read it like a seismograph, or an electrocardiogram, of nature and man. In his day, Bruegel's work was read according to the sensibilities of the day. Yet was he actually taking a stand, making a declaration? Whatever he was doing, he was lifting a veil, for his time, and for ours.

A NEED FOR SYNTHESIS

Christ Carrying the Cross and *The Alchemist* are dense, intricate works. However, as he grew older Bruegel distilled his images, pruned his subjects. Did he revisit the drawings and great landscapes of his youth? Yes and no. His early, youthful lyricism gave way to reflection, literally and metaphorically, of the world and of certain moments.

Thus *Winter Landscape with Skaters and Bird Trap*, painted in 1565 (fig. 54) might be called a meditative painting. From the same period as the famous series of *Months* and *Seasons*, like them it conveys, in a more limited format, a vision of man and nature. It is the depth of winter, but it shows a different aspect of the season from that of the famous *Hunters in the Snow* (fig. 186). There is snow and ice, but the color is less cold, the air less biting. The ocher of the sky, reflected in the trees and frozen water, seems to encourage birds to look for food and humans to enjoy themselves. At the lower right a trap awaits robins, blackbirds, and sparrows

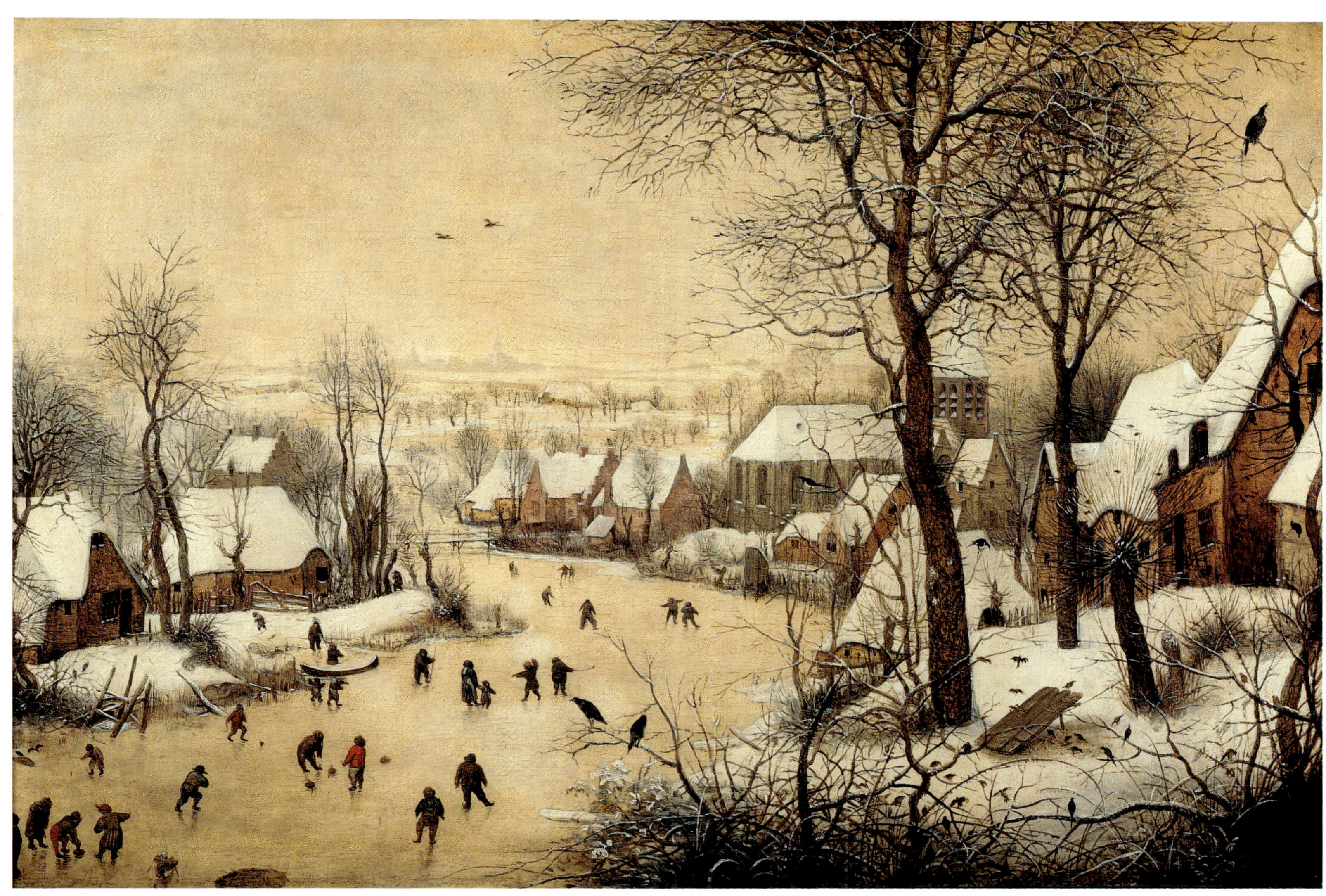

54

54–57. Pieter Bruegel, *Winter Landscape with Skaters and Bird Trap*, 1565, whole work and details. Oil on panel, 14 1/2 x 21 3/4 in. (37 x 55.5 cm). Brussels, Musées royaux des Beaux-Arts de Belgique

which emerge from the bushes or flutter down from the trees. Likewise, the ice might give way under the weight of the careless skaters; it is already melting, revealing a dark circle beneath the wooden rectangle that threatens the birds. Thus we feel a clear warning, to birds and human beings alike, of a possible fall owing to an error of judgment. The painter's intention is quite clear. The questions that a few writers still raise about the picture's significance are more about his shades of meaning and how broadly the painting can be interpreted.

Beyond the clearly visible bird trap and the excited people, beyond the bridge in front of which the most distant skaters are silhouetted, the Brabant village is caught, wrapped in a fog that is milky yet full of sunlight. This painting is the first in northern art to express an impressionist sensibility. By the interplay of materials, by the intensity of tone and translucence, everything is softened and yet everything seems to be in delicate filigree, like the silhouette of a town that we can see on the horizon (fig. 57). A moment in the year, an instant in the day, are rendered as much by the graphic tension of the trees, houses, and people in the foreground, as by the contrast in the distance, and the almost tactile softness of the paint. This was one of Bruegel's most widely copied works—but none of the copies replicates the atmosphere that is so essential to the original.

The drawing *Summer* (fig. 58), from 1568, conveys a similar impression of intensity—but this time with vigor. The season, which has literally cut a swathe

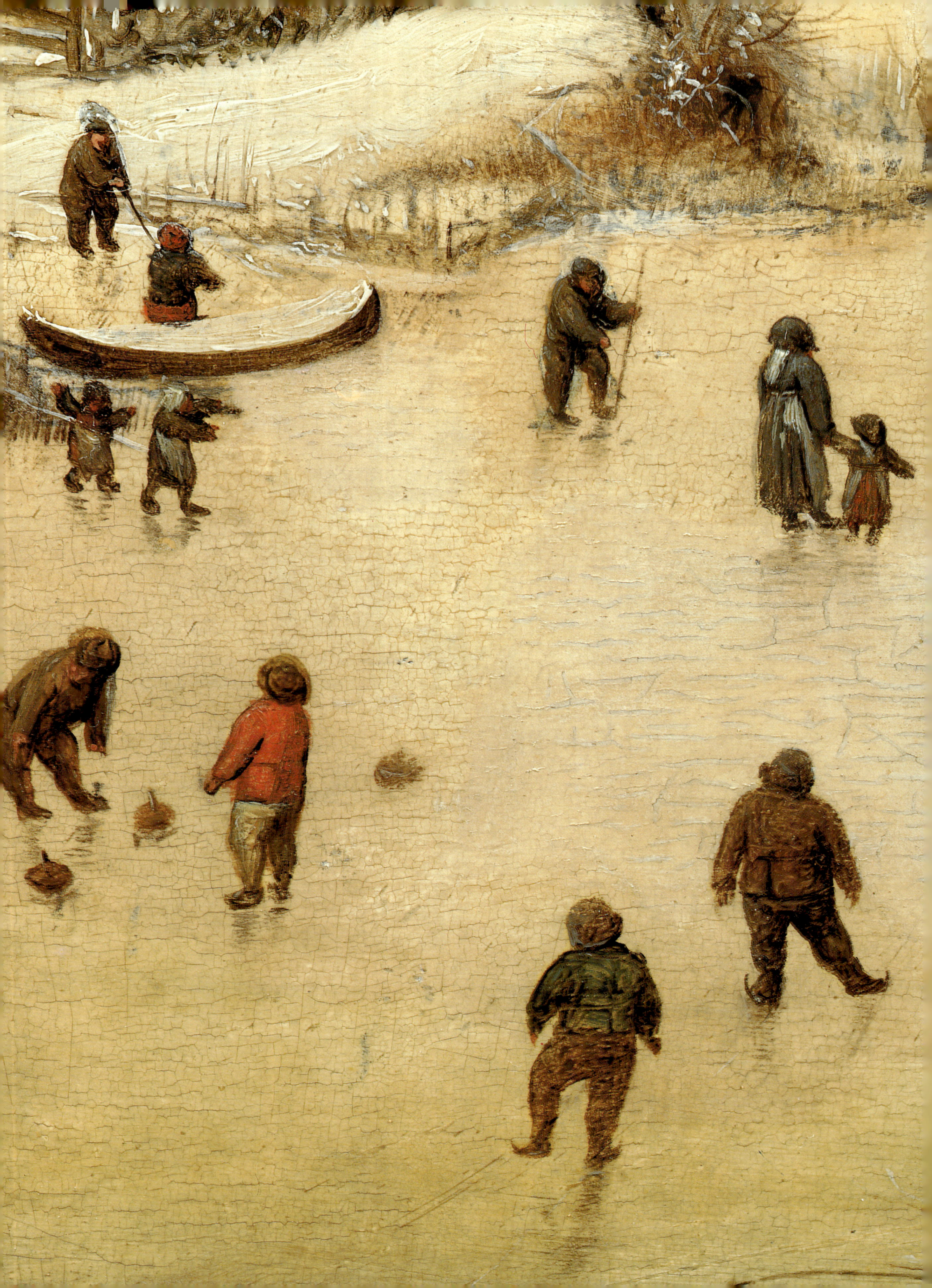

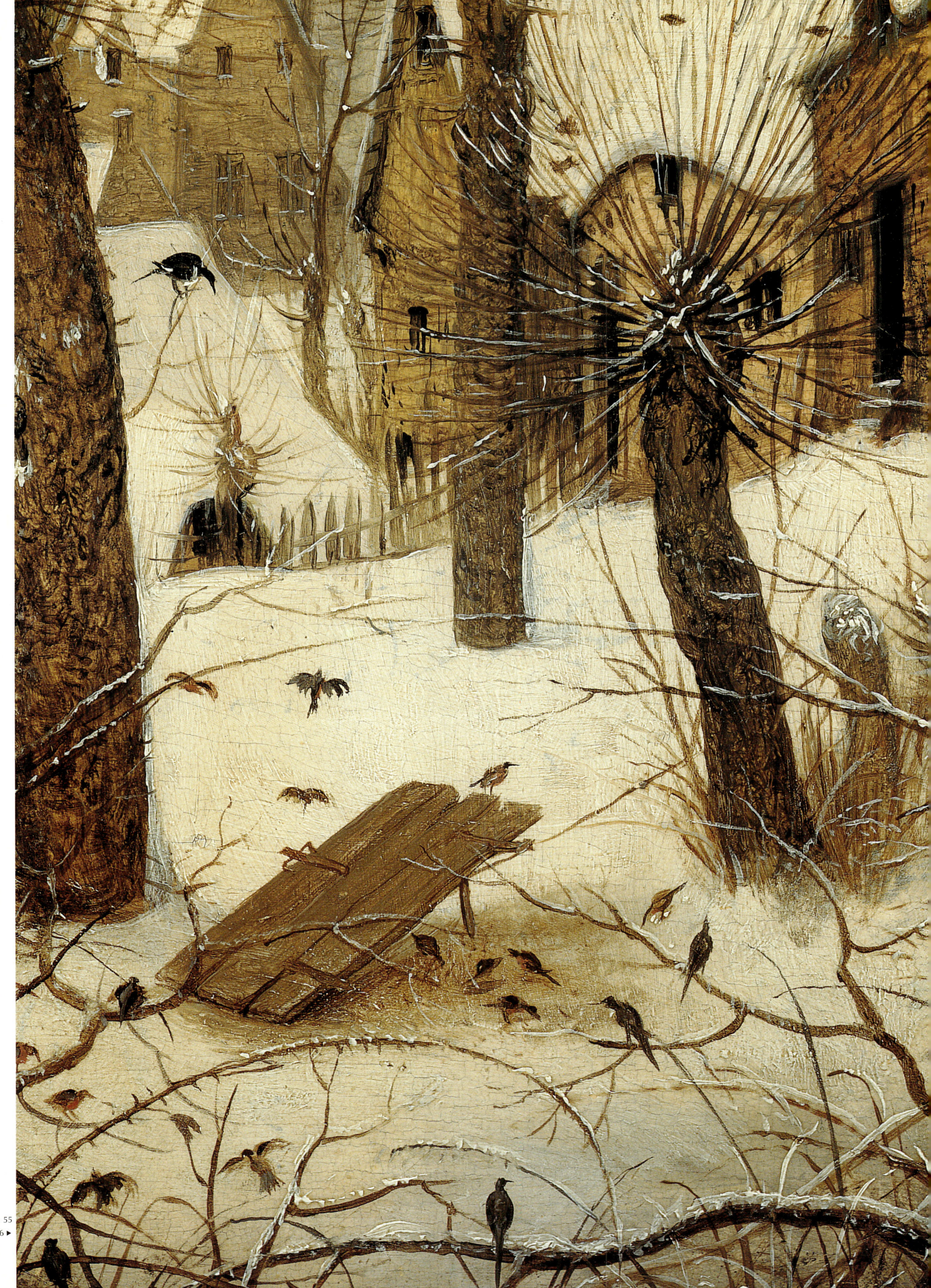

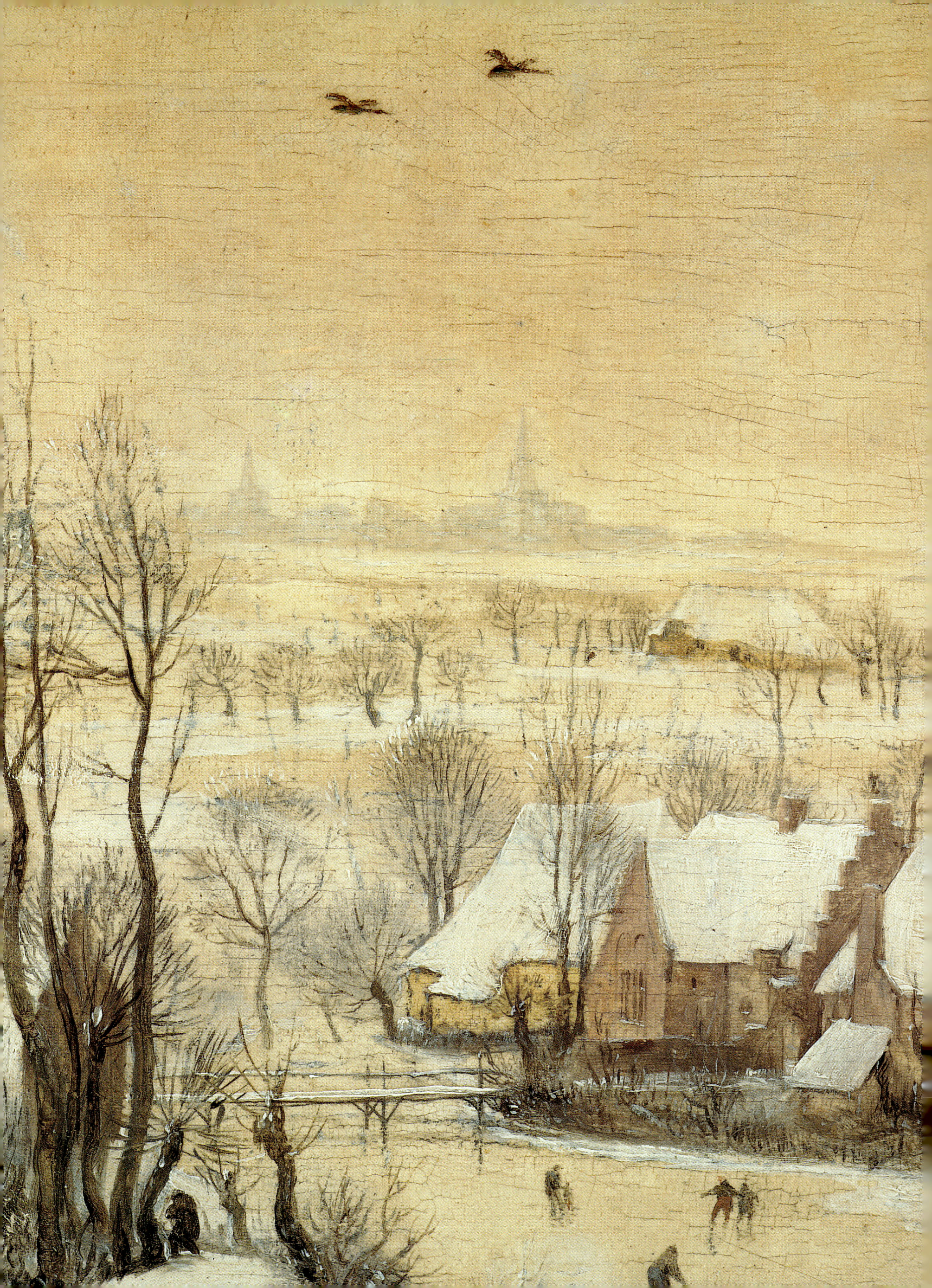

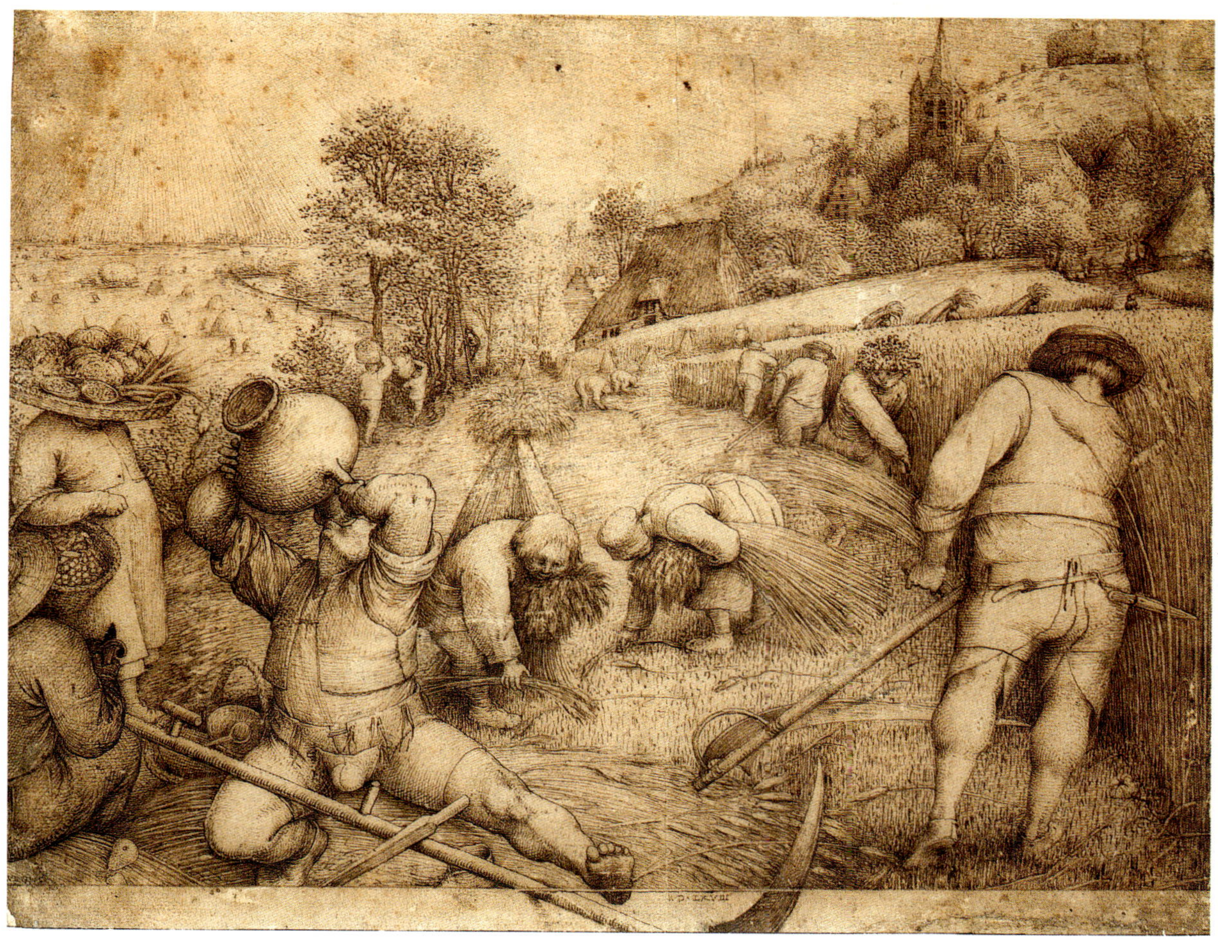

58

through the harvested grain, imposes its power as the earth's ripening bursts forth. There are human figures in the foreground—a reaper on the right, a man drinking from a jug on the left. Two pathways, lined with grain and farmhands, lead the eye into the distance: on the right, towards the shadow of the village and its church, and on the left, towards the endless fields. The engraving after this composition, which was published in 1570, after Bruegel's death, of course reproduces the composition in reverse (fig. 59). The work clearly lends itself to analysis: Some have seen the influence of mannerism in it, and it also contains comic details and references to proverbs. However, its essential quality is the expressive force of a living subject, caught in the full sun of day and backlit by it, with the distortions of light and of movement caught in time that this presentation involves. The composition is dynamic, overflowing—indeed literally, since the leg and scythe of the drinker extend beyond the picture's edge, emphasizing the monumental form of a man quenching his thirst in the midday heat.

The Bruegel image, therefore, is both multiform—because of its diversity of subjects and wealth of detail—and unique, because of the artist's personal way of seeing and his skill in painting. It ranges from inventory to synthesis, from anthology to idea, from narration to aphorism, from the *Flemish Proverbs* to *The Blind Leading the Blind*, from *Children's Games* to *The Fall of Icarus,* and from the alchemist to the reapers. While a work can be savored through its details, each of these helps to make up a whole that gives it its real flavor. However, the artist's approach evolved considerably during the course of his career, which describes a development from compositions showing a pre-eminence of detail towards a global, universal vision.

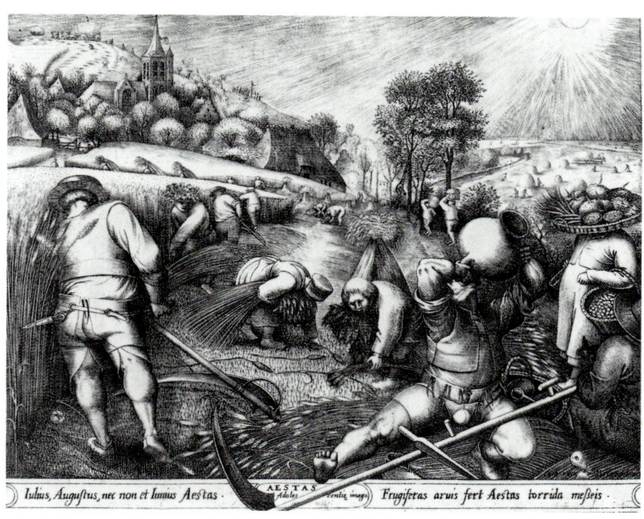

59

58. Pieter Bruegel, *Summer,* 1568. Pen and brown ink, 8⁵⁄₈ x 11¼ in. (22 x 28.6 cm). Hamburg, Hamburger Kunsthalle, Kupferstichkabinett

59. Pieter van der Heyden (attributed), *Summer,* after Pieter Bruegel, 1570. Engraving, 8¾ x 11⅛ in. (22.5 x 28.3 cm) Brussels, Bibliothèque royale Albert I, print room

LINE AND COLOR

Bruegel is not a mere maker of pictures. If his images have a resonance that is as alive today as when he created them, the reason lies not in the objects he represents but in the way he evokes them.[14] For Bruegel is above all a painter, and among the greatest. He achieves a complete union between the vision he wants to convey and the means at his disposal for conveying it; and it is from this perfect balance between mind and hand that his paintings are born. The artist's technical mastery, always present, brings to life his inner rhythm through emphasis and modulation, since it springs directly from his thoughts to punctuate his arguments.

Bruegel's pictorial vision is ahead of its time, for he is an innovator. He brings to life each square centimeter of a painting, assigning to each object its space and to each color its intensity—all done with an extreme simplicity and economy that only the greatest masters can succeed in making more forcefully eloquent than all the apparent richness of refinement.

Bruegel's painting stands out from that of fifteenth-century Flemish artists, who sought depth and power by superimposing layer after layer of transparent glazes of color—not because of any wish to break with those artists, but through a desire for simplicity. In the work of Van Eyck or Van der Weyden, for example, image, form, and color appear as if preserved beneath the surface, in the intimacy and translucence of the painting's materials. Bruegel, on the other hand, gives the ground layer of the painting a markedly active role—a development that can already be seen in the work of Bosch and Jan van Amstel. Earlier artists used the ground as the source of the painting's inner light; Bruegel makes it express his vision, and in his hands it becomes an integral part of the painting's outer skin. Its presence is a functional part of the painting, and is often animated by highlighting and by traces of fine cracking.

Bruegel's most revolutionary invention, however, is in the way that he created spatial depth simply by varying the density of tone. He often rapidly applied a dark layer of paint, which he then raised to a much brighter key by adding thin glazes of color to it. He used this interplay of media to create an illusion of space, although he never carried it quite as far as the more baroque effects that we see in the work of Rubens, who would later create visual voids in a painting's surface in order to dramatically accentuate the three-dimensionality of his foreground figures. Bruegel's pictorial space always remains firmly behind the picture plane.

Bruegel's technique of creating spatial depth is not the result of any clearly defined system, for he never repeats himself. His virtuosity was such that his skill adapted to the demands both of the scene he is depicting and of its format. Breathing, serene, answering the slow rhythm of a winter sky, the layer of paint—always thinly laid—expresses sensation by the very manner in which it is applied. *The Census at Bethlehem* (fig. 60) is a case in point. At the opposite end of the scale from *Winter Landscape with Skaters and Bird Trap*, here Bruegel's technique, charged with energy and concentrated violence, becomes more purposeful, more

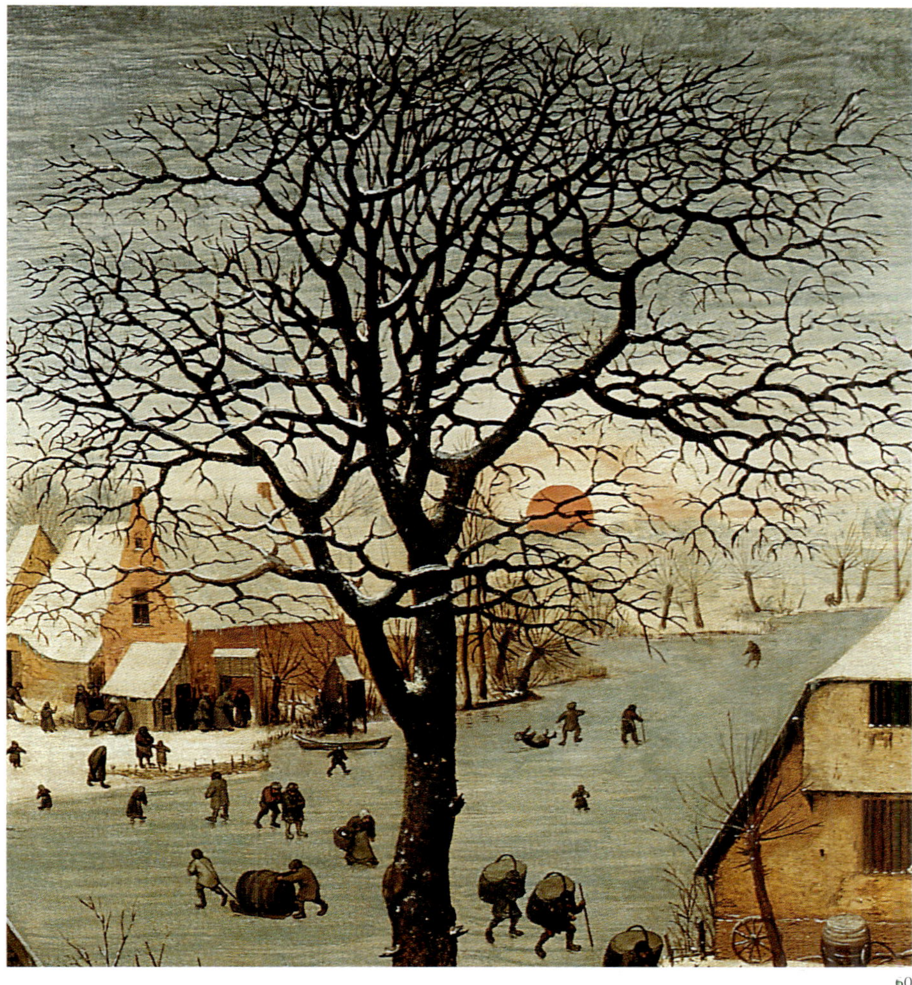

60. Pieter Bruegel, *The Census at Bethlehem*, (Brussels, Musées royaux des Beaux-Arts de Belgique): detail. The sensation of space is created through sharp graphic elements that stand out against a sky softened by diluted colors.

intellectually deliberate, in the struggle that will eventually lead to *The Suicide of Saul* of 1562, where a forest of spears literally pierces our glance (fig. 255).

It would be wrong to believe the myth of Bruegel the storyteller who communicates spontaneously, by effortless talent alone. The highly skilled construction of his works—whether achieved by the elimination of everything that does not accord with the great sweep of his synthesis in *The Harvest*, or by the accumulation of discrete elements made possible by his exceptional talent for contrasting themes in *The Fall of the Rebel Angels*—confirms that virtuosity of treatment alone is not enough to fully illustrate the weight and substance of a thought: It needs to be expressed with a complete control of painterly technique (figs. 175 and 114).

Painting, drawing, and engraving: These are the three modes of expression through which this supreme art can be appreciated. In the case of painting, a consideration of the three stages in its creation allows us to better perceive the originality, skill, and consequently, the success, of Bruegel's work.

The first stage in making an oil painting in the sixteenth century was to secure the painting's support. In Bruegel's case this might be wood panel or canvas. According to Van Mander, Bruegel had a gift for "reproducing everything in an agreeable and spiritual way, whether in distemper or in oils, for he was highly proficient in both techniques."[15] While the single adjective that Van Mander uses to describe the resonance of Bruegel's paintings— "agreeable"—is a bit jarring to us, he is certainly right about Bruegel's skill in the two media of distemper on canvas and oil on panel.

PAINTING IN OILS ON WOODEN PANELS

Oil paint—a mixture of ground pigment, quick-drying oil, and volatile spirits—dates, we know, from before Bruegel's time. Even though the medium was not invented by Jan van Eyck, as was once thought, Van Eyck certainly took it to a high point of perfection, as can be seen in his Ghent Altarpiece (*The Adoration of the Mystic Lamb*) of 1432. Van Eyck and the great artists of fifteenth-century Flanders who came after him—Rogier van der Weyden, Hugo van der Goes, Dirck Bouts, and Petrus Christus—succeeded in making the oil medium celebrated as far away as Italy. The interest Antonello da Messina showed in the art of northern Europe—even if he never visited Flanders, as Vasari claims[16]—demonstrates the technique's success, and how widely it was used.

The wood panels on which Bruegel painted following this tradition—supplemented by his own experiments—are of oak, generally from the Baltic region, and assembled to whatever format he required from several planks about ⅜ inch (1 cm) thick. *The Tower of Babel* in Rotterdam, which measures 23⅝ x 29½ inches (59.9 x 74.6 cm) comprises two vertical planks to which were later added two lateral strips about ½ inch (1.5 cm) wide.[17] On the other hand, *The Census at Bethlehem*, which measures 45½ x 64½ inches (115.5 x 163.5 cm) is made up of four horizontal planks (fig. 61).

Bruegel tended to paint thinly. The grain of the wood can sometimes be seen through the paint surface if it is examined under light falling at an angle. Even so, there are several layers between the painting's support and its outer surface. The first of these is the ground, made of chalk and animal glue, which was applied to provide a smooth, impermeable layer with a warm tone as a preparation for the paint. Bruegel sometimes allowed the ground to show through the paint layers, or even left it unpainted. In such cases it functions as a base or priming coat, and in places, it often appears to be one of the layers of paint. There are many examples of this effect, in the *Battle of Carnival and Lent* of 1559, for one example, and in the *Beggars* of 1568, for another.

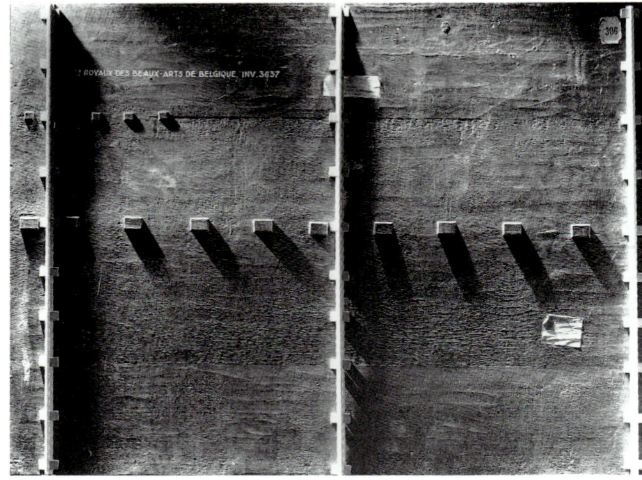

61

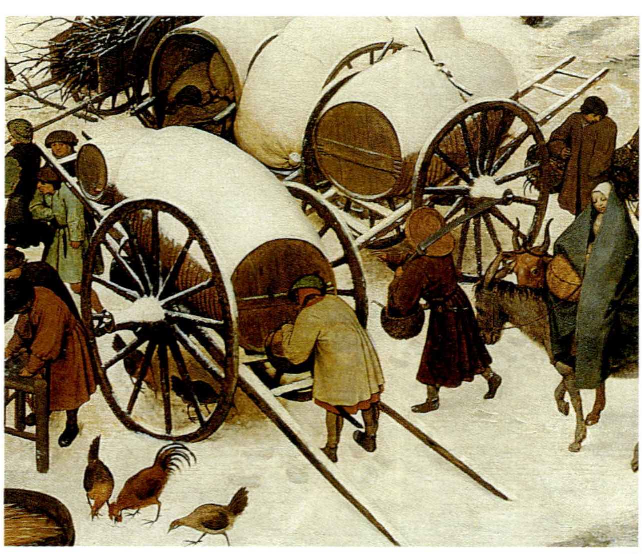

62

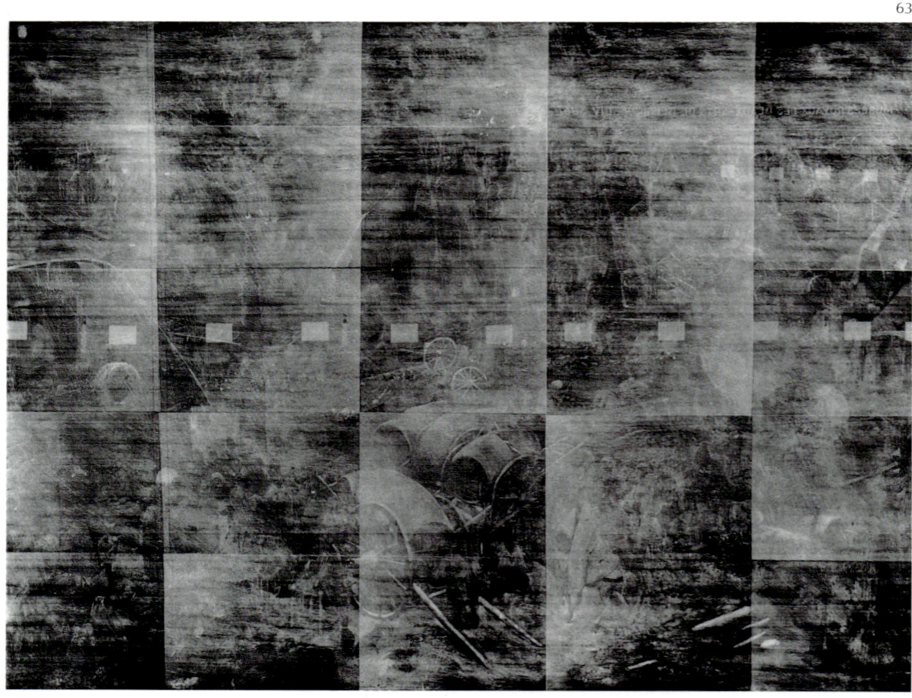

63

61. Pieter Bruegel, *The Census at Bethlehem*, (Brussels, Musées royaux des Beaux-Arts de Belgique): back, showing the assembly of the wood panel

62. Pieter Bruegel, *The Census at Bethlehem*, (Brussels, Musées royaux des Beaux-Arts de Belgique): detail of the carts, which can be seen in the foreground of fig. 63

63. Pieter Bruegel, *The Census at Bethlehem*, (Brussels, Musées royaux des Beaux-Arts de Belgique): X-ray. The X-rays, which cannot penetrate the lead white, reveal the work's internal structure, including Bruegel's unerring execution, free of corrections.

Bruegel often covered the ground with a thin brushed-on layer of lead-white paint, which can be seen clearly in X-rays. This, too, can act as a priming coat, lightening the colors above it, or it can stand as an area of color in its own right. The paintings of snowy scenes clearly make use of it. Lead white is also one of the basic pigments of oil paint, and is very useful for covering over what lies beneath it. An X-ray of *The Census at Bethlehem* (fig. 63) reveals the brushstrokes that Bruegel used to apply an overall layer of lead white, thickened in places by highlights that seem almost to create the painting's structure on their own. The freedom and apparent ease with which this has been done are a sign of the artist's extraordinarily thorough mastery of his medium.

THE PREPARATORY SKETCH

In the sixteenth-century Flemish oil technique, the initial drawing, which would become the underlying drawing of the painting once the paint was laid over it, established the general plan and the principal forms of the picture. Bruegel made his initial sketches in black chalk, either directly on the ground, or on the layer of lead white paint (fig. 64). He modified this original conception as he worked, changing the grouping of the dogs in *Hunters in the Snow* (fig. 186), for example, or the folds in Mary Magdalen's dress in *Christ Carrying the Cross* (fig. 53).

These differences between the preparatory sketch and the finished painting—adjustments made by the artist as his work progressed known as *pentimenti,* or "repentances"—reveal the painter's creative process at each stage of his work. Indeed, if we do not find these changes, if the composition of a painting seems to have been perfectly determined at the outset, we are no longer dealing with an original work, but with a copy or a studio project. Therein lies the difference not only in invention, but in vibrancy and emotion, that mark the distinction between a work by Pieter Bruegel himself and a seemingly identical one—that is, so far as the subject is concerned—by his son, Pieter Bruegel the Younger. These changes in the artist's thinking are not corrections to awkward work, but alterations necessary to adjust the composition as a whole, which the artist discovered he needed to make as he developed the work. They are almost always tiny, like the slight shift in the position of the left foot of the Magus on the right in the *Adoration* in London (fig. 146), the blurred traces of which can be seen clearly through the paint surface.

THE LAYERS OF A PAINTING

A sixteenth-century oil painting's structure was developed in a series of established stages, although these might be modified. The composition was first laid out in the preliminary drawing, which established the essential forms and positions of the major elements of the picture. When these were painted, the artist might make changes to his first idea. In *The Tower of Babel* in Rotterdam for example (fig. 274), X-ray photographs reveal that Bruegel initially drew the building's mass on a layer of lead white (fig. 65). But when he actually painted the tower, he made it larger than the drawing underneath, so that in the finished painting it is silhouetted

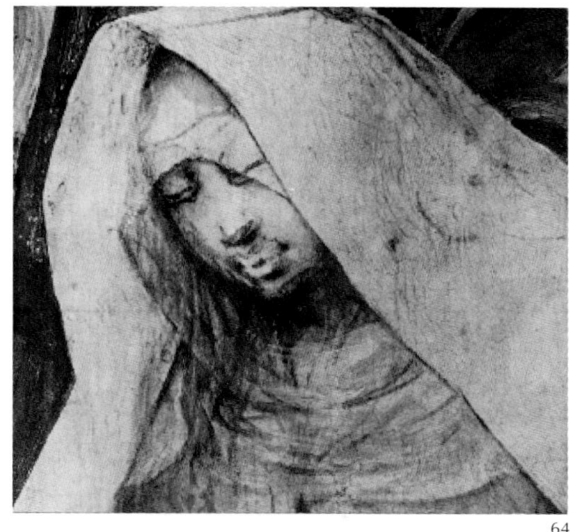

64

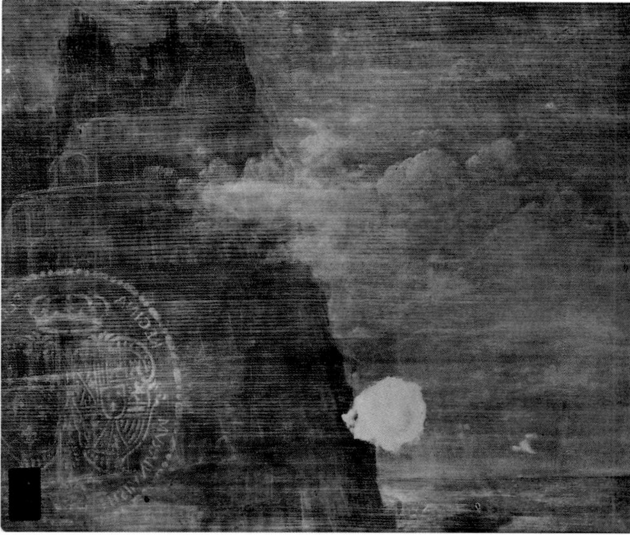

65

64. Pieter Bruegel, *The Adoration of the Magi* (London, National Gallery): infra-red photograph showing the lines of the underlying drawing, which lays out the composition and the principal forms of the painting (see fig. 147)

65. Pieter Bruegel, *The Tower of Babel* (Rotterdam, Museum Boijmans Van Beuningen): X-ray of a detail of the upper part of the tower. In the underlying drawing, the tower is confined to the ground layer of lead-white paint. Bruegel enlarged the tower beyond its original outline so that in the completed work it is more starkly delineated against the sky.

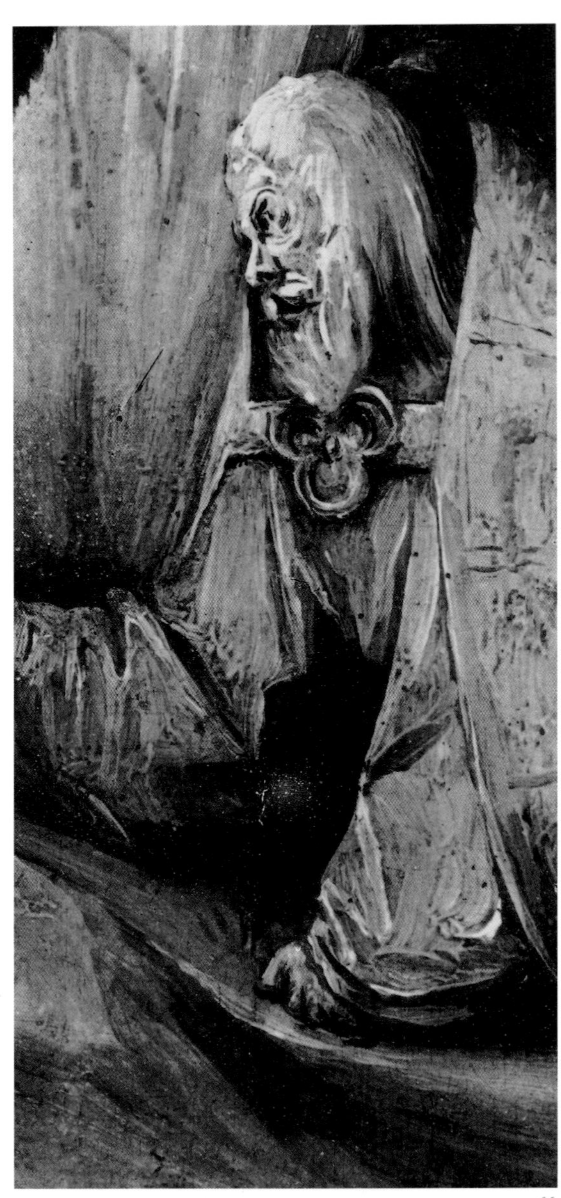

66. Pieter Bruegel, *The Death of the Virgin* (detail of fig. 152): close-up view of an apostle. The figure has been painted with a heavily loaded brush, a technique that brings out the volumes of the grisaille and accentuates the lighting.

against the sky, itself an uncovered layer of lead white paint. Was this a miscalculation at the outset, or a misjudgment at the end? Neither one. The tower appears all the more forceful, and disquieting, because it stands out vividly against the sky, its mass biting into the light. The building's volume and monstrousness are increased by the contrast between the fluid space and the rigid construction; for the latter aims to rule over, dominate, and subjugate the former. Thus by a clever use of his technique, Bruegel accentuated his work's monumental and dramatic character. While he executed certain elements in this way—the tower, or the tree in the *Census* —others, which may be just as important to the final composition, he added, superimposed, according to the demands of the picture's logic. Thus, in the center of *The Gloomy Day* (fig. 187), the clump of trees in the foreground that crosses the landscape from top to bottom, was painted after the sky, the mountains, the water, and the stormy waves, against which the trunks and bare branches are darkly silhouetted (fig. 67). This very superimposition is part of what gives them their vegetable suppleness and fragility. The shades of tone—all of them dark, but each with its own hue—that we see through these trees makes them vibrate and brings them in tune with the picture's symphonic whole.

This is equally true of details. A few square centimeters in the top right-hand corner of *The Census at Bethlehem* (fig. 200) reveal Bruegel's clarity of vision in conveying an animated scene. A small boy on the edge of the ice is raising his arms to frighten two birds (fig. 206). Between the viewer and this vignette are a pile of wood, snow-covered carts, and the slope of a roof. The way this fragment of winter is painted is astonishingly simple. The snow on the ground is the underlying layer of lead white; so is the ice, although the ice is overlaid with a thin glaze of blue. The pile of wood is painted over it in brown, through which the snow and ice are visible. Darker touches and some heightening of the snow sharpen, model, and place these elements, while also enlivening them.

A Bruegel painting cannot be reduced to contrasting plans or senses, nor to a comparison of subjects. By laying down layers of paint that fuse into one another above the white ground, the artist worked with fluid tones, sometimes with a loaded brush and sometimes with a lighter hand, according to the volume or the brilliance of the object depicted. In some cases a figure in the foreground has been rendered with great solidity in thick, viscous paint with a loaded brush; in others, something in the distance, brushed in with more liquid color in a light hue, seems almost to dissolve into the air. The man pruning a tree in the foreground of *The Gloomy Day* exemplifies the first type of rendering; the distant view of Antwerp in *Two Monkeys* is an instance of the second. The loaded-brush technique, which Bruegel uses with extreme sensitivity and whose strokes appear fine and taut under X-rays, changes and adapts to the demands of his subject. This approach to paint-handling was probably invented by Titian, and in the early seventeenth century Peter Paul Rubens would carry it to greater heights by making a dense impasto a principal feature of his brushwork. It should be noted, however, that Rubens's baroque usage was in fact a development of a vocabulary that Bruegel had mastered completely.

The few paintings by Bruegel in grisaille—that, is in shades of gray, black, and white—that have survived show his lively, heavily loaded brushwork clearly. In *The Death of the Virgin,* certain characters are painted almost entirely with white heightening (fig. 66). The grisaille technique, which was originally used to

represent sculpture, was pioneered in the fifteenth century, and it is not surprising
that Bruegel made use of it, as he probably did about 1550 on the panels of the
triptych he and Peeter Baltens painted for the Mechelen glove-makers (see p. 13).
The great freedom of rendering and modeling in his *Death of the Virgin* and *Christ
and the Woman Taken in Adultery* (fig. 155) show that he not only worked in the
technique, but that he did so with a mastery of the poetic use of chiaroscuro worthy
of Rembrandt.

The painter's diversity of expression and remarkable versatility gave him the
ability to render a wide range of materials: rough, soft, stiff, or supple; their essence,
properties, appearance—even what they sound like, if we think of *The Fall of the
Rebel Angels* (fig. 114). The same consummate skill also allowed him to convinc-
ingly create the complex spatial elements of each of his pictures.

With three or four brushstrokes he could perch a magpie at the top of a tree
silhouetted against the pallor of the sky above Bethlehem (fig. 205). The vitality of
his strokes——horizontal, short, light, or superimposed—conjures up the volume of
a tree trunk haloed by the light in *The Bird-Nester* (fig. 209). Somewhere between
material and graphic rendering, strokes of pale paint can also give body to dark
masses. The army of the Philistines takes shape in this way, snaking across the rocks
and leading to the suicide of Saul in the painting of the same name (fig. 253). In
another setting, a kind of pointillism brings to life the crests of the distant trees in
The Harvest (fig. 175). In this way every painting by Bruegel lends itself to a study
of whole composition through the techniques he used to create it, just as every
detail reveals the astonishing consonance between his ideas and their execution.

The Census at Bethlehem (fig. 200), for example, unquestionably asserts the
painter's creative power. Using all the resources of his technique, combining skill
of line with eloquence of tone, Bruegel goes beyond all anecdote, all representation, to conjure up, through the magic of a transparent sky, the deliberate rhythm
of the bare trees, the changing opacity of the snow and graduated reflections of the
frost, by the punctuating patches of color that answer each other across the space
of the picture like cries in the frozen air—the cold of the earth that the winter sun,
a watching red eye, cannot yet warm (fig. 204).

And yet, in the silence of nature itself, forces are moving; for Bruegel, as
always, has opened the door to dreams. According to what mood we are in, we
can see, in this village where people come and go, compelled by the force of
Augustus's decree, or by the necessities of their work, a peaceful scene, but one
pregnant with pain. They are unaware of what we know, that *The Census at
Bethlehem* is the prelude to *The Massacre of the Innocents* (fig. 145). If we are in
an optimistic frame of mind, we might see in this picture detached from time life
preparing to be reborn. In this mood, the census can be seen as a survey of the
vitality of humankind, and the pregnant Virgin finds her place in this rebirth of
the world, like the figure placed oddly in the middle of the painting—almost at
the intersection of the two diagonals that govern the composition—of a woman
sweeping the snow, for some mysterious reason. Is it perhaps because she wants
to help the ground receive the weak rays of a melancholy or radiant sun a little
sooner, a detail that Bruegel has slipped in for anyone who may want to make note
of it? There is a sense of space in the sky and the ice, conveyed by the dialogue
between the painting's blue tonality all over and the white ground, between the
silence of snow created in lead white and the human presence introduced by the

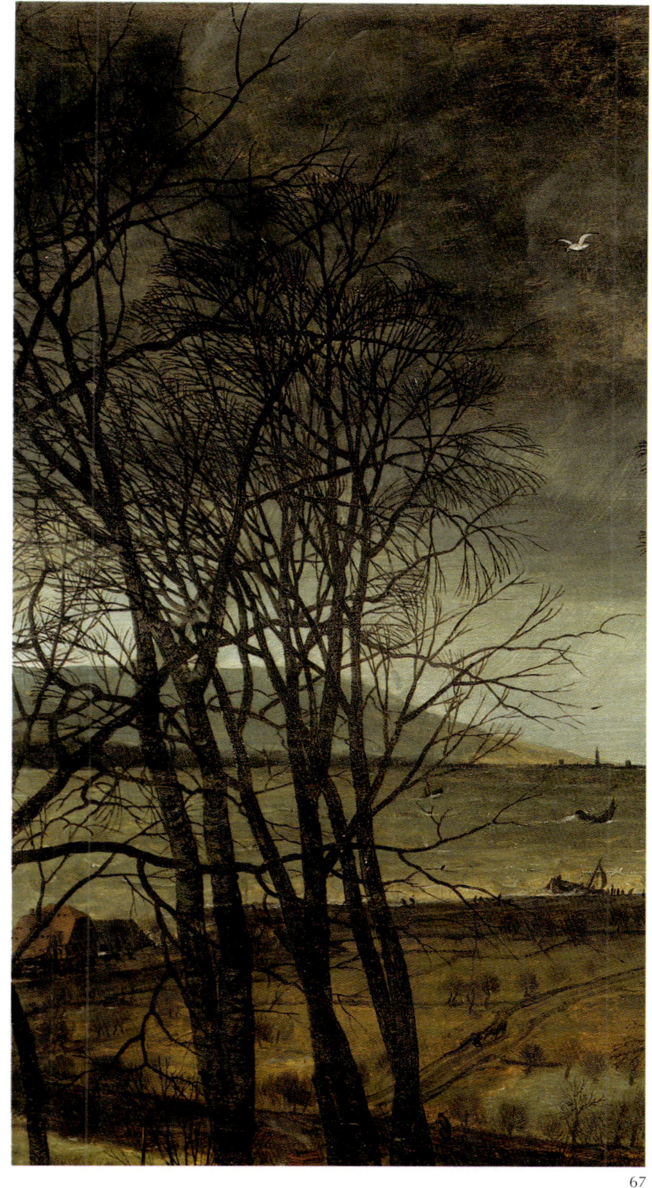

67

67. Pieter Bruegel, *The Gloomy Day* (Vienna,
Kunsthistorisches Museum): detail showing the
superimposition of the trees on the painted landscape

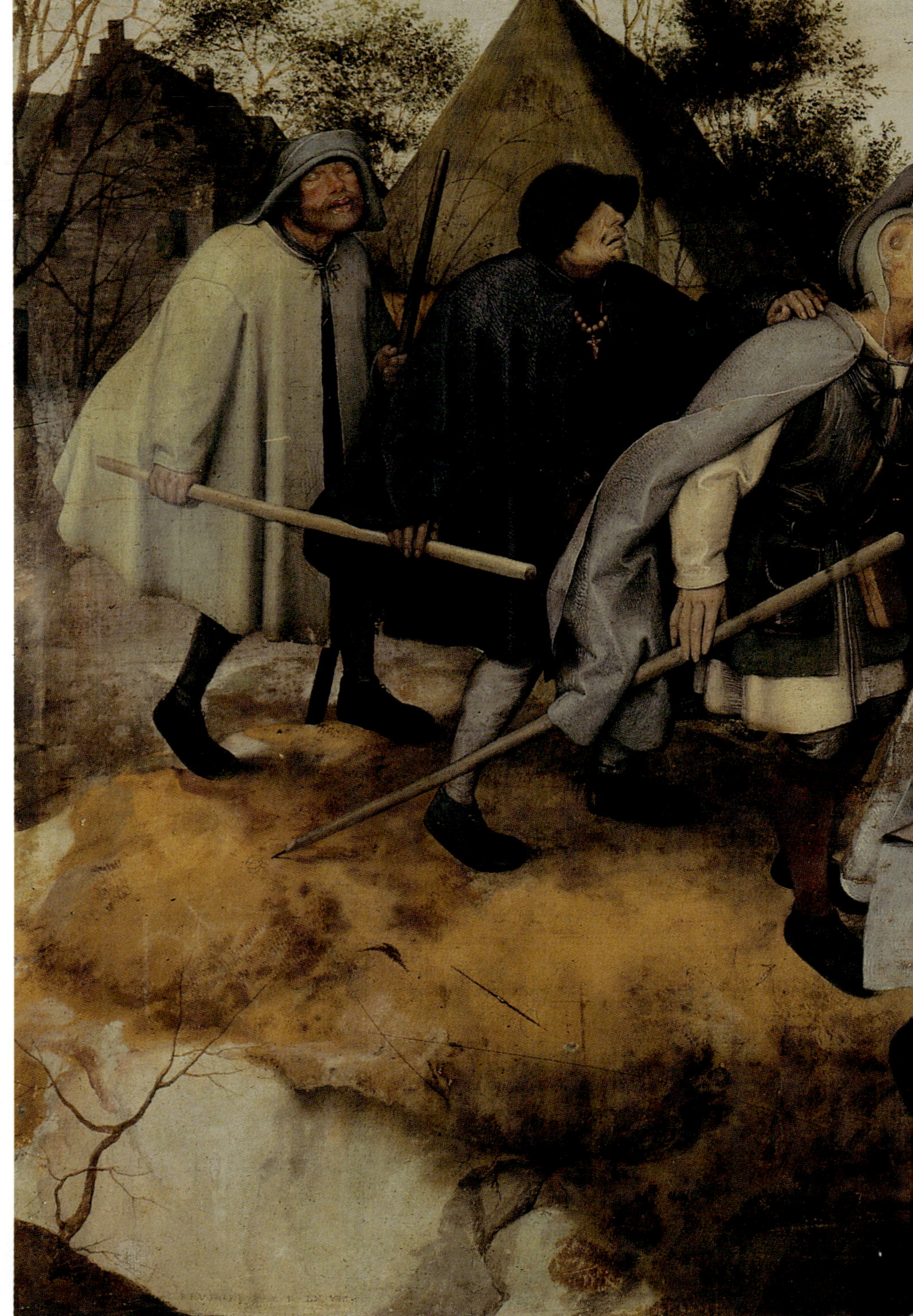

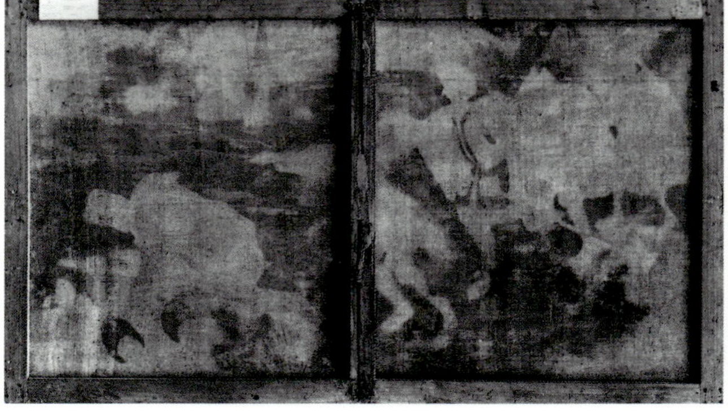

68. Pieter Bruegel, *The Blind Leading the Blind* (Naples, Museo e Gallerie nazionali di Capodimonte): reverse of the canvas

69–73. Pieter Bruegel, *The Blind Leading the Blind*, 1568: the compete composition and details. Distemper on linen, 33⅞ x 60⅝ in. (86 x 154 cm). Naples, Museo e Gallerie nazionali di Capodimonte

interplay of other colors. The elements are all there, but the art of bringing them together so brilliantly cannot be described, as Bruegel's painting demonstrates.

PAINTINGS IN DISTEMPER

Like oil painting, painting with distemper on linen was practiced in northern Europe in the fifteenth and sixteenth centuries, as we know from the works of Dirk Bouts, Hugo van der Goes, Joos van Gent, and Albrecht Dürer. The paint-

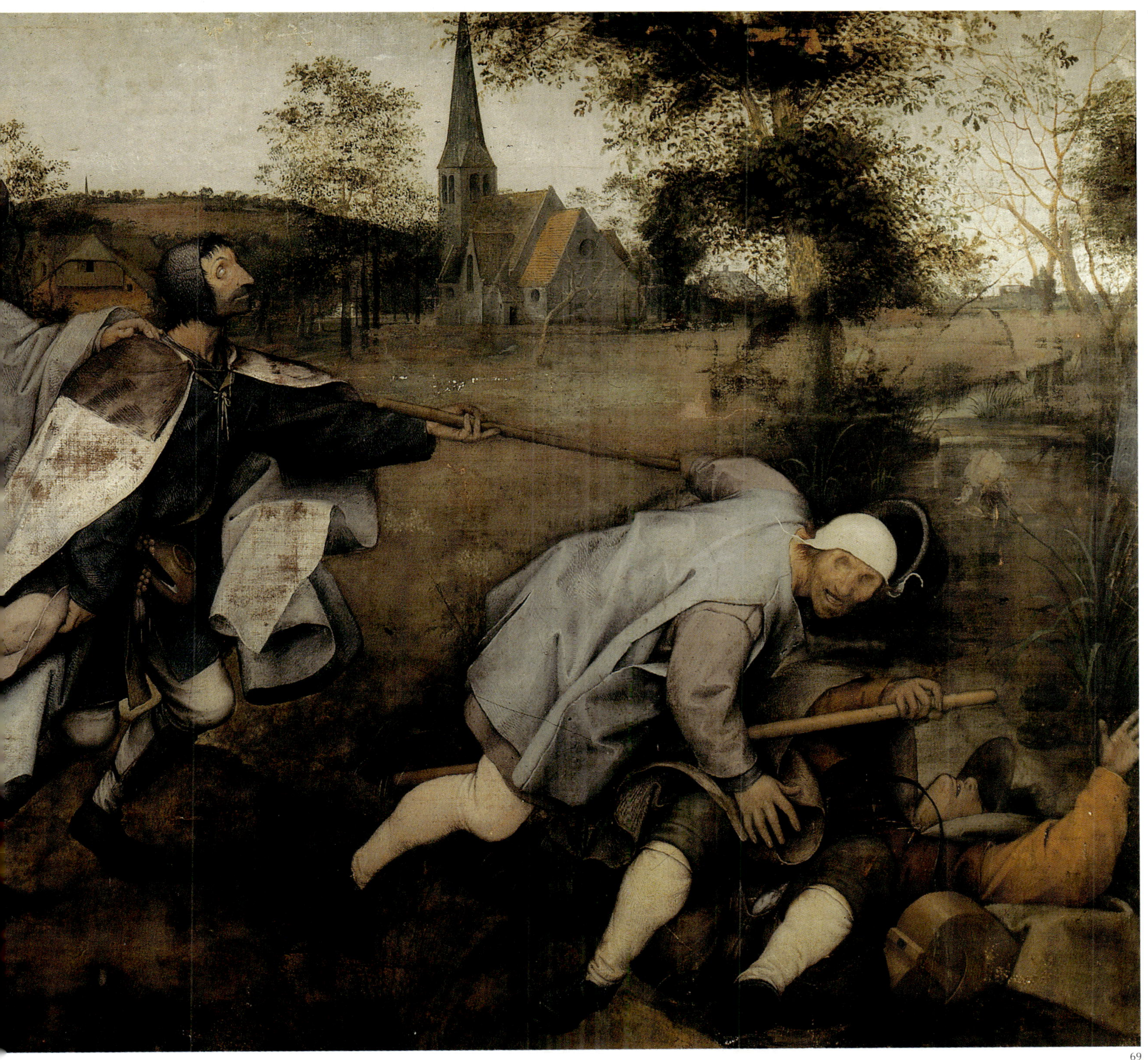

69

ings were known as *Tüchlein*, and the technique was used to make banners as well as paintings.[18] The linen used in Bruegel's distemper paintings was woven beginning in the sixteenth century. The pigments were crushed and mixed with water ("distemper" comes from the Medieval Latin *distemperare*, to soak), and the binder included an animal-hide glue. The finished paintings, which were not varnished, generally look pale and matte, because of the thinness of the paint surface, and because of the linen beneath, which is often used as the ground. Traditional distemper technique—which has been in use since the time of the ancient Egyptians—involves laying the paint on rapidly, because the linen very

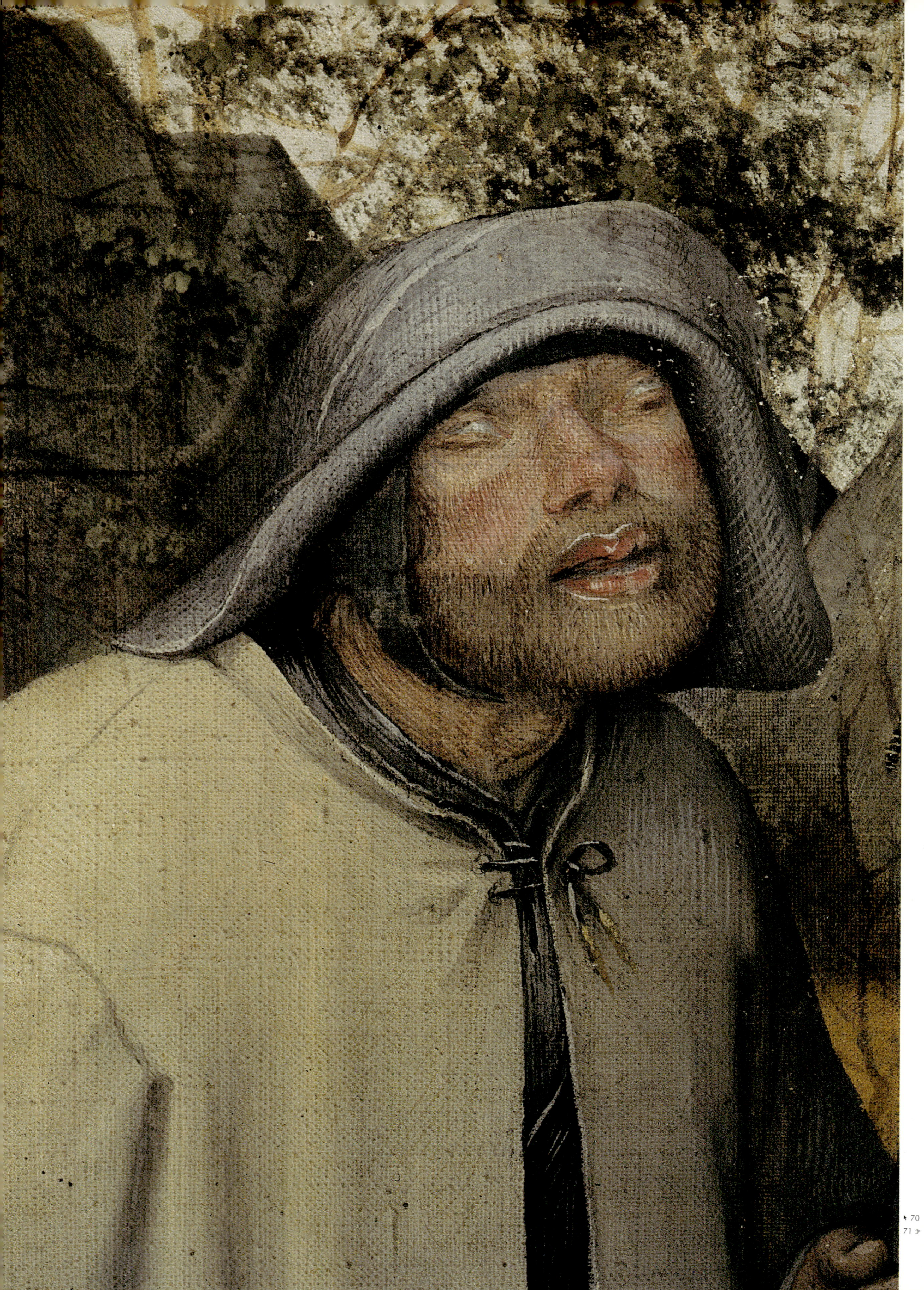

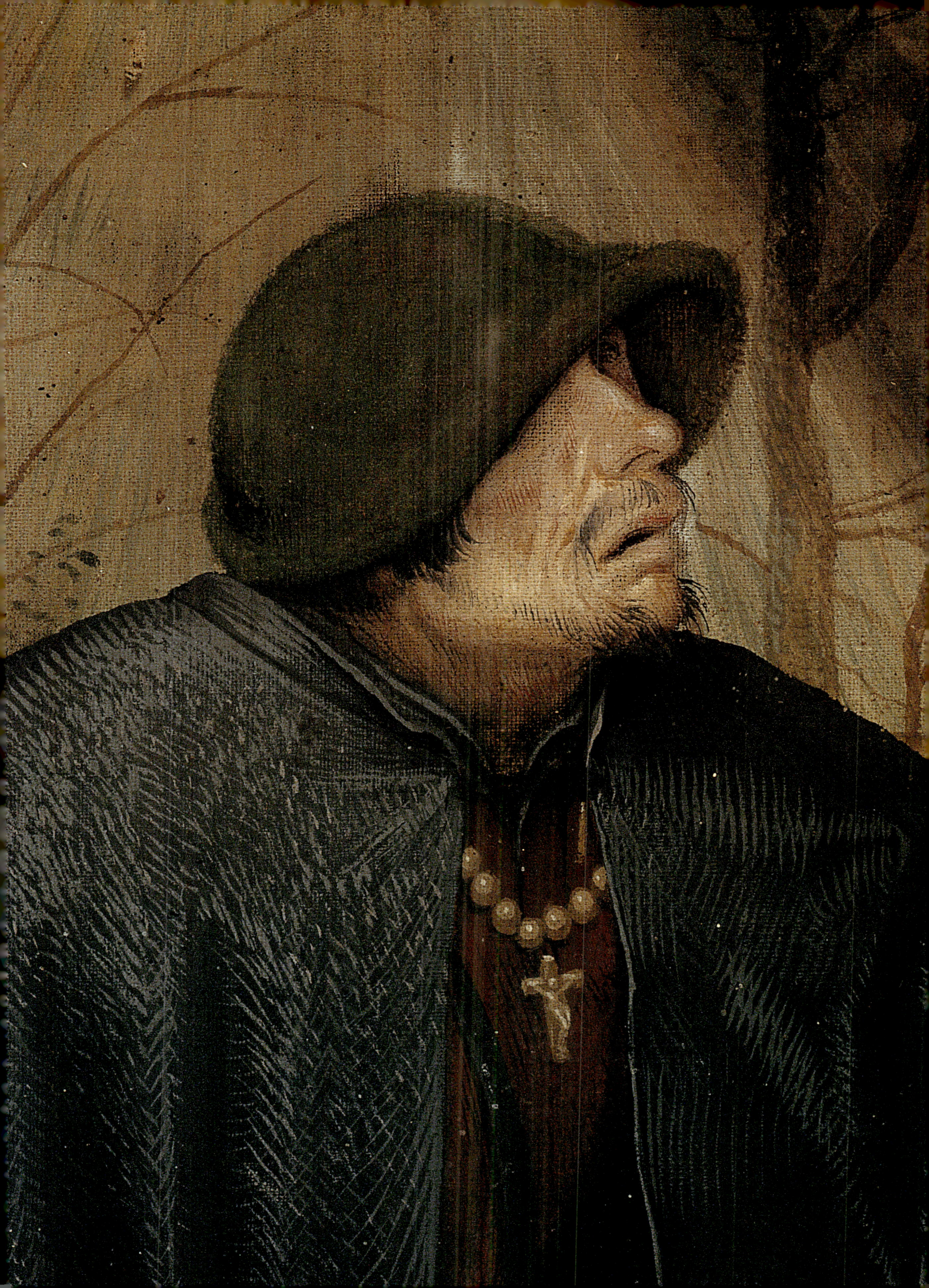

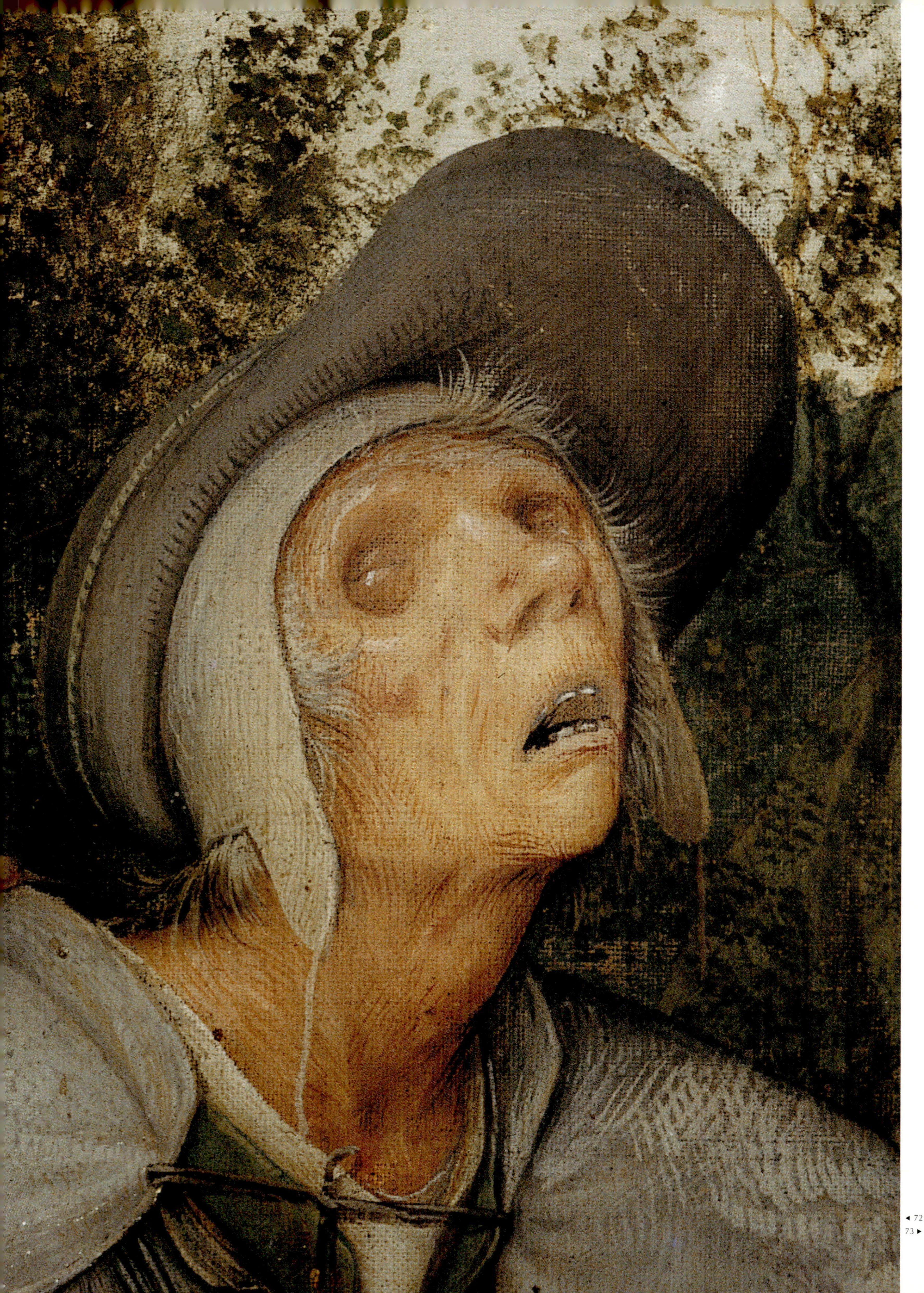

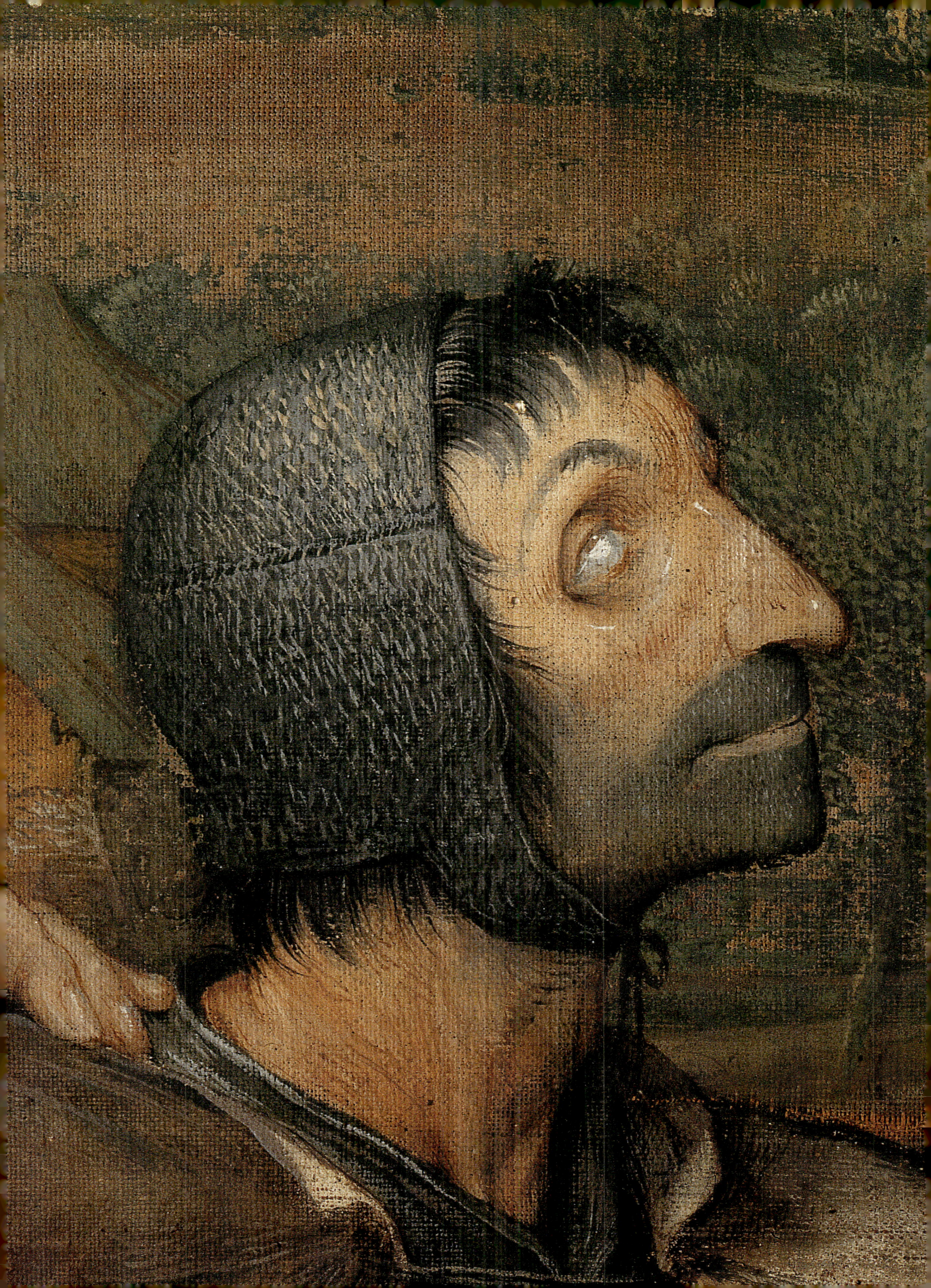

quickly absorbs the paint, and the water in which the pigment is suspended also dries very rapidly.

Bruegel produced two major paintings in distemper, both toward the end of his life: *The Misanthrope* (fig. 267) and *The Blind Leading the Blind* (fig. 69), both dating from 1568. The first of these shows a lone man in a hooded mourning cloak on a path strewn with metal spikes, being relieved of his purse by a figure encircled by a metal frame that represents the world. The canvas is painted within a round black border set on a square background, the corners of which are painted in monochrome gray. In the background, behind this scene of a man being robbed by the world, a shepherd appears to be watching his flock. In the same way, in the background of *The Blind Leading the Blind*, a church is a commanding background presence. If the message of the parable, which is drawn from scripture (Matthew 15:14), is clear, Bruegel's vision of it provokes a variety of reactions. His rendition of the subject is astonishing. The chain of blind men, with one in front who falls and drags down the others, and the way this movement is broken down, is all the more powerful because the distemper technique accentuates the major shapes of the composition, while the thinness of the paint layer, even its fading with age, retains the theme's essence.

These two distemper paintings, both of which were painted for Count Masi, an adviser to Alessandro Farnese in Parma, and which now hang in the National Museum in Naples, were probably made for export, which may explain why they are on canvas rather than on a wooden panel. To these masterpieces can be added another, *The Adoration of the Magi* (fig. 74), which has hung in the Royal Art Museum in Brussels since 1909. At the time, writers who attributed this work to Bruegel dated it, despite its poor condition, between 1555 and 1563, most preferring the earlier date. It is probably a youthful work, drawing on works in the style of Bosch—in subject matter, but not in spirit—and on a composition by Raphael first produced as a tapestry in Brussels between 1520 and 1531, and then engraved and published in that form by Hieronymus Cock. Major restoration and conservation work undertaken on the work in 1968–69, which brought out its composition and markedly lightened its tone, reinforced the generally held belief that it was by Bruegel.[19] Although the image now only shows us a vision faded by time, it nevertheless radiates a mysterious feeling of emotion.

The ground, with its dark border around the subject, recalls a tapestry, and may be connected to a style of distemper painting practiced at the time by, among others, Mayken Verhulst,[20] the widow of Bruegel's master and father-in-law Pieter Coecke, at Mechelen. While Bruegel returned to the theme of the Adoration in 1564 and 1567, this particular composition was copied many times by his sons, Pieter Bruegel the Younger and Jan Bruegel, which suggests that the original was by their father.

Pieter Bruegel's distemper painting made use of elements inherent in the technique itself. As the restoration of this work has shown, the linen acts as the base color and shows through in many places. It is lightened with white, especially in the thatch of the roofs, or reinforced with ocher, especially in the landscape. Drawing and painting are closely allied, and there is a "passing from one to the other."[21] Some heightening with color, particularly with reds and blues, vermilion and azurite (but also madder, malachite, smalt, chalk, black, and ocher) punctu-

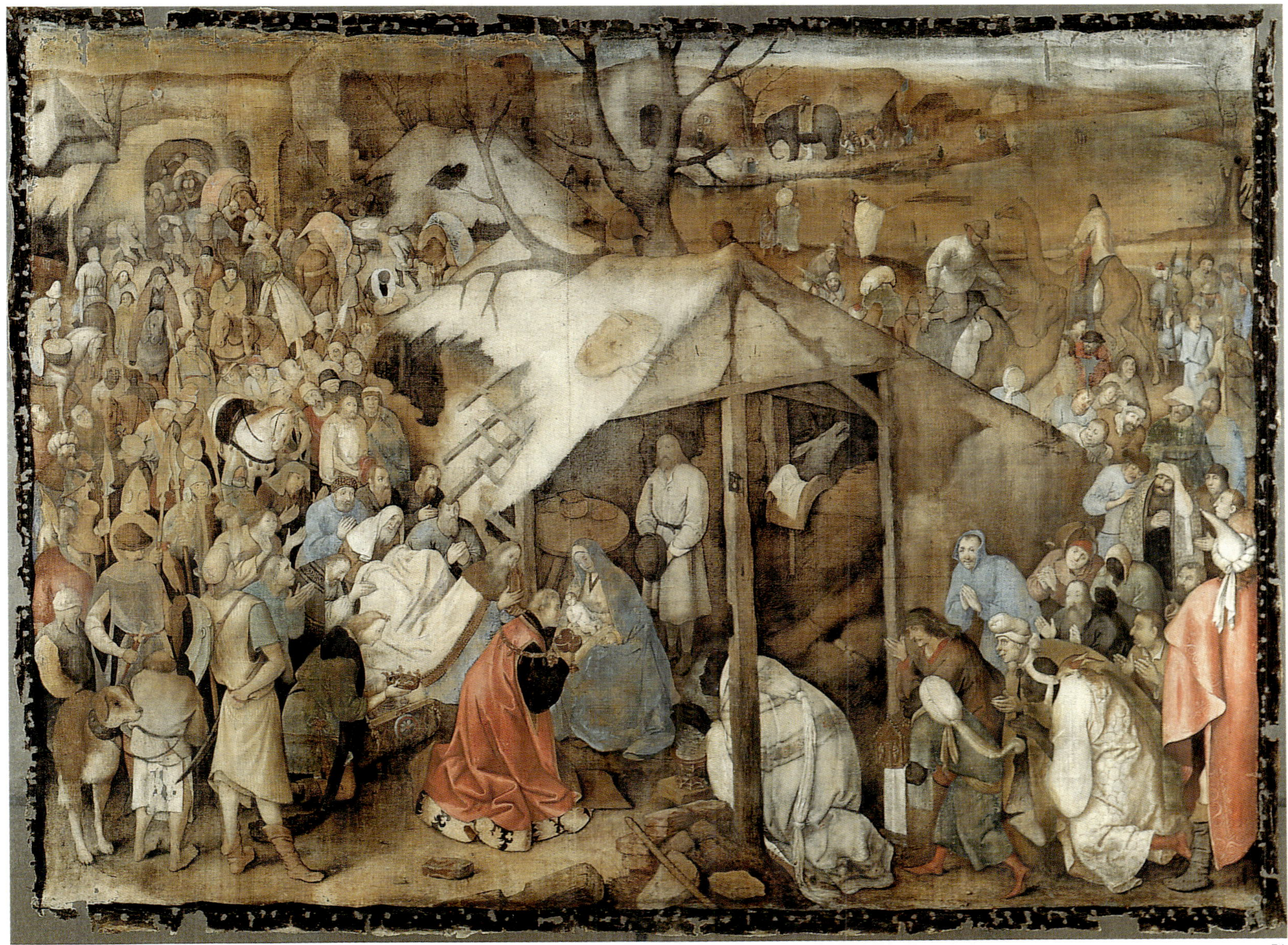

74

ates the whole and enlivens the scene, reinforcing the vitality and fervor of the characters in a spirit that expresses the presence of a creator.

Recent inventories have confirmed that Bruegel also painted in oil on canvas, and that these canvases are more numerous than had been thought.[22] But the distemper paintings also underline the expressive, fundamental strength of line in his work, and his use of cross-hatching in them demonstrates his mastery of the art of drawing.

THE ART OF DRAWING

It is unthinkable that Bruegel could have been anything but a great draftsman, as his paintings demonstrate his skill in drawing so forcefully. His drawings themselves prove it, too, although his reputation was so great that their number has sometimes been overestimated. As late as 1970 he was thought to have been the author of a group of drawings known as *naer't leven* (taken from life): exact

74–77. Pieter Bruegel, *The Adoration of the Magi*, ca. 1555–57: the complete composition and details. Distemper on linen, 48¾ x 66½ in. (124 x 169 cm). Brussels, Musées royaux des Beaux-Arts de Belgique

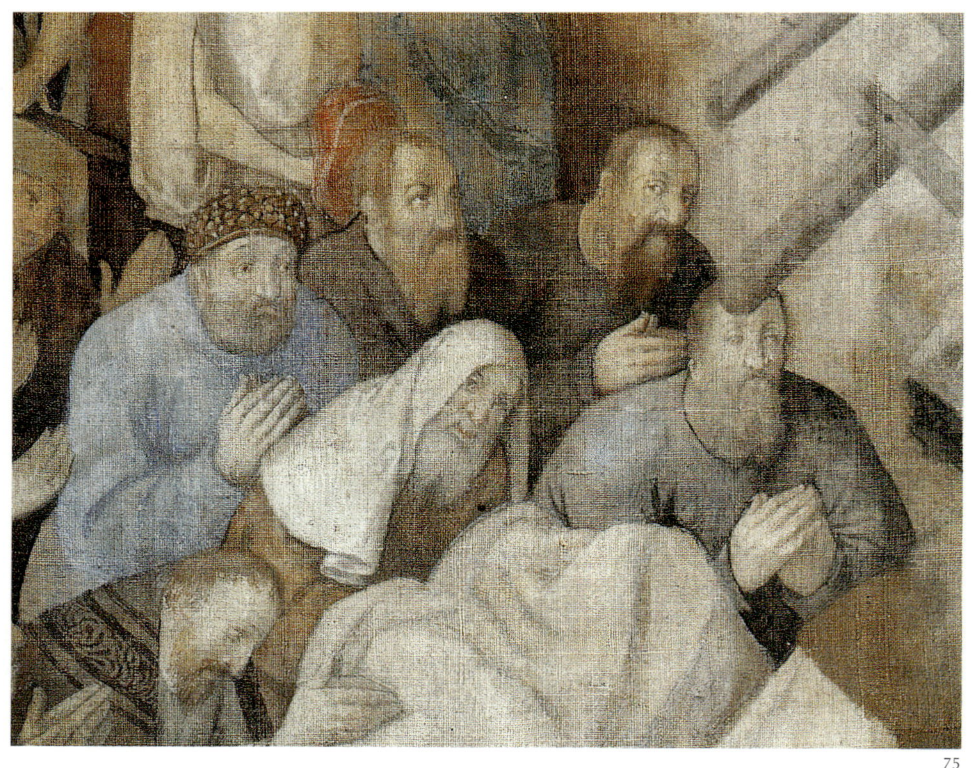

75

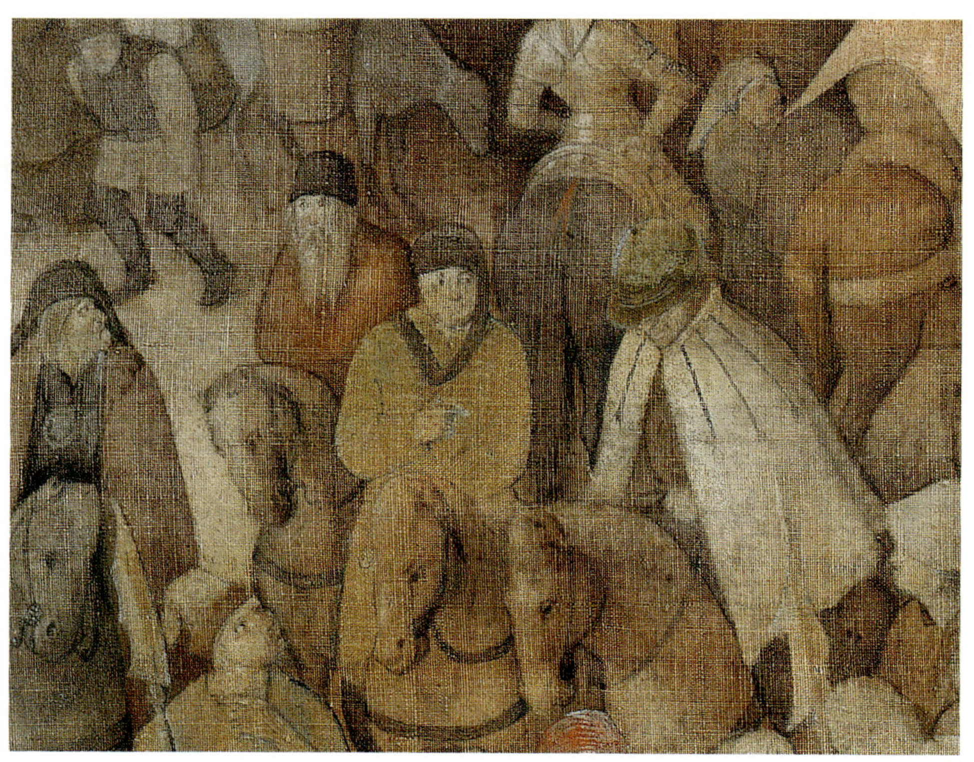

76

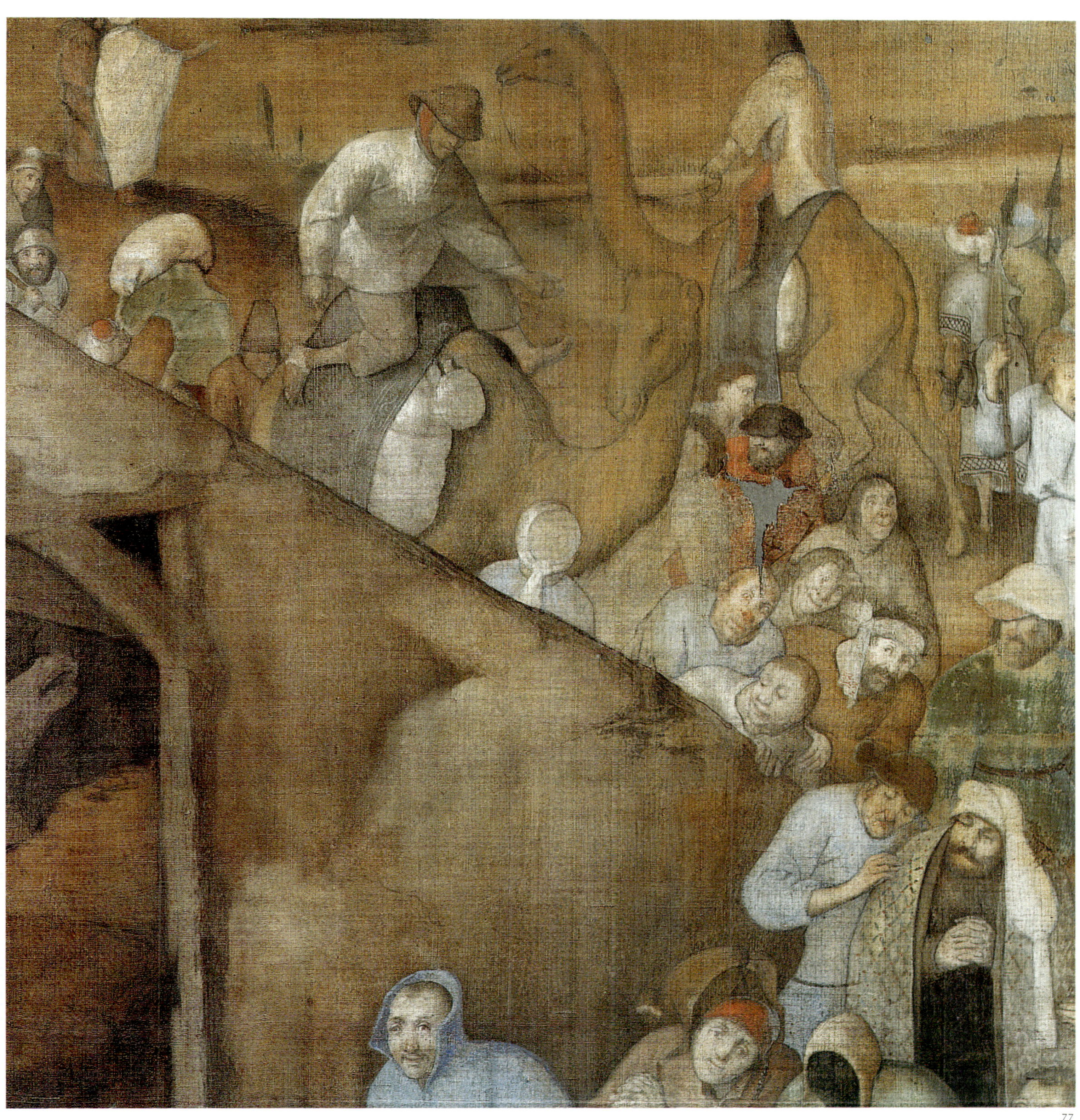

renderings of characters from everyday life, with great attention to the detail of clothing, tools, and other objects. These were long considered to be the very basis of Bruegel's approach to his art, a confirmation of the desire for accurate reproduction that is found throughout all his works. However, they are now firmly accepted as having been created by Roelandt Savery.[23]

However, we should not conclude from this that Bruegel never made sketches. High-quality drawings of figures and landscapes, dated between 1552 and 1568, show that he did. These can be divided into two groups. The first comprises drawings, chiefly landscapes, which could be described as "free" and to which he often

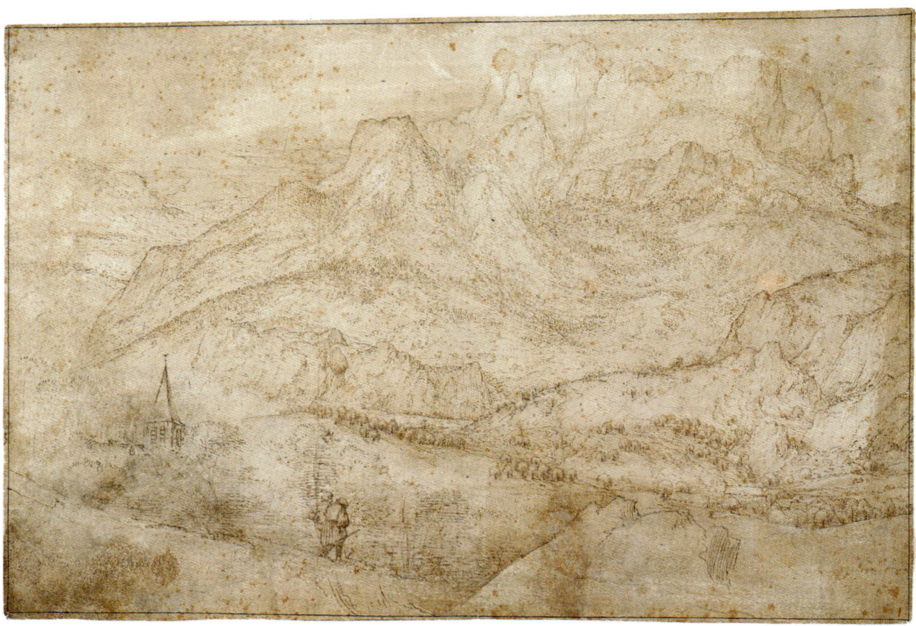

78

returned later. The second is a series of detailed drawings intended to be made into engravings. The first of Bruegel's drawings to survive are, as we know, landscapes, and many were the basis of the *Great Landscapes* series published by Hieronymus Cock in 1555–56. The earliest of these were the result of Bruegel's journey to Italy, but were often made in several successive stages: sketched in black chalk at the sites they depict, they were later finished in pen.[24] Bruegel's skill was evident from the outset. Thus, *River Landscape*, in the Louvre (fig. 80), dated 1552, has a broad sweep, and is one of his most beautiful and poetic drawings, thanks to the fineness and rhythm of its horizontal lines, which seem to follow the water's flow. This manner of modeling with parallel strokes of the pen produces—depending on the strokes' density—relief, depth, and effects of light. The technique is complemented by the effect of elements which are strong in the foreground and, fading as they get farther away, allow the eye to drift into the distance. *River Landscape* was probably executed on-site, as is suggested by many drawings or engravings that show an artist working in the open air, or seated figures looking at a view, such as *Alpine Landscape*, in the Louvre (fig. 352), and *Landscape Crossed by a River, with the Kidnap of Psyche*, which was made into an engraving by Hoefnagel (fig. 79). In *River Landscape* the economy and almost complete lack of action, details, or human figures give the scene a timeless, meditative quality similar to that of certain Oriental works of art. Its nuances and versatile language lie at the foundations of Bruegel's understanding of nature, just as the sometimes

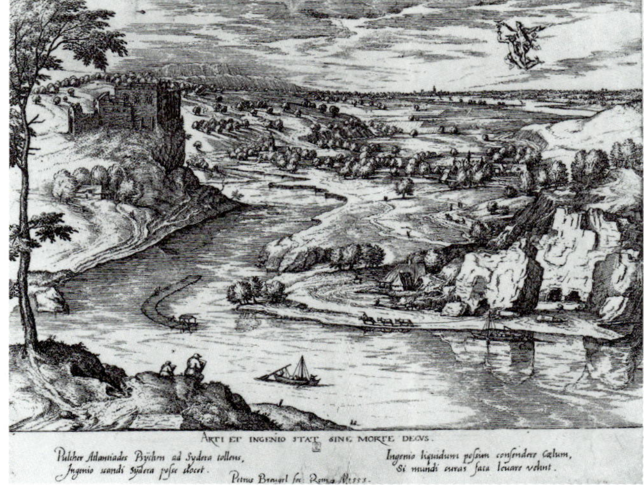

79

78. Pieter Bruegel, *Alpine Landscape*, ca. 1555.
Pen and brown ink, 12 x 17⅞ in. (30.5 x 45.6 cm).
Cambridge, Mass., Harvard University, Fogg Art Museum

79. Attributed to Georg Hoefnagel, *Landscape Crossed by a River, with the Kidnap of Psyche*, after Pieter Bruegel, ca. 1595.
Etching, 10⅝ x 13⅜ in. (21.1 x 34 cm). Brussels, Bibliothèque royale Albert I, print room

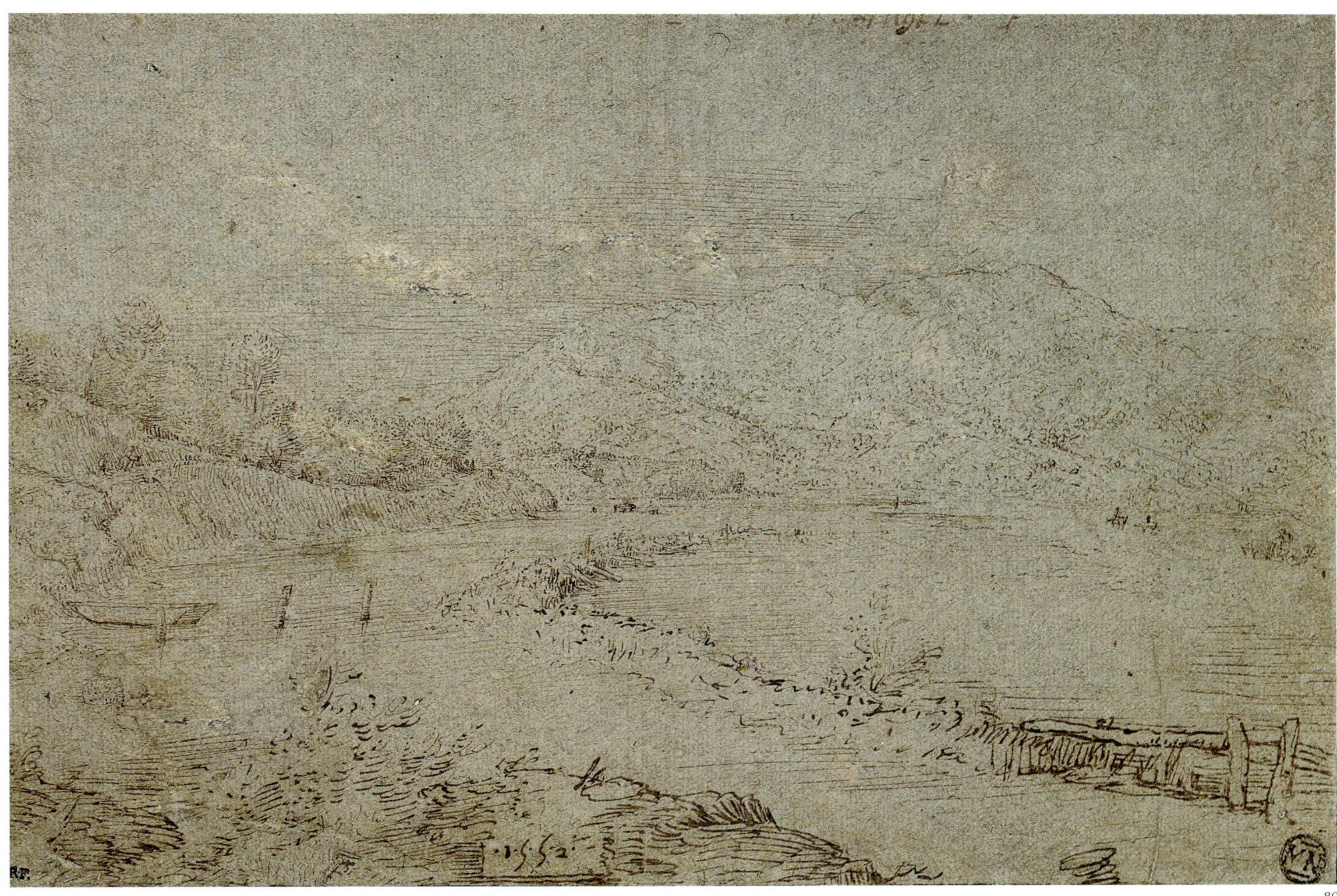

80

80. Pieter Bruegel, *River Landscape*, 1552. Pen and brown ink on blue paper, 6⅞ x 10⅜ in. (17.6 x 26.4 cm). Paris, Louvre, graphic arts department

foreboding (although not so much here) way he depicts mountains can make them appear as looming, almost architectural presences.

Alpine Landscape, now in Cambridge, Massachusetts (fig. 78), shows different stages of development. The artist started with an application of black chalk or charcoal, which was then added to in three phases: Spectrographic analysis has revealed the use of three different inks.[25] Probably the artist drew the range of mountains and the valley while he was traveling, and added the foreground after his return to Antwerp.[26] This addition seems somewhat dissonant, for the typically Flemish church on the left (which was to become an element of most of Bruegel's landscapes painted after 1563) and the two central figures are hardly in keeping with this high mountain view. The additive effect is mildly jarring, and it may be why the right foreground was left unfinished.

We need only compare *Ripa Grande* (fig. 9) with *Alpine Landscape* to see the difference between a drawing that succeeds and one that misses the mark. While the subjects are different—an urban view versus a mountain landscape—the artist proceeded in exactly the same way: by first setting out his subject in a general sense in the upper part of the sheet, and then returning to it later to fill in the foreground. The way these drawings were made, and the fact that Bruegel returned to them, indicate the importance he gave to these works, which were often destined to be made into engravings, but also, no doubt, intended to be sold as works of art in their own right. Drawing was much appreciated in the sixteenth century and

some enthusiasts practiced it for its own sake, which, at the time, seems to have
been something of a novelty.

DRAWINGS FOR PRINTS

From notations taken at a scene to the finished composition, from the sketch to
the fully realized subject, Bruegel took great pleasure in creating, but also responding to a commission for an engraving, no doubt from Hieronymus Cock himself.
From *The Ass at School* of 1556 (fig. 81) onwards, he worked with this final result
in mind. In this work he does not confine himself simply to depicting his subject in
a caustic and amusing manner—"Although the ass may go to school, being an ass,
he will not return as a horse"—but transcribes this curious masquerade, where
children have the faces of adults, into lines and hatching in a graphic language that
conveys, if not Bruegel's experience, at any rate his intimate knowledge of the
engraver's craft. The lines that criss-cross in various densities in the alcove on the
left and behind the ass are an example. It fell to Pieter van der Heyden in 1557 to
copy the original on a copper plate so as to produce an exact, mirror-imaged print
(fig. 82). This is a faithful reproduction, and yet a different one, for engraving is
the result of a process of incision which, when printed, produces a slight relief in
the inked areas. Moreover, the engraver's emphasis of the floor, which is heavily
stippled, and the deep cuts of the burin, define the volumes of the work more clearly
than in the drawing, but also darken the entire scene. Luminous in the drawing,
the engraved image seems frozen; the transcription onto the copper plate deadens
the liveliness of the work.

Bruegel's borrowings from the language of Bosch, already present in *The Big
Fish Eat the Little Fish* (figs. 16 and 17) and *The Temptation of St. Anthony* (fig. 89)
made the same year, can be seen here in various attitudes and quirks. With each
drawing Bruegel develops his repertoire, as can be seen in *Children's Games* of
1560 (fig. 246). The child stripping in the middle distance will reappear in *Lust*
(fig. 99), one of the prints in the celebrated *Deadly Sins* series. The drawings for
that series confirm that Bruegel was acquainted with the language into which they
would be transcribed, where the image would always be reversed, and which
forced him, in his drawings, to include deliberate inversions, such as the clock in
Sloth (fig. 94) and the three left-handed characters in the center of *Envy* (fig. 98).

The precision of line and the rendering of details and textures enrich these
drawings to the point of virtuosity. If the imaginary reigns supreme in the *Sins*
series, the real world asserts itself as a composite presence in the *Virtues*. Here
there is narrative, description, allusion, and enigma, giving rise to both interpretation and comment. Composition and expression always revolve around a symbolic
central figure from which a series of encyclopedic or exemplary scenes, underlin-
ing or illustrating the subject, is developed in parallel or radial planes.

The art of the miniature remains significant, despite the absence of colors.
The interplay of black and white, the shading of the grays, the illusion of movement and of textures, bring these pages marvelously to life, making them completely composed, finished works just as much as the paintings that were to follow
them, which indeed were to echo them in some ways.

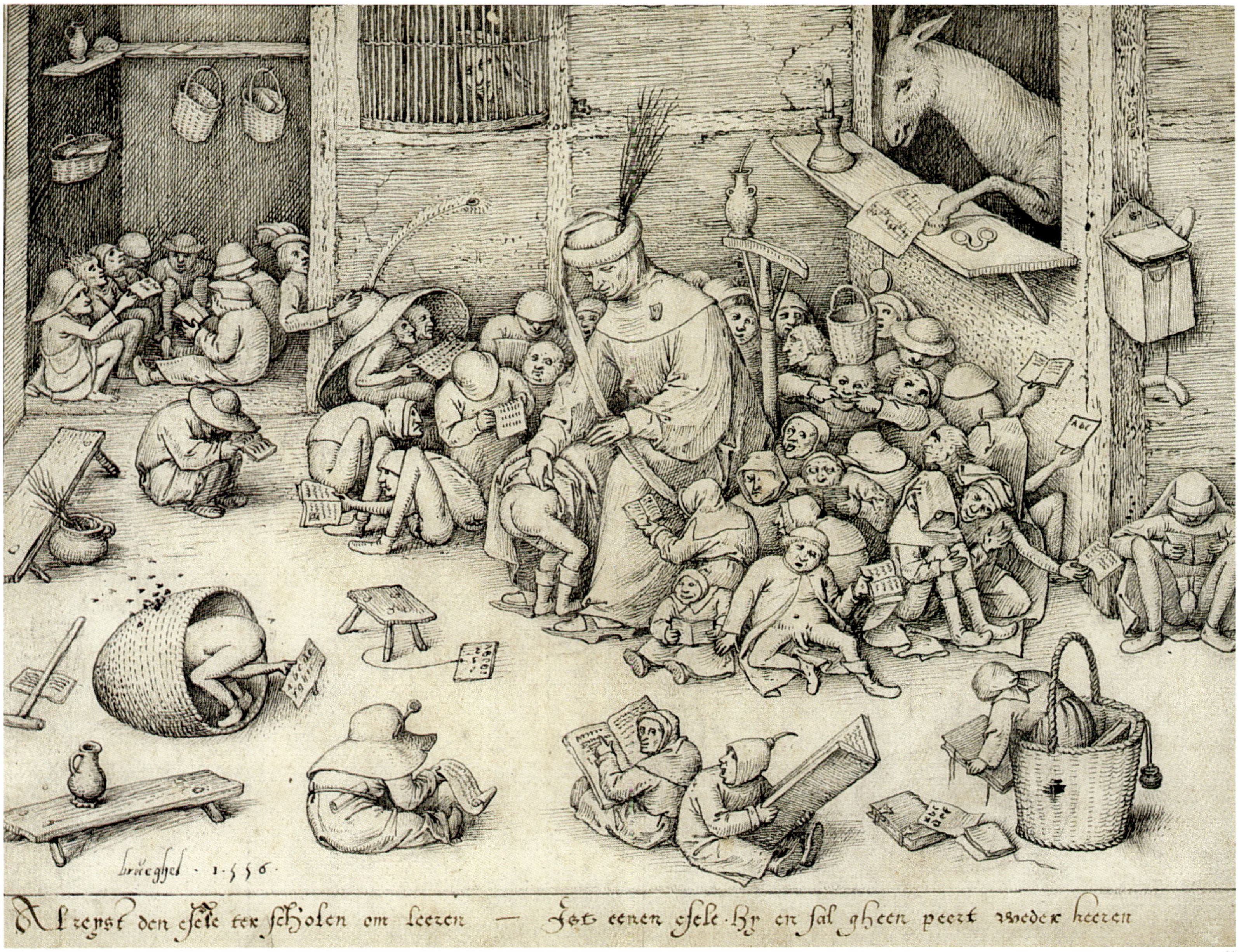

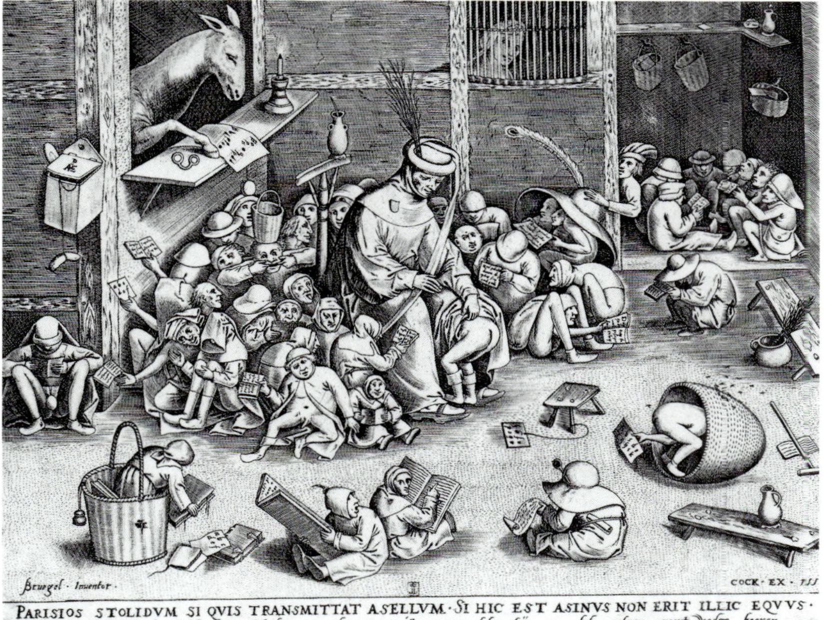

81. Pieter Bruegel, *The Ass at School*, 1556. Pen and black ink,
9⅛ x 11⅞ in. (23.2 x 30.2 cm). Berlin, Staatliche Museen,
Kupferstichkabinett

82. Pieter van der Heyden, *The Ass at School*, after Pieter Bruegel,
1557. Engraving, 9⅛ x 11⅞ in. (23.4 x 30.3 cm). Brussels,
Bibliothèque royale Albert I, print room

Bruegel, as we know, made drawings throughout his life. But while the number of drawings that survive is greatest in the period 1552–60, important works stand out as landmarks at intervals until 1568—even though roughly twenty of these, including *Views of Amsterdam*, *Landscape with Castle*, and *The Blind Leading the Blind*, have recently been attributed to Jacques Savery, elder brother of Roelandt.[27]

Bruegel once again asserted his eloquent graphic language in 1568, although, after he had moved to Brussels his production of engravings had dropped and paintings dominated his work. Nevertheless, his virtuosity was undiminished, as *The Beekeepers* (fig. 85) shows. Although no print after this drawing survives, it was surely, on the evidence, made with this end in mind: The richness of the language, the shading, and the punctuation demonstrate this clearly.

In the universe he creates, nature alone—the earth, the trees, and the man who has climbed up into one of them—appears to belong to reality. The beekeepers, the hives, and the buildings themselves, because of their shape and geometry, come from another world. Seen through twentieth-century eyes, they recall the metaphysical art of De Chirico. The image appears clear, depicting the gathering of honey. However, in the tree behind the beekeepers, hard at work in their heavy protective clothing, is a bird-nester—a well-known figure from the painting of 1568 of the same title. At the bottom of the drawing, on the left, is an inscription: *Nije den Nest Weet die weten/dijen Roft dij heeten* (He who knows where the nest is has knowledge, but he who raids it possesses it). Applying this maxim to *The Beekeepers* raises questions. Might we not simply see in it the idea that action wins out over mere knowledge? Need we look further for meaning in a work that carries an open message, as do almost all of Bruegel's creations, which, through their genius, go beyond the bounds of their age? What is particularly important here is that the inscription, in the same ink as the drawing, was made by the artist's own hand.

The breadth and quality of these pages destined to become engravings are essential to an understanding of Bruegel's oeuvre. They reveal the artist's work at an important time of his life, and his participation in an activity which was prolifically practiced at the time: engraving. Through it we can follow not only the development of his art, but perhaps also of his reputation. The audience at whom prints were aimed was inevitably larger—since they were printed in considerable numbers—than that of paintings. Furthermore, since it appears that Bruegel received only private commissions, his paintings did not appear in churches or public buildings. His route to success can be traced through the art of engraving itself.

ENGRAVING AND ENGRAVERS

The twelve *Great Landscapes* (figs. 84, 165, and 167), which are etchings and engravings, are only signed by the publisher, Hieronymus Cock. Louis Lebeer attributed them to Cock himself, but writers today assert they were mostly executed by Johannes and Lucas van Duetecum.[28] *The Temptation of St. Anthony*, made in 1556, bears no signature, and *The Big Fish Eat the Little Fish* of 1557 is signed Hieronymus Bosch, but *The Ass at School*, of the same date, and *Patience* (fig. 92)

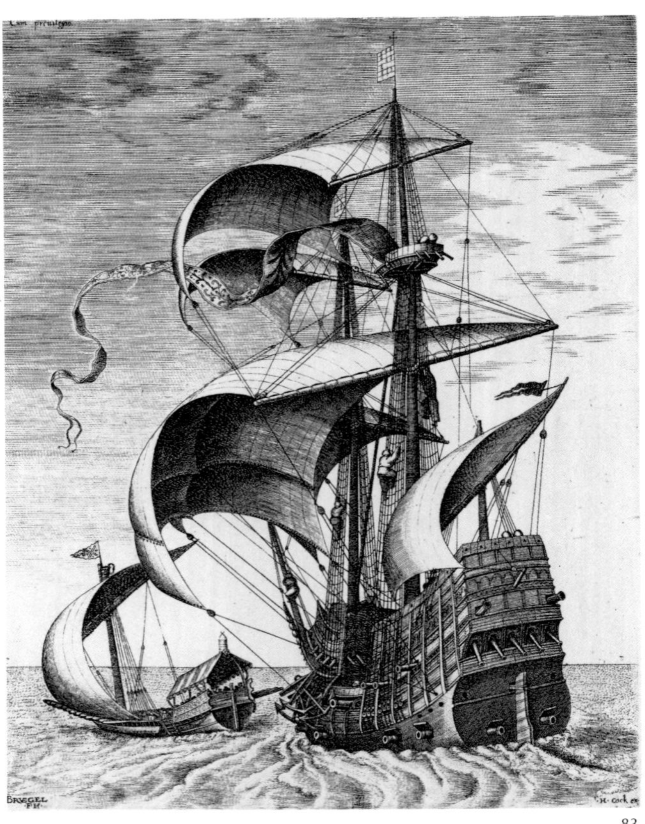

83. Frans Huys, *Three-Masted Ship with Cannon, Accompanied by a Brigantine*, from the series *Sea-Going Ships*, after Pieter Bruegel, ca. 1561–62. Engraving, 12⅜ x 9⅝ in. (31.4 x 24.5 cm). Brussels, Bibliothèque royale Albert I, print room

bear the signature of Bruegel. From that date onward his name appears on all his engravings, which were mostly made by Pieter van der Heyden (alias Petrus a Merica or Mericynus), Philipp Galle, and Frans Huys, all of whom worked for Cock at the Four Winds. There is no doubt that the most faithful, despite an occasional heaviness, was Pieter van der Heyden, to whom we are indebted for the greatest number of plates. The work of Philipp Galle, who engraved the *Virtues* series, sometimes appears drier than Van der Heyden's, but it is also lighter, since Galle rarely crosshatched, preferring parallel lines.

Since many of Bruegel's preparatory drawings have survived, the quality of their rendering as engravings can be appreciated, according to one's taste. This is not true, however, of *Naval Battle in the Strait of Messina* or the series *Sea-Going Ships* (1561–62) engraved by Frans Huys (figs. 319 and 83), the drawings for which are not extant. These beautiful engravings convey a perfect knowledge of naval weaponry, which Bruegel could have acquired simply by visiting the quay-

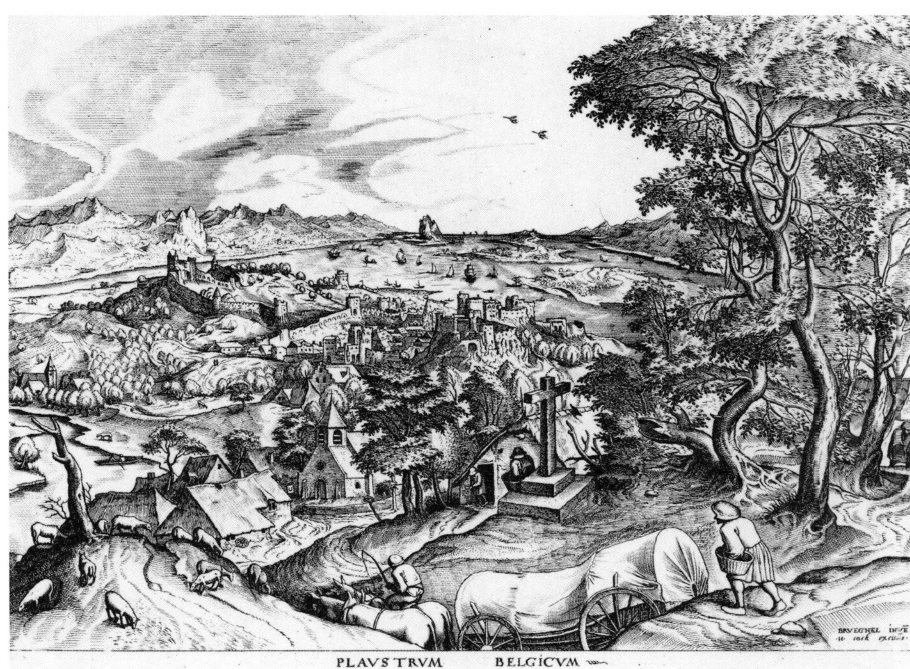

84

side at Antwerp. Such is his curiosity and love of detail in other spheres that it is not surprising to see it extended to ship design. There are also similarities with works whose authorship has been questioned, such as *View of Naples*, which can be compared to the engraving picturing the Strait of Messina. Furthermore, there is a drawing of Reggio di Calabria which has been dated about 1552, and the superb caravel in *The Fall of Icarus*, as well as two drawings, *View of Ripa Grande in Rome* (1553) and *View of Antwerp from the Scheldt River* (about 1559), which demonstrate Bruegel's interest in maritime matters.

Thanks to this profusion of engravings, Bruegel's name must have acquired the renown which explained, and justified, their publication by Hieronymus Cock. Even after 1558 more engravings were to see the light—either in the style of the master or after his drawings and paintings—engraved by Georg Hoefnagel, Pieter Perret, Jan Wierix, Pieter van der Heyden, or Philipp Galle. In the seventeenth century the Bruegel spirit can be seen in engravings by Hendrik Hondius, and by Lucas Vorsterman, who worked for Rubens.

84. Johannes or Lucas Van Duetecum (?), *Plaustrum Belgicum*, from the series *Great Landscapes,* after Pieter Bruegel, 1555–56. Etching and engraving, 12⅝ x 16¾ in. (32.1 x 42.6 cm). Brussels, Bibliothèque royale Albert I, print room

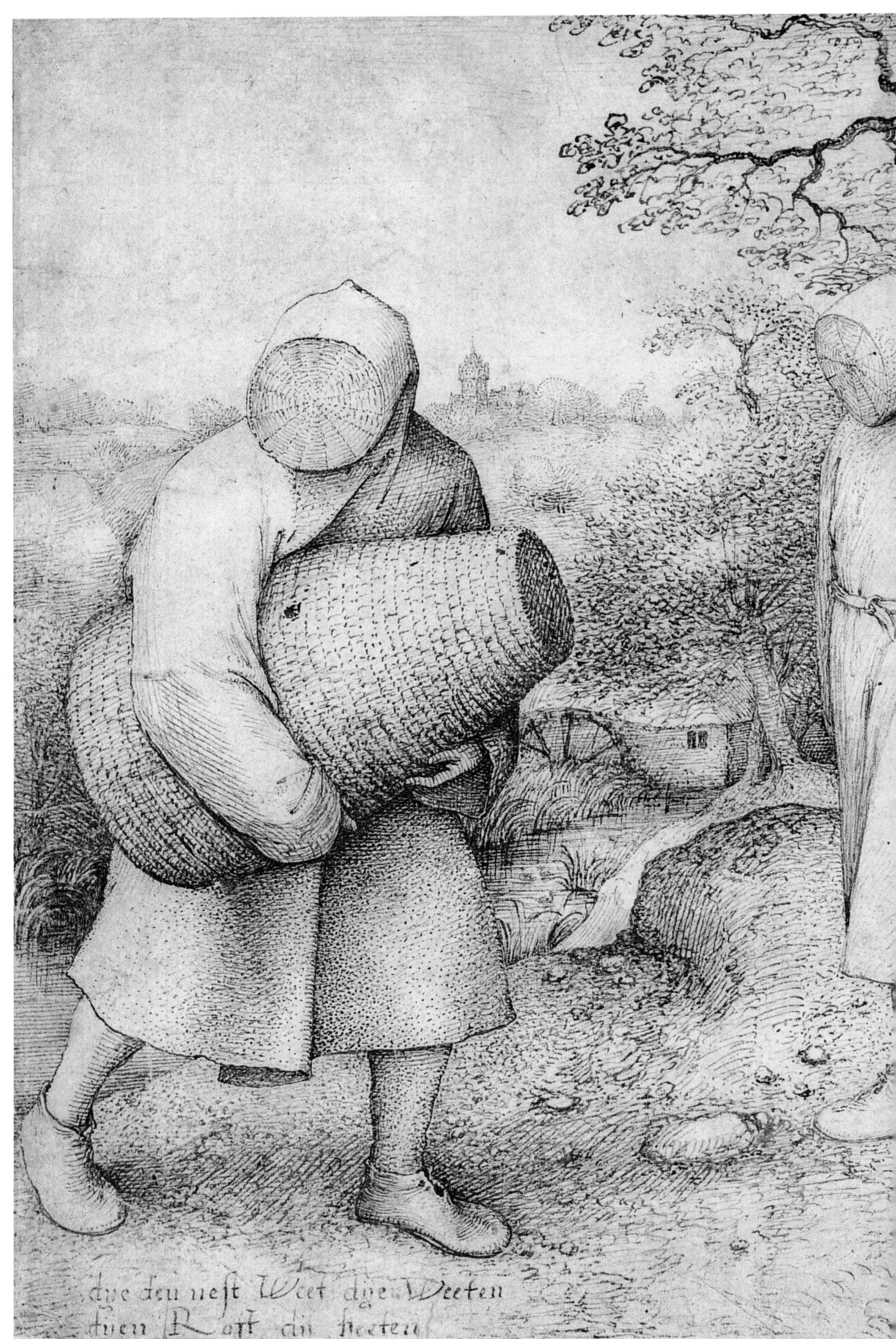

85. Pieter Bruegel, *The Beekeepers*,
1568. Pen and brown ink, 8 x 12⅛ in.
(20.3 x 30.9 cm). Berlin, Staatliche
Museen, Kupferstichkabinett

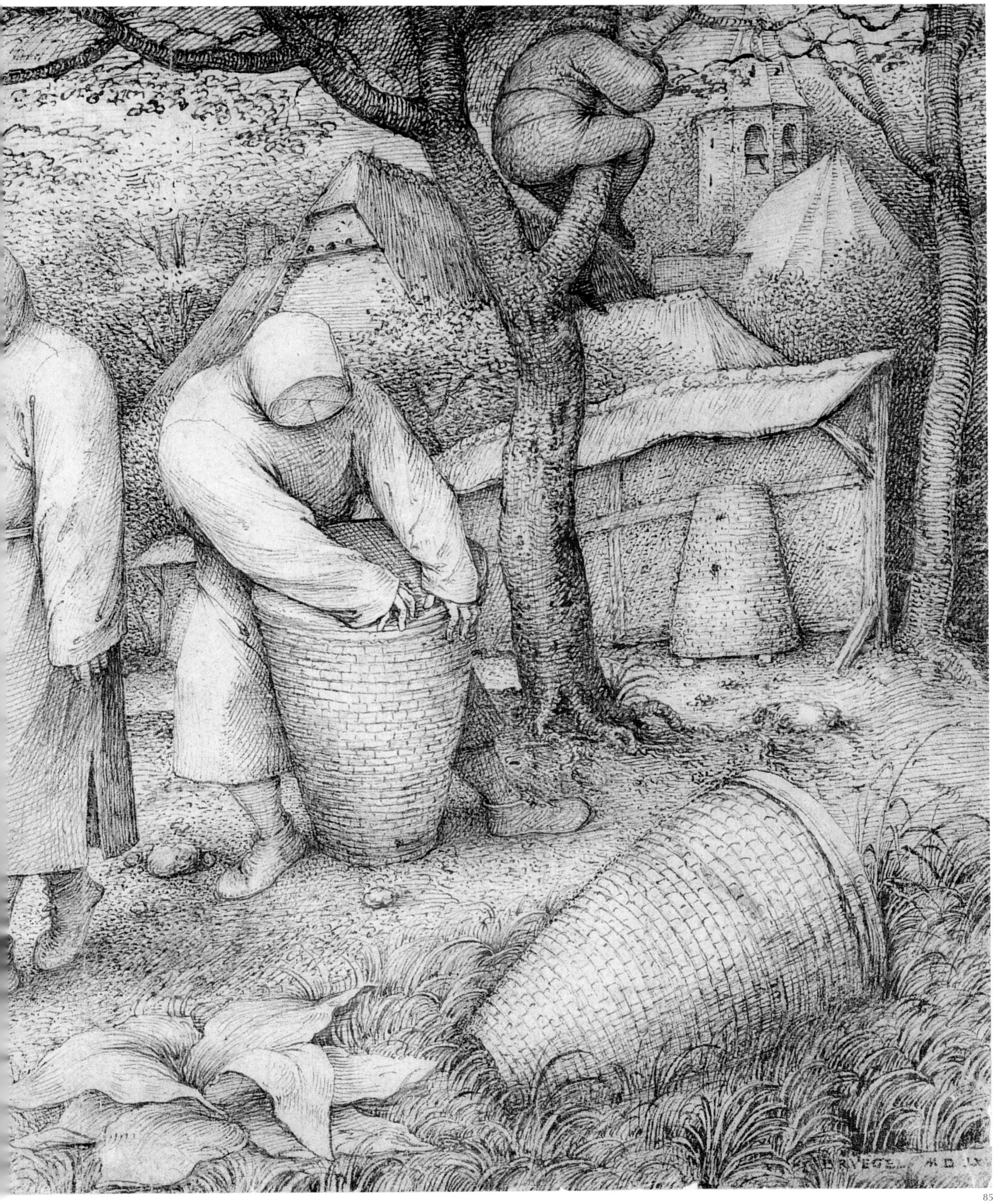
BRVEGEL M D LX

BRUEGEL THE ENGRAVER

The history of printmaking often draws a distinction between original engravings and engraved versions of other works—between Dürer's masterly creation of an immense body of work and Marcantonio Raimondi's engravings after the compositions of other artists, especially Raphael's. In theory, Bruegel belongs to the second category, but his drawings argue against this. As if he wanted to make this point himself, Bruegel produced an etching, *Hunting for Wild Rabbits* (fig. 86). It is signed, but the date, which is hard to read and looks like 1506, must, of course, be wrong. The year 1566, Louis Lebeer's reading, is possible, as this date would place the etching in the wake of the *Months* and the *Seasons* of 1565. Today, most writers agree on a date of 1560. The etching was published by Hieronymus Cock during Bruegel's Antwerp period. Aside from its striking luminosity, it illustrates in the foreground Erasmus's dictum that you should not chase two hares at once, a proverb to which Jacob Cats was to return later.[29]

Is not the hunter who is threatening the game himself under threat from a soldier rounding the tree? However, the work's essential quality lies, not in this seeming double meaning, but in the landscape, which, if we accept the date 1560, foreshadows the *Seasons* and, perhaps more precisely, *The Flight into Egypt* of 1563 (fig. 140). In this etching Bruegel conveys the effect of light by making

86. Pieter Bruegel, *Hunting Wild Rabbits,* 1560 (?). Original etching, 8¾ x 11½ in. (22.3 x 29.1 cm). Brussels, Bibliothèque royale Albert I, print room

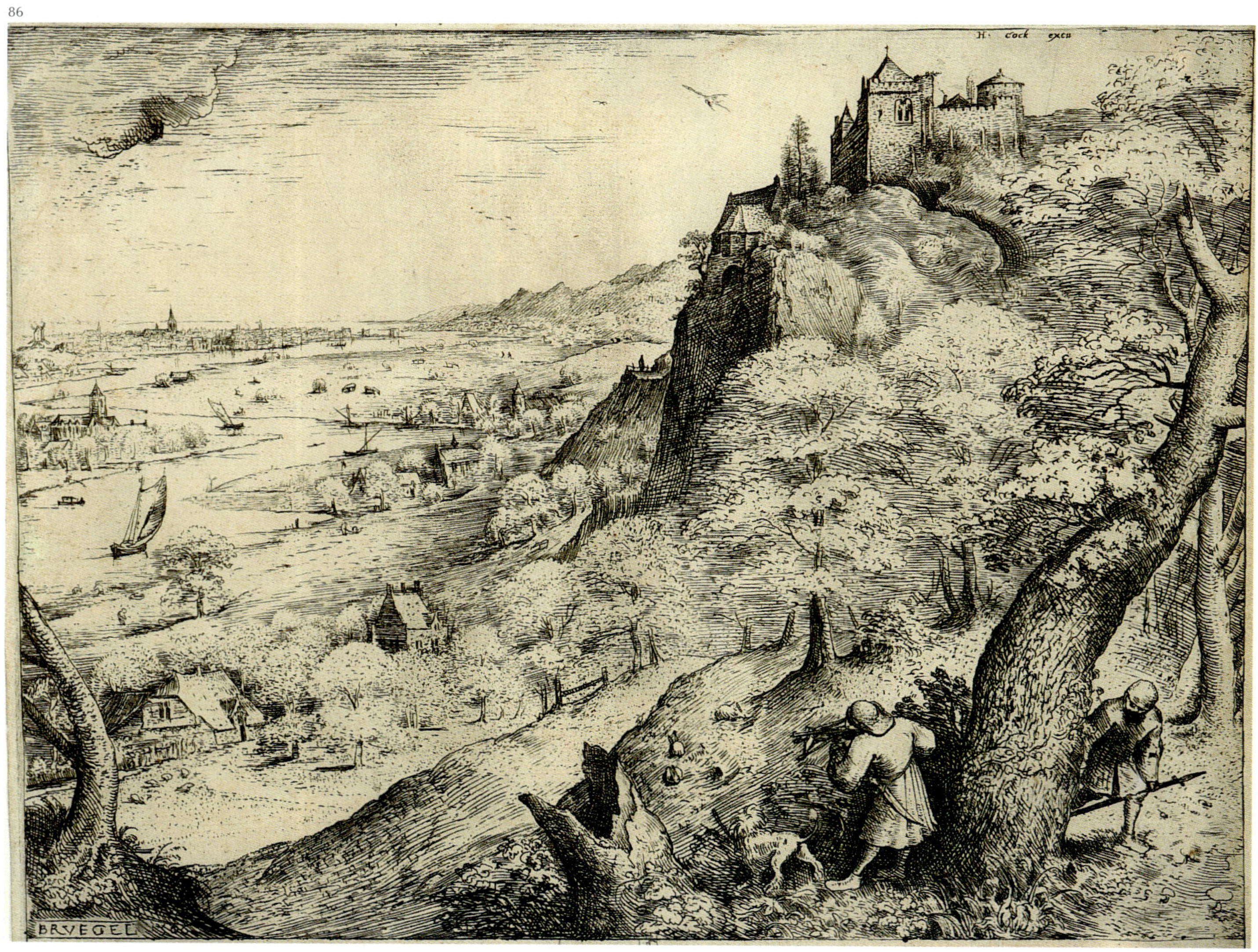

use of the underlying paper as an expressive feature, and by creating volumes using terse little lines, for example, in the foliage. Bruegel strengthened his shadows, loaded planes with ink, and sketched in the distance with a simple line. Four centuries later, Lebeer remarked: "Solely by the creative power of his hand and the acuteness of his perceptions, Bruegel here succeeds in balancing and harmonizing—in that unity of vision that characterizes all his creations—all the elements of a landscape whose living natural beauty moves the soul as much as it astounds the eyes."[30]

It is an original work, therefore. It may not be the work of a master technician, but it is that of a creator who understands the details of a craft and is not content merely to produce models to be transposed later. To complete the picture of Bruegel's contribution to the graphic world, it should be added that some engravings heightened with color were sold at the time,[31] and that two woodcuts are known of subjects drawn from his painting of 1559, *The Battle of Carnival and Lent* (fig. 125). The first, which is anonymous, is *The Masquerade of Bear Cub and Valentine* (fig. 87), dated 1566; the other is an unfinished wood block, with the drawing still on it and ready for cutting, *The Wedding of Mopsus and Nisa* (fig. 88). The latter was made into an engraving by Hieronymus Cock in 1570, the year the great print publisher died.

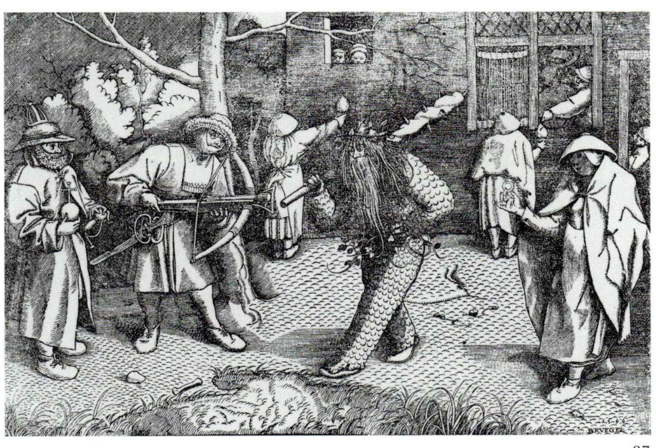

87

87. Anonymous, *The Masquerade of Bear Cub and Valentine*, after Pieter Bruegel, 1566. Woodcut, 10³/₄ x 16¹/₈ in. (27.4 x 41 cm). Brussels, Bibliothèque royale Albert I, print room

88. Pieter Bruegel, *The Wedding of Mopsus and Nisa*, ca. 1566. Pen and brown ink on panel, 10¹/₂ x 16³/₈ (26.6 x 41.6 cm). New York, Metropolitan Museum of Art, Department of Prints

88

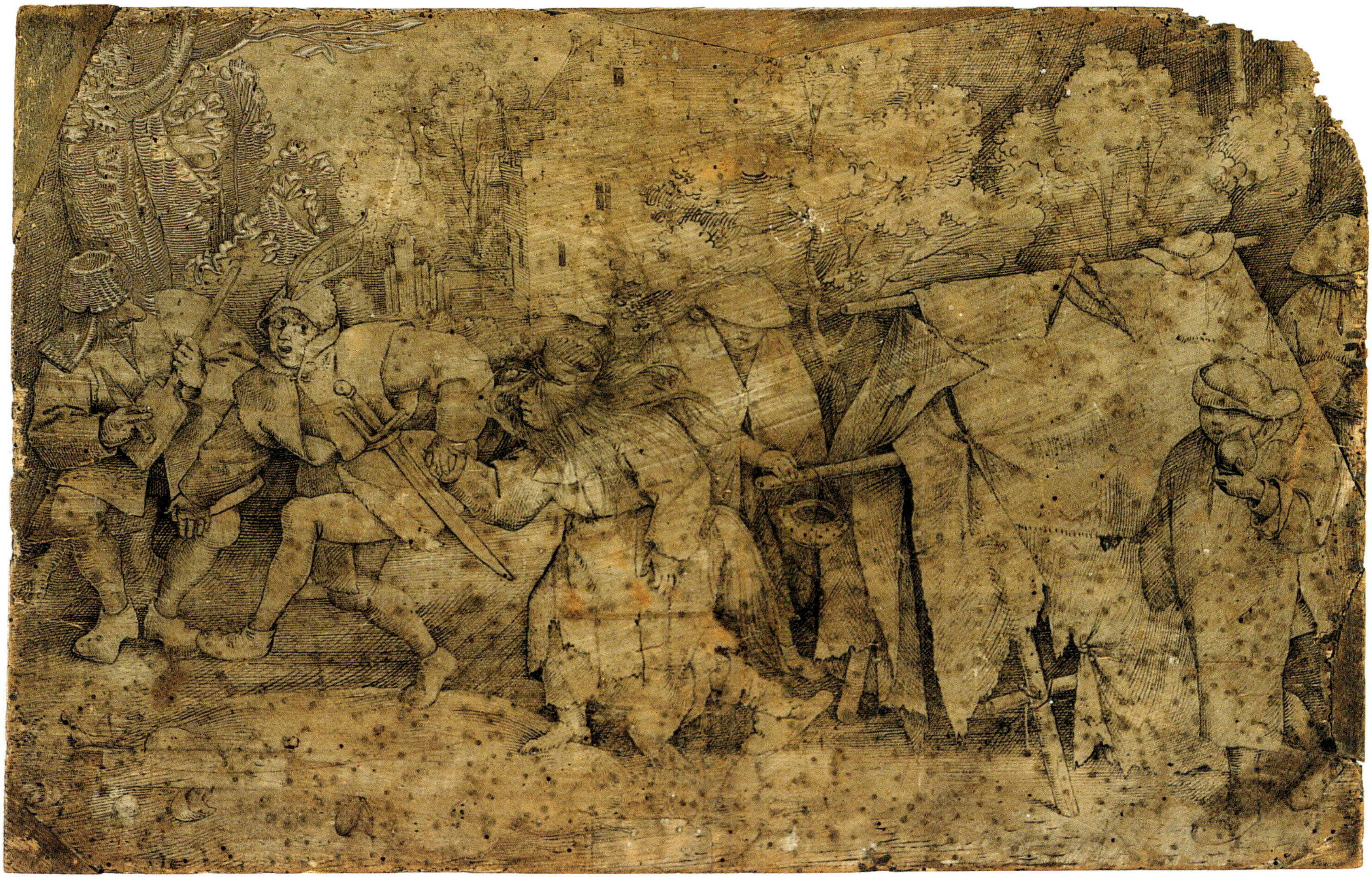

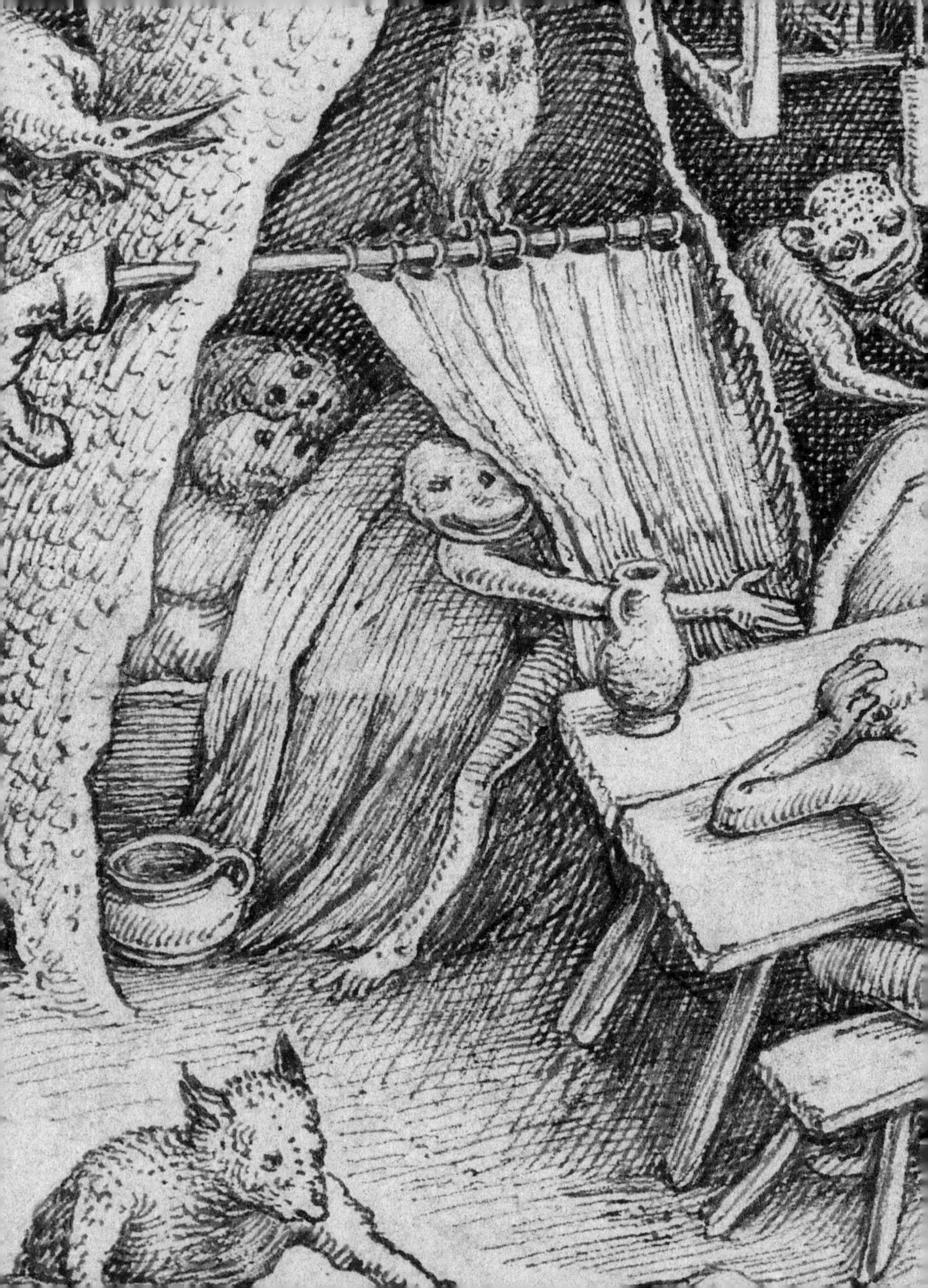

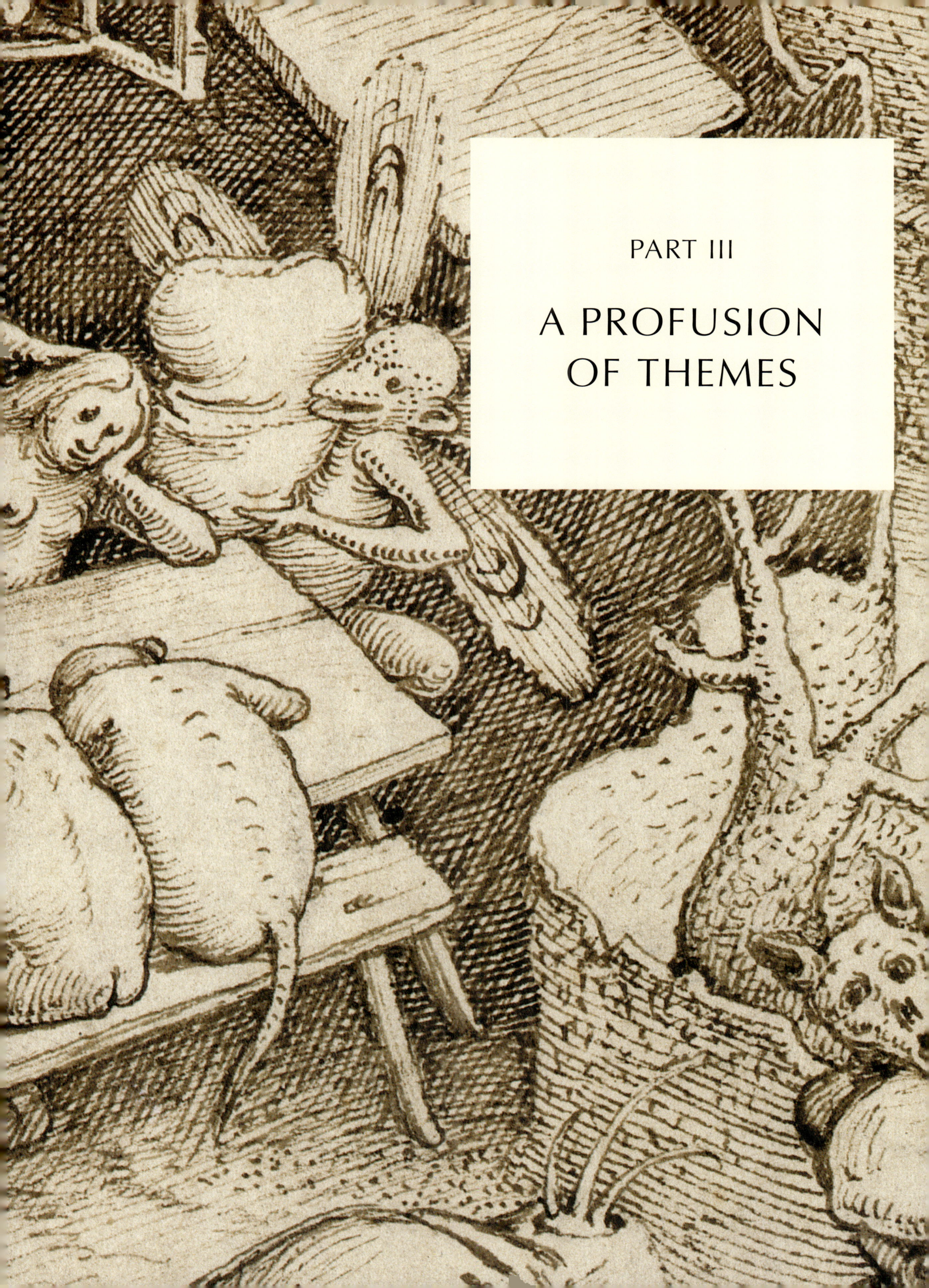

PART III

A PROFUSION
OF THEMES

HEAVEN AND HELL

Every life includes periods that are not simply one of the proverbial stages of youth, maturity, and old age, but are, aside from chance and contacts with others, also marked by tendencies, orientations, changes of course brought about by a personal quest, or by existence itself. An artist's work is therefore subject to preoccupations, obsessions, and changes of mood. This is why it is usual to identify certain stages in an artist's development, and to classify one or another group of works according to the influences on it. If good written records or literary references exist, or a precise chronology is available, analyzing the artist's work consists of checking and organizing the archival material and then making an inventory that allows the creation of a work of art or the stages of an artist's quest to be traced, with all of its innovations, corrections, discoveries, borrowings, its fixed ideas and concerns, its returns to sources, and its nostalgia. Every body of creative work feeds, in some way, its creator's sensibilities—which may be in accord with or may clash with his or her own time. Sometimes the work illustrates the story of the artist's life. From Titian to Picasso, from Michelangelo to Delacroix, Rubens to Bacon, Giotto to Cézanne, and from Grünewald to Klee, multifarious sensibilities feed into an infinitely broad visual invention that perceives the outside world and depicts a mental image. This diversity is evident in Bruegel's work, and the natural desire of all those who look at it is to seek an answer to the questions it asks of the viewer, specialist or otherwise, and to try to order the procession of images so as to group them, rightly or wrongly, according to their apparent affinities or family resemblances. Bruegel offers an incentive to do so, since he often took the trouble to date his works, which was not common practice in the sixteenth century. However, there are some problematic exceptions to this. Attempts have been made to solve these by fixing an undated work in time either according to its theme or, more commonly, its content.

Hell, earth, and heaven are the three fundamental places where beings exist and act, in reality or in the imagination. Mankind's relationship with these places, and their effect upon mankind, are inevitably studied by the painter, who is exercised by the problems this relationship raises, not because it enslaves the individual but because of the reasons, or ties, that can govern it—divine law, natural law, or human law. If Bruegel's work includes paintings in which hell, heaven, or earth show themselves to be dominant, where man is chained to infernal forces or divine will, or faces a struggle for survival, can these visions and concerns be grouped into distinct periods? The constant presence of these fundamental questions rules out, it seems, all desire for rationality on the artist's part, all the more since the very duration of Bruegel's creative output was so short.

The dates between which we know Bruegel was at work cover less than 20 years, from 1551, when he was first enrolled in the guild as a master, to 1569, the year of his death. The complexity of the themes he dealt with prevents us from making strict divisions between one overriding concern and another. While a synthesized vision of nature came to the fore about 1565, that same nature, no doubt seen from a different angle, had already caught the painter's eye when

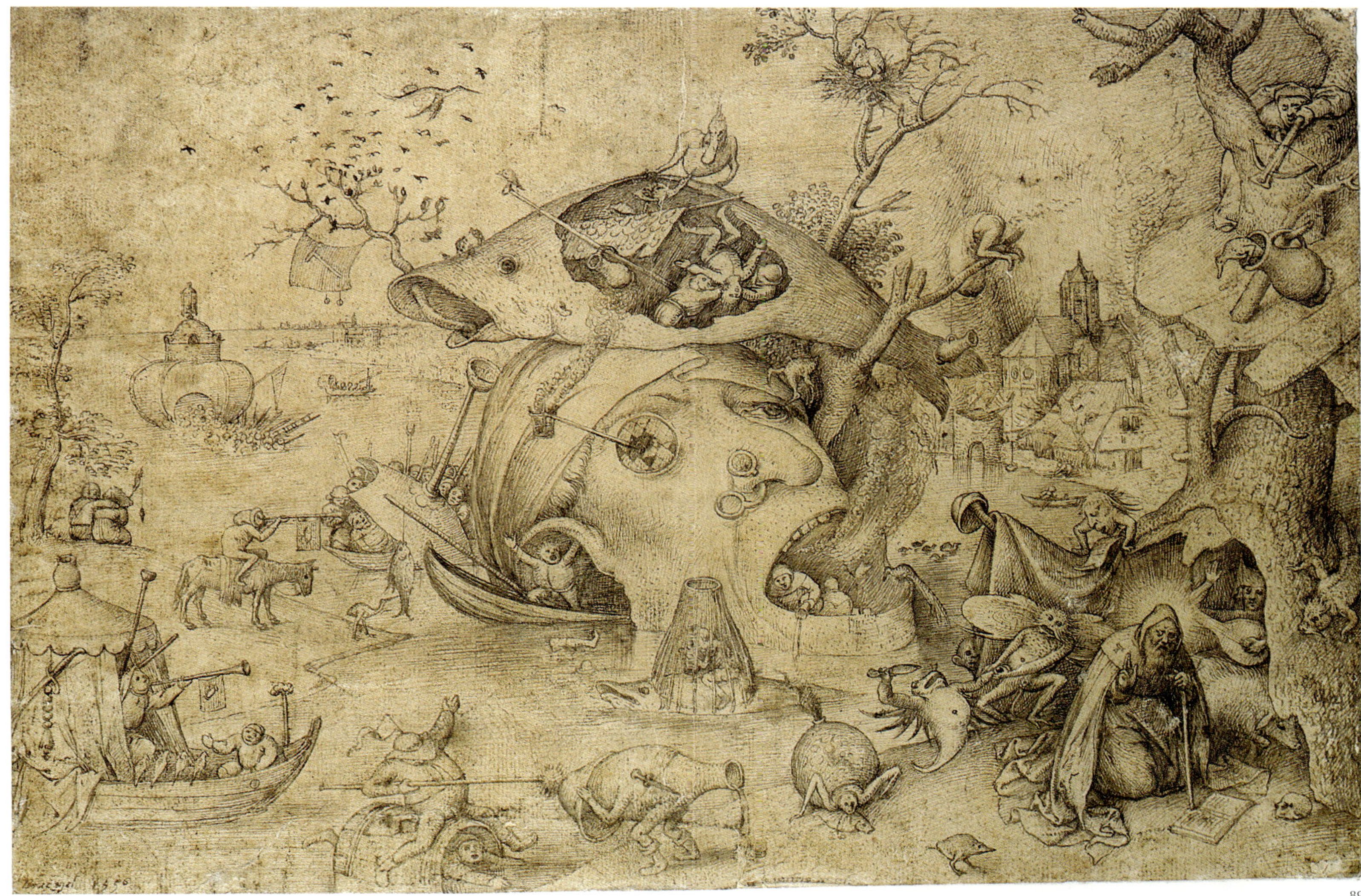

89. Pieter Bruegel, *The Temptation of St. Anthony*, 1556.
Pen and brush, with brown ink, 8¹⁄₂ x 12³⁄₄ in.
(21.6 x 32.6 cm). Oxford, Ashmolean Museum

he crossed the Alps—and, among his last statements, is not *The Magpie on the Gallows* (fig. 360) one of the most beautiful works in the history of painting? Hell and its works seem to drive Bruegel's brush during his Antwerp period—for example with *Dulle Griet* (fig. 101) in 1561—or to sharpen his quill in the *Deadly Sins* series of 1556–68 (figs. 93–100); but *St. James and the Magician Hermogenes* (fig. 133) and *The Fall of the Magician* (fig. 134), both of which are swarming with infernal, fantastic creations, date from 1565.

This suggests that Bruegel never systematically developed any particular theme at any given point of his life. While certain subjects such as proverbs, children's games, and virtues, can lead to methodical or encyclopedic analysis, often in the form of maxims, the big themes—heaven and hell, earth and mankind—are limitless, in all of his works. As fundamental elements of both the man and the artist, they are permanently in evidence and interacting with each other. *The Fall of the Rebel Angels* (fig. 114) embodies the simultaneity of heaven and hell; *The Flight into Egypt* (fig. 140) evokes the dual presence of God and nature; and *The Massacre of the Innocents* (fig. 145) is a cataclysm happening to the artist's own people, in his own time. There is no divergence of context: on the contrary, themes complement each other.

There is no dividing line between the real and the imaginary. Consequently, it is pointless to try to tie the painter to the representation of one or the other, or to think that one replaces or denotes the other. Unreal or imaginary language is as familiar to Bruegel as the real images on which his keen eye feasts. The monster is as alive as the tree. The composite, hybrid figures that he manufactures with such astonishing imagination give him at least as much pleasure as his portrayal of a stonemason in *The Tower of Babel* (fig. 275) or three peasant women in *Haymaking* (fig. 176). The full range of hellish things is as familiar to him as the characters he meets in everyday life. Monstrous figures have inhabited paintings of the Last Judgment at least since the work of Jan Van Eyck, and they appear in the work of Matthias Grünewald, Hieronymus Bosch, and Jan Wellens de Cock, the father of Hieronymus Cock, Bruegel's friend and colleague. We also see them in prints, from the woodcuts of the *Ars Bene Moriendi* of about 1450 to the work of German engravers in the first half of the sixteenth century, as well as in the work of Martin Schongauer and Albrecht Dürer. And from earlier periods, they adorn the margins of illuminated manuscripts and invade the Romanesque and Gothic bestiary from its capitals to its gargoyles, as well as the alcoves containing edifying images in which good is contrasted with evil.

In a society that has no concept of an artist's proprietorship of his creation, in which the qualities of art and imagination are based on what is already known, and which lacks any ideal of deliberately setting out to make something new or to contrive for the sake of contriving, what matters is the use of an artistic language, the created work itself, its power and beauty. This being so, it seems that hell and evil, whether for personal reasons or in response to commissions, held Bruegel's attention from 1556, when he made the drawings for the series of engravings *Deadly Sins*. The engravings were made by Pieter van der Heyden and published by Hieronymus Cock in 1558. *The Temptation of St. Anthony* (fig. 89), *The Big Fish Eat The Little Fish* (fig. 16), *The Ass at School* (fig. 81), and *Patience* (fig. 92) had all been published earlier.

The Temptation of St. Anthony (because of its title and theme) and *Patience* are peopled with diabolic characters and filled with strange scenes. Here the universe of the unreal is part of the natural world, and the fantastic invades the earth, though without taking it over. St. Anthony will hold out, we suspect, just as Patience has its resources—but this will not make the world any less disturbing or nightmarish with its hallucinations, its meaninglessness, and the absurdity of the acts and scenes that take place. The particular kind of inventiveness, simultaneously droll and devilish, bears the clear marks of Hieronymus Bosch. The similarity between the two artists was already clearly established at the time, by both Guicciardini and Vasari. The day after Bruegel's death Lampsonius said: "What is this new Hieronymus Bosch [bestowed upon the] world, who can imitate, with brush or crayon, the inspired dreams of his master with such skill that sometimes he even surpasses him?"[1]

A distorted scale of objects and beings, a proliferation of hybridized creatures, polymorphous yet apparently viable monsters from humanoid tree trunks to body-less heads, and sexual and esoteric symbols abound in the work of both painters, from the hollow tree to the alchemical egg. Indeed, outright quotations from Bosch are numerous in Bruegel's work, particularly in his *Deadly Sins* series, and these have been pointed out and commented upon many times. Starting with *The Temptation of St. Anthony*—whose protagonist is almost overshadowed by the hollow tree—we can see obvious borrowings, such as the odd ovoid-shaped vessel

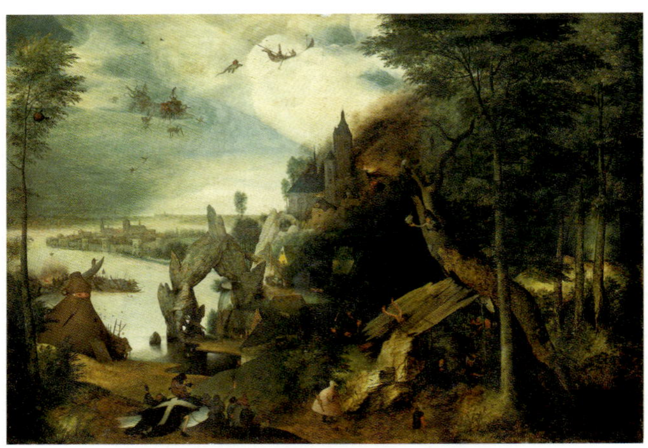

90

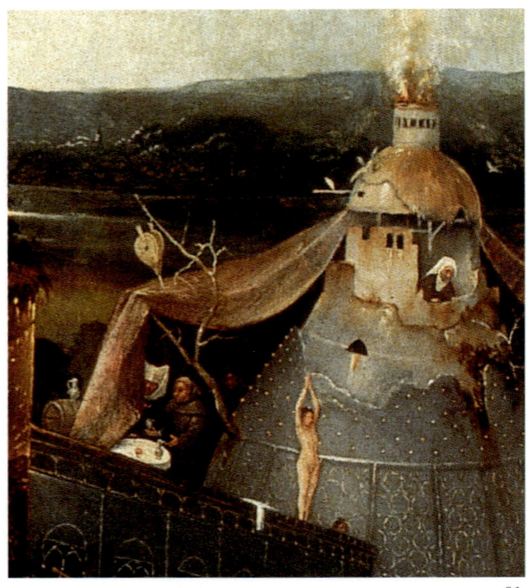

91

90. Follower of Peter Bruegel, *The Temptation of St. Anthony*, ca. 1550–75. Oil on panel, 23 x 33¾ in. (58.5 x 85.7 cm). Washington, National Gallery of Art, Samuel H. Kress Collection

91. Hieronymus Bosch, *Triptych of the Temptation of St. Anthony* (detail of central panel), 1505–06. Oil on panel. Lisbon, Museu Nacional de Arte Antiga

in the left background, with its crowd of figures, which has been compared to the giant egg, also full of people, in *The Garden of Earthly Delights*.[2] However, Bruegel also developed his own vocabulary. Does not the figure astride a barrel in the foreground, who is attacking with a spear a strange character—actually a pitcher spilling its contents—foreshadow the hero of *The Battle of Carnival and Lent*, painted in 1559? In the water behind this scene, is not the naked man trapped in a cage carried on the back of a fish one vision of "the world upside down"? There are many ways to read the *Temptation of St. Anthony*. The hollow, one-eyed head that dominates the scene is sometimes interpreted as a corrupt church, sometimes as the Spanish government of the Netherlands. When it is seen as the state, the fish surmounting the head is then taken to be the church, the very seat of the struggles rending the body politic during Bruegel's lifetime.[3] And yet, beyond these visions, in which the shoreline perhaps represents reality, rises a stone church such as can be found throughout Bruegel's work.

The subject of St. Anthony was very popular at the time; a painting on wood panel (now in the National Gallery, Washington) which is in the spirit of both Bosch and Bruegel, was, until 1976, attributed to Bruegel (fig. 90). It has since been attributed to a follower of Bruegel's as a result of a scientific study that concluded that the painting has a composite character and contains "heterogeneous material."[4]

Patience (fig. 92), engraved by Pieter van der Heyden in 1557, is equally enigmatic, and shares the character, complexity, and the presence of certain elements with work that Bruegel was to produce later. It already contains, like the later *Deadly Sins* and *Virtues* series, an allegorical figure: a woman of classical appearance, holding a cross, and seated on a block of stone used at the time for exhibiting condemned people, on which a chain and shackles can be seen. The real world— or the world we see as such—is pushed into the background. This distant view of the mouth of the river where the sun sets could be a landscape from Norse mythology. In the middle distance seethes another world, peopled with gnomes, monsters, and various invented beings, also disquieting, and representing the errors of nature and of human vice. There is humor too: The pilot of a fish-boat dangles a smaller fish in front of its nose, as others might use a carrot to tempt a donkey forwards. Farther away, on the left, an egg-man crawling on all fours is being ridden by a figure wearing a cardinal's hat. The rear end of the egg-man is being attacked by a gang wielding an enormous knife, while a barren tree appears to be sprouting from the rider's back. Behind these two apparently hollow creatures a church is on fire. On the right, a hollow tree is inhabited on all levels. On the ground floor of this insalubrious place, little monsters are dancing the sarabande. Upstairs, a monk and a woman are about to taste the drink an innkeeper is pouring them. The same scene can also be found in Bosch's *The Temptation of St. Anthony* (fig. 91). Bruegel was therefore not breaking new ground in portraying a scandalous relationship between a monk and a prostitute.

Many details and objects adorn the trunk of the tree whose branches, toward the top right of the picture, are reminiscent of those in the winter landscape of *The Census at Bethlehem*. Other elements are equally evocative, such as the figure on the left, lying on its back with its legs in the air, which recalls a similar one in *Lust* (fig. 100). A little higher up, another figure, seated with its knees apart, is the brother of the pupil on the far right of the drawing *The Ass at School* (fig. 81).

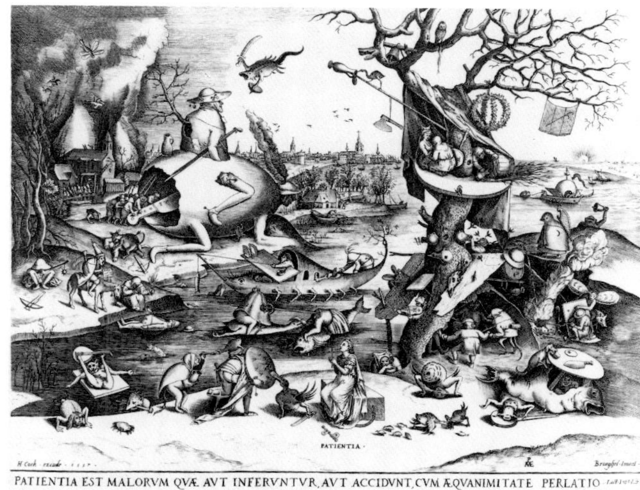

92

92. Pieter van der Heyden, *Patience*, after Pieter Bruegel, 1557. Engraving, 13 3/8 x 17 1/4 in. (34 x 44 cm). Brussels, Bibliothèque royale Albert I, print room

Moreover, these works are contemporary, the drawing dating from 1556, the two engravings from 1557.

At the center of the engraving, on a tongue of land in line with the allegorical figure of Patience and the distant town, are some fishermen and an inn, from which a drunkard is being ejected: Here we catch a glimpse of the everyday world. Thus *Patience* is a hybrid of real and imaginary scenes, unlike the compositions in the *Deadly Sins* and *Virtues* series, which, apart from the allegorical personifications themselves, confine themselves to one or the other. This hybrid character makes *Patience's* meaning all the more complex. It seems to be saying more than simply that we must bear blows wherever they come from, as the legend indicates. For one thing, there is a strong element of satire. Does it refer—as some have argued— to those in power, and, in particular, to the religious authorities? Whatever the meaning, it is not innocent; but we should be wary of reading more into the image than it actually intends. Some have deduced, for example, that the letter A on the knife that is probing the egg is an allusion to the Duke of Alva, but he only came to the Netherlands ten years after the print was made.[5] The engraving is all the more difficult to judge aesthetically because Bruegel's original drawing is no longer extant. As it is, because of the juxtaposition of the elements and the lack of a link orchestrating them, the difference between the work's creator and his borrowings appears all the clearer. Hieronymus Bosch created a world of his own, autonomous and existing alongside the everyday world, a surreal place in which individuals sometimes lose their way. Bruegel, on the other hand, integrates Boschian elements in the universe of humans, creating a composite world where ambiguity rules. Thus *Patience* becomes multiform, through the coexistence of the normal and the strange.

THE *DEADLY SINS*

Unity, both of spirit and of representation, reigns in the *Deadly Sins* series. The title is more consistent with its subject than in the case of the *Vices*, whose number is not so clearly defined, as it refers specifically to *Anger, Sloth, Pride, Avarice, Gluttony, Envy*, and *Lust*, a series of engravings by Pieter van der Heyden, published by Hieronymus Cock in 1558. Bruegel's preparatory drawings are extant (figs. 93–98 and 100), and their graphic quality and inventiveness are remarkable. The figures draw on the language of Bosch, but the landscapes obey the laws of Bruegel himself, and this time fantasy has the upper hand. The work's unity is thus assured, and the scenes, which the viewer sees from above—in a bird's-eye view—assert their space and depth. Their elements are not distributed or arranged simply in order to fill gaps but are set on roughly parallel lines leading to vanishing points on the high horizon line. These are arranged along the central axis, where each allegorical figure stands. The various groups and anecdotes are thus governed by a composition that allows for rhythm, structure, and movement. The drawings, according to the dates that have been established, were not made in the same order as the series of engravings: *Avarice* is dated 1556, the rest 1557.

Anger (fig. 93) is personified by a woman in armor holding a sword and a torch and preceded by an aggressive bear, her attribute. Here there is only violence, cries, and horror. A human is being roasted on a spit over a fire, and a couple are

93. Pieter Bruegel, *Anger*, from the series *Deadly Sins*, 1557. Pen and brown ink, 9 x 11¾ in. (23 x 30 cm). Florence, Uffizi

94. Pieter Bruegel, *Sloth*, from the series *Deadly Sins*, 1557. Pen and brown ink, 8⅜ x 11⅝ in. (21.3 x 29.6 cm). Vienna, Graphische Sammlung Albertina

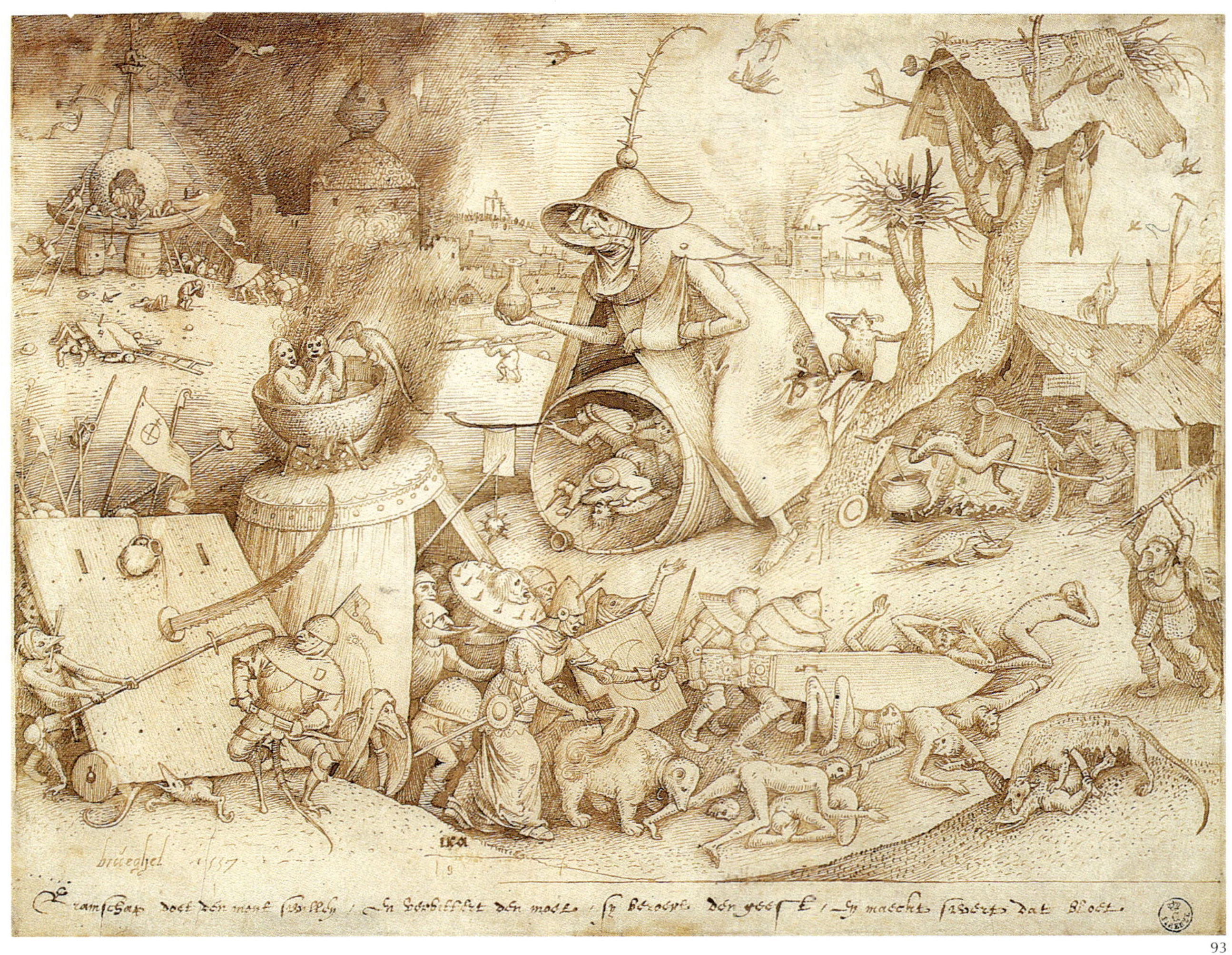

93

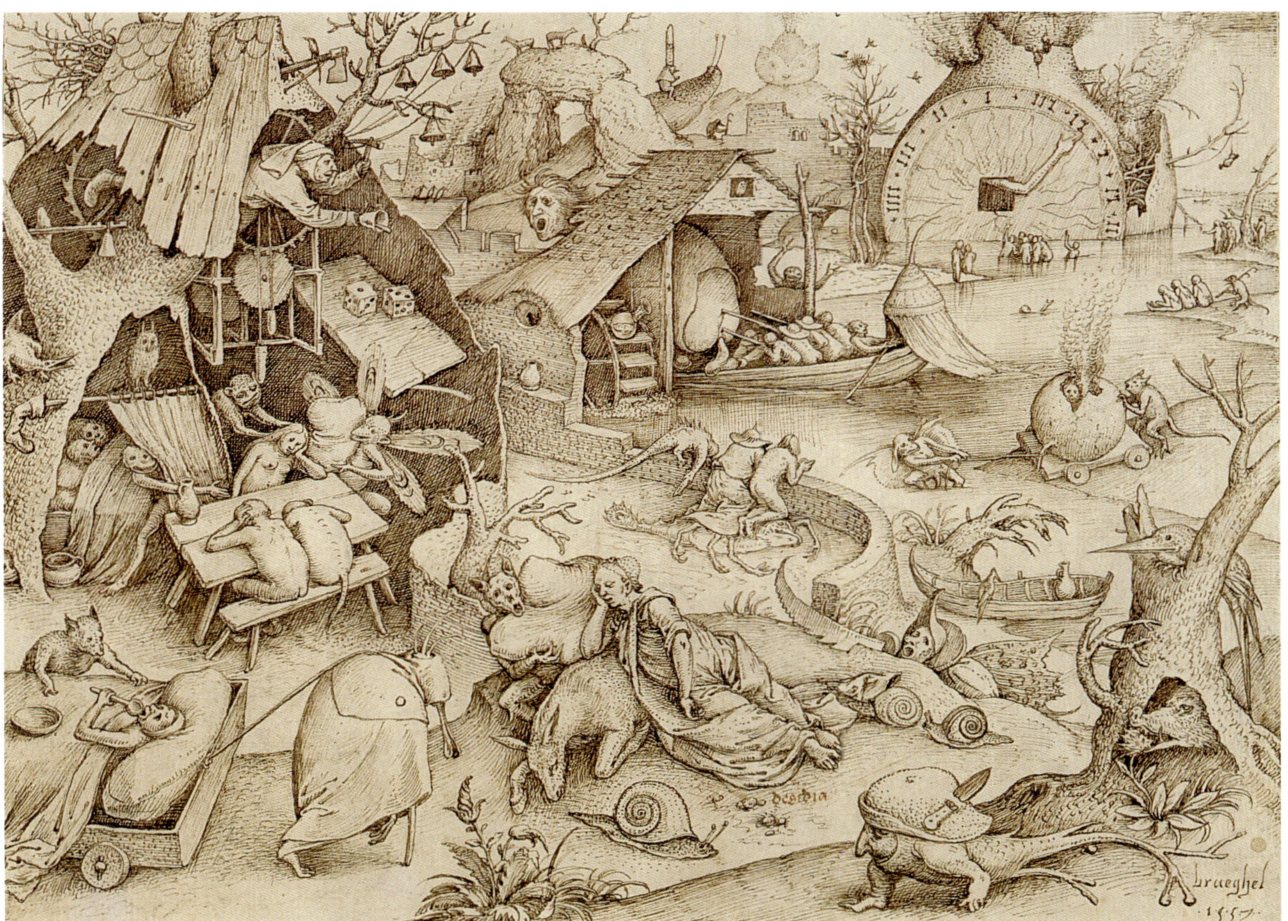

94

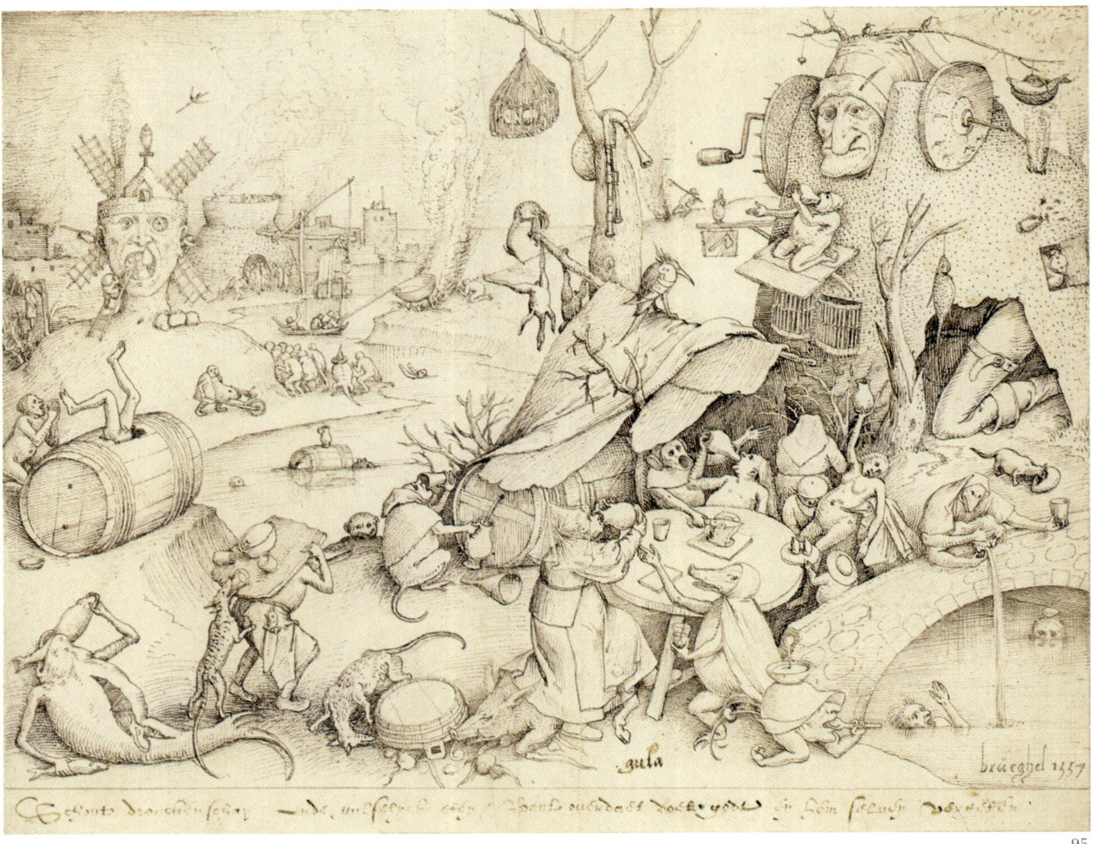

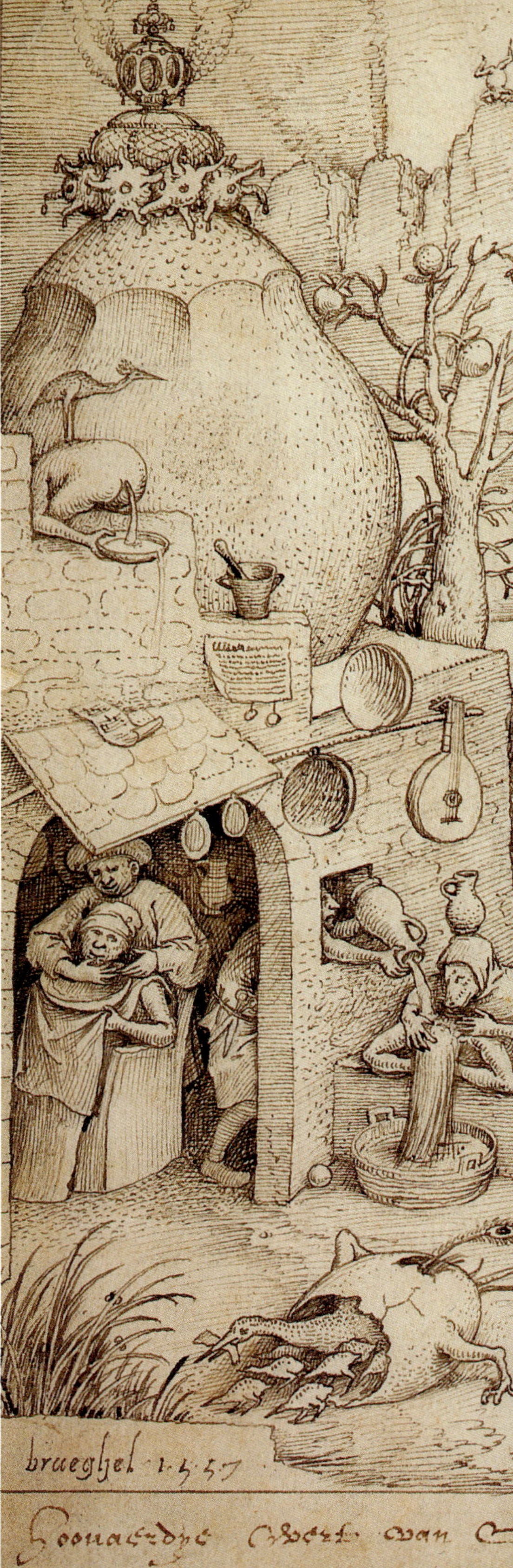

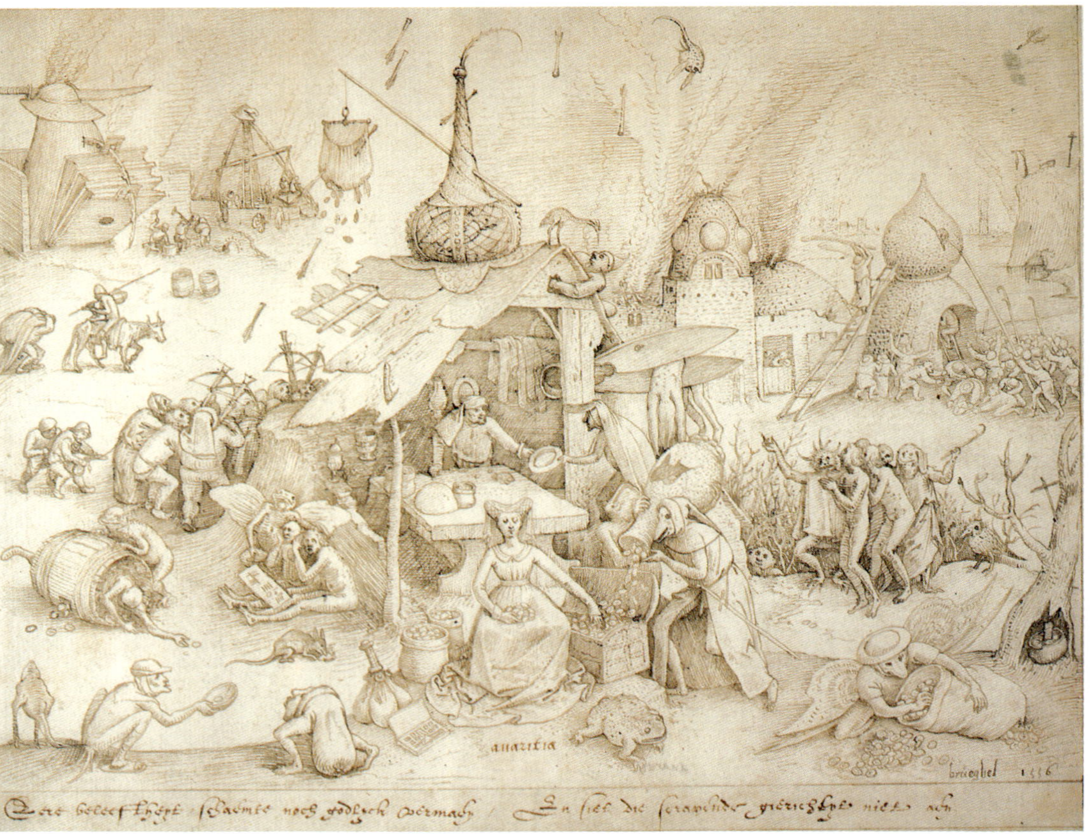

95. Pieter Bruegel, *Gluttony*, from the series *Deadly Sins*, 1557. Pen and brown ink,
9 x 11¾ in. (23.1 x 30.1 cm). Paris, Institut néerlandais, Fondation Custodia, F. Lugt collection

96. Pieter Bruegel, *Avarice*, from the series *Deadly Sins*, 1556. Pen and brown ink,
9 x 11¾ in. (22.8 x 29.8 cm). London, British Museum, Department of Prints and Drawings

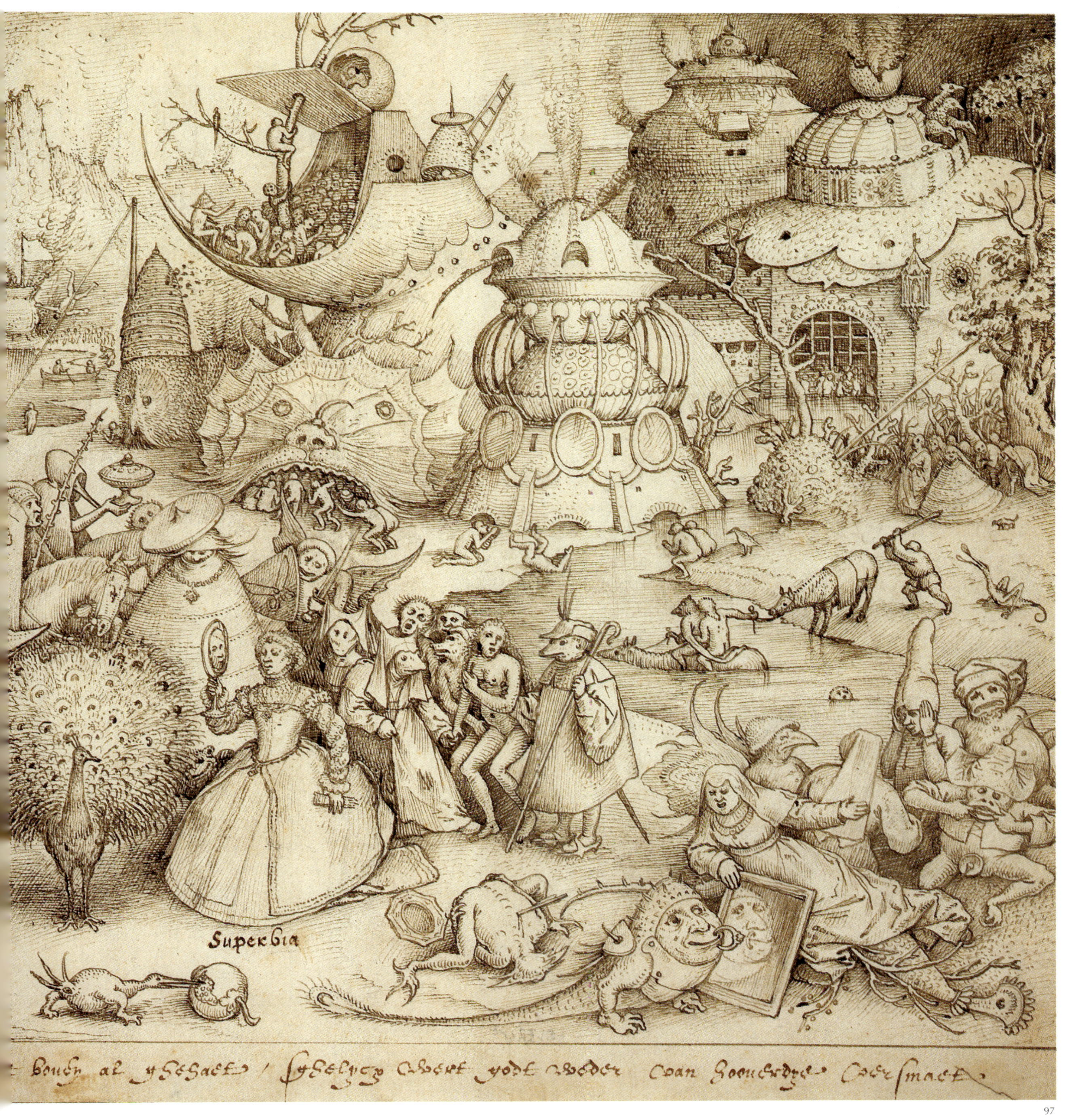

97. Pieter Bruegel, *Pride*, from the series *Deadly Sins*, 1557. Pen and brown ink, 9 x 11¾ in. (22.9 x 30 cm). Paris, Institut néerlandais, Fondation Custodia, F. Lugt collection

being boiled in a cauldron, people and animals kill each other, and fire ravages the background. "Anger swells the mouth and embitters the heart, it clouds the mind and blackens the blood," the Dutch saying goes. Many quotations from Bosch have been pointed out in this work: the man being roasted on the spit, others slitting each other's throats, and the curious boat carrying a sphere—here supported by two barrels—forming an extraneous scene in the left background. Bruegel also returns to personal themes: for example, the giant knife carried by soldiers that cuts and crushes everything before it was already slicing open the belly of the *Big Fish* of 1556. More importantly, Anger herself will become the figure of Dulle Griet (fig. 101) in the painting of the same name.

Sloth (fig. 94) is a vice that weakens the mind and the muscles. The woman who incarnates it lies sleeping on a donkey, surrounded by the snails that are also her attributes. The clock, which is shown backwards here so that it will appear the right way round in the engraving, is a reminder of time being wasted. The demon can only rejoice: he is handing out pillows to comfort the sleepers, both Sloth herself and the woman seated in what appears to be a gambling-den, judging from the dice there. "Ledigheid is des duivels oorkussen" (Idleness is the devil's pillow) as the Dutch saying goes.[6] Laziness—Sloth—is also personified by the character eating while lying in a wheeled bed, which a figure with a long beak is hauling behind him; by the intestinal laziness of the defecating man, who is too lazy to sit up even for this elementary task; and by the monstrous slug at the top of the composition.

Pride (fig. 97) admires herself in the mirror, flanked by a peacock spreading his tail. Into another mirror a monster gazes at the reflection of his buttocks, and a third glass is held up by a nun-siren, with a deformed face and a peacock's feather for a tail. The barber shop/beauty parlor at the left is doubtless an allusion to the care of one's physical appearance. The Boschian constructions in the background no doubt evoke luxury, fantasy, ostentation, castles in the air. And in the distance, just to the left of the hedgehog wearing a beehive on its head (an allusion to the church) is a figure that, like prideful Icarus, tumbles from the sky.

Avarice (fig. 96) is a woman who is scooping gold out of a chest in order to pile it up in her lap. In front of her, her attribute—a toad—can also be associated with lust. Indeed, many details in the *Deadly Sins* series are ambiguous and refer to each other. These sins are deadly and likewise indifferent: in the case of avarice, indifferent to honor, to wisdom, to decency, to God's commandments. Behind the allegorical figure rises the dilapidated house of a pawnbroker whose sign is a pair of sheep-shears: these, in an eloquent image, have caught a naked man between their blades. In the right background a dwelling in the shape of a money box is besieged by a crowd. Behind the moneylender's shack, men with crossbows are shooting at a suspended purse from which gold coins are falling, without realizing that they themselves are being relieved of their money by thieves—a scene that is repeated in *The Misanthrope* (fig. 267). The purse is dangling from a pole that connects to an transparent ovoid object in which a bird is trapped. Some have suggested an alchemical link between this spheroid and the gold that Avarice is collecting, perhaps an allusion to the transmutation of base metals.[7] And one cannot help wondering if the weighing instrument hanging from the gallows in the left background an allusion to the Last Judgment.

Gluttony (fig. 95), seated on a pig that is collapsed under her weight, drinks avidly. Drinking to excess leads to licentiousness, as the two naked women at the

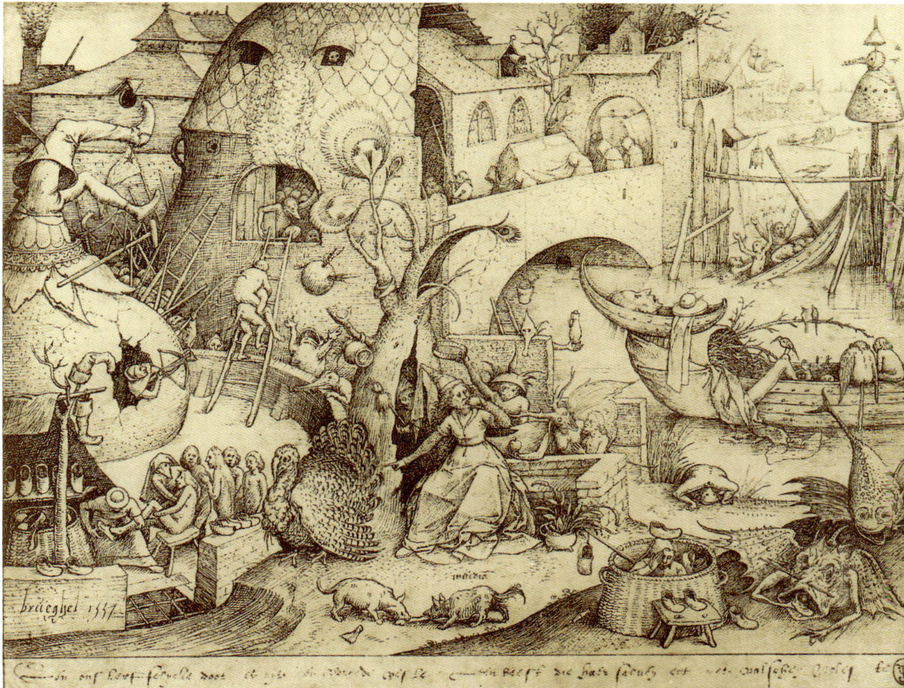

98. Pieter Bruegel, *Envy*, from the series *Deadly Sins*, 1557.
Pen and brown ink, 8⅝ x 11¾ in. (22 x 30 cm). Switzerland,
private collection

table show. Another figure, supported by an evil spirit, regurgitates his drink over
the railing of a bridge, splattering a man who has already fallen into the water.
On the right a kneeling giant is imprisoned in an oven, his head literally skewered,
apparently enslaved by an obsession with food. On the left a windmill with a
human face is being carefully force-fed. Slightly lower down from this in the
composition, a man is carrying his large belly in a wheelbarrow, while in the foreground a big fish eats little fish (another reference to that proverb), its abdomen
so distended that it has split and has to be held together by a lace. All is excess;
even a building is transformed into a vast cooking-pot. "Excess makes man forget
God and himself," reads the legend. Oddly, on the left edge of the picture, a man
hangs from a gallows.

Envy (fig. 98), wearing a pointed headdress (old-fashioned in Bruegel's time),
gnaws at her own heart while pointing to a turkey-cock, which would appear to be
her attribute. The presence of a shoemaker's shop on the left, and on the right of a
woman sleeping in a basket surrounded with shoes and even wearing one on her
head—as well as a shoe-eating monster—evoke proverbs such as "living on a large
foot (i.e., lavishly)"[8] and "knowing where the shoe pinches."[9] There is, indeed,
plenty here that is a matter for envy and torment. But, says the legend, Envy is also
a sort of death, even a sort of self-destruction. Thus a funeral is crossing the
bridge, under which a man-boat lets himself drift with the current, in a state close
to perdition. In the right foreground a winged fish, foreshadowing *The Fall of the
Rebel Angels* (fig. 114), appears greedy. On Envy's left is a demon with breasts,
tempting the man at her side with an apple.

Lust (fig.100) "stinks, she is full of shamelessness," reads the legend. Naked,
with a cockerel standing over her, she allows herself to be titillated by a demon sitting in a hollow tree—a place hollowed out by vice. Here, everything is fornication,
exhibitionism, even self-mutilation. There are many borrowings from Bosch, from
the crystal sphere which imprisons and exposes to view the lovers at the top of the
tree—a doubly Boschian evocation in that it is caught in a giant shell—to Bruegel's

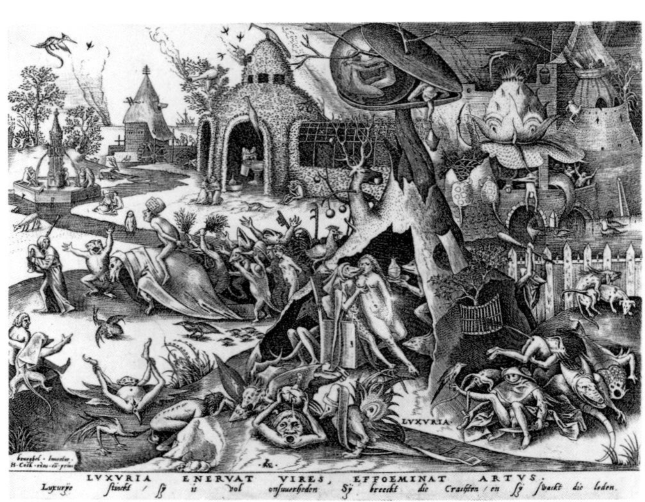

99. Pieter van der Heyden, *Lust*, after Pieter Bruegel, 1558.
Engraving, 8⅞ x 11⅝ in. (22.5 x 29.5 cm). Brussels,
Bibliothèque royale Albert I, print room

own version of the garden of earthly delights with its fountain and embracing couples, which takes up the whole background on the right. As for the strange procession in the middle ground, in which a man with his hands tied behind his back rides a strange quadruped, preceded by a bagpiper, it has elicited much comment and given rise to various theories. The man, seen by some as representing adultery,[10] wears a miter, and could thus be a bishop. In the engraving, however, his headgear has become round, losing its ecclesiastical dignity. This has inevitably been seen as revealing the artist's religious views. This line of thought need not be pushed too far, for the image in itself is not surprising. By the mid-sixteenth century, Netherlandish paintings and prints had a long history of showing crowned heads and high church dignitaries mingling in the cauldrons of Hell with common people, just as people of all stations were admitted to Heaven. Woodcuts illustrating incunabula—for example, those after Vrancke van der Stockt in the *Exercitium Super Pater Noster*, which was published about 1450 at the abbey of Groenendael near Brussels—and being printed matter, addressed to the largest possible audience, bear witness to this.

Hieronymus Cock modified Bruegel's drawing when he had it engraved (fig. 99), possibly because he wanted to avoid trouble. Religious controversies were raging in the late 1550s, and edicts and placards denouncing heresy were everywhere. This may explain certain precautions taken—in this case the change of a hat—or the suppression, as in the second state of *Patience*, of certain religious allusions.[11] The existence of these details in the original drawings, however, does not imply that Bruegel was necessarily involved in any religious or political debate, and there is no evidence to suggest that he was. Bruegel observed mankind and recorded its acts, its suffering, its joys, its condition; he put his finger on the problems of the time—among them, misery and hatred—just as he presents an inventory of sin in his series. Should we deduce his religious opinions from the presence (or not) of a miter? Does he become anti-Catholic by putting it on a man's head, or side with the authorities in suppressing it? Does an egg—possibly an alchemical one—in the foreground of *Lust*, confer on the work some esoteric significance? If, as Van Mander writes, "when he was on his deathbed" he asked his wife to burn some of his drawings because their subjects and legends were "too biting or ridiculous,"[12] it was probably to protect her. Indeed, the circumstances at the time, with the Duke of Alva's army in Brussels, justified this. Whatever the case, the *Deadly Sins* present many problems, even enigmas, because of their details that allude, covertly or not, to sayings and proverbs, and to literary references, as well as to the free-thinking, religious, and esoteric tendencies of the time. The often encyclopedic character of Bruegel's work in the late 1550s—a quality also characteristic of his paintings of around 1559–60, such as *Flemish Proverbs* (fig. 223), *The Battle of Carnival and Lent* (fig. 125), or *Children's Games* (fig. 246)—loads these works with intellectual and religious emblems, or references to knowledge or customs of the time, which are either indecipherable or whose implications cannot be fully understood today. It should not be forgotten that Bruegel's paintings were aimed at wealthy humanists, and that his engravings could only be understood by a relatively limited number people with a certain level of education. Many of the allusions of that time are unknown to viewers four centuries later, but this in no way diminishes the vigor of Bruegel's perception and creation.

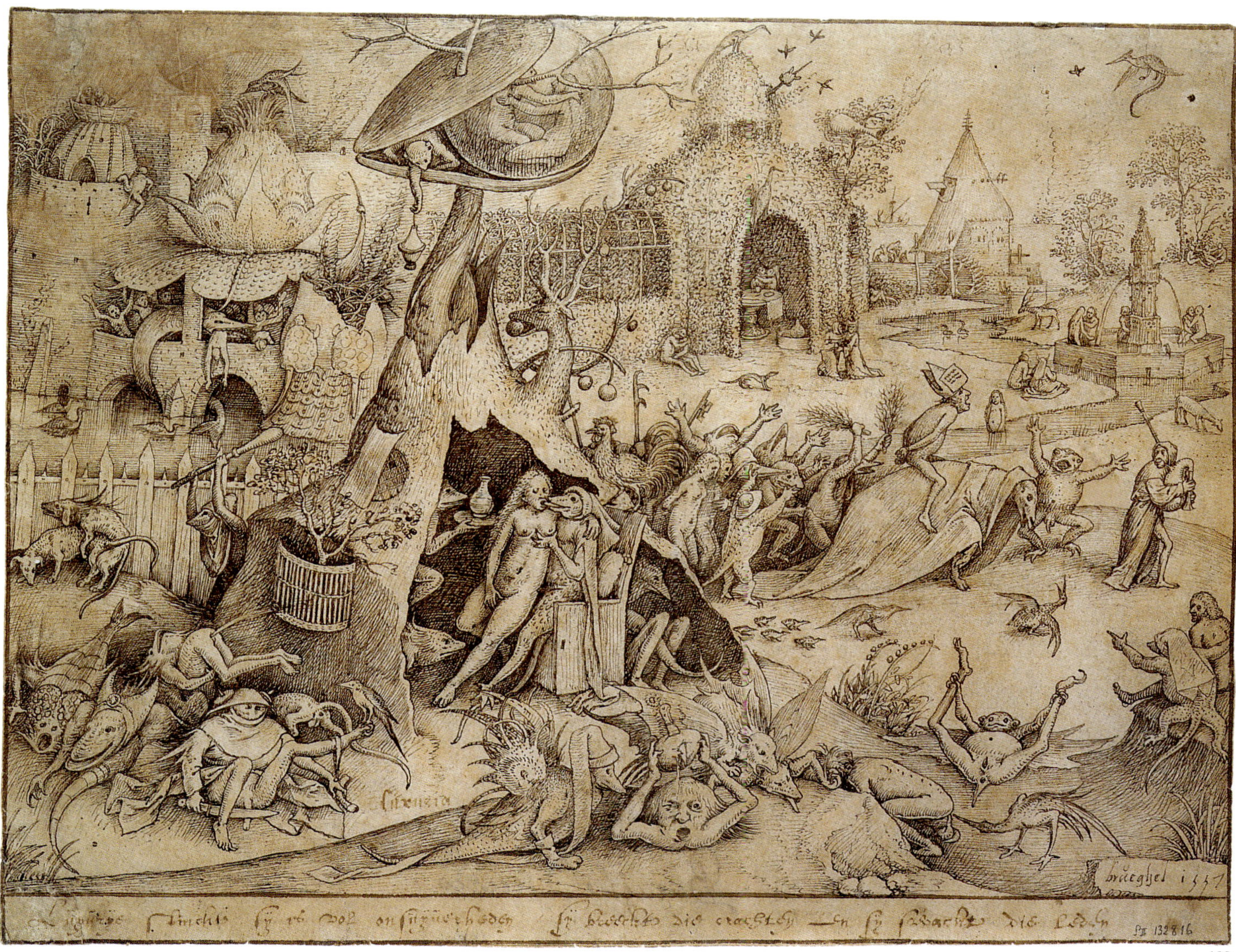

100

100. Pieter Bruegel, *Lust*, from the series *Deadly Sins*, 1557. Pen and brown ink, 8⅞ x 11¾ in. (22.6 x 29.7 cm). Brussels, Bibliothèque royale Albert I, print room

DULLE GRIET, OR *MAD MEG*

Fantasy, a Boschian vision, and a hellish spirit animate the whole of this painting, in which the elements of Bruegel's graphic world are drawn out and amplified. It seems clear that the central figure in *Anger* gave birth to that of *Dulle Griet,* or *Mad Meg* (figs. 101–05). Other motifs from *Anger* also reappear, modified to varying degrees: the curious ship carrying a sphere and resting on two barrels is here, this time containing a transparent bubble and resting on the back of a bent-over figure in the center of the painting; and the cauldron holding a couple makes a comeback, but now it is filled with soldiers. Thus there is a continuity in the vocabulary, which is adapted to suit the new work, and also in the feeling of unreality, which echoes the paintings of Hieronymus Bosch, with the harp, the egg, and the glowing sky whose forceful color conveys the intensity of the conflagrations painted by that master.

Many studies have noted these resemblances, allusions, and quotations, which it would be tedious to repeat here. The work's date was uncertain for a long time; even though the painting was signed and dated, the date was indistinct.

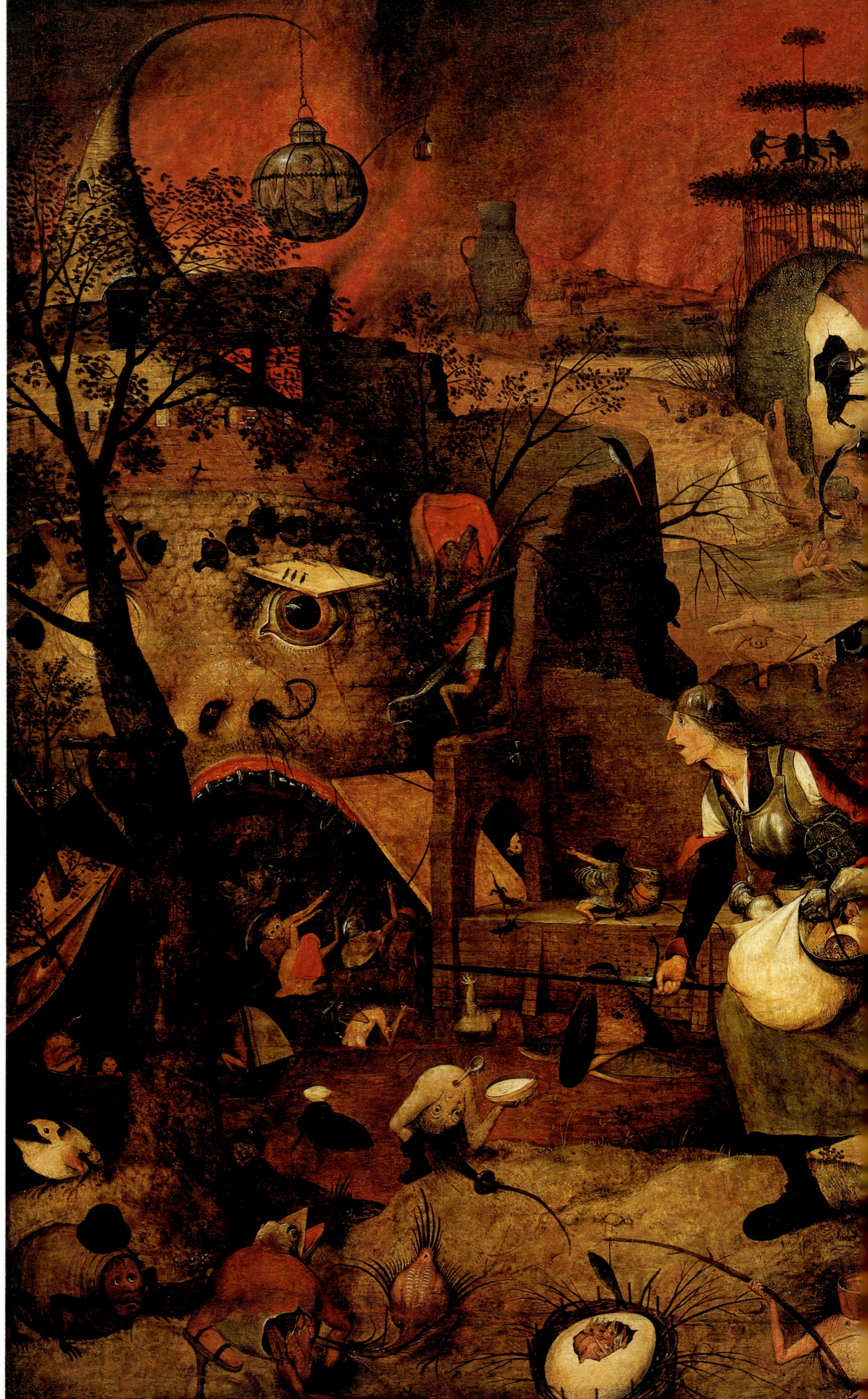

101–105. Pieter Bruegel,
Dulle Griet or *Mad Meg*, 1561:
whole work and details.
Oil on panel, 46¼ x 63¾ in.
(117.4 x 162 cm). Antwerp,
Museum Mayer van den Bergh

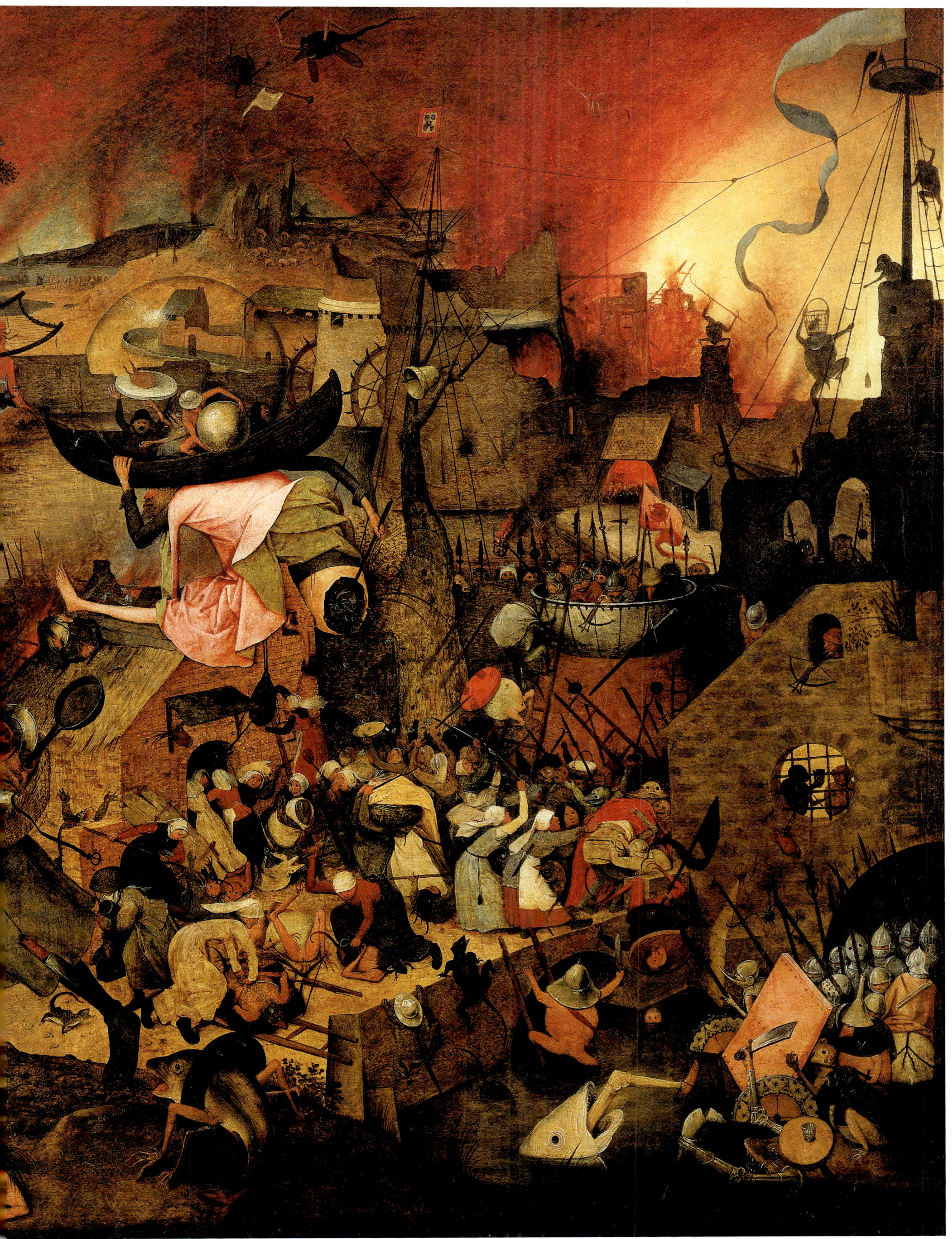

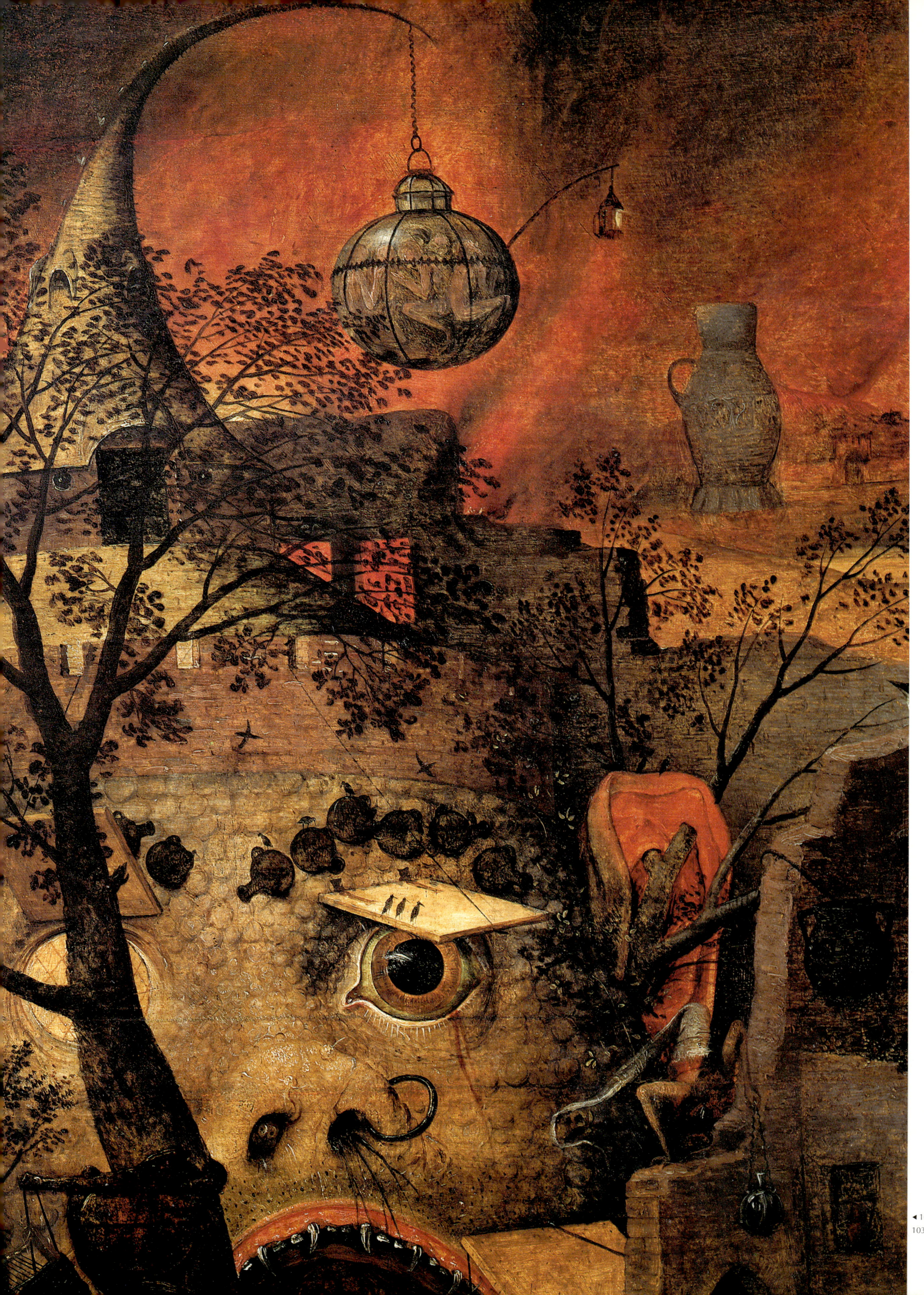

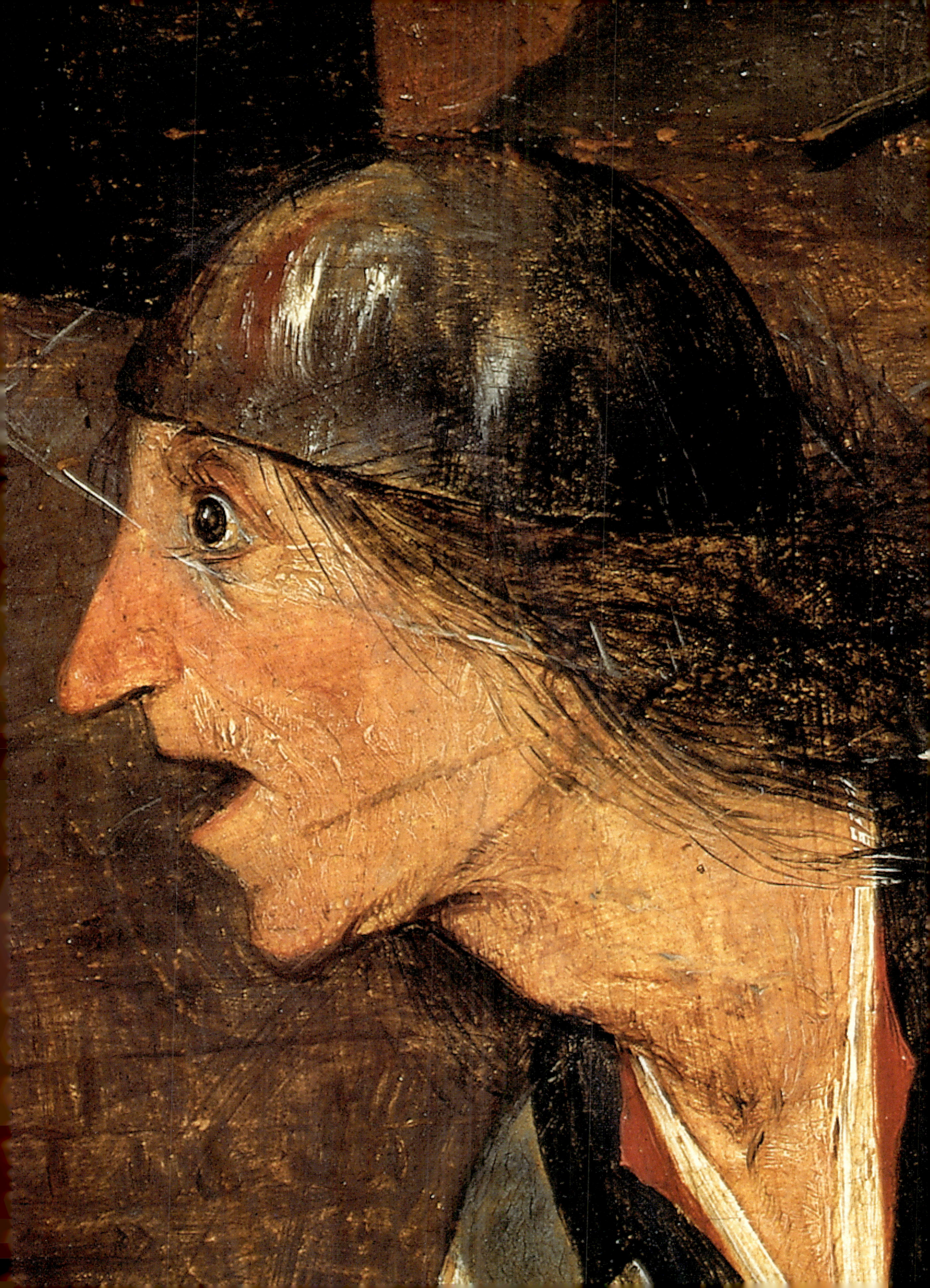

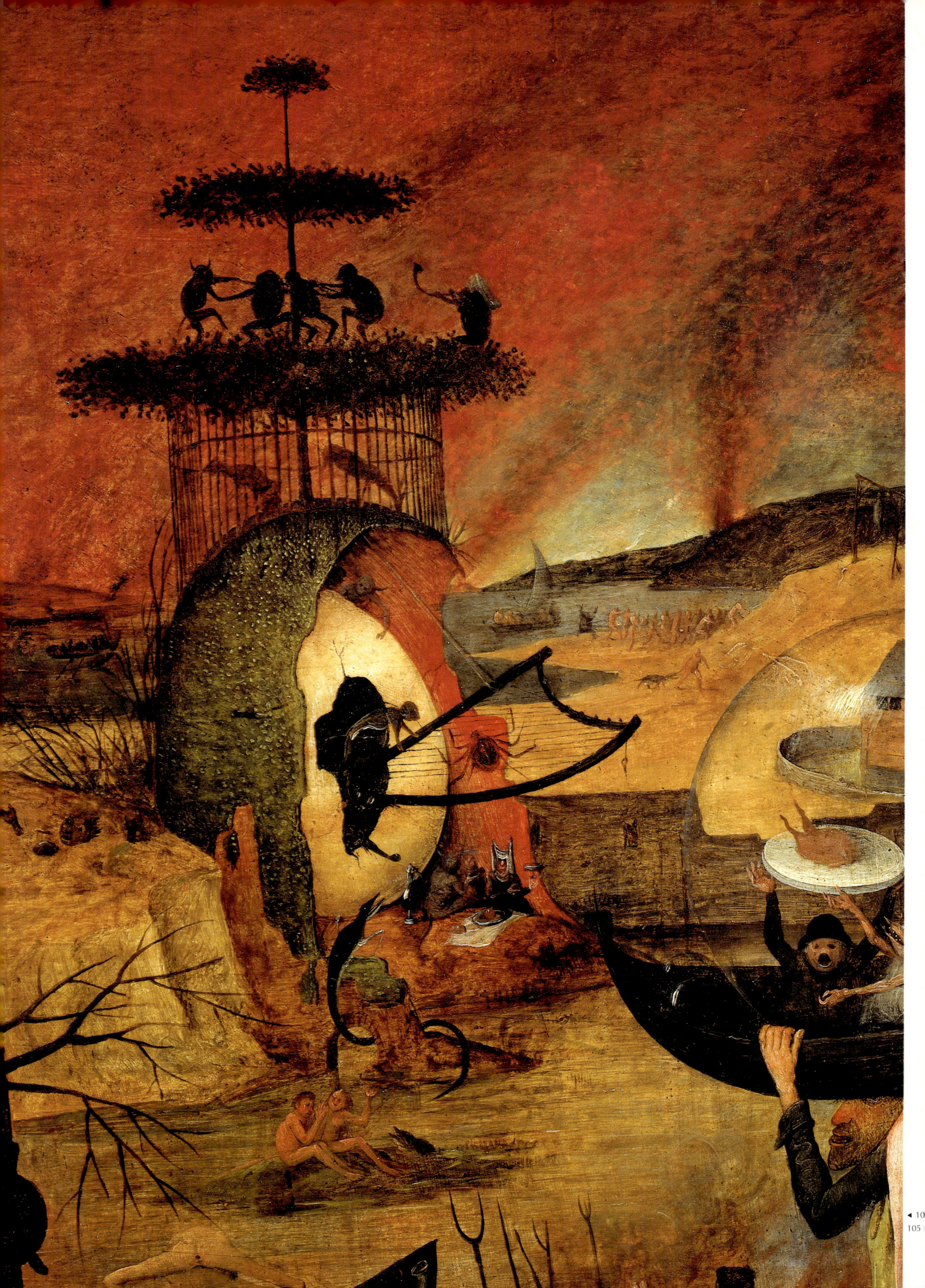

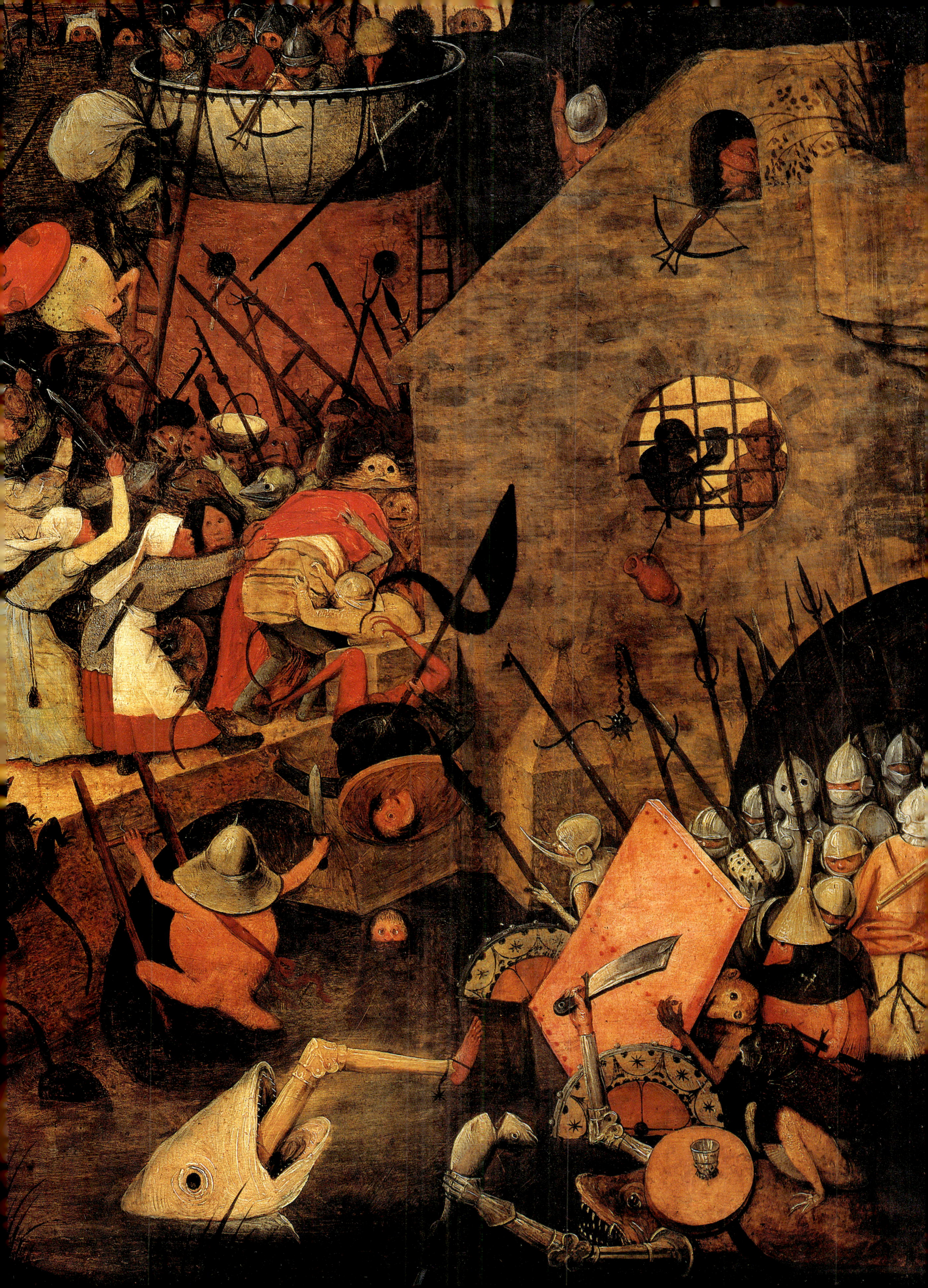

However, a recent scientific examination using infrared reflectography has confirmed the date as 1561.[13] This would place the painting in Bruegel's Antwerp period, and the subject, so reminiscent of the *Deadly Sins* series, confirms this. While this date rules out any theories that depend on its having been painted later, it does not eliminate interpretations of the work's meaning.

The painting shows a warlike woman—Dulle Griet herself—in the foreground, a sword in one hand and the spoils of pillage in the other. On the left gapes the maw of Hell. She is not marching toward it, but has crossed a bridge leading out of a beleaguered town where chaotic battles between women, soldiers, and demons are raging. Karel van Mander described the painting, which in his time was in the collection of Rudolf II, thus: "He [Bruegel] has also painted a Dulle Griet, rampaging in front of Hell, with the eyes of a madwoman and dressed up in odd, multicolored clothes. I believe this and other works too are found in the Emperor's palace."[14] This description is an assumption by the chronicler, not an established fact. The work must have passed through many hands, under different titles, before it was finally bought by Fritz Mayer van den Bergh in Stockholm in 1894, and it was after this, in 1897, that the name Dulle Griet was assigned—or restored—to it.[15]

Ever since then, it has been fashionable to try to interpret the painting. The name, and the resemblance to Bruegel's own *Anger*, have made her a formidable harridan—an "untamed shrew," according to one writer, and a "witch" in the eyes of another.[16] We might see in her the devil personified, were she not standing outside Hell rather than inside it, and were it not for the fact that she is not doing the devil's work but, according to Van Mander, "*een roof voor de hell doen*"—an often misinterpreted phrase that means "laying waste in front of hell."[17] It is worth noting that the depiction of Hell in *Dulle Griet*—already portrayed by Bruegel in two drawings, *The Last Judgment* of 1558 (fig. 106) and *Christ in Limbo* of 1561 (fig. 138)—resembles the latter, and is of the same date.

These details do not exhaust the subject, for while the Dulle Griet character appears as a shrew in texts from the fifteenth century onwards in Germany, Roger Marijnissen writes that a play, *En Griete die den Roof Haelt Voorde Helle* (And Meg Seizing her Loot in Front of Hell) was performed by the Iris, a society of rhetoricians in Mechelen, during a *Landjuweel*—a festival that featured a dramatic contest—held in 1561.[18] The coincidence of dates is again intriguing, particularly when we consider that Bruegel was familiar with the town of Mechelen. Beyond Griet herself, beyond Hell (fig. 105) with its gaping maw, its eyebrows made of starling-traps, and its cap from which hangs the emblem of lust (the same transparent bubble as in the drawing of 1557), there is all the rest too: the quotations from Bosch, fire everywhere on the horizon, the battle on the bridge and on the ramparts. This battle in fact pits other, smaller Megs against a bizarre force of warriors and monsters (fig. 105). Are these Megs smaller because they are farther away from the viewer? Probably. But they are also smaller than another figure that hangs over them, at the same distance—the bent-over one carrying the boat and sphere—and who is ladling a shower of coins from its rear end. This part of his body is in the form of a broken egg, which may again be a reference to alchemy and transmutation. Perched on a roof, he is dressed in pink and must be at least as large as the gray-clad Dulle Griet herself. While Griet is pillaging, he is throwing

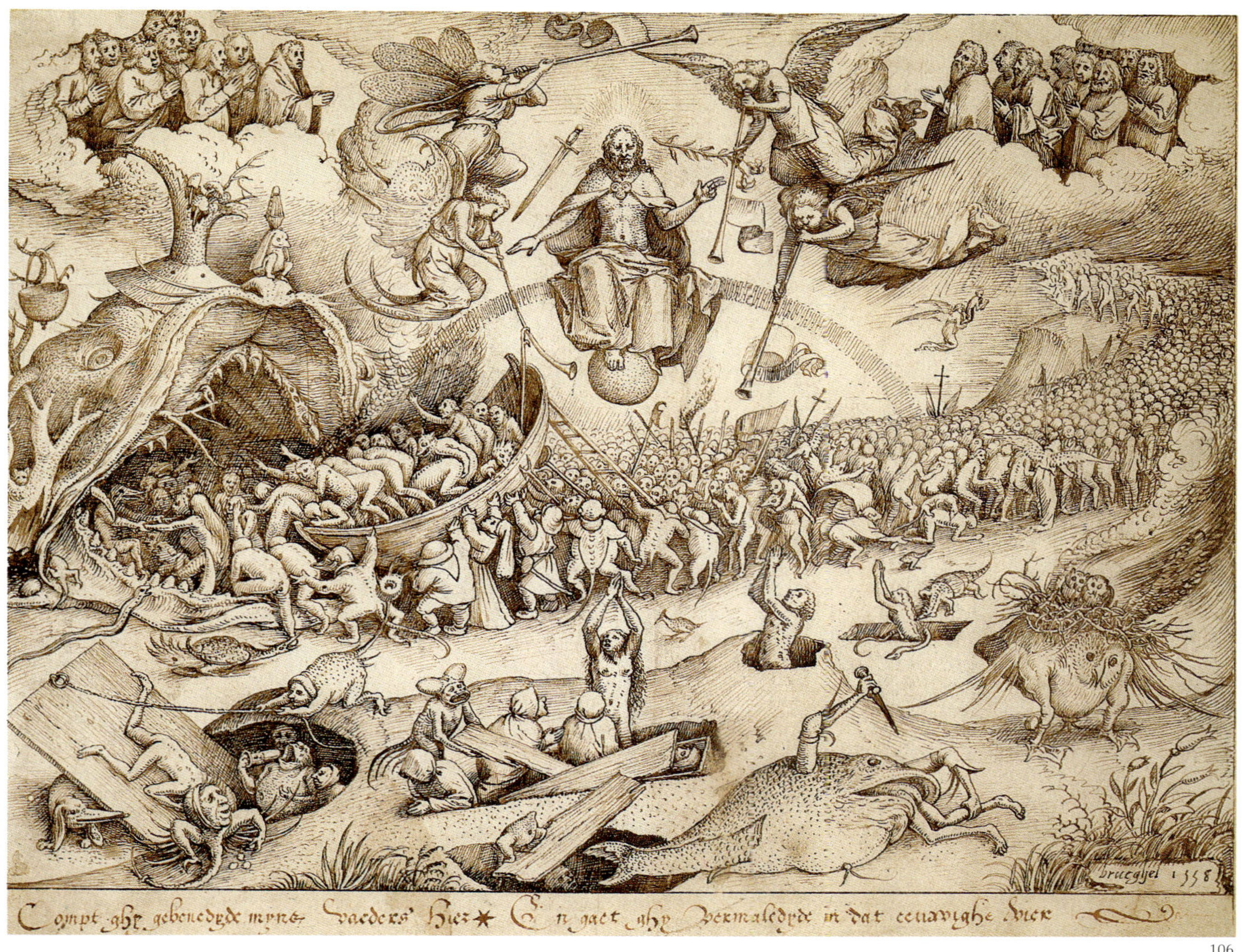

106. Pieter Bruegel, *The Last Judgment*, 1558. Pen and brown ink, 9 x 11¾ in. (23 x 30 cm). Vienna, Graphische Sammlung Albertina

his substance away. Are these two meant to be complementary emblems of greed and prodigality? If the work is rooted in the oral tradition and the images readily understandable at the time, this would not be surprising. However, the breadth the artist gives this work, the transformation—never mind alchemy—that he works on it allows each of us to read it according to our own fears or our own feelings. Thus from a simple narration we can pass to a diabolic evocation, to the drama of war, to the extremes of fantasy, to heresy, anti-feminism, madness (with a typical case of schizophrenia),[19] and of course, to all the misery and social and religious strife of the time.

Before this work, which evokes so many things and which, as always with Bruegel, goes from comic detail to dramatic vision, we are faced with the eternal question: How far can genius go in using a subject as a vehicle for something far more intense? This question underlies a recent study which sees in *Dulle Griet* an illustration of the ninth chapter of the Apocalypse, in which humanity and the earth, once the seventh seal has been broken, are ravaged by evil, while anger, greed, licentiousness, and ruin are rampant.[20] The Apocalypse, it will be remembered, was a theme that interested many artists in the sixteenth century, from Dürer to Duvet.

THE TRIUMPH OF DEATH

The vision of *Dulle Griet* connects with that conjured up by *The Triumph of Death* (figs. 109–11). Although unsigned and undated, this painting nevertheless leaves no doubt about its authorship. On the other hand, dating of the work has led to disagreements. Its format, certainly, and its range of colors are, according to some writers, close to those of *The Fall of the Rebel Angels* of 1562 (fig. 114),[21] and the sophistication of its language recalls *The Suicide of Saul* (fig. 253), of the same year. Other specialists however suggest a later date, some even seeing it as a late work of 1568 or 1569.[22] Unlike *Dulle Griet*, this work is unambiguous: There is no infernal demon or ruinous shrew here. The traditional subject of death, however, is here in all its aspects and effects. Hieronymus Bosch-style monsters have disappeared, except—and the exceptions confirm the rule—for the evil geniuses of this infernal place, in the center of the painting. Humans and skeletons alone face each other. The reason is clear, despite a few startling elements. Death is the leveler. If there is resistance, its legions and horsemen—all skeletons—are there to reinforce Death, a skeletal figure on an emaciated horse at the center of the composition, who swings his scythe and drives the herd of humanity toward the final trapdoor. Above the throng, and behind the door, stands another skeletal figure beating a set of drums.

Some writers have linked the painting to a phrase of Van Mander's, in which he refers to a painting "where all remedies for death are used."[23] That would hardly seem to refer to this painting, for its real subject is all the ways of dying. It is a sort of inventory of the different forms of death. There is genocide, and accidental death—a man falling from a rock—as well as illness, shipwreck, and execution. These are not chance occurrences—even the fall from the rock appears to have been assisted—but there is struggle and revolt against them. Is the *Triumph* also a Last Judgment?[24] Perhaps, but this is not certain. It draws on a tradition that embraces *The Triumph of Death* in the Palazzo Sclafani (fig. 108) in Palermo (which Bruegel might have seen on his journey to Italy; and indeed, there is a similarity between the two paintings' depictions of Death's horse), as well as the numerous medieval *danses macabres*, the death-preoccupied frescos in the Campo Santo in Pisa, the engravings of Dürer (fig. 107) and Holbein, the illuminations in *The Battle Between the Living and the Dead* by Giulio Clovio,[25] and even *The Hay Wain* by Bosch, which is in a different spirit, but has points of similarity. In modern art this same theme resurfaced in Henri "le Douanier" Rousseau's *War*.

The Triumph of Death depicts "The immensity of the battlefield," as one art historian commented.[26] This is indeed what strikes us at first glance: a wrecked landscape, scorched earth ravaged by the final scourge. All pass through it: women and children, people of all races and from all social classes—princes, bishops, monks, priests, peasants, and townsfolk—even the dead are exhumed. Is the woman in the left foreground who has fallen in front of a skeletal figure on a horse—and in falling, cuts with her shears the thread from her spindle—one of the three Fates?[27] Indeed, a second woman, who has fallen just in front of her, is clutching a distaff. But if these two represent the Fates, the third is nowhere to be seen. To the right, a couple appear to have been spared, perhaps for a moment.

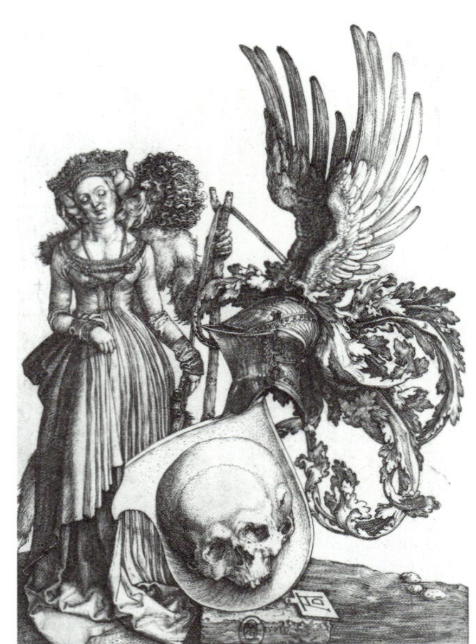

107

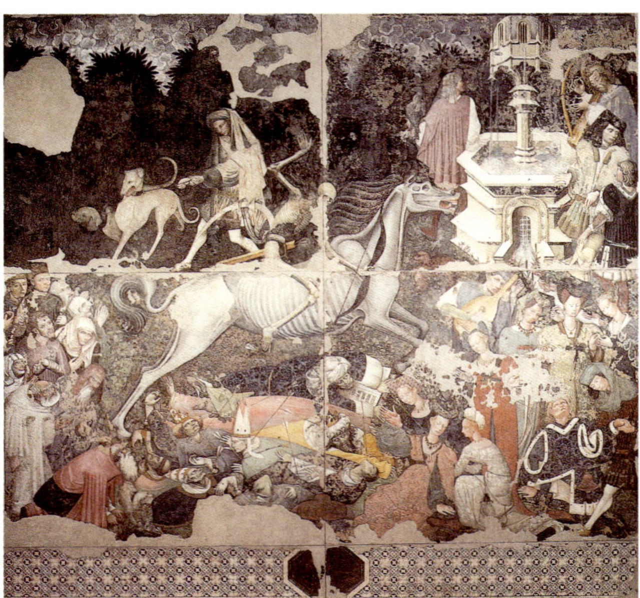

108

107. Albrecht Dürer, *Death's Coat of Arms*, 1503. Engraving, 8 ⅝ x 6 ¼ in. (22 x 15.8 cm). Paris, Bibliothèque nationale de France, print department

108. Anonymous Italian artist, *The Triumph of Death*, ca. 1450. Fresco from the Palazzo Sclafani. Palermo, Galleria Regionale della Sicilia

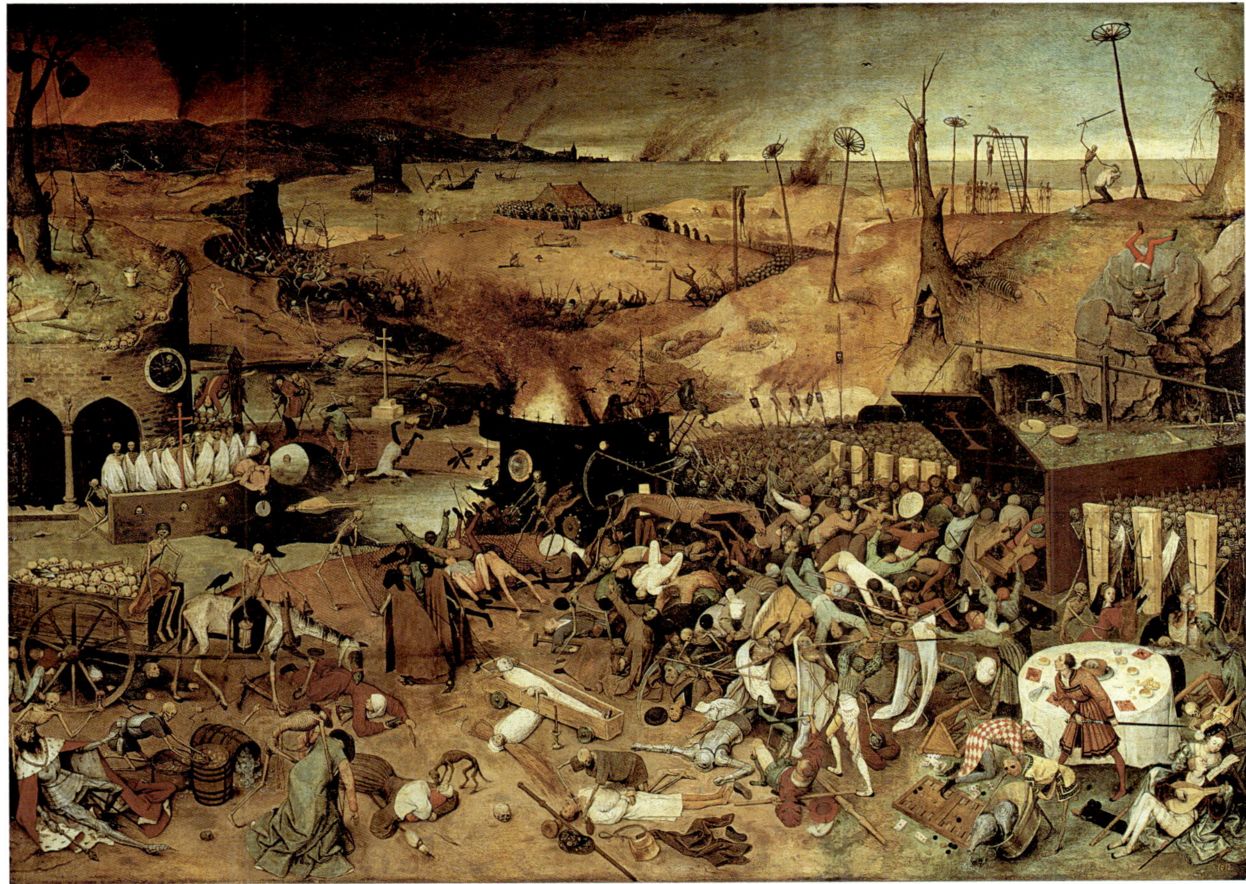

109

But is that moment just a hope? Music and, one presumes, love unites them. Are
they making a final appeal? We should not raise our hopes too high, even though
a humorous note is sounded close by, where a joker hides under the table. The
painting is a grandiose and lasting vision, a sister image to Goya's *Disasters of War*,
to Picasso's *Guernica,* and to the daily horrors of totalitarian regimes everywhere.
Everything here is dreadful, and yet fascinating: the ranks of skeletons behind
their shields; on the left, the cart full of skulls on the front of which a skeleton
playing a hurdy-gurdy sits, pulled by an emaciated horse ridden by another
skeleton carrying an hourglass; and behind them, a strange balconylike structure in
which stands a file of skeletons wearing shrouds, some playing trumpets. A horse
and a dog, both starved to the bone, and a bird are here too: All life meets the
same fate. Here the four elements have been reduced by Bruegel to their most
ruinous forms: arid earth, thin air, polluted water, and all-consuming fire.

One recent theory has suggested that this work belongs to the very end of
Bruegel's life, and links it to the rhetorical societies suppressed by the Duke of
Alva in 1568, and to a phrase in Van Mander's biography of Bruegel that speaks
of a painting "in which truth triumphs," which the artist considered the best he
had ever painted.[28] We might ask, however, whether "truth" can be said to be
the central theme of this work.[29] Other opinions have been put forward, too.[30]
Rhetorical societies celebrated the spirit of the country and of those who exemplified that spirit, men who included several of Bruegel's friends and perhaps Bruegel
himself. Did the suppression of these societies, their "burial"—which the painting
represents according to one line of argument—deserve such a grandiose work?

109–11. Pieter Bruegel,
The Triumph of Death,
ca. 1562: whole work
and details. Oil on panel,
46 x 63¾ in. (117 x 162 cm).
Madrid, Museo del Prado

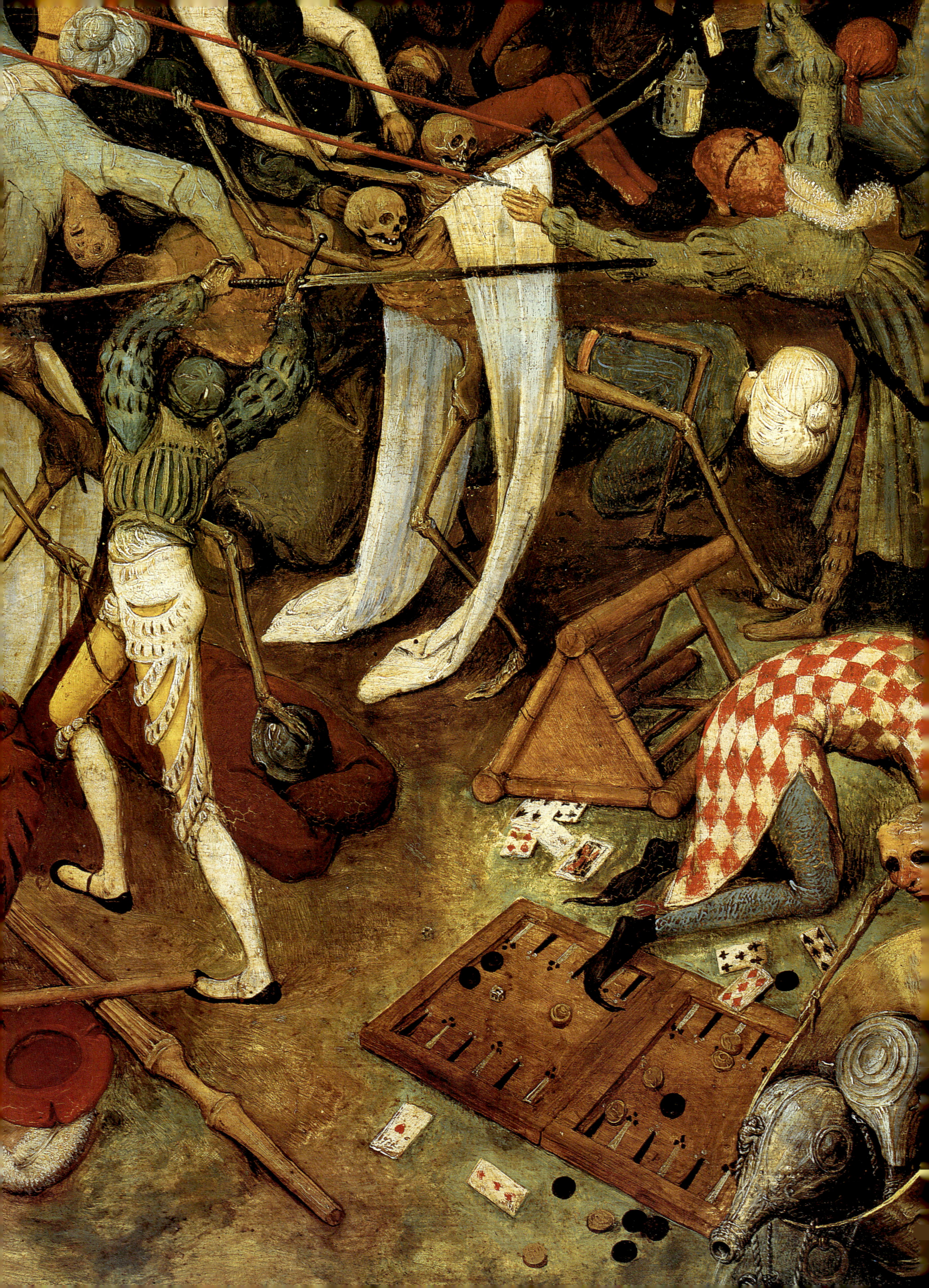

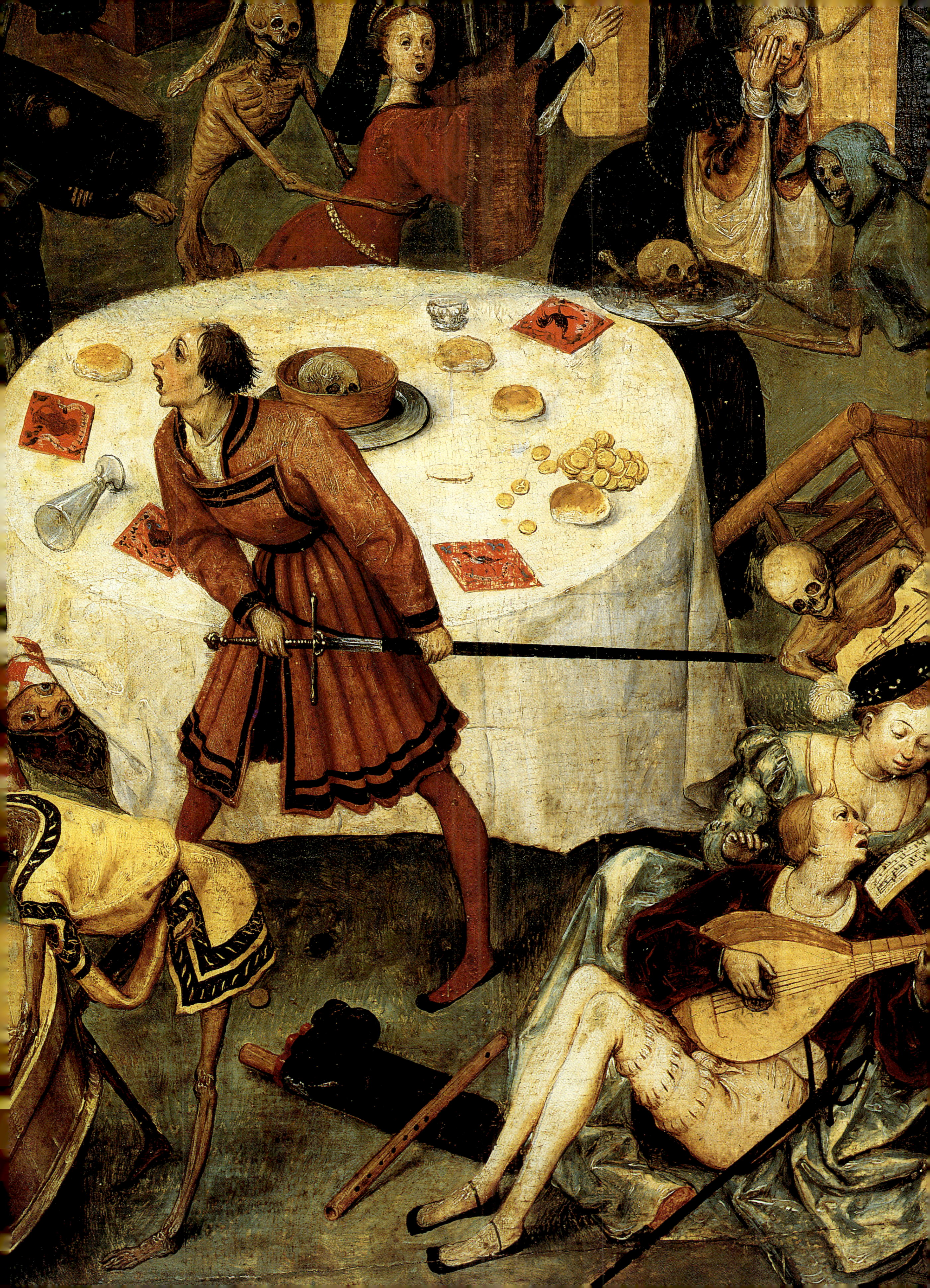

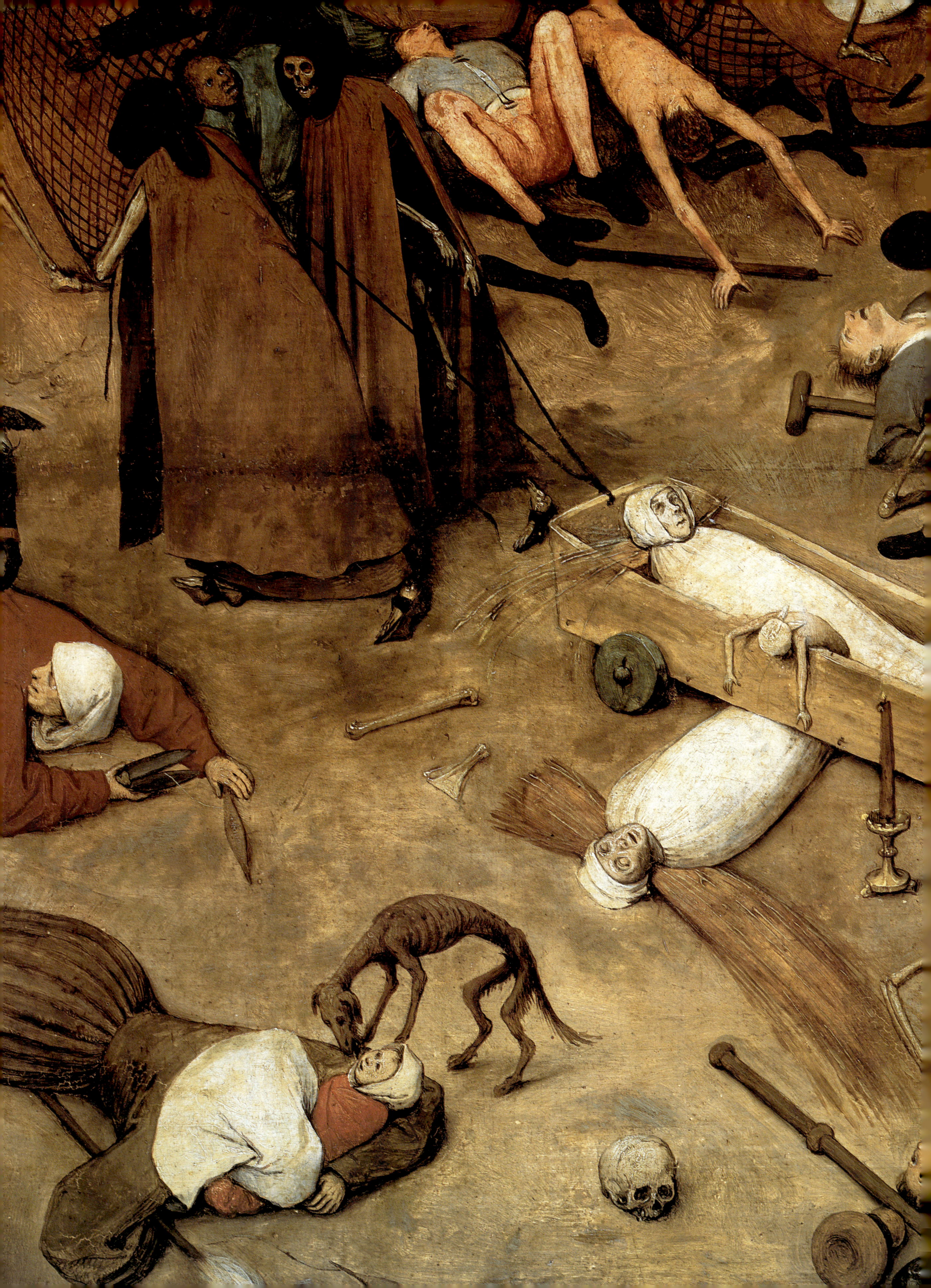

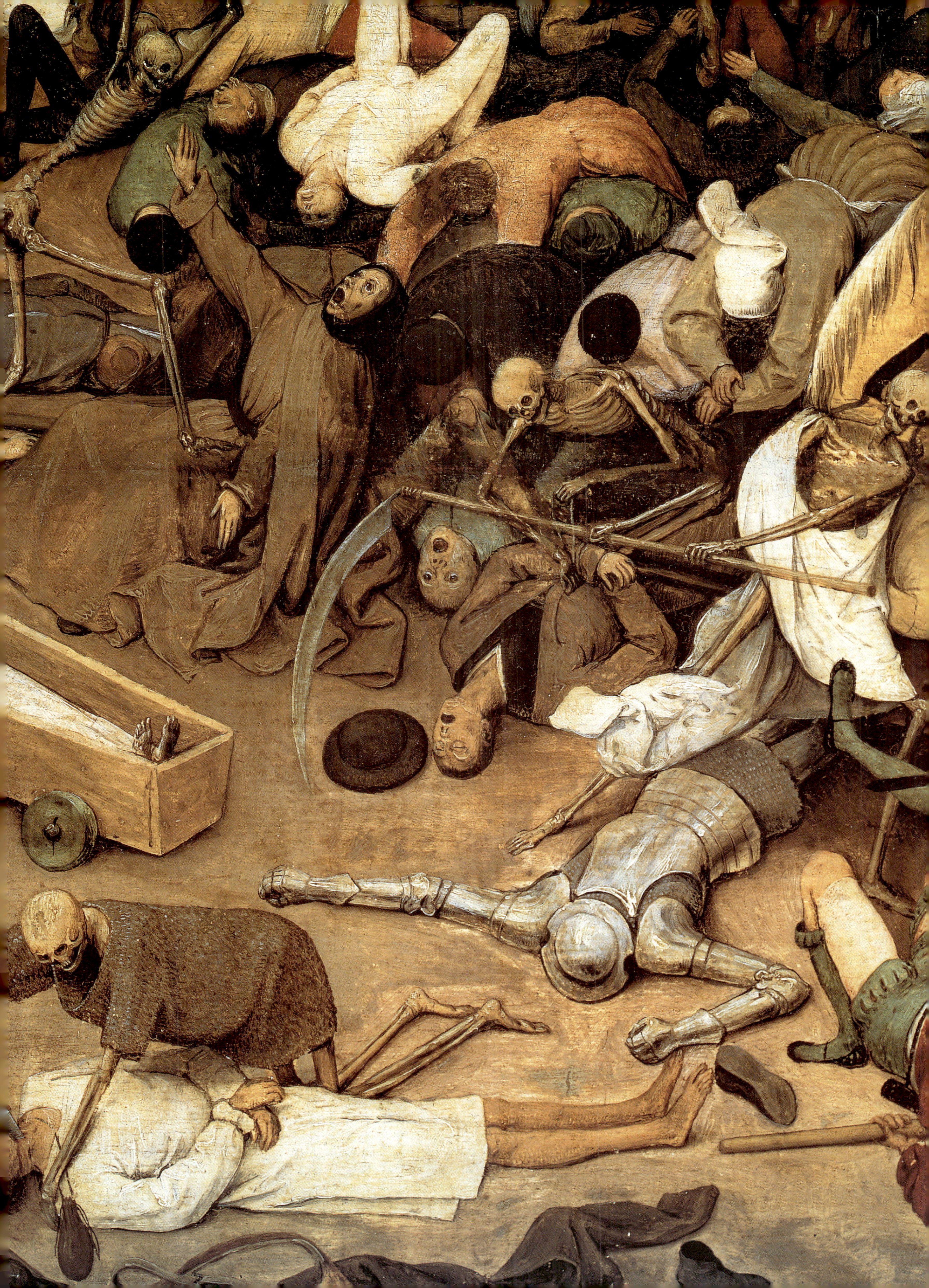

It is worth noting the elements borrowed from the theater, such as the stage-Hell, an articulated structure on wheels that occupies the picture's geometrical center, and the theatrically posed trumpet players. However, the painting's depth and the spaciousness of the landscape in no way recall a theater backdrop. Rather, they foreshadow the panoramic scope of *Haymaking* (fig. 173) and the painter's triumph over a composite reality. It scarcely seems possible that Bruegel would have painted, on the eve of his own death, a work of such breadth, and such despair, for reasons strictly tied to his personal circumstances. The *Magpie on the Gallows* (fig. 360) seems to fit in better with the sequence of the works, and its melancholy is less macabre. If it were a theatrical creation, there would doubtless be a reference to the Last Judgment and to the house of God. But this scene is filled with triumphant skeletons. There is surely no paradise here on earth in this *Triumph of Death.*

BETWEEN HEAVEN AND HELL

A very different spirit can be seen in a Last Judgment. Bruegel provides a convincing example in a drawing from 1558 (fig. 106), which was made into an engraving by Pieter van der Heyden the following year. Christ reigns in Heaven, surrounded by angels. With a gesture he separates the chosen, who climb the heavenly slope beneath a lily branch. With his outstretched hand—above which hovers a sword—he orders the literal and metaphorical disembarkation of the damned into the maw of the leviathan. The drawing, which was intended to be made into an engraving, reverses left and right. The composition is a classical example of a type directly descended from the conventions of the Flemish fifteenth century, although the artist has embellished the scene with fantastic creatures, particularly in the foreground, where the resurrection is taking place. While the damned still have faces, the features of the chosen fade the further they proceed in their ascension. However, the work is no less full of surprises for all that. Thus the gate of Hell is crowned by a strange, opening plantlike structure, rather like an agave, from which sprout mushrooms that are no doubt poisonous.

The work is connected to the *Deadly Sins* series for theological reasons, of which Hieronymus Bosch had already given an example in his own *Seven Deadly Sins*. Bruegel's vision is often governed by tradition. Although a highly creative innovator in painting, he nevertheless did not seek a drastic break with the past. His *Last Judgment*, destined for engraving, and therefore for a wider audience than a painting, is a case in point: it would have to be readable, despite the ironic presence of an owl and its fledglings. The same is true of the paintings.

Most notably in *The Fall of the Rebel Angels* of 1562 (figs. 114–22)—where good and evil struggle, with the certainty that Heaven will be victorious over Hell— iconographic tradition prevails, as a page from the *Mayer van den Bergh Breviary* demonstrates (fig. 112). If we compare Pieter Bruegel's treatment of this subject with a nearly contemporary composition by Frans Floris (fig. 113), we can see that Bruegel's work still relies on a medieval painterly language, while the one by Floris aspires to Italianism: imaginary monsters on the one hand, sinister hominids on the other. Bruegel could thus be accused of archaism, of being closer to Bosch than to the southern European style by then in fashion. The work—bought in

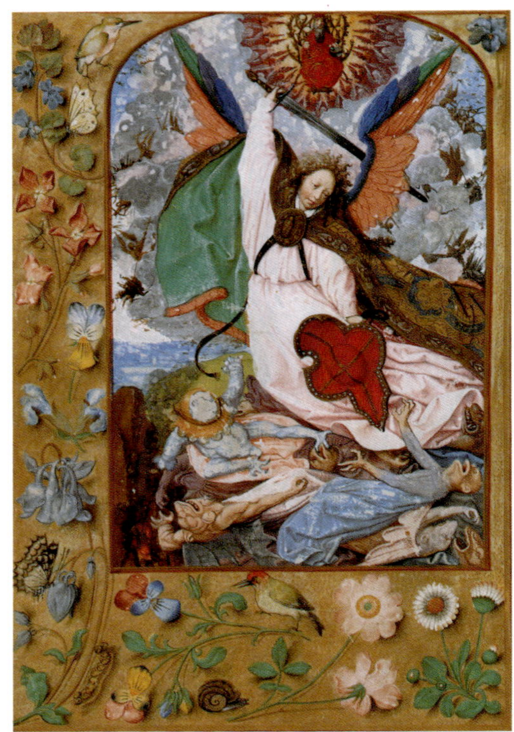

112

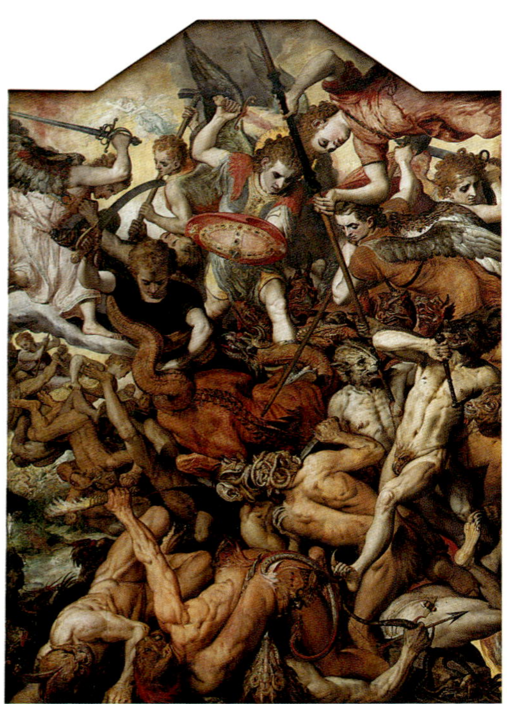

113

112. Attributed to Simon Bening, *The Fall of the Rebel Angels, Mayer van den Bergh Breviary,* ca. 1510, fol. 552, verso. Miniature on parchment, 8⅞ x 6¼ in. (22.4 x 16 cm). Antwerp, Museum Mayer van den Bergh

113. Frans Floris, *The Fall of the Rebel Angels,* 1554. Oil on panel, 119¼ x 86⅝ in. (303 x 220 cm). Antwerp, Koninklijk Museum voor Schone Kunsten

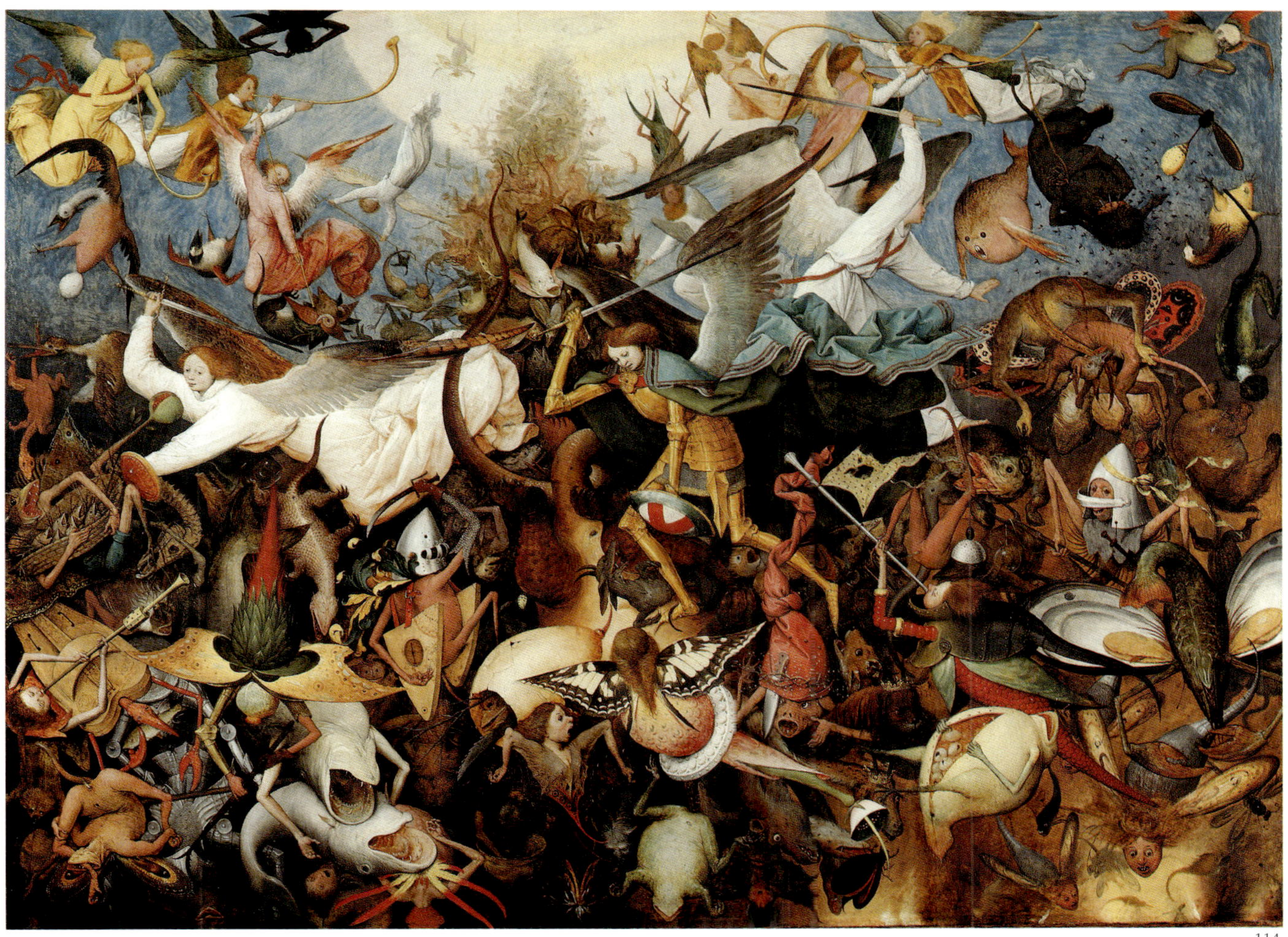

114

114–22. Pieter Bruegel, *The Fall of the Rebel Angels*, 1562: whole work and details. Oil on panel, 46⅝ x 64 in. (118.5 x 162.5 cm). Brussels, Musées royaux des Beaux-Arts de Belgique

1846 by the Musées royaux des Beaux-Arts in Brussels as a work by "Bruegel d'Enfer" ("Hell" Bruegel, that is to say, Pieter Bruegel the Younger), before the original signature was discovered under the side of the frame—was attributed in the 1880s to Hieronymus Bosch. The nightmarish details, the coming together of the human, animal, and vegetable kingdoms, all associated with unusual objects, and astonishing, amusing, or terrifying creatures, could excuse such an attribution, as could the luminous hemisphere in the upper part of the painting, which recalls Bosch's *The Ascension of the Chosen*. Bruegel, on the other hand, revisits elements of his own vocabulary: the angels are those of the *Last Judgment* drawing, and many details are drawn from the *Deadly Sins* series, the drawing *Christ in Limbo* of 1561, or *Dulle Griet*.

What is striking, and what makes the work exceptionally original, is its unity of action. This chaos is a perfect illustration of a passage from the Apocalypse (XII, 3–9), which relates the battle between St. Michael, seen here in his golden breastplate, and evil: "He was cast down, the great dragon, the ancient serpent, he who is named Devil and Satan, the seducer of the whole world, he was cast down on to the earth, and his angels with him." From the moment they were painted, they have not stopped falling; coming from elsewhere, they have not stopped cascading, sliding under our gaze, well to our side of the frame that marks the painting's border, in an agonizing rhythm marked with sharp colors. After the darkened varnish was cleaned off, which showed the work more clearly, it was remarked that "a unique spatial perspective" had been revealed.[31] Some have seen the painting

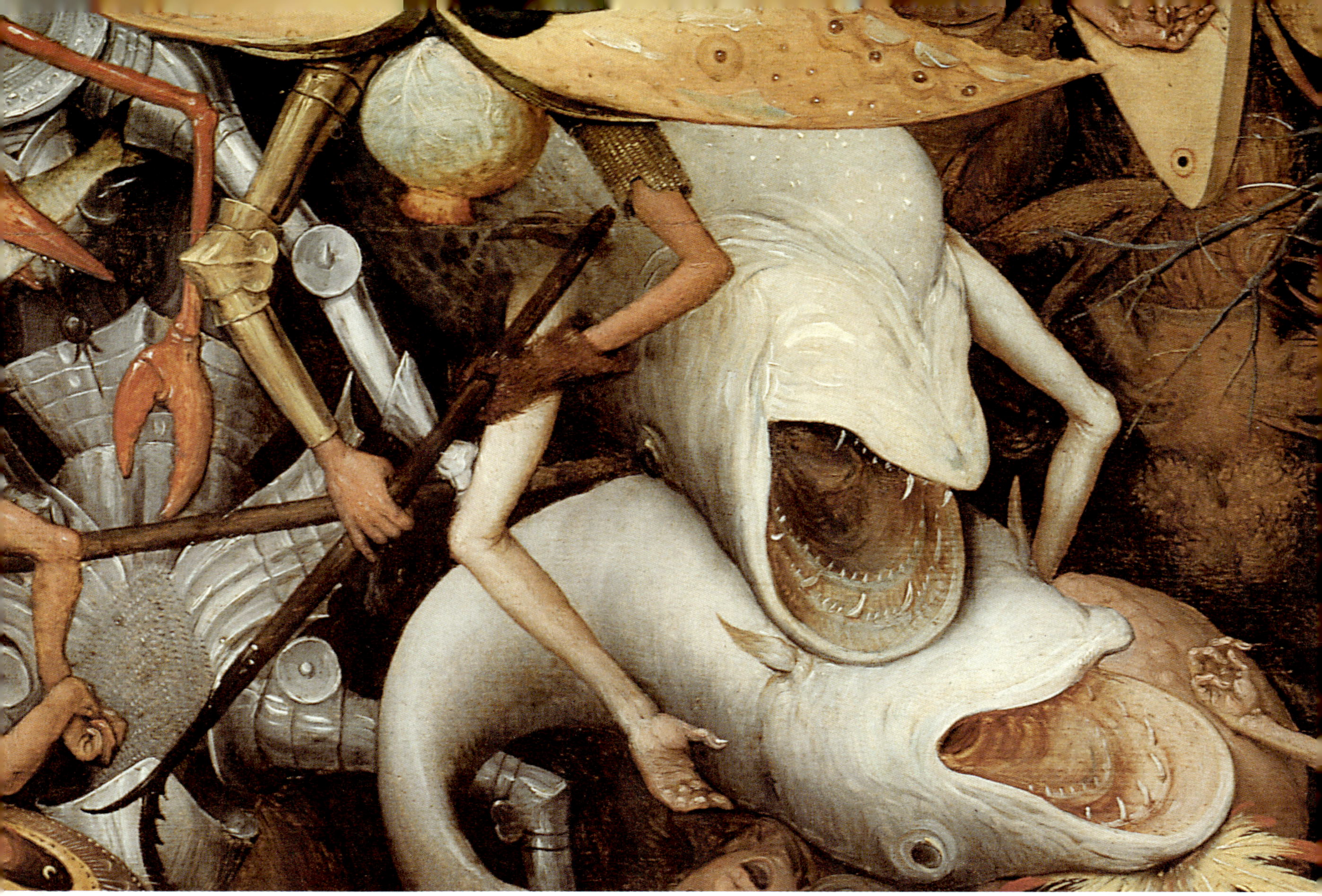

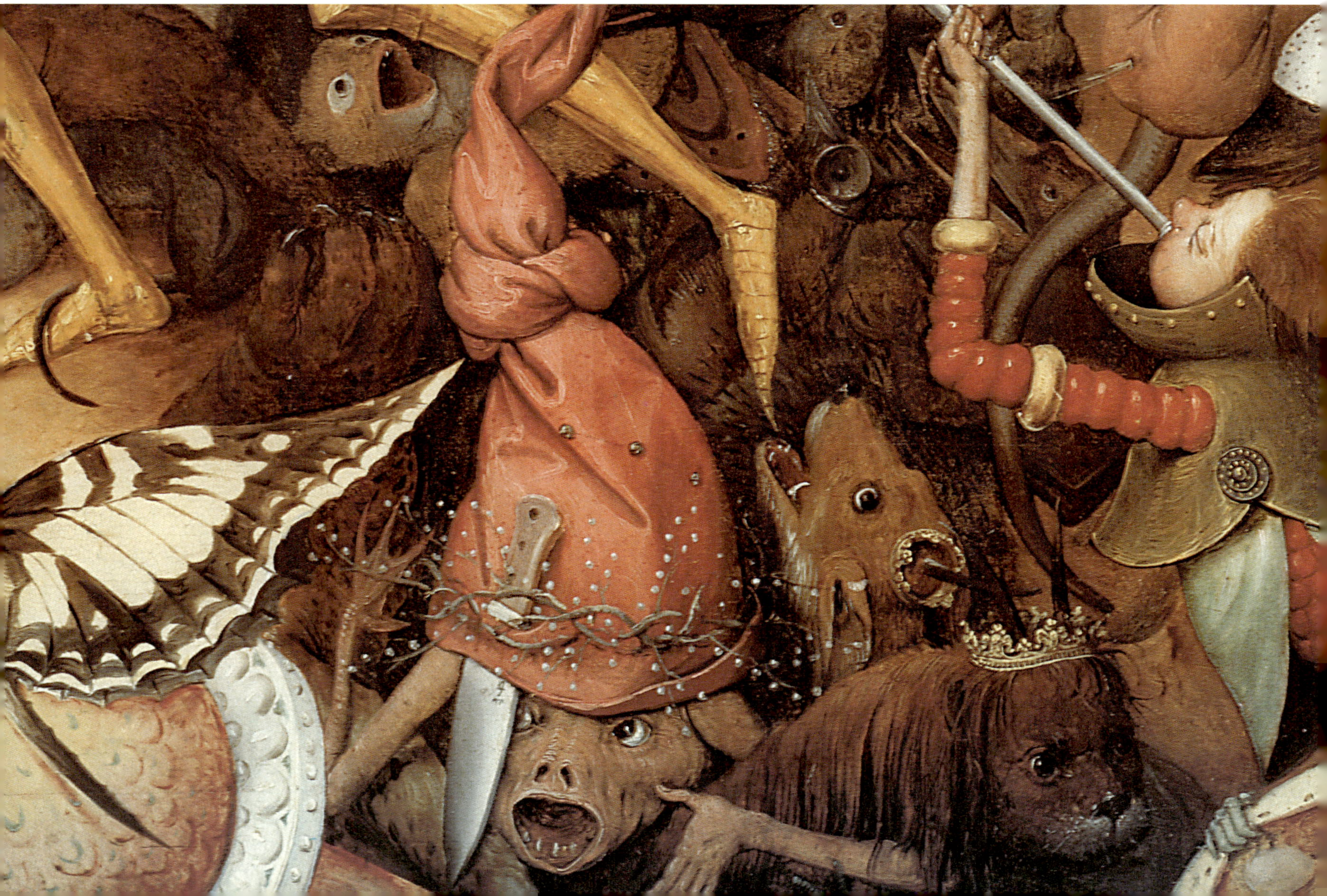

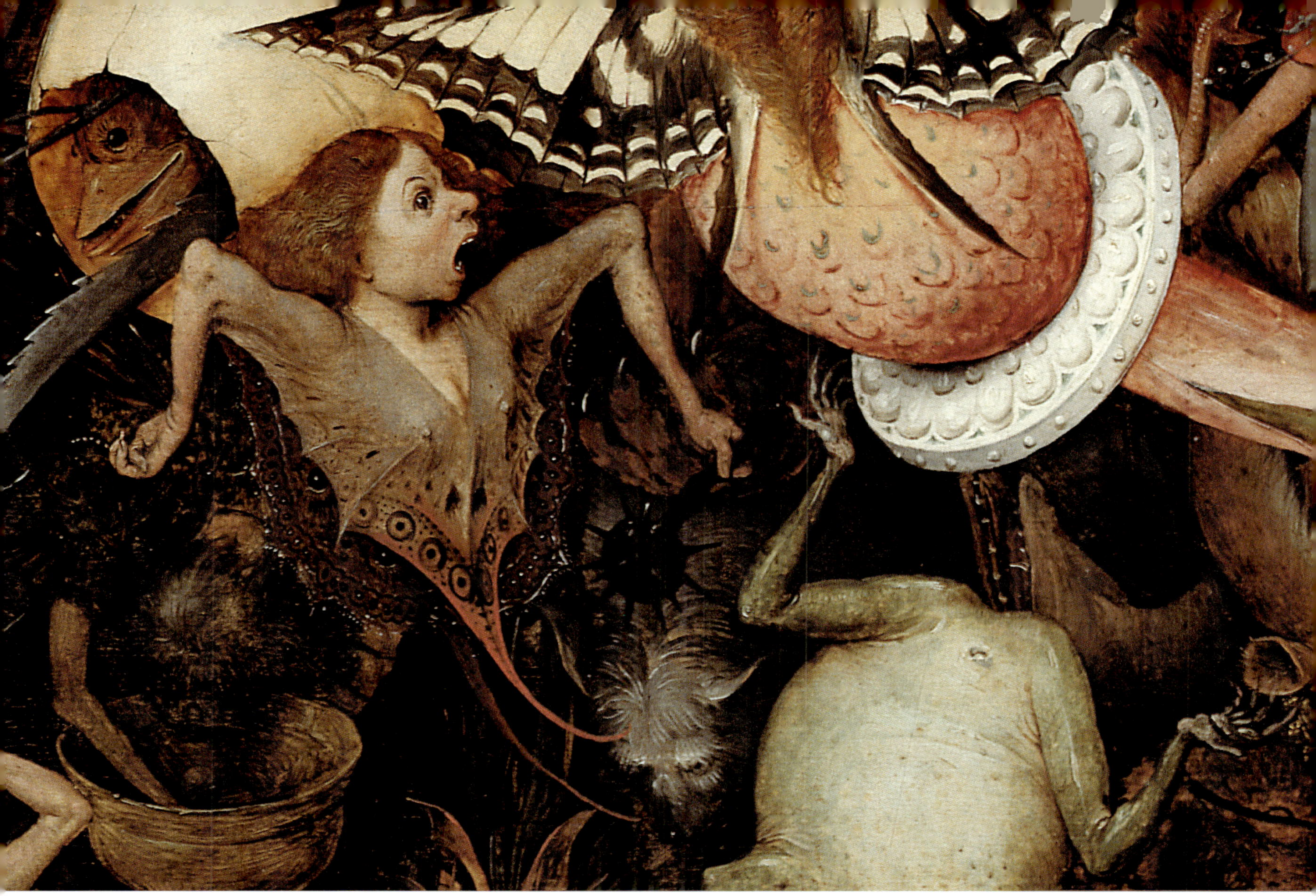

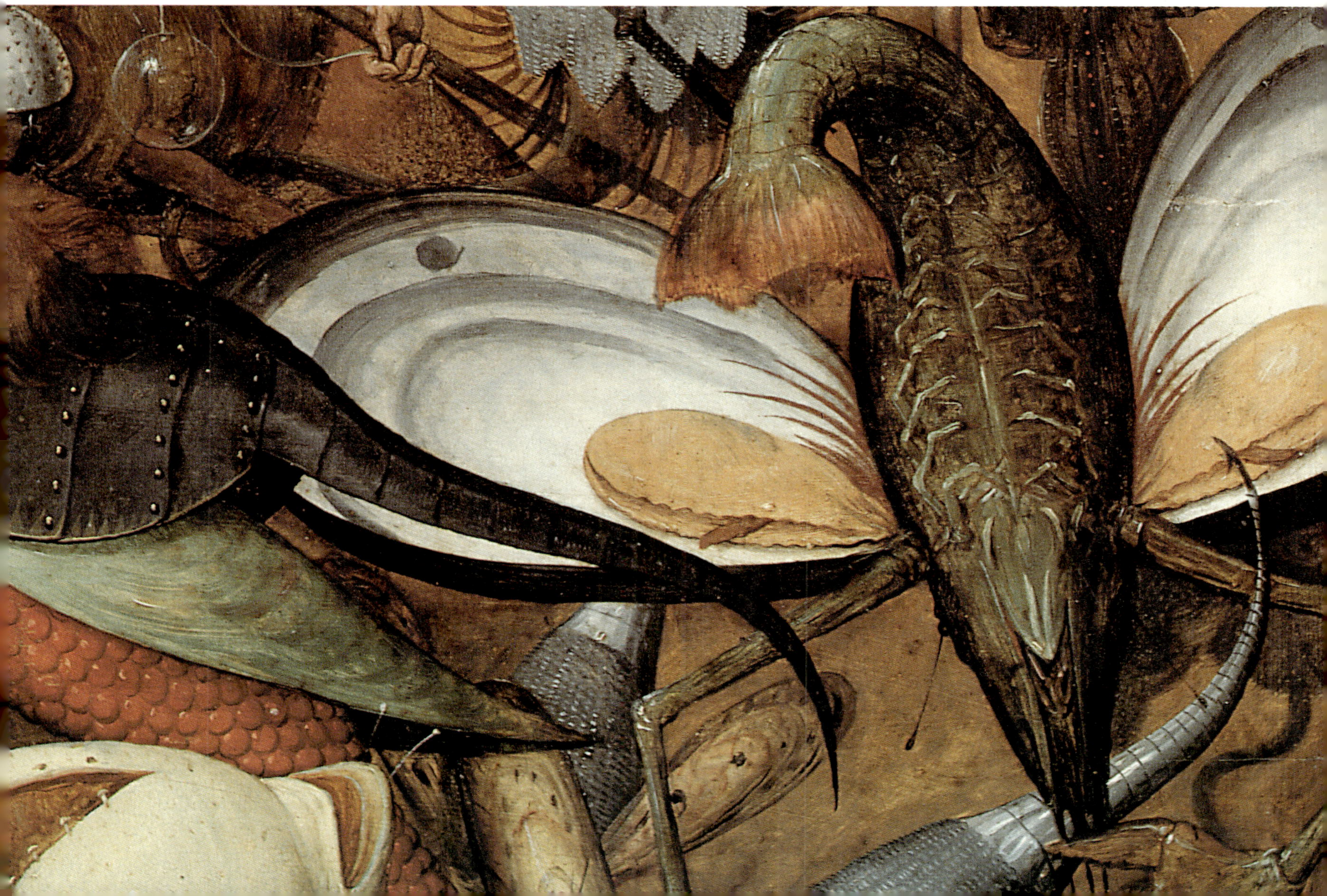

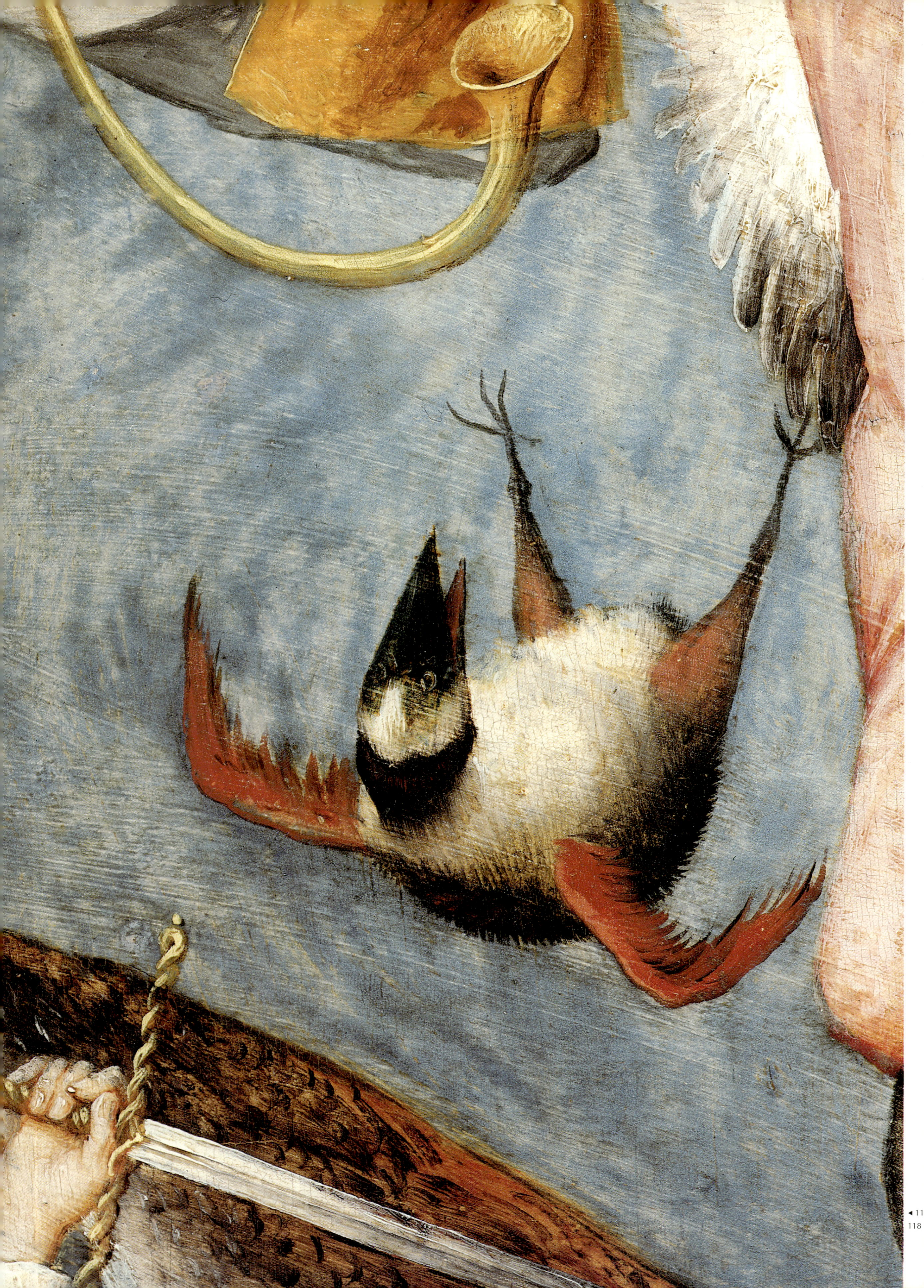

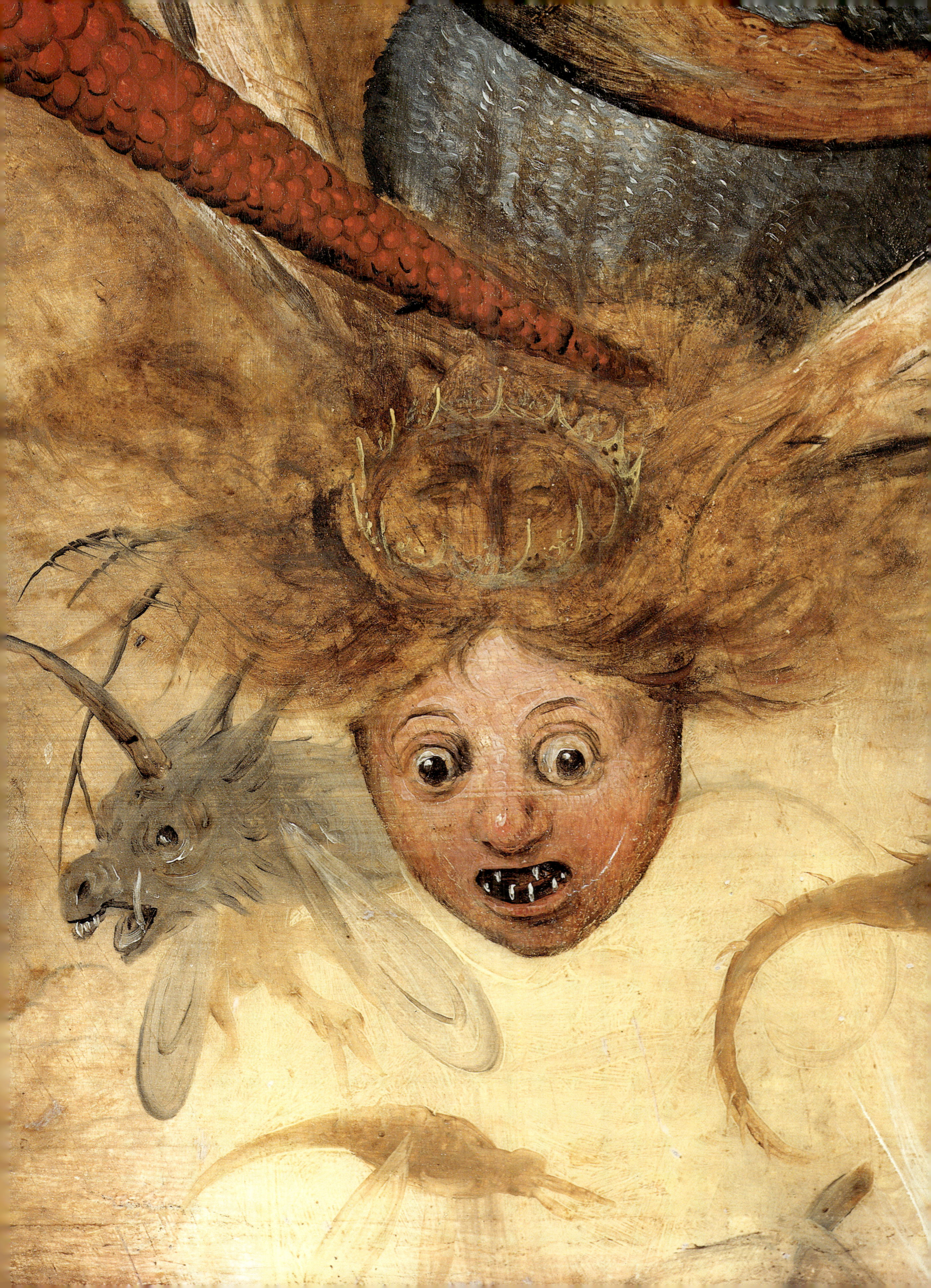

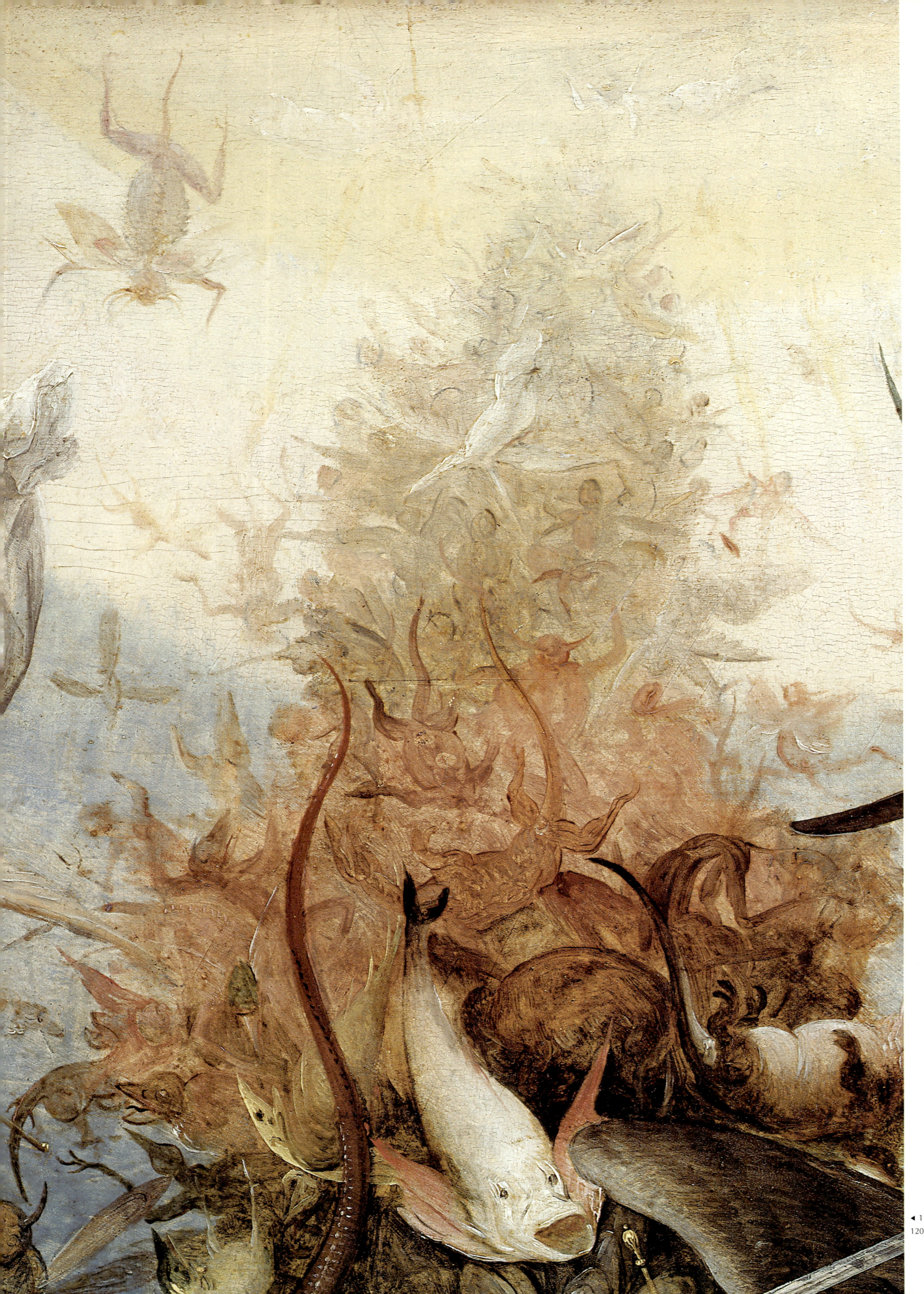

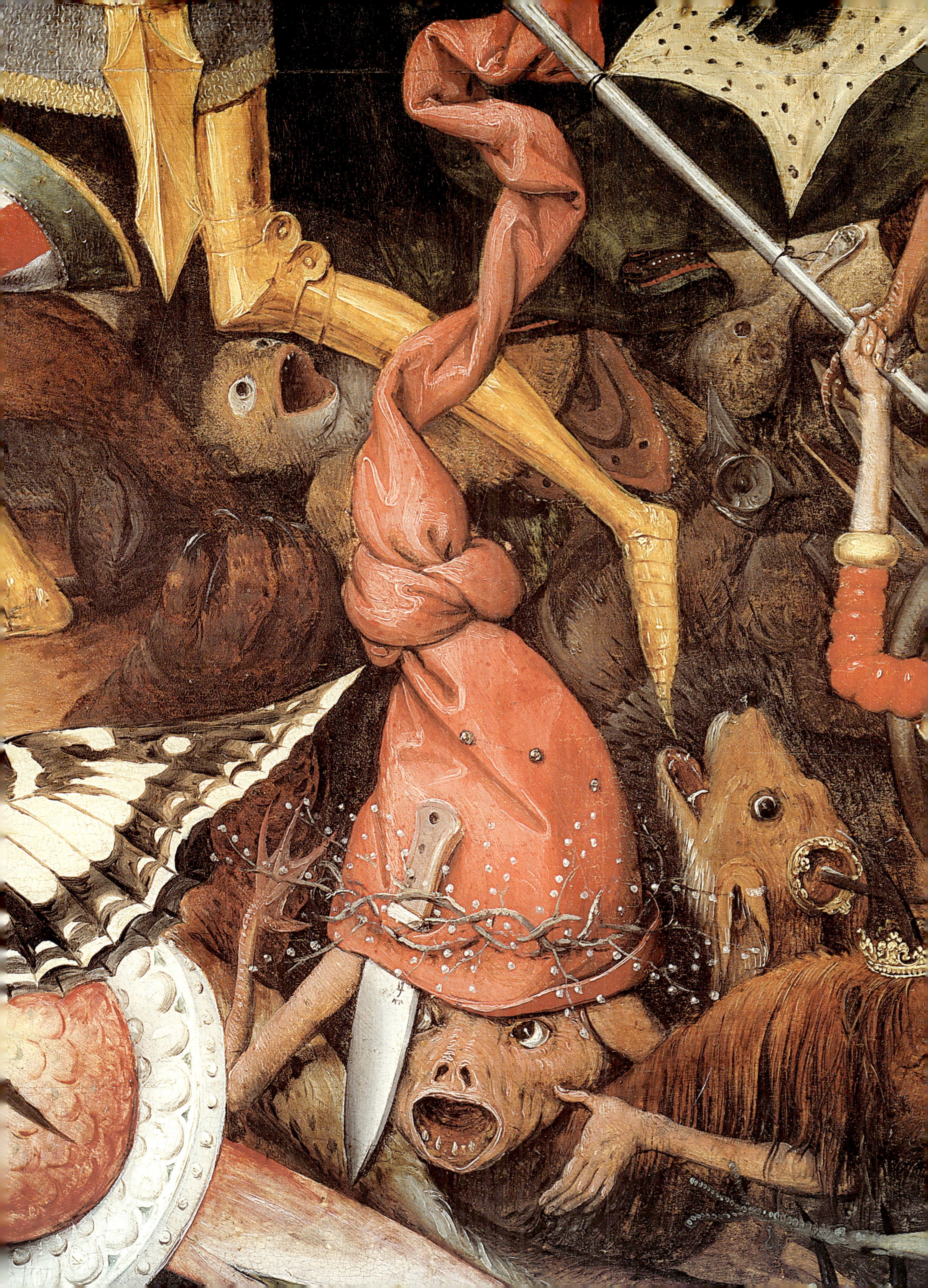

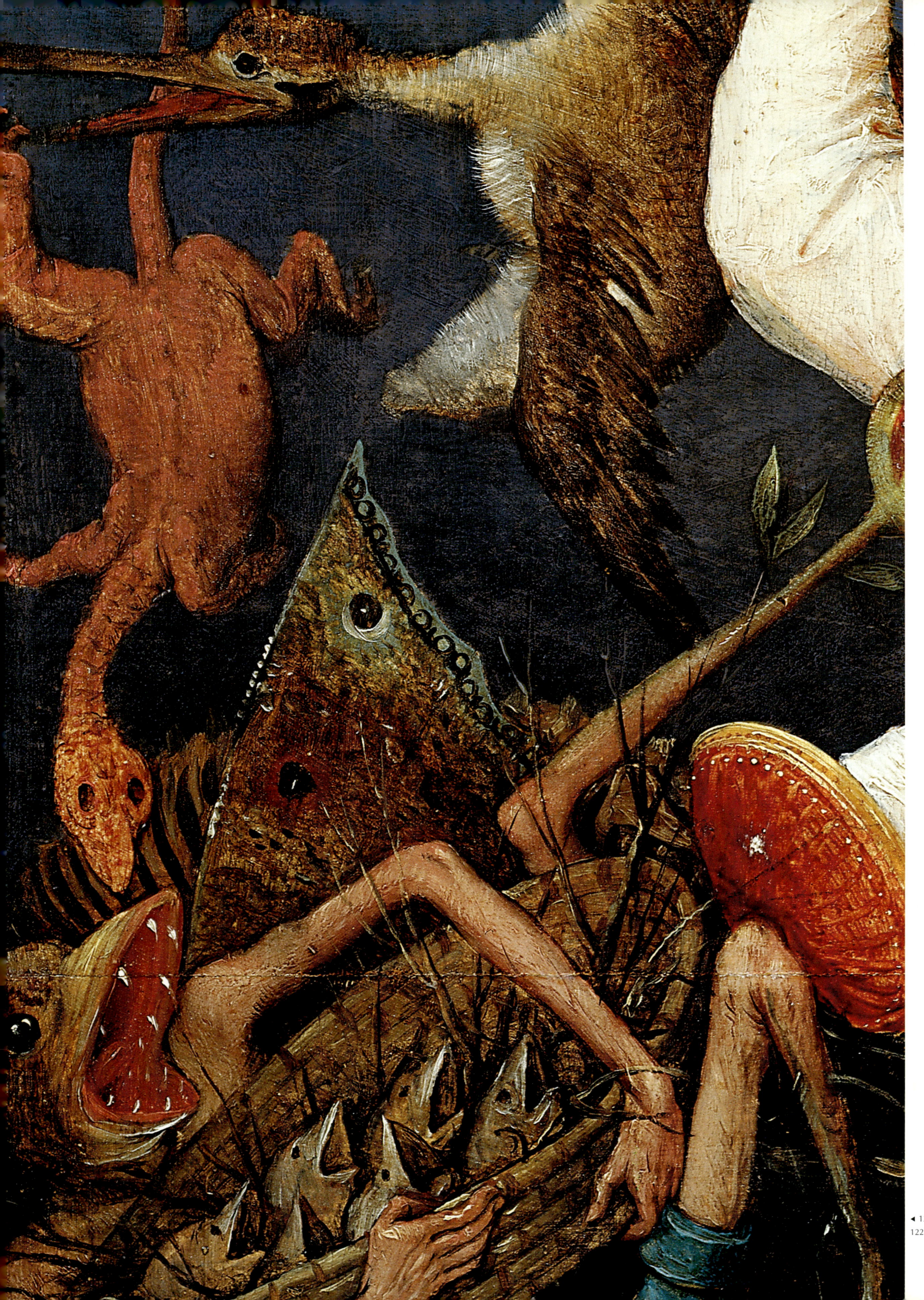

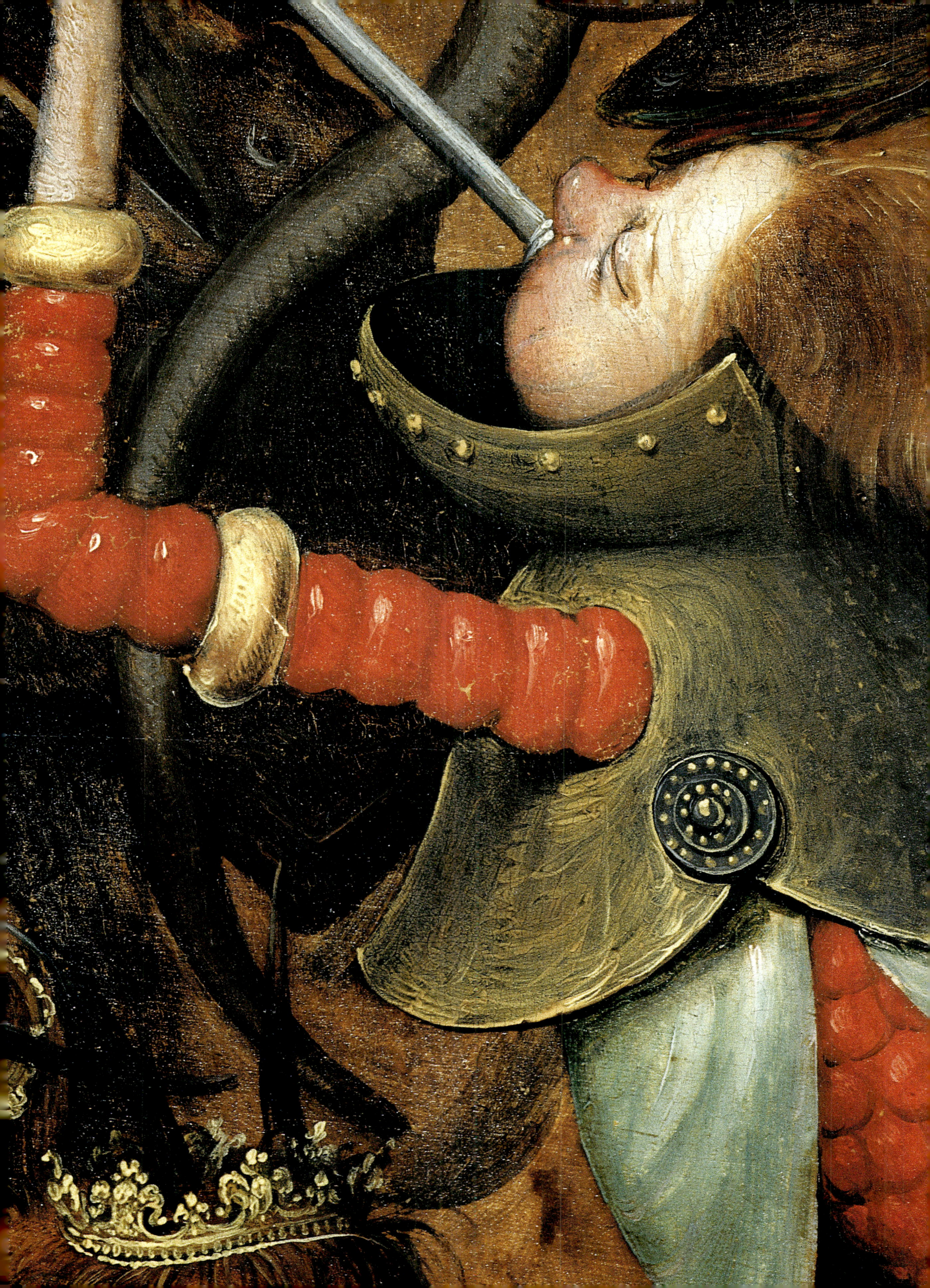

only as entertainment, others as a meditation on the end of time.[32] Meditation here is creative, and creation is fascinating. While in the upper part of the composition there is freedom and sweeping curves, and while disorder is to be seen in the rest of the picture, a triangular movement orchestrates the lower part, starting from the corners and culminating above the head of St. Michael, in an area marked by a pink and silver fish. This archaic-looking contrivance actually appears almost baroque in its movement and liveliness of line. Bruegel thus asserts his genius in defining and contrasting each element in the chaos through color and texture, and producing, by these same means, an ordered composition and a synthesized vision of a universal theme. An analysis of X-ray photographs of the under-painting has confirmed the vibrant work of its creation.

The coexistence of good and evil, the battle between them, and the eventual defeat of one—as well as the danger of evil's possible triumph and the absence of a guaranteed victory for good—permeate all Bruegel's works, because his profound humanity is the driving force behind them.

FROM CARNIVAL TO LENT

In *The Battle of Carnival and Lent,* the two seasons come face to face. While one follows the other, each brings its joys and its miseries. When Bruegel brings them together, light is not to be found only in the church square, nor ruin only at the tavern's threshold. The theme is medieval and draws on farce, satirical comedies, and mystery plays. The excesses of carnival remind us perhaps of Rabelais and *Gargantua,* but also of Hieronymus Bosch. The duality of the two is inherent in human nature, alternating the idea of revelry and penitence, whose essences themselves imply confrontation. In 1558 an engraving by Frans Hogenberg, published by Hieronymus Cock, illustrated this (fig. 123): The carnival procession perched on its barrel, on the left, and the Lent procession on the right, grapple in front of a backdrop of a pleasant, tree-lined village grouped around a church. Some of the people have already come to blows; battle is joined.

Things go quite differently in Bruegel's work, painted a year later. The artist has presented the two protagonists, who appear similar but are placed in a completely different context, with such breadth of vision that Hogenberg's image is reduced to the level of mere anecdote. In *The Battle of Carnival and Lent* (figs. 125–30), fighting has not yet begun: the protagonists and their forces are approaching each other and are about to meet. While a parody of a joust is hinted at in the foreground, this is but one element—albeit no doubt an important one— of an animated crowd that swarms all around it. Bruegel plunges the viewer into a town square bustling with activity. The architecture of the houses and church, a late Gothic building, takes up three sides of this human theater, allowing only a scrap of sky to peep through in the distance. The streets, the church loggia, and its side entrance act as stage scenery, enlivening the action unfolding within it.

Two opposing and contradictory processions are coming together. The first, led by Carnival, seems to come from the back of the painting, from the left, drawing in its wake a series of groups and events. Starting in the distant background from a fire where an effigy of Winter is being burned, we see (coming forward through

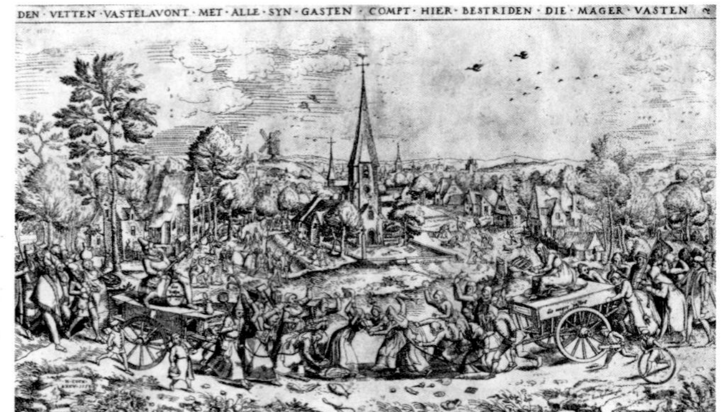

123

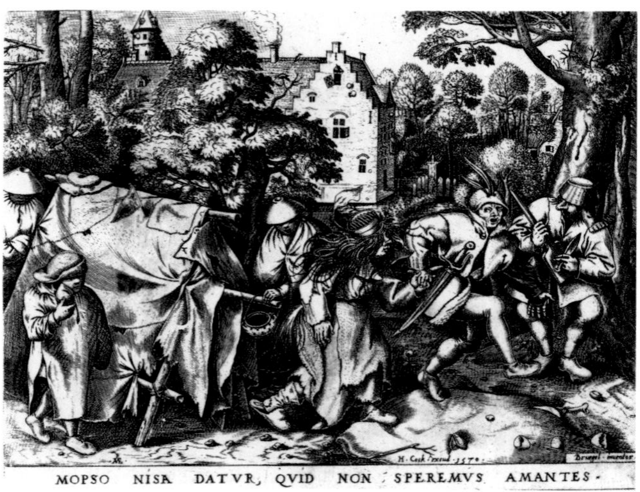

124

123. Frans Hogenberg, *The Battle of Carnival and Lent,* 1558. Etching, 12⁷⁄₈ x 19⁷⁄₈ in. (32.7 x 50.5 cm). Brussels, Bibliothèque royale Albert I, print room

124. Pieter van der Heyden, *The Wedding of Mopsus and Nisa,* after Pieter Bruegel, 1570. Engraving, 8³⁄₄ x 11³⁄₈ in. (22.2 x 29 cm). Brussels, Bibliothèque royale Albert I, print room

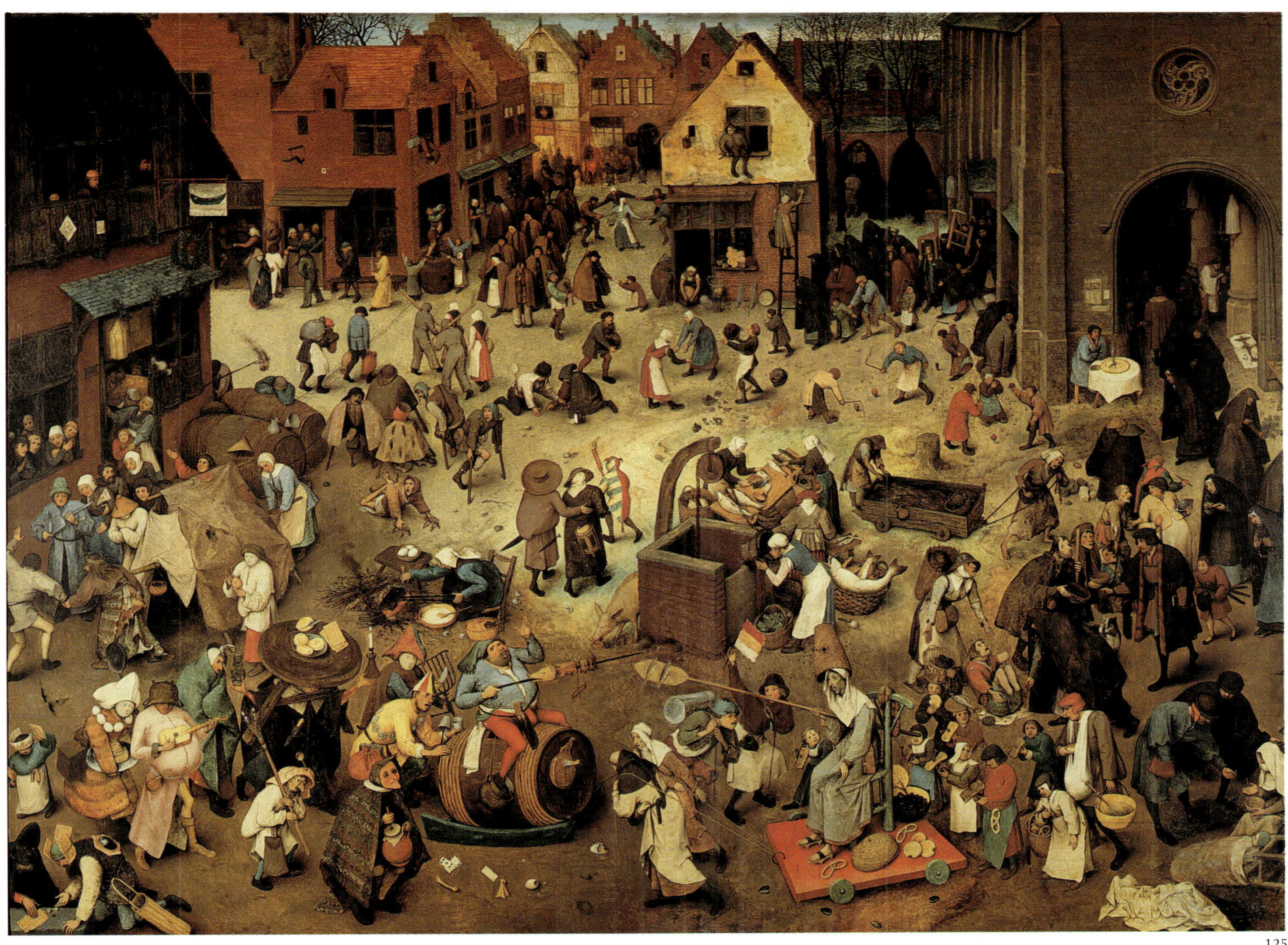

125

125–30. Pieter Bruegel, *The Battle of Carnival and Lent,*
1559: whole work and details. Oil on panel, 46$\frac{1}{2}$ x 64$\frac{3}{4}$ in.
(118 x 164.5 cm). Vienna, Kunsthistorisches Museum

the painting's space) a procession of lepers, a tavern with the sign of a dragon
where *The Masquerade of Bear-Cub and Valentine* (a theme Bruegel later returned
to in an engraving, fig. 87) is being performed, another line of cripples (from
whom Bruegel would fashion his *Beggars* of 1568), wine barrels at the corner of
the De Blauwen Schuit (The Blue Ship) tavern—before which another folk farce,
The Wedding of Mopsus and Nisa (see fig. 124), also known as *The Dirty Bride,* is
being performed—all lead to the masked retinue of Carnival himself, who rides a
barrel being hauled along on a blue barge. Opposite, on the church side of the
picture, Lent is being pulled on a wheeled platform by a nun and a monk. Crowned
by a beehive, the figure of Lent resembles the allegorical one of Hope in the
Virtues series (fig. 214), but is emaciated and stooped by hardship. The painting's
two symbolic characters are thus seen in opposition, as caricatures; the rotundity
of the one and the frailty of the other are pushed to ridiculous lengths to emphasize
their excesses. Lent's retinue includes children, their foreheads marked with
crosses of ash, a man carrying holy water, and some notables who, leaving the
church, perform acts of charity between two rows of beggars.

 If we consider that the picture shows "simultaneously scenes of rejoicing
and penitence, its theme is thus the illustration and representation of traditions
and customs […] from Epiphany to Ash Wednesday, the passage from winter to

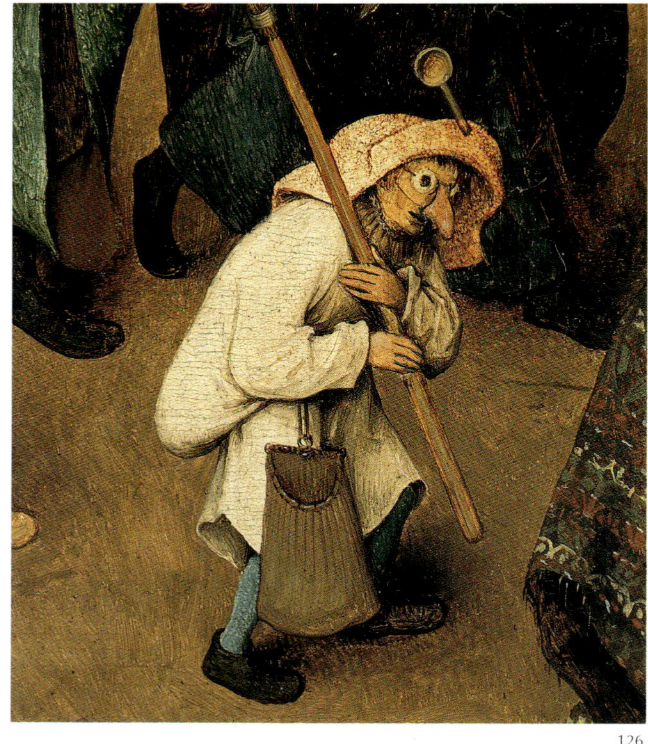

126

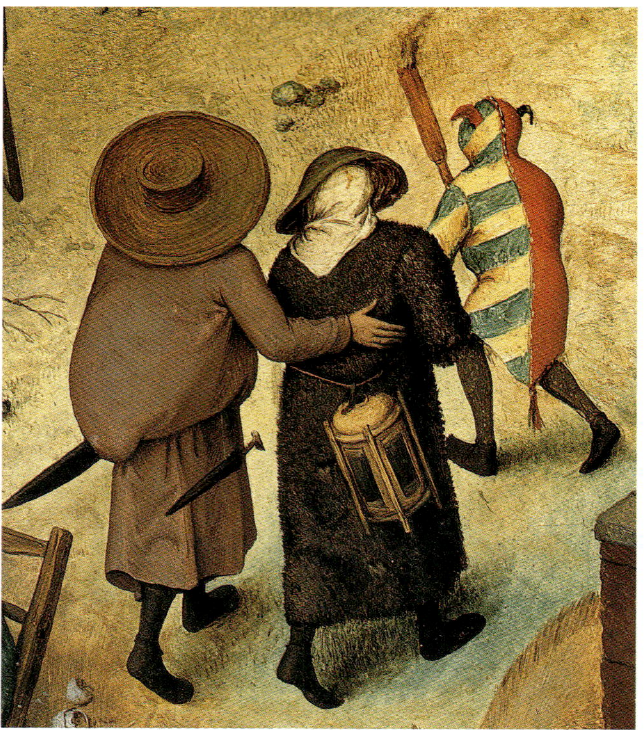

127

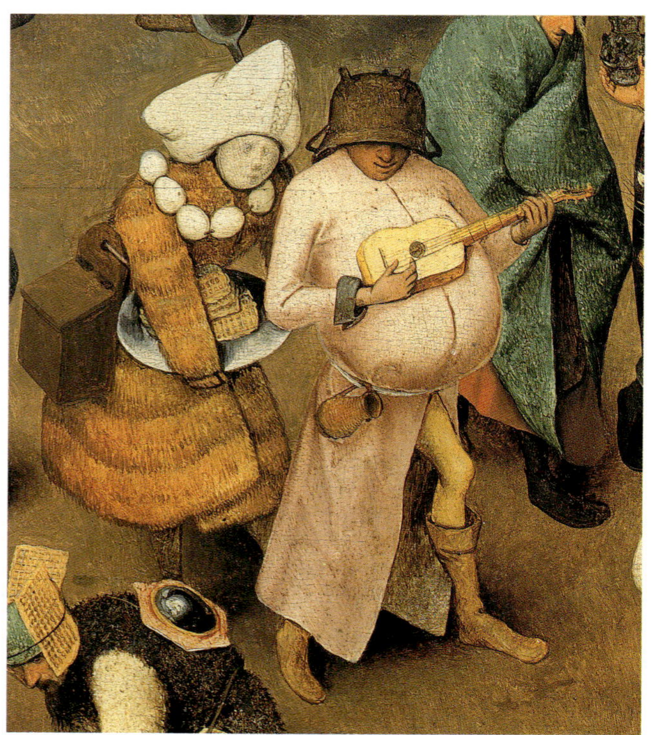

128

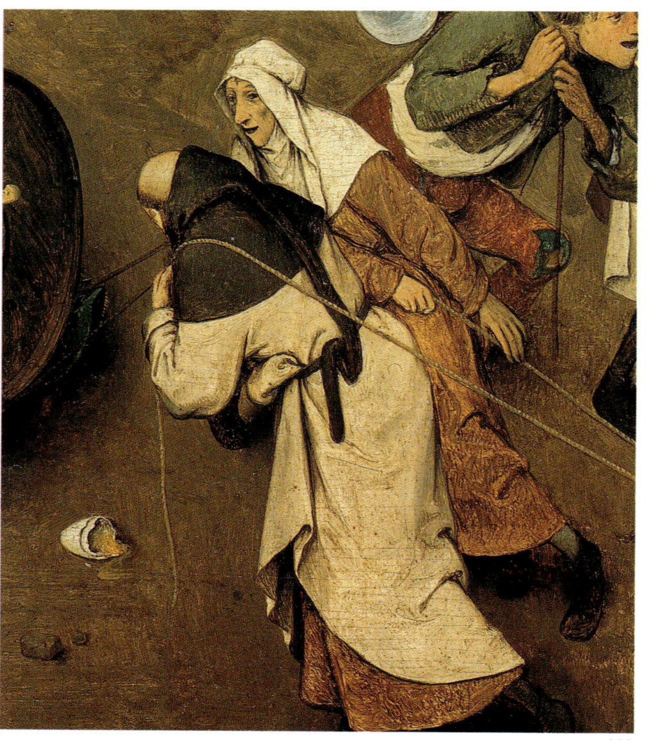

129

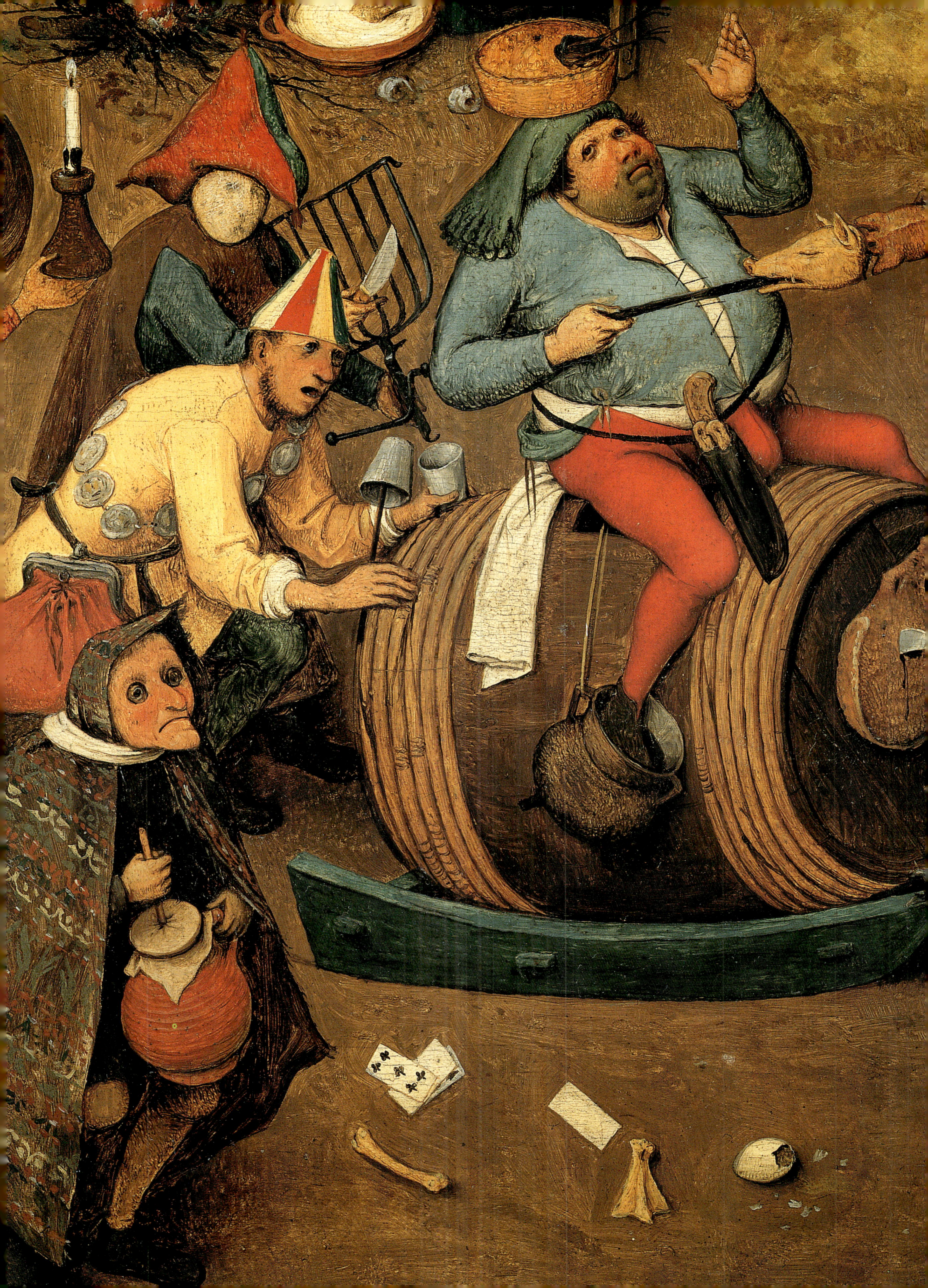

spring"[33]—a single place evokes elements that are separate in time. These scenes have been the subject of systematic studies, which have allowed the composition and meaning to be mapped out.[34]

Bruegel painted bare branches against a patch of sky on the left and branches with leaves on the right, presumably to convey the passing of the seasons, and the brightly colored house in the center may represent Easter, but it is hardly likely that the artist confined himself merely to listing evocations and anecdotes, prodigious though his accomplishment in doing just that might be. All of these myriad events are brought together in an overriding order; and therein lies Bruegel's genius. The work has an encyclopedic quality, like that of two paintings from the same period, *Flemish Proverbs* and *Children's Games*, and also like that of the *Deadly Sins* and *Virtues* series—but it remains a picture of life nonetheless. If we focus on a group of figures, we lose sight of it a moment later, such are the demands made on our attention by the teeming life on all sides. Events and daily life are constantly interfering with each other. Next to the cripples on the left, a man is slumped on a case to sleep off his drunkenness. On the other side of the picture, urchins play with spinning tops next to the church. Even though this game might be symbolic,[35] it still conveys the children's simple pleasure in it. Happiness, like misery, does not respect boundaries. There are miserable people at Carnival as in Lent—and Bruegel had indeed depicted more of them on the side of the latter. A copy of the painting by his son, Pieter Bruegel the Younger, reveals three elements "blotted out by overpainting in the original in Vienna: the children lying down at the church door, the old woman curled up in the trolley drawn by a woman in rags, and the bloated body of the drowned man, of whom all that is visible is the folds of his shroud in the foreground on the far right."[36] These sinister elements can be seen, from another angle, as being balanced by a sort of ironic humor. For example, in the same context, a woman with a basket on her back draws the attention of a devout woman to the sorry state of her maimed companion. A moving scene: but in the basket hides a monkey—symbol of deceit. At the back of the square, level with one of the side streets, two crouching men

131. Pieter van der Heyden, *The Thin Kitchen*, after Pieter Bruegel, 1563. Engraving, 8⅝ x 11⅜ in. (22 x 29 cm). Brussels, Bibliothèque royale Albert I, print room

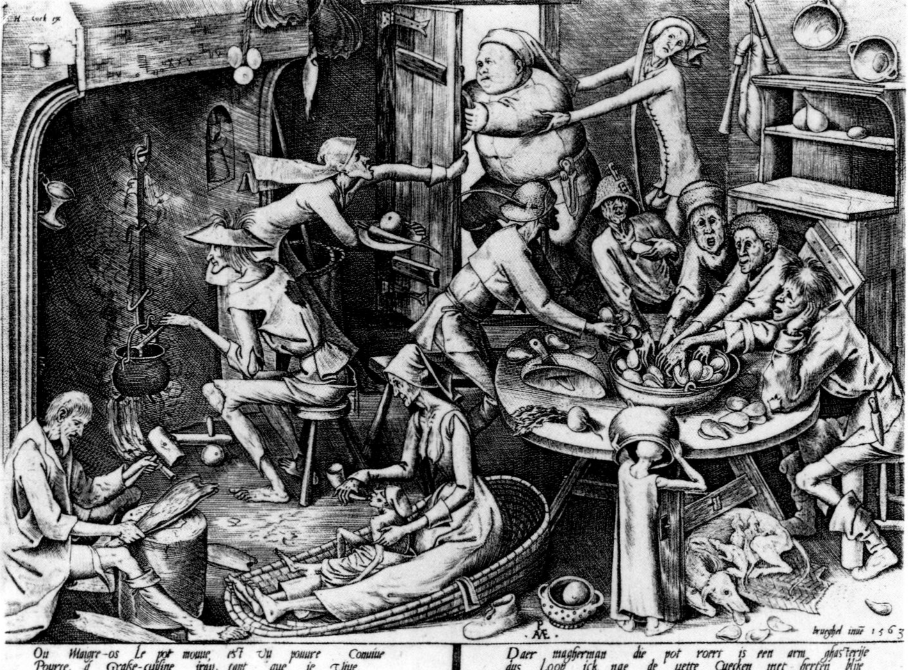

are playing dice—and the one in the pale shirt, who is picking up the money, has a skimmer thrust into his belt.

Bruegel also seeks to produce contrasts: in the center, to the left of the well, a pig is feeding on rubbish. On the other side, a woman with her basket of fresh vegetables is drinking the fresh water. The fish stall offers Lenten food that is very appetizing—as are the Carnival waffles a woman is cooking nearby, if we are to believe a contemporary recipe: "they are well spiced, delicious, and succulent [...] inside them there are cloves, cinnamon, and many other spices"; and we are told that the mixture needs "twelve eggs for every bowl of flour."[37] Have these eggs' shells been used to make the necklace worn by Carnival's companion?

These details, exchanges, and echoes that seem to respond to each other across the painting give it its playful liveliness. For some, drinking fresh water from the well might mean drinking from a spring, implying a return to nature and to the Scriptures; for others, the battle itself could be an allegory of the struggle between Lutherans and Catholics.[38] From the look of the protagonists, which camp should we choose? The painting acquires, indeed imposes, its intensity merely by being looked at just as it is: an extraordinary concentration of vitality that goes from farce to suffering, from the child-king in his paper crown on the far left to the drowned man on the far right.

By no means the least of these questions and mysteries is the jester in the center of the picture, who is guiding a couple; all three have their backs to us. Is he leading them on? Is he reference, witness, or arbiter? Are we to believe Sebastian Franck in *The Book of the World*: "In broad daylight they seek with torches and lanterns, and on Ash Wednesday they ask themselves with doleful cries where Carnival has gone"?[39] But what about the jester seated on the windowsill on the brightly colored house at the back of the square? Is he some sort of malign spirit, or the personification of Easter?[40] He could be either.

The Battle of Carnival and Lent is a complex and multifarious painting, which the artist dominates with his vision and which his gift brings to life through expanses of light and shade—often subjective, sometimes unreal—through the interplay of

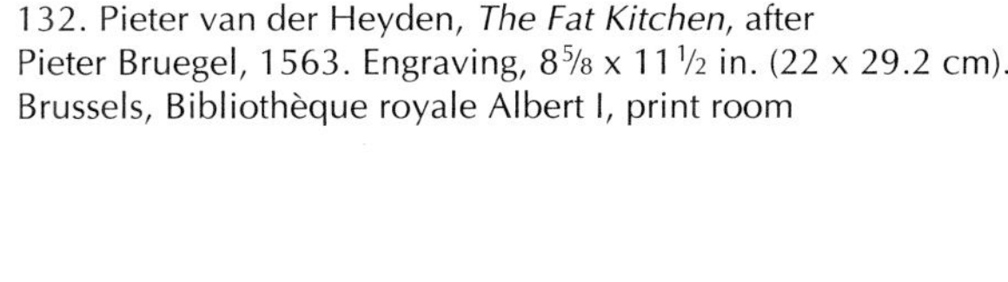

132. Pieter van der Heyden, *The Fat Kitchen*, after Pieter Bruegel, 1563. Engraving, 8⅝ x 11½ in. (22 x 29.2 cm). Brussels, Bibliothèque royale Albert I, print room

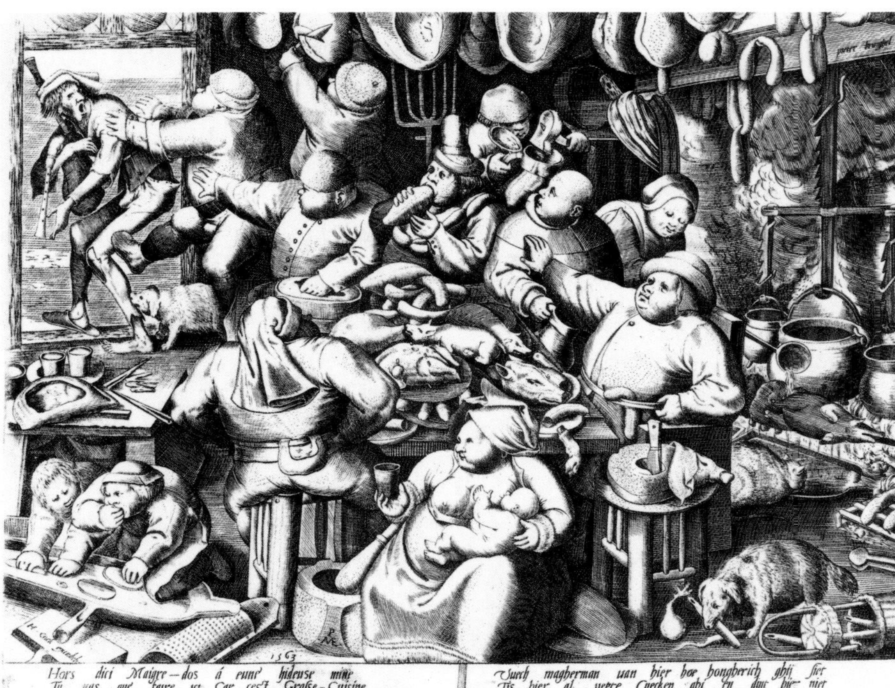

132

white, red, and blue areas of color, and through grays, browns, pinks, and the ocher that seems to be almost everywhere. The forms are well defined, and sometimes swollen with impasto—heavily laid on areas of paint—which give force to the characters' gestures in their roles, their clothes, and their disguises, just as they define objects, structures, and textures. With this painting, which dates from 1559, the artist has not yet acquired the compositional fluidity of *The Fall of The Rebel Angels* (fig. 114), painted in 1562, but he has already mastered a language that he had not when he painted *Flemish Proverbs* (fig. 223). One accomplished work is not necessarily followed by others of equal value. Thus *The Thin Kitchen* (fig. 131) and *The Fat Kitchen* (fig. 132), two engravings by Pieter van der Heyden after drawings by Bruegel and published by Hieronymus Cock in 1563, continue the theme of abstemiousness versus prodigality. However, they emphasize the comic

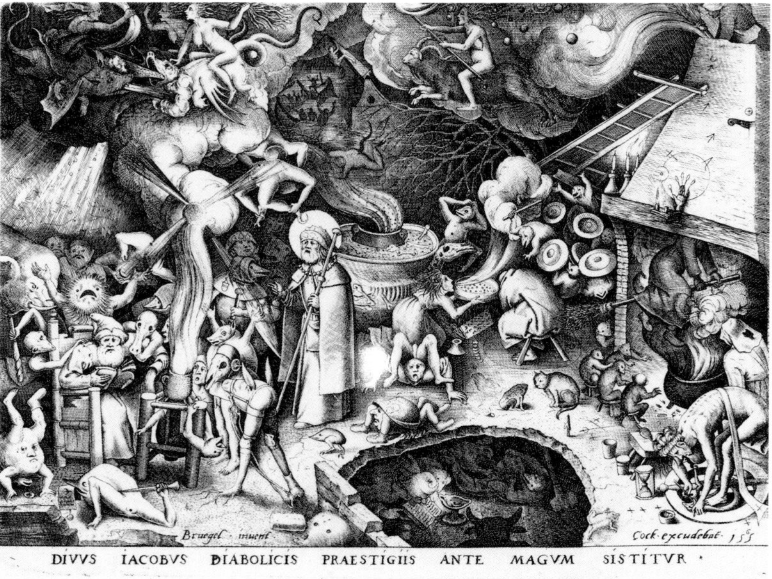

133

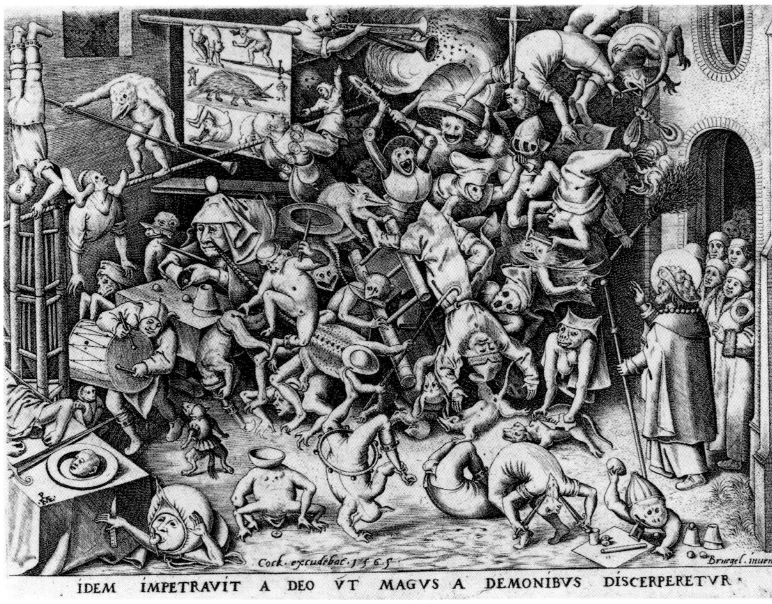

134

133. Pieter van der Heyden, *St. James and The Magician Hermogenes*, after Pieter Bruegel, 1565. Engraving, 8¾ x 11⅜ in. (22.2 x 29 cm). Brussels, Bibliothèque royale Albert I, print room

134. Pieter van der Heyden, *The Fall of the Magician*, after Pieter Bruegel, 1565. Engraving, 8¾ x 11⅜ in. (22.2 x 28.8 cm). Brussels, Bibliothèque royale Albert I, print room

aspect of this duality, and as the titles indicate, the contrast between the well-fed and the undernourished, which induces laughter by the simple comparison between fat and thin. Curiously, these plates are signed "BRUEGHEL INV. 1563," although the artist had dropped the "h" from his name about 1558. It may be, therefore, that Bruegel made the drawings some time before the engravings were published, when he was still spelling his name as he had originally. This cannot be established for certain, however, since the preparatory drawings do not survive, although certain stylistic comparisons can be made with engravings from 1558–59. For example, the features of the person at the cooking pot in *The Thin Kitchen* resemble those of the alchemist at his furnace in the engraving of the same name (fig. 45). Likewise, the shape of the fat people can be compared to some of the debauched characters in the *Deadly Sins*.

These works were clearly intended as entertainment, rather than to be seriously thought-provoking. They were highly popular and were republished several times, while pastiches and copies were also made.[41] They should not, however, be underestimated for this reason. The comic device is the same in both works: a fat man pushes his way in among the thin people, and an emaciated one appears at the door of the house of the fat. The contrast is certainly funny—but the fat person is

120

welcomed and even invited to share the thin people's frugal meal of turnips, carrots, mussels, and a slice of dry bread, while the poor thin man is driven away as an intruder by the guzzling fat ones. We can thus find a social statement in these two engravings: welcome and sharing on one hand, rejection and selfishness on the other. Is there irony in the first picture? Could a fat person imagine eating so sparingly? Perhaps he has made a mistake and knocked on the wrong door. The opposite case is inevitably different, and the contrast is eloquently portrayed. In the fat people's house, everything is rounded and curved, and there is such an accumulation of plenty that it seems to be about to overflow the tables and shelves. Among the thin people, the sheer emptiness of space gives the objects themselves a meager, sharp, and distressing appearance. The image of the thin child in the foreground, who has thrust his head into an empty pot, is a poignant emblem of human want.

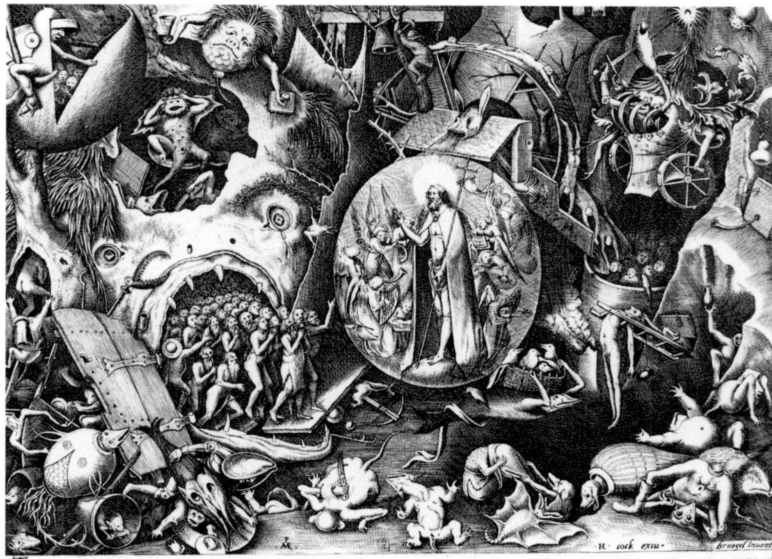

135

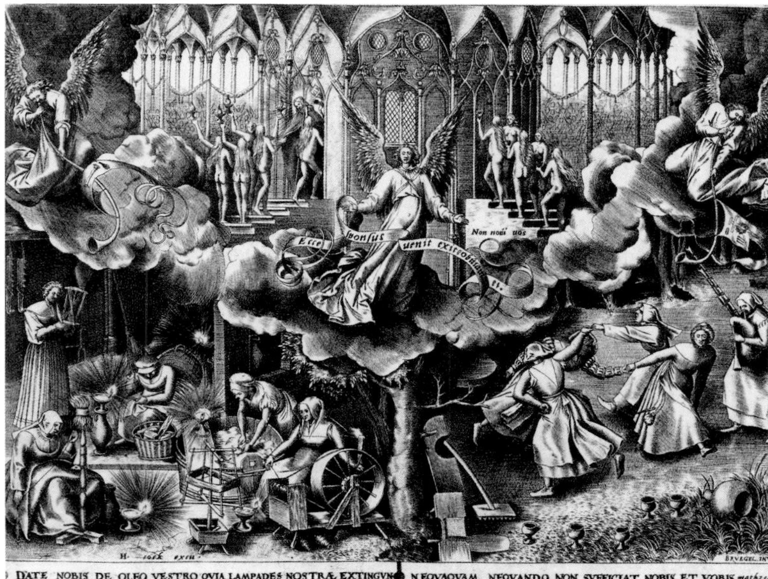

136

The difference between the subjects dealt with in paintings and those rendered in engravings may indicate the different audiences for whom these works were intended. Some engravings from 1565 depict devilish scenes that are nevertheless far removed from those in the paintings from about 1562. The comparison between good and evil, which *The Fall of the Rebel Angels* (fig. 114) illustrates so triumphantly, is returned to in a related but more anecdotal and less universal theme, borrowed from the *Golden Legend* of Jacques de Voragine, which Pieter Bruegel could easily have read in Flemish translation.[42] This episode that Bruegel took from the book contrasts St. James of Compostela with the magician Hermogenes, and it was made into two engravings by Pieter van der Heyden. *St. James and the Magician Hermogenes* (fig. 133) is set in the magician's lair, where we see witches' revels and other scenes from an infernal bestiary that stretches from the sky to a cave deep within the earth. The image conjures up the torment and anguish of emptiness. In the companion engraving, *The Fall of the Magician* (fig. 134), whose original drawing, dated 1564, survives, depicts the triumph of good, the downfall of evil, and the victory of faith over magic, with images of acrobats, circus acts, and illusionists. The collapse is no less real for that: a falling monster bites its own tail—a detail repeated from *The Fall of the Rebel Angels*, and spectators observe the scene

135. Pieter van der Heyden, *Christ in Limbo*, after Pieter Bruegel, ca. 1561 (?). Engraving, 9 1/8 x 11 1/2 in. (23.2 x 29.1 cm). Brussels, Bibliothèque royale Albert I, print room

136. Attributed to Philipp Galle, *The Wise and Foolish Virgins*, after Pieter Bruegel, ca. 1560–61 (?). Engraving, 8 3/4 x 11 1/4 in. (22.1 x 28.6 cm). Brussels, Bibliothèque royale Albert I, print room

through a gap in the wall on the right of the drawing. A similar acknowledgment of the viewer is already present in Bruegel's *The Ass at School*, and can be seen in several paintings, such as *Christ Carrying the Cross* (fig. 51) or *John the Baptist Preaching* (fig. 284).

Two other engravings should be mentioned in the context of good and evil, and of a diabolic presence. *Christ in Limbo*, whose original drawing dates from 1561

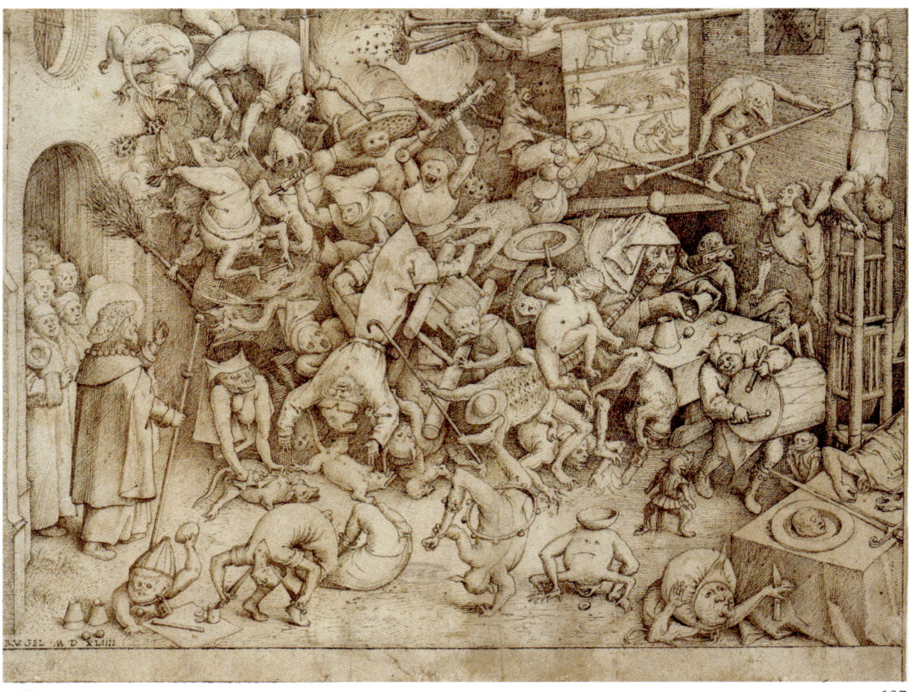

137. Pieter Bruegel, *The Fall of the Magician*, 1564. Pen and brown ink, 8¾ x 11⅝ in. (22.3 x 29.6 cm). Amsterdam, Rijksmuseum, Rijksprentenkabinet

(fig. 138) but was probably added to later,[43] belongs to the line of development that runs from the *Deadly Sins* to the *Magician Hermogenes*, and shows points of similarity with *Dulle Griet*, as well as such astonishing invented images as the helmet on wheels, which bursts out of a cave on the left, echoing the figure of Satan on the right. *The Wise and Foolish Virgins* (fig. 136), a parable of lost and saved souls, depicts a subject popular at the time. Bruegel has confined himself to showing the image in a medieval idiom, with elements of Gothic architecture on either side of a tree, dominated by the figure of an angel. The wise virgins are carefully spinning wool, while the foolish ones dance to the bagpipes, an instrument of sensuality, played by one of their companions. This work, which is of a high quality despite being conventional, no doubt reflected the tastes of the clients who bought prints from its publisher, Hieronymus Cock. The theme is illustrated with only human figures, with no allusion to devilry.

HEAVEN

About 1563, a breath of fresh air in Bruegel's work seems to have blown away the droll, fantastic, and obsessional presence of the devil and his companions. Did *The Fall of the Rebel Angels* really take place within the painter's mind? He was increasingly preoccupied by great religious themes, though the subjects depicted and the motivations behind them need to be analyzed. The presence, more or less visible, of a theme in a painting presents a problem with Bruegel—as in the work of other artists—which cannot be resolved in general terms, but must be addressed

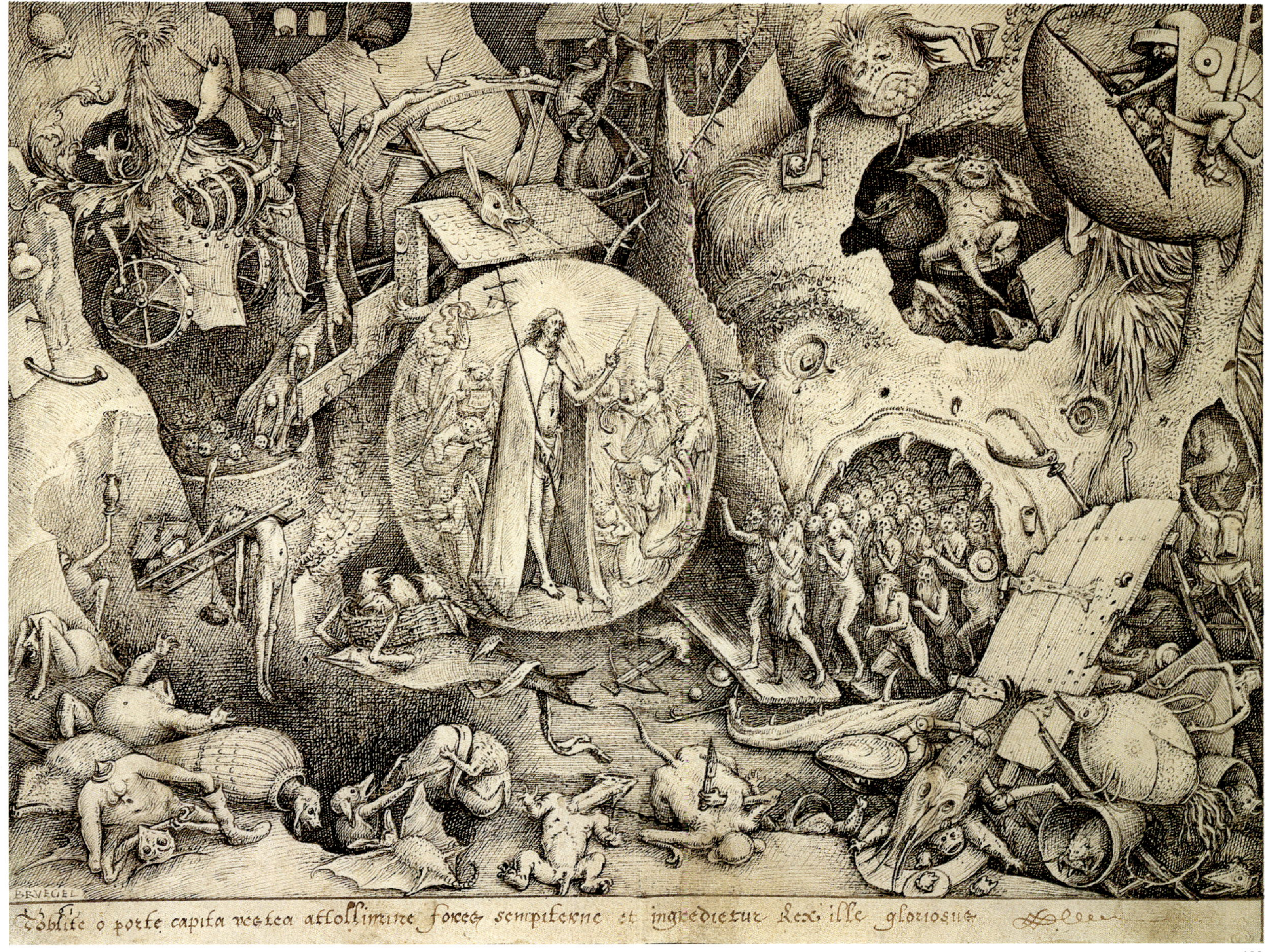

138

138. Pieter Bruegel, *Christ in Limbo*, 1561.
Pen and brown ink, 9 x 11⅞ in. (23.1 x 30.1 cm).
Vienna, Graphische Sammlung Albertina

case by case. The artist's new vision is already hinted at in a work whose authorship is sometimes disputed: *Landscape with the Parable of the Sower* (fig. 139), which shows a wide estuary and a figure that evokes not only the parable (Matthew XIII, 3–8) but also a living scene of rural life. Small figures here and there—one large group of them gathered around Christ, who is preaching on the shore in the far distance—enliven the painting's great space which, punctuated by trees, farms, a church tower, the buildings of a town, and the high line of the mountains, stretches beyond the horizon. The painting has rightly been compared with a preparatory sketch made in about 1555 for an engraving in the series *Great Landscapes, Solicitudo Rustica* (fig. 142).[44] Indeed, it has the same composition, with a river and a mountain range crossing the picture diagonally—a parallel pointed out by the collector who owned the painting in 1930. In a letter to the museum in Brussels, the Antwerp collector Fernand Stuyck del Bruyère revealed that he had bought the painting in 1924, at which time was it attributed to Joos de Momper and was "covered by centuries-old grime." Cleaning, he explained, had uncovered "at the lower right the signature and date 'BRUEGHEL 1559'."[45] The Timken Art

Gallery in San Diego, which acquired the work in 1965, gives the date 1557, not 1559. First mentioned by Friedländer in 1931, the painting's state of repair has caused some concern. Nevertheless, what we know about its purchase supports the buyer's perhaps too confident belief that this is "one of the earliest surviving works by the master." Charles de Tolnay, who acknowledges the attribution without giving "a definitive verdict," given the work's condition, writes of "an overall impression that is almost *monochrome.*"[46]

Nuances suited Bruegel's purpose. So did brilliance, and this is fully demonstrated by the landscape of 1563, *The Flight into Egypt* (fig. 140). Hell may have given way to Heaven, but mankind's lack of faith has caused the departure of the Virgin and her child. Coming after the tumultuous works of Bruegel's Antwerp period, this painting—which belonged to Cardinal de Granvelle and perhaps also to Rubens—marks a moment of peace. Its setting is one of the most beautiful landscapes Bruegel ever painted, and it has an accomplished sense of unity. The scene, with its wide, mountain-ringed estuary, seems to recall Bruegel's journey to Italy. The light and the colors of the earth as much as of the water and the sky give this landscape a breadth of space that the art of northern Europe, despite the achievement of Joachim Patinir, had yet to come to know. The subject in itself is

139. Pieter Bruegel, *Landscape with the Parable of the Sower,* 1557. Oil on panel, 29⅛ x 40⅛ in. (74 x 102 cm). San Diego, Timken Art Gallery

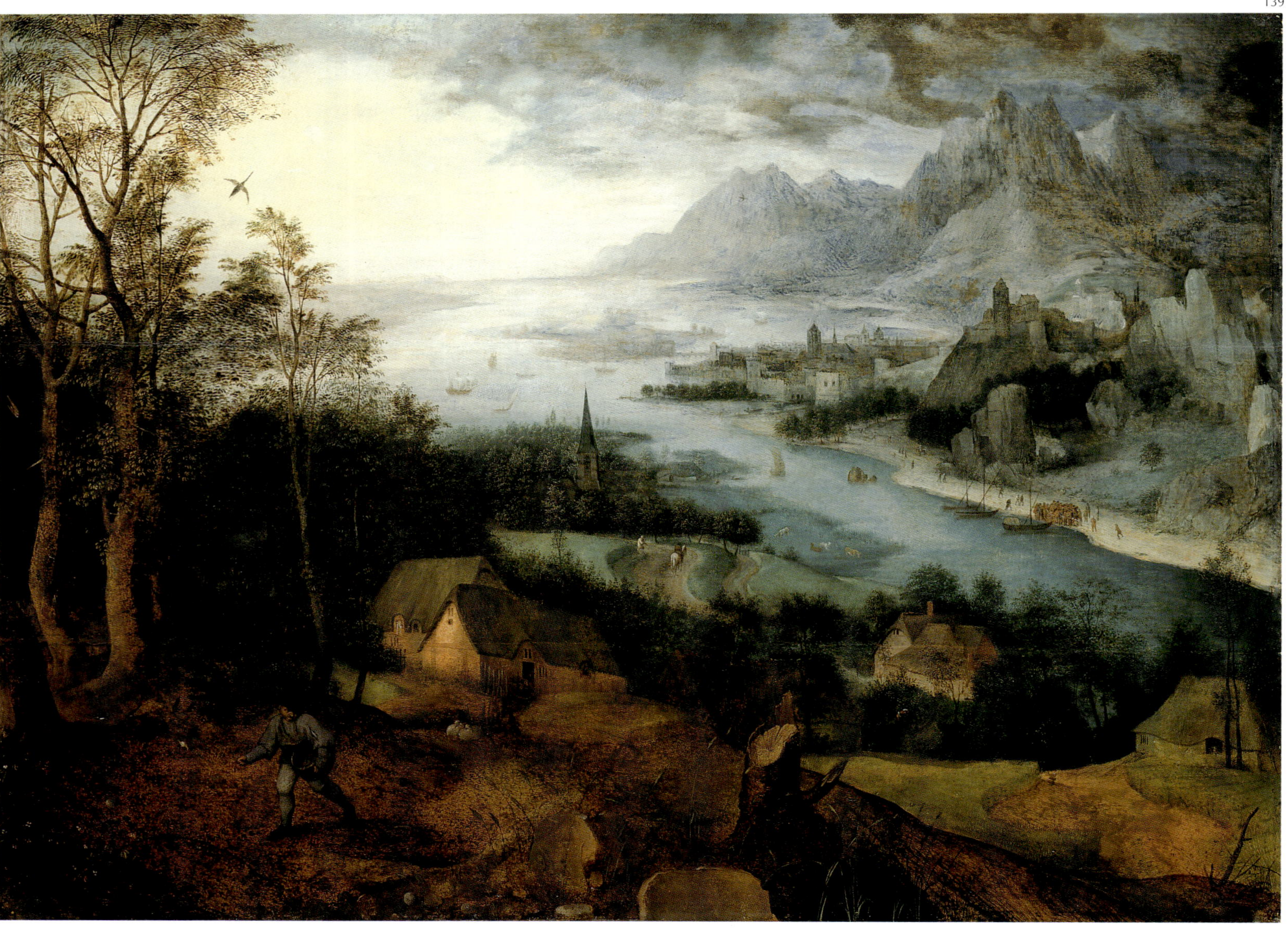

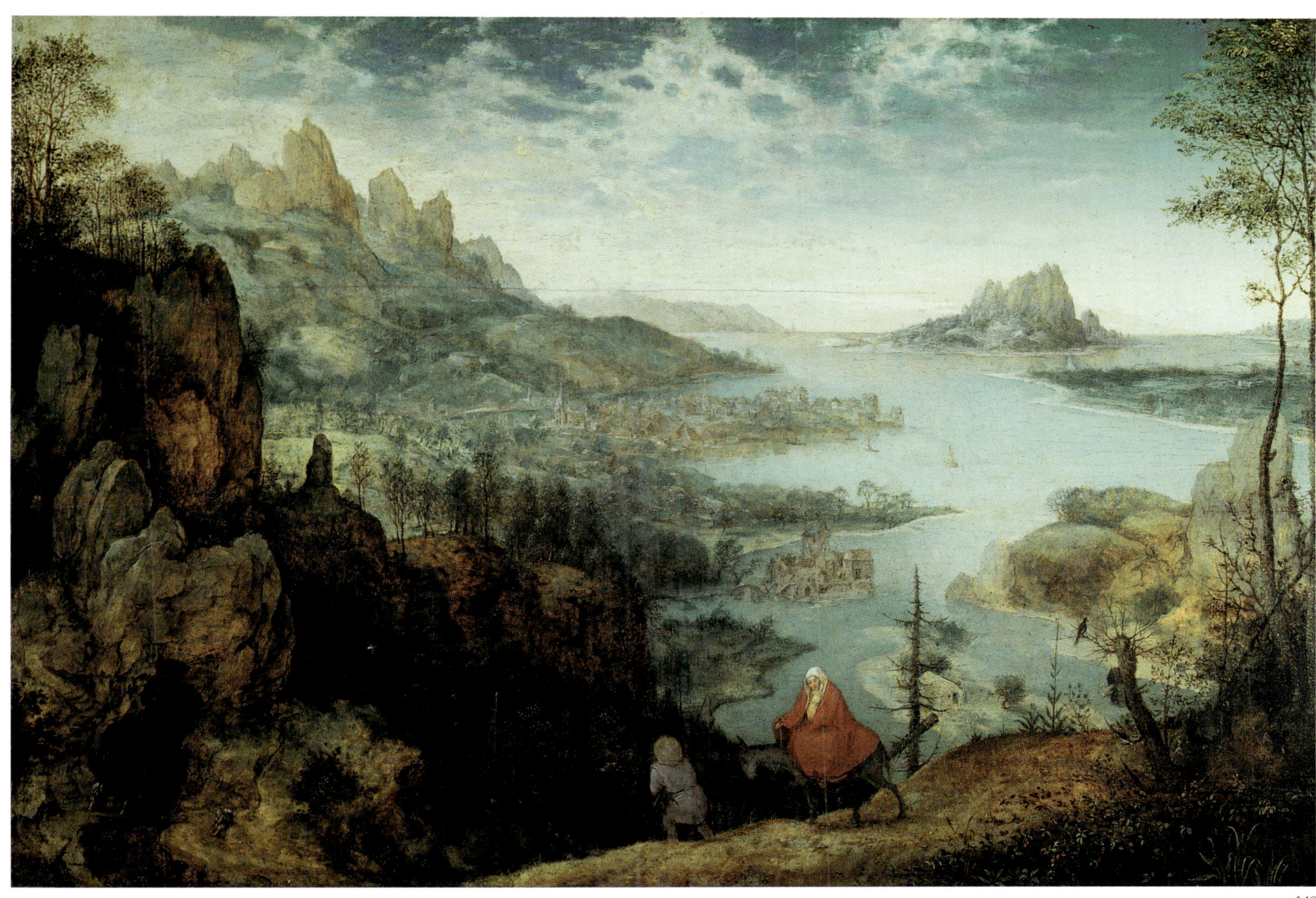

140. Pieter Bruegel, *The Flight into Egypt*, 1563. Oil on panel, 14⅝ x 21⅞ in. (37.2 x 55.5 cm). London, Courtauld Institute of Art, Count Antoine Seilern Collection

not new: It was often depicted during the sixteenth century, by the Cranachs, by Patinir, and Van Cleve in the form of a Rest on the Flight into Egypt. Bruegel, too, had already made a drawing of the subject about 1553–54, in his *Italian River Landscape with the Holy Family and a Cloister* (fig. 141). The water and rock are already there, but the drawing, also known as *The Rest on the Flight into Egypt,* lacks the painting's harmony and integration of subject and landscape. As with other drawings Bruegel made at that time, we sense that elements have been added later.

Although there are obvious parallels between the two works, the horizon in the drawing is broken by rocks, while the painting's planes are modulated toward an open horizon that is in line with the figures. One element alone disturbs this great peace: on the right, inside a small shrine attached to a tree, is a small pagan idol that was overturned as Christ passed it—a time-honored symbol of the Christian triumph over paganism.[47] This detail, and the red color of Mary's cloak, as she follows Joseph into the valley, load the scene with significance. The painting's atmosphere is thus different from that of the landscapes of Patinir, where figures and events seem to be used simply as "filling," to quote Gustav Glück,[43] who rediscovered Bruegel's work in 1939. The painting is thus indeed a *Flight into Egypt*, in a superb landscape, a variation on the theme of nature, which the painter was to treat with genius, from his *Seasons* to the *The Fall of Icarus*.

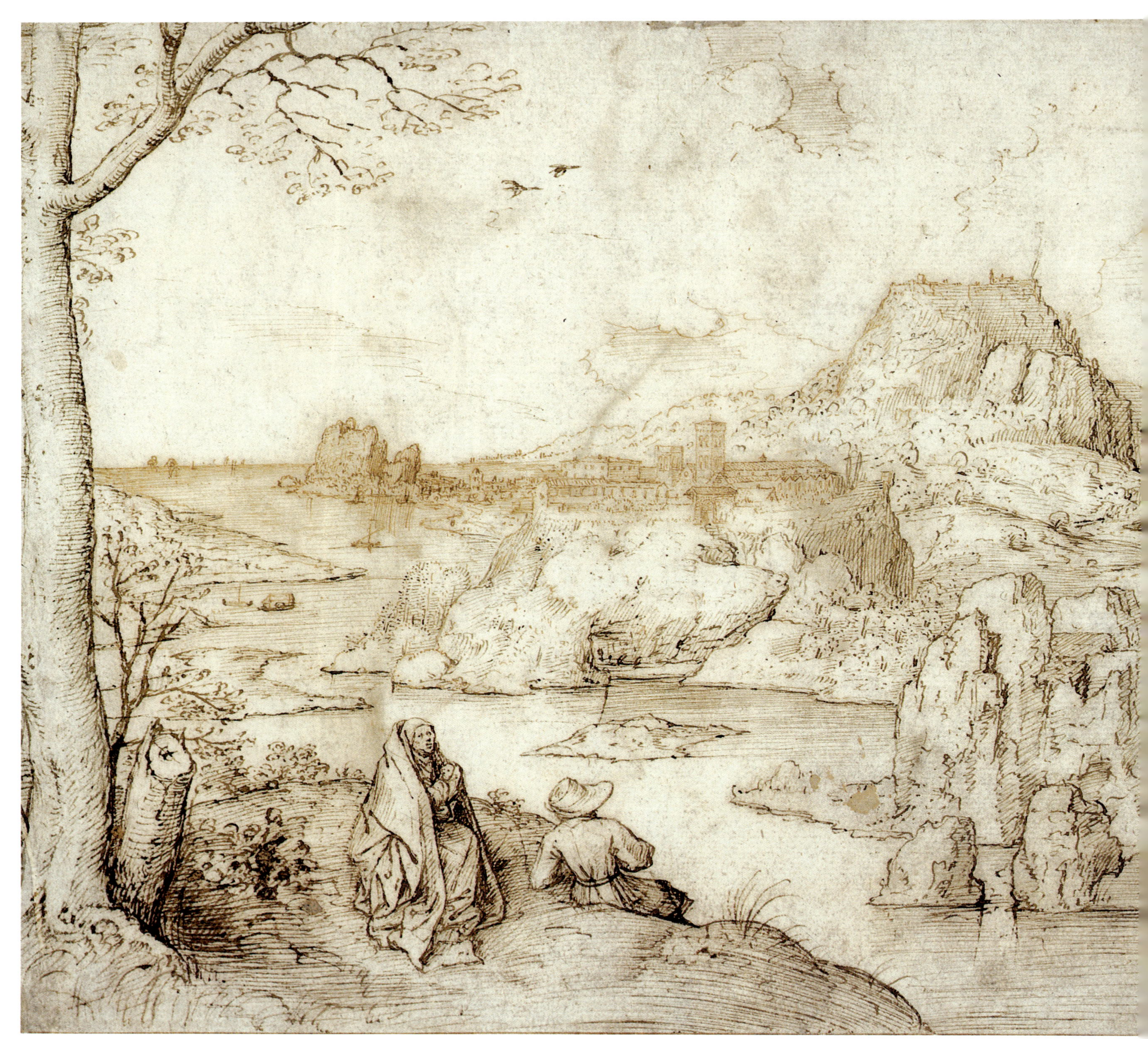

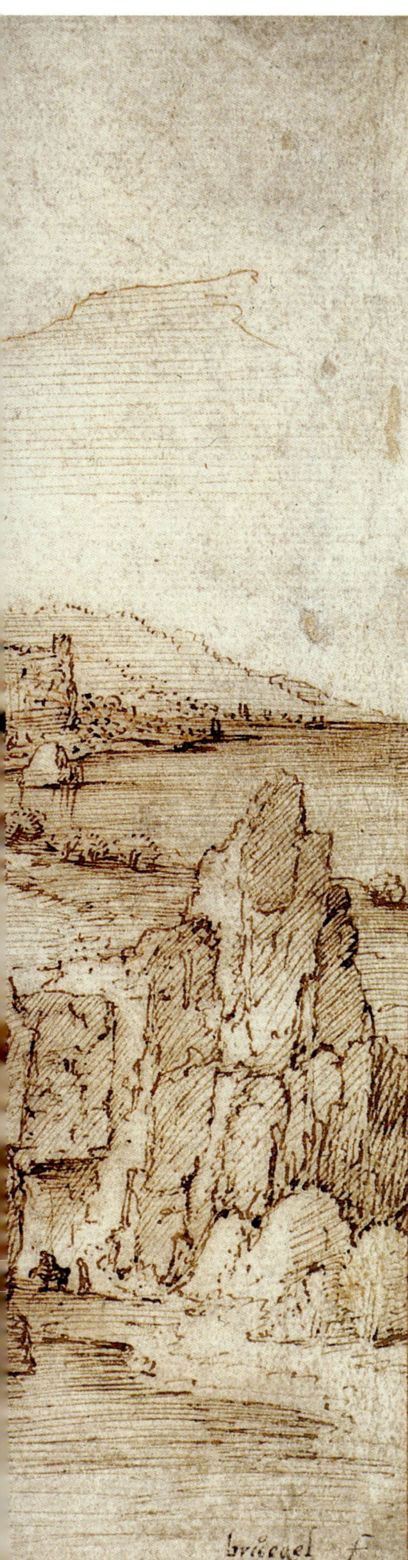

141. Pieter Bruegel, *Italian River Landscape with the Holy Family and a Cloister* or *Rest on the Flight into Egypt*, ca. 1553–54. Pen and brown ink, 8 x 11 in. (20.3 x 28.2 cm). Berlin, Staatliche Museen, Kupferstichkabinett

142. Pieter Bruegel, *Solicitudo Rustica*, 1555, preliminary sketch for the *Great Landscapes* series. Pen and brown ink, 9⅝ x 13⅞ in. (24.2 x 35.2 cm). London, British Museum

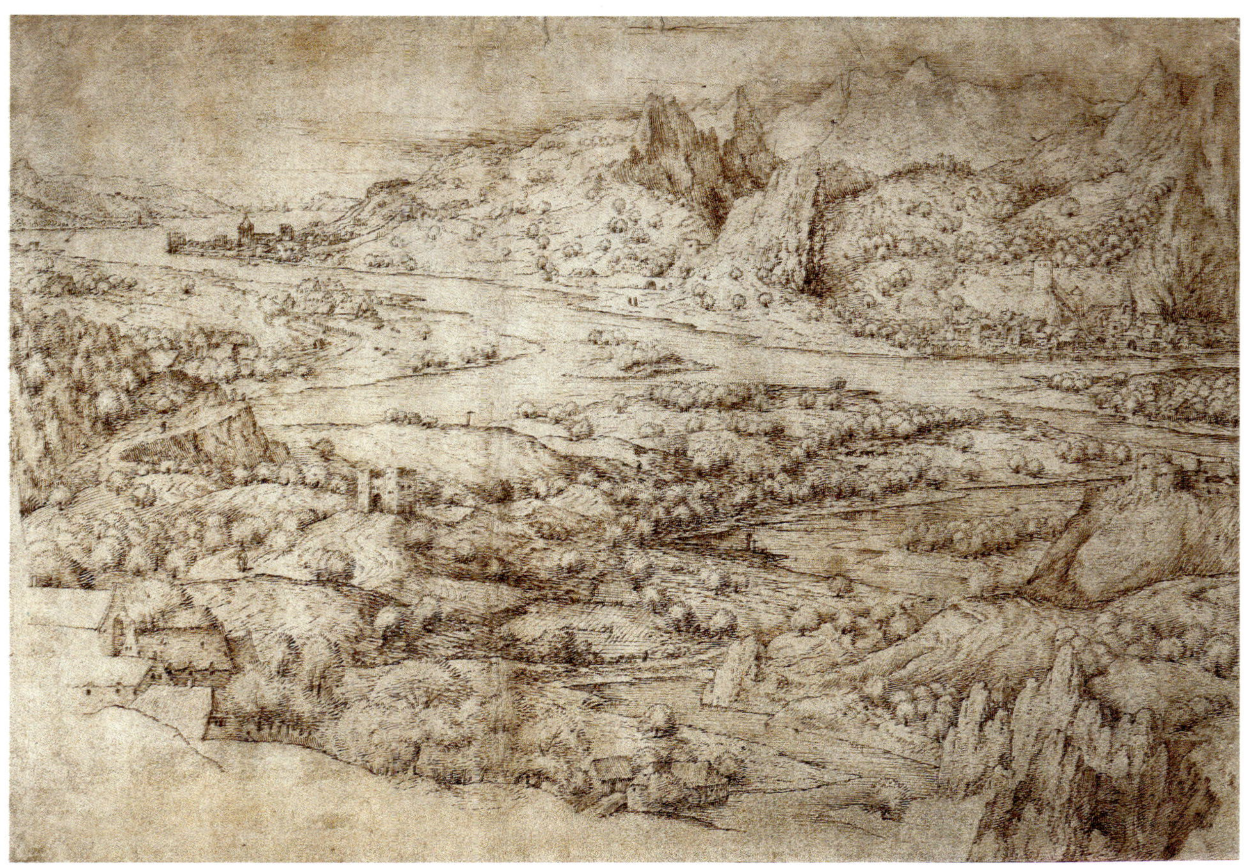

RELIGIOUS SUBJECTS

The *Adoration of the Magi* of 1564 (figs. 146–49) leaves us in no doubt about its subject, which the painting's vertical format and composition make all the more dominant. This work, which is exceptional in Bruegel's oeuvre in being vertical, returns in a monumental manner to a subject the painter had already depicted in distemper. The accent here is on the actors in the scene, which strikes us with its directness, the boldness of its contrasts of texture, and the direct contact it makes with the viewer, almost at head height. The variety of human types, and the almost caricatured coarseness of some faces and of the soldiers, reinforce the strangeness of the slender Moorish king, whose mysterious majesty, quiet demeanor, and restraint contrast with the gift he is bearing—an elaborate nautilus-shaped vessel, worthy of Benvenuto Cellini.

Many possible sources of inspiration for the painting's composition and details have been suggested, from medieval miniatures to Michelangelo, via Bosch, Parmigianino, and Correggio.[49] Some Mannerist elements are noticeable, such as the graceful appearance of the infant Jesus, which contrasts sharply with the realism of the faces made clearly individual by the artist. Similarly, Bruegel has skillfully captured, in the private conversation St. Joseph is having with a young man who is speaking into his ear, a lifelike detail that gives this solemn subject its human scale. The Virgin herself underlines this with her femininity and motherliness as she presents the child whom all have come to adore.

The vertical composition, shored up by the diagonal mass formed by two of the kneeling Magi, leads the eye from the brightness of the foreground toward the shadow of the stable, where the ass is visible, although the ox is not. While the panel has been cut down on three sides, the bottom remains uncut, the signature is clear, and the date, 1564, would appear to be beyond doubt.[50] A vigorous, far from conventional, and highly personal image, its religious feeling is unmistakable. Bruegel's faith must have been deep and sincere, even though his religious subjects sometimes seem to be intended to express other themes entirely. For example, *The Adoration of the Magi in the Snow*, from 1567 (fig. 195), gives more prominence to the weather than to the happy event itself. This work—which is masterly—is probably the first picture in the history of Western painting that shows the snow actually falling. What we are shown is a village in the grip of winter, where the Adoration happens to be taking place.

The grip of winter prevails as well in *The Massacre of the Innocents* (fig. 145). The snow has fallen, the freeze has set in, and the killing is on. The contrast between the wintry quiet of a Brabant village and its invasion by the blind violence of men is striking. The episode—drawn from the Gospel of Matthew (II, 16), where King Herod orders the killing of all newborn boys in Bethlehem—is remarkably evoked. Van Mander mentions the work twice, emphasizing "the despair and the fainting of the mothers, and other moving and affecting images."[51] A number of versions of this work exist today, including several copies made by Pieter Bruegel the Younger (fig. 353). The work's original conception is clearly that of Pieter Bruegel himself, however, given the links it has with other paintings by him that convey similar contemporary settings of biblical scenes, such as the *Census at Bethlehem* (fig. 200), which is sometimes considered a companion picture to it.

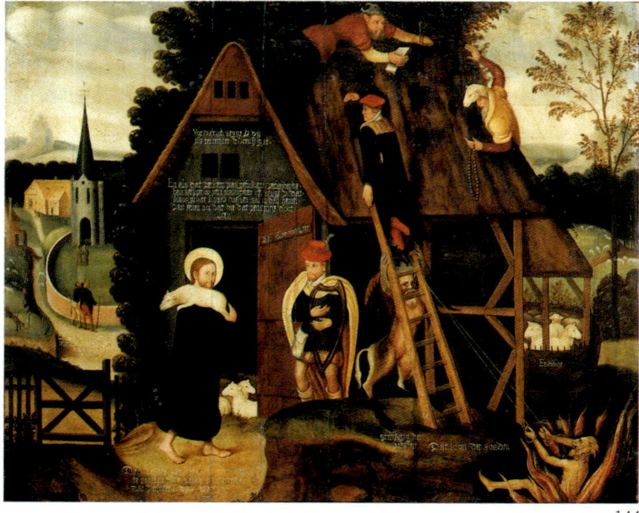

143. Philipp Galle, *The Parable of the Good Shepherd*, after Pieter Bruegel, 1565, second state signed Theodor Galle. Engraving, 8⅞ x 11⅝ in. (22.5 x 29.5 cm). Brussels, Bibliothèque royale Albert I, print room

144. Anonymous artist, southern Netherlands, *The Good Shepherd*, third quarter of the sixteenth century. Oil on panel, 30¾ x 37¾ in. (78 x 96 cm). Brussels, Musées royaux des Beaux-Arts de Belgique

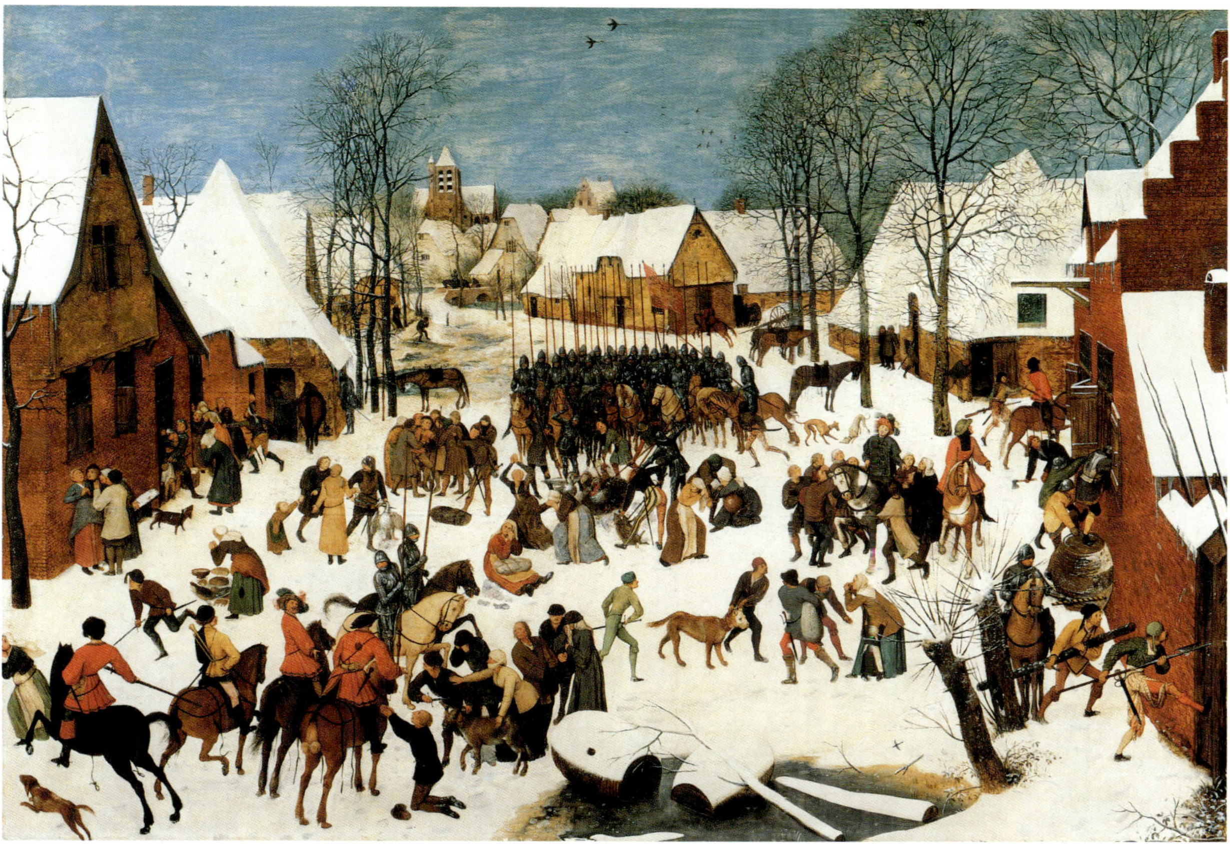

145. Possibly by Pieter Bruegel, *The Massacre of the Innocents*, ca. 1566–67. Oil on panel, 43 x 62¼ in. (109.2 X 158.1 cm). London, Hampton Court Palace, Royal Gallery

It is possible, however, that one of the extant versions may be the original. The version in the Kunsthistorisches Museum in Vienna has been ruled out by dendrochronology—an examination of the growth-rings of the wood panel on which it was painted—which in this case shows that the tree from which the panel was cut was felled after the artist's death.[52] Another version of the composition is in the British royal collection, and is housed at Hampton Court Palace. This panel was bought by Charles II in 1660,[53] but by then it had already been repainted so as to transform it into a picture of a village being sacked by soldiers. All the children had been overpainted, and replaced by animals, objects, or parcels. Other elements were also changed, such as the banners and the sign *Dit is in de ster* (At the Sign of the Star) at the inn where the Virgin and Joseph had lodged and which the soldiers on the right are attacking. The intention was clearly to suppress the painting's true subject and to turn it into a scene that, although still violent, was devoid of religious significance.

Restoration of the Hampton Court painting (fig. 145) and study of the undisturbed areas have revealed, both in the execution and in the underlying drawing, a sensitivity and freedom of expression that strongly suggest that this is an original work by Bruegel.[54] Even in its damaged state, the painting retains the memory of the emotions that led to its creation. The drama is still there, with its foreground broken up into groups, weeping or attacking, glancing toward the compact mass of horsemen almost in the picture's center. Force of arms thus dominates, contrasting darkly with the white surface of the landscape. Some writers have seen in it a condemnation of the Spanish regime, and in the soldiers' commander, a direct allusion to the Duke of Alva. The figure was overpainted in the Hampton Court

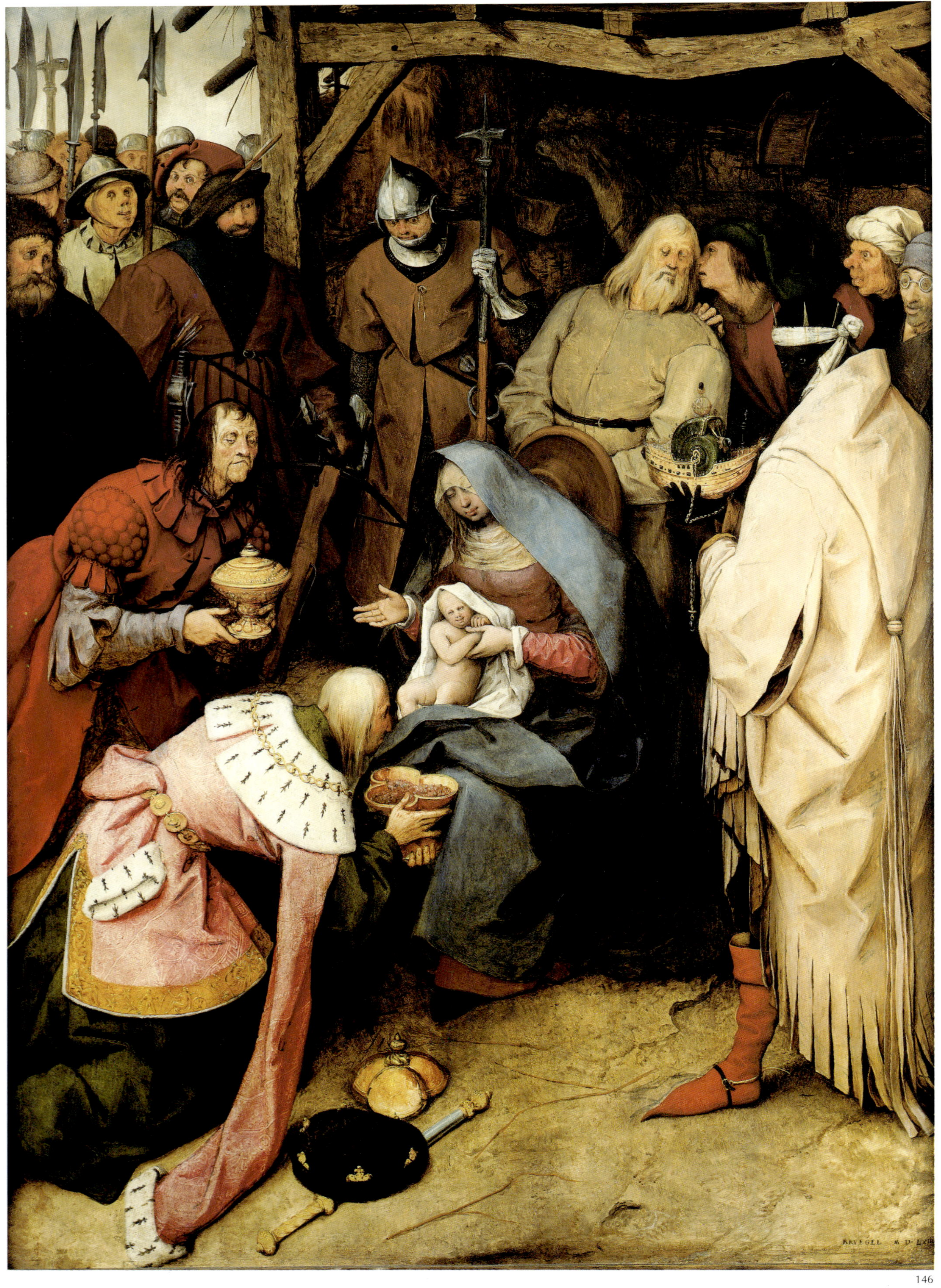

146–49. Pieter Bruegel, *The Adoration of the Magi*, 1564: whole
work and details. Oil on panel, 44 x 33 in. (111.5 x 84 cm).
London, National Gallery

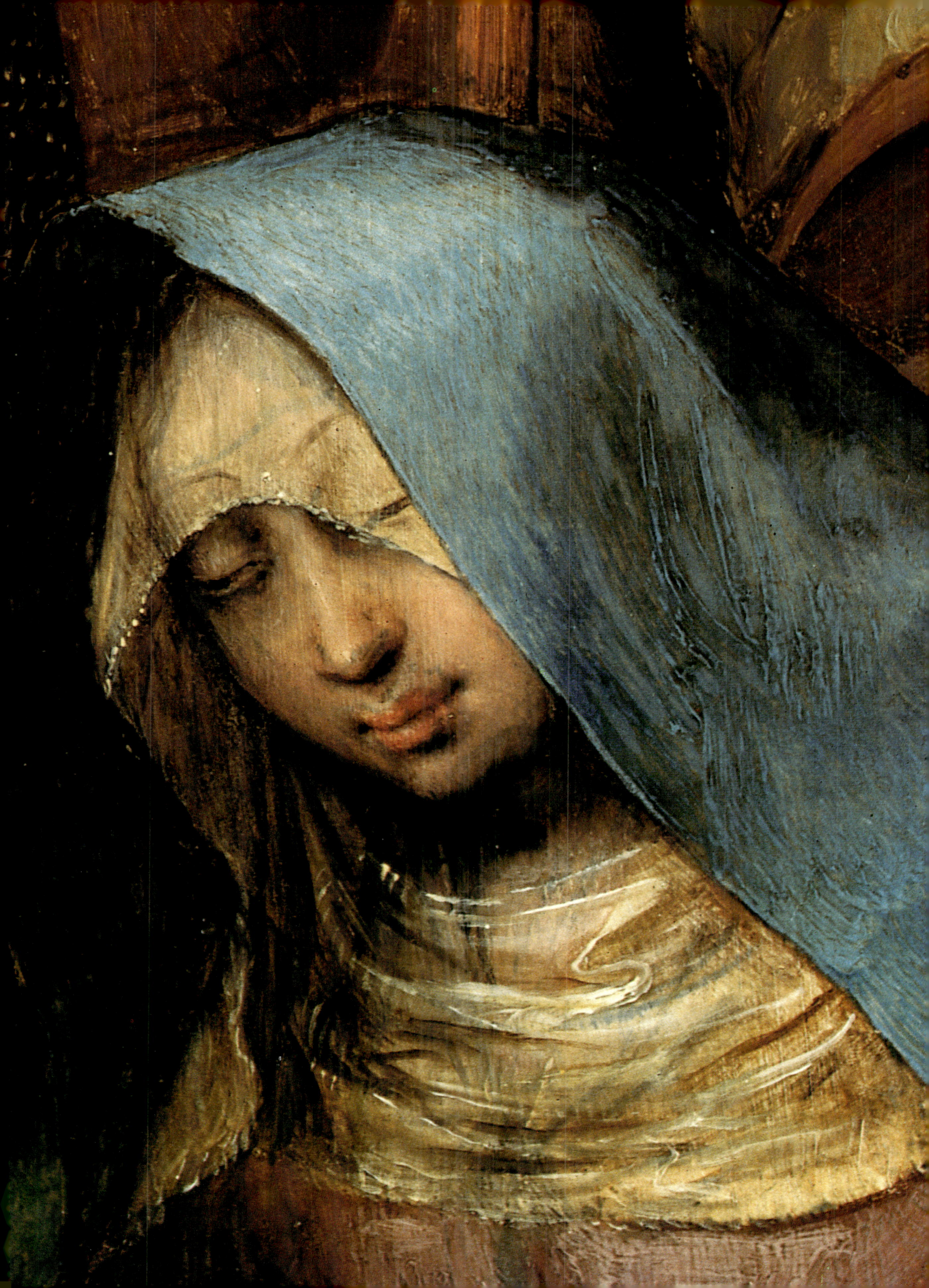

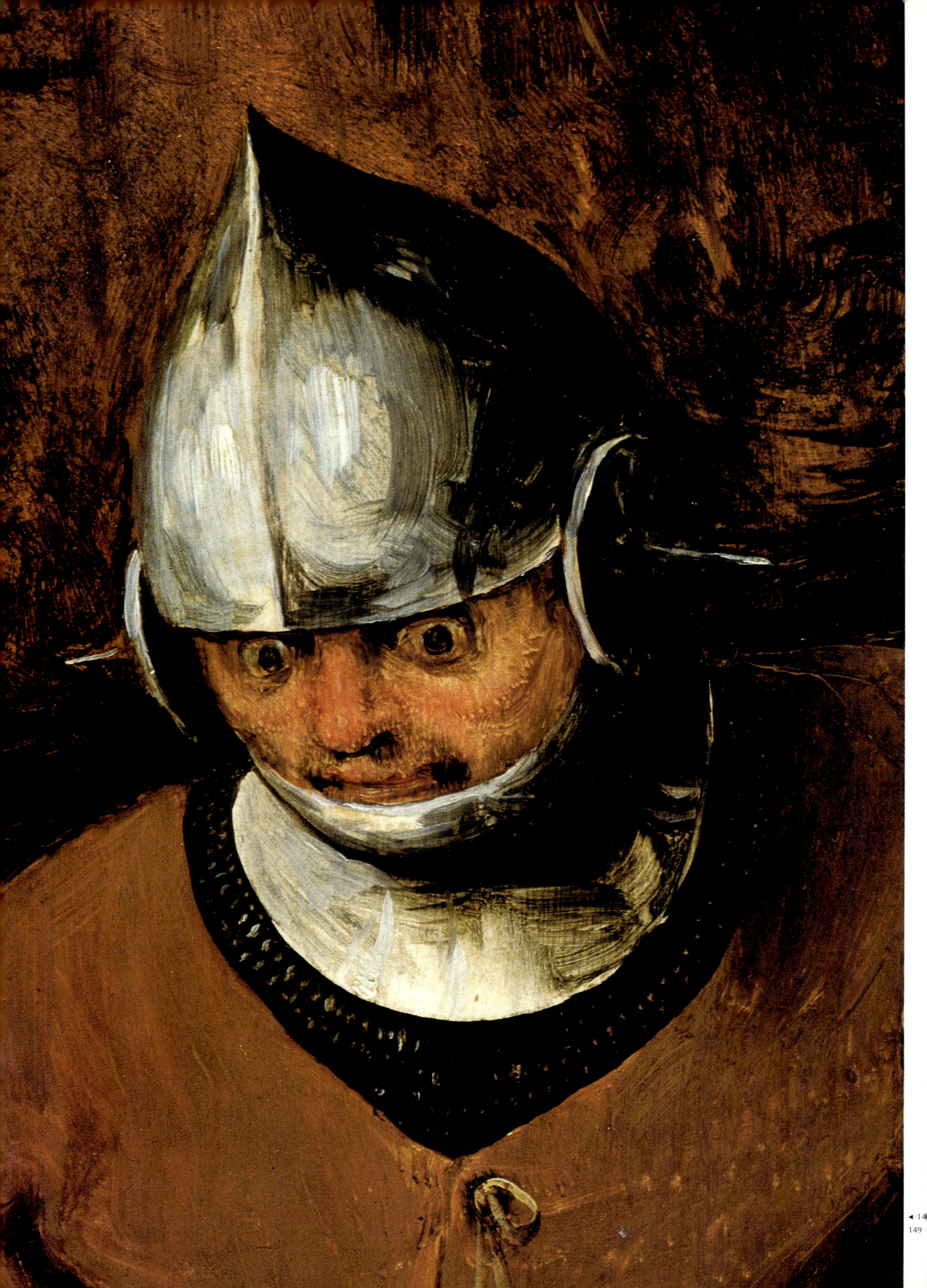

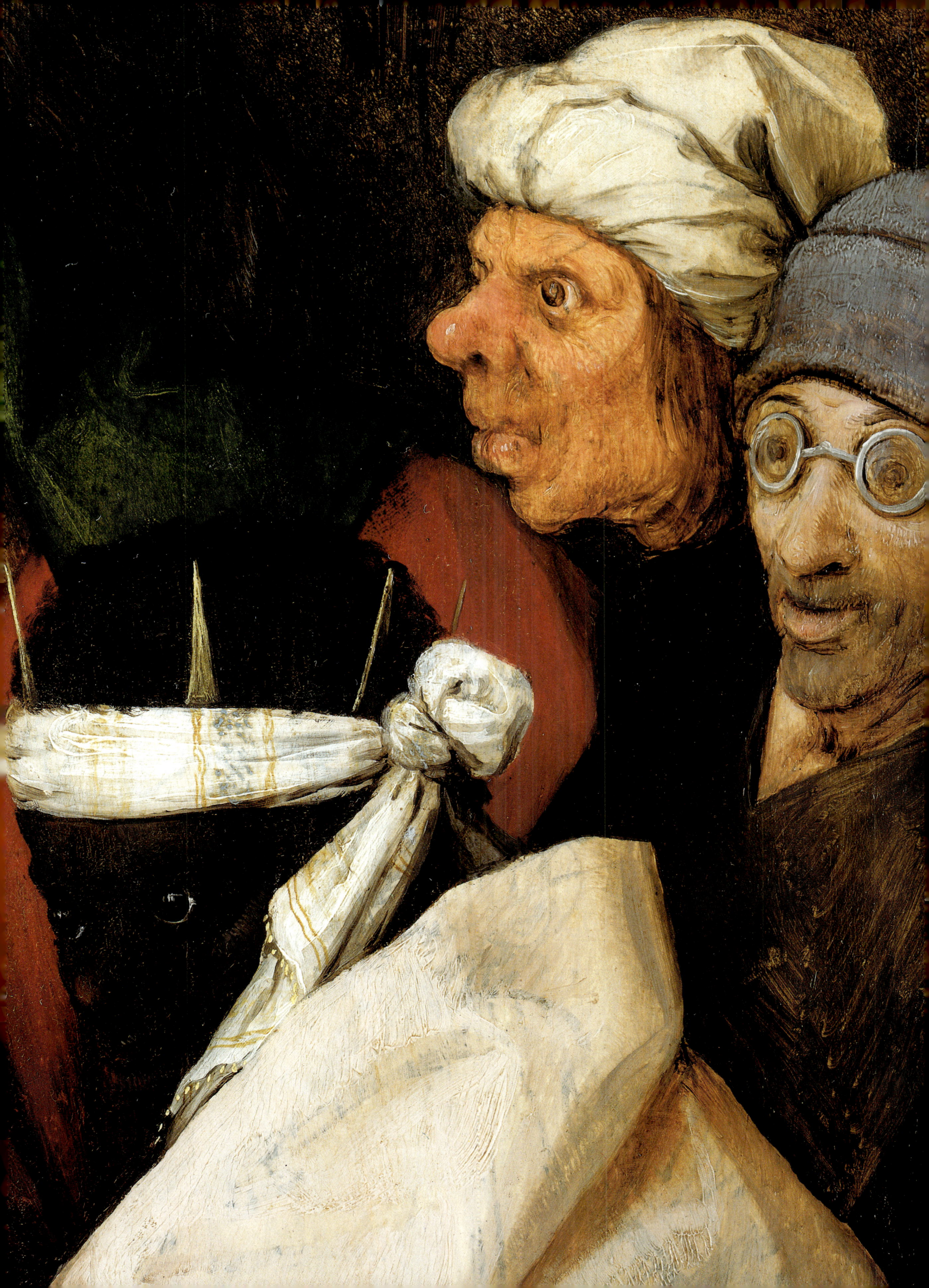

version of the painting, but in the Vienna picture this figure, with his great gray beard, does indeed resemble portraits of the duke. The theory of this identification seems unlikely, however, because the Spanish troops had only arrived in the Netherlands in August 1567, while the painting, judging from the spirit in which it is painted, seems to belong to a period slightly earlier than that, about 1565–66. Perhaps it would be more apt to see Herod in the figure.[55] The painter may well have witnessed severe repression and even carnage in those troubled and unstable years; however, the episode became a subject in its own right in paintings by artists such as Roelandt Savery or Sebastian Vrancx.

While Bruegel conjured up sins and devilry for engravings, he also conveyed his own convictions through them. *The Parable of the Good Shepherd*, engraved in 1565 by Philipp Galle (fig. 143), is as monumental as many of Bruegel's paintings. The artist, who drew on the Gospel of John (X, 1–16), depicts Christ in the conventional manner (as an engraving, it must be clearly readable), carrying a sheep on his shoulders and standing in the doorway of a shelter on whose lintel is the legend EGO SUM OSTIUM OVIUM (I am the sheep's doorway). The building is being attacked on all sides by thieves and brigands, who break through the walls and roof. In the upper left corner a shepherd is defending his flock against a wolf; on the right another is fleeing, and abandoning his animals. The theme of the shepherd resurfaces as a side element in both *The Misanthrope* (fig. 267) and in *The Fall of Icarus* (fig. 325) and, in the shape of a bad shepherd, in compositions attributed to Bruegel and in copies (figs. 346–47).

The engraved image is both powerful and dense. Some have seen in it political comment and allusions to Margaret of Parma or the Duke of Alva. The events involving these historical figures did not take place until 1567, two years after the engraving was made, but religious and political tension were already present in 1565.[56] Whether or not Bruegel's intention was simply to convey the image of the good shepherd, and whether or not the engraving was interpreted thus at the time, the double interpretation should not be dismissed. The theme of the sheep fold attacked by heretics occurs in several works of the period from the southern Netherlands, one of which shows Philip II guarding the door and the roof, while the brigands are Martin Luther, John Calvin, and possibly Ulrich Zwingli (fig. 144).[57]

PAINTINGS IN GRISAILLE

Very different in its refinement and mystery, *The Death of the Virgin* (fig. 152), surprises us with its vision. Painted in grisaille, not in tones of gray but in a warm brown monochrome that heightens the sense of contemplation, this small panel— measuring only 14⅛ x 21⅝ inches (36 x 55 centimeters)—conjures up, through its nuances, and above all, its effect of artificial light that seems almost proto-Caravaggesque, an atmosphere that prefigures much that we see in seventeenth-century art, especially in the work of Rembrandt and Georges de la Tour. The painting was quite possibly made for Abraham Ortelius, who had it engraved— without the image being reversed—by Philipp Galle in 1574 (fig. 151).

Ortelius, a celebrated geographer, was also a lover of the arts, and from 1547 onwards a member of the guild of St. Luke in Antwerp, as a cartographer, as well as a member of the De Violieren chamber of rhetoric. He considered his own art

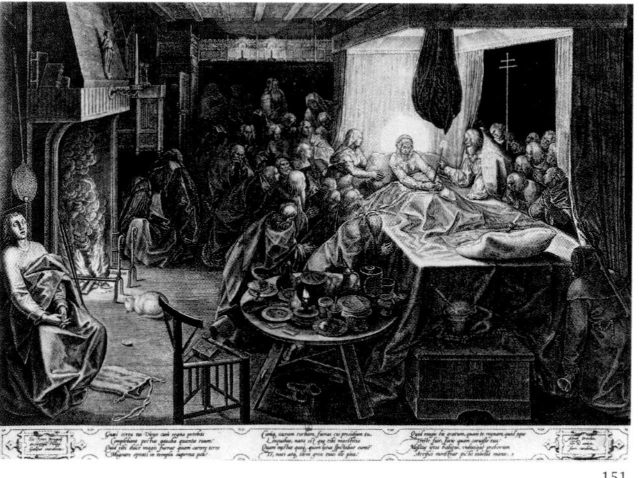

150. Martin Schongauer, *The Death of Mary*, ca. 1470–73. Engraving, 10 x 6¾ in. (25.5 x 17 cm). Paris, Bibliothèque nationale de France, print department

151. Philipp Galle, *The Death of the Virgin*, after Pieter Bruegel, 1574. Engraving, 12¼ x 16⅜ in. (31 x 41.7 cm). Brussels, Bibliothèque royale Albert I, print room

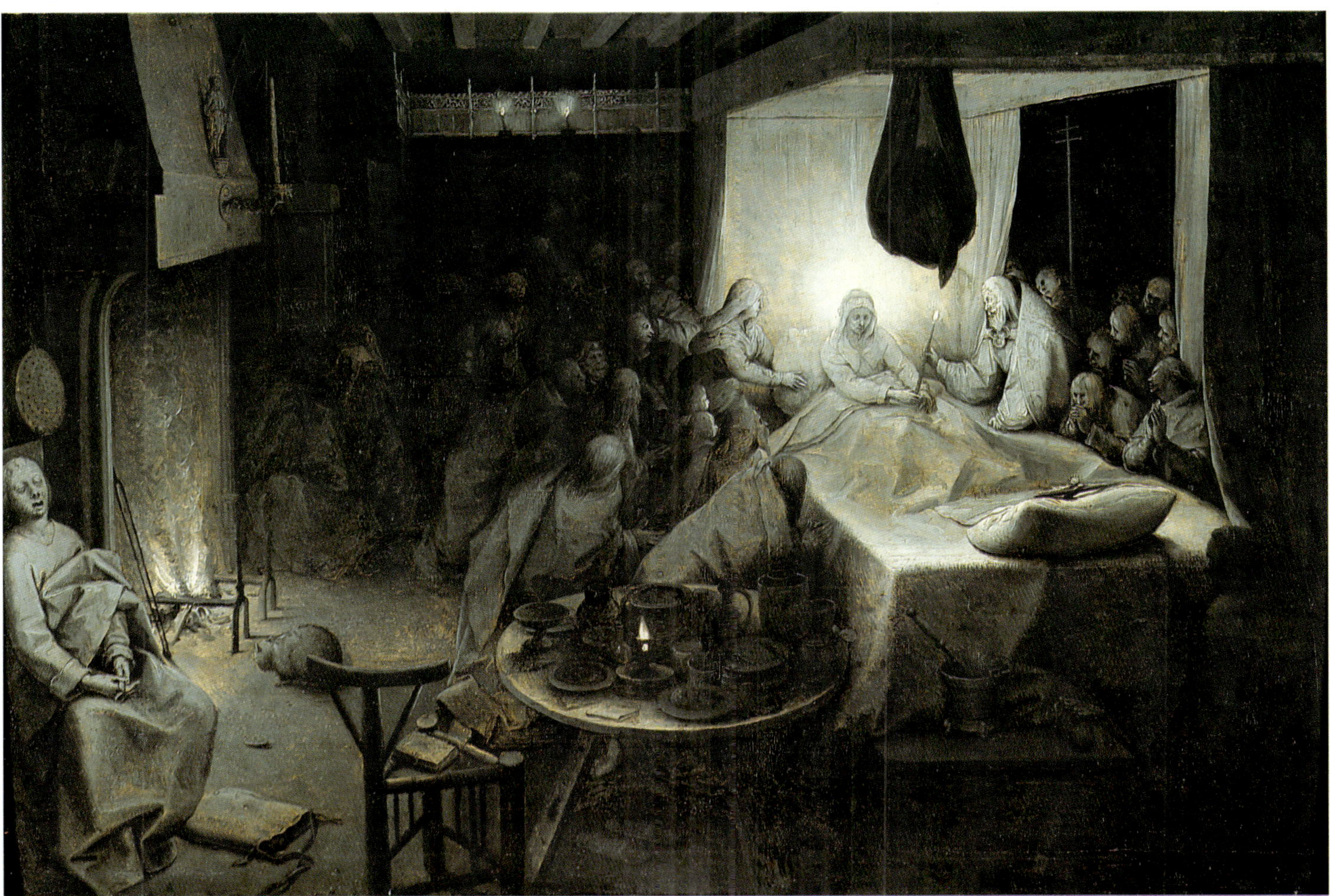

152. Pieter Bruegel, *The Death of the Virgin*, 1564–65. Oil on panel, 14 1/8 x 21 5/8 in. (36 x 55 cm). England, Banbury, Upton House

collection "a museum" and even published a catalogue whose first volume came out in 1573.[58] After his death the painting passed into the hands of Isabella Brant, and then to her husband, Peter Paul Rubens, under the title *The Death of Our Lady Black and White*.[59] Born of a Protestant family, Ortelius made a show of being a Catholic, but belonged to a group of Antwerp humanists that included the printer Plantin, the engraver Galle, and Coornheert, an engraver and philosopher. When the engraving was published, Ortelius gave prints to some friends including Coornheert, who expressed his appreciation thus: "I have examined it with pleasure and admiration from top to bottom for its drawing skill and care in engraving. Bruegel and Philipp have excelled themselves. Neither could have done better." He added that the work would "survive for art lovers of all times to come."[60] Ortelius lived with his mother, whom he loved dearly, and which may explain his liking for the work's subject: virtuous, pious death, as already illustrated in fifteenth-century woodcuts and in *Ars Bene Moriendi* (The Art of Dying Well), a devotional book for people near death. *The Death of the Virgin* is drawn from the *Golden Legend* of Jacques de Voragine[61]—which, as we know, was also the source for *St. James and the Magician Hermogenes* and which inspired sermons and religious plays at the time.[62] Iconographically the subject dates from the previous century; the intimacy of the bedroom is also found in the art of the Primitives, and one of the first masterpieces depicting this subject is an engraving by Martin Schongauer made before 1475 (fig. 150). Did Bruegel remember it? Others who dealt with the theme include Hans Memling, Joos van Cleve (formerly known as the Master of

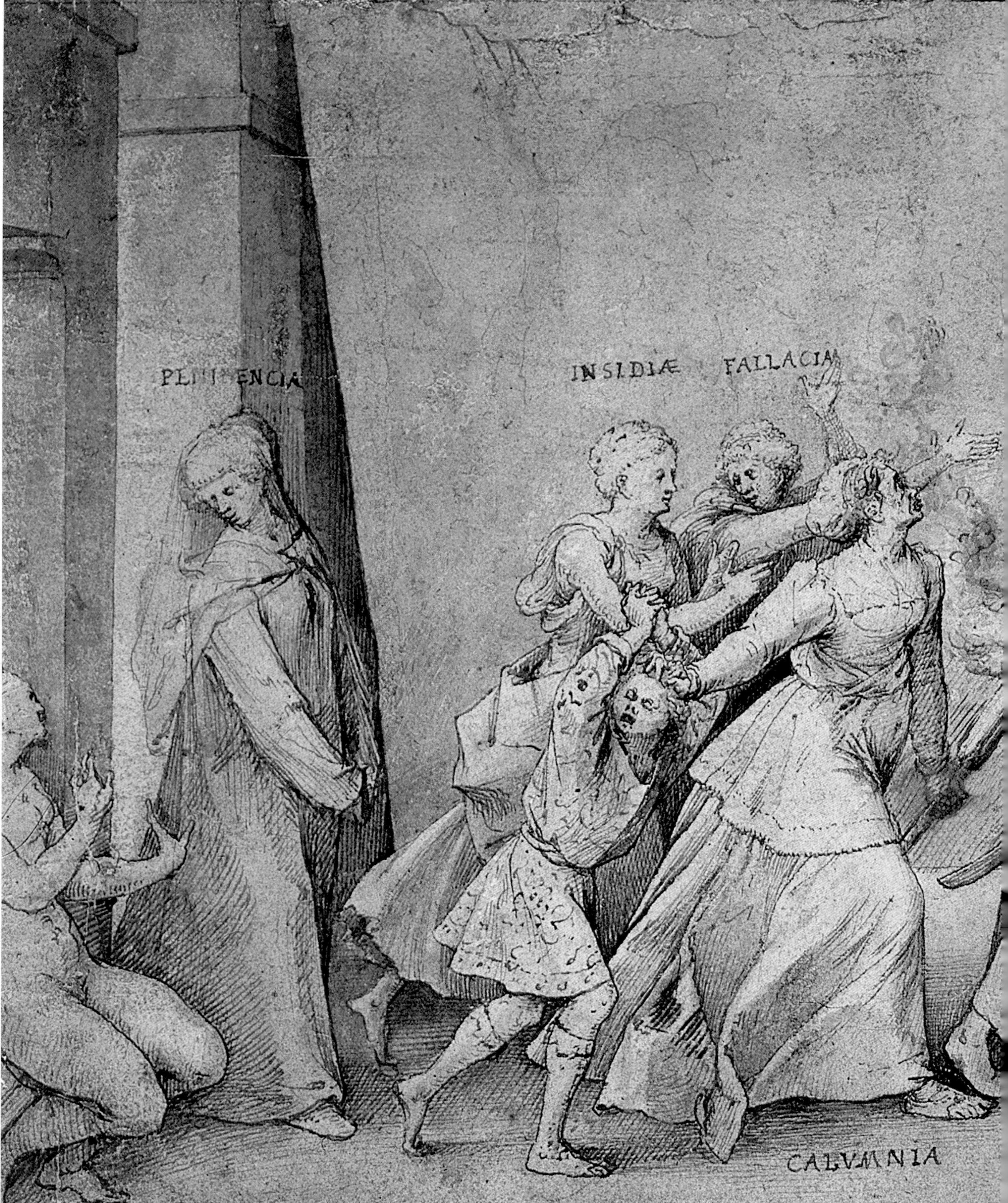
PLVI ENCIA
INSIDIÆ FALLACIA
CALVMNIA

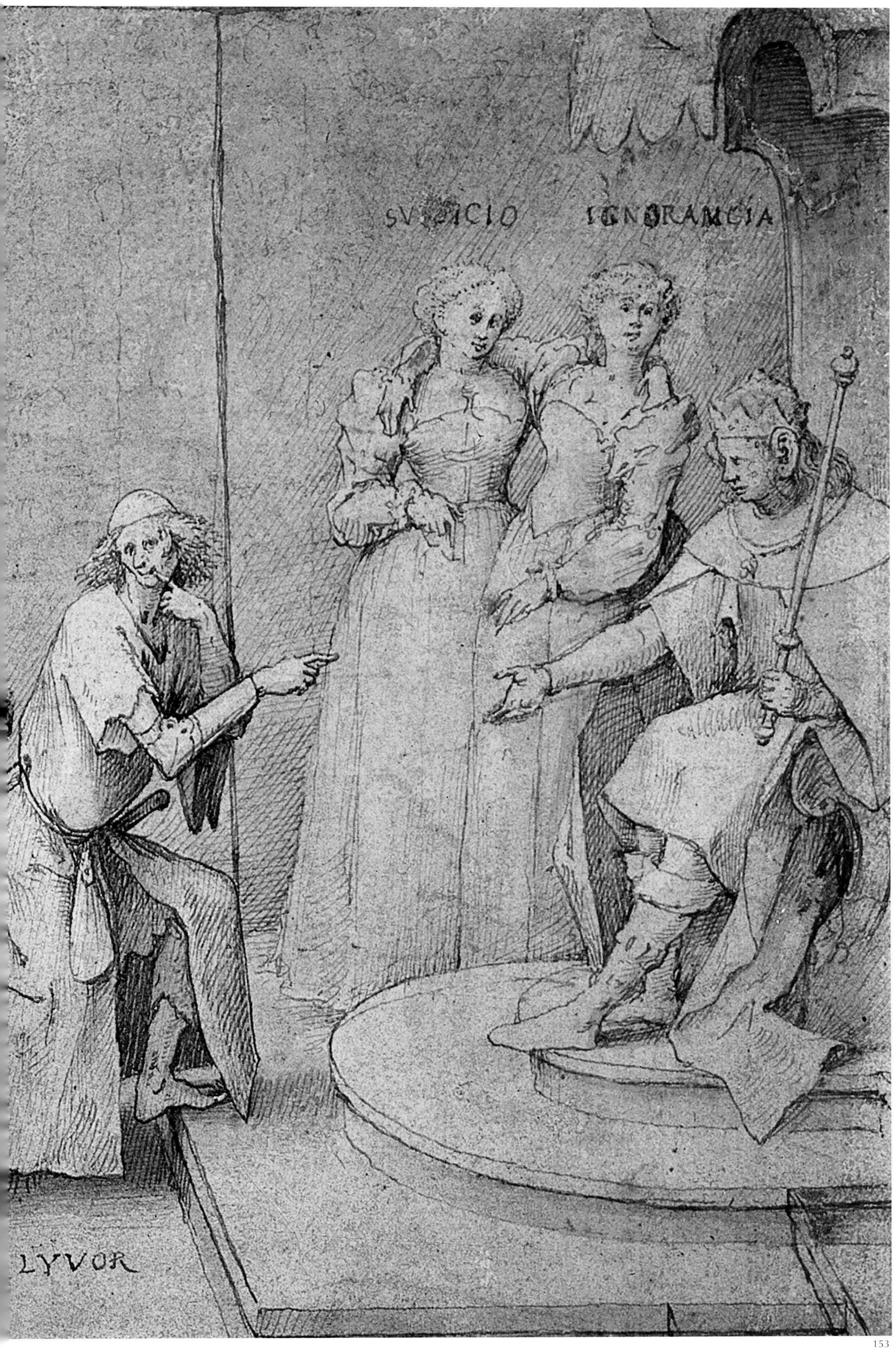

153. Pieter Bruegel,
The Calumny of Apelles,
1565. Pen and brown ink,
brown wash, and white
heightening on tinted paper,
8 x 12 in. (20.4 x 30.7 cm).
London, British Museum

the Death of Mary), and Bernard van Orley. Bruegel's rendering, while it appears simple on the surface, is none the less complex. The spiritual and the everyday are closely linked. The laid table and the cat crouching in front of the fire contrast with the supernatural light that envelops the Virgin. The figure asleep on the left, separated from the main scene, could be St. John, dreaming of this event, of which he had a premonition.[63] Sleep and death have long been associated in Western thinking, from the time of the ancient Greeks, who conceived of them as the twin gods Hypnos and Thanatos. Furthermore, the traditional iconography of the Death of the Virgin includes other examples of sleepers; for example, in a painting of this subject attributed to Petrus Christus, and in another, painted by Bernard van Orley for the Beguine convent in Brussels about 1520.[64]

These parallels seem to correspond to something Bruegel's version is striving for. The deformation in the perspective of the chair in the foreground, "corrected" in Philipp Galle's engraving and seen by some as an error could, on the contrary, be a deliberate device intended to link the composition's two main elements. In this intense, fervently religious work, Grossmann believed that Bruegel was manifesting his confidence in the resurrection and in the salvation of the just, and that his expression of it here acquires a "miraculous" quality.[65] Whatever Grossmann meant by "miraculous," the term surely referred above all to the work's aesthetic completeness.

The Death of the Virgin is thought to date from 1564 or 1565.[66] Pieter Bruegel the Younger made three copies—one of these, oddly, in color, a change that deprives it of all its emotion and spirituality. Even more copies—more than a dozen—were made of another of Pieter Bruegel's grisaille works, *Christ and the Woman Taken in Adultery*. One of these is possibly by his son, Jan Bruegel, who kept the original (fig. 155) throughout his life. The work was made into an engraving by Pieter Perret in 1579. The grisaille resurfaced in London in 1952, and was brought to public attention the same year by Fritz Grossmann, who made a study that was both technical—taking account of Bruegel's alterations—and aesthetic, emphasizing the influence of southern European art. Indeed, in front of the group of figures that forms the work's structure, as is traditional in Italian or Italian-influenced painting, the main characters stand out, more intensely lit and grouped around Christ, who is writing his famous message of charity: "Let he who is without sin cast the first stone." The effect of the monochrome, heightened by an underlying ground in warm tones as in *The Death of the Virgin*, accentuates the work's sculptural style. The contrasts between light and shade, between the Pharisees and Christ—as well as the complete absence of scenery—remove all superfluous material and emotionally imbue Bruegel's work with all the radiance of St. John's text. The restrained beauty of the female figure, and Christ's gesture, look like a plea for tolerance in a time of religious strife.

At this point we should consider a drawing, *The Calumny of Apelles*, which can be dated, like *Christ and the Woman Taken in Adultery*, about 1565 (fig. 153). The two works are not only roughly contemporary, but of similar format: the former measures 8 x 12 inches (20.4 x 30.7 centimeters) and the latter 9½ x 13½ inches (24.1 x 34.4 centimeters). Both show a series of figures arranged from left to right against a neutral background; the first is a grisaille in oil on a wood panel, the second is a brown wash heightened with white on tinted paper. They also share a stone floor, interrupted by a step. In the first work, Jesus judges and forgives; in the other, Calumny appeals to King Midas who, surrounded by bad

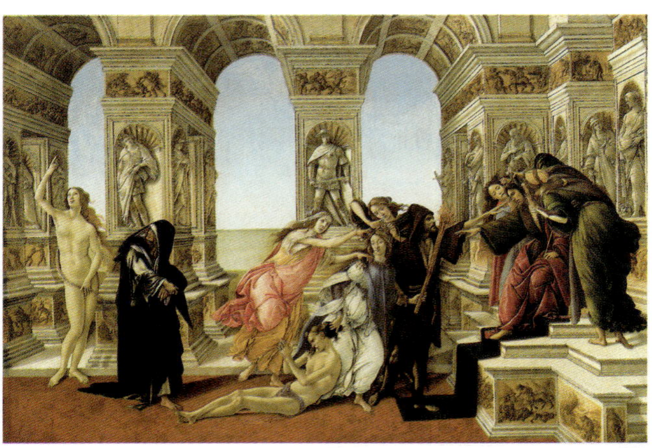

154. Sandro Botticelli, *The Calumny of Apelles*, 1495. Distemper on panel, 24³⁄₈ x 35⁷⁄₈ in. (62 x 91 cm). Florence, Uffizi

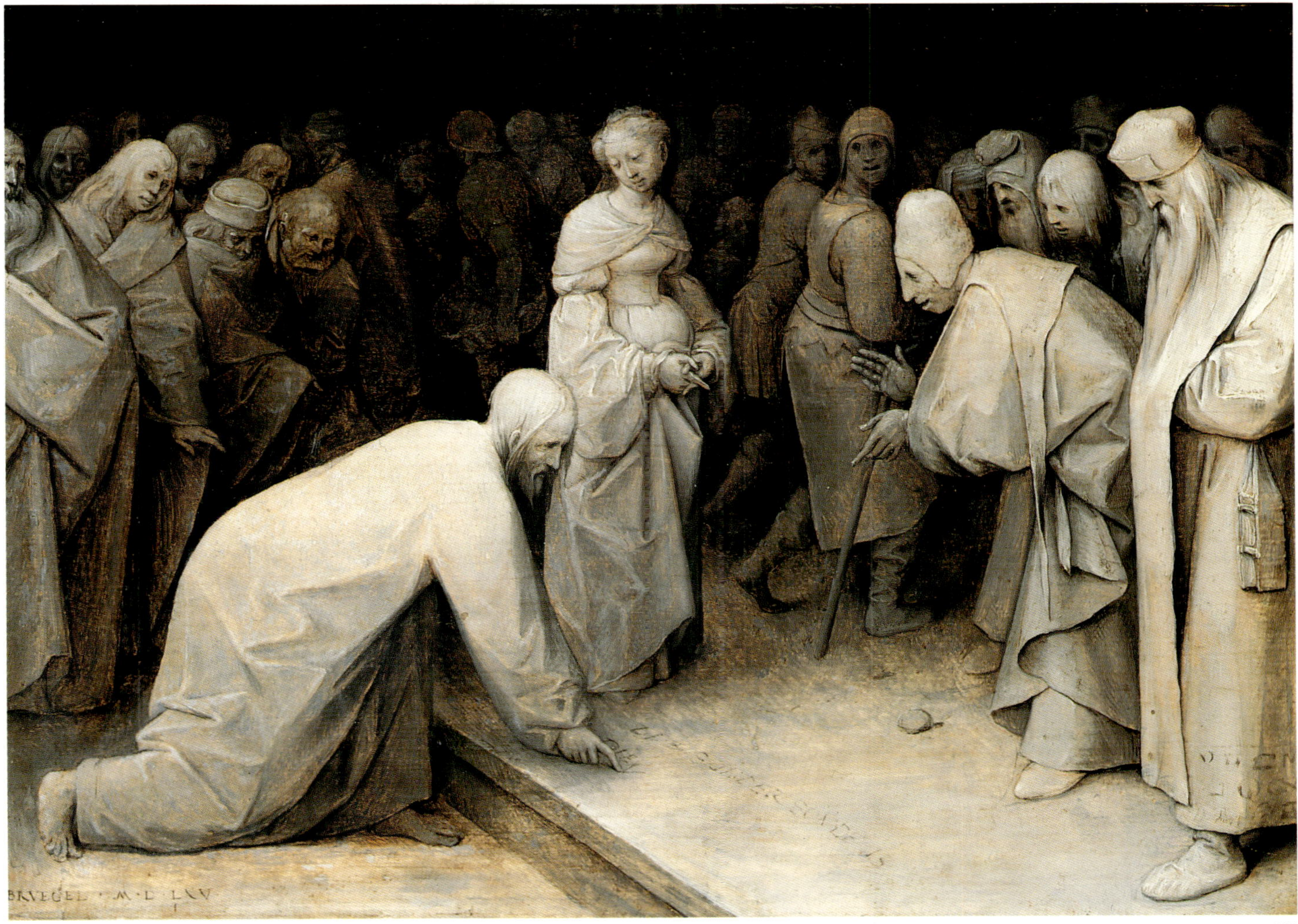

155. Pieter Bruegel, *Christ and the Woman Taken in Adultery*, 1565. Oil on panel, 9½ x 13½ in. (24.1 x 34.4 cm). London, Courtauld Institute of Art, Count Antoine Seilern Collection

counselors, appears to be listening to them. Both works, therefore, hinge on the theme of justice. On the one hand is its Christian interpretation, on the other a pagan evocation. While we should not consider these works as a pair (there is no painting of *The Calumny*), they were perhaps linked in the artist's mind, since they were made the same year.

Calumny is a theme from antiquity—the only one that we know of, apart from the fall of Icarus, that Bruegel painted or drew. The drawing refers to the painter Antiphilus's jealousy of his rival Apelles, whom he accused of having plotted against King Ptolemy in Alexandria in the fourth century B.C. The episode was painted by Apelles and the work described by Lucian of Samosata in one of his dialogues, as well as by Alberti in his *De Pictura* of 1435. The Renaissance saw a revival of interest in the subject on the part of, among others, Botticelli (fig. 154) and Raphael in Italy, and Caron in France.[67] Bruegel in turn shows Italian influence in the work's severe structure, against which figures with Mannerist proportions stand out, as in a frieze.

Calumny, a torch in her hand, is dragging by the hair a child who is wringing his hands—is he meant to represent Innocence?—and which she seems to have snatched from the arms of Truth, who—shown naked, as tradition demands— is seated on the left. Other allegorical figures are arranged from left to right: Penitence, Betrayal, Deceit, Envy, Suspicion, and Ignorance. By their presence or their gestures they support Calumny before the throne of King Midas who,

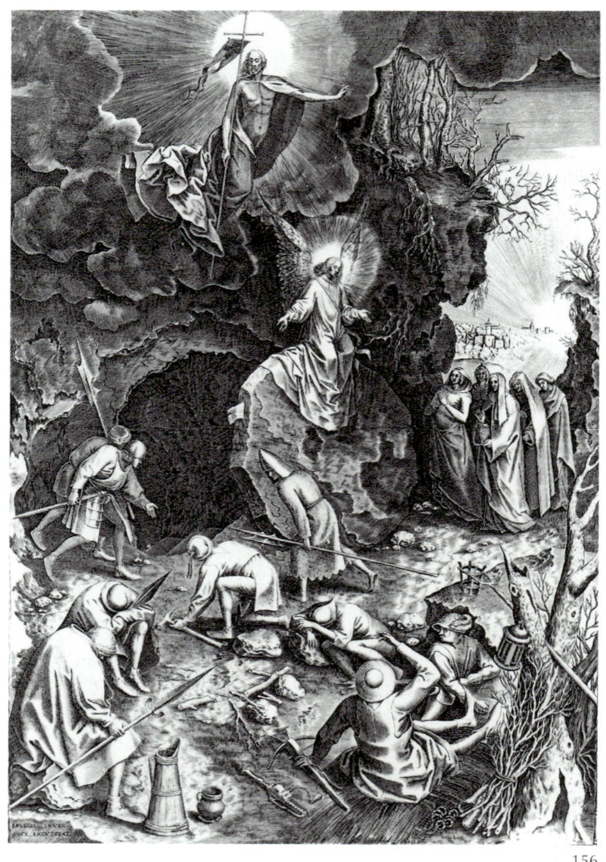

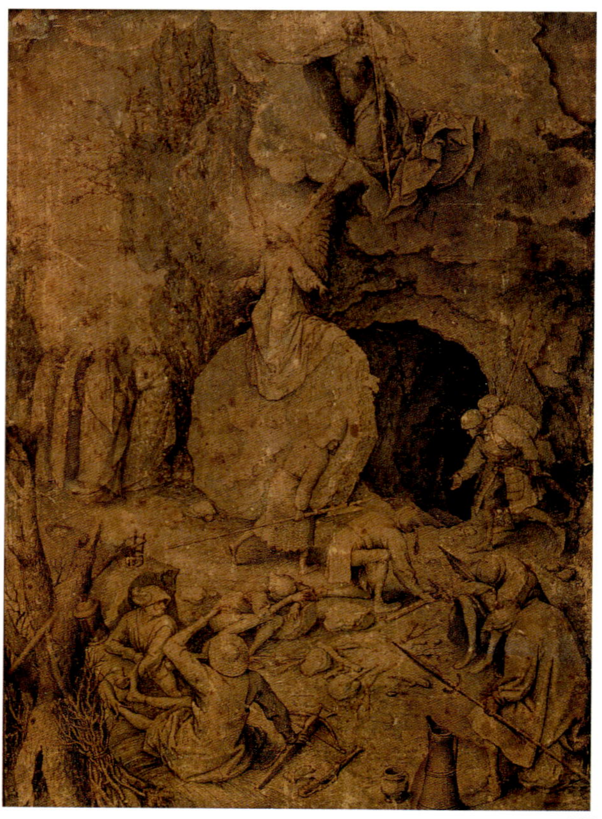

according to legend, had the ears of an ass. The same characters, similarly arranged, are present in Botticelli's painting (fig. 154), but they are presented in a highly ornamented Renaissance setting and are animated by lyrical, even theatrical, gestures. In Bruegel's drawing, the figures are far less idealized, despite their elongated bodies and small heads. The robust nudity of Truth (one of the few nudes in Bruegel's body of work) contrasts with the slim proportions of Truth in Botticelli's painting. The reserved attitude of Penitence also contrasts strongly with the captivating, friendly demeanor of the elegant women who represent Suspicion and Ignorance. The character denoted as Lyvor—an astonishing caricature of a man eaten away by Envy—links Calumny with Midas, simultaneously accusing and turning his face away. Vasari considered Botticelli's *Calumny* an exceptional painting, and described its meaning at length. The work's owner, a noble named Fabio Segni, asserted: "This small painting reminds the kings of the world not to attempt to punish others on the basis of false witnesses."[68] If originally the subject was a warning based on a personal experience—that of Apelles—in Botticelli's hands it becomes a form of moral tale, and that larger content is no doubt also present in Bruegel's work, bearing witness to his humane outlook at a time of religious and political conflict. Could this drawing be the preparatory sketch for the painting mentioned by Van Mander "in which truth triumphs," and which Bruegel himself considered his best work?[69] Perhaps. However, while denouncing calumny may help the cause of justice, it does not guarantee the triumph of truth.

The Resurrection of Christ (fig. 157), a drawing in brown ink heightened with white, also bears some similarity to the two grisailles. This work, which has been mounted on a wood panel, has suffered considerable damage, and not everyone agrees that it is by Bruegel.[70] The attribution, accepted by some,[71] is supported by the existence of a print published by Hieronymus Cock under Bruegel's name, the engraving for which is attributed to Philipp Galle (fig. 156). The scene, in vertical format, drawn from the gospels of Mark (XVI, 1–7) and Matthew (XXVIII, 1–8), shows, on the right, Roman soldiers dozing while others wake to find the tomb of Christ empty, with the great slab of rock that sealed it pushed aside. On the left, Mary Magdalene and the other Holy Women approach the tomb to anoint the body of Christ. He, unseen by all, floats in the air, surrounded by a nimbus of light, making a gesture of blessing with his right hand and carrying a banner in his left. In the engraving, which reverses the image of the drawing, Christ, of course, is shown raising his left hand, which makes no sense unless all he is doing is pointing to the rising sun.[72] This anomaly has naturally given rise to various interpretations and suggested to some a view of the work as deliberately esoteric. The presence of a hollow tree, which may represent an athanor, or alchemical furnace, has been thought to suggest a reading of the work in the light of the theories of alchemy.[73] As for the drawing's stylistic sources, Dirck Bouts and Hans Memling have been mentioned, along with Albrecht Dürer and Simon Bening's *Grimani Breviary*.[74] Whatever the problems raised by the reversal of the drawing's composition, the *Resurrection* is a powerful image which was regarded by the engraver with considerable respect,[75] for he made a copy of it in oil (although reversed like the engraving), a fragment of which survives in the Musées royaux des Beaux-Arts in Brussels.[76]

The Resurrection is a traditional image, and therefore less surprising than *The Conversion of St. Paul*, of 1567 (figs. 160–62). This subject, drawn from the

156. Attributed to Philipp Galle, *The Resurrection of Christ*, after Pieter Bruegel, after 1562. Engraving, 18⅜ x 12⅞ in. (46.5 x 32.8 cm). Brussels, Bibliothèque royale Albert I, print room

157. After a drawing by Pieter Bruegel, *The Resurrection of Christ*, ca. 1562. Pen and brown ink heightened with white using a brush, 17 x 12⅛ in. (43.1 x 30.7 cm). Rotterdam, Museum Boijmans Van Beuningen

Acts of the Apostles (IX, 3–4) had already inspired Pieter Coecke and Frans Floris;
a drawing by Floris was the original for the celebrated majolica made in Antwerp
in 1547 and now in the Vleeshuis there (fig. 159). Bruegel approached this subject
with matchless formal and dynamic mastery. In the right foreground of a rocky,
mountainous landscape a horseman has come to a halt and has turned to look
toward the center of the composition. In the middleground, slightly in front of the
first horseman, a second man riding a white horse with powerful hindquarters has
also stopped to look back. Both figures are gazing toward the painting's subject: a
man who has fallen from his mount and lies on the ground surrounded by soldiers.
This is, of course, Saul of Tarsus—soon to rename himself Paul—who has been
struck by divine insight on the road to Damascus. The path that climbs the mountain on the left and the two horsemen form a triangle at the apex of which, slightly
to one side of the picture's center, is this fallen rider. Placing the subject of a work
at a distance from the picture plane is common in Northern sixteenth-century art:
Lucas van Leyden made use of the same device in an engraving of 1509 of the same
subject (fig. 158), in which soldiers are also shown straggling through a similar
rocky setting. Bruegel may have even known that work. The painting's feeling of
movement, however, which gives a sense of crossing the mountains from the
narrow gorge on the left to the cloudy summits on the right—which the flourish of
a red flag seems to want to ward off—is Bruegel's alone, as is the sudden stillness
in front of the tall larch trees. The composition is masterly in its originality.

All the details—animals, men, rocks, the distant sea, the mountain (the color
of which changes, as in *Christ Carrying the Cross*, from blue to darkness), the
straight lines and diagonals, the jagged ridges, the volumes, the colors ranging
from the horse's coats to the punctuating accents of the clothes and weapons—
everything seems to unite man and nature. Here Nature completely dominates the
scene and seems to express the will of God, which has struck Paul down. This
work, like others, has not only been admired but has given rise to a great deal of discussion. That it was admired in its own time is proved by Van Mander's mention
of it,[77] and the fact that in 1595 it was bought in Brussels by Archduke Ernest of
Austria, before becoming part of the collection of the emperor Rudolf II. As with
other paintings by Bruegel, some scholars have seen in it allusions to contemporary
political events, particularly the arrival of the Duke of Alva in the Netherlands in
1567, the year the picture was painted. But to interpret it simply in this way
would be a mistake, reducing a profound and powerful work to the level of a mere
topical picture. With an artist of Bruegel's greatness, the time in which he lived
naturally sharpened his creative powers. But if creativity is to retain its resonance
it must be transcendent. *The Conversion of St. Paul* exists in its own right, outside
any temporal context.

Among other readings of the painting, one suggested by Klaus Demus deserves
to be quoted: "This painting is therefore—and this is the only explanation for
the painter's choice of the Alps—a symbolic visualization of men going astray,
losing their way and trapping themselves in plans that are as absurd as they are
impossible; it is a metaphor for crisis, for wandering about aimlessly, from which
'conversion' means return."[78] Is the painting a lesson in faith, in morality a page of
philosophy? No doubt. But above all, it is a great visual creation where man
and nature are mingled, and where a landscape painter of genius re-creates one to
express the other.

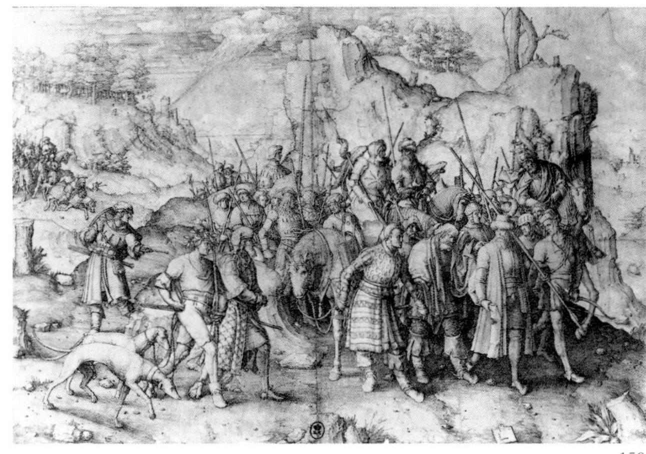

158. Lucas van Leyden, *The Conversion of St. Paul*, 1509.
Engraving, 11 ¼ x 16 ⅜ in. (28.5 x 41.7 cm). Paris, Bibliothèque
nationale de France

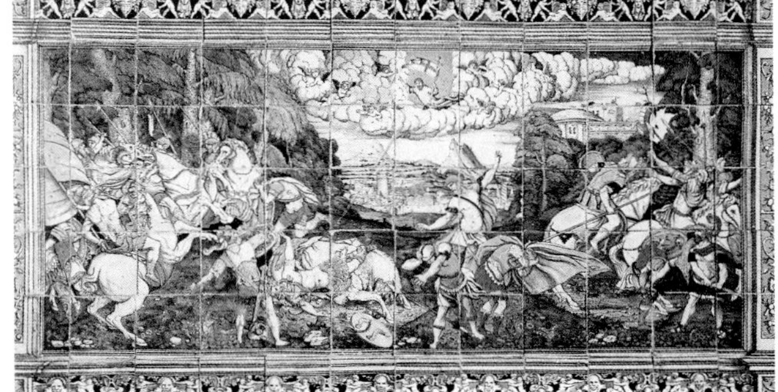

159. After Frans Floris, *The Conversion of St. Paul*, 1547.
Majolica. Antwerp, Museum Vleeshuis

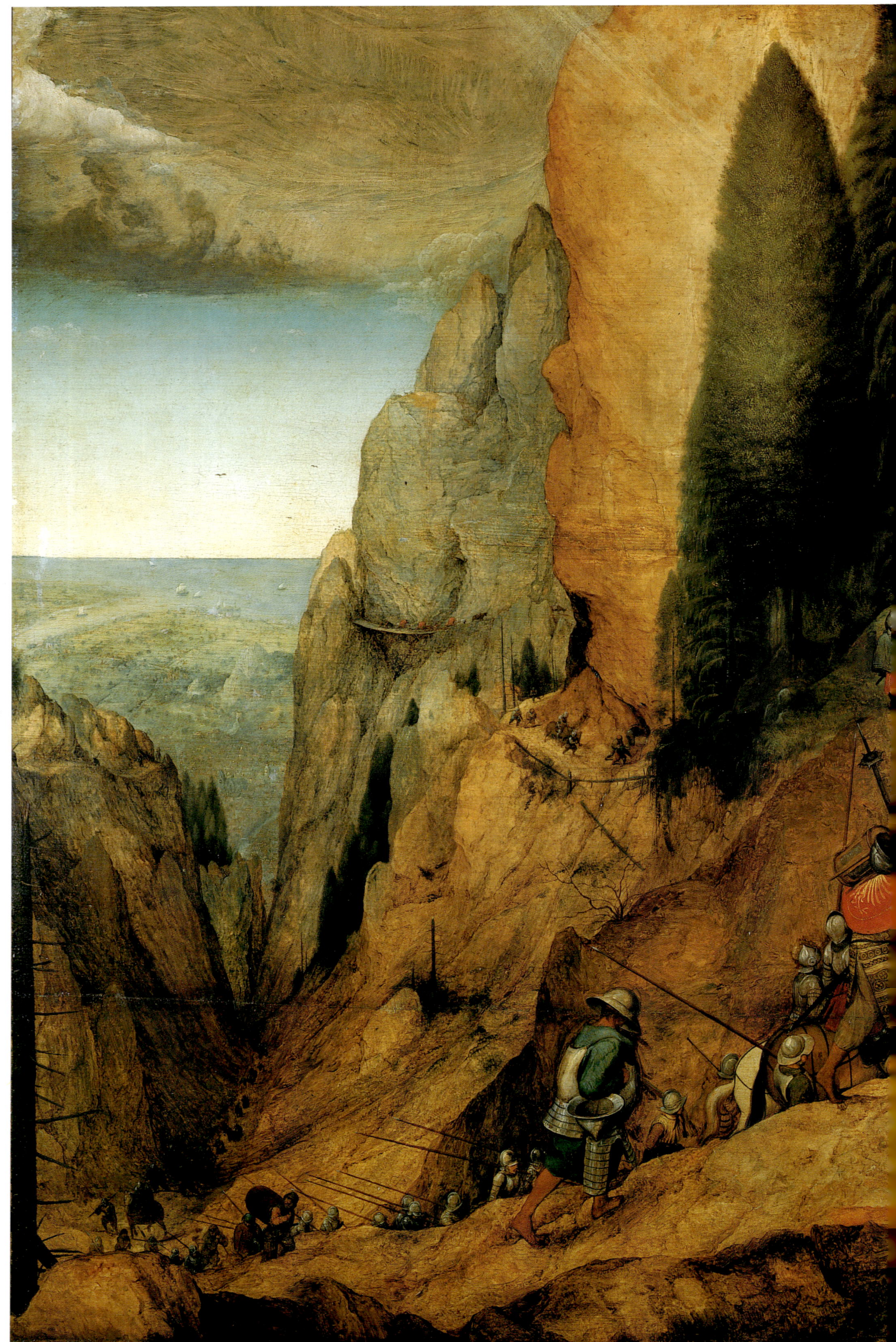

160–62. Pieter Bruegel,
The Conversion of St. Paul,
1567: whole work and details.
Oil on panel, 42½ x 61⅜ in.
(108 x 156 cm). Vienna,
Kunsthistorisches Museum

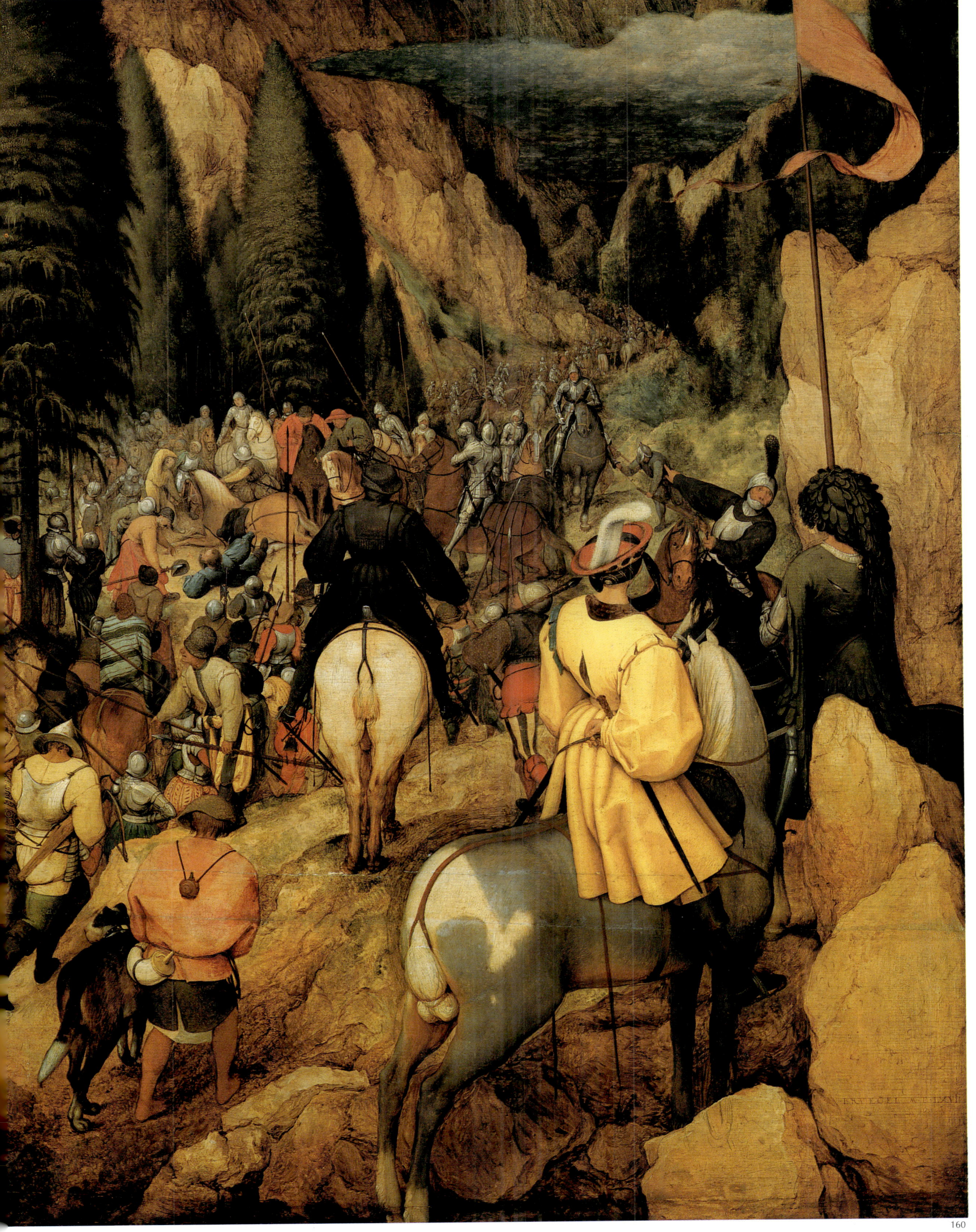

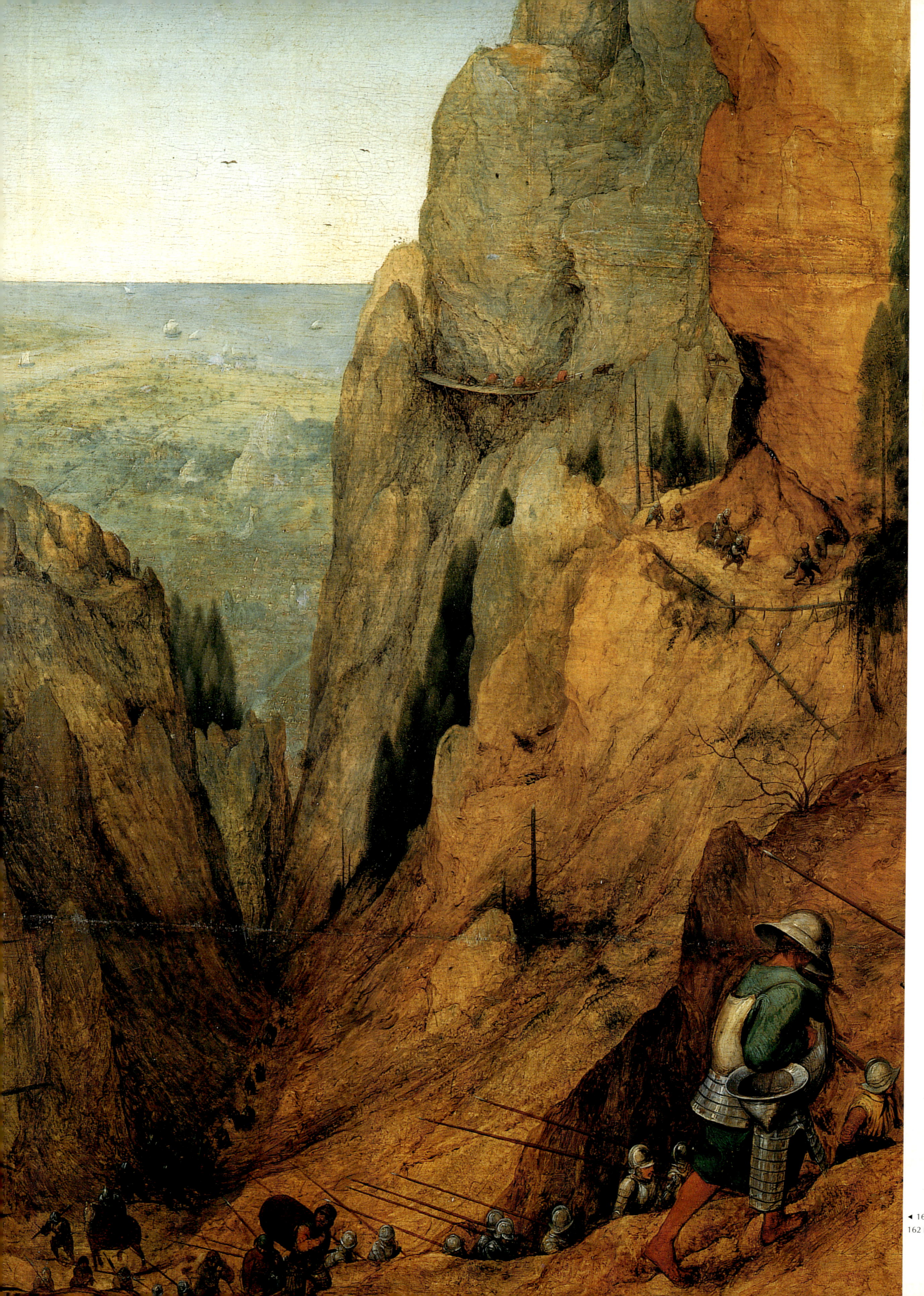

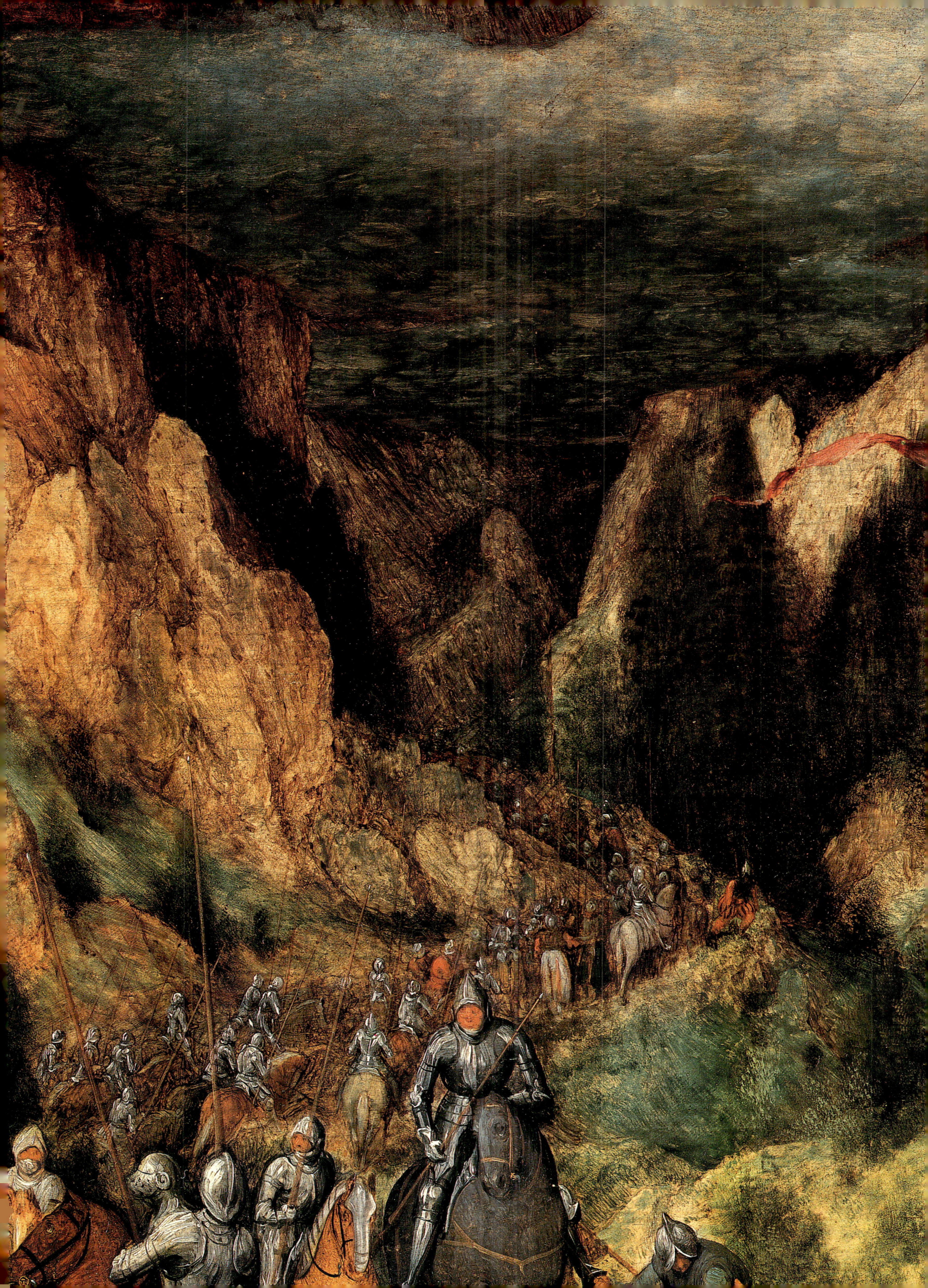

MAN AND NATURE

Describing Pieter Bruegel in his *Librum Amicorum*, the geographer Abraham Ortelius says: "I always say that his paintings speak not of artifice but of nature. And in truth I could call him not the best of painters, but 'nature's painter.' This is why I feel he is worthy of being imitated by all."[79] This return to a contemporary account gives a measure of the true resonance Bruegel's works encountered among the humanists of his day.

From this eulogy one fundamental idea asserts itself: the complementarity, even the fusion, of painter and nature. Ortelius's judgment, which makes a choice among the artists of his time, defends authentic works and contrasts them with those that might be governed by fashion. Those who want to add "a certain seductiveness and grace," he declares, "completely ruin their work." This opinion should not be seen as betraying a conventional attitude that demands purely traditional images, for the geographer and cartographer from Antwerp makes for Bruegel the same claim that Pliny made for Apelles: "In all his works, there is always something to understand beyond what is depicted."[80] This sentence has often been misused, to justify the search for hidden or reversed meanings, and esoteric or political allusions. Ortelius's opinion alludes to the Italianist tendencies that were widespread among so-called "Romanist" painters. But it could be used to justify the comments of those who see in Bruegel a champion of the spirit and style of the Netherlands and, in *The Fall of the Rebel Angels* of 1562, a vigorous riposte to Frans Floris's more Michelangelesque painting of the same subject. Even if well founded, this theory does not mean we should see Bruegel as a traditionalist, however great, or forget his extraordinary innovations. And all this—his experience as much as his creations—is expressed in the painter's relations with the world around him. Mankind and nature are contrasted or associated in the artist's personal approach. In Bruegel's work nature exists in its own right, as a subject for study or an object of contemplation.

NATURE: LANDSCAPE

Nature is portrayed throughout Bruegel's work and permanently holds his attention, from the *Great Landscapes* series of drawings and engravings to the *Seasons* series, and to the painting *The Magpie on the Gallows*. The drawings made between 1552 and 1556 are an early sign of this: The skillful product of a keen eye, they also have the movement and tension of life.[81] The characters that appear in the series published by Hieronymus Cock in 1555–56 are only present to reinforce nature's vitality, and to give it scale. The artist's glance, made permanent by the marks of black chalk or pen, combines the eloquence of detail with the spirit of synthesis. In 1604 Van Mander noted that "he had swallowed all the mountains and rocks so that, once he had returned home, he could pour them out onto his

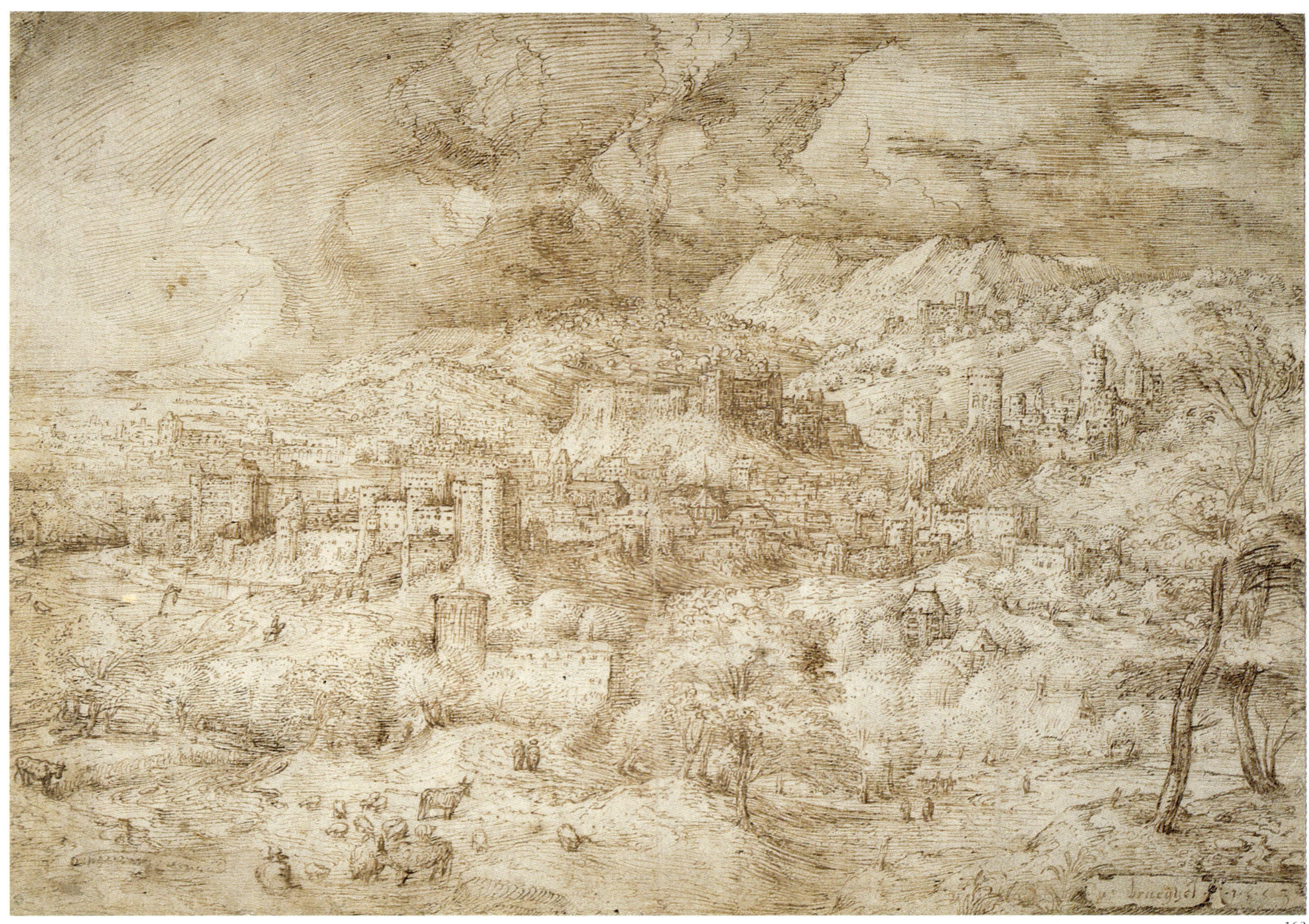

163

163. Pieter Bruegel, *Mountain Landscape with Fortified Town*, or *Heroic Town*, 1553. Pen and brown ink, 9¼ x 13⅛ in. (23.6 x 33.5 cm). London, British Museum

canvases and panels, so faithfully did he follow Nature there as elsewhere."[52] This is undeniable: The graphic memories Bruegel left us have allowed us to retrace his Italian journey. This fidelity has a different quality, however, in his paintings. There, respect for nature is still complete, but without the need to depict a place as such. We cannot merely call these painterly, for we are left speechless in the presence of space, land, water, and sky. The earliest known drawings are revealing. Whether these are jottings made on the spot, or preliminary drawings for the *Great Landscapes* series of engravings, the sense of space, the arrangement of planes, the synthesis, all transcend the painterly and enter into a dialogue between mankind and nature. Thus a *River Landscape* (1552, fig. 80) or an *Alpine Landscape* (1553, fig. 352) convey the meditative mood of a walk at the water's edge or contemplation of the mountain peaks, while a *View of Reggio di Calabria* (fig. 320), possibly heightened by Claude Lorrain in the seventeenth century, looks down on the town which is bursting into flames. The date of the last work is uncertain. It is not clear whether the drawing was made as a finished work during Bruegel's Italian journey, or if it was a preparatory sketch for *Naval Battle in the Strait of Messina*, made into an engraving by Frans Huys in 1561 (fig. 319).

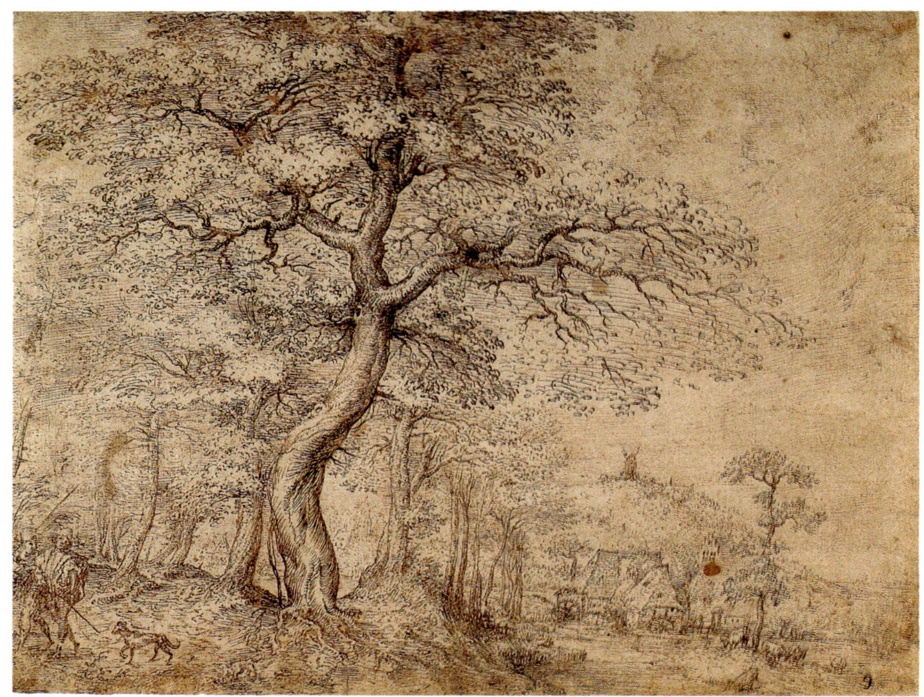

164

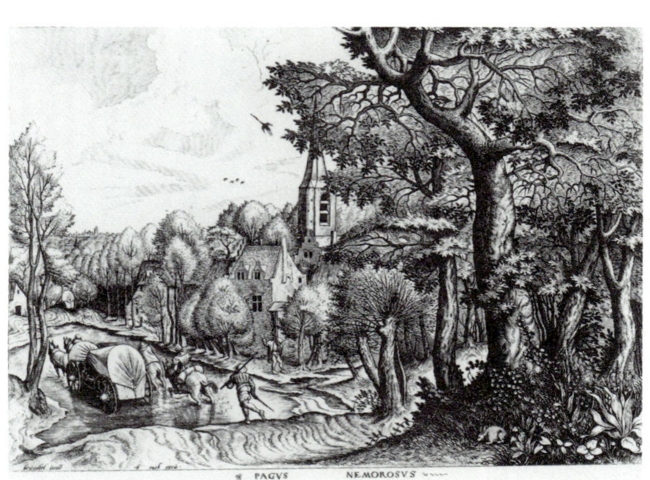

165

164. Pieter Bruegel, *Wooded Landscape with Three Windmills*, 1552. Pen and brown ink, 8⅜ x 11 in. (21.3 x 28.1 cm). Milan, Biblioteca Ambrosiana

165. Johannes or Lucas van Duetecum (?), *Pagus Nemorosus*, from the series *Great Landscapes*, after Pieter Bruegel, ca. 1555–56. Etching and engraving, 12⅝ x 16¾ in. (32.2 x 42.7 cm). Brussels, Bibliothèque royale Albert I, print room

FACING PAGE
166. Johannes or Lucas van Duetecum (?), *Great Alpine Landscape*, after Pieter Bruegel, ca. 1558–59. Etching and engraving, 14½ x 18⅜ in. (36.8 x 46.8 cm). Brussels, Bibliothèque royale Albert I, print room

167. Johannes or Lucas van Duetecum (?), *Milites Requiescentes*, from the series *Great Landscapes*, after Pieter Bruegel, ca. 1558. Etching and engraving, 12⅝ x 16⅜ in. (32.1 x 42.4 cm). Brussels, Bibliothèque royale Albert I, print room

Whether *Wooded Landscape with Three Windmills* (1552, fig. 164) was a chance to magnify a tree, whose majesty can also be seen in *Pagus Nemorosus* or in *Milites Requiescentes* (figs. 165 and 167) from the *Great Landscapes* series, as well as in the drawing *The Pilgrims of Emmaus* (fig. 331) for the same series, or whether *Undergrowth with Five Bears* (1554; fig. 333), which Hieronymus Cock used for *The Temptation of Christ* (fig. 334),[83] unveils the mystery and life of a forest, Bruegel always uses pen and ink to re-create the land in its different guises. These range from the depiction of a spot that is apparently natural but has been reassembled in the engraving—*Alpine Landscape Crossed by a Deep Valley* (about 1555)[84]—to a place enlivened by a religious scene—*Landscape with St. Jerome* (1553, fig. 171), in which the figure is merely a pretext or a reference to human scale—to a vision of nature perhaps enriched by the imaginary—*Mountain Landscape With Fortified Town* (1553, fig. 163), also known as *Heroic Town*. All these works combine tradition, the geographical and stylistic discoveries Bruegel made on his Italian journey, and above all a true genius for landscape which came to the fore from the start of the 1550s. With Bruegel, the conception of the Flemish landscape evolves and deepens. That conception is already present in the earliest works of that tradition; from the *Baptism of Christ* in *The Turin-Milan Hours* to Van Eyck's *Madonna with Chancellor Rolin*, from Robert Campin's *Nativity* to Van der Weyden's *St. Ivo*, and from Petrus Christus's *Pietà* to the right panel of the *Portinari Triptych* by Van der Goes, the fifteenth century is rich in finely chiseled backgrounds. Nature began to be treated as a subject in its own right in the sixteenth century, beginning with an artist from Dinant, Joachim Patinir, described as "der gute Landschaftmahler" by Dürer, who met him in Antwerp in 1521[85] and was invited to his wedding. The evolution of the genre cannot be examined in detail here, but the main stages and its principal exponents can be described. What is immediately striking

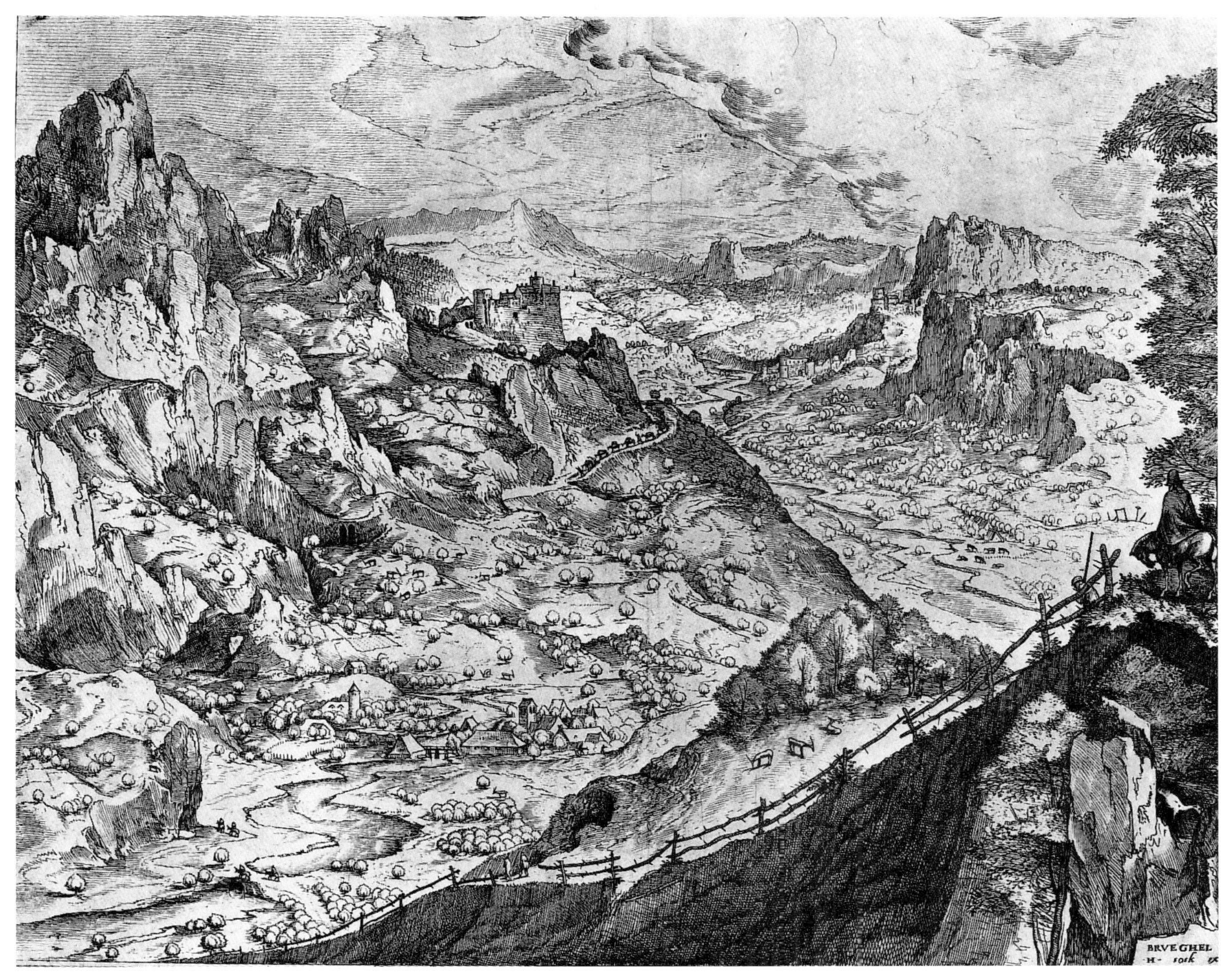

166

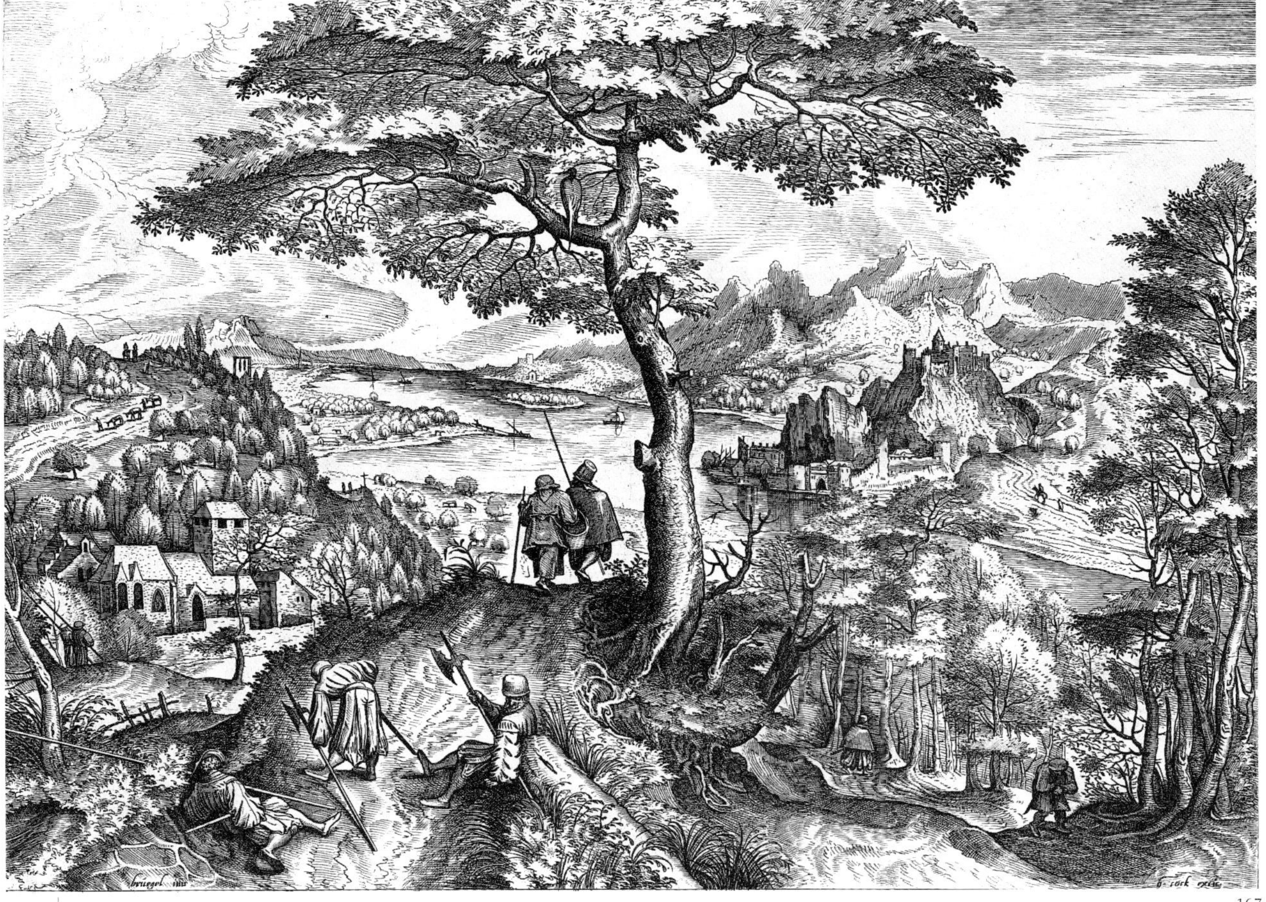

167

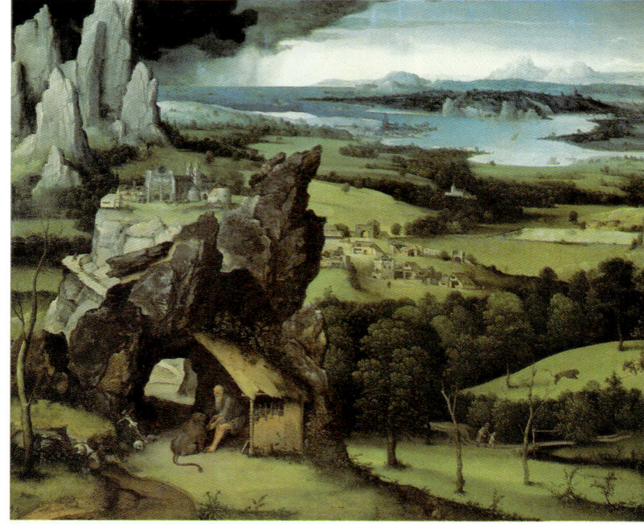

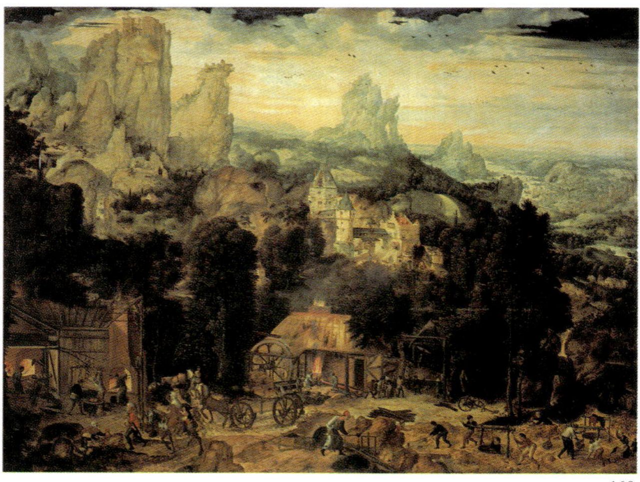

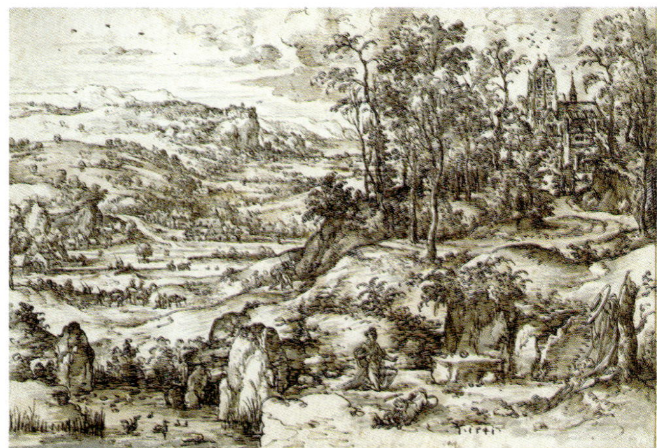

168. Joachim Patinir, *St. Jerome*, ca. 1520. Oil on panel, 29⅛ x 35¾ in. (74 x 91 cm). Madrid, Museo del Prado

169. Herri met de Bles, *Landscape With Mine Scenes*, ca. 1540. Oil on panel, 32⅝ x 44½ in. (83 x 113 cm). Florence, Uffizi

170. Matthijs Cock, *Landscape with St. Jerome*, 1541. Pen and brown ink with gray wash, 8⅛ x 11¾ in. (20.7 x 29.7 cm). Berlin, Staatliche Museen, Kupferstichkabinett

about Patinir's work is his viewpoint, that is·to say, the bird's-eye view. Patinir wanted to seize, as it were, the sphere of the earth—space and its contents—with one glance (fig. 168), an approach variously referred to by art historians as "world landscape," or "cosmic landscape." Patinir was nevertheless also attentive to detail, always and everywhere, and produced the effect of distance by creating three zones of color: brown, green, and blue. The raised horizon line, strongly emphasized, implies a sort of flattened reading, as if the painting were a map. The far distance, which appears to recede into infinity, rests upon the meanders of a waterway and its mouth, which stretch perspective, or it makes use of the masses of rocks and trees which guide the eye and make it rebound or glance off them.

Patinir's masterpieces are powerful—he was indeed the first to give the landscape priority over a painting's subject[86]—but the paintings that were probably made by artists working under his supervision, to which he added the finishing touches, revealed a process that others could follow, too, often pleasingly and with character. These included Quentin Metsys and Joos van Cleve in Antwerp, Adrien Isenbrant in Bruges, Bernard van Orley in Brussels, and the Master of the Half-Lengths. The generation who were active between 1530 and 1540, including the landscape painters Lucas Gassel, Cornelis Metsys, Jan van Amstel, and Herri met de Bles (fig. 169)—who is believed to have been Patinir's nephew—tried to soften Patinir's harsh execution and, in order to express space, made greater use of curves and variations in tone. Their paintings are often repetitive, and their repertoire relatively limited. Bruegel thus differed sharply from his immediate predecessors. Nevertheless, Vasari reported in 1547 that few Italian interiors lacked a Flemish landscape "with pleasant views and far distances."[87]

Growing interest in travel, exploration, and discovery, the development of geography, cartography—in which Ortelius and Mercator in the Netherlands won fame—printing and publishing, by Hieronymus Cock, among others, from 1551: all of these help to explain the evolution of landscape painting. Bruegel's eye would probably also have been influenced by the drawings of Matthijs Cock (fig. 170), brother of Hieronymus, and by contemporary works such as those contained in the *Album Errera*.[88] The illuminations of Simon Bening, who illustrated the *Grimani Breviary* and the *Hennessy Hours*, should also be mentioned, for in his hands miniatures ceased to be illustrations and became works of art in their own right. Likewise, we should mention *Maximilian's Hunts* by Bernard van Orley, tapestries that give an important role to the landscape and the seasons, and of which the great eighteenth-century French collector Mariette, who possessed the preliminary sketches for these works and also admired Bruegel, said: "They contain parts of landscapes which Titian would not disown."[89]

Engraving, too, played an indispensable part, and the works of Dürer, such as *The Cannon* (fig. 172) or *The Peasants' Dance*, as well as those of Lucas van Leyden (especially the plates he made between about 1505 and 1520), may have been familiar to Bruegel. Neither should we overlook, in the schooling of his eye and the apprenticeship of his hand, which were the foundations of his universe, Bruegel's contact with Italian art through Titian's Venetian landscapes and the

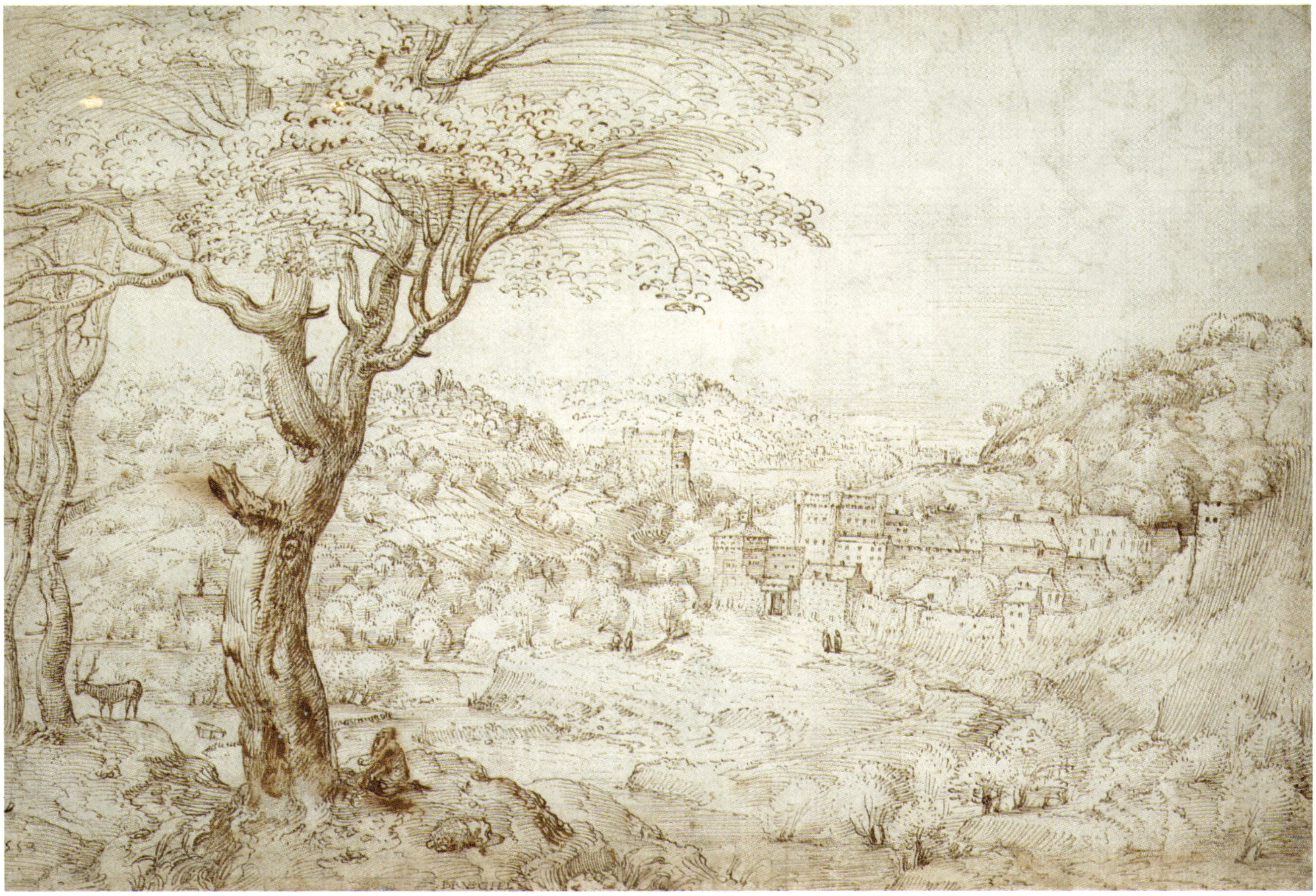

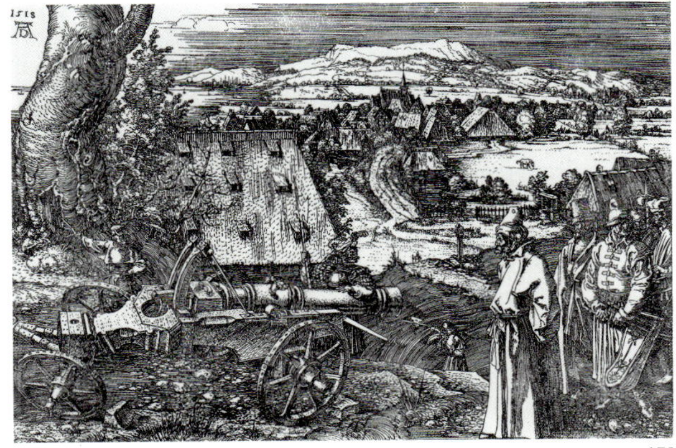

171

engravings of Domenico Campagnola and the landscapist Girolamo Muziano, who was in Rome from 1548 and whom Bruegel may have met in 1553, even though he was then but 21 years old.[90]

Whatever may be the basic ingredients, and the various influences that contributed to them, Bruegel's vision is at once composite and synthesis, combining elements of northern European art and his memories of the south. Every person is made up of multiple elements. An artist experiences a moment of crystallization—the work of art—whose creation is the final consequence of personal genius. Realism and imagination are closely bound up with it.

While some see the Flemish landscapes that preceded Bruegel as the source of seventeenth-century Dutch landscape painting, and others see only contrivance in them, it is clear—as Walter Gibson rightly emphasizes[91]—that Dutch seventeenth-century realism only depicts a diminished version of nature, observed or invented. Focusing the view limits the field of vision and dictates the composition. Flemish painters in the sixteenth century wanted a panoramic view which, in photography, would be achieved with a wide-angle lens. There is therefore no progress, either in one direction or in the other, but only a fundamental difference of opinion. While the one can be fully perceived in one glance, the other requires a reading, a route to be followed as on a map.

172

171. Pieter Bruegel, *Landscape with St. Jerome*, 1553. Pen and brown ink, 9¼ x 13¼ in. (23.5 x 33.8 cm). Washington, National Gallery of Art

172. Albrecht Dürer, *The Cannon*, 1518. Etching on iron, 8⅝ x 12⅞ in. (22 x 32.7 cm). Paris, Bibliothèque nationale de France, print department (reserve collection)

The bird's-eye view, in Renaissance terms, corresponds to a philosophical concept, which, placing humans at the center of the universe, allows them to contemplate it. Neither Erasmus nor Ortelius was to resist this idea. Did this also betoken a sense of detachment, a desire to see things from on high? Sometimes, no doubt, it did represent a certain distancing. But Bruegel creates and takes part in nature and in mankind. He summarizes the outside world not by reducing it or by juxtaposing typical elements, but by literally bringing to life a universe whose unity and complexity are overwhelmingly eloquent.

Bruegel's *Seasons* are to visible resonances what Vivaldi's *Four Seasons* are to the colors of musical themes, but with perhaps even greater symphonic breadth, for their links and echoes intertwine and answer each other ceaselessly with trees, estuaries, birds, and clouds.

THE SEASONS OF THE YEAR

This series, one of the masterpieces in the history of landscape painting, was made for an Antwerp merchant, Nicolas Jongelinck, who already owned sixteen paintings by Bruegel, including *De Twelff Maenden* (The Twelve Months). On 21 February 1566, these works were placed for security with the town of Antwerp (fig. 22).[92] Five panels survive today. Six panels of Bruegel's *The Twelve Months* are mentioned in the inventory made in 1595 by the Archduke Ernest, to whom the town had given them a year earlier. They then passed by succession from Rudolf II to his kinsman, the Archduke Leopold William, whose inventory, made by David Teniers, mentions only five of the panels, "which represent the diversity of the twelve Months of the year."[93]

A certain amount of confusion, and the evident muddling of one work or scene with another, have provoked discussion and a number of theories about the significance of the series, which is now owned by several museums: the Kunsthistorisches Museum in Vienna (*Hunters in the Snow*, *The Gloomy Day*, *The Return of the Herd*), The Metropolitan Museum of Art in New York (*The Harvest*), and the Národní Galerie in Prague (*Haymaking*). Identification of the months is problematic, and exacerbated by the liberties Bruegel took with convention, as well as by the possible confusion between the months themselves.

The problem, meticulously studied by Klaus Demus,[94] centers on the idea—felicitous and apt—of "seasons," or more precisely, of "periods of the year," rather than actual months. Demus turns to Robert Genaille's formulation: "The characteristic moment of each season is the theme of the painting."[95] The sequence therefore envisages an order that is natural to the northern and central regions of Europe, making a distinction between the period before spring, spring itself, the beginning of summer, high summer, autumn, and winter. If the content is thus made clear, the same cannot be said for the order of the works themselves. Demus keeps it just as it is, basing this, furthermore, on each work's dominant color: dark brown for the period before spring (*The Gloomy Day*, fig. 187); a "hypothetical" blue for the spring panel, which does not survive; pale green for early summer (*Haymaking*, fig. 173); yellow for summer (*The Harvest*, fig. 175); golden ocher for autumn (*The Return of the Herd*, fig. 174); and white for winter (*Hunters in the*

Snow, fig. 186). Without disputing either the order or grouping of the works, Marijnssen points out that the year 1565, the pivotal date in these works' creation, began at Easter according to the calendar in use at that time, and not in January, which was only instituted as the beginning of the year in 1576.[96] None of this changes the meaning or quality of the paintings, but it does affect their order. For all that the order in which they were made is the same as that of the seasons depicted, *Haymaking* has an archaic appearance, especially if compared, for example, with *The Gloomy Day*.

Haymaking (figs. 176–79) covers the months of June and July, when hay is cut and fruit and vegetables—beans, cherries, broad beans, and peas—are gathered, and it is particularly outstanding for its luminous spaciousness. The painting's depth is produced by a diagonal from left to right. This starts from a man who is sharpening his scythe and is integrated in the geometric shape formed by the tool, his gestures, and the planks of a fence, and ends with the fluid meanders of a river on the horizon. On the way, we meet a group of three women (fig. 176), the incarnation of haymaking, who all look different—the central one as graceful as the adulterous woman in the grisaille of *Christ and the Woman Taken in Adultery* of 1565. Next, a line of figures carrying baskets, walking parallel to a horse in harness, passes in front of the vertical axis of a post which bears a small shrine containing a statuette of the Virgin. This vertical, displaced to the right, accentuates the movement of the basket-carriers, who are descending into the painting's middleground. The disjunction between the foreground, middleground, and background is accompanied by other elements, which draw on the conventions established by Joachim Patinir: for example, his system of three tones—brown, green, and blue—in modulated zones receding into the distance; the mass of rock that dominates the distance; and many small details. The middleground of the painting is rich in anecdote: There are groups of people making hay, and further out, houses animated by people shooting arrows, jumping over a fence, and driving a flock of geese.

The main activity is, of course, haymaking, the various activities of which radiate outwards from the hay wain in the middle distance. Gesture and texture are carefully observed: the hay lifted by the pitchfork is darker than that in the outer layer, which is already dry. This attention to detail is confirmed by X-ray and infrared examination, which reveal the freedom and the beauty of line, modifications and alterations, and even figures that have been painted over. Bruegel thus pruned the details in this happy work, dotted with living portrayals, shafts of light, daisies, cornflowers, and poppies, and thus gave it the timeless quality that a poet of the twentieth century, William Carlos Williams, commemorated in a series of poems about Bruegel's work.[97]

The Harvest (figs. 180–82), signed and dated 1565, is remarkable for its almost sculptural unity. The powerful, billowing mass of the wheat separates the foreground from the distance, which is lost in a haze of heat. The oppression of summer, heightened by the strength of color, is counterbalanced by a peaceful composition that is flattened—like the man stretched out in the foreground, a motif that Bruegel would return to in *The Land of Cockaigne*, of 1567—by the horizontals of the fields and their piles of ears of grain, mirrored in the distance by the flat lines of what some have suggested may be Lake Geneva, perhaps a memory from Bruegel's journey to Italy.[98] The great tree asserts the painting's

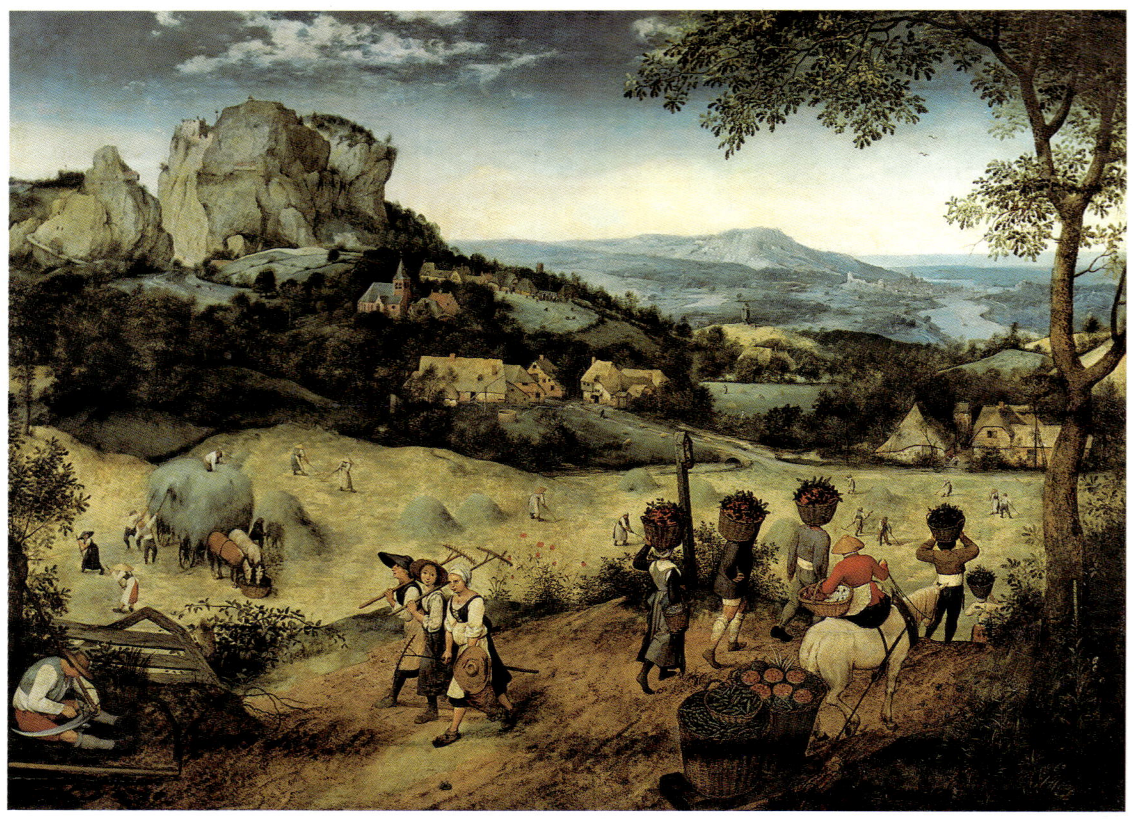

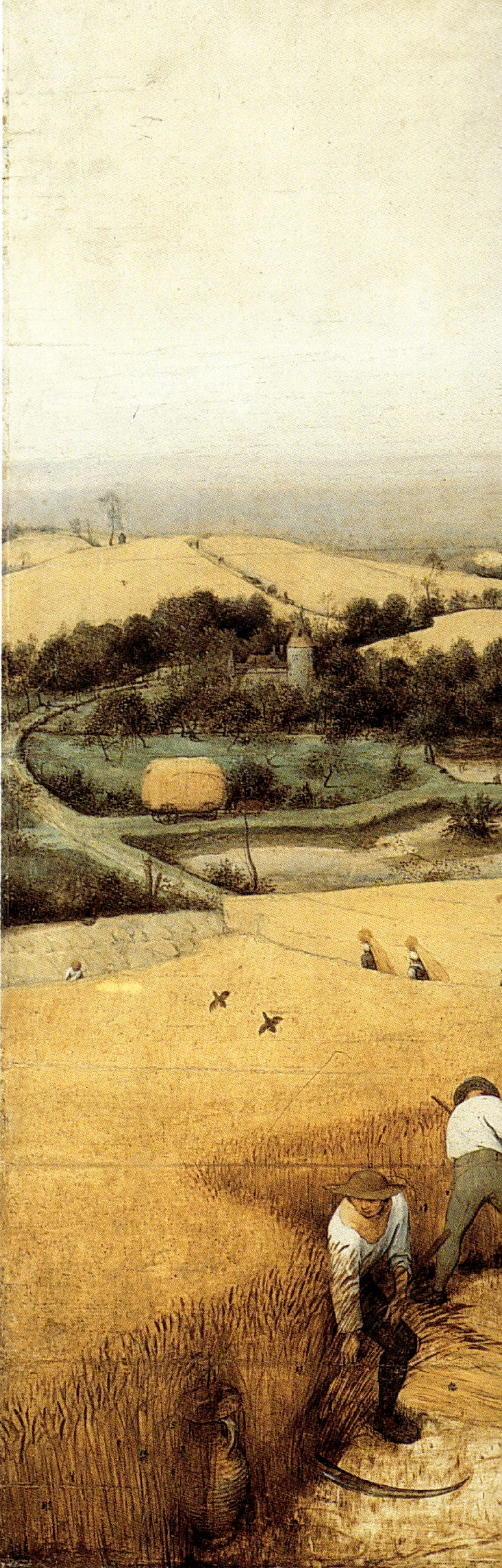

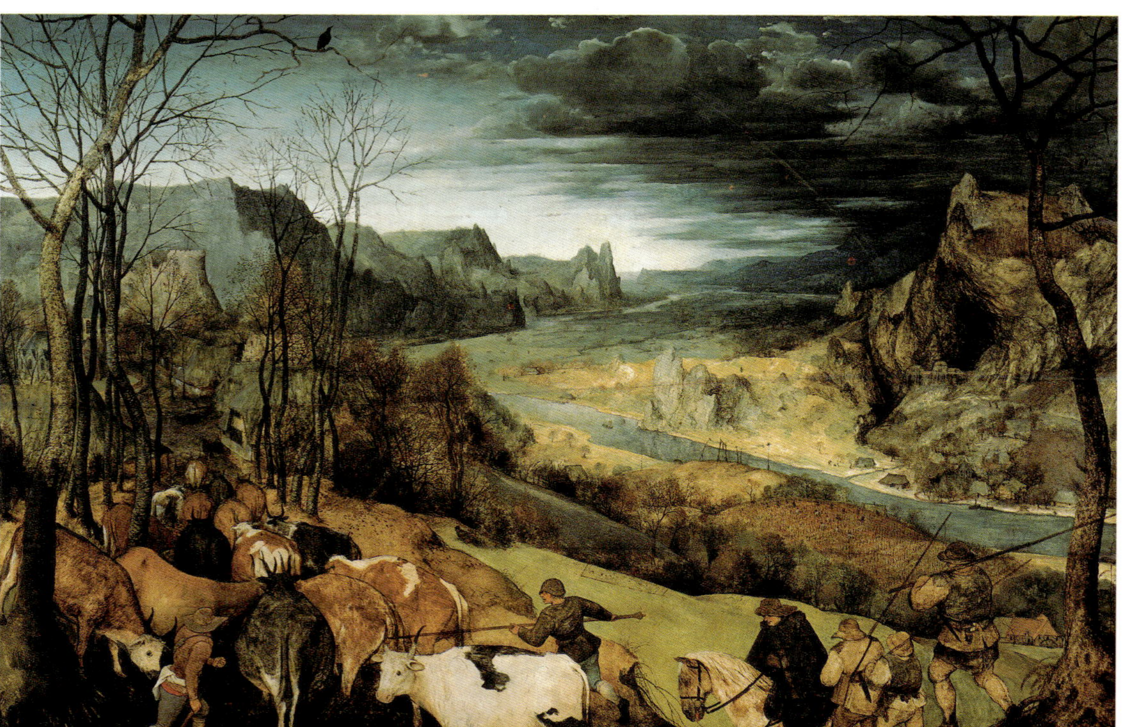

173. Pieter Bruegel, *Haymaking*, 1565. Oil on panel,
44⅞ x 62¼ in. (114 x 158 cm). Prague, Národní Galerie

174. Pieter Bruegel, *The Return of the Herd*, 1565. Oil on panel,
46 x 62⅜ in. (117 x 159 cm). Vienna, Kunsthistorisches Museum

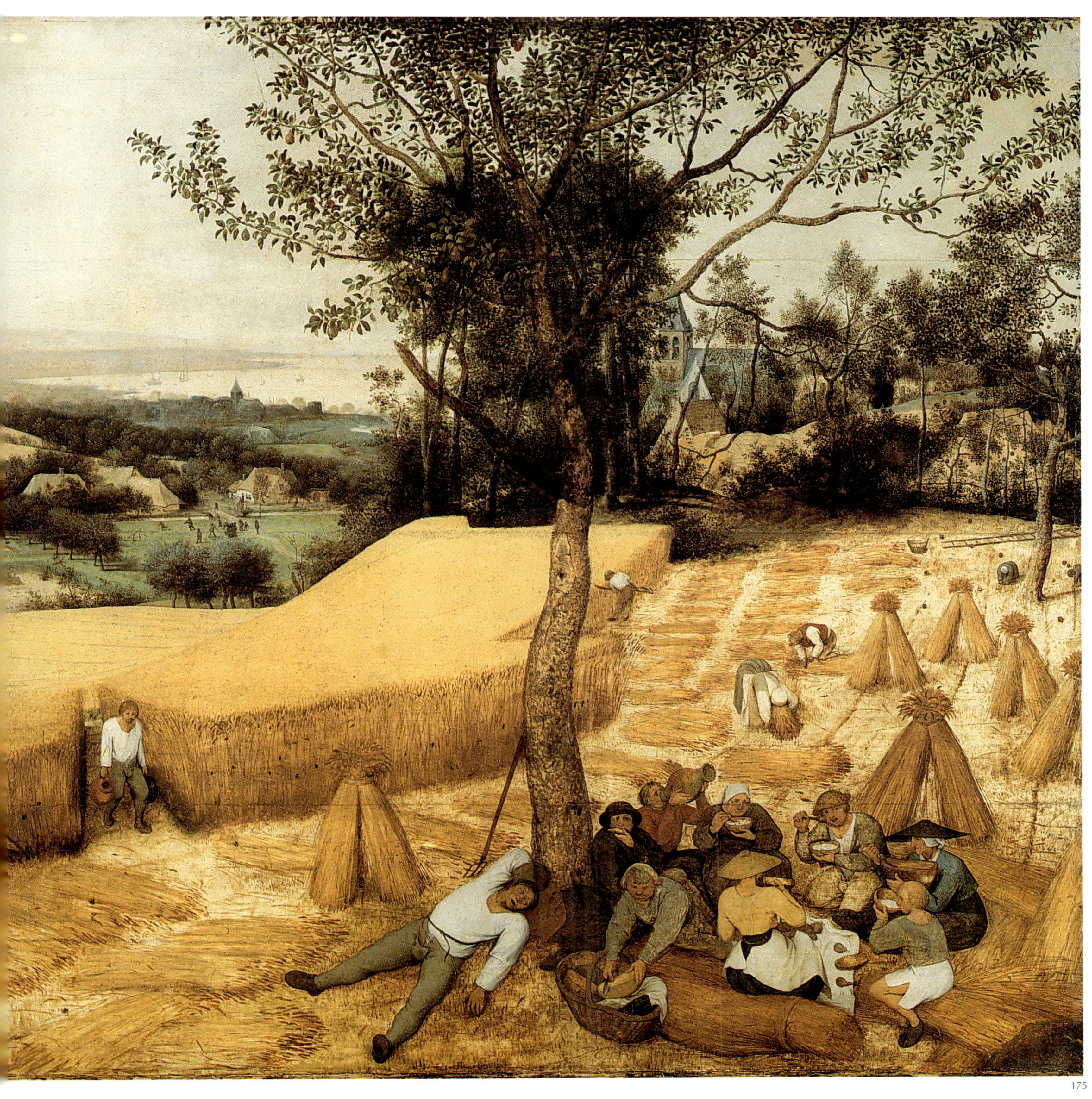

175. Pieter Bruegel, *The Harvest*, 1565. Oil on panel, 46½ x 63¼ in.
(118 x 160.7 cm). New York, The Metropolitan Museum of Art

176–79. Pieter Bruegel, *Haymaking*, 1565: details. Oil on panel, 44⅞ x 62¼ in. (114 x 158 cm). Prague, Národní Galerie

180–82. Pieter Bruegel, *The Harvest*, 1565: details. Oil on panel, 46½ x 63¼ in. (118 x 160.7 cm). New York, The Metropolitan Museum of Art

structure by its presence, and the tasks of summer—harvesting grain or gathering pears—convey once again the active strength of mankind. The shade-giving foliage invites rest, the lunch in the fields depicts the pleasures of eating and drinking, and the women's hats echo the shape of the stacks of wheat sheaves.

The Return of the Herd (figs. 183–35) shows the life of the country after the harvest, in October and November, when the dark ocher of autumn dominates the foreground. The season imposes movement: there is a threat in the form of a buildup of clouds on the right that will soon cast their shadow over the still luminous river, which broadens as it approaches its mouth. The animals are leaving the freedom of the pastures for the narrowness of their stables, but also for the safety of the village on the left, which, still sunlit, looks welcoming. There are other signs of change and uneasiness. Between the movement of the cattle and the flow of the river, the trees are reddish or bare. People are harvesting grapes or gathering vine shoots, but they are also laying bird nets and beyond, in the distance beside the river are wheels of torture, and a gallows with a hanged man on it. Life, death, the village, the rocks and hills, the flow of life and of time—*The Return of the Herd* makes a synthesis of all these. Bruegel presents a transposed, imaginary image, unlike those he would have seen where he lived and worked, since it is set not in flat country, but in some place where livestock moves from the high pastures to the valley at the approach of winter. Klaus Demus, while suggesting the northern Rhine valley as a setting, rightly says: "On its own his utter mastery of nature, which leaves far behind the clumsiness of the earlier 'world landscapes,' makes us forget that he was not a realist, but a poet."[99]

This skill of transposing from reality, of creating in order to convey an essential meaning, allows the artist to escape the immediate setting and make from it, in a reinvented context, an object of contemplation without limit in time or space. Bruegel's supreme skill is taken further in *Hunters in the Snow* (figs. 186, 188). The season is far removed from what we have seen thus far: it is December and January, the depth of winter. This time the composition moves from left to right, following a diagonal that starts from the group of hunters and their pack of hounds, is reaffirmed by a line of trees and a bird in flight, and is supported by other lines between a roof and the river, a bush, and the mountain. But the impression of movement is stabilized by an oblique, from the bottom right-hand corner to its opposite, and by the line from which rise the distant mountains.

This work, also known by the title *The Return of the Hunters*, presents a synthesis between the infinity of the world the eye embraces—as winter embraces nature—and the scale of people in their everyday surroundings: On the one hand, snowy expanses on several planes stretch as far as the icy peaks; on the other, people are playing on the ice, performing their winter chores before a house where a pig is being singed and, in the distance, fighting a chimney fire. It is a picture of nature plunged into inertia, where life is none the less present—if sometimes precariously: There is a bird trap—like that in *Winter Landscape* (fig. 54), painted the same year, 1565—in just where the hill drops off, just to the right of the center of the foreground (fig. 188). The picture contains warnings, but humor, too: A dog with long ears in the left foreground looks out at the viewer with its round eyes, rather as the cow in the left foreground does in *The Return of the Herd*, or the white horse in *Christ Carrying the Cross*. Though they look more gaunt, the dogs by their precision of

176 ▶

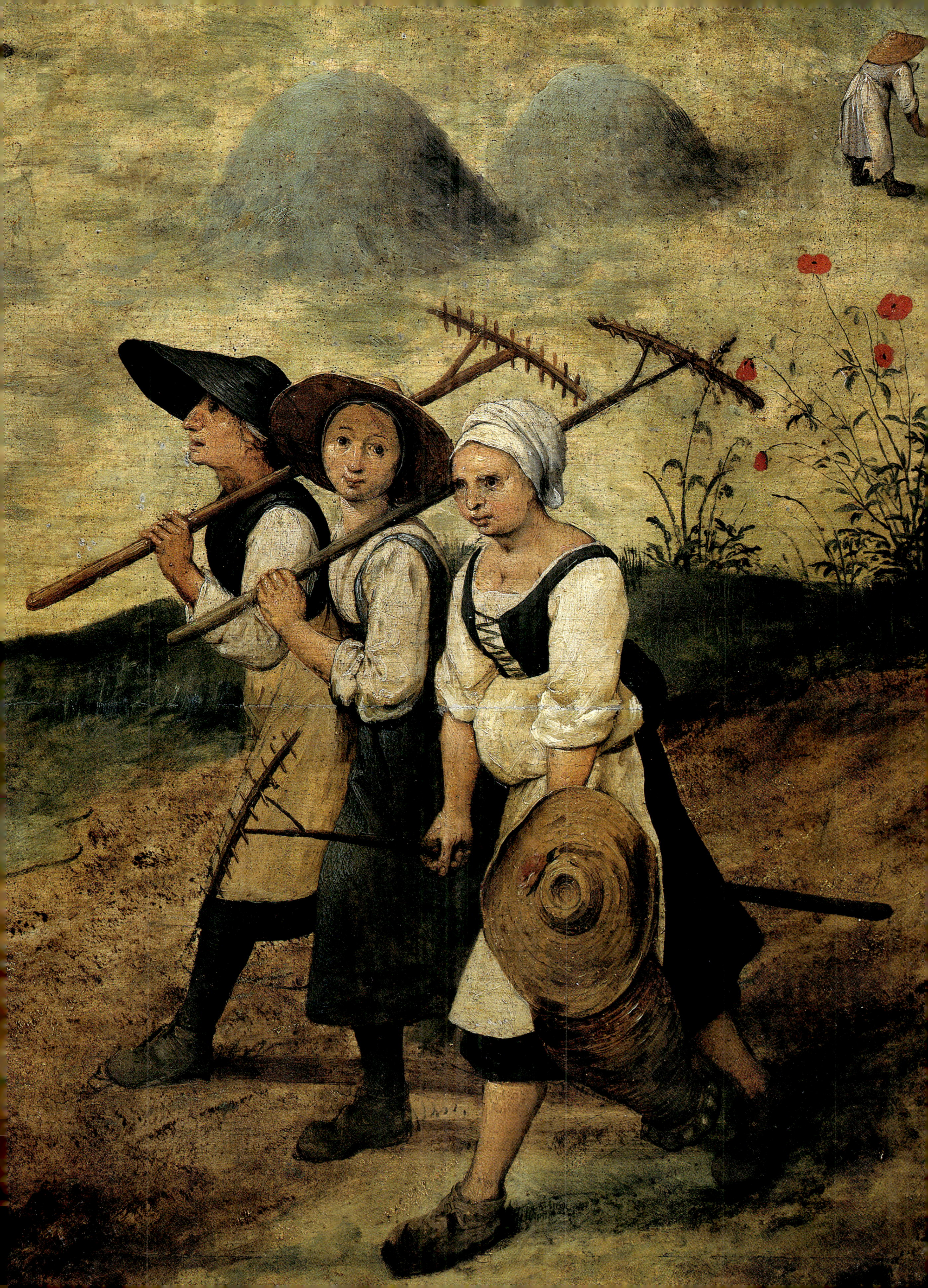

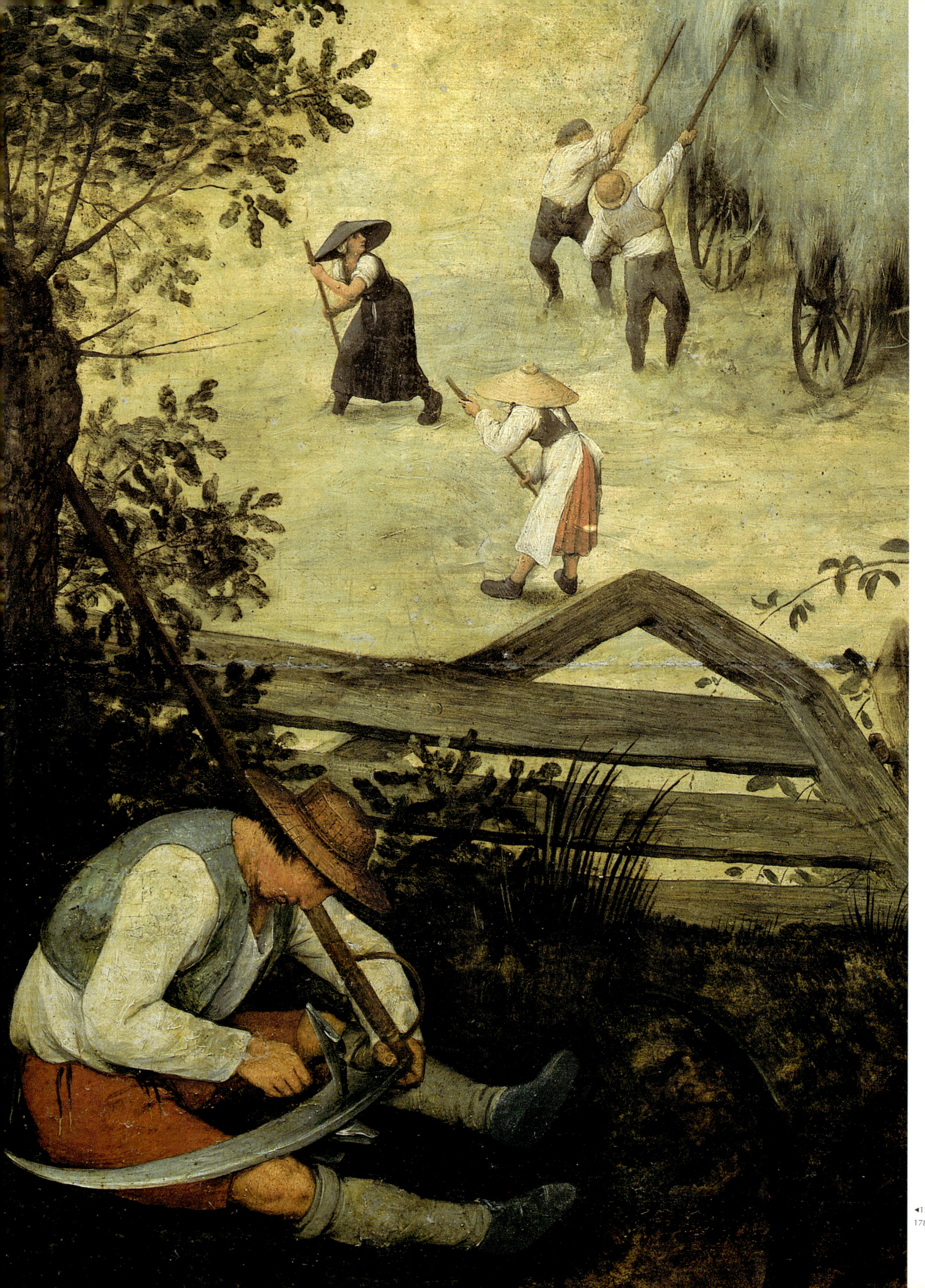

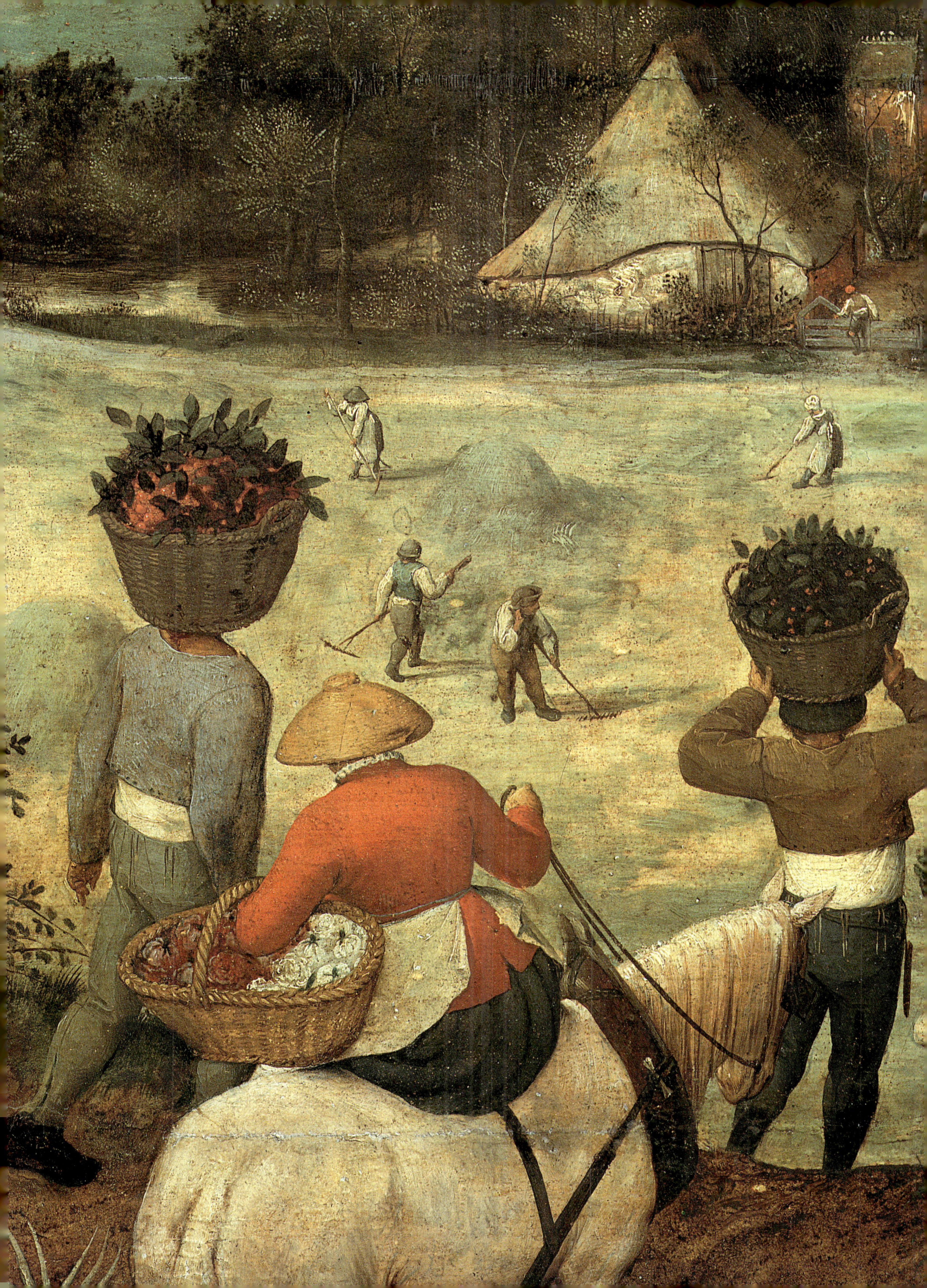

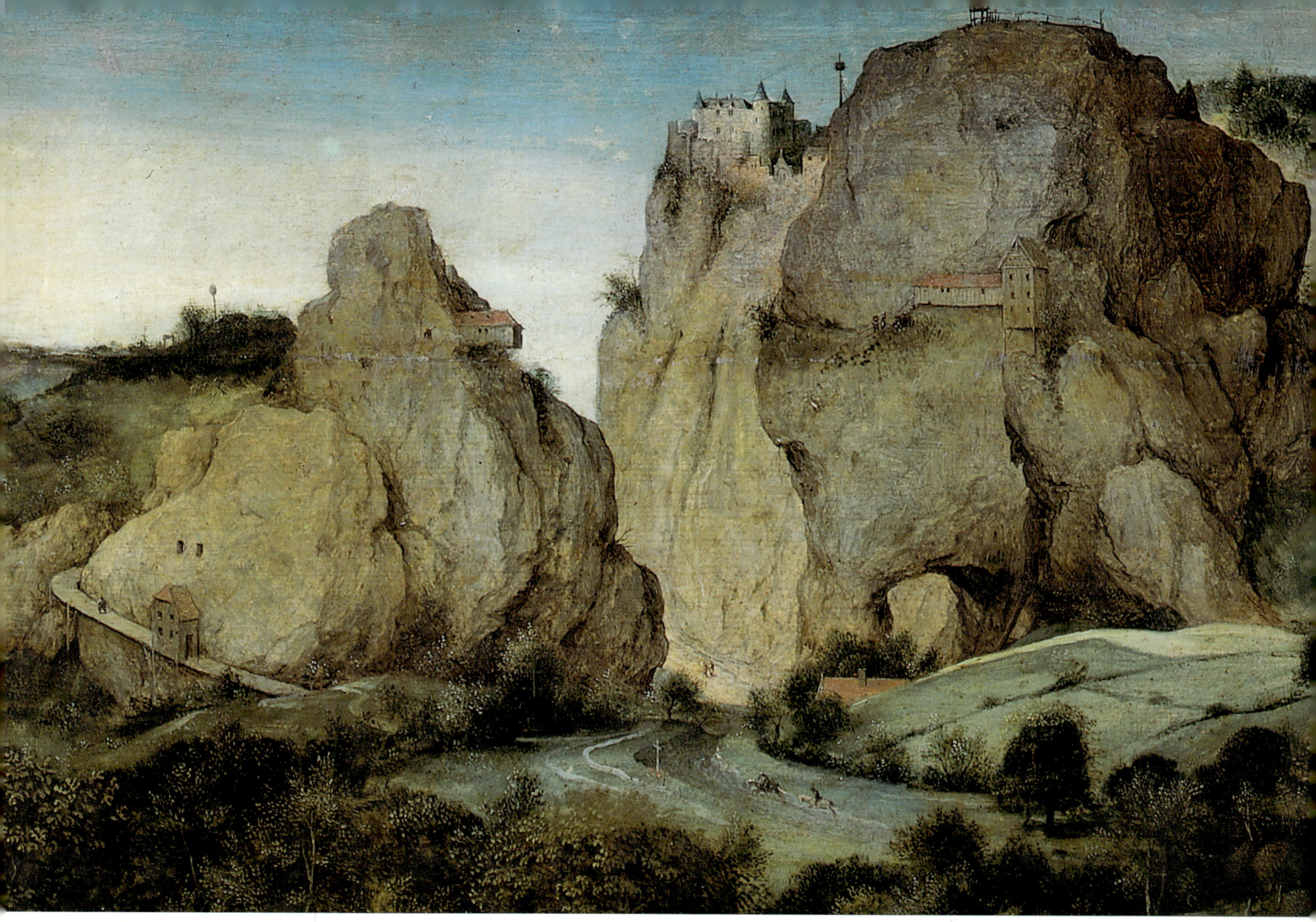

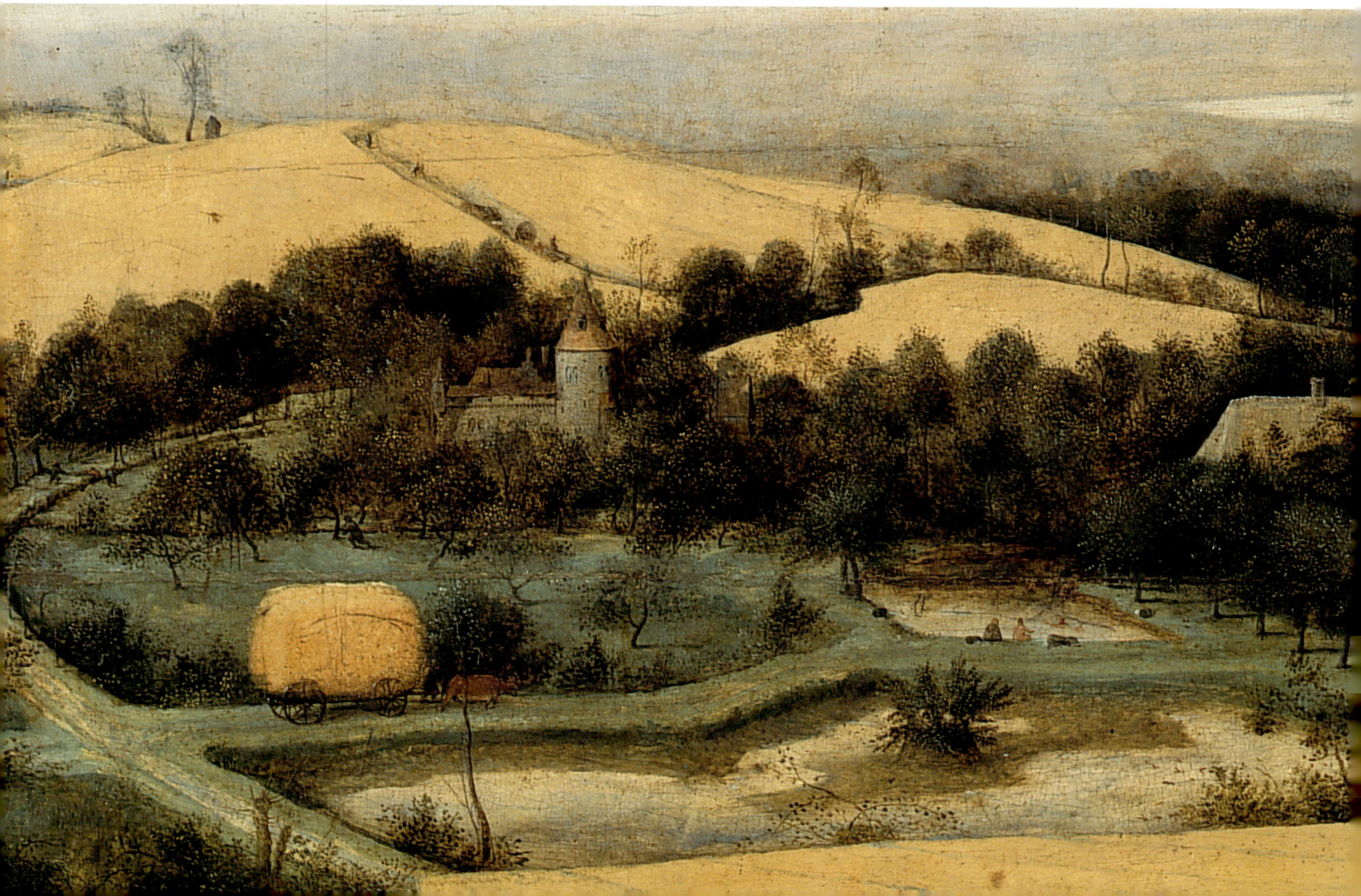

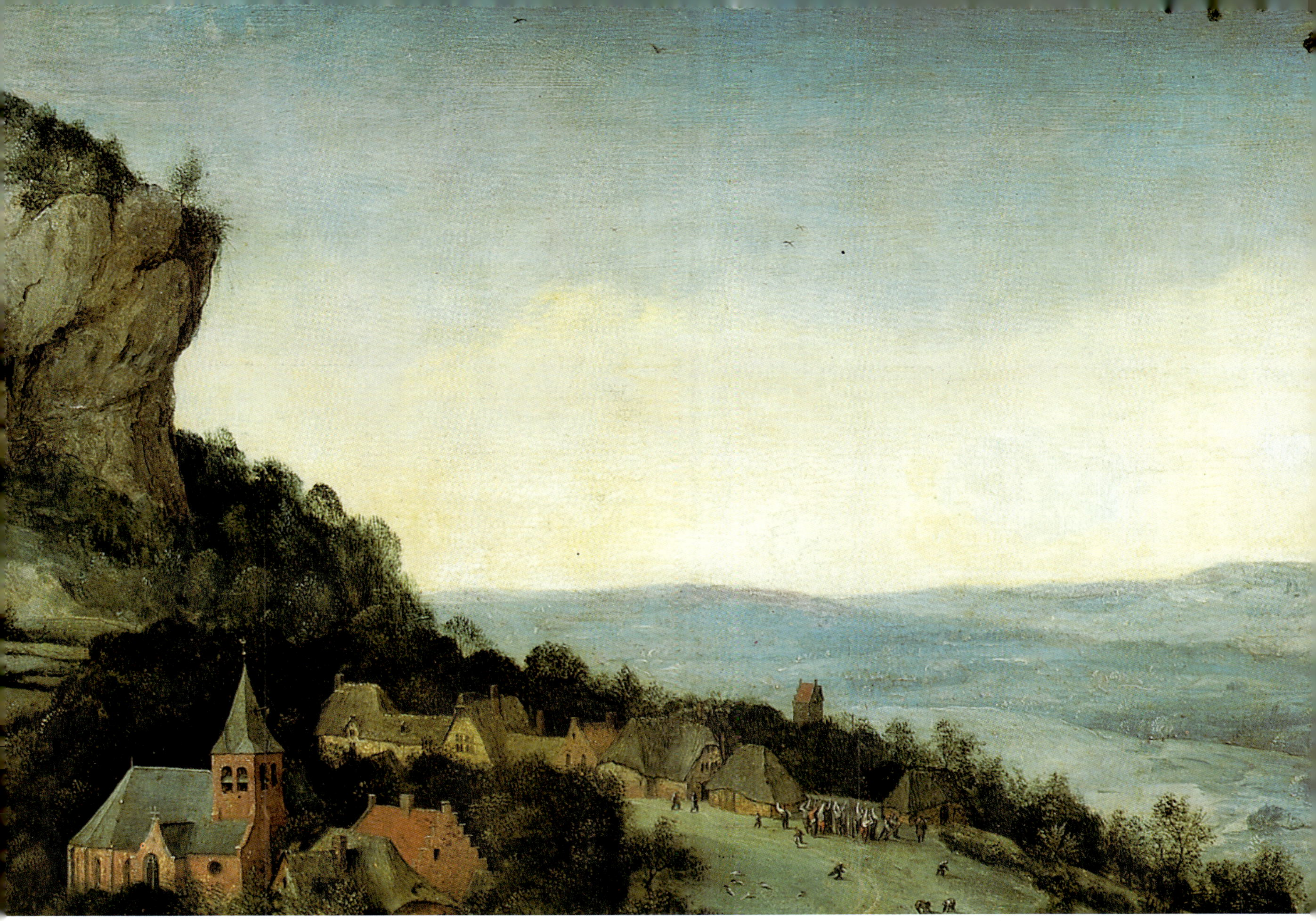

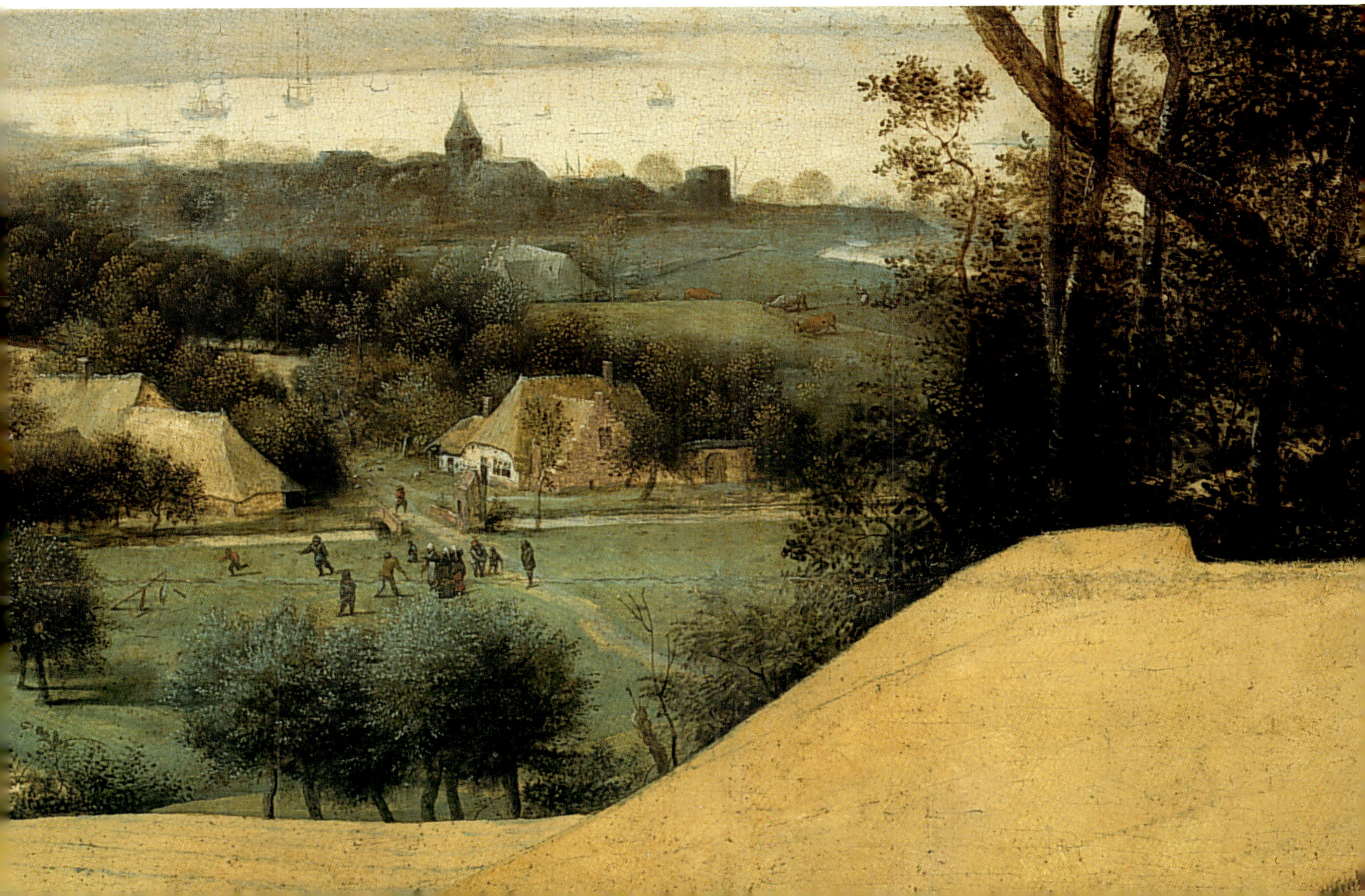

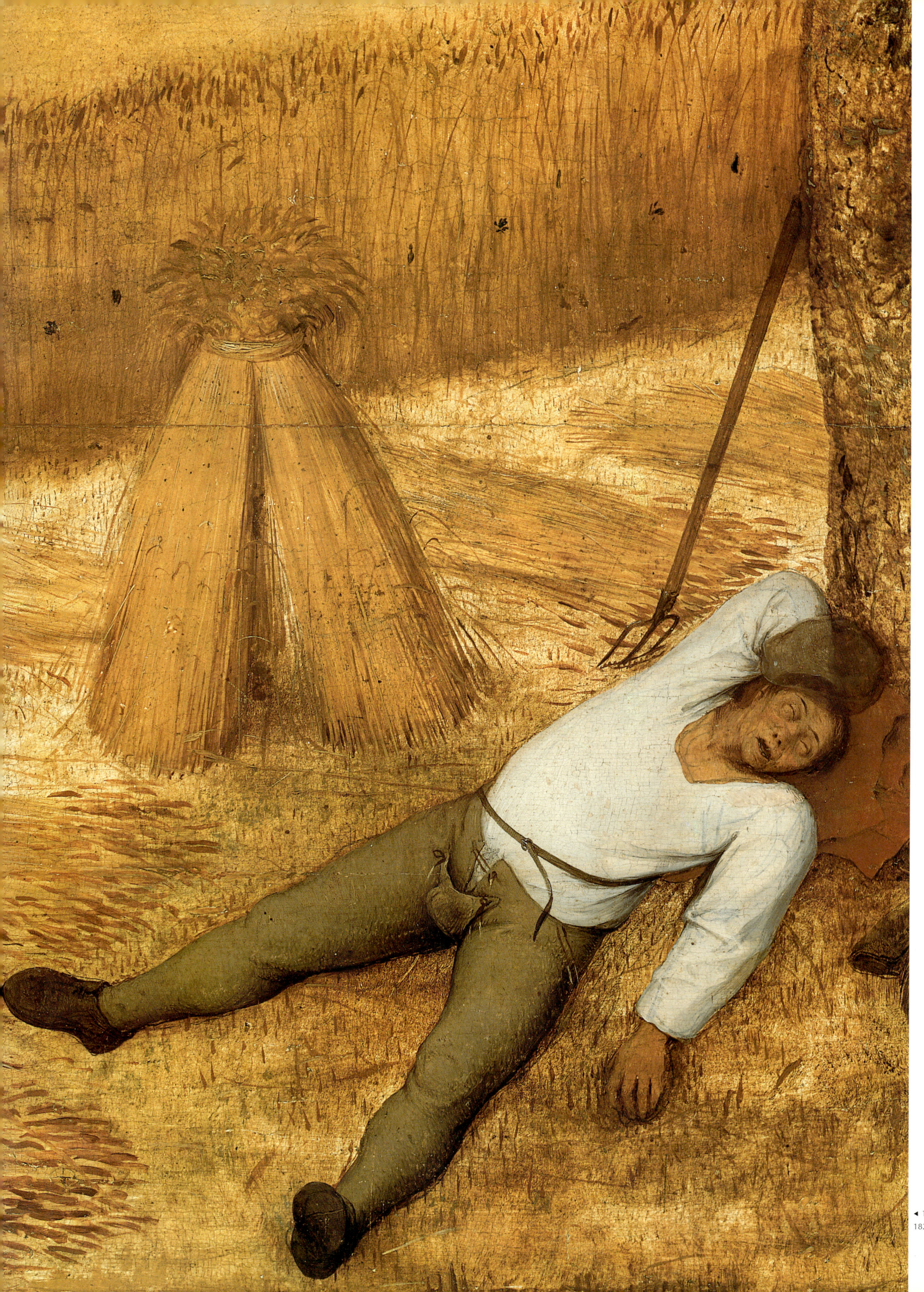

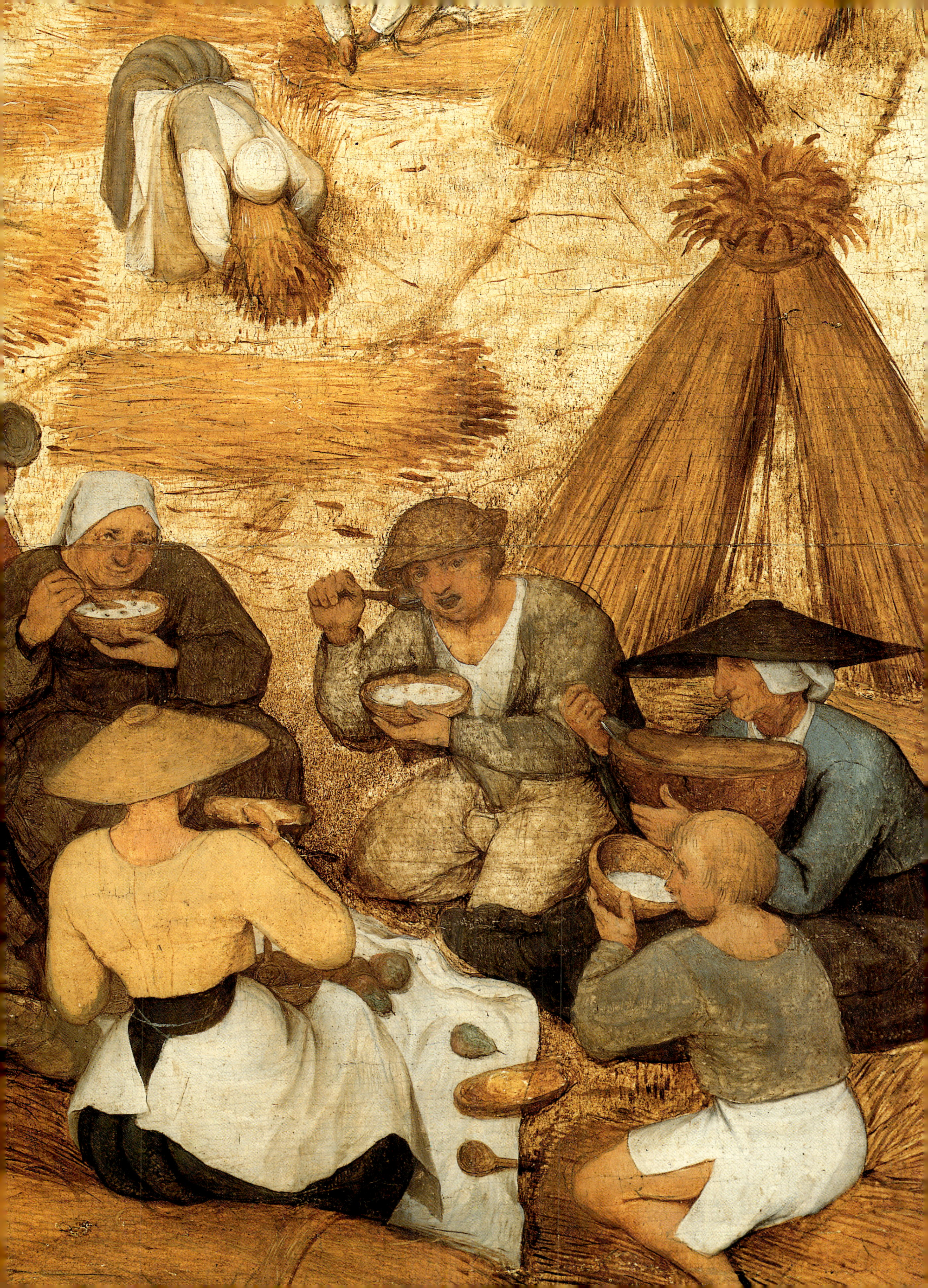

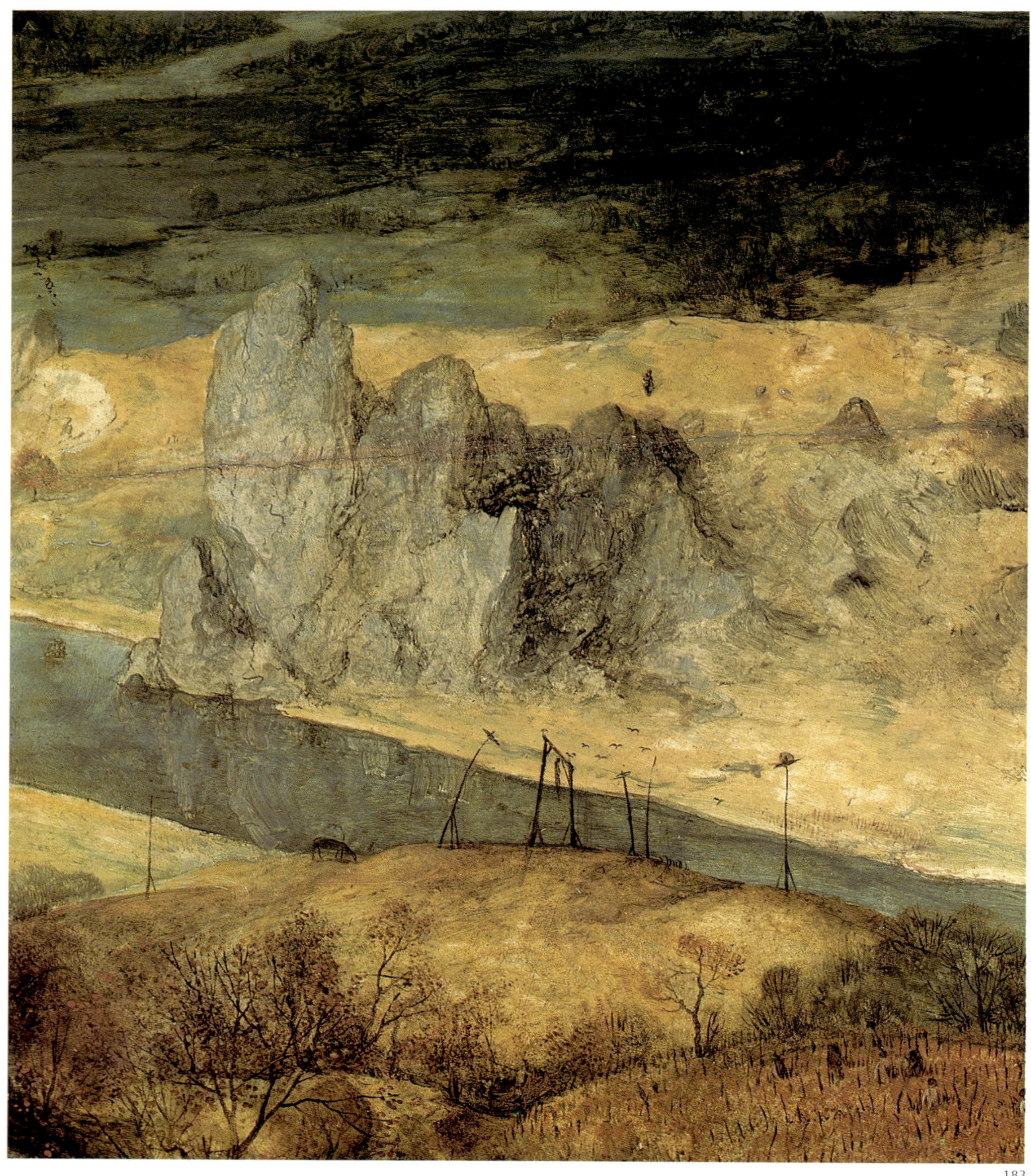

183

183–85. Pieter Bruegel, *The Return of the Herd,*
1565: details. Oil on panel, 46 x 62⅝ in. (117 x 159 cm).
Vienna, Kunsthistorisches Museum

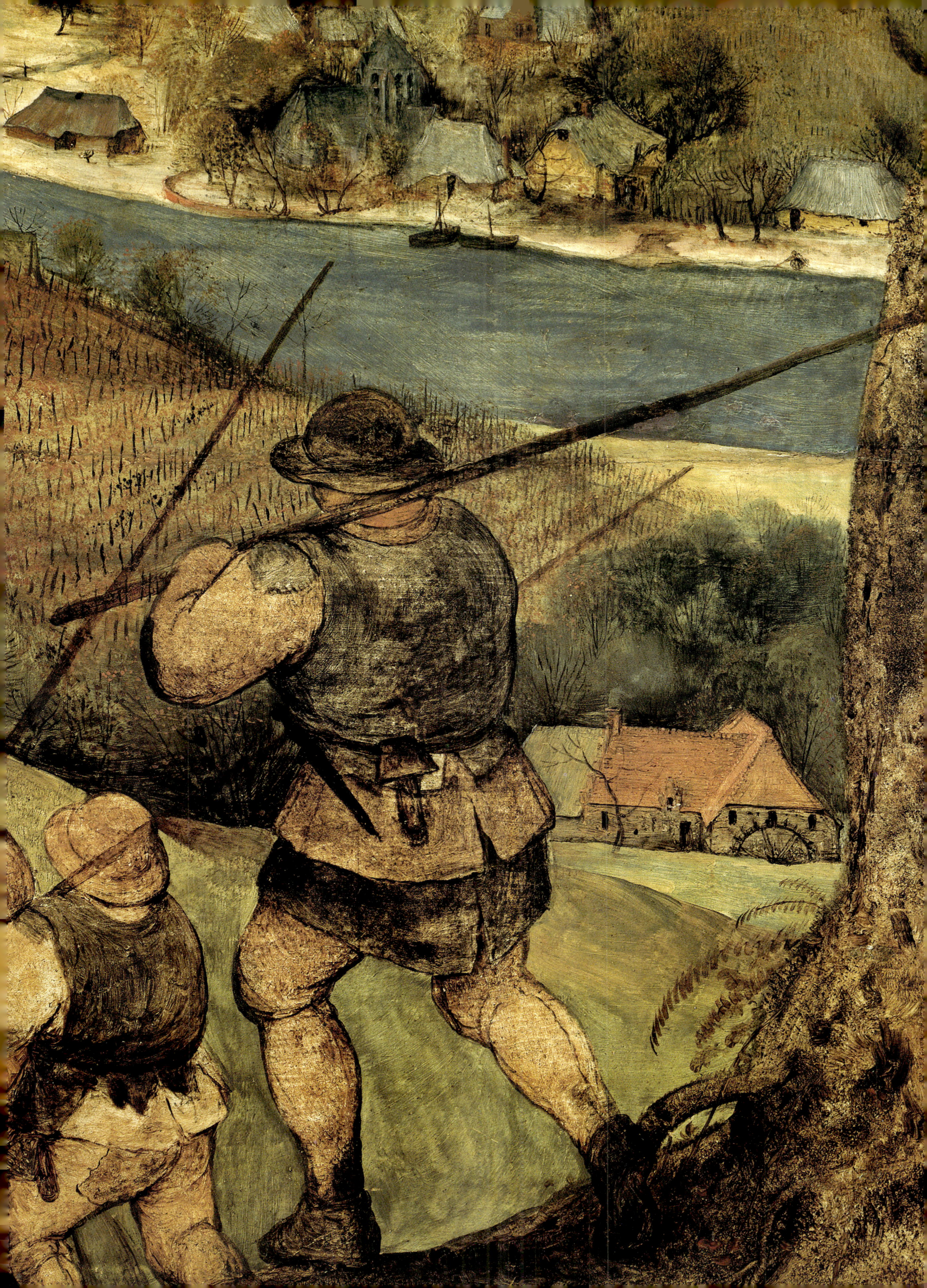

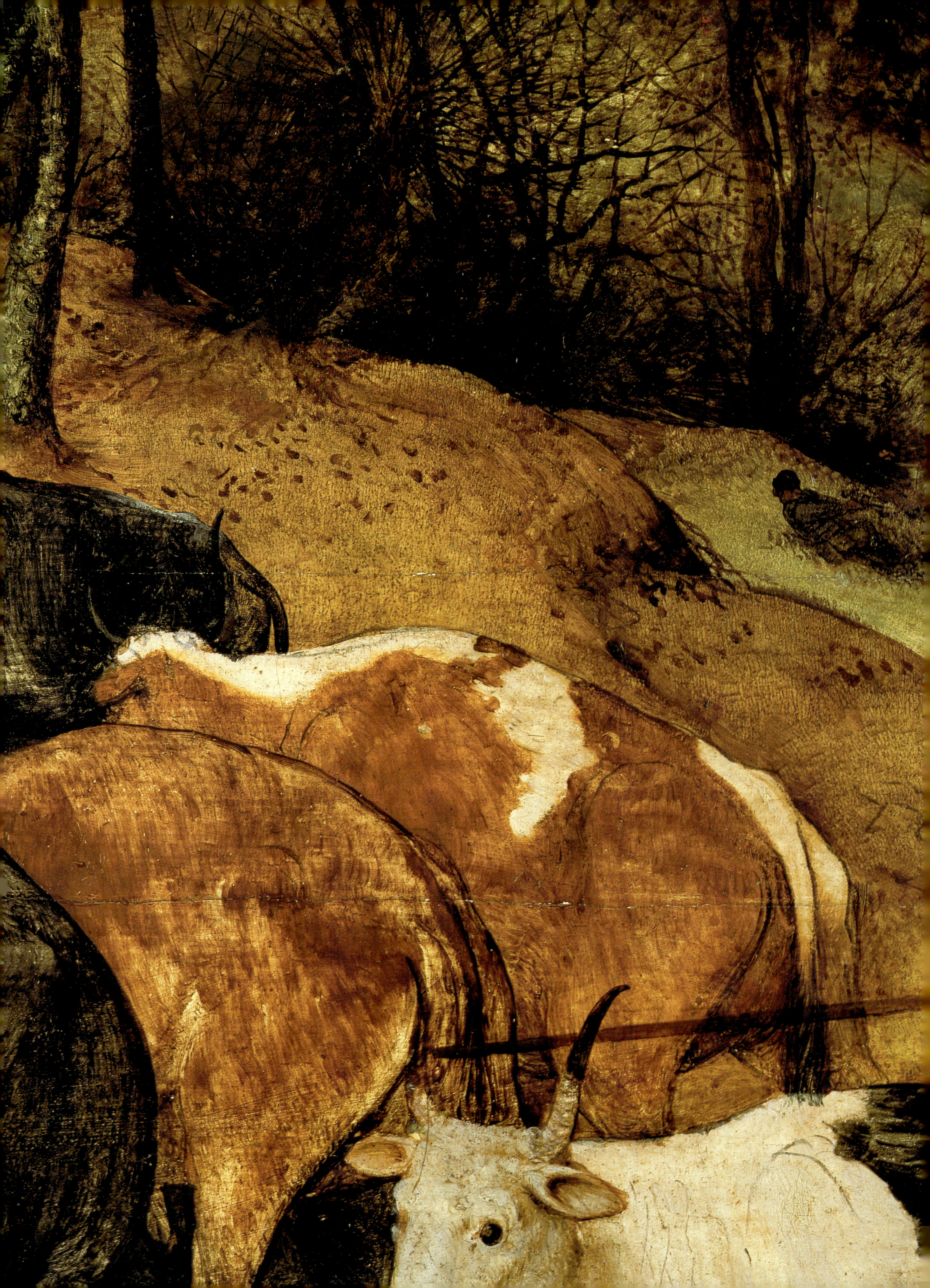

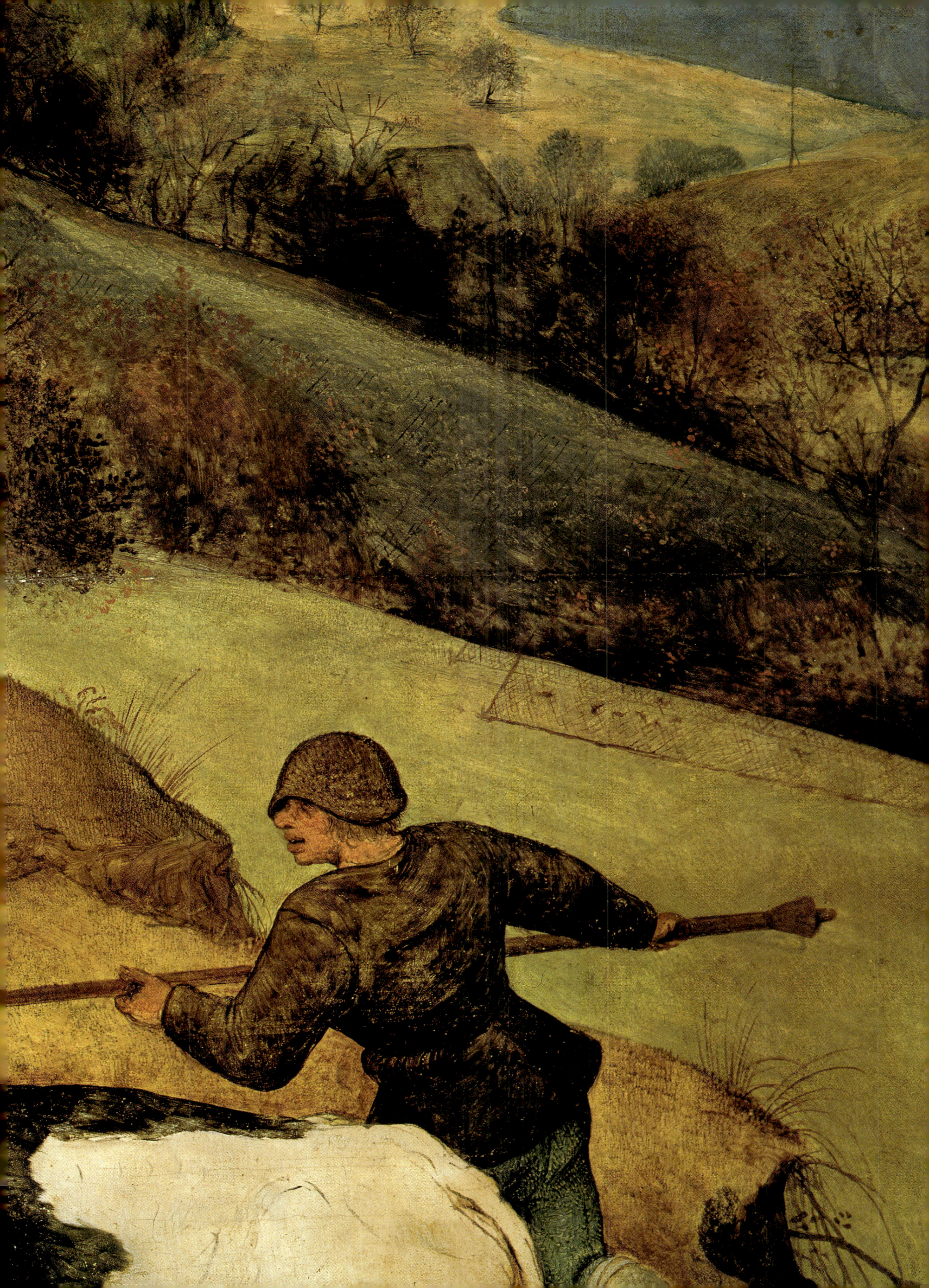

line and position recall the dogs that Dürer engraved in about 1501 in his engraving of *St. Eustace*. Curiously, the hunters are passing in front of an inn whose sign displays that very saint: *Dit is in den Hert* (At the Sign of the Stag).

The snow is far from uniform. Not only does Bruegel sign his name in it, at the center of the rock under the bush, but snow can be dirty, muddy on the road, hardened on the strip of earth that separates the two pools, and it can vary depending on whether the roofs face the sun or not. This subtleness of textures contrasts with the almost abstract precision with which the willow branches are painted, more or less black against the gray blur, and with the rhythm of the figures on the ice. The execution is rapid and extremely precise, capturing the child and his spinning top on the ice of the pool beyond the bridge, with the reflection of his stick, of his feet, and even of the top.

If winter has frozen nature here, she comes to life again in *The Gloomy Day* (figs. 187 and 189–92), whose title does not properly express the idea of a dawn.[100] A white bird in a heavy sky echoes the black bird against the icy background in *The Hunters*. Melting snow, the hint of a break in the clouds, a storm blowing the ships aground, ground drenched under a lowering sky, branches in the shape of forked lightning, bustle on the edge of the village: everything proclaims life being reborn after the torpor of winter. The new year begins in March, and Bruegel portrays it in a manner that could be described almost as expressionist. In the foreground a child, wearing a paper hat that recalls a similar one in *The Battle of Carnival and Lent*, carries a lit lantern, a reference to the short daylight hours. The crown and the biscuits the man is eating may suggest Epiphany. These biscuits can also be seen in *The Battle of Carnival and Lent*.

The peasant who is coppicing the willows, the other gathering the wands, and the man who is repairing the house convey confidence in the face of the unpredictability of nature. On the edge of the village at the lower left a man can be seen relieving himself against a wall, another is playing the hurdy-gurdy in front of an inn, others dance, a roof is being repaired, carts are ready, and the church belltower seems to mirror the masts of the ships broken by the tempest. The light strikes the mountains on the left, and the front of the house on the right; the painter emphasizes the pale highlights of the icy crests, as well as the child's crown, the mother's cap, and the father's codpiece. Thus life expresses itself high in the heavens, and in the hollow of the tree blown down by winter.

One picture from the series is missing: spring; April and May, when nature blooms and lovers' bonds are forged. Can we imagine it? Probably not, for Bruegel always surprises. It could be suggested that the drawing made in 1565 entitled *Spring* (fig. 193) gives us some indication. A fine work, certainly, with its flower beds being replanted, sheep being sheared, and sweet talk under the arbors, in the tradition of the fifteenth-century gardens of love or of a Renaissance engraving by the French artist Etienne Delaune (fig. 194). Is this a valid approach? If we compare *The Harvest* with *Summer* (fig. 58), which makes a pair with *Spring*, we can see the clear, and understandable, distance between a monumental composition and one intended to be made into an engraving. Both are admirable, but each in its own register. No doubt the missing *Spring* shared common elements with the drawing, as *Summer* does with its corresponding painting. As to what it was like, we can only guess.

186, 188. Pieter Bruegel, *Hunters in the Snow*, or *The Return of the Hunters*, 1565: whole work and detail. Oil on panel, 46 x 63¾ in. (117 x 162 cm). Vienna, Kunsthistorisches Museum

187, 189–92. Pieter Bruegel, *The Gloomy Day*, 1565: whole work and details. Oil on panel, 46½ x 64⅛ in. (118 x 163 cm). Vienna, Kunsthistorisches Museum

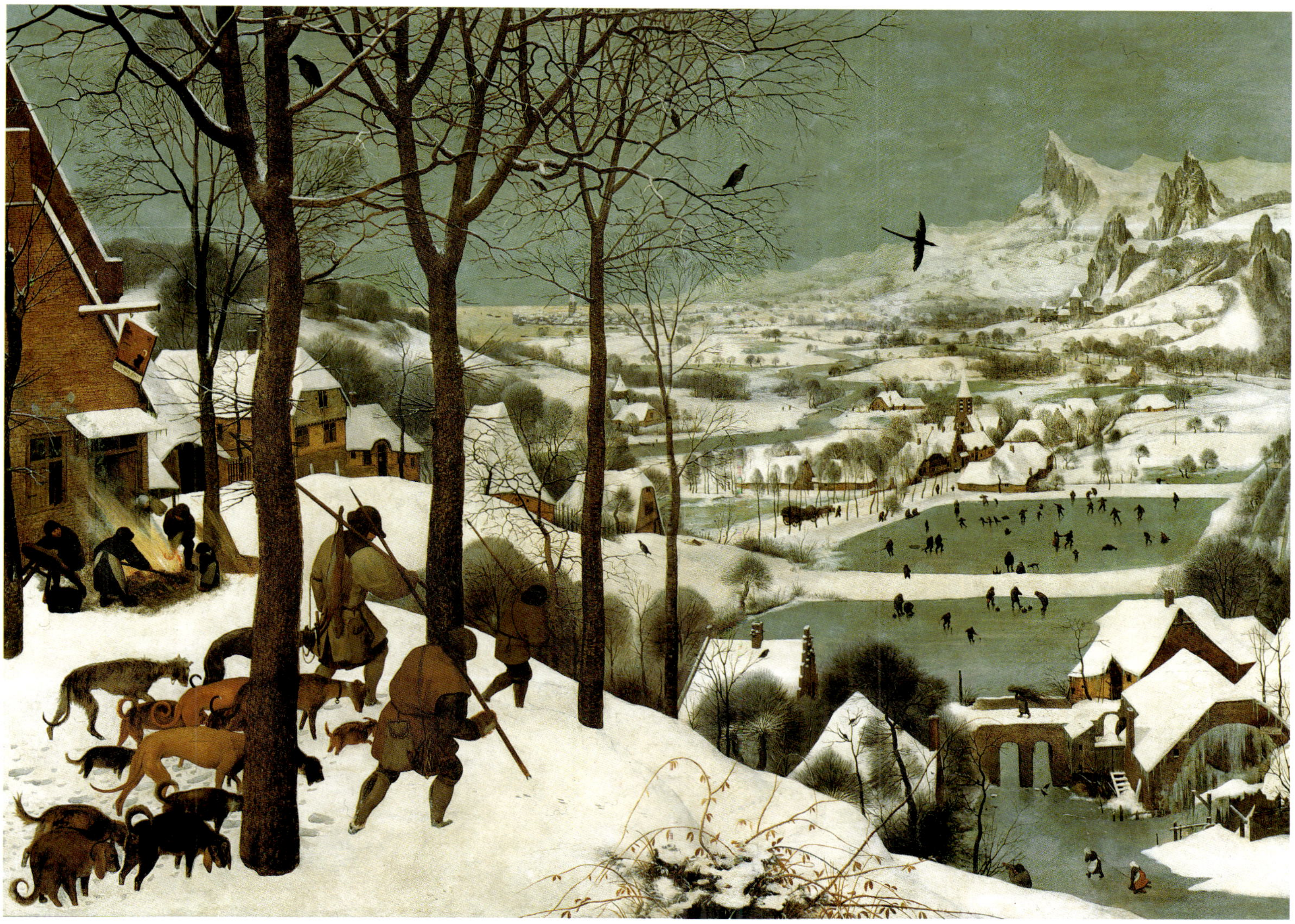

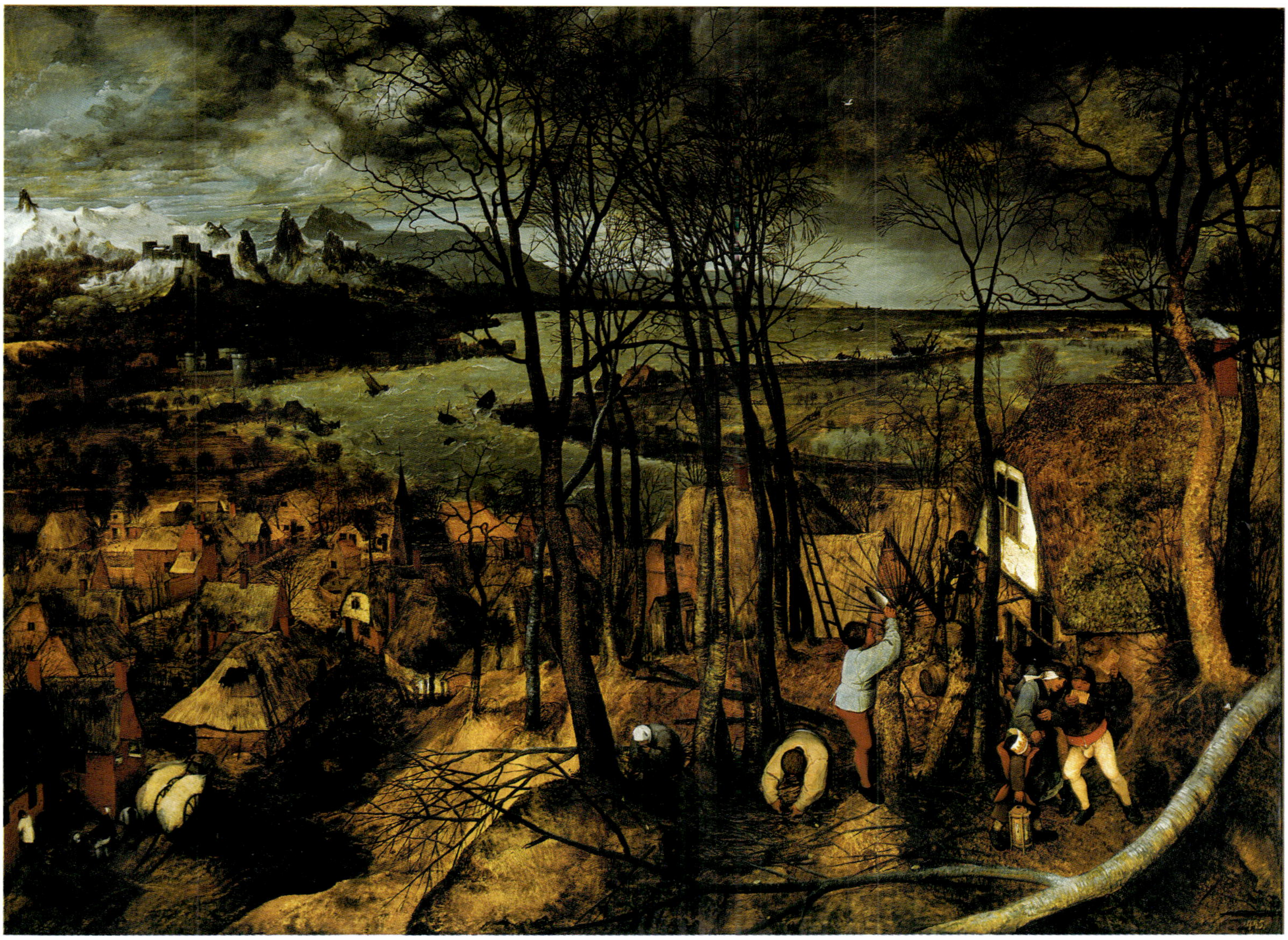

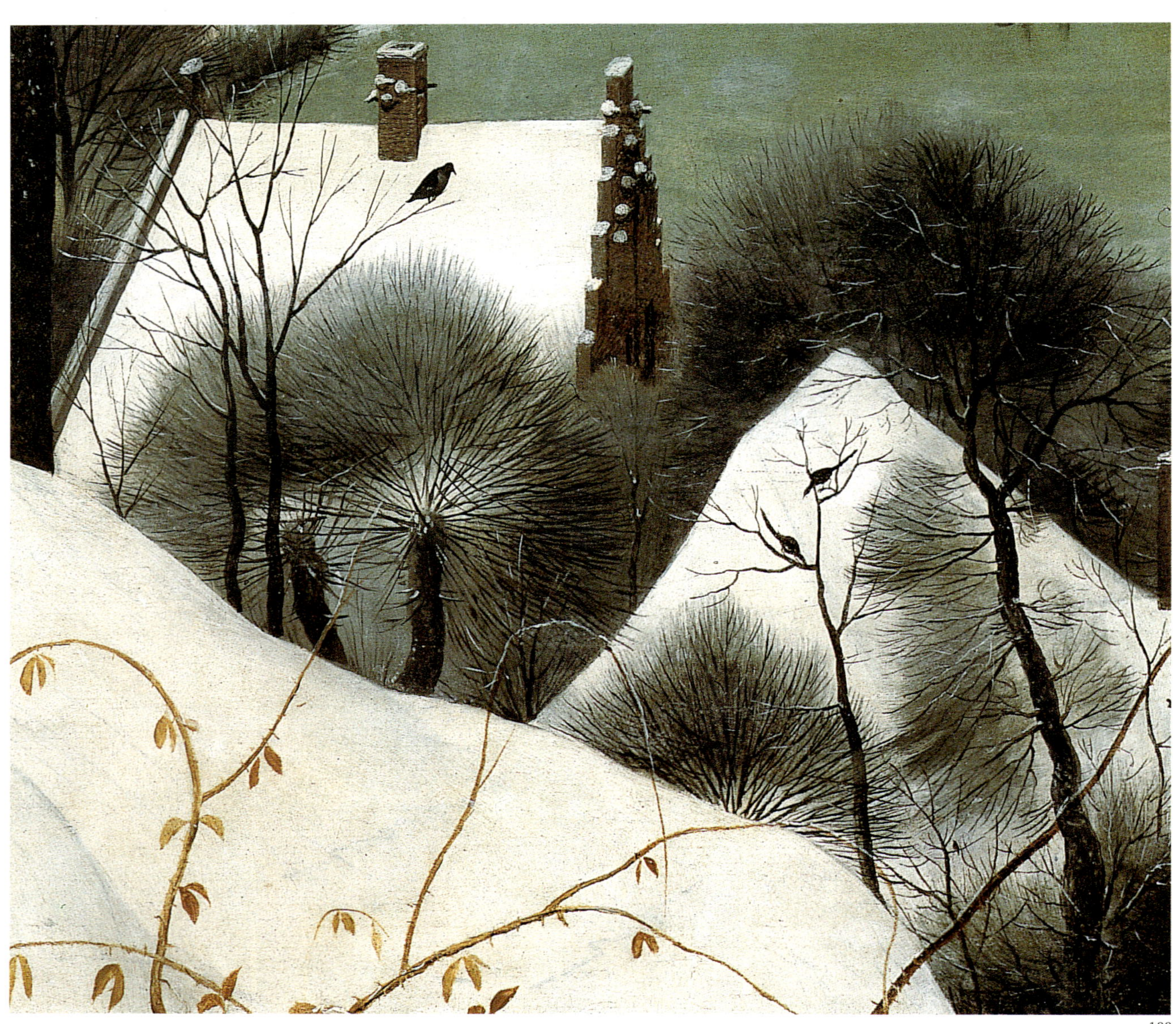

188

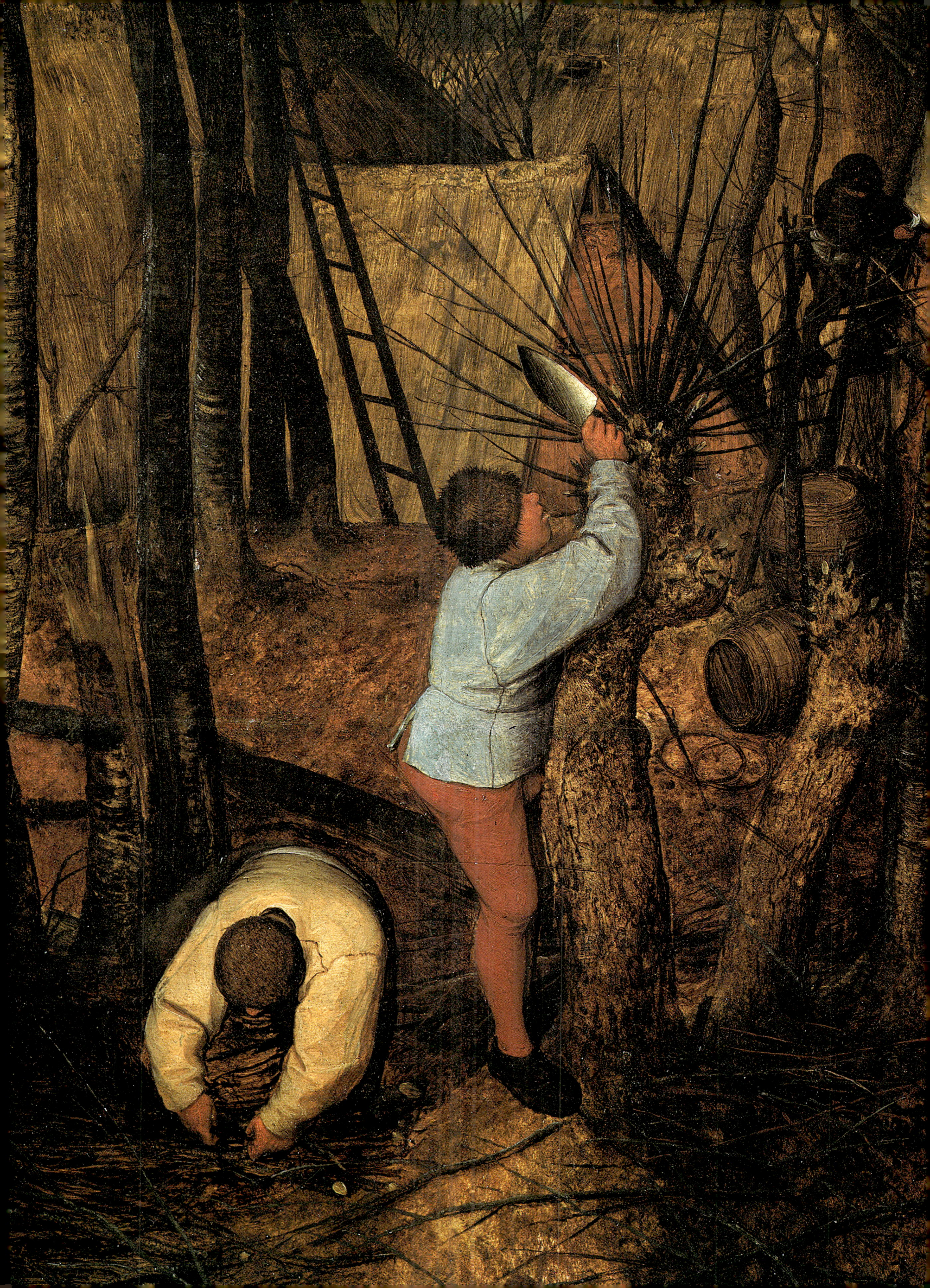

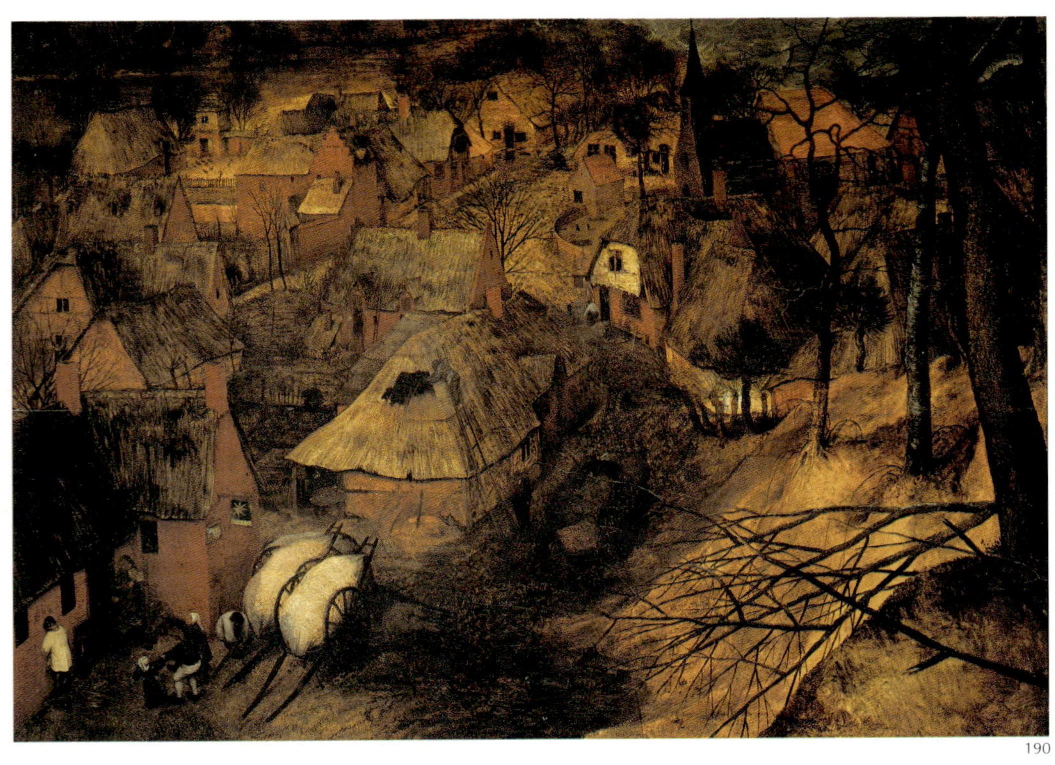

190

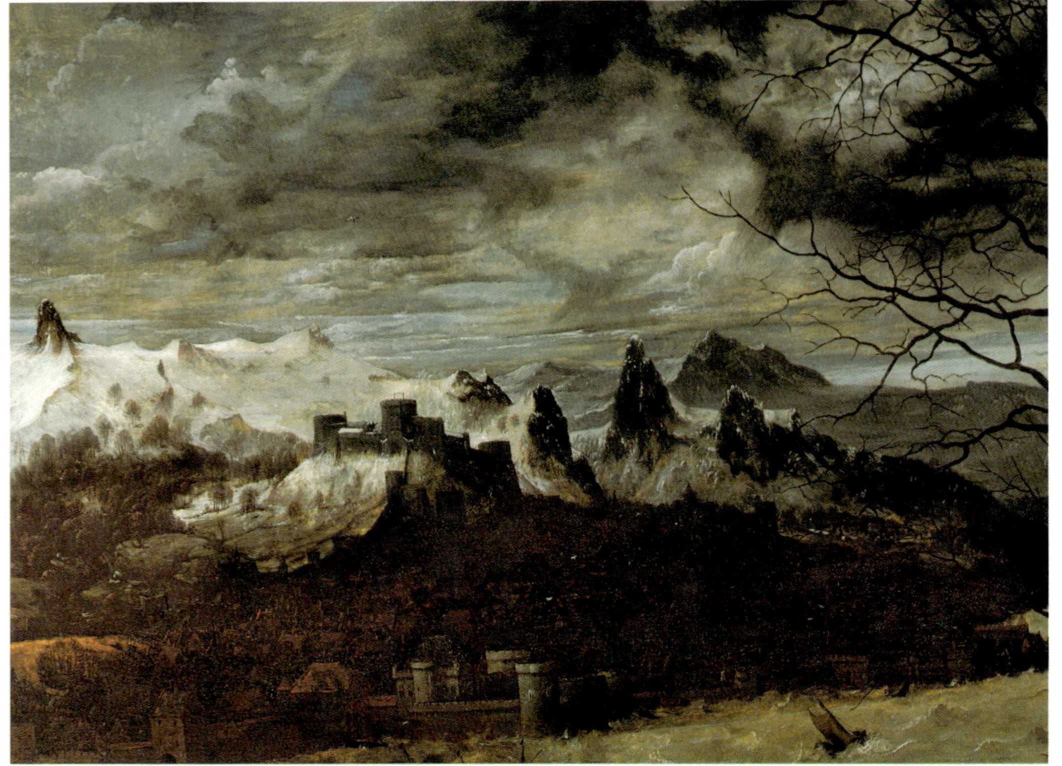

191

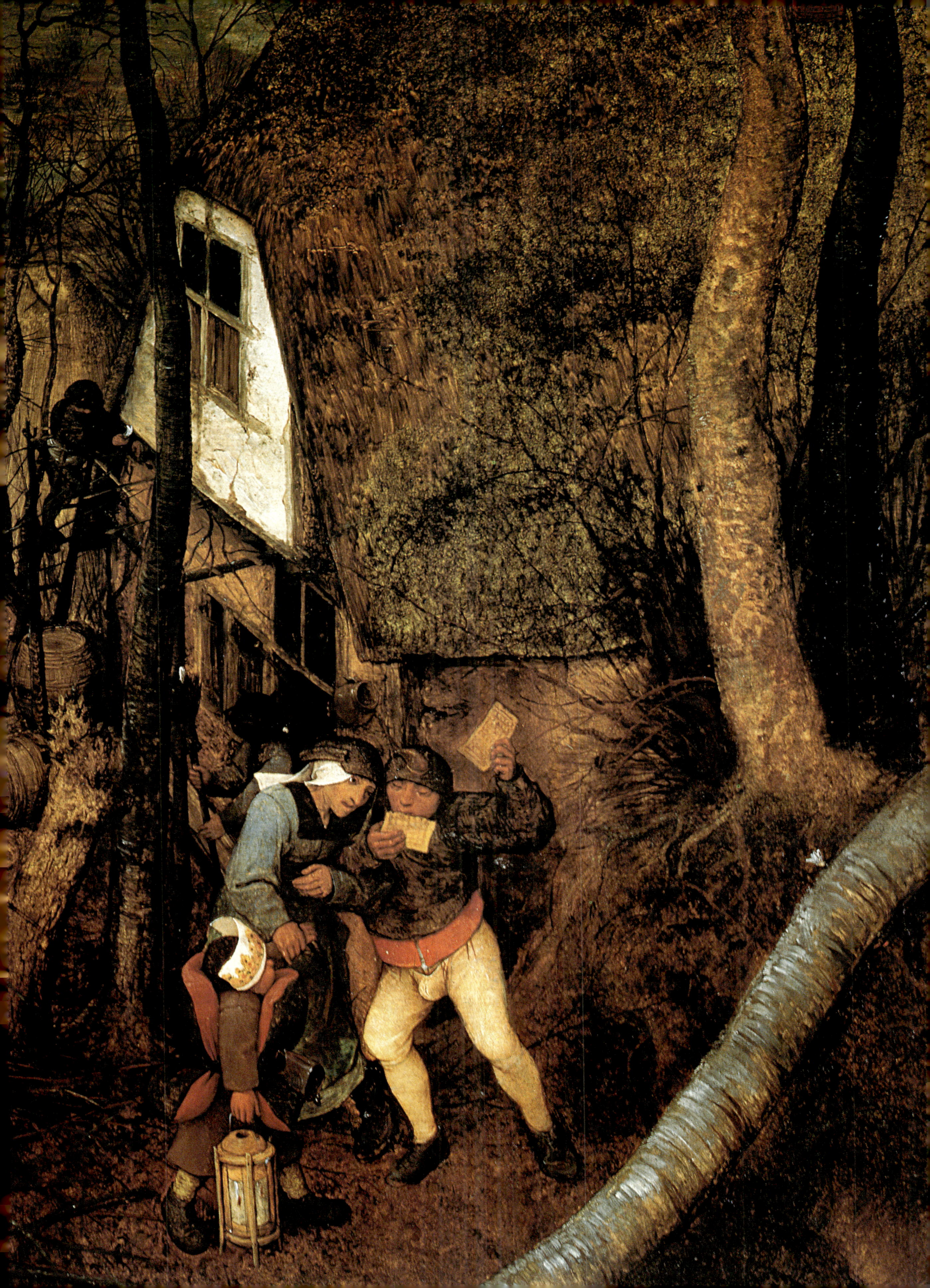

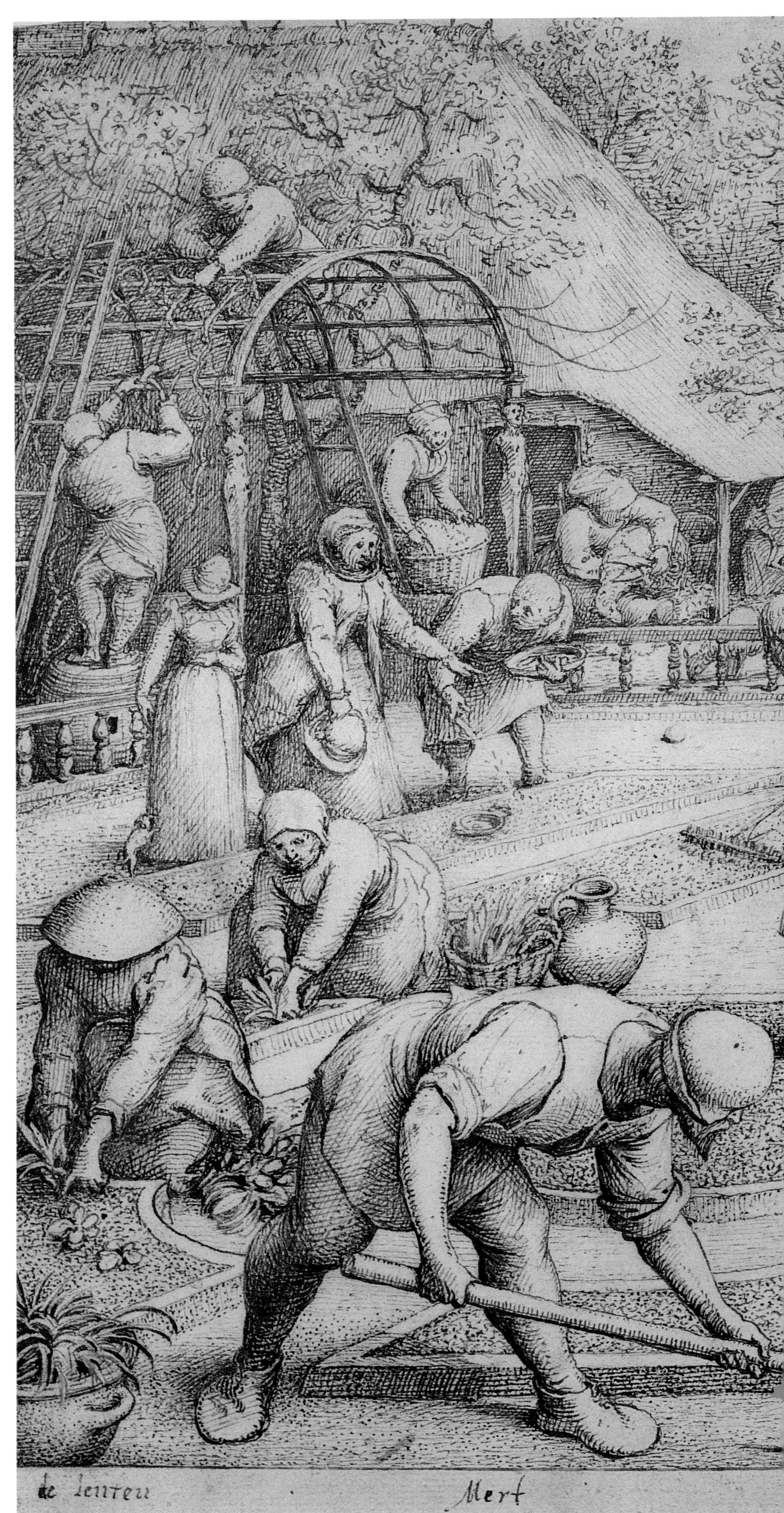

193. Pieter Bruegel, *Spring,* 1565. Pen and brown ink, 8¾ x 11⅜ in. (22.3 x 28.9 cm). Vienna, Graphische Sammlung Albertina

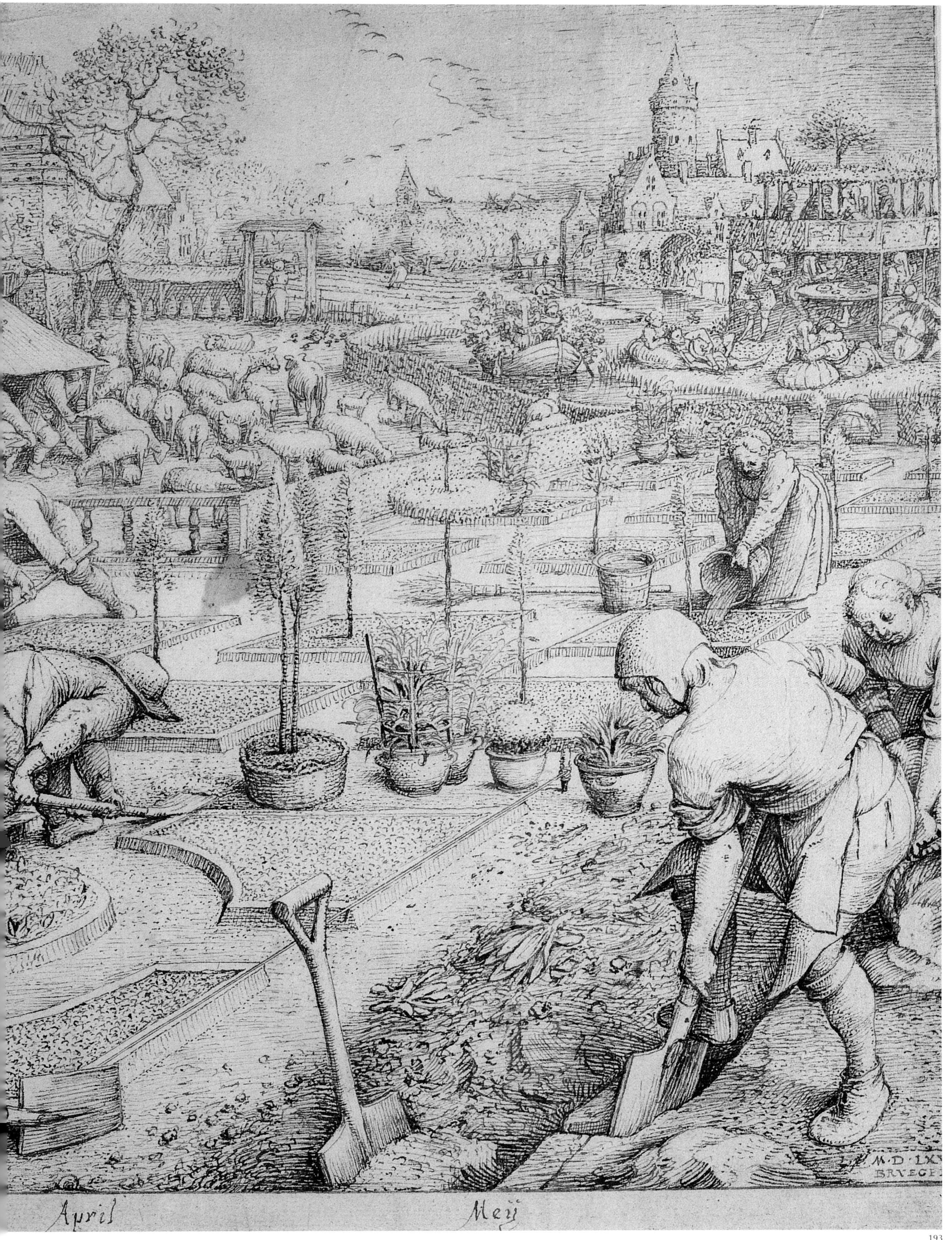

193

THE AGE OF MATURITY

With the *Seasons* series, the year 1565 proved an auspicious one. The painter's maturity reached its zenith. The power of his expressiveness reached a balance between form and content: evocation, synthesis, and suggestion, all working together perfectly to reconstruct the world. As well as this series and other works made the same year, such as *Christ and the Woman Taken in Adultery*, several drawings date from this period, including *The Calumny of Apelles*, *Four Men Standing in Conversation*, *The Goose Keeper*, and *The Painter and the Art Lover*. Better still, the year 1565 produced *Winter Landscape With Skaters and Bird Trap* (fig. 54). This vision of the world, in which white and gold answer each other, is a now-familiar landmark in Bruegel's art. The small format gives this work an intimate feel,[101] and the unity of the place depicted contrasts with his often composite landscapes. The painting opens a window onto nature: a Brabant landscape, possibly the village of Pede-Sainte-Anne. Our gaze first lingers on a bramble patch, then slides over the water's frozen surface and, from snow-covered roofs to modulated expanses of tone, climbs to the horizon, where a town rises from the mist. Everything is drenched in a warm, muted light that even the great trees leave unbroken. There would be total peace, were not the birds, on the right, threatened by a trap, and careless people, on the left, by the fragile ice, already holed in the foreground.

Does the work therefore contain a message? Several writers have sought a proverbial meaning in *The Bird Trap* (as it is sometimes called, erroneously, as this places too much emphasis on the trap), or tried to find an essentially philosophical significance in the work.[102] This would not go against the essence of the painter's works, but this one invites happy contemplation more than anything else. The painting was the prototype for a series of copies and variants of which some fifty—most of them by Pieter Bruegel the Younger and his workshop—have been identified by Georges Marlier;[103] and it already prefigured, as Friedländer points out,[104] the Dutch genre paintings of winter scenes of the following century. More importantly for present-day viewers, this snowy landscape conveys a sensitivity to nuances of light that was to be heightened in the nineteenth century. It is probably the first landscape in its own right that freezes a moment, both naturally captured and contrived. Bruegel demonstrates his innovative approach via a new genre: the perception of the world through what renders it visible—the phenomenon of light. Here are the first seeds of what will one day be known as impressionism. Therefore beyond, or rather in addition to, the work's meaning, there is painting purely for its own sake. The format—14½ x 21⅞ inches (37 x 55.5 centimeters), a third of the area of the synthesized views—lends itself to this approach. Impressionism would have to await the arrival of Monet's *Waterlilies* to become monumental; Corot, Boudin, Sisley, and Pissarro, right up to the haystacks by the painter of *Impression, Sunrise*, kept to an easel format.

Bruegel thus brings a new approach, which he continues with *The Adoration of the Magi in the Snow*, of 1567 (figs. 195–96), a village landscape where snowflakes, like people, are frozen instants, speaking for eternity in a place where there is building and life—Bruegel is sometimes closer to Cézanne than to

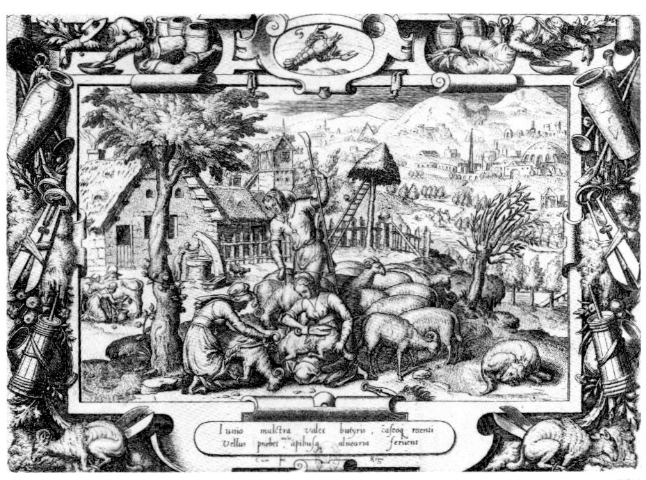

194

194. Étienne Delaune, *The Month of June*, 1558. Engraving, ca. 6⅞ x 9¼ in. (17.5 x 23.5 cm). Paris, Bibliothèque nationale de France

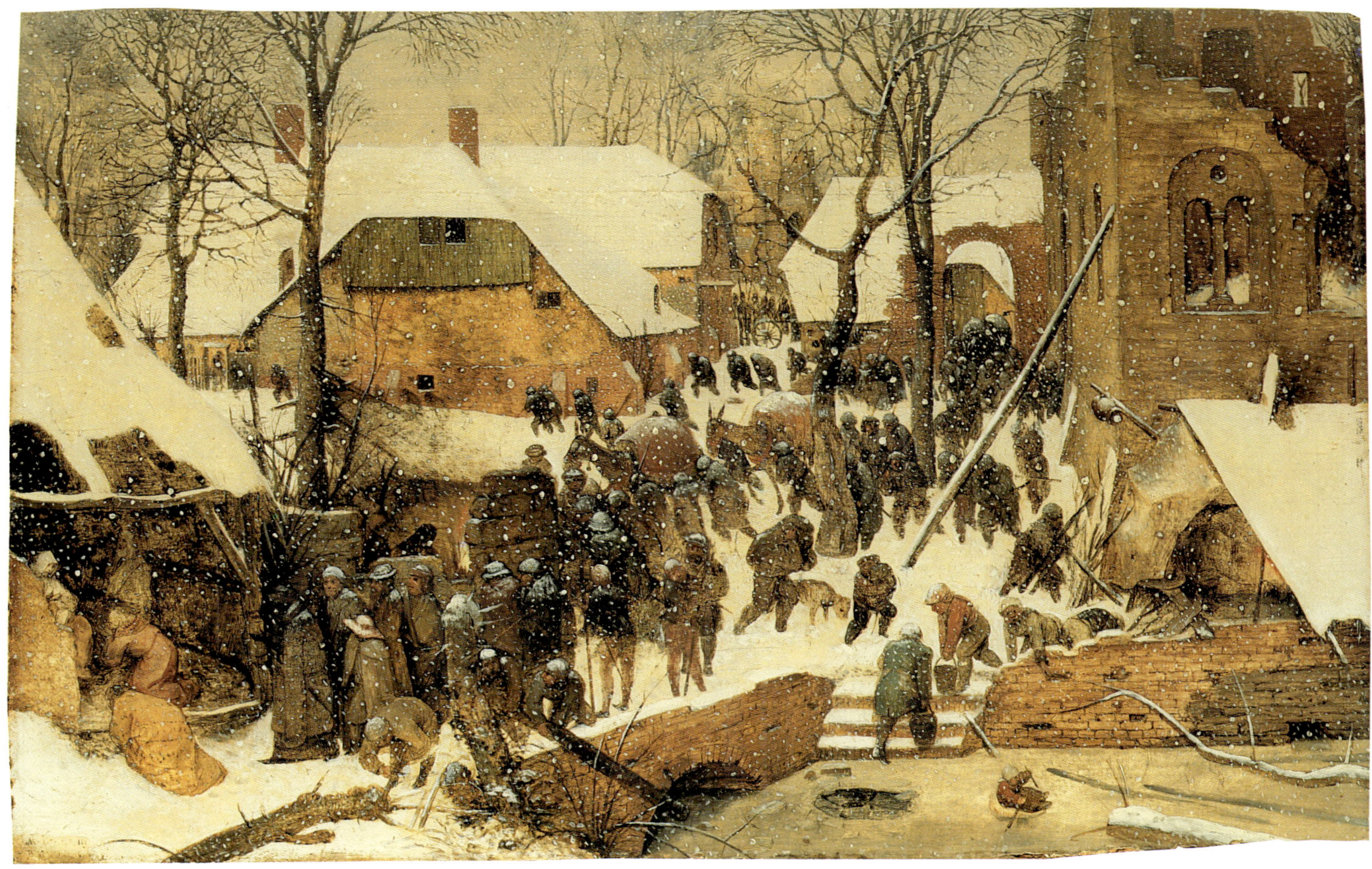

195

195–96. Pieter Bruegel, *The Adoration of the Magi in the Snow*, 1567: whole work and detail. Oil on panel, 13¾ x 21⅝ in. (35 x 55 cm). Winterthur, Oskar Reinhart collection

Monet—even though the snow falls according to its own, random rules. Aside from the religious scene, the hole in the ice—beneficial because water is drawn from it—resembles the one that lies in wait for the skaters in *Winter Landscape with Skaters and Bird Trap*. Both have more than a hint of the infernal hole in *St. James and the Magician Hermogenes*.

This luminous sequence ends with *The Magpie on the Gallows* (figs. 197 and 360), which Van Mander tells us was bequeathed to Bruegel's wife, with the words: "with the magpie he was referring to gossiping women, whom he was sending to the gallows."[105] This explanation hardly seems plausible. The bird remains on its perch, in the painting's exact center. Behind the gallows, a cross evokes torture. In 1568, this might well have been an allusion to repression, and thus to the Spanish forces who were on the rampage in Brussels, a theory that many writers have endorsed.[106] On the left, peasants are dancing: is joie de vivre winning? However, there is also a man defecating, a natural enough action, but an incongruous one in this spot. Is this meant to convey the contrast of life and death?[107] Or the foolishness of peasants before a magpie, a bird of Satan, symbolizing sin and defiance?[108] Could it be a depiction of a proverb, or an

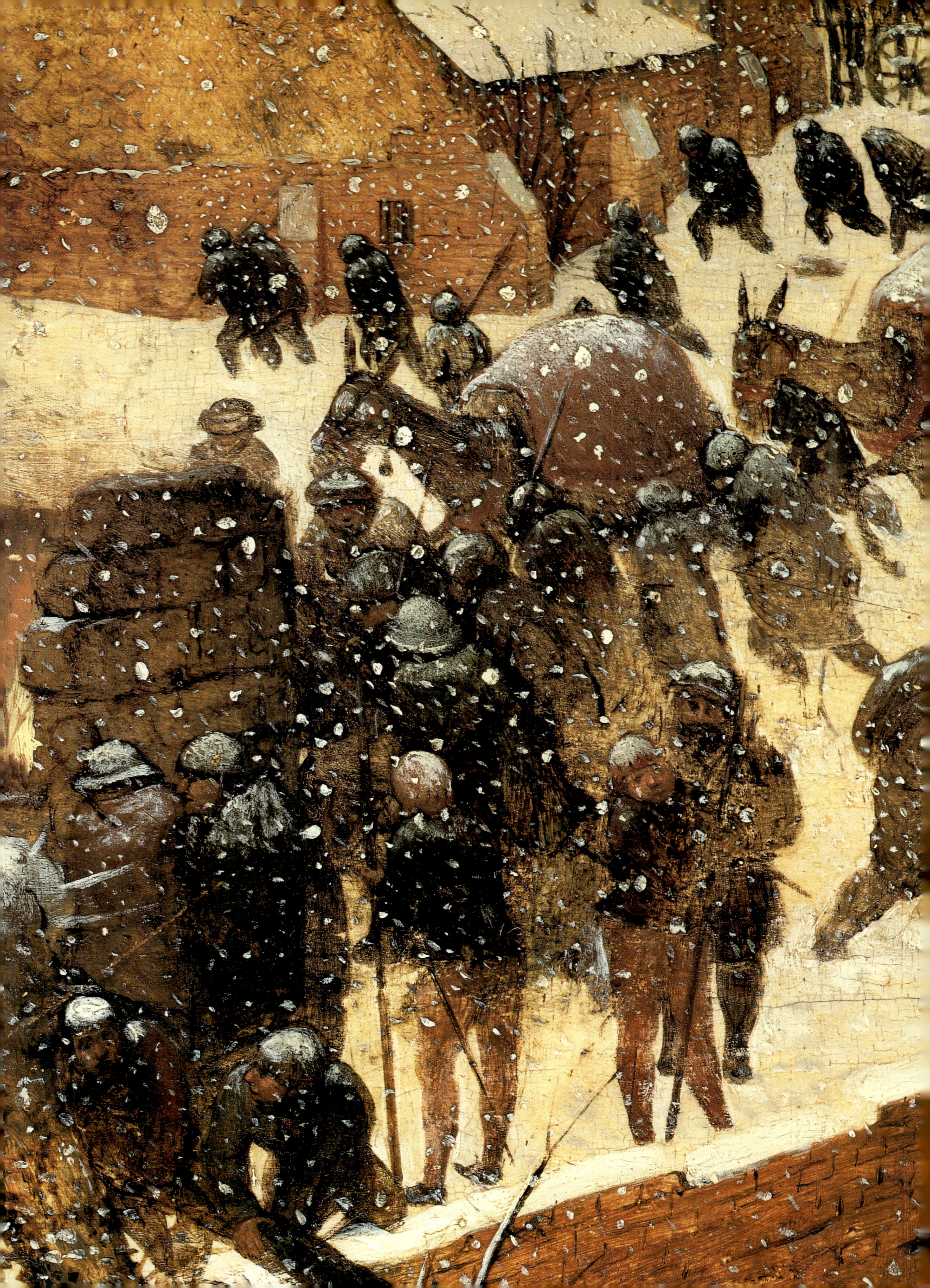

allegory? There are plenty of other things here to feed the imagination. Why not see, in the carefree circle of peasants, an echo of the watermill wheel, the inexorable passage of time? Might not the two trees framing the gallows be the two robbers on either side of the Cross? Nothing here either defines or restrains creation and our responses to it. *The Magpie on the Gallows* summarizes everything: joy, death premonition, flight, earthiness, wit. And the river flows on. As for the landscape, it exists in its own right purely by virtue of the light that goes from the rock in the foreground to the horizon, and well beyond the mist and the clouds. Lyrical the work certainly is, down to the shimmering of the leaves in the trees. While this is beyond question, some have commented that the painting's composition has a quality that predates the *Seasons*, and that it is thus obsolete—an opinion that is hard to share.[109]

While this work is testamentary, it inevitably sums up the elements of a life. Its form is not surprising for a work painted in 1568, but its lighting transcends all incidental detail. The scene, which is emphatically present with all its weighty questions, is set against the most extraordinary landscape Bruegel painted, the infinity of the world is lost in the most subtle nuances of the atmosphere. Color, which becomes light, foreshadows future centuries. In 1935 the playwright Michel de Ghelderode ended his play of the same name as the painting, with these words: "Then, as quiet returns to the spot, the magpie twitches on the crossbeam, black against the yellowing sky. It seems to chuckle, joining in the universal joy. Then it cries out bitterly: 'It's too beautiful!…' And the curtain falls; the farce is over."[110]

These three landscapes—*Winter Landscape with Skaters and Bird Trap, The Adoration of the Magi in the Snow,* and *The Magpie on the Gallows*—constitute an astounding chapter in the history of art. As early as 1562 the vision that would give birth to them was heralded by *Two Monkeys* (fig. 213). These animals—realistically depicted, allegorical, and no doubt tragic too—are silhouetted against a luminous landscape, already conveying a comforting impression of life and freedom. Light, the miracle of painting! Bruegel's palette was nature itself.

The master's special technique—freer, simpler, in which variations of tone density go beyond the sensitive play of colors to take on a spatial dimension—revolutionized the art of painting and, at the same time, that of molding volumes. Bruegel's landscapes are always alive; people are always present. Such is the landscapes' perfection that he could dispense with figures, yet, even were such a move imaginable, it would be mortal, and would make this wonderful world freeze. In nature, but with nature, Bruegel has shaped the natural life of men.

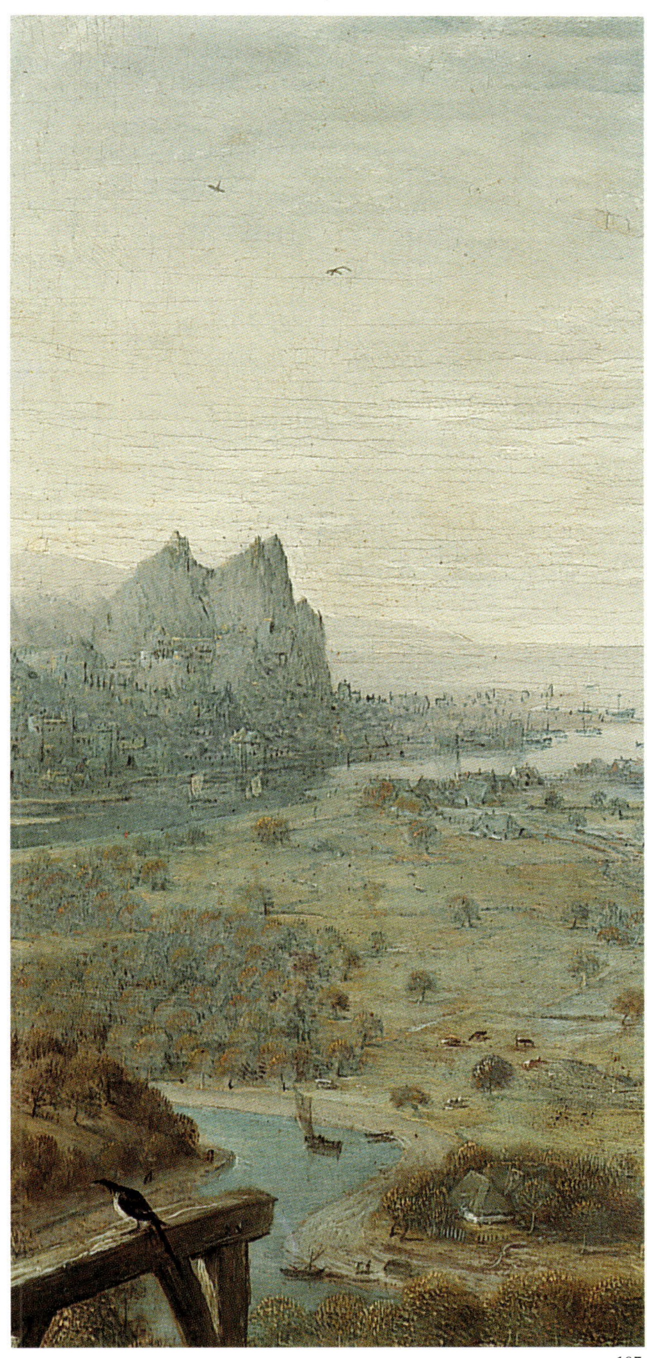

197

197. Pieter Bruegel, *The Magpie on the Gallows* (detail), 1568. Oil on panel, 18 x 20 in. (45.6 x 50.8 cm). Darmstadt, Hessisches Landesmuseum

THE HUMAN PRESENCE

In the Netherlands, before and during Bruegel's time, painters such as Aertsen (in *Return from a Pilgrimage to St. Anthony*, fig 198), Beuckelaer (in *A Day at the Fair*, fig. 199), Van Hemessen, and Van Amstel—who is identified with the Monogrammist of Brunswick—paid remarkable attention to everyday, working-class life and to realistic depiction of faces. This attention has often been underestimated, but it is based upon theatrical effects or picturesque anecdote. Intimate participation, integration, is not accomplished; we simply see animated scenes. Bruegel, on the other hand, achieves this integration to the full, from a *Haymaking* that links the fruits of the earth to human happiness, to *The Triumph of Death,* which connects the reign of the skeletons to the scorched earth. Man and nature have common cause; one is the mirror of the other. Human nature is rooted in it, just as the perennial movement of the sap and the sun inevitably crushes individual ambition. *The Tower of Babel*, in Rotterdam, is both a spiral of knowledge, a fatal anthill, and the image of pride. It is a figure in its own right, a powerful and terrible incarnation of the human, just as Mad Meg scours the countryside amid blood and fire, and as the laborer in *The Fall of Icarus* doggedly continues his toil. Here the laws of nature prevail over individual destiny, which is engulfed by the waves amid general indifference.

These are just some of the elements that forge the cellular, organic unity, the undivided depth, and multiple resonances of Pieter Bruegel's paintings. Has this lesson been learned or understood? Often, this is doubtful. A comic incident, an illustration of a popular proverb, a caustic detail, or a realistic depiction have caught people's eye, but without the reflective universe Bruegel proposes reaching the mind or the imagination. Did not Van Mander, while praising the artist, prefer the painter of country people? And is this surprising, given that the artist's contemporaries, and especially his own son Pieter Bruegel the Younger, copied and developed, not without talent, that aspect of his work?

The Census at Bethlehem (figs. 200–07) takes place neither in Judea, as St Luke's Gospel (II, 1–5) describes, nor in an imaginary setting, but in a small village of Brabant, gripped by snow and ice in the year of our Lord 1566. The previous year was particularly harsh, according to contemporary accounts.[111] Nevertheless, the painter has stepped back from the event itself, which he observes in detail, in a bird's-eye view, and which he simultaneously orchestrates with many allusions, contrasts, and ambiguous signs. We know that this biblical text is surrounded by doubt, because it only appeared in the Scriptures several years after the birth of Christ. Paintings of the episode—in which, following the edict of the emperor Augustus, Joseph travels to Bethlehem with the pregnant Mary—are rare, and Bruegel's is the most important example. It was, furthermore, copied by several artists.[112]

Why did Bruegel choose this theme? Was the biblical subject a pretext? It might well be, given the incidental nature of the protagonists, lost with the ox and the ass in the center of the composition, amid a crowd of other figures. The Virgin is in the same position in the painting as in *The Flight to Egypt*, but in that work she is alone with St. Joseph, and all the more visible because she is dressed in red.

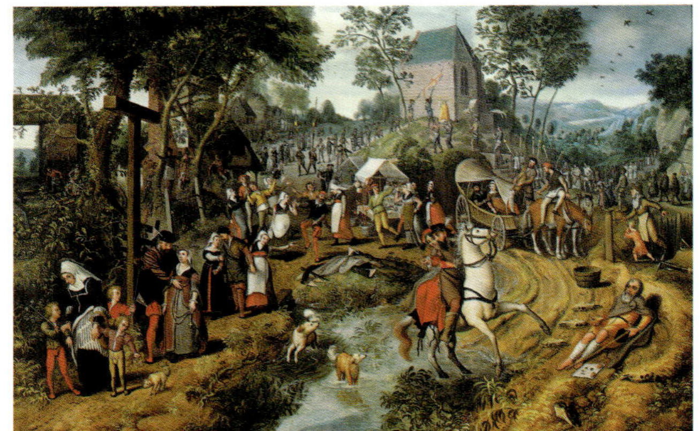

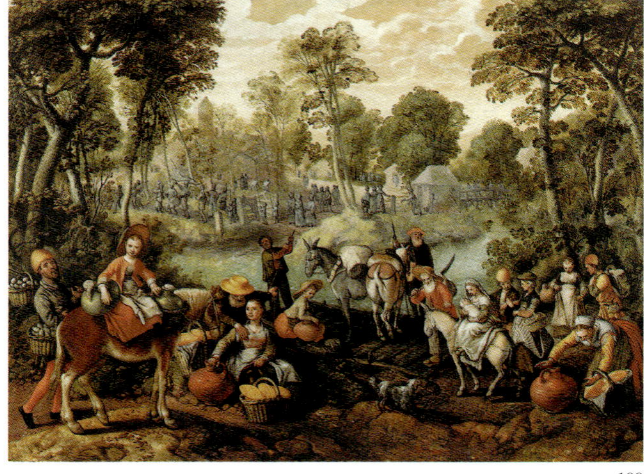

198. Pieter Aertsen, *Return from a Pilgrimage to St. Anthony*, ca. 1550. Oil on panel, 43¼ x 66⅞ in. (110 x 170 cm). Brussels, Musées royaux des Beaux-Arts de Belgique

199. Joachim Beuckelaer, *A Day at the Fair*, 1563. Oil on panel, 44¼ x 60⅜ in. (112.5 x 153.5 cm). Brussels, Musées royaux des Beaux-Arts de Belgique

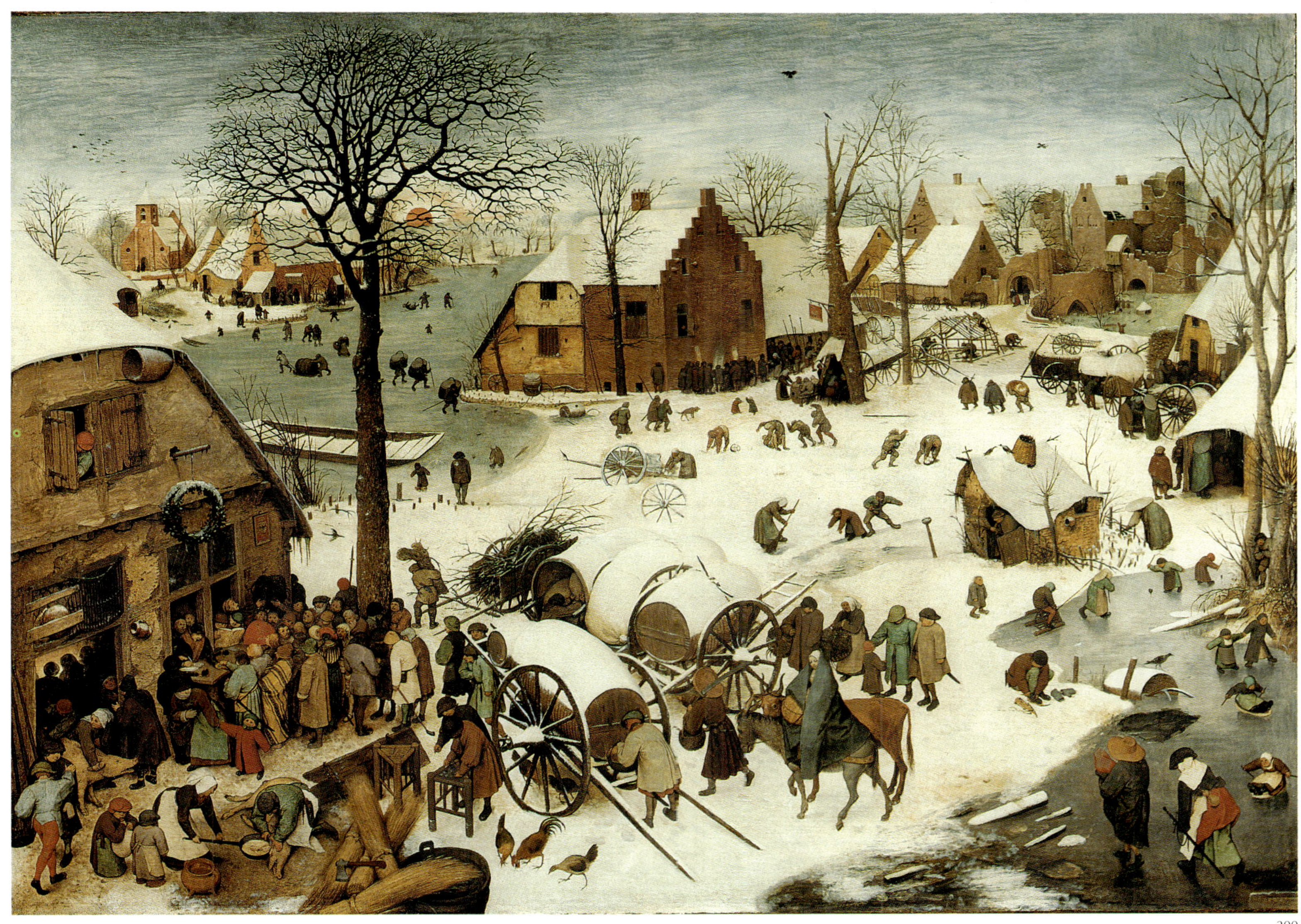

200

200–207. Pieter Bruegel, *The Census at Bethlehem*, 1566: whole work and details. Oil on panel, 45½ x 64⅜ in. (115.5 x 163.5 cm). Brussels, Musées royaux des Beaux-Arts de Belgique

Did the painter want to make the religious scene contemporary so as to endow it with more force for the people of his day? It seems not; more probably he simply used a chapter from the Scriptures to illustrate a slice of life. Indeed, the painting faithfully depicts taxes being collected, for which reason it is sometimes known under the title *The Payment of Tithes*. Gathered in front of an inn, whose sign shows a green wreath and a placard bearing the coat of arms of Charles V, a group of people do their duty as taxpayers. The tax collector is a common theme in the sixteenth century, when monetary matters were a concern, and in the Netherlands artists such as Quentin Metsys, with his famous *The Money-Changer and his Wife*, and Marinus van Reymerswaele painted it.

Bruegel does not however limit his painting to just two meanings: a religious one, perhaps rooted in medieval mysteries,[113] and an economic one, clearly aimed at those in power. Both are elements in a composition with many sides, which lends itself to many theories and stimulates the curiosity of the ordinary viewer and scholar alike. Thus the solid-looking church, on the upper left of the picture—an anachronism, for the Savior is not yet born—contrasts with the dilapidated hovel

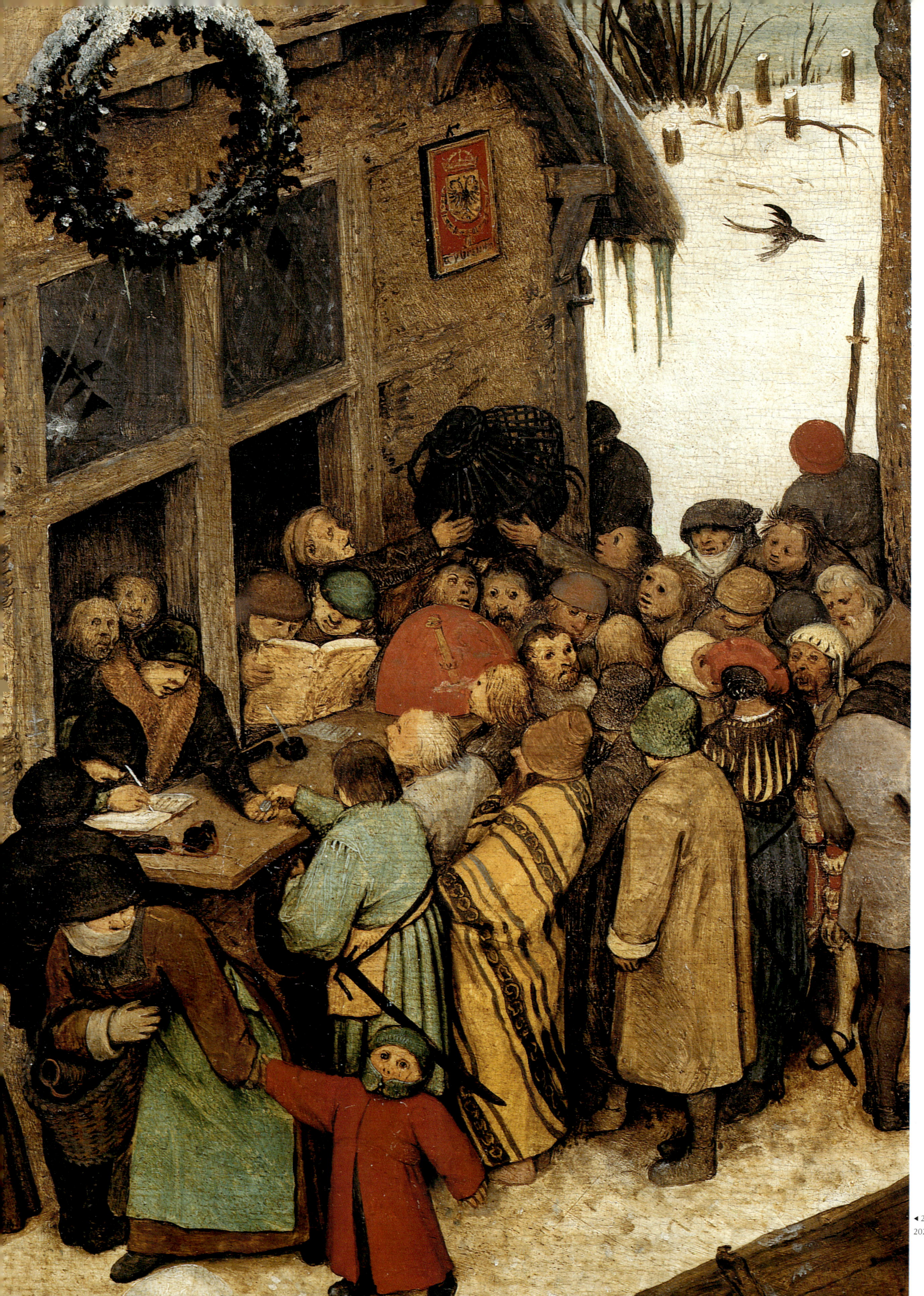

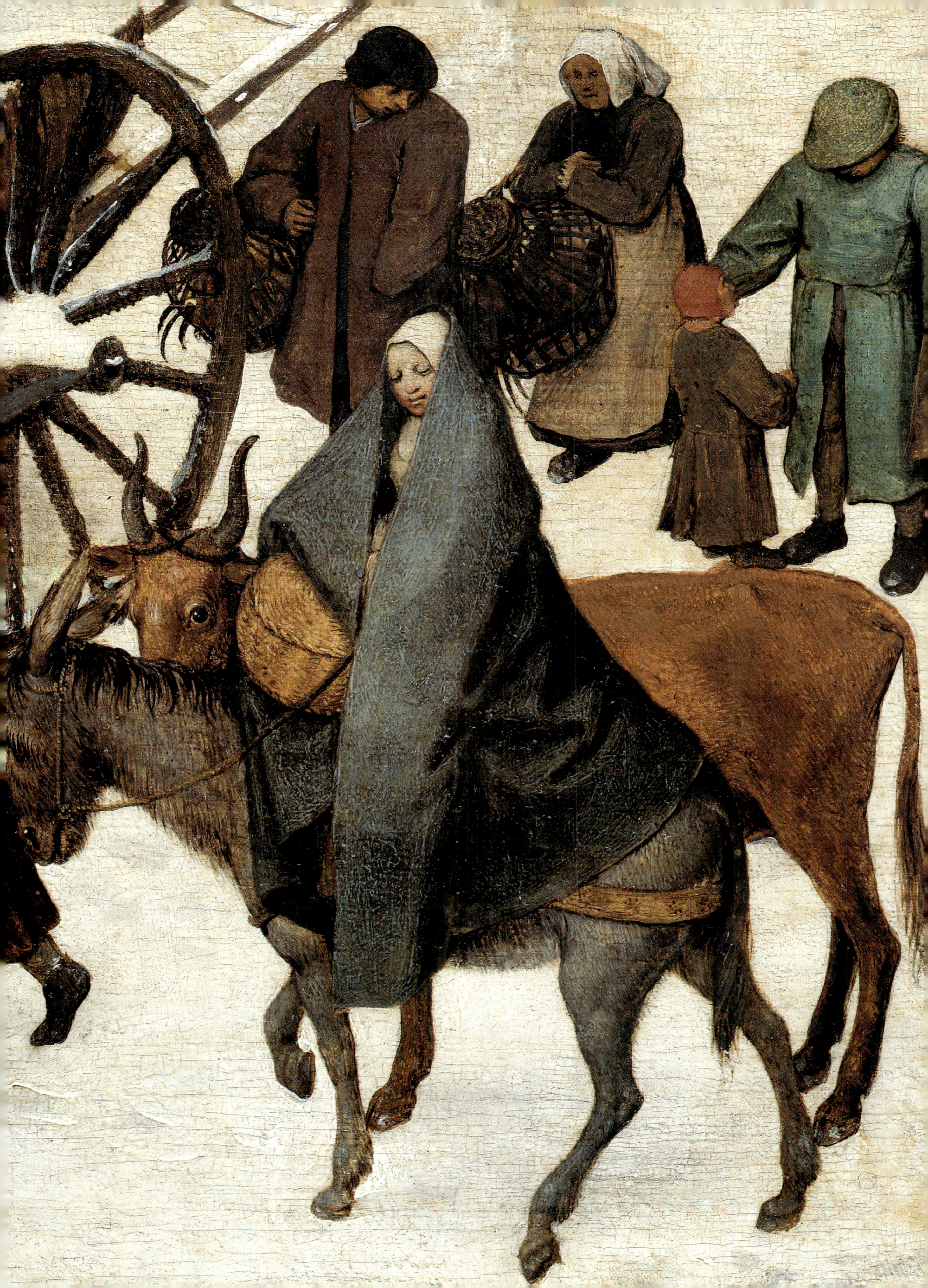

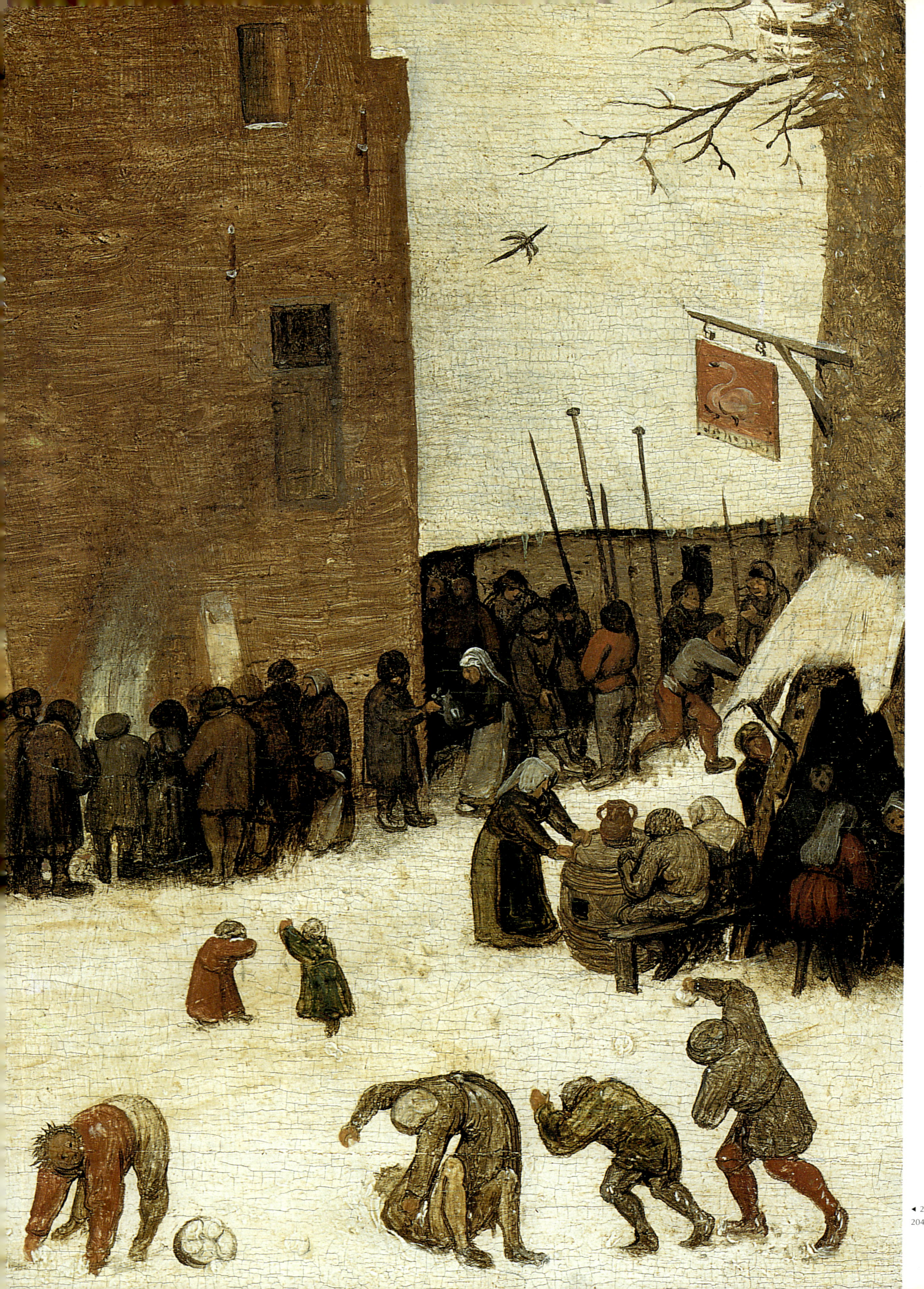

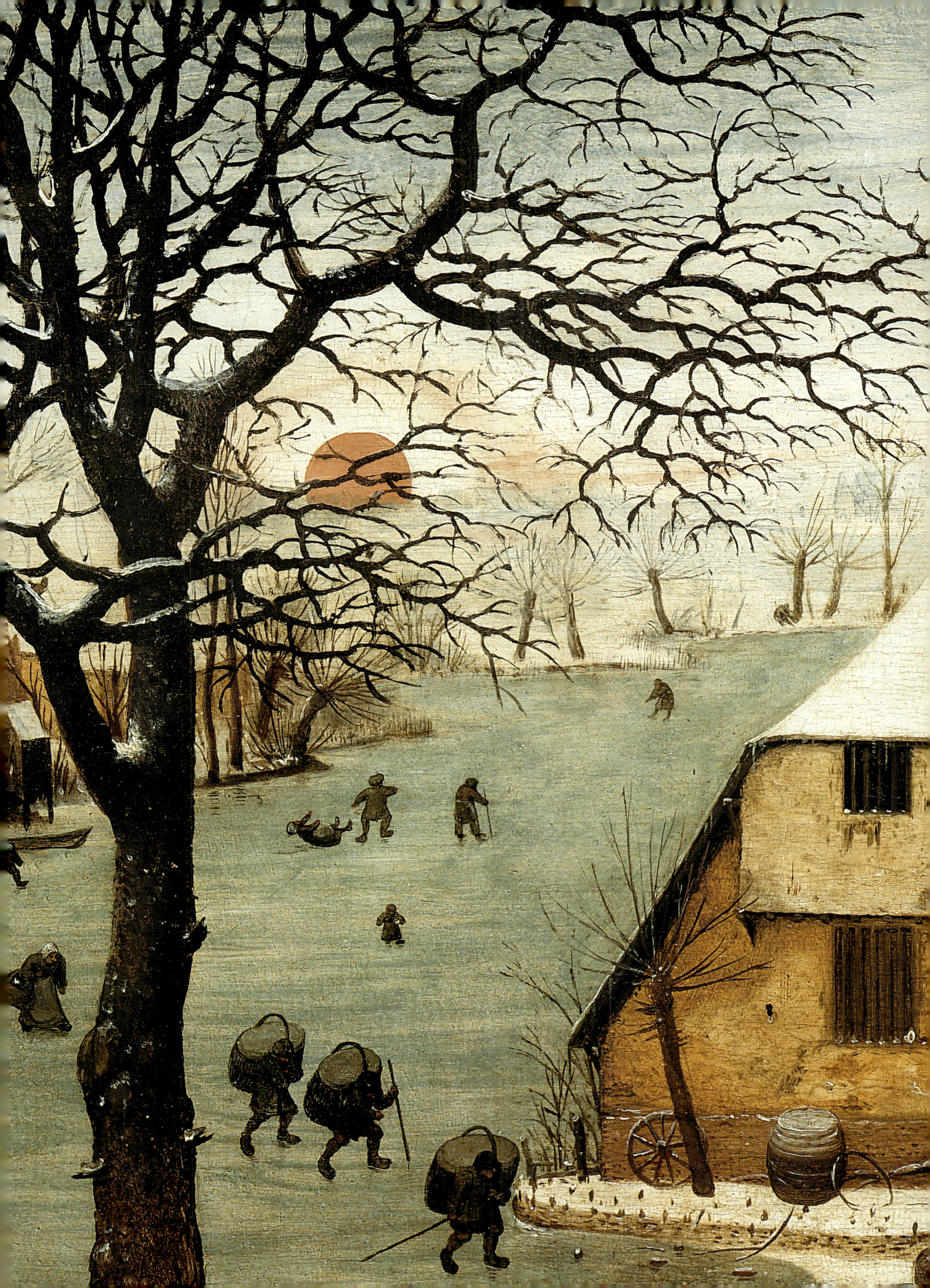

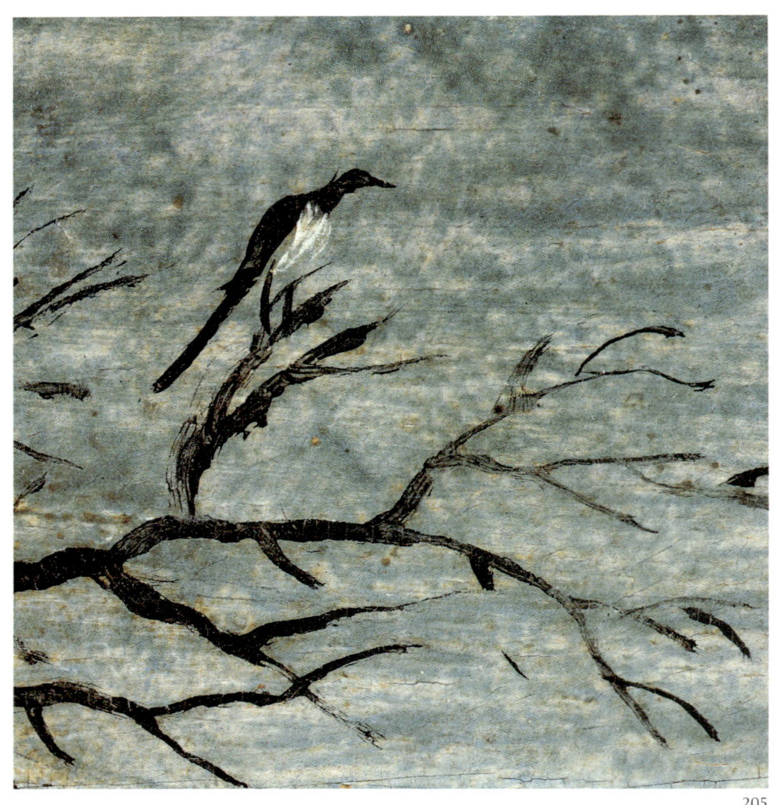

205

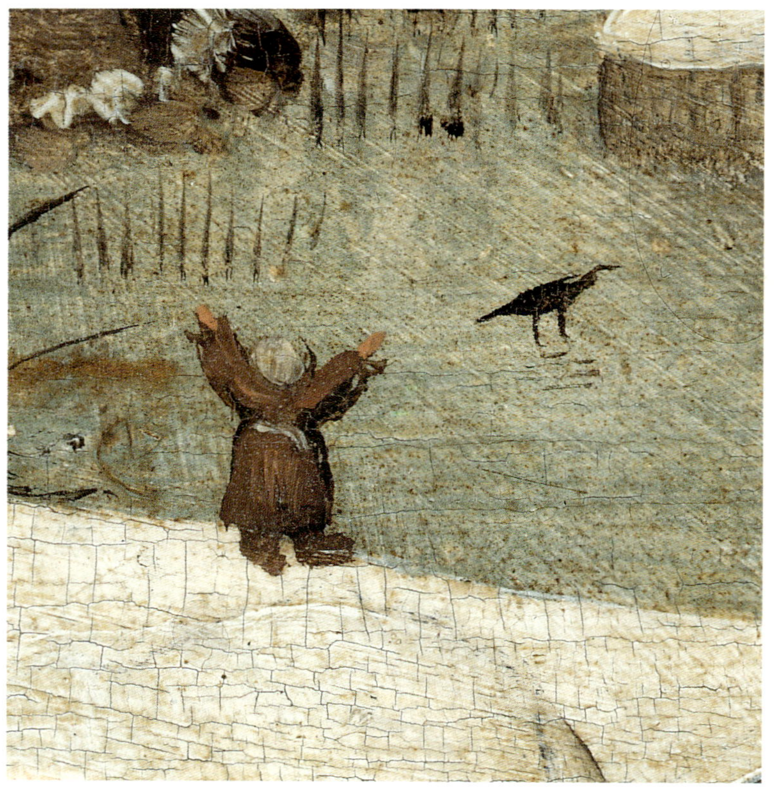

206

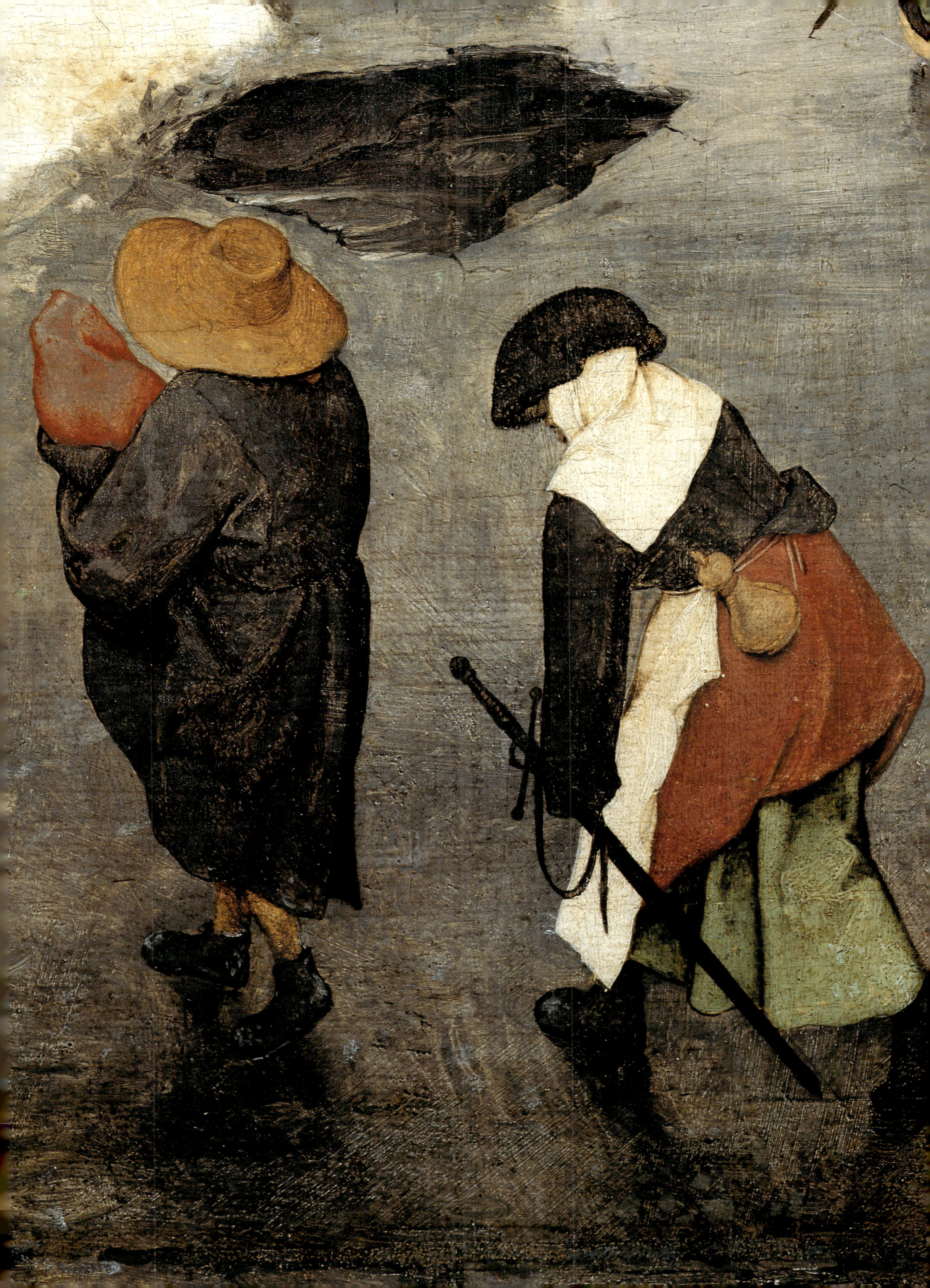

of the plague sufferer on the right. The inn, on whose threshold a pig is having its throat cut (a familiar theme in illuminations such as those of the *Mayer van den Bergh Breviary*, fig. 208),[114] finds an echo, in the middle distance, in a hollow tree with a sign of a swan, a place of disrepute which, in the work of Hieronymus Bosch, conceals a woman who symbolizes sin. In the distance are the ruins of a town which some have wrongly assumed is Amsterdam—on the basis of drawings from 1562, previously attributed to Bruegel, depicting the ramparts of that city— and which for others symbolize the downfall of paganism.[115] (This theory can be compared to that advanced regarding the dilapidated building on the right of *The Adoration of the Magi in the Snow*).[116] In front of the ruins in the *Census* people are busy erecting a new building, presumed symbol of a new religion, in which case the wooden outhouse could even be the stable in Bethlehem.[117] Thus we could tirelessly stroll around this painting, identifying everywhere signs that reflect the religious, political, and social concerns of the time. Moving around it we come across a wealth of episodes from daily and rural life: men at work with their tools, children playing, household tasks, loaded, empty, or overturned carts, and, scattered across the entire painting, about forty spoked wheels.

Some have seen a companion painting to the *Census* in *The Massacre of the Innocents*,[118] consequently stressing, by intuition, the anxious feeling of the open, spacious, animated composition. Tolnay even saw, in the right-hand group in which a man carries a child over the ice, an allusion to the flight into Egypt,[119] perhaps because fifteenth-century illuminations sometimes combine the massacre and the flight on the same page.[120] The painting lends itself to such prolonged pondering and numerous diversions. The details it contains and the thoughts it awakens are an emphatic statement of the richness, diversity, and complexity of Bruegel's world, and above all, objectively, of the interpenetration of man and nature.

While the *Census* could be described as panoramic, *The Bird-Nester* (figs. 209–10) narrows down its subject. A large figure in the foreground points accusingly at someone who is up a tree, robbing a nest. There are tree trunks, leaves, flowers, and a peaceful farm and its ponds in the background, fed by a stream that flows at the feet of the first character who, absorbed by the act he is denouncing, is about to fall into it. He is not blind, but someone who thinks he can see: the mote and the beam, in a sense. A proverb, therefore: but what lesson is to be drawn from it? Should we see didacticism here, because some of Bruegel's works can be read thus? If so, what idea is depicted? We are inevitably reminded of *The Beekeepers* (fig. 85)—where there is also a robber of birds' nests, and whose inscription underlines the difference between knowing where the nest is and possessing it:[121] the difference between passivity and action. But such an exegesis is only partly satisfying. The work may contain symbols—the bramble bush, the iris, the falling hat[122]—as well as references to the poems of Anna Bijns, Sebastian Brant's *Ship of Fools*, or to *The Mirror of Love*.[123]

There are other examples of bird's nest robbers in art aside from *The Beekeepers*: a drawing in the Uffizi in Florence, a work by David Vinckboons, and some copies of it.[124] While most historians agree that Bruegel's painting of the peasant shows the influence of Michelangelo, none can offer a convincing

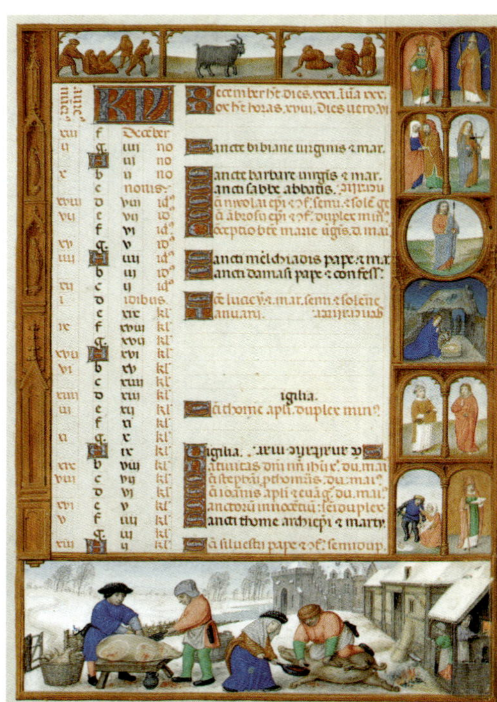

208. Attributed to Simon Bening, *The Month of December*, Mayer van den Bergh Breviary, ca. 1510, fol. 7. Miniature on parchment, 8¾ x 6¼ in. (22.4 x 16 cm). Antwerp, Museum Mayer van den Bergh

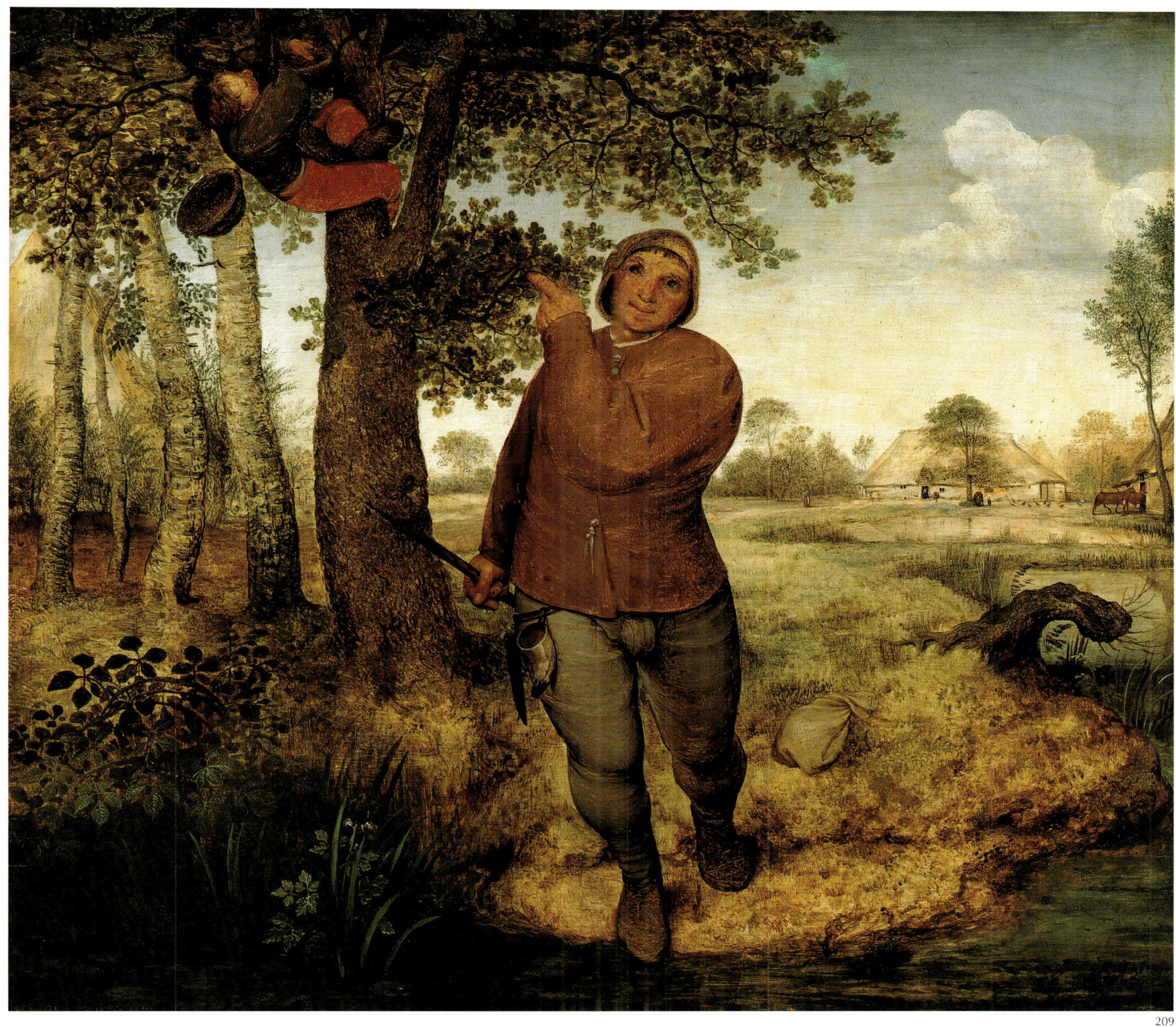

209–10. Pieter Bruegel, *The Bird-Nester*, 1568: whole work and detail. Oil on panel, 23⅜ x 26⅞ in. (59.3 x 68.3 cm). Vienna, Kunsthistorisches Museum

explanation of this scene. Is one even necessary? Is it not enough to find in it an ancient and eternal wisdom according to which, if we denounce the transgressions of others, we overlook our own destiny? Nevertheless, given the difference of scale between the two characters (which is not justified by the distance between them, and which no one seems to have noticed), doesn't this amusing scene also show an adult taking aside a spectator and mocking a youthful escapade, while not looking where he himself is going? Pierre Francastel wrote: "We can indeed interpret it just as much from the peasant's point of view as from the boy's or the spectator's. For, in the final analysis, is it always desirable to possess the nest? It might be

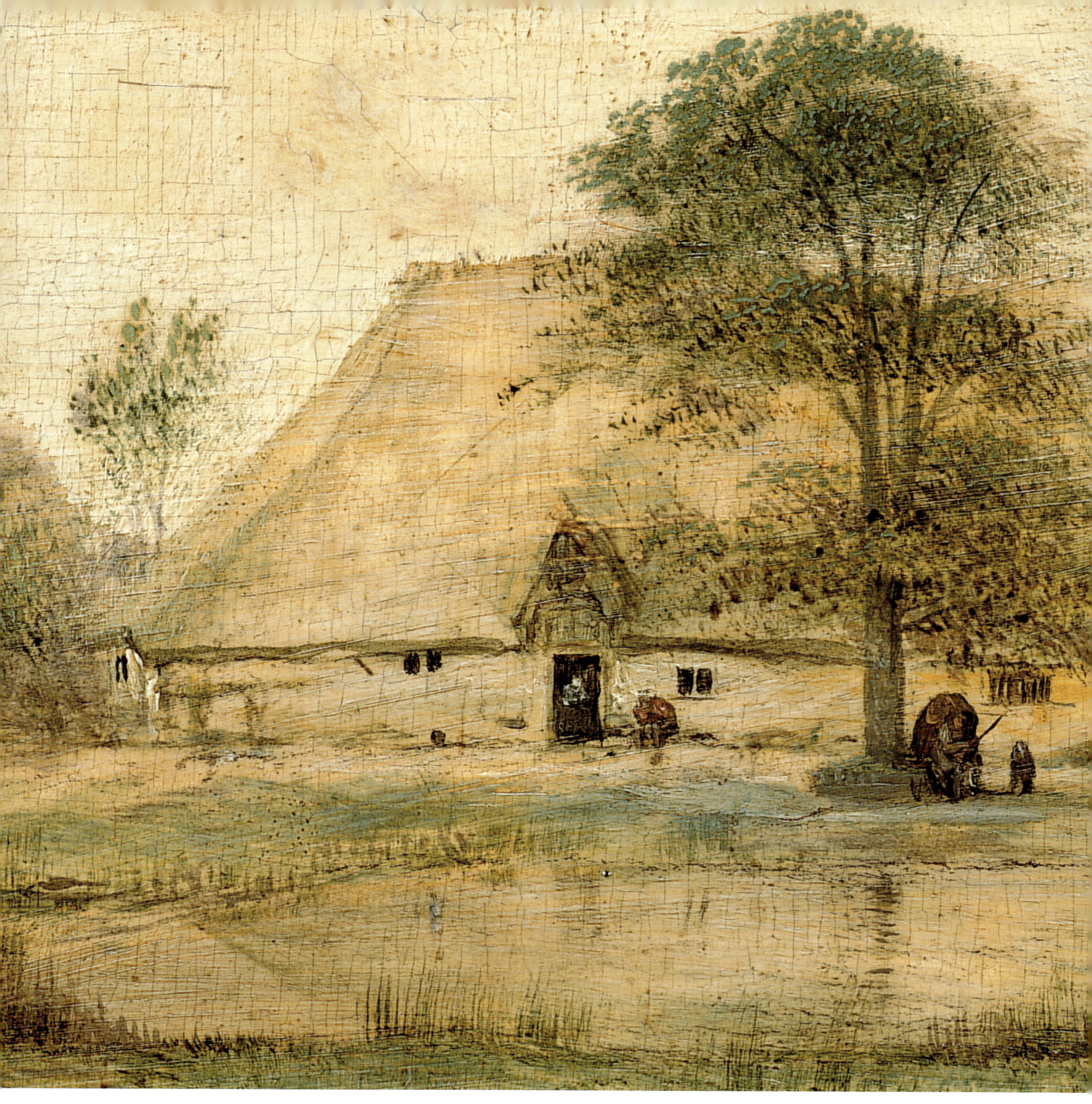

compromising. Or it might be more interesting to let the young birds grow up. Every act is ambiguous, every episode serves different purposes for different people. What is important is to capture the signs and set them within a problem structure that suits each case."[125]

Perhaps this demonstrates that a work by Bruegel always remains marvelously open. This one intimately links man and nature, and shows that the mistake of the one can be sanctioned, not without humor, by the other. This painting, made in 1568, was part of the Archduke Leopold William's collection. It has been

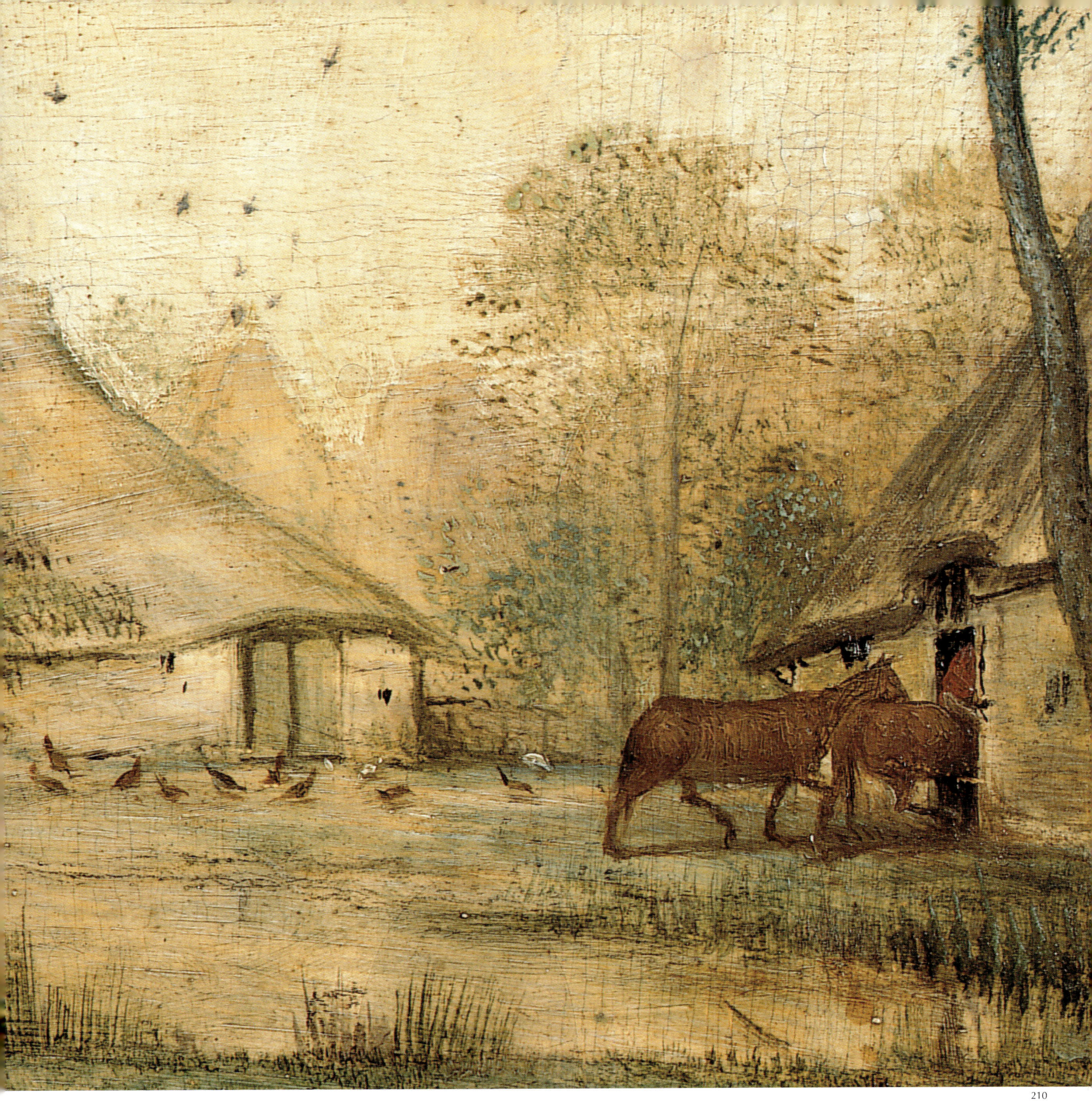

trimmed along the bottom, and especially on the right edge, by some 4 inches (10 centimeters).[126] It displays wonderful technical skill, with broad touches and unity of color: gray (the peasant's trousers), reddish brown (his face, jacket, the tree, the wood), green (dark in the marshy areas, gentle elsewhere), and the red note of the bird nest robber. The masterliness of form rules out all discussion, emphasizing mystery and poetry instead. We sense something, but we don't know why. Something luminous, timeless, and which concerns us because, here, man is the greater.

SOCIETY AND THE HUMAN CONDITION

Do the *Two Monkeys* (fig. 213) in the arched embrasure represent chained men? This painting from 1562 seems to represent power and refinement at the same time. The animals trace a perfect spiral from the central ring to the arch and, despite the small size of the work—it measures 7⅞ x 9⅛ inches (19.8 x 23.2 cm)— these are Bruegel's first monumental figures. They are silhouetted against a bright background, harmoniously painted with an impressionist feel, where we glimpse the Scheldt river, the city of Antwerp, and its cathedral. In its dimensions, and by its contrast between the animals' captivity and the freedom of the landscape, the painting could be said to foreshadow *The Beggars* (fig. 258) of 1568, where the men's physical wretchedness contrasts with the spring greenery.

The theme of the captive monkey is a common one, and Bruegel may have been inspired by the engravings of the German artist Israel van Meckenem (fig. 212), whose work has been linked to the drawings of Pisanello.[127] The theme appears in Brabant itself, in the church of Notre-Dame de Lombeek, in the carved altarpiece depicting the life of the Virgin (1512–16), where the monkey is also depicted chained under an arch (fig. 211). In Bruegel's work a monkey can be seen playing on the shoulder of one of the faithful in *The Adoration of the Magi*, the painting in distemper in the Brussels museum. Some have seen the Berlin painting as symbolic of something historic[128]—of the subjugation of the Flemish provinces,[129] for example, of despair,[130] of the human soul, blind and unhappy[131]— or even as a satire of the character of the citizens of Antwerp.[132] Others have simply seen it as a realistic depiction of a rare and clearly identifiable simian species: the red-headed colobus.[133]

In 1983 Adolf Monballieu gave a precise exegesis of the work that gave it a humorous dimension and linked it to a historical event. Robert Genaille took it up, and summarized it thus:

> In the language and usage of the Low Countries, as archive documents prove, there existed a similarity of sound that allowed a pun between the French "singerie" [monkey tricks] and the Brabant corruption of the French word "seigneurie" [lordship, or sovereignty]. From the fourteenth to the sixteenth centuries there was constant competition for the "singerie" of the Scheldt between the count of Flanders (allied with France) and the duchy of Brabant (which, with the marquisate of Antwerp, was part of the German Empire): one ruling on the left bank, the other on the right. In Bruegel's time the situation changed: the Count of Hoorn, lord of the left bank, ran into financial problems and found a buyer in the city of Antwerp. But the ruling power opposed this and, in 1562 the Emperor, master of the game, maintained in effect the status quo which gave him absolute power, and removed all room for maneuver from the two rivals, thus *chaining* them.[134]

In its own time, therefore, this work might have raised a smile. However, one explanation does not necessarily rule out another. A precise meaning, limited to

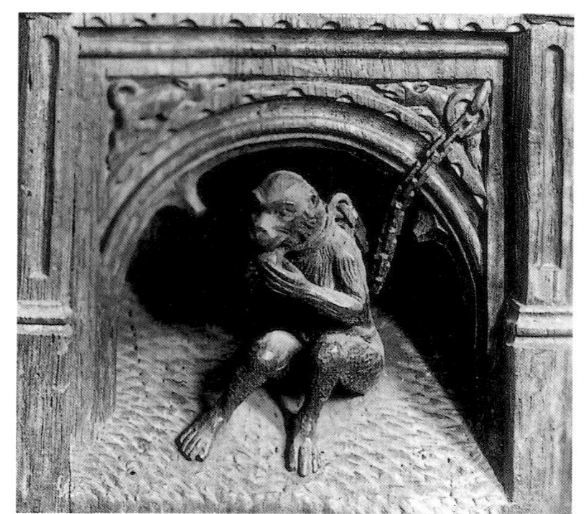

211

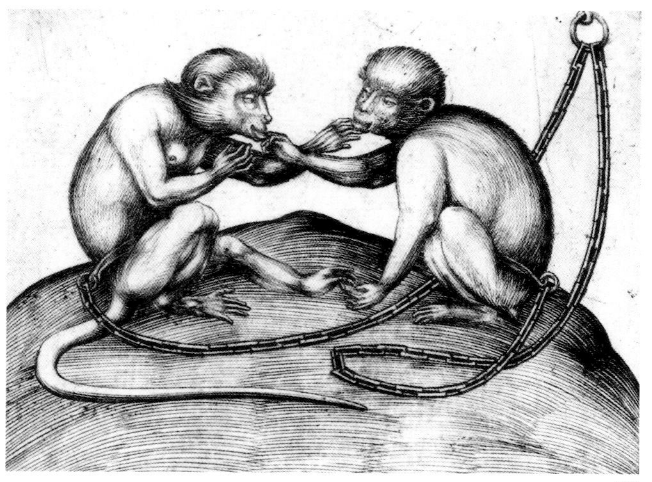

212

211. Anonymous, *Altarpiece of the Life of the Virgin* (detail), ca. 1520–30. Wood. Lombeek, Church of Notre-Dame

212. Israel van Meckenem, *Two Chained Monkeys*, ca. 1500. Engraving, ca. 3¼ x 4⅜ in. (8.3 x 11.3 cm). Paris, Bibliothèque nationale de France, print department, reserve collection

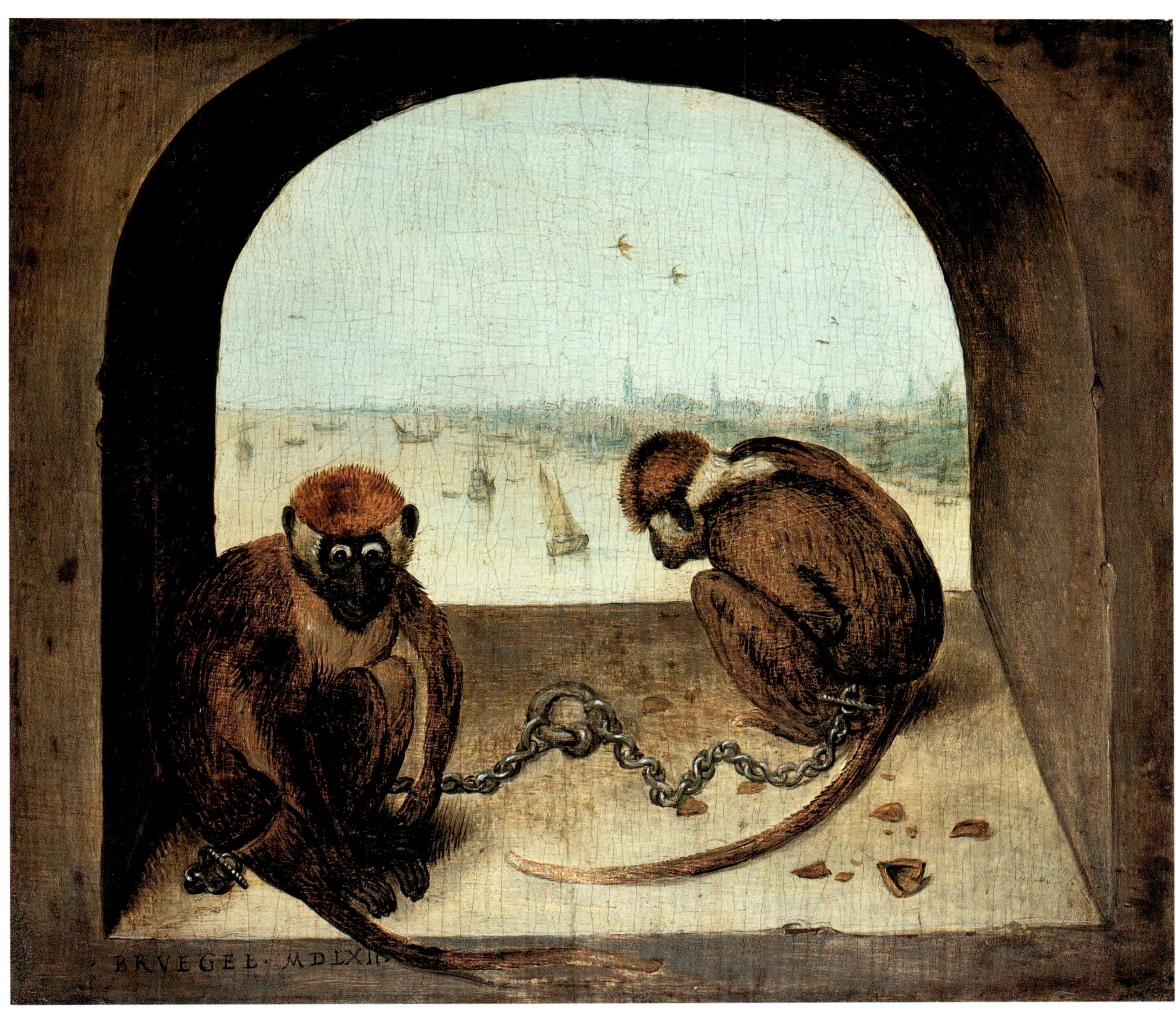

213. Pieter Bruegel, *Two Monkeys*, 1562. Oil on wood, 7⅞ x 9⅛ in. (19.8 x 23.2 cm). Berlin, Staatliche Museen, Gemäldegalerie

one event and to the eyes of those in the know, is charged here, as with all works that transcend events, with an image that seems to communicate a universal meaning. Without going too deeply into the symbolism that the work might have evoked in the sixteenth century, a sentence from Carl Gustav Stridbeck bears quoting: "The two monkeys represent humanity living in a way that is in itself a punishment and a misfortune."[135] Perhaps Bruegel found this subject in a local event, but he went beyond it to create a masterpiece from the close relationship of its formal expression and its emotional power.

The condition of the two monkeys is in any case very "human" if we compare it to that of the two chained and shackled men in a similar composition, which also has an arched embrasure, although with a dark background: This is a prison, which can be seen at the right of *Hope* (fig. 214), a drawing Bruegel made in 1559. It belongs

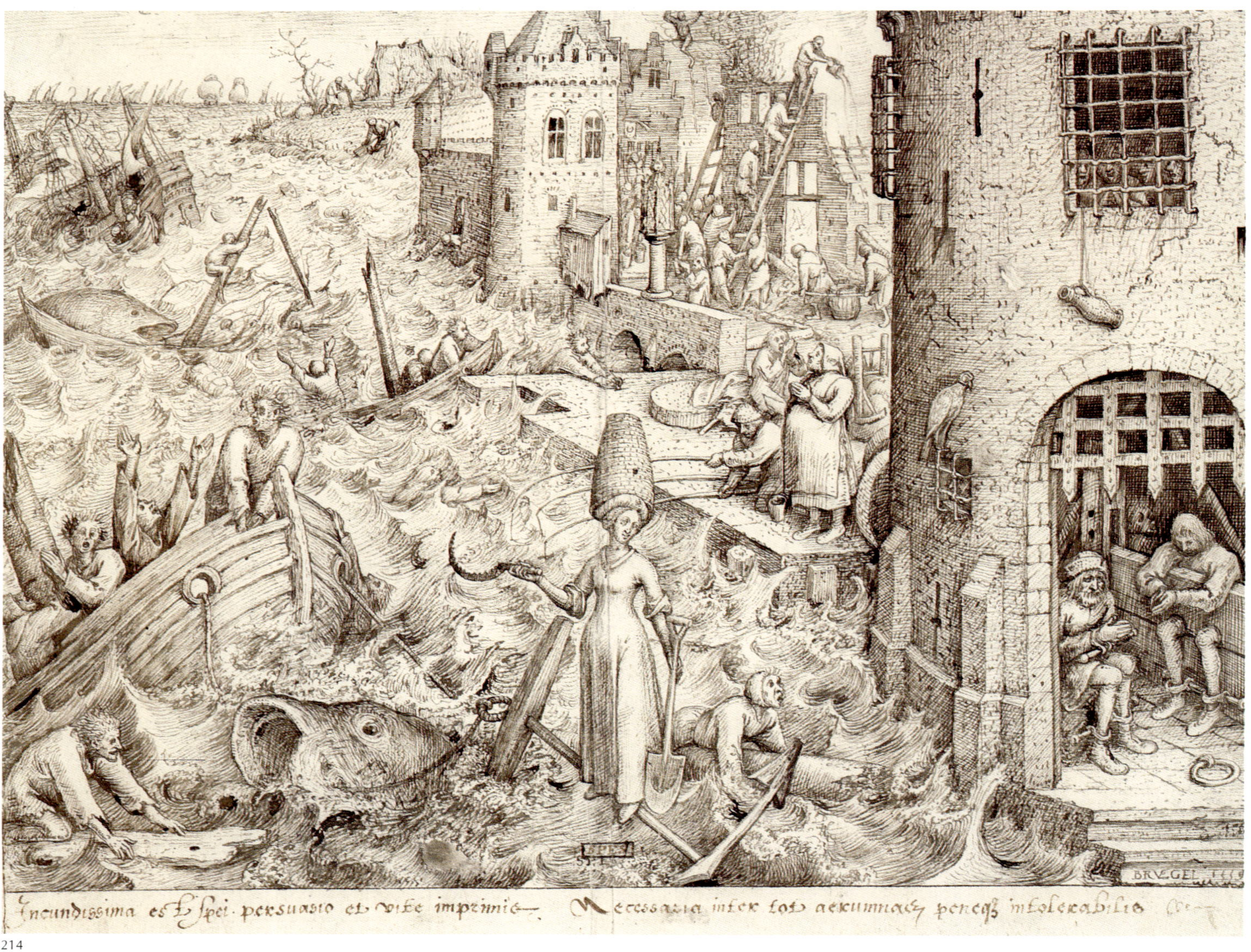

214

214. Pieter Bruegel, *Hope,* from the *Virtues* series, 1559.
Pen and brown ink, 8¾ x 11⅝ in. (22.3 x 29.5 cm).
Berlin, Staatliche Museen, Kupferstichkabinett

to the series of seven drawings in pen and brown ink that the artist made in 1559–60 for the *Virtues,* another series published by Hieronymus Cock. The engravings made from these drawings can be reliably attributed to Philipp Galle.

THE *VIRTUES*

While humans are threatened by their sins—and Bruegel has demonstrated the horror and fear of this in his *Deadly Sins*—the *Virtues,* which we might expect to be serene, are demanding and sometimes distressing works. The figures representing *Spes,* or *Hope* (fig. 214), indeed seem besieged, swamped by an angry sea that is wrecking ships and pounding the fortifications of a town where other dramas are unfolding.

These threats are clearly identifiable, and the *Virtues* series in general differs from the *Deadly Sins* in that it alludes to real situations. Great and voracious fish, sinking, dismasted boats, and men in peril of drowning dominate the left side of the picture. There is a chance of survival, but sheer terror makes the desperate sailors' hair literally stand on end. In the fortified town battered by the waves on

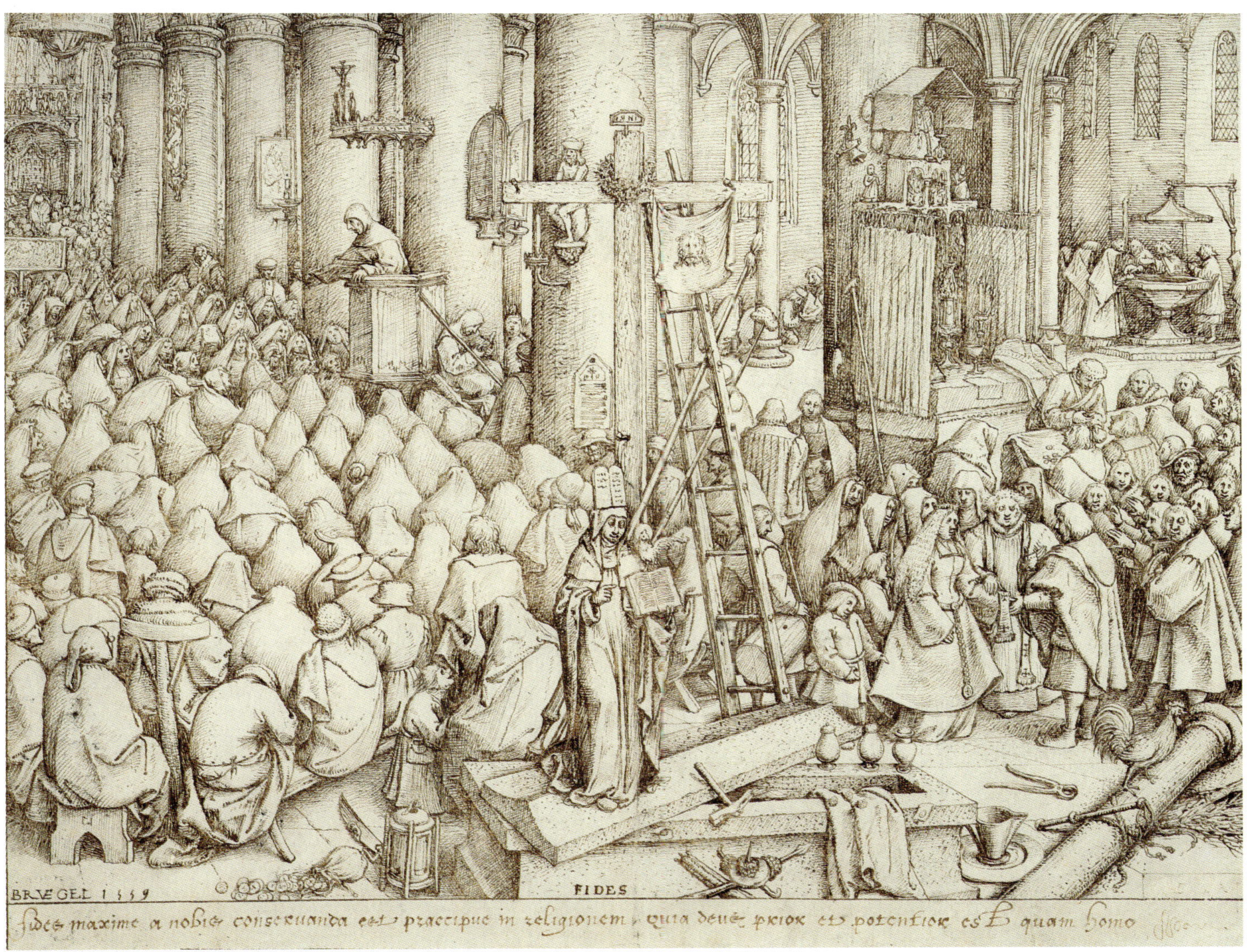

215

215. Pieter Bruegel, *Faith*, from the *Virtues* series, 1559. Pen and brown ink, 8⅞ x 11⅝ in. (22.5 x 29.5 cm). Amsterdam, Rijksmuseum, Rijksprentenkabinet

the right, prisoners are praying for delivery. The hooded falcon perched on the wider grate may refer to the hope of light following darkness.[136] A pregnant woman standing on the mole prays for a successful delivery, while a fisherman beside her is hopefully casting his lines in the water; in the near distance, men are busy putting out a fire. Although in the far distance two men appear to be calmly working the land, and a fleet of ships in a fair wind can be seen on the horizon, the hope embodied by them is vague and far off.

Bruegel humanizes the virtues, while he demonizes the vices. This is a real distinction, but there are inevitably nuances to it. Where he depicts depravity, he shows it in action, giving the leading role to the bestiality that carries his protagonists away. When he portrays the virtues, he tries to show how they can serve humanity, and presents circumstances where they are useful to it. The two series are thus parallel but different, describing cause and effect in each case, with varying degrees of realism and fantasy, optimism and pessimism. While they contrast in spirit and in subject matter, their compositions demand to be read in an identical manner. In both series, figures and scenes are grouped around a personification of the intended virtue or sin, always a female figure, who is accompanied by her attributes. The surrounding scenes are related to the allegory represented; they

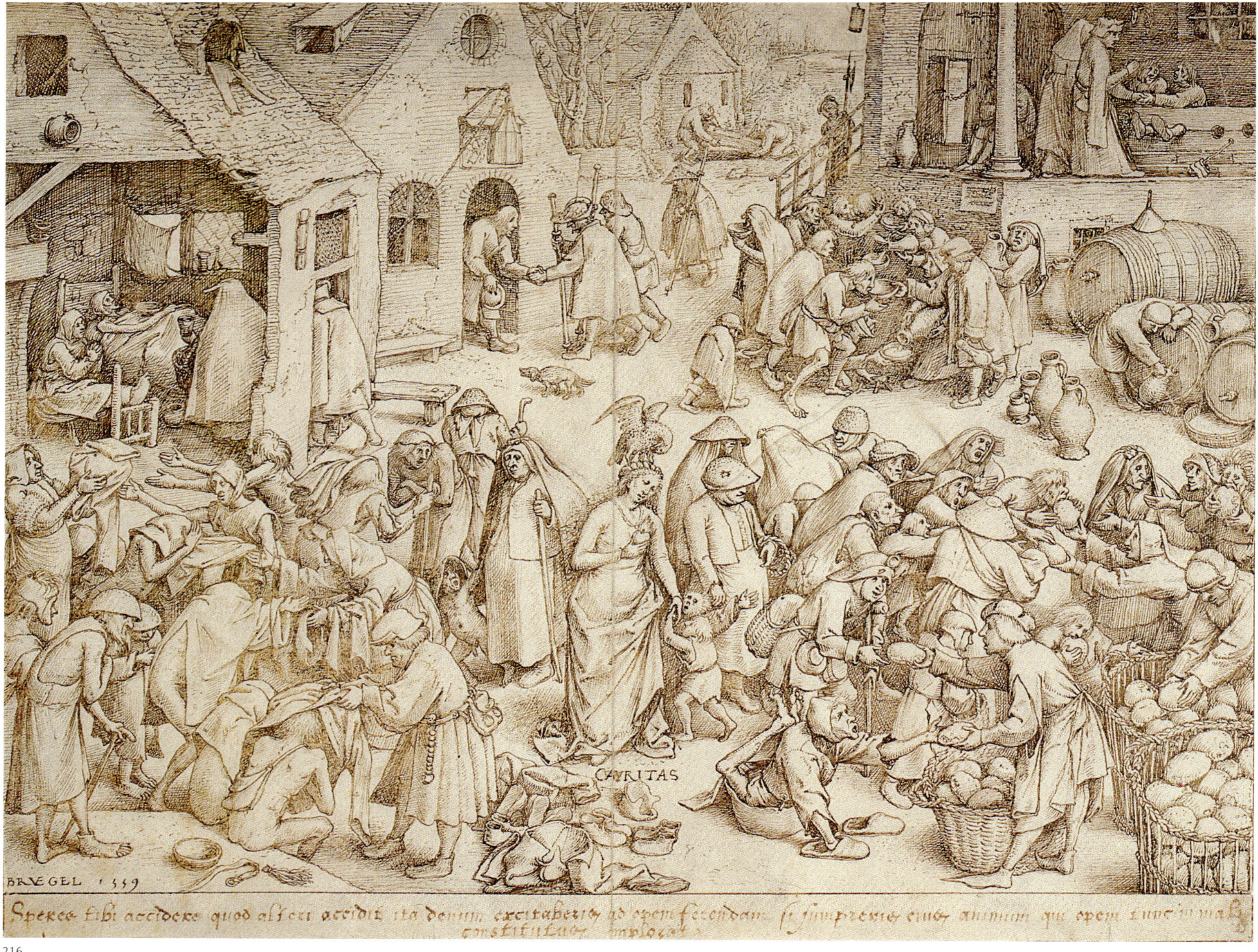

216. Pieter Bruegel, *Charity*, from the *Virtues* series, 1559.
Pen and brown ink, 8⅞ x 11¾ in. (22.4 x 29.9 cm).
Rotterdam, Museum Boijmans Van Beuningen

FACING PAGE
217. Pieter Bruegel, *Justice*, from the *Virtues* series, 1559.
Pen and brown ink, 8⅞ x 11⅝ in. (22.4 x 29.5 cm).
Brussels, Bibliothèque royale Albert I, print room

218. Jacques Callot, *Tortures* (detail), ca. 1630. Black chalk and
bistre wash, 4½ x 8⅝ in. (11.3 x 22 cm). London, British Museum

unfold panoramically and encyclopedically, with clear didactic intent and arranged
with pleasing harmony. The *Sins* refer chiefly to the imaginary; the *Virtues* are
more concerned with reality—although there are reciprocal references too. The
two series form a whole, in a sense weighing up good and evil, warnings and advice,
dangerous dreams and painful reality.

The *Virtues* are seven in number: first, the three theological virtues, Faith, Hope,
and Charity, followed by the four cardinal virtues, Justice, Prudence, Temperance,
and Fortitude. *Fides,* or *Faith* (fig. 215), comes first. Each plate is accompanied by a
saying or motto in Latin, in this case the reminder that as God came before all things
and is more powerful than humanity, we should all keep the faith and observe our
religious duties. Faith is represented by a figure dressed as a nun standing on the
cover of Christ's tomb and bearing on her head the Tablets of the Law. She holds a
copy of the New Testament, on which is perched the dove of the Holy Spirit, the incarnation of faith. Around her are objects relating to the Passion of Christ: Judas's
pieces of silver, Peter's sword, the Cross, the crown of thorns, the veil of St. Veronica,
the lance of St. Longinus, the column of the flagellation, the cockerel, the bowl in

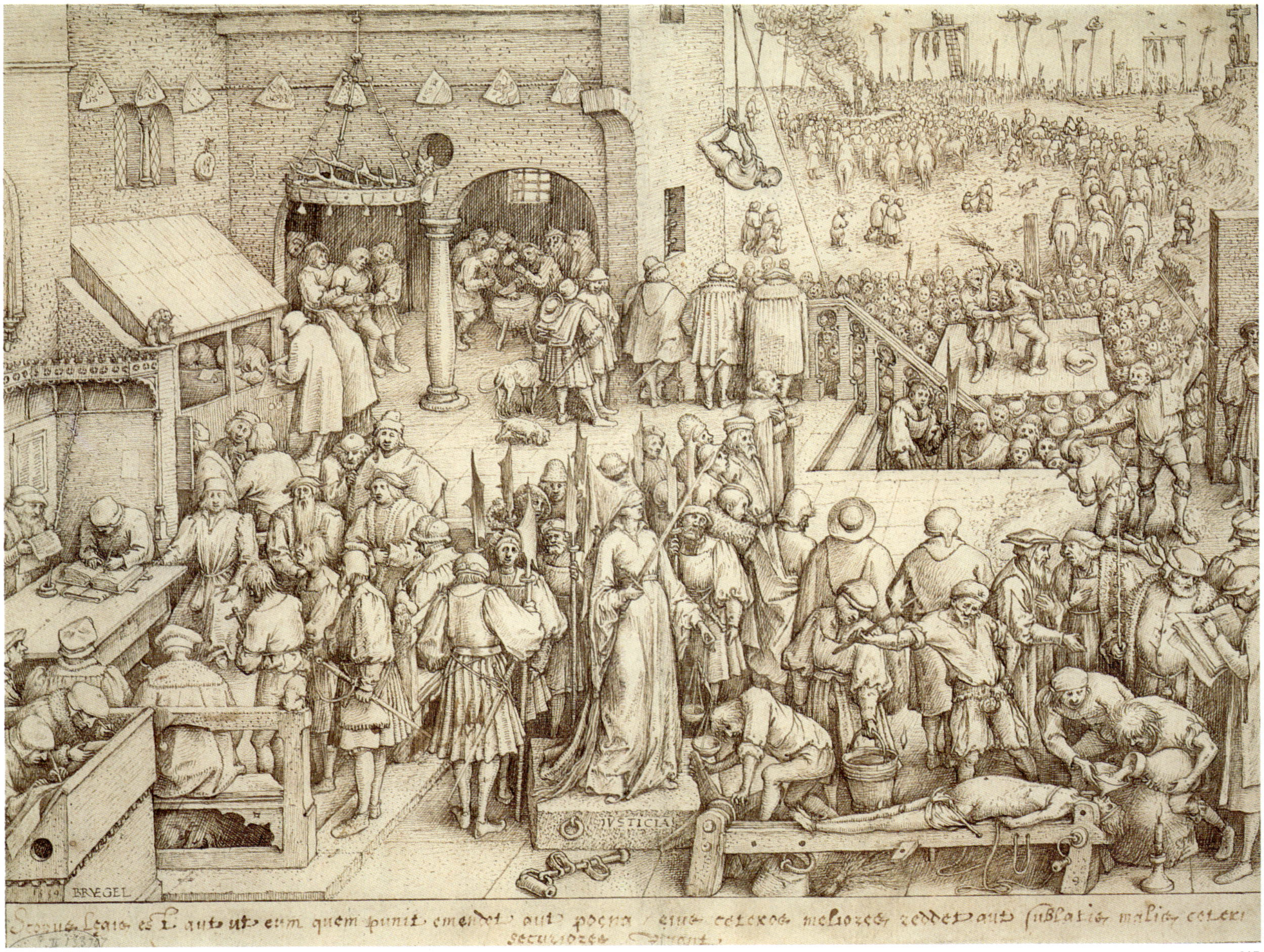

217

which Pontius Pilate washed his hands and, on the open tomb, Jesus's graveclothes, the soldiers' dice, and the pots of ointment brought to the grave by the Holy Women.

The scene is set in the church itself, in whose right-hand section the sacraments are being enacted: marriage, communion, baptism, and confession. The elevation of the Host can be seen in the background on the left. In the left middleground, a priest is delivering a sermon. In the foreground, the shapes of the backs of the congregation turned toward us form an abstract pattern, while the attentive faces of others are turned forward from the middle distance. The drawing's curious, double-oblique view shows us the scenes the faithful would have seen when attending Mass. According to some writers the importance given to the sermon suggests a sympathy for the Reformation, which is later confirmed by Bruegel's *John the Baptist Preaching* (fig. 284) in the open air. On the other hand, the drawing also shows the sacrament of confession, a practice rejected by Protestants. Bruegel may simply have wanted to convey the idea of faith by depicting its rites and teachings. Certainly this vision would reach a wider audience than a representation of the religious differences of the time.

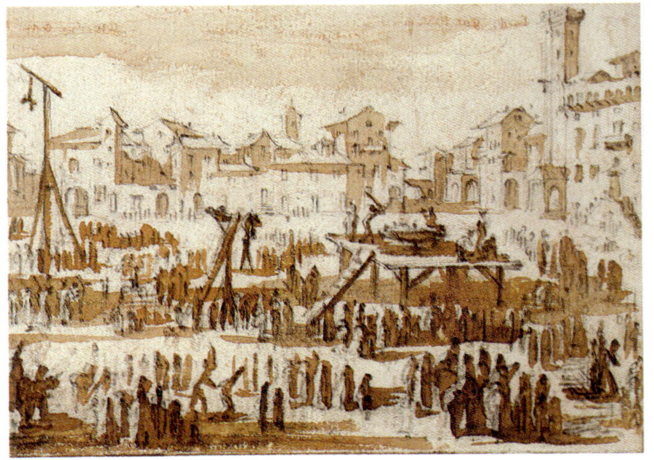

218

After *Faith* comes *Hope*. This page, already described, states explicitly that hope is necessary in a life whose suffering is "almost intolerable." The allegorical figure standing on an anchor, Hope's attribute, is also armed with a spade and a scythe, symbols of harvest, and crowned with a beehive, like the figure of Lent in the painting depicting its battle with Carnival.

Next comes *Caritas,* or *Charity* (fig. 216). The woman that incarnates this virtue is dressed in the old Netherlandish style, with a headband holding back her waves of hair. A pelican perched on her head feeds its young with its own blood. In one hand Charity holds a burning heart, the symbol of God's love; she holds the other out to some impoverished children. Around this central figure the Seven Acts of Mercy are being put into practice: feeding the hungry, offering drink to the thirsty, clothing the naked, nursing the sick, offering shelter to the homeless, visiting the imprisoned, burying the dead. The inscription written below the scene in Latin reads: *Speres tibi accidere quod altere accidit* (You hope that what happens to others will happen to you).

Justitia, or *Justice* (fig. 217), according to the drawing and the engraving, emphasizes the need to be severe, to make an example of wrongdoing, and thus to secure the security of others. The picture contains an inventory of punishments, from torture to death, as well as a number of judicial practices of the time. Contemporary documents confirm Bruegel's summary of these.

Justice, like Charity, is also dressed in old Netherlandish style in a double-pointed headdress. She stands on a square stone that was used for presenting, committing to jail, or executing prisoners (it can also be seen in *Patience,* fig. 92). She holds a sword in one hand, a set of scales in the other, and she is blindfolded, not because justice is blind but because it must be impartial. Various ordeals and manners of execution are shown here: the rack, the water torture, the cutting off of a hand, and others. Such subject matter must have been popular. In about 1630 Jacques Callot, in a large engraving (fig. 218), made an inventory of all the tortures used judicially to extract confessions and punish the guilty. In the foreground of Bruegel's drawing, to the left and to the right, two lawyers carry long, spiny wands, symbols of their authority. In the *Deadly Sins* series these same symbols are used again, this time to condemn pride. According to Bruegel, therefore, justice appears to be severely repressive and in tune with the times. Strangely, however, behind the flagellation scene in the middle distance, a procession is setting off toward the gallows in the distance. This inescapably conjures up—perhaps misleadingly— the walk to Calvary, all the more so because, in the top right corner, is the outline of Golgotha.

After Justice comes *Prudentia,* or *Prudence* (fig. 219). The Latin motto along the bottom of the drawing reads: *In futurum prospectum ostende* (Be mindful of the future). There is intense activity in the scenes surrounding the allegorical figure: people are gathering in harvests of grain and bundles of firewood, salting pork, carrying heavy sacks to storehouses, repairing a house; others are looking after the health of their bodies and souls, saving money; a child at the lower left is even putting a coin in a bank. *Prudentia,* according the literature, "has three meanings: wisdom, foresight, and prudence."[137] Indeed, Prudence is endowed with many attributes and symbols. On her head she bears a sieve to separate the wheat from chaff; in her hand is a mirror, not that of *Pride,* but that of self-knowledge. With her other hand she embraces a coffin marked with a cross. Beneath her feet

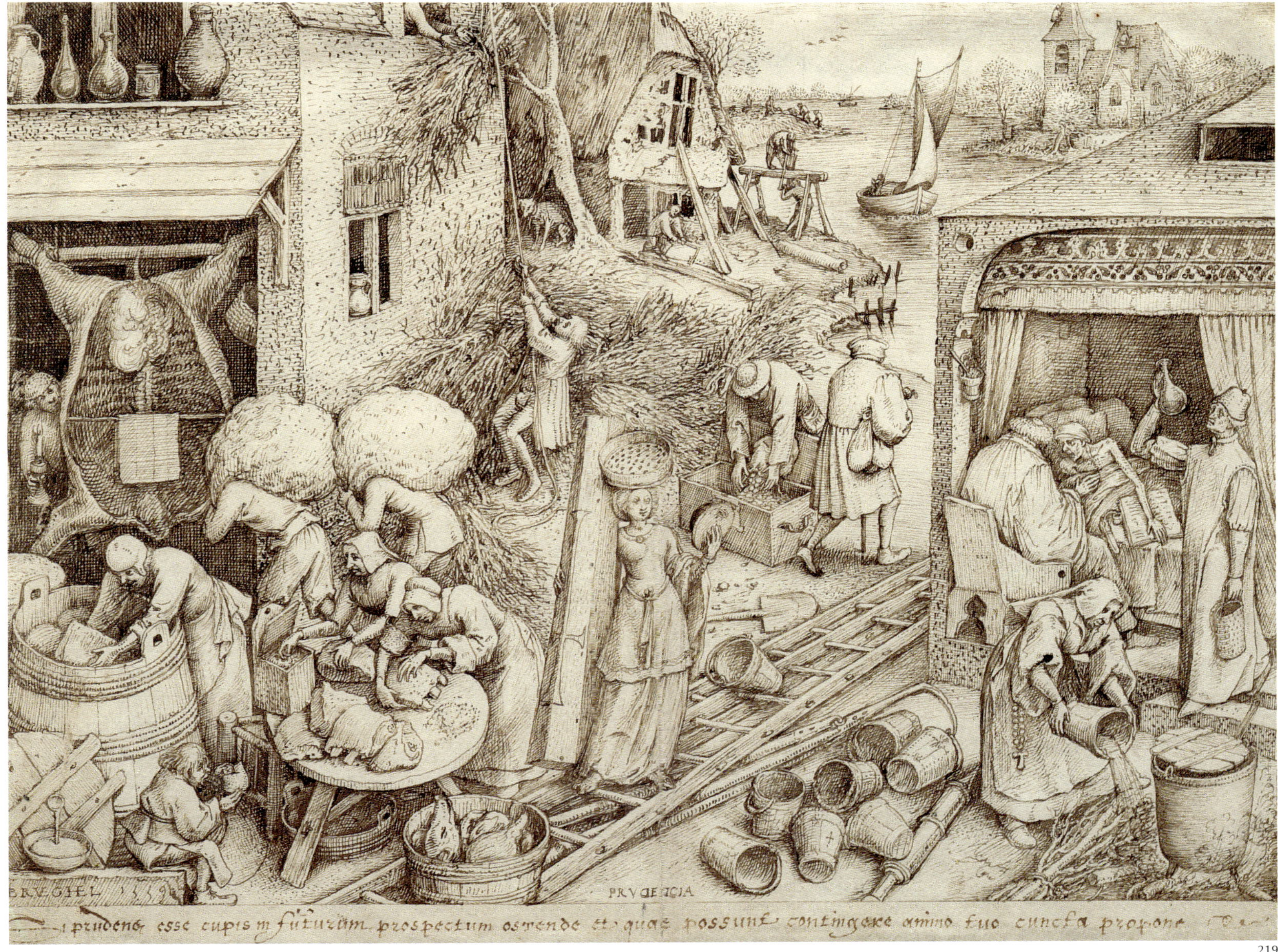

219. Pieter Bruegel, *Prudence*, from the *Virtues* series, 1559.
Pen and brown ink, 8⅞ x 11¾ in. (22.5 x 29.8 cm).
Brussels, Musées royaux des Beaux-Arts de Belgique

ladders, buckets, and a pump are signs of precautions against fire, a scourge that
Bruegel depicts in many of his works. Some have seen this elegant representation
of Prudence as a personification not so much of precaution as of miserliness.[138]
But the background landscape shows, beyond the feverish toil, a serene beauty,
and a boat returning to shore.

Fortitudo, or *Fortitude* (fig. 220), consists of restraining our instincts, our
anger, our humors—in other words, controlling ourselves. Bruegel's image
contrasts Good and Evil. *Fortitudo* here has the wings of an angel, and a warrior's
breastplate adorned with a lion. She has chained the dragon she is trampling, and
she steadies herself with an erect column, while the anvil on her head demonstrates her strength. Around her Bruegel has brought back to life, as if for a final
battle, the beasts who represent the *Deadly Sins:* the peacock of *Pride,* the pig of
Gluttony, the cock of *Lust,* the ass of *Sloth,* the turkey-cock of *Envy,* the bear of
Anger, and the toad of *Avarice.* The monsters that we saw in the earlier series,
too, have reappeared, but the outcome of the battle is in no doubt as the horsemen
of Good, helped by the peasants on the right, will prevail. In the background a

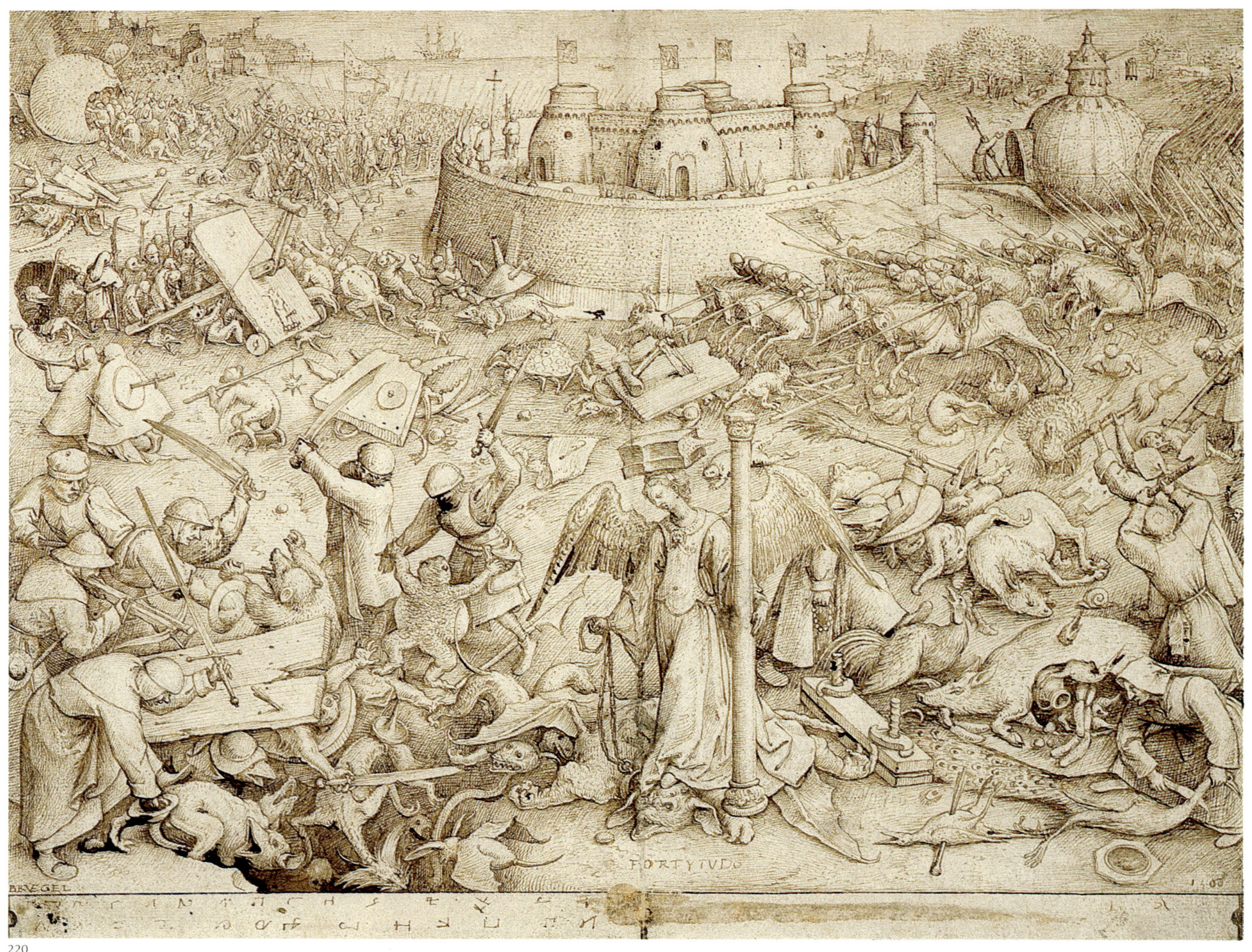

220. Pieter Bruegel, *Fortitude*, from the *Virtues* series,
1560. Pen and brown ink, 8⅞ x 11⅝ in. (22.5 x 29.5 cm).
Rotterdam, Museum Boijmans Van Beuningen

castle, over which fly the flags of the Evangelists, represents Faith before a broad
expanse of open water, perhaps representing the oceans and the far-flung explo-
rations of the sixteenth century. Curiously this work, in which two of Bruegel's
tendencies, fantasy and realism, come together, prefigures both the *Fall of the
Rebel Angels* (with the monsters falling on the left) and *The Suicide of Saul* (with
the cavalry charge on the right). *Fortitudo* thus represents the victory of the
Virtues over the Sins, and, in its triumphant language, stands out from the other
drawings in its series.

Temperantia, or *Temperance* (fig. 221), suppresses the excess of pleasure that
leads to sensuality, and holds at bay the baseness of Avarice. The figure in the
center bears a clock on her head, a symbol of an ordered life. One hand holds
the reins to the bridle that she wears with the bit in her teeth, to demonstrate that
she can control her tongue; the other holds a pair of spectacles, no doubt with the
same meaning applied to her eyes. One of her feet rests on the sail of a windmill,
which evokes the regular rhythms of work, and a snake tied round her waist

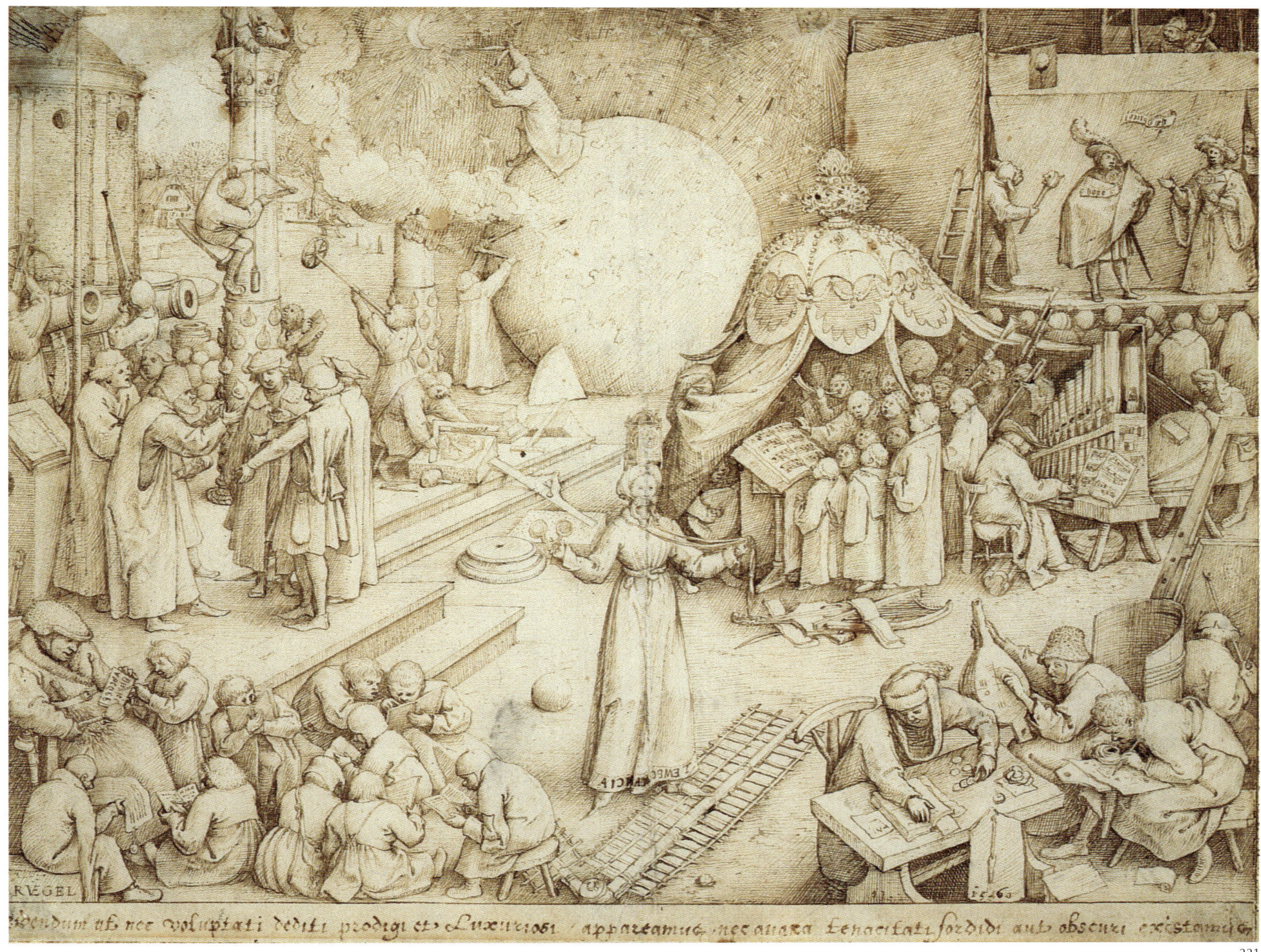

221

221. Pieter Bruegel, *Temperance*, from the *Virtues* series, 1560. Pen and brown ink, 8¾ x 11⅝ in. (22.2 x 29.5 cm). Rotterdam, Museum Boijmans Van Beuningen

symbolizes her control of her own desires.[139] Thus, Bruegel links the idea of Temperance "with human activities governed by the observance of the rules of moderation"[140] by associating it with the Seven Liberal Arts. *Grammar,* in the foreground on the left, is represented by a class of children practicing reading and writing; *Arithmetic*—mathematics, commerce, and finance—is represented on the right. In the middle distance is *Music.* Between commerce and harmony Bruegel had placed, perhaps ironically, an artist—himself?—in the shape of a painter working at his easel. Painting did not, in Bruegel's day, figure among the liberal arts. As for music, it occupies a prime spot with, from right to left, an organ, symbol of religious music, a group of instrumentalists, a choir, and a lutenist, an example of secular music, and the last survivors in *The Triumph of Death* (figs. 109–110). More instruments of the period lie on the ground. *Rhetoric* appears in the distance on the right: the art of eloquence, practiced at the time in societies of rhetoricians, taking the stage as a man who represents hope and a woman who represents faith. Their conversation is interrupted by the intrusion of the fool, under a flag showing the world upside down, a sign that also appears in Bruegel's painting, *Flemish Proverbs* (fig. 224). *Astronomy* appears at the back of the drawing, with the sphere of the earth, which one astronomer is measuring, while another calculates with a set of compasses its distance from the moon. Further to the left, *Geometry* is represented by architecture and the arts of war. Finally, before the column in the left middle distance, are the five men who represent *Logic.* They appear to be all talking at once, or at least barely listening to each other. Some observers have seen in them the representatives of religious faiths: Catholics and Jews on the left, and three members of reformed churches on the right.[141] The column before which the logicians stand and its companion have also been interpreted as a reference to the columns on the coat of arms of the emperor Charles V,[142] but since the emperor had abdicated four years before the drawing was made, it seems unlikely.

The richness of all of Bruegel's works, the multiplicity of elements in each image—what today would be called the semantic content—inevitably leads to a variety of interpretations and theories about the images. The game of hunting for references is amusing, and sometimes stimulating. But without resorting to elaborate, and often specious, theories, Bruegel's meaning is almost always clear if we consider his work in the context of the customs and the common objects and details of his time, taking into account also his own manner of creation, his angles of view, his sense of humor, and his profoundly human response to what is cruel and moving. There is almost never any the need to look further.

If we compare Bruegel's *Justice*, *Faith*, or *Temperance* with similar images by his contemporaries, for example, an ink drawing of *Temperance* by Maerten van Heemskerk,[143] dated 1556 (fig. 222), Heemskerk's rather ponderous symbolic figure, here reduced to a single human form with the virtue's attributes set against a background that vaguely suggests a landscape, seems a world away from the sheer inventiveness and caprice—dated but apt terms here—that mark the universe of Bruegel. In Van Heemskerk's work, Temperance also holds a bridle and bit and, behind her, a horse gallops toward a barely outlined city. His drawing of Justice shows her equipped with the inevitable sword, scales, and blindfold, in front of a few classical ruins and a village in the distance. Faith holds the Tablets of the Law, rather casually, in one hand and a perfume pan in the other. These good-natured, matronly figures have their qualities, but in no way do they embody what they are intended to represent.

FLEMISH PROVERBS

The *Virtues* series on its own demonstrates that Bruegel's world is not limited to the study of a given social class or type of person. The multiplicity of scenes and activities of the characters in them proves that the painter's eye wandered everywhere, precisely identifying behavior that reveals the human condition as he experienced it, but that he also brought out its most profound and essential aspects. He then highlighted it, either in a realistic manner or in a synthesized vision, defining, through acts or faces, what best conveys a character, an ambition, or a weakness. The limits of symbolism, allegory, parody, and satire are soon reached—and sometimes breached when the opportunity arises or it is necessary to do so. The

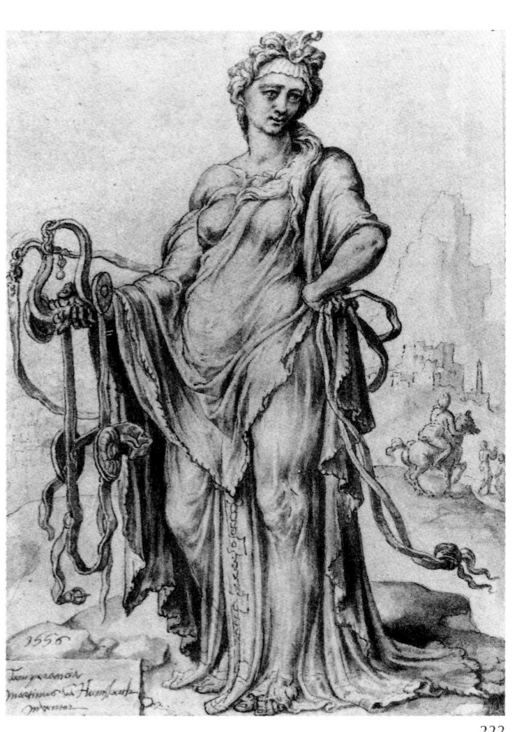

222. Maerten van Heemskerk, *Temperance*, 1556. Pen and brown ink, gray-brown wash, heightened with pink gouache, 11 5/8 x 8 1/4 in. (29.7 x 21.1 cm). Paris, Institut néerlandais, Fondation Custodia

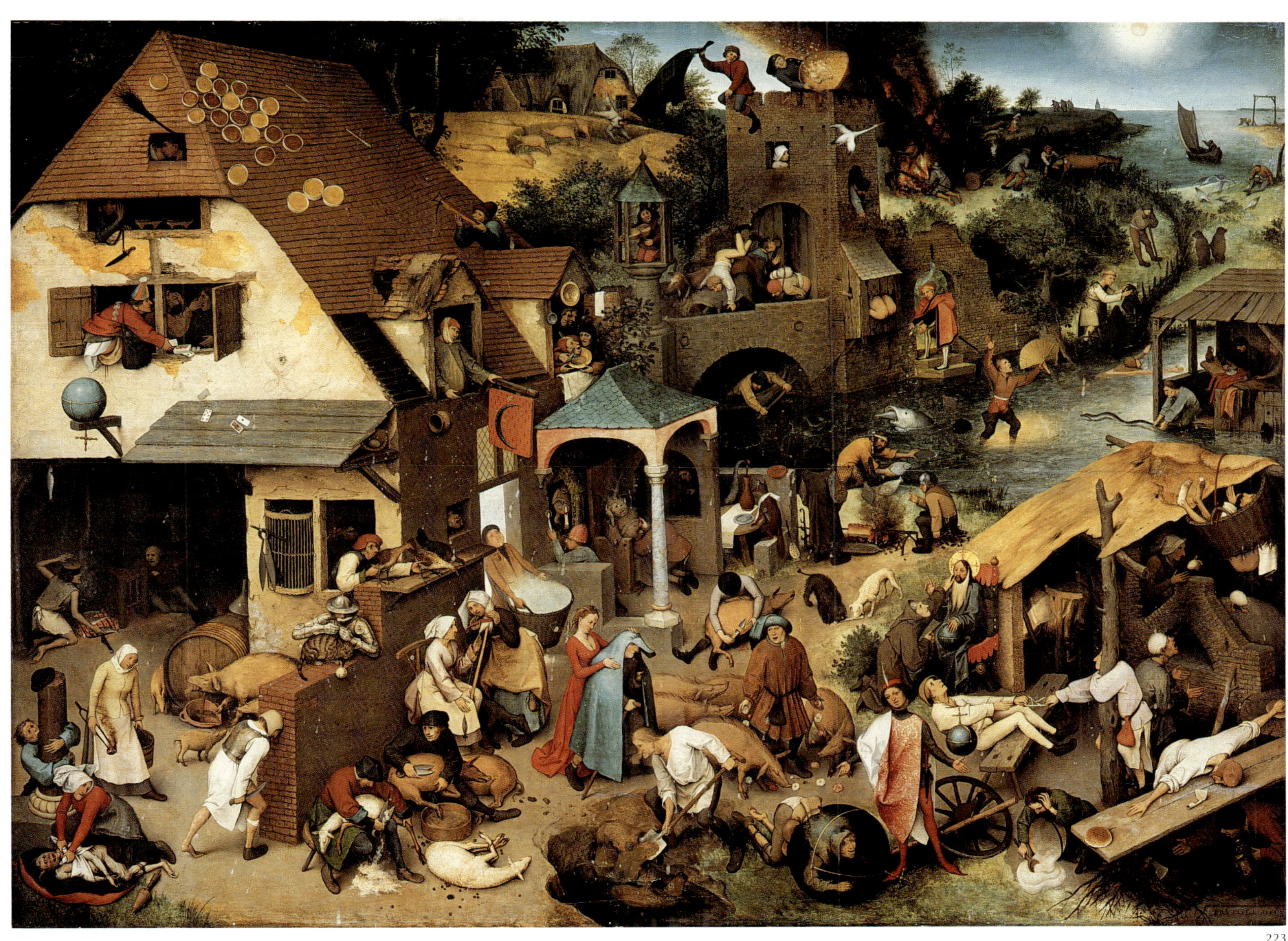

223

223–29. Pieter Bruegel, *Flemish Proverbs*, 1559: whole work and details. Oil on panel, 46 x 64⅜ in. (117 x 163.5 cm). Berlin, Staatliche Museen, Gemäldegalerie

famous painting *Flemish Proverbs* (fig. 223) is an illustration of this. To have gathered together and pictured eighty-five proverbs—or even as many as 118 according to some authors[144]—on a single panel measuring 46 x 64⅜ inches (117 x 163.5 cm) is not so much a masterpiece as a tour de force. To have carried off such an encyclopedic treatment of the subject while avoiding any effect of congestion or clutter is a feat of virtuosity. There are other works that rise to this challenge of abundance: *The Battle of Issus* by Bruegel's younger son, Jan Bruegel, musters several hundred figures, and is a direct descendant of his father's *Suicide of Saul* of 1562 (figs. 253 and 255), though it is amplified by the baroque inspiration that governs Jan's work. But the subject's unity of action, time, and place induce the creation of a space which, though at saturation point, remains readable, owing to the astonishing skill of its execution.

Flemish Proverbs, for its part, while it makes similar demands, boasts almost 100 discrete elements—one per proverb—that the artist had to orchestrate in such a way that the various figures retain their separateness and yet inhabit the same painting, whose composition is not only clearly legible, but harmoniously arranged. At first sight, this painting of 1559, the first large work signed and dated

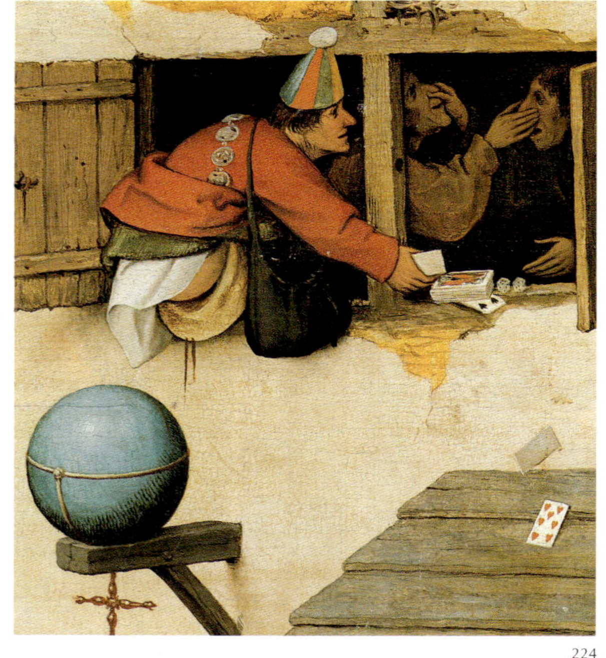

224

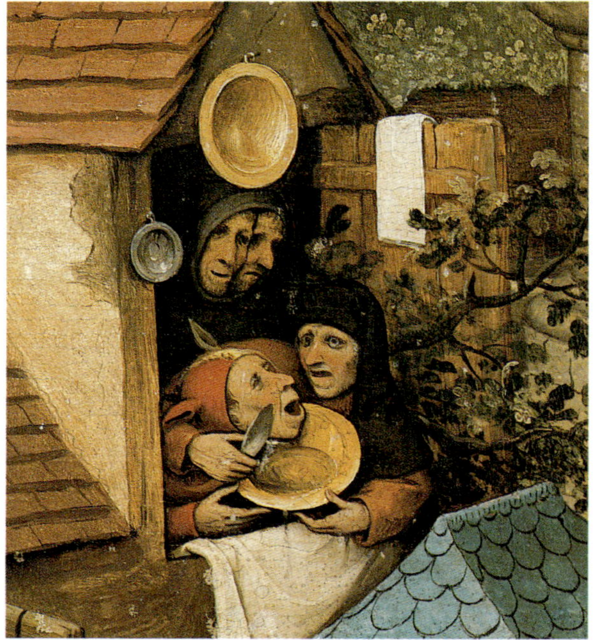

225

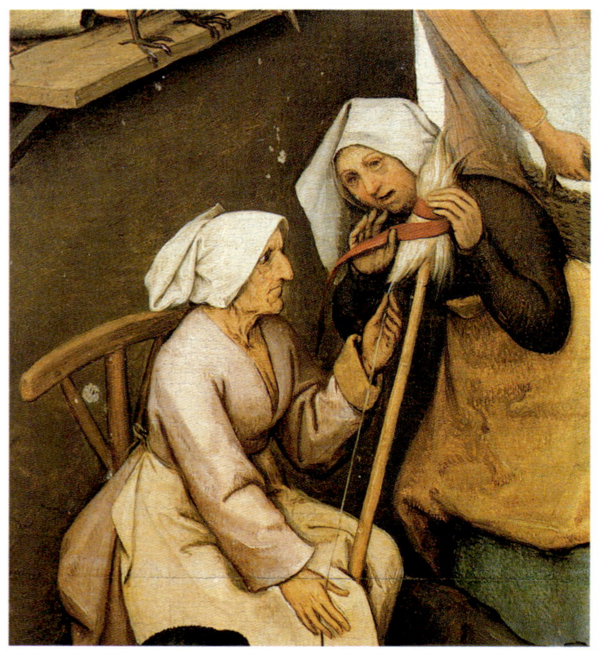

226

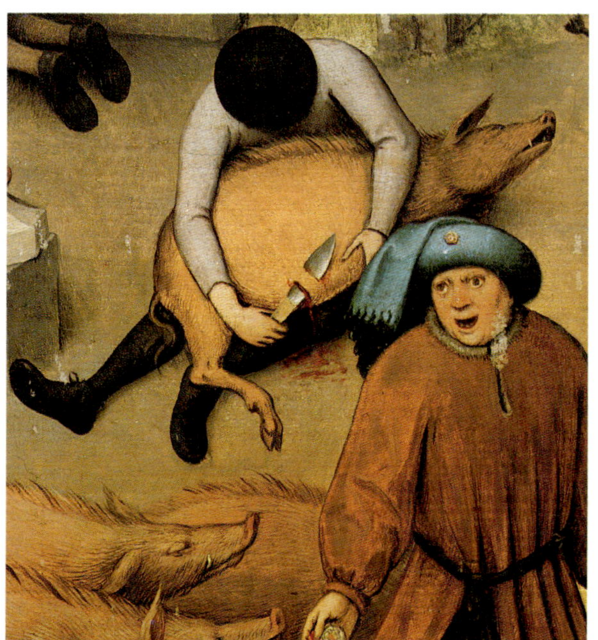

227

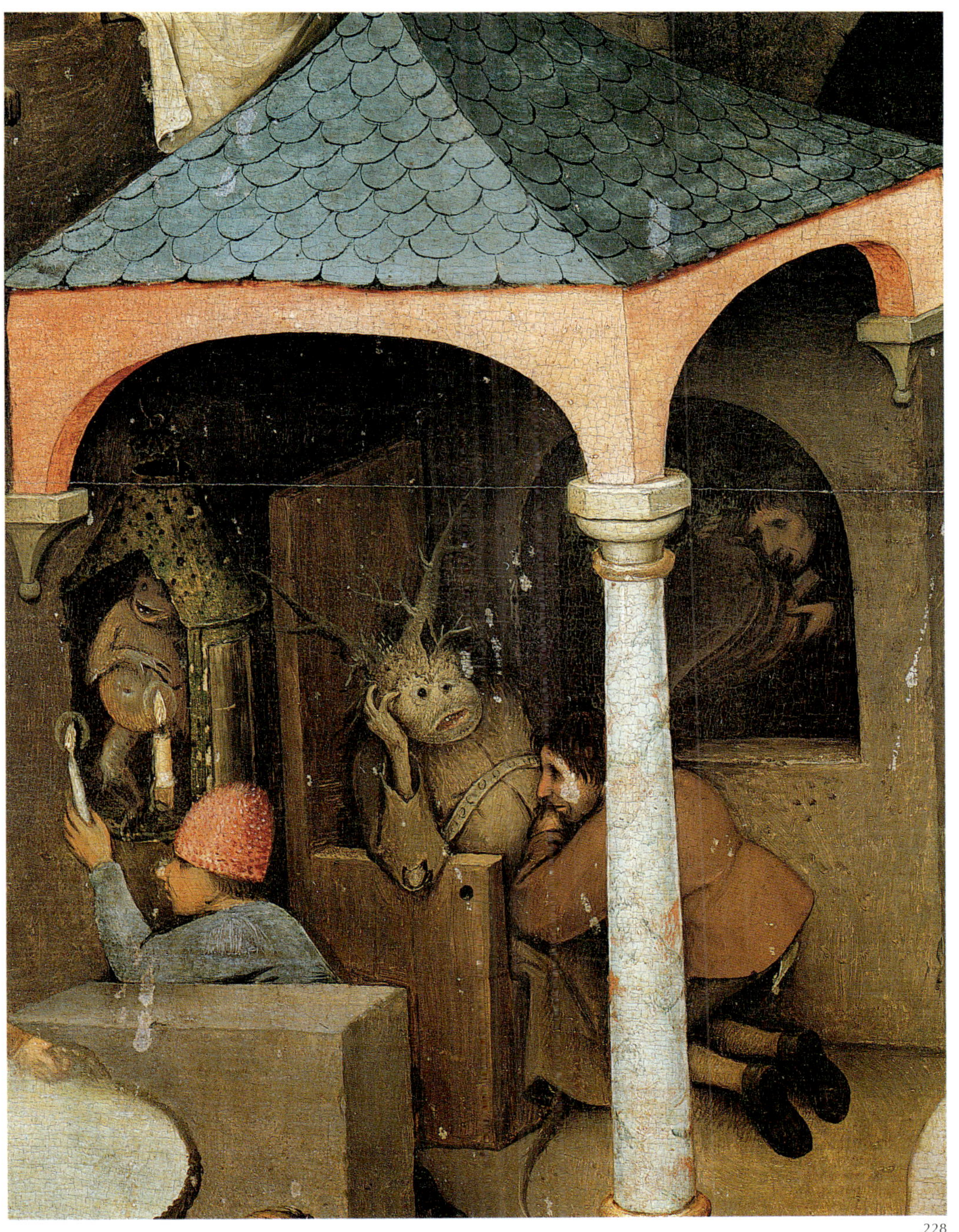

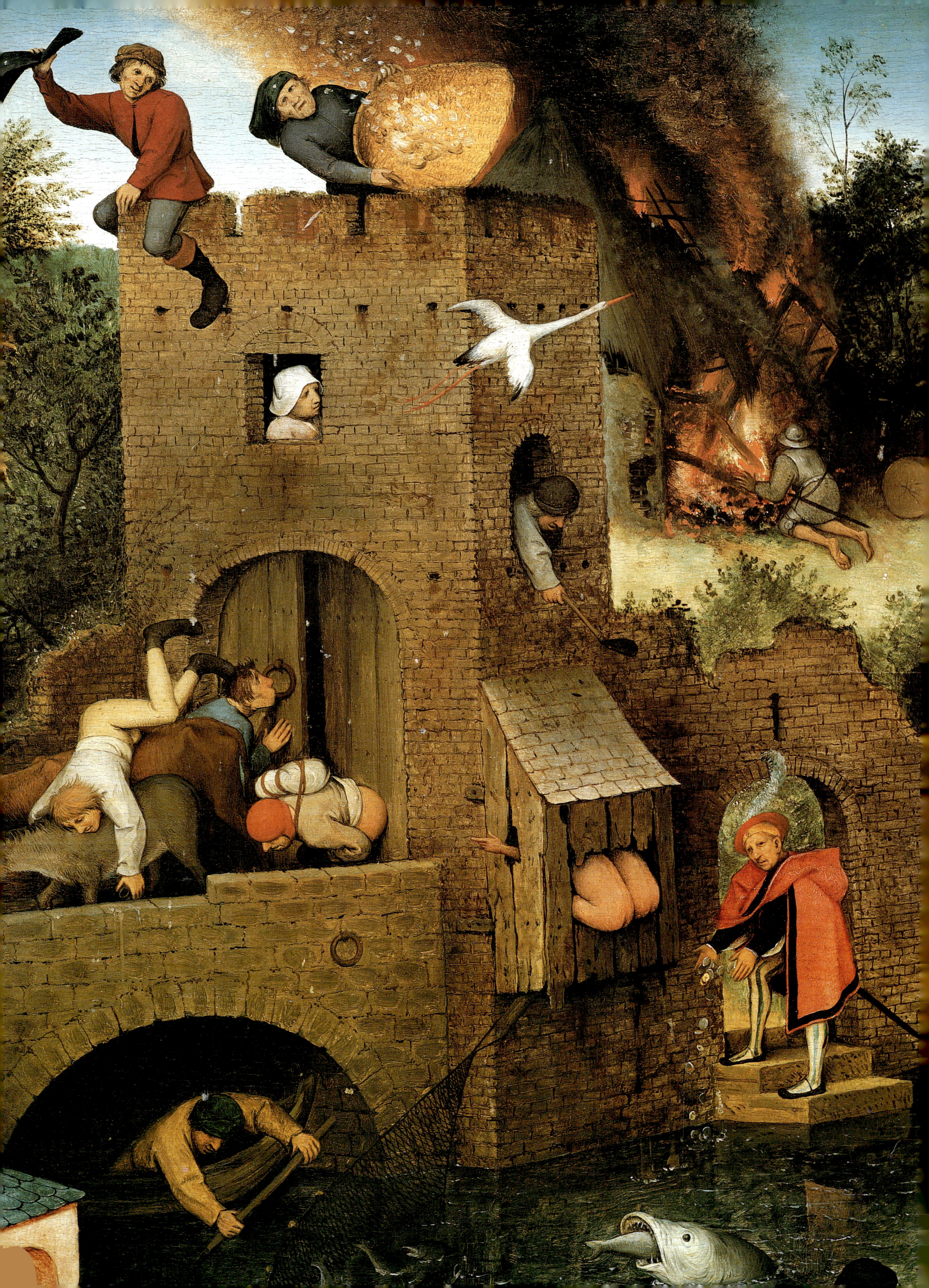

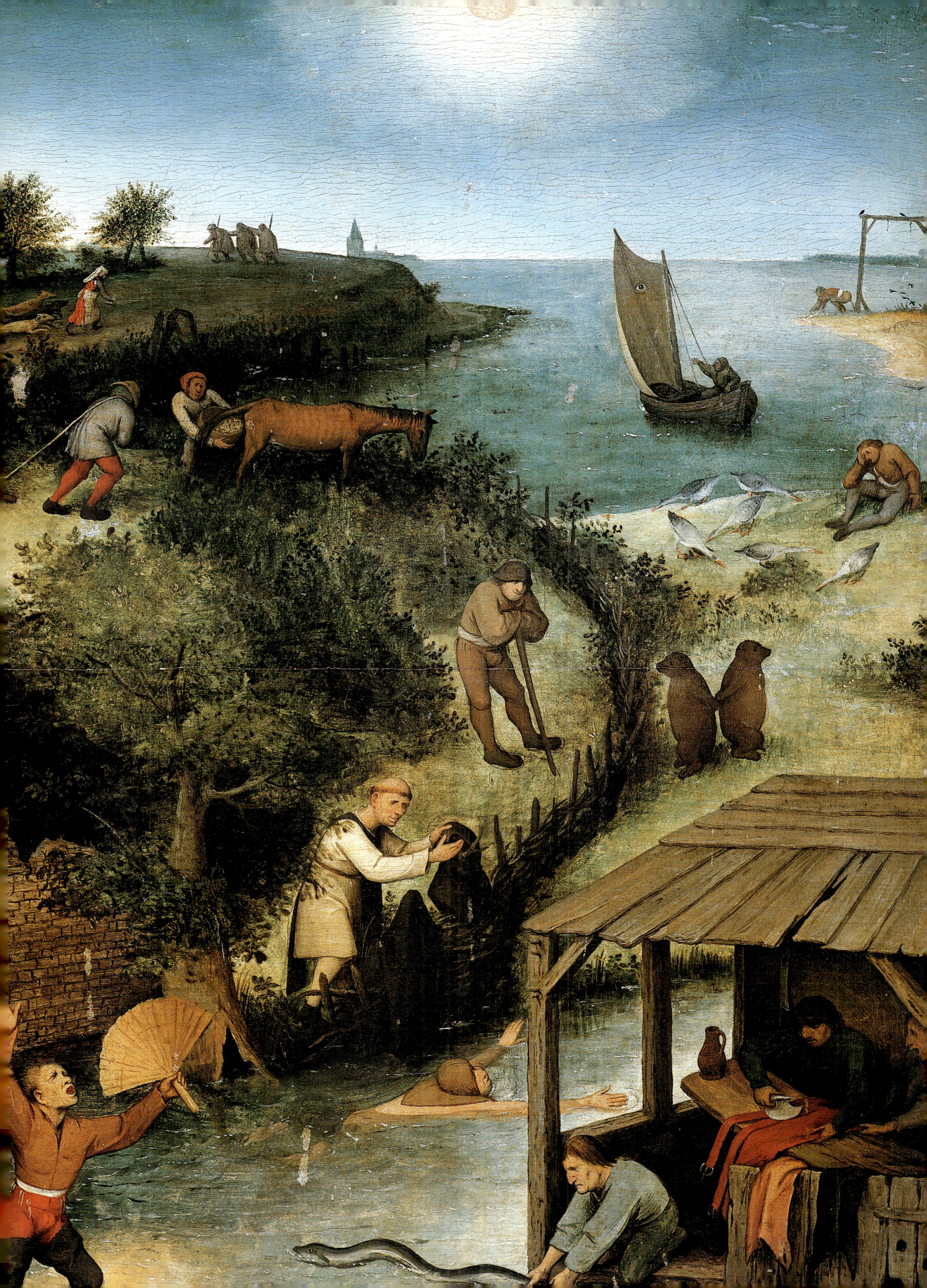

by Pieter Bruegel, could almost be a landscape bustling with people. It is the crowd that first catches our attention. But while there is movement and rhythm, there are no reciprocal links. Each character or group—none of these ever numbering more than three people—is enclosed within its own world, in an activity that has no relation to those of its neighbors.

Proverbs, sayings, popular expressions: these utterances have both an epigrammatic quality because of their brevity, and a resonance because of the images they have produced. They can appear as statements, warnings, or moral precepts, ranging from the ironic to the wise, from wordplay to philosophical maxims. Throughout history, proverbs have played an important role in writings and thought: Writers in antiquity made use of them, as did the Scriptures. They became increasingly popular, reaching their height in the sixteenth century. In various languages of the time, and in various forms, from Luther to Rabelais, the proverb became a genre. The *Adages* of Erasmus, first published in 1500, which appeared later in many editions, are an erudite collection bringing together thousands of proverbs, maxims, and mottoes, drawn from Greek, Roman, and Hebrew literature, whose origins, use, and meaning the philosopher from Rotterdam studied. Sebastian Brant's *The Ship of Fools* (*Das Narrenschiff*), published in Nuremberg in 1494 and translated into Latin, French, Dutch, and English during the following century was, as its title suggests, a rich source of strange ideas, allegories, and maxims, all the more eloquent because the work was illustrated with engravings. In 1535 Rabelais, with *La Vie Inestimable du Grant Gargantua*, (The Inestimable Life of the Great Gargantua) parodied proverbs in his chapter dealing with his hero's adolescence. While François Villon wrote *Ballade des Proverbes* (The Ballad of the Proverbs), the English dramatist John Heywood also composed a poem entitled *Proverbs in the English Tongue*.[145] There were therefore many inventories in various European languages—a sign of their success—right up until 1568, the year before Bruegel's death, when François Goedthaels's *Proverbes Anciens Flamengs et François* (Old Flemish and French Proverbs) was published in Antwerp by Christophe Plantin.

These maxims and proverbs, which, fed by a realistic and popular vitality, say so much in so few words, gave birth to a type of short morality play that was presented by itinerant actors, of the very sort that Bruegel depicted in the right background of his drawing of *Temperance*. These short plays, known as *sinnekens* or "little allegories," are mentioned by Van Mander,[146] and were also performed in the rhetorical societies. They were, among other things, visualizations of fundamental truths, but also of human folly, and of illogical behavior that today we would call nonsensical. The proverbs illustrated by actors were also depicted in images, enlivening manuscript illuminations,[147] and in one case, a tapestry made in about 1500, which shows a number of the vignettes that appear in Bruegel's painting, including the blue cloak, a man seated between two chairs, a second man licking or gnawing a pillar—an image of a hypocrite—a third about to tie a bell around a cat's neck, and a fourth who is lighting a candle for the devil (fig. 230).[148] In the field of sculpture, there were proverbs depicted in reliefs or on carvings decorating church stalls, notably in the church of St. Catherine in Hoogstraten, near Antwerp on the old Leuven-Breda road. The church, built between 1525 and 1550, is decorated with stained-glass windows of the period, and it also contains the tomb, attributed to Jean Mone, of Antoine de Lalaing, Charles V's favorite, and of his

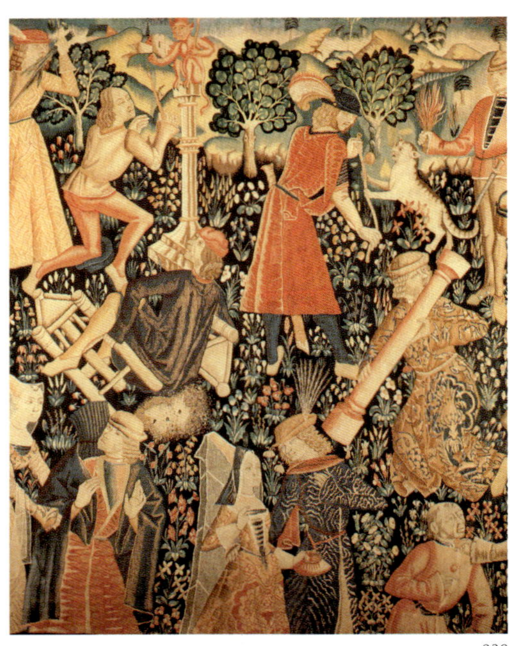

230

230. Flemish artisans, *Proverbs*, end of the fifteenth century. Tapestry in wool and silk, 111 x 86⅝ in. (282 x 220 cm). Boston, Isabella Stewart Gardner Museum

wife. The choir stalls, carved by Albrecht Gelmers between 1532 and 1548, represent approximately 60 proverbs in a lively style (fig. 231). "The 16th century loved the language of images: it is the century of the proverb," according to one writer.[149] The church in Hoogstraten is contemporary with, and geographically close to, Bruegel. The Flemish proverbs would seem to have been omnipresent.

Bruegel had already used such proverbs, both as a independent subjects—*The Big Fish Eat The Little Fish*—and as elements in the *Deadly Sins* series. They continued to inspire him, and he gave them exceptional breadth and resonance in *The Bird-Nester* (fig. 209) and *The Blind Leading the Blind* (fig. 69) in 1568. But in 1559, *Flemish Proverbs,* which is now in Berlin—and which has sometimes done the painter a disservice by reducing him to a mere inventor of popular images—in fact profoundly reflects the spirit of Bruegel's age. This world seen from above, from an angle Bruegel favored all his life, is that of an observer of human beings. As Tolnay rightly notes: "The line of the ground takes on a convex curve and gives the impression that the scene is taking place on a section of the earth's sphere."[150] The supreme achievement here is to have created, by means of the compositional elements—line, color, arrangement of figures and other forms—an organic unit that depicts approximately 100 proverbial sayings. Fundamentally composite in the sense that it is made up of accumulated elements, the work exhibits that quality in every area: earth, sky, and water; animals and fish; peasants, merchants, and aristocrats; working women and ladies of leisure; soldiers and priests; angels and demons; in tower, farm, hovel, and classical column. There is consequently no unity either of place or of time. The only thing all these have in common is a certain absurdity of behavior. The painting has sometimes been criticized for lack of balance[151]—but that is precisely what it is portraying. Given the challenge of the subject, the painting is arranged in a remarkable and readable manner. If we compare it to paintings of the same subject before and after him, Bruegel does it better, to use a modern expression. He did not invent the idea of an anthology of proverbs. At least two engravings appear to predate the painting: one by Frans Hogenberg, published by Bartholomeus de Momper in Antwerp in about 1558 (fig. 232), and the other, anonymous and made in about 1550, entitled *Sloth*.[152] Both show, in an undulating landscape, random characters and elements, representing or acting out proverbs, and each is accompanied by a descriptive note. What the sayings are is clearly stated; thus, there are fewer demands on the viewer's knowledge and imagination, and the acuity of the artist's invention is less important than in Bruegel's picture.

Hogenberg's engraving is especially interesting. First, a work of his was probably the inspiration for Bruegel's *The Battle of Carnival and Lent*, made the next year,[153] which gives weight to the theory that there was some contact between the two artists; second, the engraving depicting the proverbs bears an inscription: "This is generally called the Blue Cloak, but would more accurately be named the abuses of the world." Thus the meaning we can attribute to this collection can be stated precisely.

Bruegel is not content merely to arrange his characters more or less in groups with the sole aim of filling the available space. Instead, he has built his composition around a principal oblique line running from left to right, on which hinge other, secondary lines. The anonymous engraving of about 1550 had made a timid attempt at doing this: it shows a village, with proverbs relating to sloth, but it is the details, rather than the style, that hold our attention. Bruegel, on the other hand,

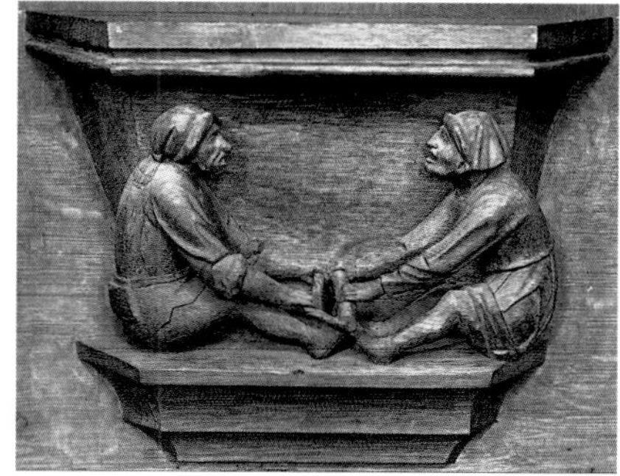

231

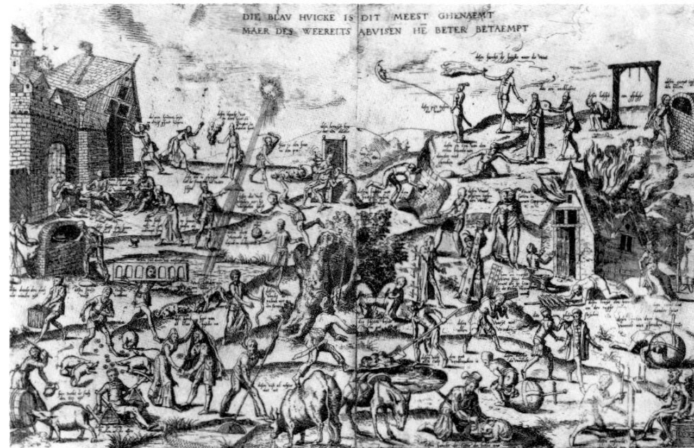

232

231. Albrecht Gelmers, *Each Pulls his Way*, 1532–48. Carved wood choir stall. Hoogstraten, Belgium, Church of St. Catherine

232. Frans Hogenberg, *The Proverbs*, ca. 1558. Etching and engraving, 14⅜ x 22 in. (36.5 x 56 cm). Brussels, Bibliothèque royale Albert I, print room

asserts the authority of his composition. On the oblique line, almost in the center, and seemingly the focal point of the scene, is an enactment of the proverb of the Blue Cloak. Indeed, "The Blue Cloak" has sometimes been given as the title of the painting. The cloak, which symbolizes the deceived husband, and here is significantly hooded, is being draped about him by his beautiful young wife, who is dressed in red. Another important element in the picture is the signboard that projects from the front of the house on the left, which represents the world turned upside down, that is, the world of abuses and absurdity. A traditional symbol of power, the globe surmounted by a cross, which Charles V, for example, is shown holding in his left hand on Flemish florins, is here literally turned on its head. Furthermore, above it is a character seated on the window ledge, perhaps a fool telling fortunes from cards, who is exposing his buttocks to it. Is the image Bruegel gives us in *Flemish Proverbs* therefore the expression "of a philosophical reflection on the meaning and necessary evolution of human life, the realm of the mad—the opposite of the life of nature, the realm of reason,"[154] as Tolnay suggests? As far as it goes, we can concur, but the idea of the world turned upside down, and which shows the opposite of what should be, cannot sum up the artist's genius. *Flemish Proverbs* certainly shows aberrations and human madness, set out in a contemporary context that is strikingly summarized.

A similar, but transparent, globe—the glass's fragility showing the vanity of all things—is being crawled into by a figure in the right foreground, "for we must bend down if we want to make our way in the world". The scene is repeated in 1568 in *The Misanthrope* (fig. 267), in which the world, or its representative, a man hunched within a transparent sphere, steals the purse of the cloaked man who turns away from it. In *Flemish Proverbs,* all is vanity, deceit, satire, and mockery. Next to the man crawling into the glass globe, an elegantly dressed young man "spins the world on his thumb." In the middle of the work, in the shadows, we can see man making his confession to the devil (fig. 228). Not far away, a monk "attaches a beard of tow to the face of the Lord."

While this triumph of a painting is in accord with a humorous, ironic vision that was typical of its time, it is in no way superficial, as its inventiveness and portrayals show. Bruegel might have added *mutatis mutandis* to the words of Erasmus who, in 1508, wrote to Thomas More in the preface of *In Praise of Folly*, which he dedicated to him:

> Each of us can freely take our rest from the toils of life; what an injustice to deny this right to the work of the mind alone! Especially when trifles lead to serious things, and specially when the reader, if he has a little understanding, finds more to his purpose there than in many a serious and grand dissertation. The one may compose a eulogy of Rhetoric or Philosophy, another a panegyric to a prince or a call to arms against the Turks. There are writers for predicting the future, others for dreaming up questions about the hair of goats. Nothing is more foolish than to treat frivolous things seriously; but nothing is more spiritual than to put frivolous things to serious use. It is for others to judge me; however, unless pride has led me astray, I think I have praised Folly in a way that is not at all foolish.[155]

In his treatment of the *Flemish Proverbs*, as in the meaning they contain, Bruegel is not content merely to adapt tradition or to confine himself to humor.

He creates images, some of which inhabit his work throughout his life, as they
are integrated in their meaning or their appearance into his language. Thus, for
example, the two elements at the ends of the large diagonal in the painting are, on
the left, a powerful, bellicose woman who is tying up the devil himself, and, high
up on the right, a man who is exposing his buttocks to a gallows. The first image
can be seen, a few years later, in *Dulle Griet*, where, on the bridge, a cohort of
warlike women are thrashing an army of demons. As for exposing one's buttocks
to the gallows, whether through bravado or through contempt,[156] this act would
seem to throw some light on one of Bruegel's last works, *The Magpie on the
Gallows* of 1568, where a crouching man is emptying his bowels not on the gallows
themselves, but close to them. Another recurring element, though this is only a
detail, are the pies spread out on the roof of the house at the left, which reappear
in *The Land of Cockaigne* of 1567 (fig. 269). And the lovers kissing in the attic,
illicitly no doubt, will do the same in broad daylight in *The Peasants' Dance*.
Thus there are nuances and variations, both in the proverbs themselves and in
the behavior of the people who act them out, or who are conditioned by them.
Parallels between the works of painters and writers demonstrate this amusingly, as
they draw on common roots.

While Rabelais's Gargantua "pissed against the sun,"[157] the moon on a red
signboard near the center of the painting gets this treatment in Bruegel's *Flemish
Proverbs*; while the one "turned the sows out into the hay," the other lets the
swine run through the wheat (in the far distance, at upper center). Whatever the
differences of context or meaning, the visual image is similar: when, in one as in
the other, someone sits between two chairs, they each end up "backside on the
ground" or in the ashes, as in the case of the man in the house at the left. Humor,
present in Rabelais as much as in Bruegel, is not a matter of place, time, or way of
seeing. It is more cutting, no doubt, in the work of the painter, whose vision draws
on a caustic sense of comedy and conveys a judgment. The characters portrayed
are closer to *commedia dell'arte*, as later depicted by Jacques Callot, than to a real-
life situation. The human dimension soon appears, just a few years later. The idea
is no less pessimistic for that, hovering between the world turned upside down
and the blue cloak, either of which could be a title or a subtitle, but both images
of deceit. The isolation of each proverb from the others, and its personification,
result from the fact that each is a closed world, no doubt with its own ramifications,
conjured ideas, similarities, and parallels; but each nevertheless conveys a choice, a
trait, a particular obsession.

Bruegel clearly shows that the juxtaposition of these obsessions makes up
the world, though there is no communication because each person is a prisoner of
his or her own self, of this *Elck*, or *Everyman* (fig. 238), which the artist drew in
1558 and had made into an engraving. However, before we turn to moralizing idea
that the artist made into engravings we must linger on the *Proverbs*. In 1668 the
painting was mentioned as being in the collection of Peter Stevens, one of the
most important Flemish collectors of the seventeenth century, under the title *The
World Turned Upside Down, Portrayed in Several Proverbs and Morals*.[158] Stevens,
who lived in Antwerp, owned ten other paintings by Bruegel. The painting was
mentioned again in 1669 by the art dealer Guilliam Forchoudt, under the name
De Blauwe Huyck. On 11 June 1676, Constantin Huygens remarked in his journal:
"The day before, I saw at the house of Mr Stevens, whose father once owned a fine

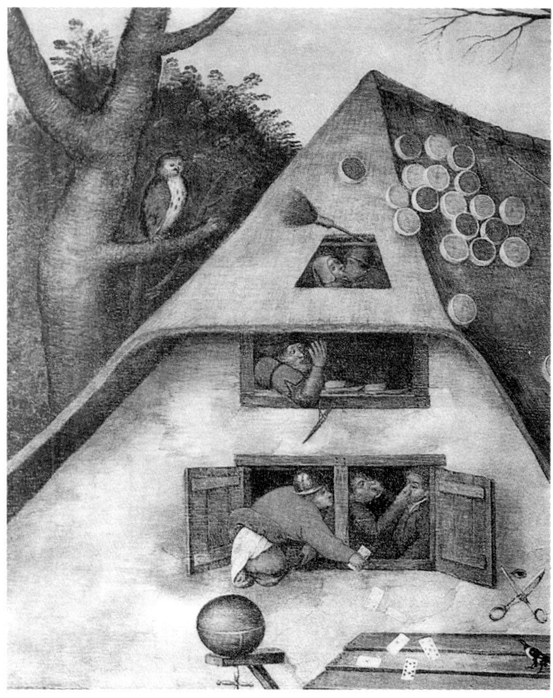

233

233. Pieter Bruegel the Younger, *Flemish Proverbs* (detail),
first quarter of the seventeenth century. Oil on panel,
47¼ x 66⅛ in. (120 x 168 cm). Belgium, private collection

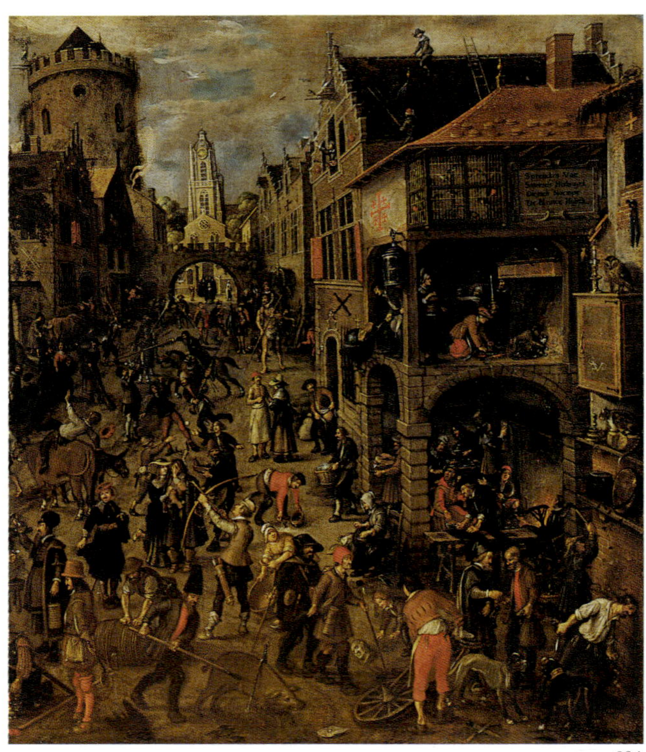

234

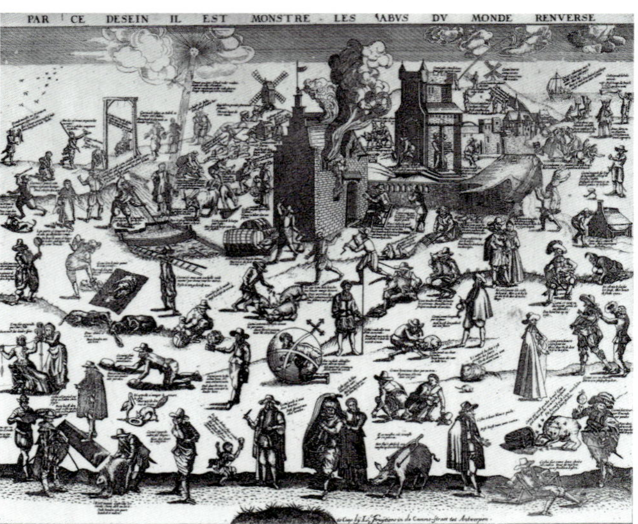

235

234. Attributed to Sebastian Vrancx, *The Flemish Proverbs* (detail), ca. 1630. Oil on canvas, 46½ x 96⅞ in. (118 x 246 cm). Brussels, Musées royaux des Beaux-Arts de Belgique

235. Lodewijk Fruytiers, *The Flemish Proverbs*, eighteenth century. Etching, 18⅜ x 22¼ in. (46.6 x 56.7 cm). Brussels, Bibliothèque royale Albert I, print room

collection of paintings, the work by the elder Bruegel which they call *De Blaeuwe Heuijck*, which represents the literal meaning of several proverbs and which is certainly very beautiful."[159] The work was therefore known and appreciated; from 1614, two copies by Pieter Bruegel the Younger were to be found in one collection—and these were among about sixteen produced by the painter's workshop, which are listed by Georges Marlier in his book published in 1969. The copies are faithful, with the exception of one or two details. One variant, however, alters the portrayal of the proverbs, and increases their number to 132.[160] The bird's-eye view is inevitably retained in the son's versions, and this distancing is curiously reinforced by the addition, in the top left-hand corner, of an owl that appears to contemplate the scene of this upturned world beneath the tree where he is perched (fig. 233). This may refer to the familiar expression "as wise as an owl" (*wijs als een huil*). Perhaps the son, consciously or unconsciously, meant to emphasize the position of his father as the artist observes, but does not take part.

Be that as it may, this world of aberration, this encyclopedia of human folly, where characters end up looking like puppets or automata, was to be portrayed by others than Pieter the Elder and the Younger. The theme was taken up several times in engravings, by Johannes van Duetecum, Theodor Galle, and Lodewijk Fruytiers (fig. 235),[161] and also in paintings by Sebastian Vrancx, Cornelis Saftleven, and David Teniers the Younger, who was, in a sense, a grandson of Bruegel's by marriage, since he married the daughter of Jan Bruegel. Vrancx's *Proverbs*, or at any rate the painting attributed to him (fig. 234), deserves some attention. Although based on the original, it aims for profusion—202 proverbs have been counted in it![162]—and the result is a certain confusion. The picture is interesting for another reason. Bruegel's *Proverbs* has sometimes been considered a companion piece to his *Children's Games* (fig. 246);[163] the dimensions of the two paintings are almost identical. Now, Vrancx's *Proverbs* takes up the theme of Bruegel's, but not its composition, which instead draws on that of *Children's Games*. "Some out of nothing made great things, and made great things return to nothing," as Rabelais said in his *Fifth Book*, published posthumously about 1565.[164]

The number is less important than the ambiguity, and Bruegel's *Proverbs* leaves us dreaming. No matter how broad and exact the research undertaken by commentators, the analysis of sayings, even if it makes them yield their secrets, does not necessarily reveal how the painter meant them and pictured them. Here is an example: The man handling the hens just left of the center of the painting could refer to a "ladies' man," or he could be someone "counting his chickens," depending on whether the proverb the artist had in mind was about women[165] or about eggs not yet laid.

We cannot leave the subject of proverbs without mentioning two other series of works by Bruegel, both of paintings. The first is *Twelve Proverbs* (fig 236): these are circular, and may have originally been wooden plates with painted figures on them of a type common in the southern Netherlands between 1530 and 1570. If so, they were later filed down to make them into medallions, which were set into a single panel in the seventeenth century,[166] under a title that reads: "These scenes of daily life are lavish with irony and advice, and cleverly mock human behavior."[167] All the sayings except the first—a seller of waffles who drinks and plays[168]—appear in the *Flemish Proverbs* of 1559, from the man who shakes

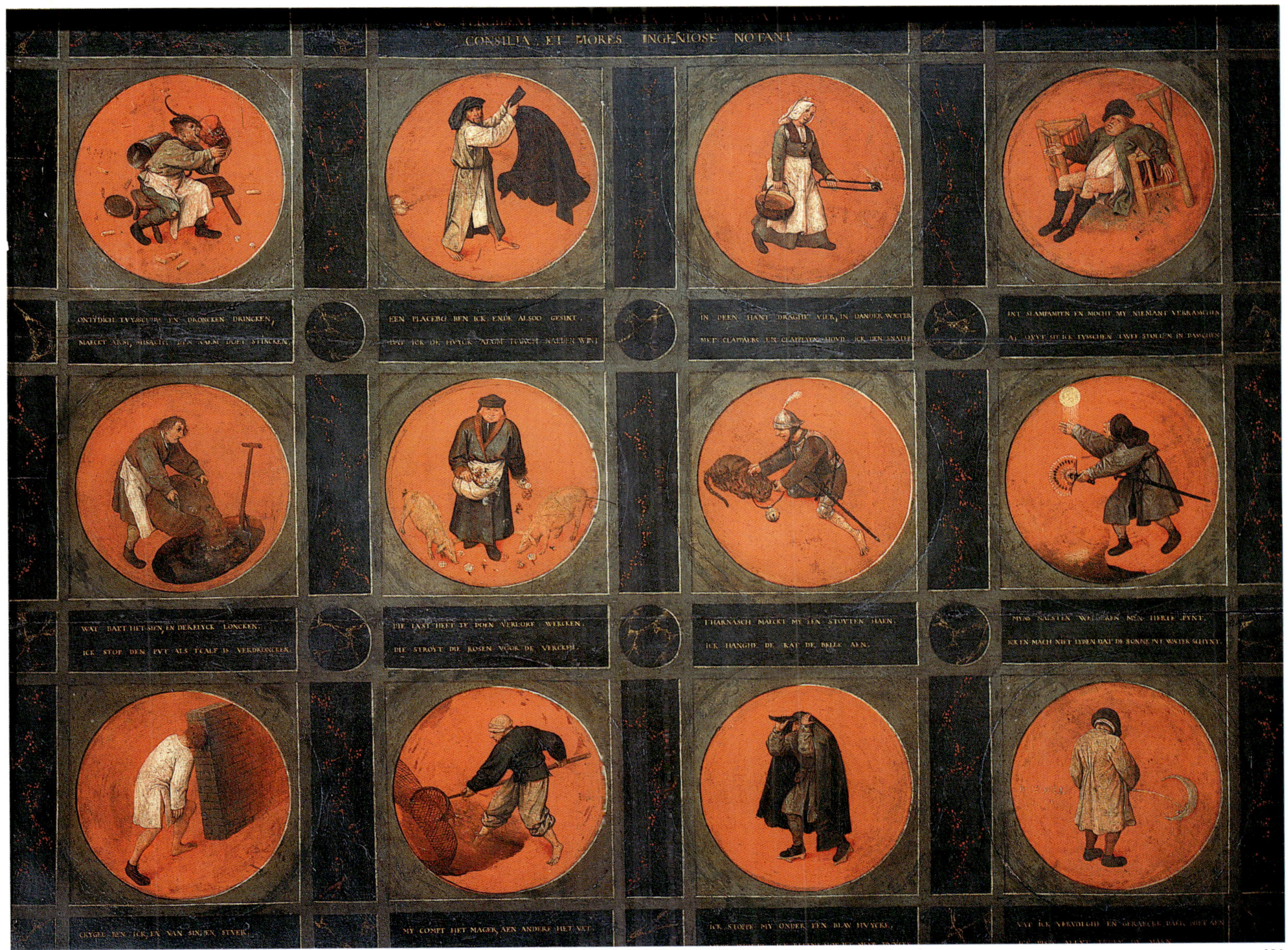

236. Pieter Bruegel, *Twelve Proverbs*, ca. 1558–60 (?).
Oil on panel, each medallion 8¼ in. (21 cm) in diameter.
Antwerp, Museum Mayer van den Bergh

his cloak to the four winds, to the one who is urinating on the moon, to the one throwing roses to swine (a parallel saying to our "pearls before swine"), to the one wearing a hooded blue cloak. These figures stand out against a monochromatic vermilion background, and this very lack of detail gives them great plastic power. However, the attribution to Bruegel, despite a signature and a fragmentary date, has been questioned. A study by Jozef De Coo, which accepts the work, points out that the estate inventory of Nicolaes Cornelis Cheeus, an Antwerp collector, mentions, in 1621, twelve plates painted by Pieter Bruegel the Elder.[169]

The other series (figs. 259 and 266), also of twelve images, consists of engravings of different subjects (though the images are still circular), which can also be seen in *Flemish Proverbs*—for example, the man warming himself at the house on fire (far distance, upper right) and the crossbowman wasting his arrows (on the roof above the half-moon signboard)—or are the subjects of entire paintings, such as the *Misanthrope* (fig. 267) and *The Blind Leading the Blind* (fig. 69).

The engravings, seven of which are signed with the initials of Jan Wierix (the other five may be by Pieter van der Heyden)[170] contain no reference to Bruegel. Neither is any preliminary sketch known. Of varying quality, they bear legends that describe what is portrayed. Louis Lebeer has defended the attribution to Bruegel on the grounds that they are rooted "tightly in inventions and creations whose spirit and formal qualities would be inconceivable without Bruegel's influence."[171] We can accept this argument, applied to this case but also applicable to some of the paintings. It confirms, or at least supports, the attribution of the *Twelve Proverbs*, but also the inventiveness of *The Fall of Icarus* (fig. 324), which is also a morality tale, although in this case, a universal one.

ELCK, OR *EVERYMAN*

Is morality part of the human condition, or a lesson we are to draw from it? No doubt everyone seeks their own answer, in the world or in themselves. A drawing dated 1558, made into an engraving probably by Pieter van der Heyden, presents an image of it that is both odd and striking (fig. 238). It is called *Elck*: the name appears seven times in the engraving, on or beneath figures which are identical (fig. 237). Elck is the Flemish Everyman. Elck goes everywhere, searching, with or without glasses, often carrying a lantern, always the same person, looking for something in a bag, a basket, a barrel, in the distance by an encampment and its forest of spears, or farther still on the edge of a village and its church.

In the center of the image, amid a confused mass of bundles, packing cases, and various other items such a writing desk, pitchers, scales, distaff, a pair of compasses, hatchet, trowel, checkerboard, dice, and cards—all material possessions and distractions in a world of vanity—the main character, in his search, steps over a globe with a cross that has a hole in it. The engraving bears two Latin couplets in the margin and, in certain editions, quatrains in French and Flemish, which say: "In the world Everyman looks everywhere/And wants to find himself in all things/ Everyman therefore is always seeking himself/Might someone be lost forever?"[172] Behind the central figure, two of his fellows quarrel over a length of cloth, a scene the second quatrain explains: "Everyman pulls for the longest piece/One strains upward, the other down/No one knows himself, almost, in this world/We should take careful note, and wonder." In the background a framed image, a picture within a picture, shows a fool looking at himself in a convex mirror, amid various items of bric-a-brac that reflect the confusion of the main image. A legend in Flemish below this narcissistic fool reads: "No one knows himself." In the original drawing, level with the fool's face, NEMO (no one, in Latin) is written backward. The picture seems to be an allegory of selfishness, a satire on covetousness (the central Elck carries a bulging bag under his arm), a depiction of folly, even a pessimistic reply to Socrates's exhortation "Know thyself." This world shown here is not one of poverty, but of plenty; it might be Antwerp, a great commercial metropolis. The packages and bundles of goods indeed bear imaginary trademarks, either cabbalistic or real, which identify them. Thus, on the lower part of the case between the two quarreling characters we see the mark of Hieronymus Cock: the four points of the compass and the letters I W C, the initials of Jan Wellens de Cock, Hieronymus's father.[173]

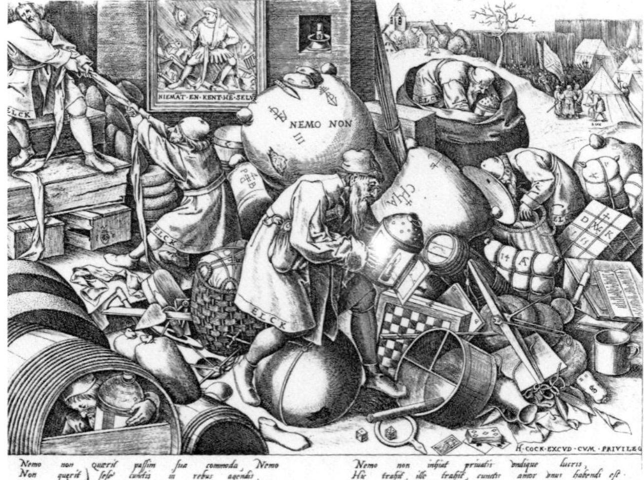

237. Pieter van der Heyden (attributed), *Elck,* or *Everyman,* after Pieter Bruegel, ca. 1558. Engraving, 9 x 11½ in. (22.8 x 29.4 cm). Brussels, Bibliothèque royale Albert I, print room

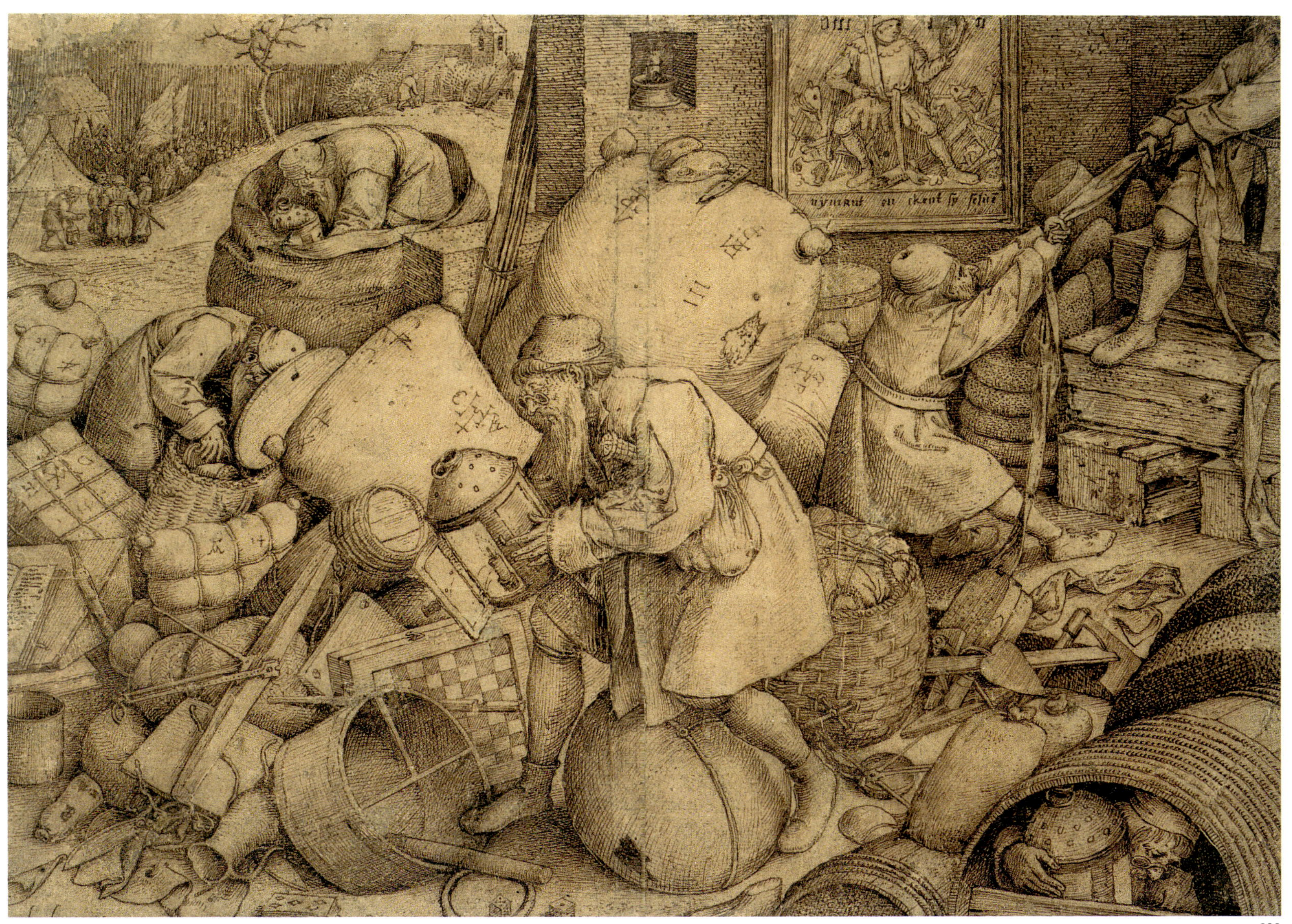

238. Pieter Bruegel, *Elck*, or *Everyman*, 1558. Pen and brown ink, 8 1/4 x 11 1/2 in. (21 x 29.3 cm). London, British Museum

The drawing perhaps contains other proverbs, which Bruegel was to introduce the following year into *Flemish Proverbs.* In that painting, the man with the lantern in the lower right corner who is looking for a hatchet could be Elck (who in the drawing is turning his back on the tool). In the painting, the two men near the lantern-carrier who are arguing over a pretzel, each pulling against the other, immediately recall the pair in the drawing who are having a tug-of-war over a piece of cloth; and the world-upside-down lies on the ground, not with someone inside it this time, but stepped over and ignored by Elck. Some commentators have compared the subject of *Elck* with a Flemish morality play, *Elckerlyc*, published at the end of the fifteenth century, but the theory seems to have been abandoned today.[174] However, the character of Elck appeared frequently in plays and readings presented by the rhetorical societies during Antwerp festivals, the theater and poetry competitions of the 1561 *Landjuweel*, and the *Ommeganck* procession of 1563.[175] Elck is thus a well-known character of the time and, in pursuit of his quest, with his lantern lit in broad daylight, he also echoes Diogenes seeking, under similar conditions, "an honest man."[176] The image's fascination endures because of the ambiguity of Everyman and "no one"; its combination of repetition with unusual events creates a composition that holds the imagination much as Dürer's *Melancholia* does. Here, disorder replaces the German master's enigmatic order and, while Dürer addresses the feelings of the individual, Bruegel speaks more to man as a social being.

OF MONEY, MADNESS, AND MONKEYS

Reflections on morality, man, and society are behind many of Bruegel's drawings and engravings. Besides *Elck* and *The Alchemist* (fig. 45), which has already been discussed for the excellence of its conception and execution,[177] others should be mentioned: *The Battle of the Money-Boxes and the Safes*, *The Witch at Mallegem*, *The Dean of Renaix*, *The Madmen's Festivities*, and *The Haberdasher Robbed by Monkeys*. If *The Alchemist*, beyond its richness of content, denounces penury and despair, what are we to say of *The Battle of the Money-Boxes and the Safes* (fig. 239)? The engraving is by Pieter van der Heyden and was published by the Four Winds; the creation was Bruegel's, but the original drawing no longer exists. The date is subject to debate and has been variously estimated as early as 1558[178] and later than 1570.[179] As for the work's style and spirit, Louis Lebeer rightly dates its creation about 1563.[180]

The Battle of the Money-Boxes and the Safes is a magnificent battle, astonishingly chaotic, and full of prodigious pile-ups: the last two aspects recall *Elck*, with the same composition hinging on two intersecting diagonals. Nevertheless, while the piling up of elements appears more lopsided in *Elck*, here it pitilessly conveys action and power. The legend reads: "We money-boxes, barrels, and chests, it is for money and possessions that we brawl and quarrel." The turmoil is conveyed by lines and masses, in which we can discern the shapes of the combatants, whose armor protects their precious, jangling cash, but which pours out, where they are broken, like blood from a wound. The subject, then, is money. An eternal subject, undoubtedly, and one very relevant to the times: Antwerp was, as we know, a bastion of world trade. Money inevitably ruled there, but the city suffered an economic crisis in 1552 and, five years later, bankruptcy. In 1557 silver replaced gold as the currency. Special taxes were levied constantly, first by Charles V in 1552, then by the Duke of Alva in 1569. Throughout the painter's life he was aware of the acute problem of earning a living, which separated the well-off from the destitute. Some have seen in *The Battle of the Money-Boxes and the Safes* a contrast between the rich and those earning a pittance, but in fact everyone here is fighting for himself. Furthermore, a later, trilingual, edition bears the legend in Latin, French, and Flemish: "Riches make thieves/Gold and silver have destroyed many of these." The moral is clear: Bruegel is attacking the realm of money, which sinks into strife. Cupidity and greed hold sway over the battle.

Can madness be cured? So *The Witch at Mallegem* (fig. 243) maintains. A legend in Flemish explains: "I, lady witch, wish that all here should love me the same, I have come to cure you…" With the help of her assistants, she is removing the stone of madness that is swelling in a man's head. The growth of this stone was popularly believed to be a symptom of the illness, hence the need to remove it. This takes place in Mallegem, a place invented by Bruegel and "made up of the word *mal*, meaning mad, and the ending *gem*, meaning dwelling place."[181] The work was made into an engraving by Pieter van der Heyden and published by Cock in 1559; there were several later editions. The image is highly animated: A large crowd is milling around to be cured. Various scenes are grafted on to the main one. A madman, in the lower right corner, is going under the surgeon's knife in a giant, hollow egg—seen by some as an allusion to the philosopher's stone.[182] Spectators at the upper right are lifting a shutter; at the lower left, a face appears behind a grille. Is he a prisoner, a hospital inmate, or a symbolic figure?

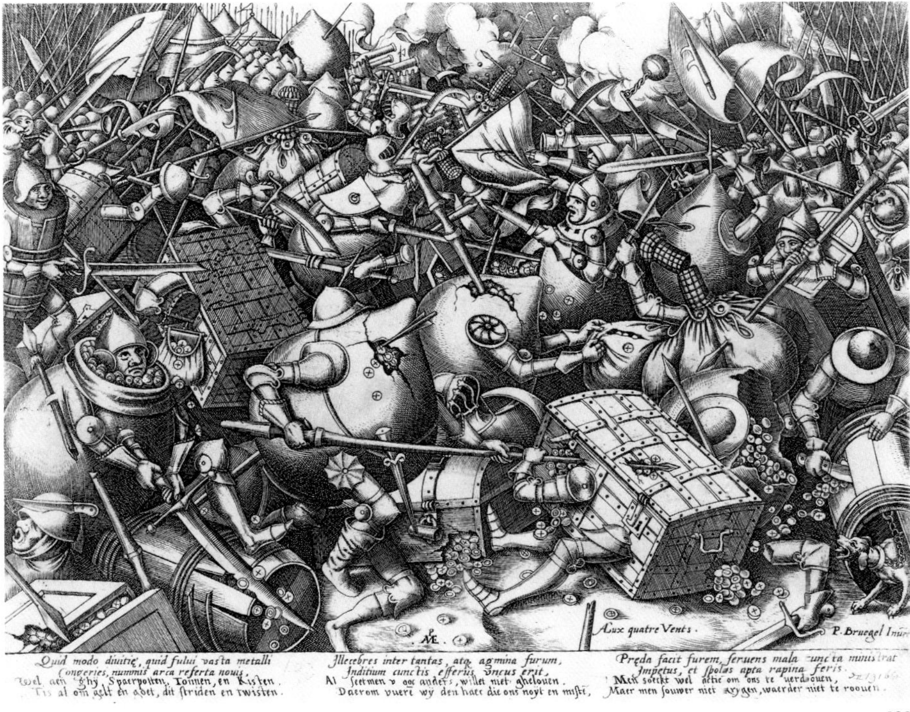

239

239. Pieter van der Heyden, *The Battle of the Money-Boxes and the Safes*, after Pieter Bruegel, ca. 1563. Engraving, 9 1/4 x 12 in. (23.6 x 30.4 cm). Brussels, Bibliothèque royale Albert I, print room

At the top left corner a watermill appears to be peacefully grinding flour. In the center are some echoes of Hieronymus Bosch, and some figures, wearing cloaks, remind us that this work is contemporary with *Flemish Proverbs*. Is this why, in the far distance, a ship sails toward the sun, as it does in the painting? It seems to be saying that we must "keep our sail in the eye of the wind," that is, look out for squalls, and that "everything comes out in the end."

One of the witch's helpers holds a lantern to shine a light on the operation. We are reminded that Elck, too, searches with a lantern among a labyrinth of objects. Here, is it a labyrinth of ideas? The heroine of Mallegem brandishes the extracted stone. In the legend to another edition she compares herself to the "Italian operators" who remove stones from the bladder, and concludes: "They only cure the kidneys/And I cure the brain."[183] But under the table a man, his mouth held shut by a padlock, seizes from a tub another stone, no doubt destined for the next client! The presence of cloaks in the crowd proclaims deceit. A satire of madness then, but also of charlatans.

217

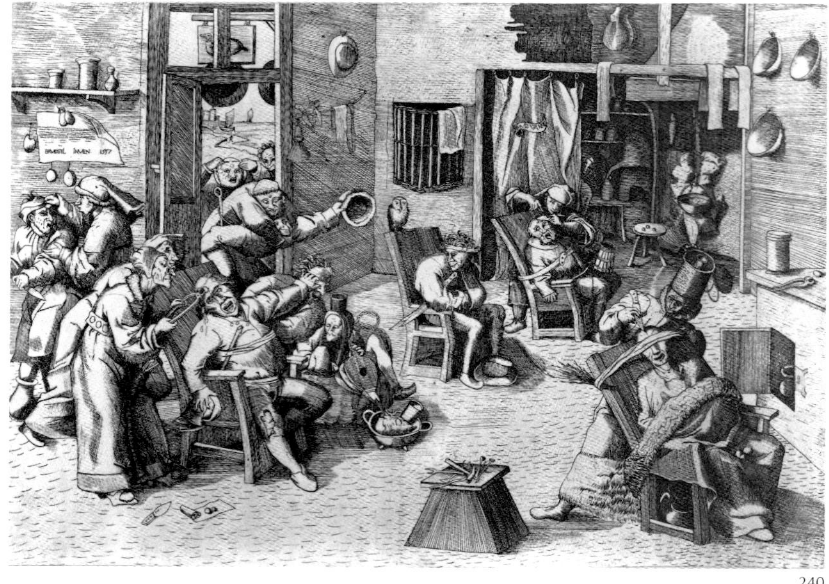

240

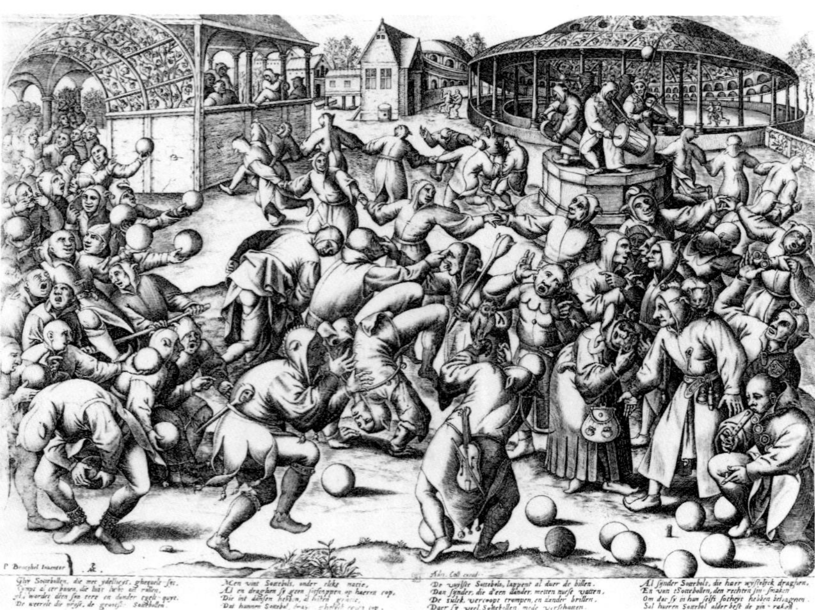

P. Brueghel Inuentor

Ghy Sottebollen, die met ydelheyt, ghequelt, zyn,
Compt al eer haeuen, die haer liefs al rollen,
Jck, wordet dten zen tere en dander tgelt quyt.
De weerelt die vryst, de grootste Sottebollen.

Men vint Sottebols, onder elcke natie,
Al en draghen sy geen jossenppen op haeren cop,
Die int dansen hebben, al hebben gracie,
Dat hunnen Sottebol, fray, ghelyst een cop.

De wyse Sottebols, lappent al duer de billen.
Dan synder, die d'een dander, metten nuese vatten.
De sulck, vercoopt trompen, en dander brillen.
Daer sy veel Sottebollen mede verschatten.

Al synder Sottebols, die haer wystelyck draghen,
En van tSottebollen, den rechten sin smaken
Om dat sy in hun selfs sotheyt hebben belnaghen
Sal haeren Sottebol alder best de pin raken.

Adr. Coll excud.

241

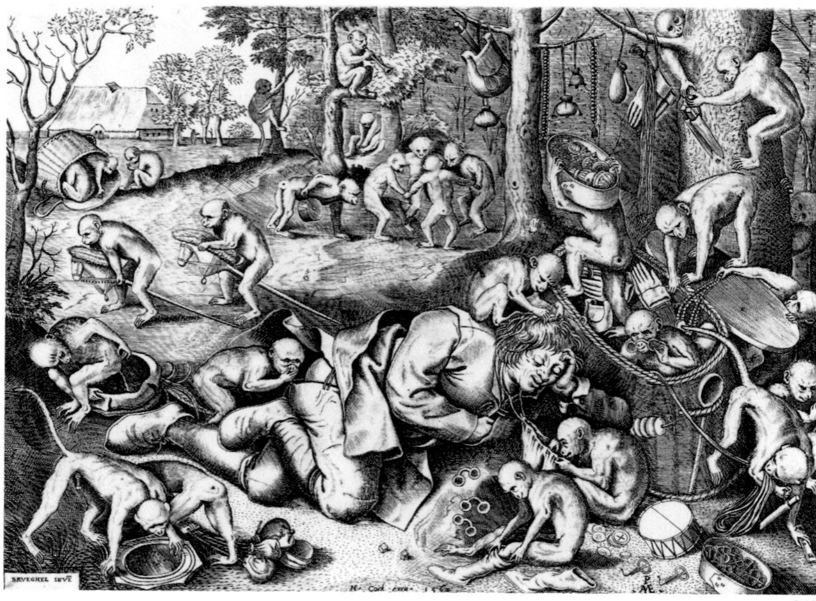

BRVEGHEL INVE
H. Cock excu.

242

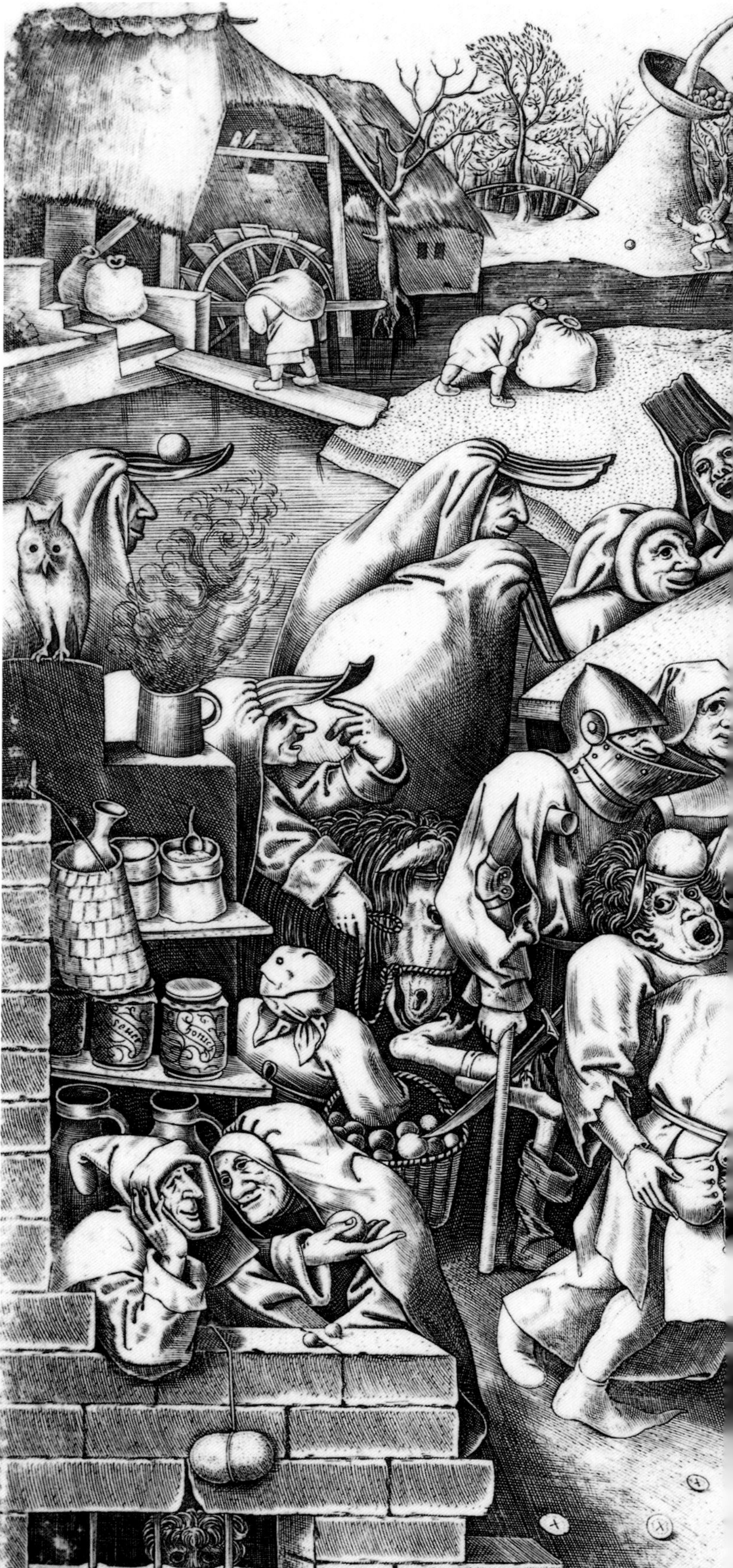

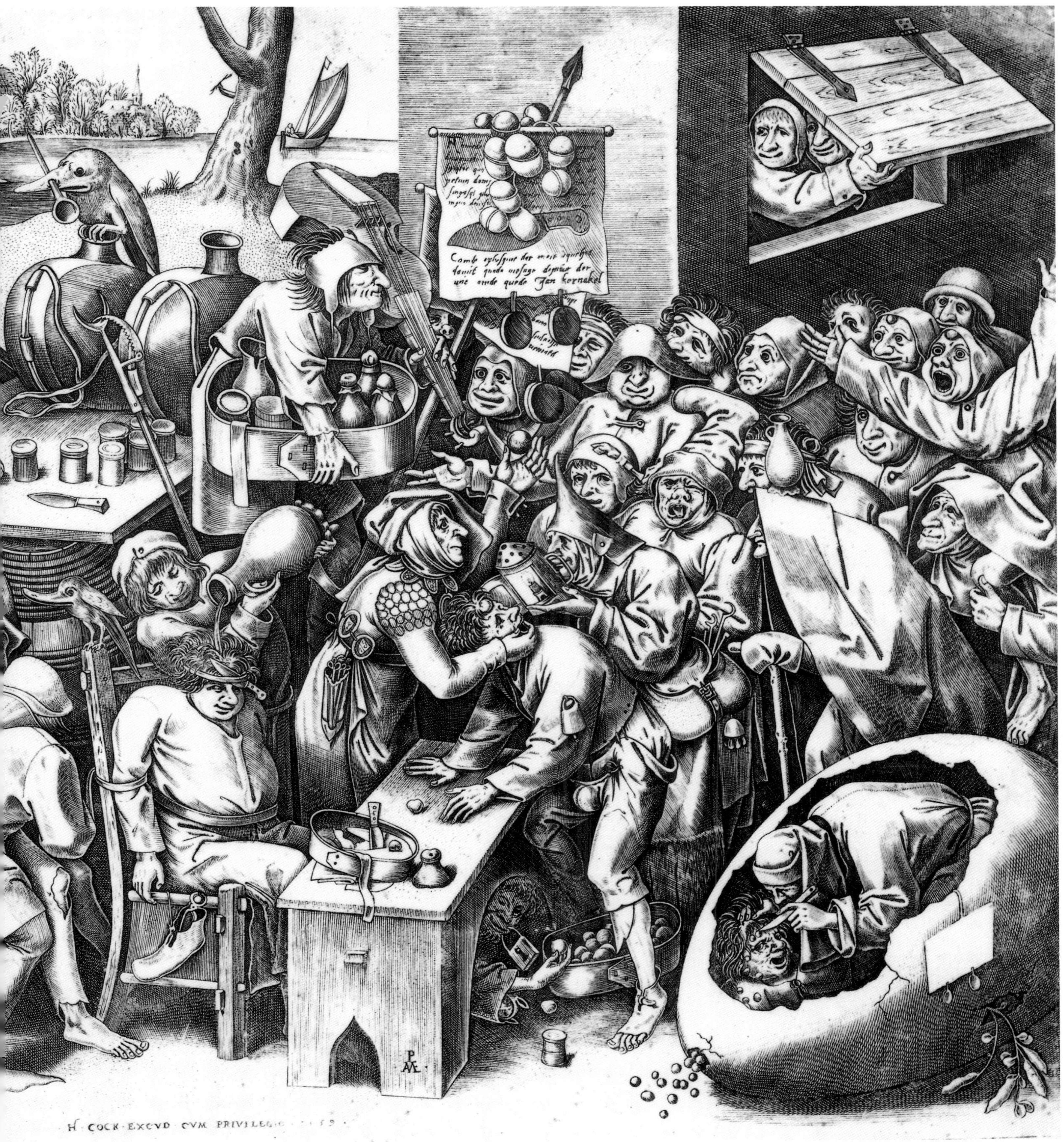

243

240. Anonymous, *The Dean of Renaix*, after Pieter Bruegel (?), 1557 (?). Engraving, 11 1/8 x 16 in. (28.3 x 40.6 cm). Brussels, Bibliothèque royale Albert I, print room

241. Pieter van der Heyden, *The Madmen's Festivities*, after Pieter Bruegel, ca. 1559. Engraving, 12 1/2 x 17 1/4 in. (32.5 x 43.7 cm). Brussels, Bibliothèque royale Albert I, print room

242. Pieter van der Heyden, *The Haberdasher Robbed by Monkeys*, after Pieter Bruegel, 1562. Engraving, 8 7/8 x 11 3/8 in. (22.5 x 29 cm). Brussels, Bibliothèque royale Albert I, print room

243. Pieter van der Heyden, *The Witch at Mallegem*, after Pieter Bruegel, 1559 (?). Engraving, 14 x 18 7/8 in. (35.5 x 48 cm). Brussels, Bibliothèque royale Albert I, print room

Another engraving, *The Dean of Renaix* (fig. 240), similarly depicts the removal of the stone of madness but, although it bears the inscription BRUEGEL INVEN 1557, its quality is mediocre and its lack of flair hardly worthy of the master. Its authenticity therefore appears doubtful.[184] On the other hand, the antics are lively in *The Madmen's Festivities* (fig. 241), an engraving by Pieter van der Heyden—after an original by Bruegel, now lost—published by the Four Winds in about 1559. In the foreground, a game of bowls alludes to a Flemish play on words: a madman can be referred to as *sottebol*, the term *sot* meaning mad and *bol* either bowling ball or head. Indeed, on the left, a madman is trying unscrew his own head in order to bowl with it. Others are dancing, sometimes in circles, doing somersaults, playing music, thumbing their noses or holding each other by the nose (allusion to another proverb—to be led around by the nose); others are selling each other spectacles or pulling faces at each other. In the background are buildings that are neither urban nor rustic, but rather decorative: a large carousel-like structure with an ornamented roof, a summer house with an arbor and columns. The engraving has been compared to a woodcut by Hans Sebald Beham (fig. 244), which has itself been linked to *The Wedding Dance* by Bruegel, now in the Detroit Institute of Arts.[185] The quatrain inscribed on the engraving in another edition reads: "You madmen who incessantly play with your heads/Whose brains are filled with vanities/Come, and run to join this band/Losing both honor and possessions, The world orders you to."[186] This invitation to dance, and the later editions of the engraving, bear witness to the popularity of such entertainments and to the role played by "Madness" in the rhetorical societies and the performances of the *Landjuweelen*. It is, after all, a fool who leads the dance in *The Battle of Carnival and Lent*, which Bruegel painted in 1559.

The verses on *The Madmen's Festivities* go on to explain: "All leading each other by the nose, selling spectacles/Resembling by their Madness the gallant merchants." This recalls another work, *The Haberdasher Robbed by Monkeys* (fig. 242); here, the merchant is certainly not gallant, but fast asleep! He will regret it. Dozing on the edge of a wood after a good meal, drinking bout, or other amusement enjoyed in the nearby house, the traveling salesman is being robbed by a band of monkeys that empty his baskets, spreading around and carrying away various objects. The subject is an amusing one, which occurs in images from the end of the fifteenth century in Florence and in Swabia.[187] In 1532 Hans Weiditz used it in an illustration for a translation of Petrarch published in Augsburg (fig. 245), and Karel van Mander mentions a painting on the same theme by Herri met de Bles, which he saw in Amsterdam and on which, reportedly, was inscribed a satire against the pope.[188]

Nothing however suggests such an interpretation in the engraving by Pieter van der Heyden after Bruegel, published in 1562 by Hieronymus Cock. The same year, the painter made *Two Monkeys* (fig. 213), a masterpiece of a different kind of intensity. As for *The Haberdasher*, it draws on popular entertainment: the itinerant salesman is a well-known figure of the time. He appears in *Christ Carrying the Cross*, for example, and in other engravings; an inventory of his wares is displayed by the animals, which unwrap them, scatter them about, or hang them from trees. As for monkeys, they often appear in works ranging from illuminations to the paintings of David Teniers the Younger and his followers, who seized on them as a way of imitating humans in the form of "monkey tricks."

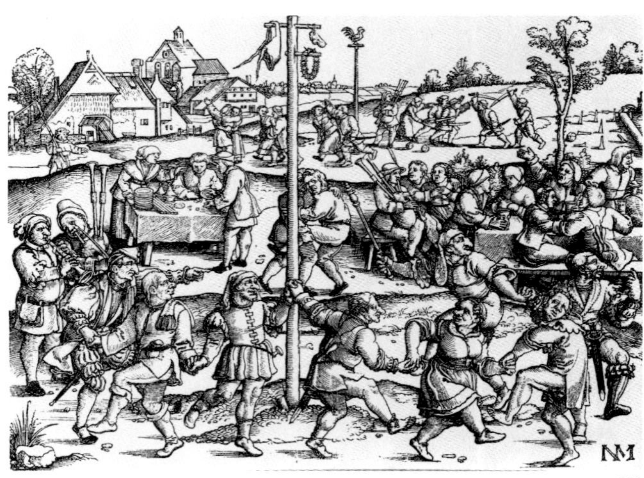

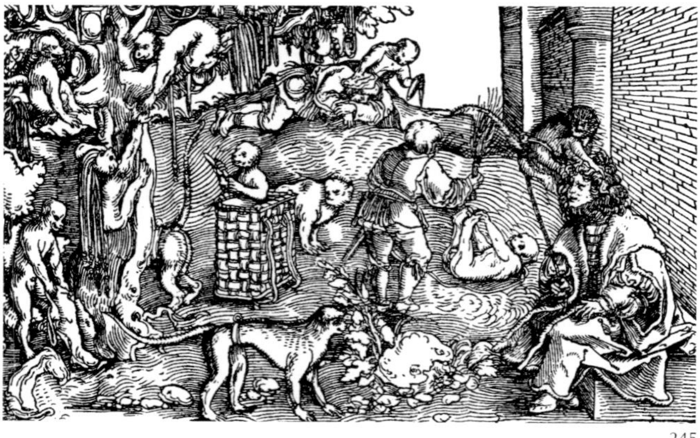

244. Hans Sebald Beham, *The Dance of the Nose at Gümpelsbrunn* (detail), 1534. Woodcut, 15½ x 14¼ in. (39.3 x 36.3 cm). Formerly at Gotha, Schlossmuseum (now destroyed)

245. Hans Weiditz, *The Haberdasher Robbed by Monkeys*, illustration in Petrarch, *Das Buch der Artzney beider Glück*, Augsburg, 1532. Paris, Bibliothèque nationale de France

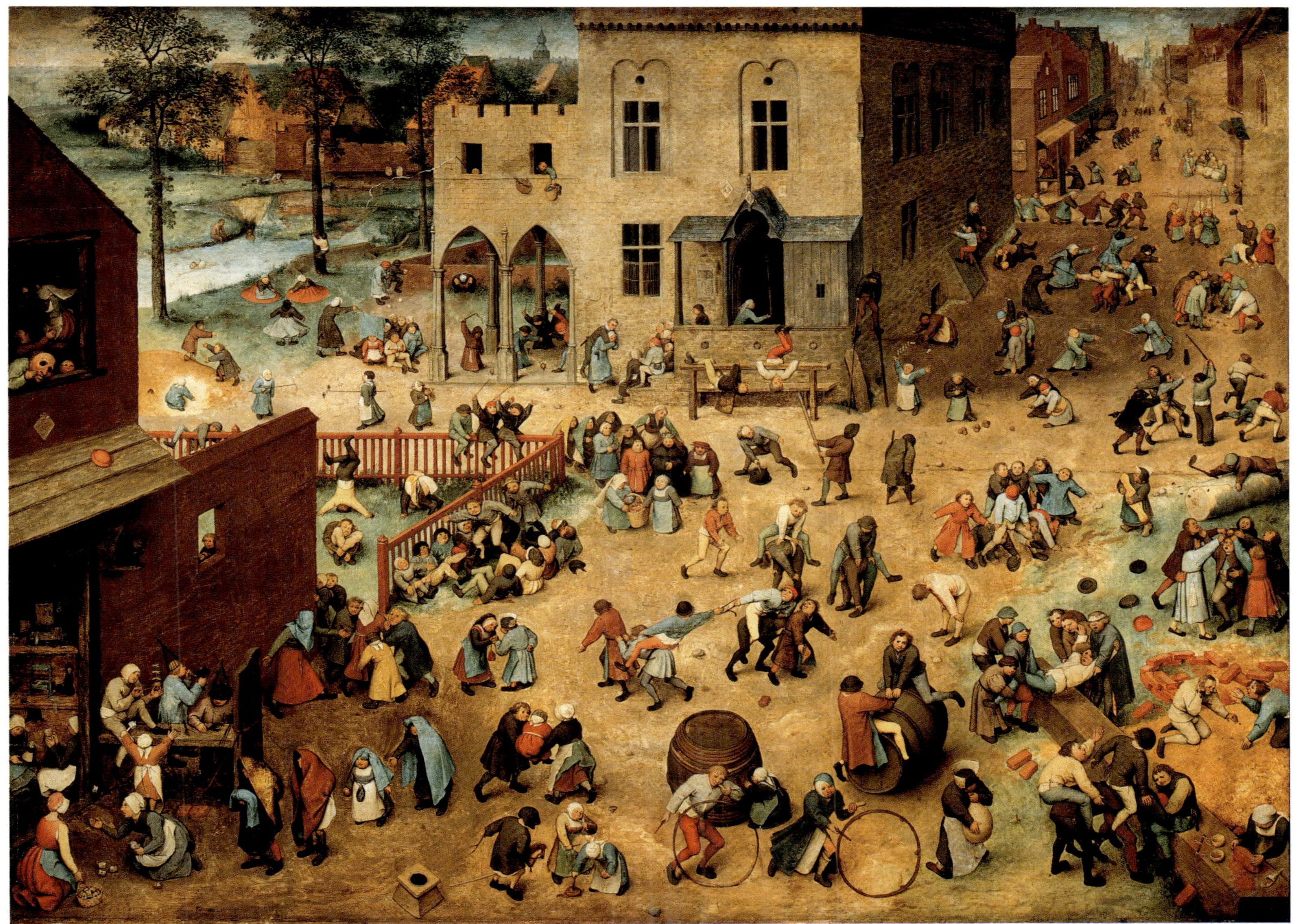

246

IMAGES OF CHILDHOOD

Children's Games (figs. 246–50), painted in oil on wood panel in 1560, is striking
for the way it is constructed—buildings with clear lines, a deliberate effect of perspective, which has been seen as recalling Italian art or that of Vredeman de Vries
in Flanders—and for the joyous childhood world that takes shape in every sense,
which could be contrasted with the terrifying vision presented by *The Triumph of
Death* a few years later. The theme, which is repeated in breviaries, books of hours,
and calendars, parallels sixteenth-century allegories of *infantia* or *innocentia*,[189]
and is renewed here through the astonishing way this urban scene is brought to
life by the invasion of some 230 children. No adults are to be seen, with the
exception of a woman throwing a bucket of water over two fighting boys, as over
two over-excited dogs.

While the games themselves can be identified (one count has enumerated a
total of 91) the children are barely pictured as individuals: They are brought to
life by an attitude or an expression, and movement springs from a line, a shape, a

246–50. Pieter Bruegel, *Children's Games*, 1560: whole
work and details. Oil on panel, 46½ x 63⅜ in. (118 x 161 cm).
Vienna, Kunsthistorisches Museum

221

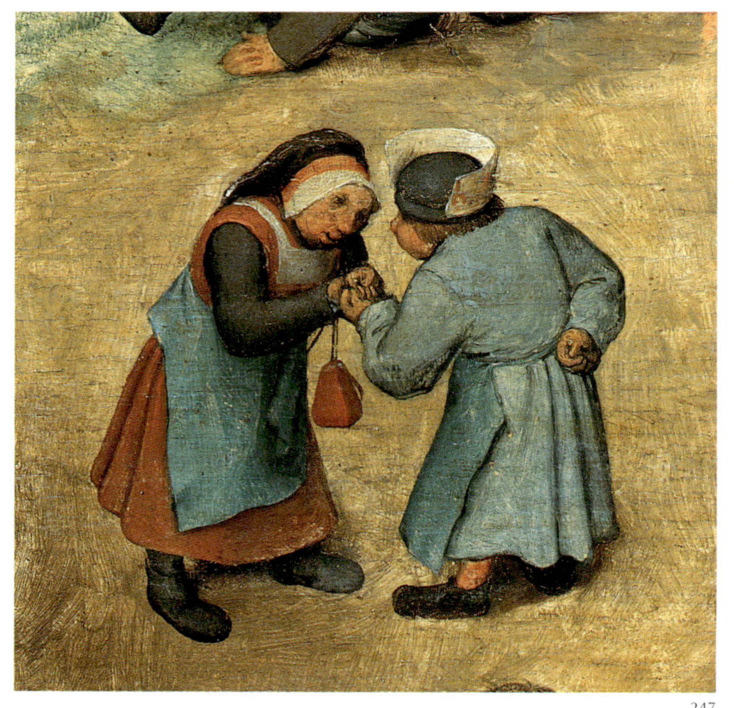

247

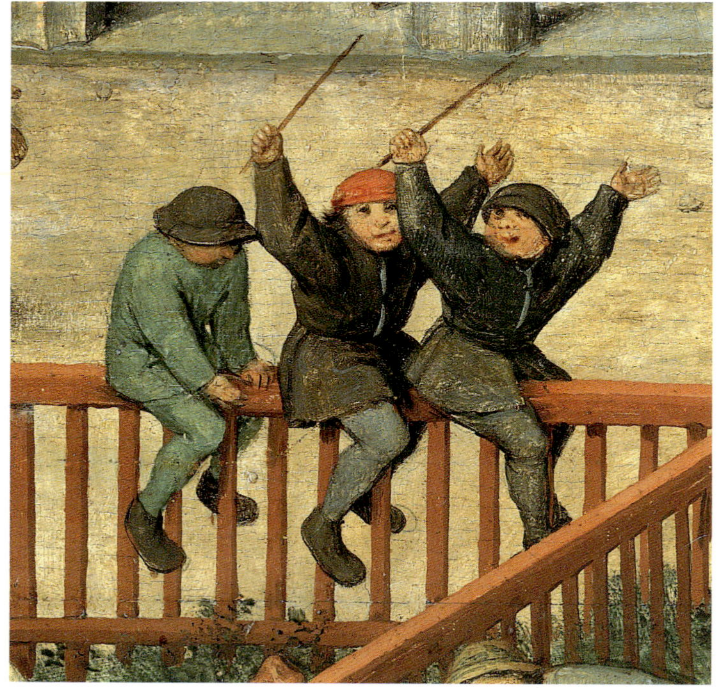

248

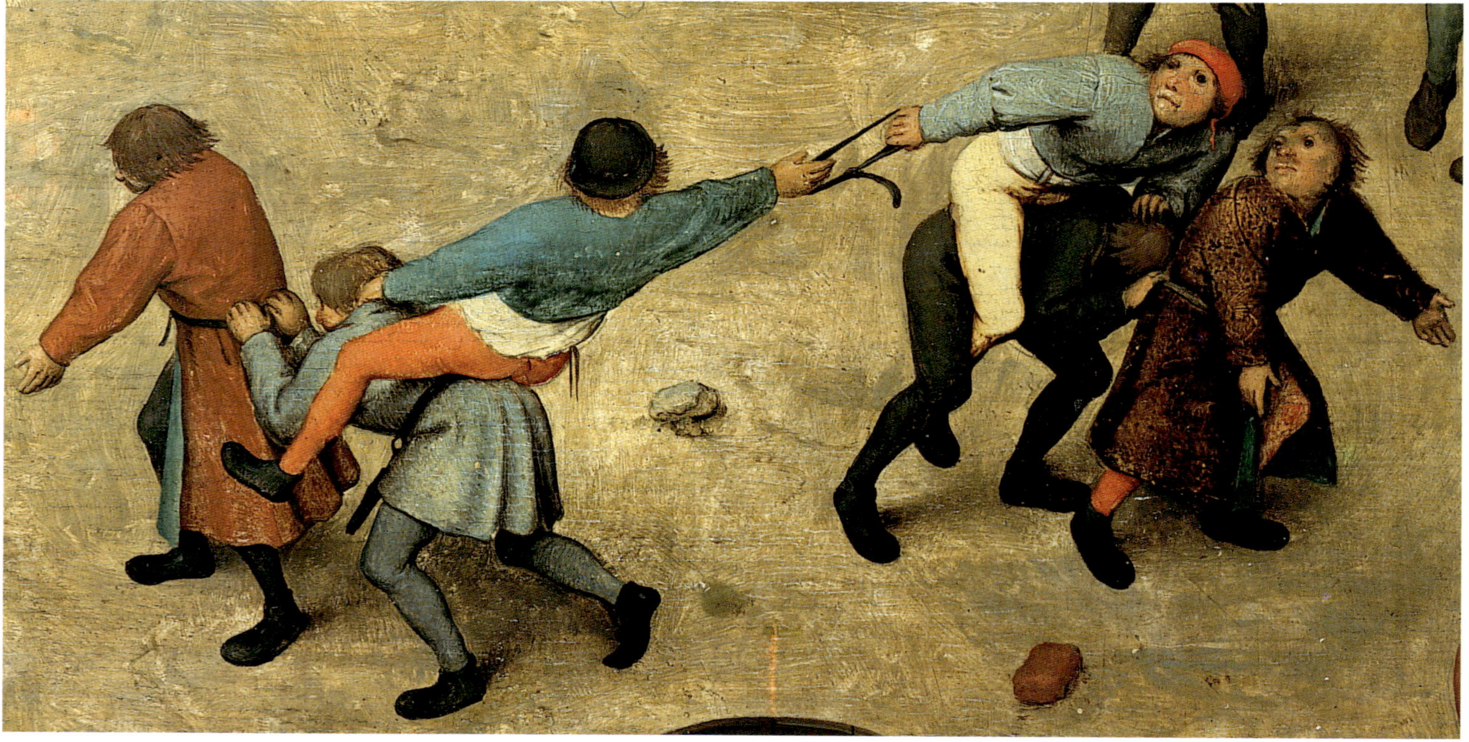

249

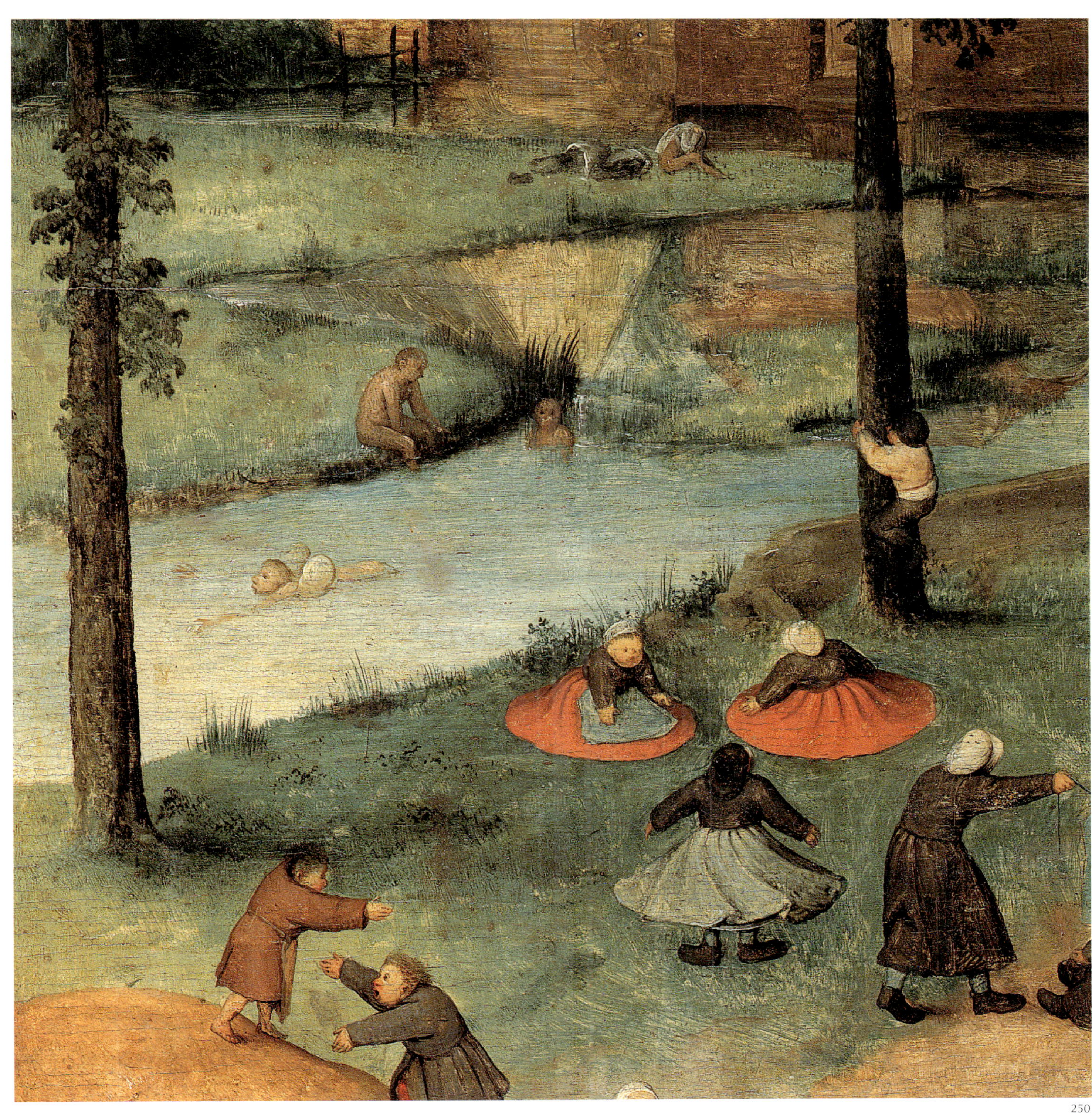

patch of color. Such is perhaps the positive side of this large painting whose title, *Khinderspill von Bruegel*, appears in 1595 in the succession inventory of Habsburg Archduke Ernest, who had bought it the previous year in Brussels.[190] Karel van Mander also mentions a work "with all the games of children, and countless little allegories."[191] The latter phrase, which could equally well describe the painting or be the final item in a list, opens the door to a number of readings. In contrast to the simple, and clever series of the 218 amusements of Gargantua listed by Rabelais,[192] some have seen Bruegel's painting as a means to denounce human folly. For example, he captures the parody of marriage in the center of the painting, a game of chance at the bottom where a little girl plays with knucklebones, and a blue cloak worn by a child in the baptism procession. An attempt to interpret one or other of these groups, in isolation from the rest, could open the way to a satirical reading.

Yet what could be more innocent than to play with dolls, run after a hoop, play leapfrog, walk on stilts, or turn somersaults? Certainly, these little characters are facially anonymous: we cannot tell Peter from Paul or Catherine from Mary; the child's world is barely personalized, and clothing, colors apart, is virtually uniform, though different between the sexes. This universe of childhood seems real enough, and the impression it gives is reinforced if we compare it with that depicted in *The Ass at School* (fig. 81), where the supposed children have a rather old look about them, closer to the appearance of adults than to the denizens of a primary school. The marriage scene in *Children's Games* is roughly where the compositions's two large diagonals intersect: Is this a denunciation of the sacrament? Is it not, on the contrary, the true place, the very source, of the child? And if there are references to proverbs, what could be more natural, since these always summarize a human attitude or action. Besides, since children imitate their parents, the painter is giving the viewer a knowing wink. Here is Bruegel in 1560— after *Flemish Proverbs*, *The Battle of Carnival and Lent*, the *Virtues*, *Elck*, *The Alchemist*, *The Witch at Mallegem*, and *The Madmen's Festivities*—going on to make allusions and references, even quoting himself. For by this time he had at his command a wide range of images, and he naturally made use of them. As for the blue cloak, here it is less a case of mockery than, perhaps, a warning. Irony always lurks in Bruegel's work in the 1560s, and its mood does not change overnight. If *Flemish Proverbs* often condemns, and if the *Battle of Carnival and Lent* emphasizes the ridiculous, might not *Children's Games* represent a pause for breath? Innocence may imitate madness, but only in appearance, not in reality. This appearance is no more than a game, which could be seen as a warning addressed to adults, without, for all that, defiling the world of children. This world is in no way simplistic; its very diversity is exemplary. The hoops and barrels in the foreground give the feeling of movement; the children at the bar and the stilt-walker in front of the large building, in the middle distance, combine construction with instability; the children at the windows on the left make a game out of the unusual; and the vista in the background appears to abolish time and space.

The painting has sometimes been interpreted as embodying the season of spring. It was exhibited in this spirit in Vienna after the death of Rudolf II,[193] with *The Massacre of the Innocents,* which represented winter, *The Harvest* (summer), and *The Return of the Herd* (autumn). Despite the view of some commentators,[194]

this great public square before a building——perhaps Antwerp's town hall[195]—
which on the left opens out on to a waterway and lush countryside, and straight
ahead into a long street that rises to a church in the distance—this living place
does not personify a single moment in the year. It contains, indeed, some celebrations of summer such as the midsummer's day fire, but also, on the left, a child
carrying a Christmas and new year loaf and, on the left, at the window, a mask
for carnival, such as we have already seen in the latter's battle with Lent. Different
times are mingled and combined, as are the games themselves—the only ones
missing are those that require snow, depicted in *The Census at Bethlehem* (fig. 200)
and *Landscape with Skaters and Bird Trap* (fig. 54).

   Children's Games cannot, therefore, be reduced to a single aim on the part
of the artist. The work is more akin to a burst of energy than to a moral lesson,
more a picture of life than an inventory of a time and place—but it has its notes of

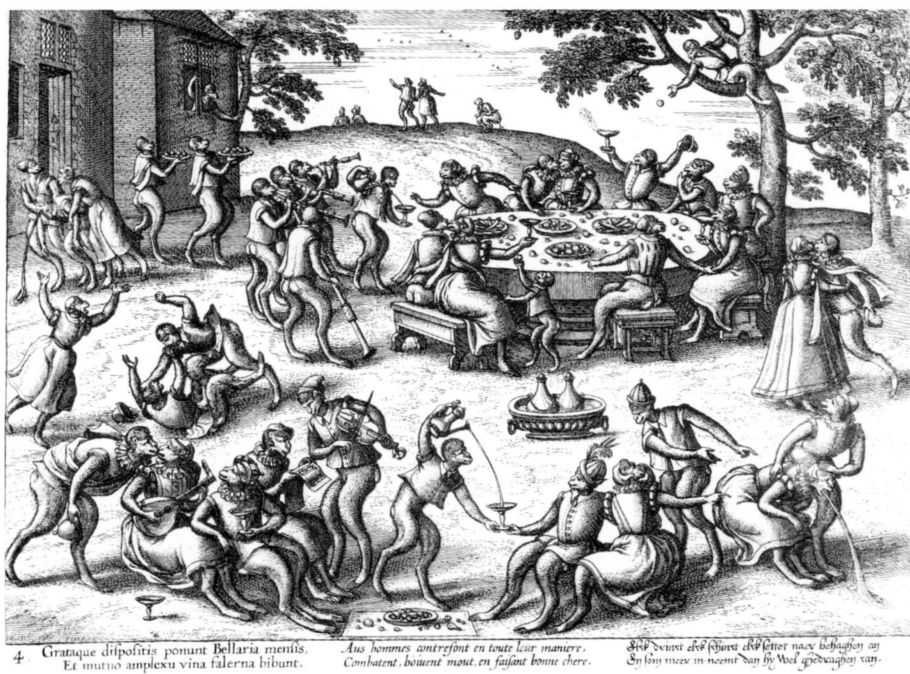

251

humor too. Thus the arrangement of the hats thrown to the ground on the right—
three black, one red—forms an ironic-looking face, as Tolnay points out;[196] as for
the little girl who is playing at being a shopkeeper in the lower left corner, she is
scraping a red brick in order to make a painter's pigment, and beneath her the
artist, as Sandra Hindman points out, has signed himself BRUEGEL 1560.[197]

   Historically the work has its forerunners: images in illuminations, writings by
Froissart, Rabelais, and the Spanish humanist Juan Luis Vivès, who wrote treatises
on education in Latin. And we might also recall Sebastian Brant's remark in his
Ship of Fools: "All children resemble/their parents to some degree."[198] Posterity,
was to remember this painting. While some inventories mention copies by Bruegel
the Younger,[199] these versions have disappeared. However, others exist, such as
one by Martin van Cleve; several parodies, in the form of monkeys' games, by
Pieter van der Borcht, a native of Antwerp and follower of Bruegel (fig. 251); and,

251. Pieter van der Borcht IV, *The Monkeys' Game.*
Etching, 8½ x 11½ in. (21.5 x 29.3 cm). Brussels,
Bibliothèque royale Albert I, print room

equally closely associated with the master, an engraving by Nicolas de Bruyn after a drawing by Martin de Vos,[200] who was in Italy at the same time as Bruegel. The following century, the Flemish poet Jacob Cats did much to promote a non-realist reading of the painting. He wrote: "The world is nothing but a children's game" and added: "You will find, I know/your own madness in the game of children."[201] No doubt. Everything can be seen in anything, of course; but, to quote Klaus Demus: "It is certain that Bruegel, in this work as in others, is 'showing' something as an artist (by 'creating' and not 'lecturing')." To this we can add that interpreters bring with them their own formulae.[202] Thus, the children's games become adults' games. And youthful imagination sometimes has firmer foundations than reason. If some have been able wrongly to transform this childhood world into a parody, it is that they have omitted its colors. These—vibrant, joyous, to the point of giving a feeling of spring or summer, with their reds, blues, greens, and yellows, arranged and above all punctuated——suggest a positive, even expansive vision of this world. Indeed, in formal terms the groups and patches of color occupy the painting's space, taking possession of it in all senses, in town as in the country, on the ground floor as on the second floor, in the secular as in the religious. This is indeed the seat of the child, literally and figuratively: the former is clearly visible in the foreground. Bruegel perfectly adapts his chosen theme to the space in which he expresses it. He unites, to cite Paul Philippot's apt formula, "narrative demonstration and spatial unity."[203] The choice of format is in some ways surprising. We have no way of knowing whether it follows the wishes of a client, or the artist's own inspiration, for no information on this question survives.

SOLDIERS, BEGGARS, AND THE BLIND

If the sheer number of children, as of proverbs or of characters in Carnival and Lent, is striking in the larger paintings, what can we say of the multitude of spears, and therefore of soldiers carrying them, in *The Suicide of Saul* (figs. 253–55)? The painting refers to the battle of Mount Gilboa between the Philistines and the Israelites, after the biblical account to which Bruegel specifically refers next to his signature and the date 1562: SAVL. XXXI. This is a small panel, measuring just $13\frac{1}{8}$ x $21\frac{5}{8}$ inches (33.5 x 55 centimeters), and literally crammed with figures. For this reason, and because of the shifting accents of the awe-inspiring and tragic battle, the work has been compared to Altdorfer's *The Battle of Issus* (fig. 252). While the comparison seems inevitable, the differences are significant. In Bruegel's work the drama is resolved, so to speak, on the far left of the painting, where King Saul has fallen on his sword in order to elude the enemy, followed by his faithful armor-bearer. While this is the outcome of the episode, all the events preceding it are still happening: the clash of the armies, the dead and the living, archers on a rocky spur, a river which the troops are crossing by boat, battalions with dromedaries climbing to attack a citadel. In the distance on the left is a town open to the sea, or the sky, or perhaps both, with a great, mysterious fire. The vastness of the landscape fits the magnitude of the event, and its fractured character corresponds to the different episodes portrayed. We are almost forced to contrast the human

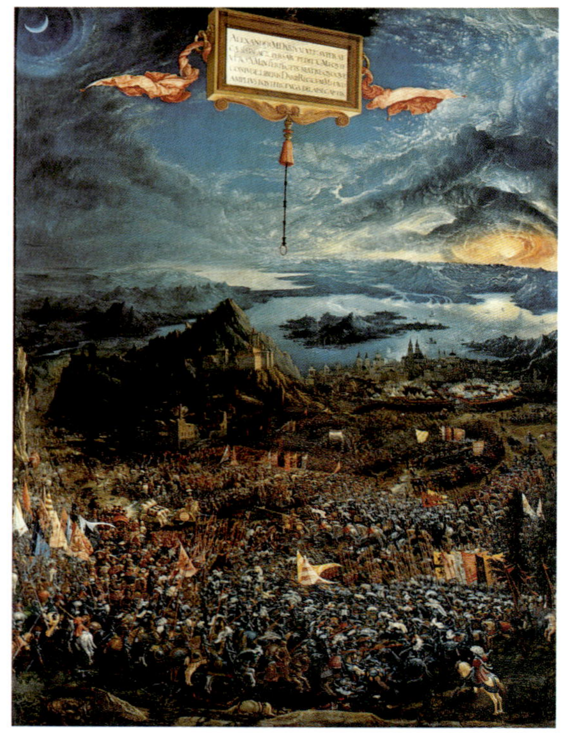

252

252. Albrecht Altdorfer, *The Battle of Issus*, 1529. Oil on panel, $62\frac{3}{8}$ x $47\frac{3}{8}$ in. (158.4 x 120.3 cm). Munich, Alte Pinakothek

226

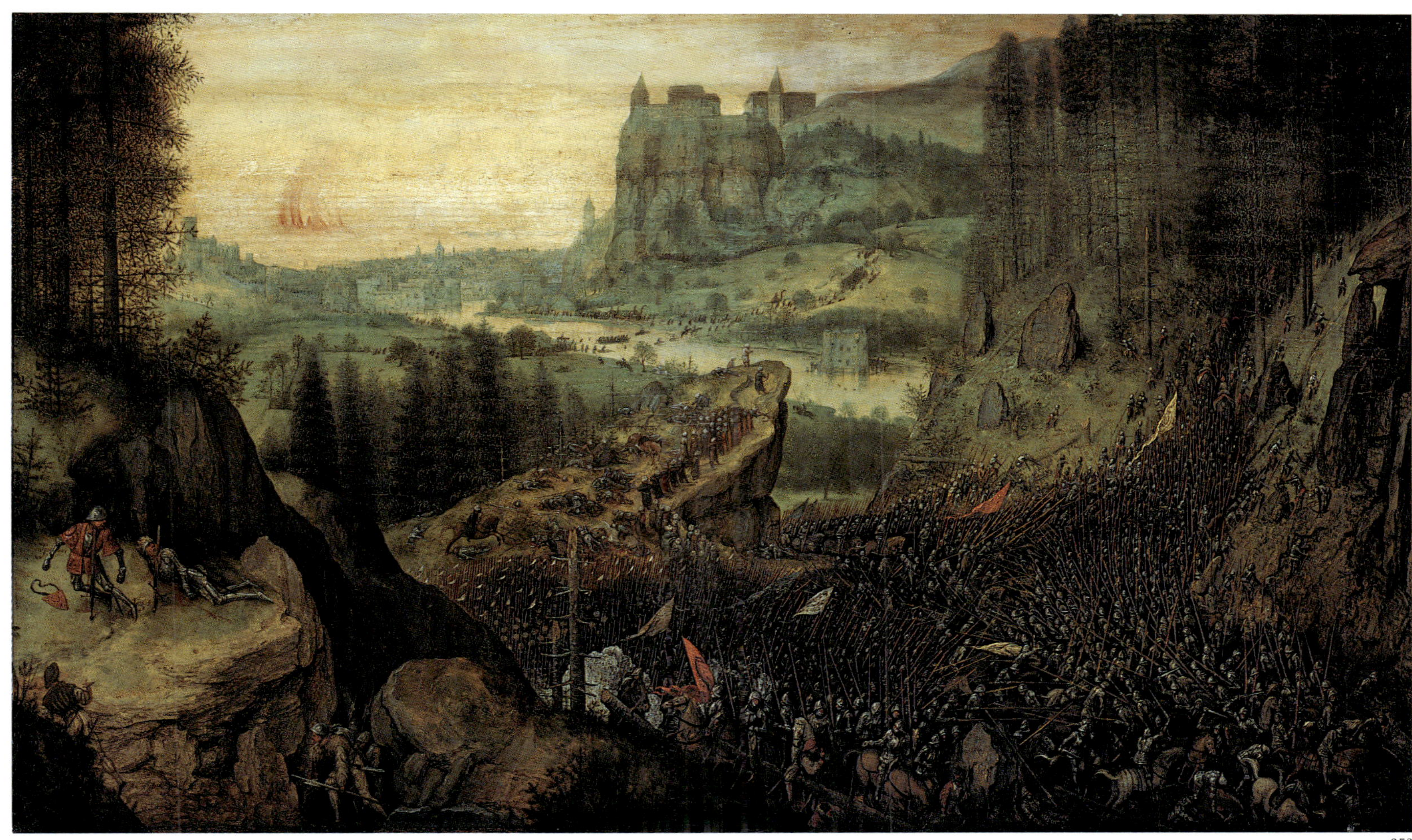

253

turmoil with the peace of nature. The labyrinthine landscape, with its rocks and conifers, foreshadows the wider one in *The Conversion of St. Paul* of 1567 (fig. 160).

The fall of Paul was the work of God; the suicide of Saul the image of his own defeat. Solitary and proud, it has been said of Saul that he was "one of the most extraordinary characters in the Bible, divided between the mystery of God and that of evil."[204] The consonance of the theme with the place, and prominence of the death of the hero—who in Bruegel's work is often lost in the composition, as in the case of St. Paul himself—here may convey an anguished dialogue between the individual and the world, a questioning which the fire on the horizon, as in the Apocalypse, would seem to answer. A mere hypothesis no doubt, among the many that arise from the human condition. Because of its concentration and the resulting expressive power, this painting goes significantly beyond the idea of a miniature, often mentioned, because it is outside all the refined and illustrative notions that this technique can imply. The broken composition is tense; the keen, extremely precise touch creates and brings to life its volume, defines detail, and punctuates the painting's space by endowing it with rhythm, breadth, and depth.

If the spears are smashed—and Bruegel knows them well, for he raises them aloft in *Elck* (1558), and lowers them to charge in *Fortitudo* (1560) as, later, in

253–55. Pieter Bruegel, *The Suicide of Saul*, 1562: whole work and details. Oil on panel, 13⅛ x 21⅝ in. (33.5 x 55 cm). Vienna, Kunsthistorisches Museum

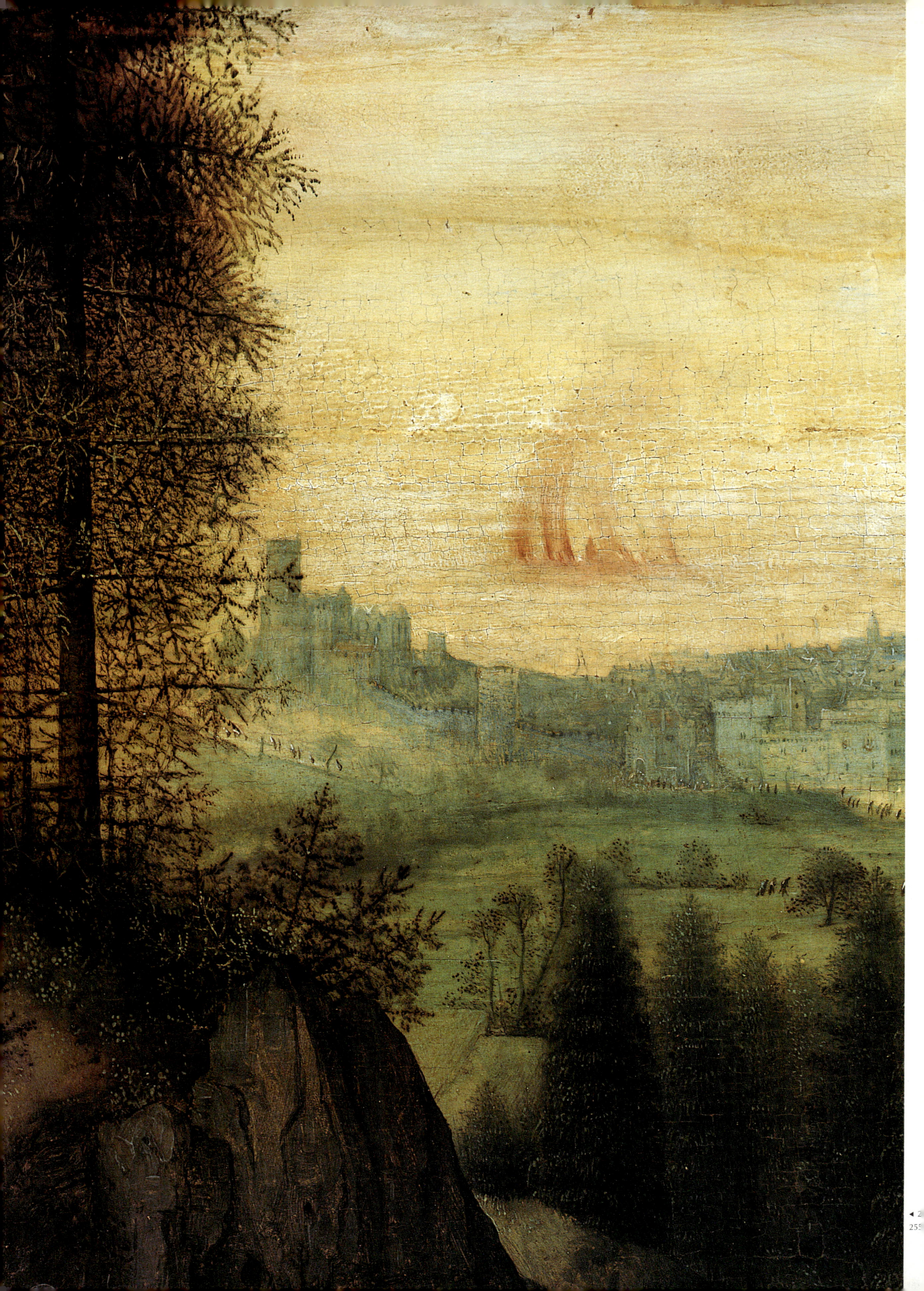

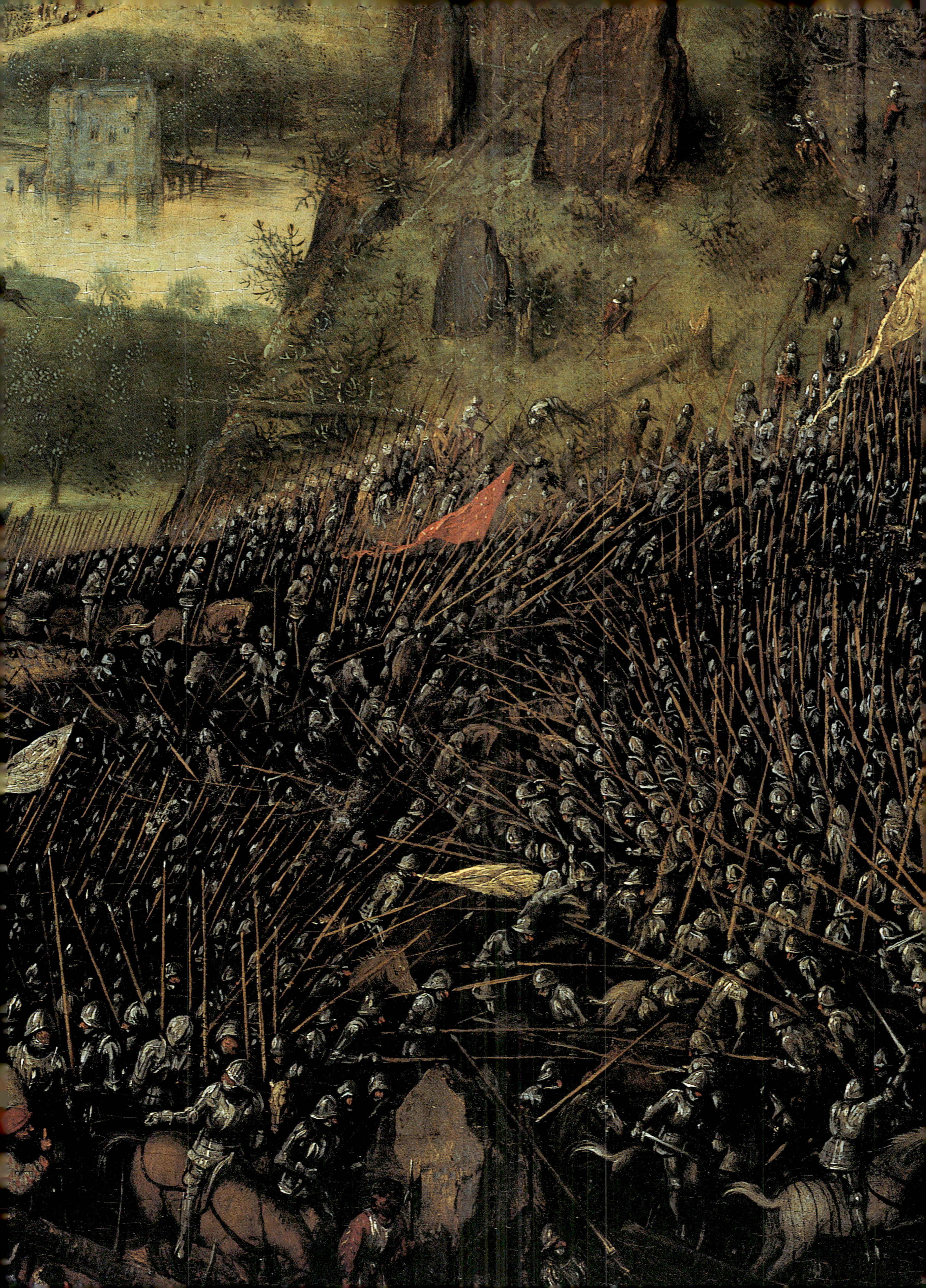

The Triumph of Death—the clash of weapons causes death and injury, maiming people for life. The infirm, the deformed, the legless, and various other cripples join forces to form bands of beggars who excite pity during public celebrations or at church doors. The theme is an old one, occurring in illuminations, church stalls—such as those of Diest in Brabant, which were made in a Brussels workshop at the end of the fifteenth century (fig. 256)—and in the drawings of Bosch, which were reproduced in engravings published by the Four Winds (fig. 257).

Bruegel's *The Beggars* (fig. 258) is a very small panel, measuring just 7¼ x 8½ inches (18.5 x 21.5 cm), dated 1568 and showing five figures variously dressed, with different types of headgear and differently colored clothing. Ocher, green, red, blue, brown, black, white, and pearl gray are mingled. Lines, which are embedded in the colors, define each mass, and the interplay of the crutches gives the composition its rhythm. The figures are on a space of closely cropped grass, surrounded by areas of bare brick wall. A figure on the right holds a wooden bowl. In the background, between the angled walls, there is a doorway behind which trees in an impressionist-style landscape are green against a blue sky. There is a deliberate contrast between the group of beggars, which is a structure of truncated pyramids, almost Cézanne-like in appearance, and the vista toward a no doubt peaceful countryside. A partly obliterated inscription in Dutch on the back of the panel wishes that the cripples' circumstances may improve. Another inscription (two Latin distichs) reads: "There is nothing in nature that is beyond our art,/ So great is the favor granted the painter./Here nature, transformed into painted images, and seen in its cripples,/Is bewildered to find that Bruegel is its equal."[205] The compliment echoes that of Ortelius, but the work is remarkable in itself, and in a way that goes beyond mere realism. Many writers have been tempted to read a message or hidden meaning in it. Early on, the fox or badger tails that the beggars wear as a distinctive mark of their condition were interpreted as a political allusion to the signatories of the Compromise of Breda. The nobles who opposed Margaret of Parma, and thus Spain, in 1566 were proud to be called "beggars."[206] According to this view, the painting is the act of a partisan.[207] Disguised as the beggars are, one with headgear shaped like a miter (already used by Bruegel in his drawing of *Lust*), and others with hats shaped like a crown or a flower-pot holder, they are not dressed as beggars, in brown serge, but on the contrary in various colors, better to attract attention to their misery and excite pity. Moreover, these excluded people are already on the scene, with the same attitudes and clothing, on the left of *The Battle of Carnival and Lent* of 1559 (fig. 125), and thus long before political resistance was organized and provoked the wrath of Philip II and the dispatch of the Duke of Alva to the Netherlands.

But are these real beggars? Probably—because when they cheat, Bruegel tells us. A fine example is to be found on the side of Lent, where people are coming out of the church: the monkey hidden in the basket on the back of the woman who is pleading in the name of her maimed husband speaks volumes. Should we therefore see a symbol of hypocrisy here? Probably not. There is a sense of parody, which the beggars themselves emphasize by various aspects of their clothing in order to coax a smile, and goodwill, from passers-by. Perhaps Bruegel used this misery in order to denounce society and to make a pastiche in which each beggar

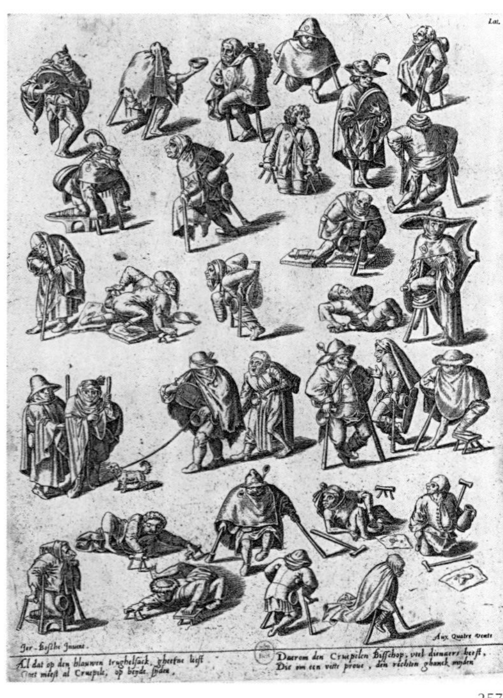

256. Brussels workshop, *A Beggar*, ca. 1491–1500. Carved wood choir stall. Diest, Church of Saint-Sulpice

257. Anonymous, *Cripples, Madmen, Musicians, and Beggars*, after Hieronymus Bosch. Engraving, 11¾ x 8⅝ in. (30 x 21.8 cm). Paris, Bibliothèque nationale de France, print department

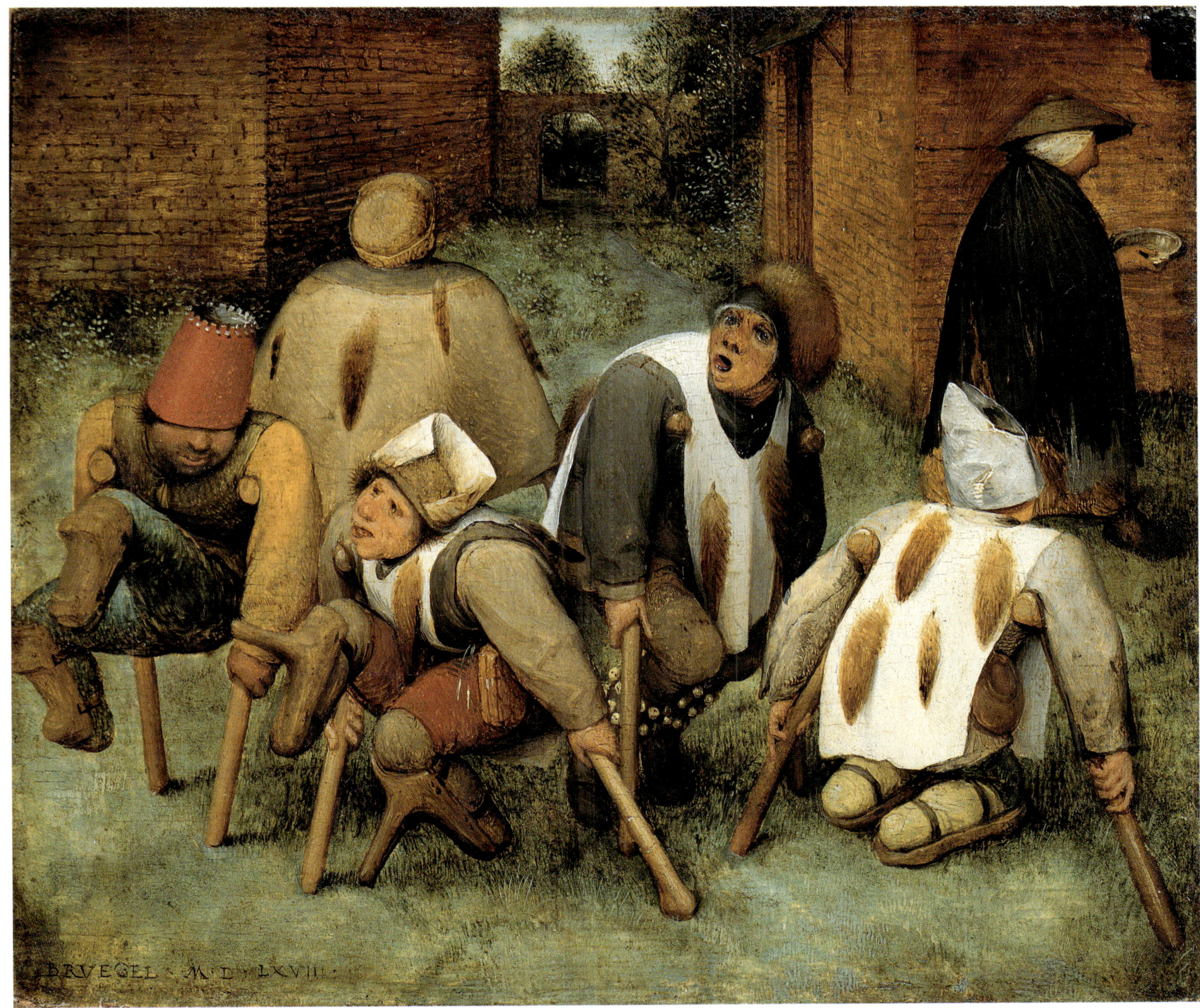

258. Pieter Bruegel, *The Beggars*, 1568. Oil on panel, 7¼ x 8½ in. (18.5 X 21.5 cm). Paris, Louvre

represents a social class.[208] It might, too, refer to a collection of alms at Epiphany[209] (hence their presence, already, in *The Battle of Carnival and Lent*). Similar works exist by Pieter Aertsen and Martin van Cleve, contemporaries of Bruegel, who dealt with the same subject. The persistence of this theme is noticeable. A painting by Van Cleve dating from 1579, now in the Hermitage Museum, and which is in a sense a companion to Bruegel's *Carnival* of 1559, makes a precise historical reference even less likely. Be that as it may, the beggars, who haunt the court of miracles, are common in the iconography of the period. With or without political or social allusion, reference to folklore or even to religion,[210] Bruegel's work is essentially an artistic achievement of the highest quality, and a statement about humanity.

The emotion contained within a little more than seven square inches (46 square centimeters) does not get diluted on a surface forty times that size, as is demonstrated by *The Blind Leading the Blind*, which Bruegel painted in distemper in 1568 (fig. 69). Six monumental figures drag each other to the ground, in the midst of a rustic and apparently indifferent landscape. The subject is drawn from the Gospels: "They be blind leaders of the blind. And if the blind lead the blind, both shall fall into the ditch."[211] This idea, which was taken up in other writings—those of the poet Anna Bijns among others—inevitably takes the concrete form of an image. A version by Bosch, published by Cock, and another after Bruegel, part of the series *Twelve Flemish Proverbs* (fig. 259), are both more anecdotal than arresting, and contain just two figures. A small engraving made by Cornelis Metsys in about 1540 (fig. 260) contains, on the other hand, four blind figures. The subject can already be seen in Bruegel's *Flemish Proverbs* of 1559 (fig. 229), where three figures are silhouetted on the horizon to illustrate the saying: "Als de ene blinde de andere bidt, vallen ze beiden in de gracht" (When a blind man leads another, both fall into the ditch). The subject therefore had time to mature within the artist's mind before it was reborn, magnified into a masterpiece, nine years later (the drawing of 1562 that depicts it is no longer attributed to him). Although the painting has suffered the ravages of time—some of the paint has been lost and it is worn—the composition, the spirit, and the tones of the whole have retained all their force.

A large diagonal, accentuated by the painting's considerable width, is the axis along which the action unfolds, from the upper left corner to the bottom right, directing the six figures toward their final fall. The movement thus created is conveyed by a progressive overbalancing. Although the latter is put into question by the slope of the ground, its progressive acceleration is rendered by a series of oblique lines that begin from the slopes of the roofs and are echoed by the sticks that link the blind men to each other. These lines—like dashes between printed words—are sometimes pushed upward and sometimes stretched, increasing the

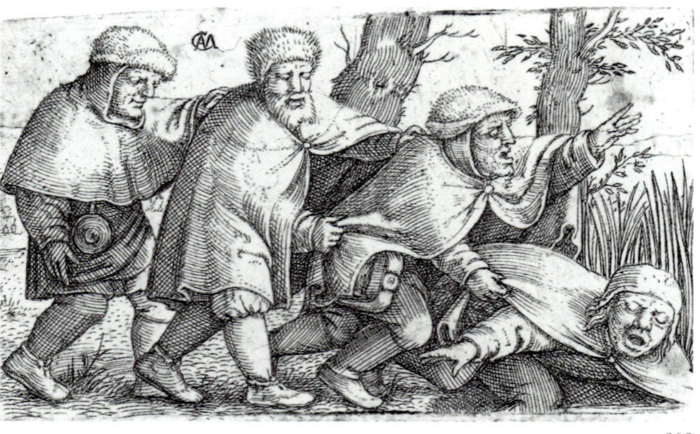

259

260

261. Jacques Villon, *Marching Soldiers*, 1913.
Oil on canvas, 25 5/8 x 26 1/4 in. (65 x 92 cm). Paris,
Centre Georges Pompidou, Musée nationale d'art moderne

259. Anonymous, *Two Blind Men Leading Each Other*,
from the series *Twelve Flemish Proverbs*, after Pieter
Bruegel, ca. 1568. Engraving, diameter 7 in. (17.7 cm).
Brussels, Bibliothèque royale Albert I, print room

260. Cornelis Metsys, *Four Blind Men Falling*,
ca. 1540. Engraving, 1 3/4 x 3 in. (4.5 x 7.8 cm).
Brussels, Bibliothèque royale Albert I, print room

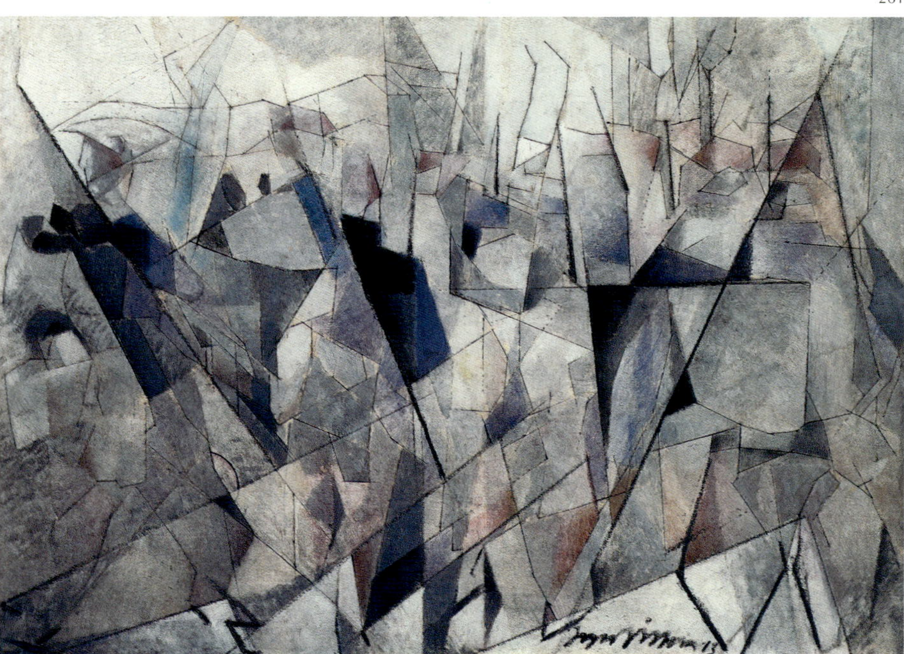

261

impression of discord. The analysis of this linkage, which we can already see in the procession of figures on the Panathenaic frieze from the Parthenon, prefigures that exploited by Watteau in his *Embarkation for the Island of Cythera*, and those used in the twentieth century by the Futurists: Marcel Duchamp in *Nude Descending a Staircase* or, better still, Jacques Villon in his *Marching Soldiers* (fig. 261). The last of these dates from 1913, three and a half centuries after Bruegel, and strikingly mirrors *The Blind Leading the Blind* in its proportions and color, though the movement is in the opposite direction. Paul Claudel might have been talking of Bruegel's work when he said: "Everything that exists is a symbol—everything that happens is a parable."[212]

The work's resonance goes beyond the mere depiction of a parable. Without entering into a debate on orthodoxy—which has no foundation, only differing interpretations[213] arising from a painting, which are always open—and without giving too much importance to the distance separating the character who is falling from the one who senses he is about to, between whom rises the steeple—probably that of the church of Pede-Sainte-Anne (fig. 262)—we can ask ourselves whether Bruegel here is not portraying the blindness of the world he lives in. He gives the work a force which is both temporal and spiritual and, as a result, universal. Besides a physical and visual analysis, a reading of the figures' facial expressions would seem to be essential. Apart from remarking on the realism of the eye ailments that afflict them,[214] we can also read on their faces the psychological reactions of those who are prisoners of a movement that is beyond their control. Without making a subjective interpretation, and starting from the left (figs. 70–73), the two first blind men seem, if not confident, at any rate passive; the third, straightening his neck, appears to be responding to a call: is he sensing something? The fourth, his knees already buckling, is clearly worried and tense; curiously, he seems to be gesturing toward the church with his head. As for the fifth, who is falling, he calls the world as his witness and looks at the viewer with his empty eye sockets. The sixth has fallen, and plunges into the water of the marsh, into which the treacherous, sloping path leads, and from which a solitary, magnificent iris rises in full flower. Neither the Church nor the world is absent: All people, whatever their individual form of blindness, are implicated here. Certain copies confirm this, precisely because they lack this painting's intensity. One example is in the Louvre. In a larger format (fig. 263) and an apparently faithful copy, even though the landscape is more heavily overgrown with bushes, it is not known which of Bruegel's sons—Pieter the Younger or Jan Bruegel—painted it. The sense of drama is less tangible, less gripping. There is, as Georges Marlier rightly remarked, a "dispersion of interest";[215] the fall gives less of an impression of inevitability. Indeed, a copy never reinvents an invention, that is to say, the emotion that created it. Nevertheless, according to historians of the subject,[216] numerous other copies were made, from the engraving attributed variously to Van der Heyden and Wierix[217] that is part of the *Twelve Flemish Proverbs* (fig. 259) to the copies of Pieter Bruegel the Younger and Martin van Cleve. This edifying theme also appears in the writings of rhetoricians and poets,[218] but most often in the sense made clear in the engraving: "Always walk with prudence, be faithful, do not trust anyone, but only God in all things." Bruegel's parable is not so simple, or so easily challenged. The fall of the blind, and that of Icarus, like that of the angels are all like the falls of men.[219]

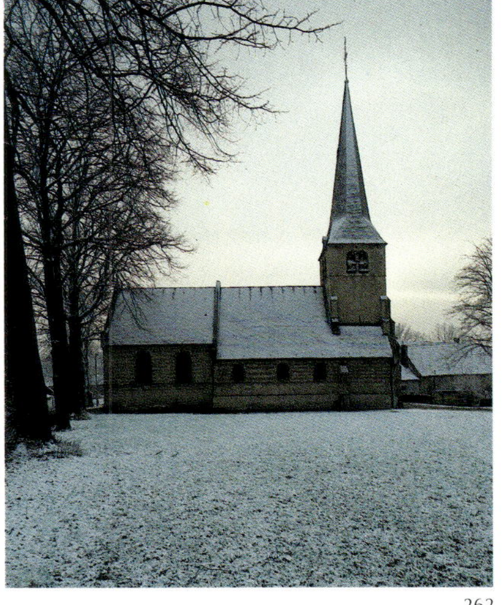
262

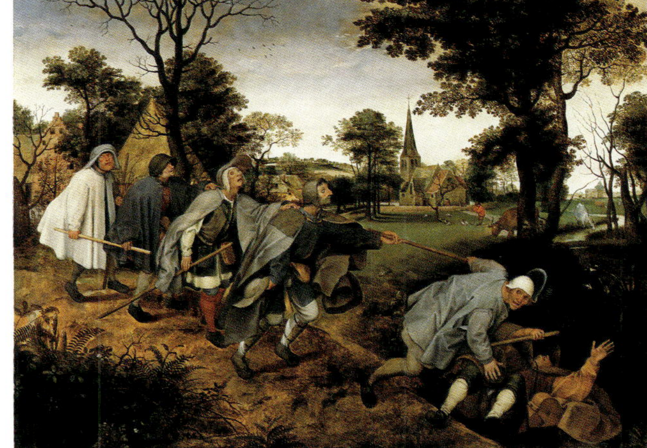
263

262. View of the church of Pede-Sainte-Anne, late thirteenth century–sixteenth century

263. Pieter Bruegel the Younger or Jan Bruegel, *The Blind Leading the Blind*, first half of the seventeenth century. Oil on panel, 48 x 66⅞ in. (122 x 170 cm). Paris, Louvre

CREATOR OR MISANTHROPE

Bruegel painted two images of the human condition—one positive, the other negative—during the years 1565 to 1568: *The Painter and the Art Lover* (fig. 265), and *The Misanthrope* (fig. 267). Both are on a large scale, considering the materials of their supports. The first is a drawing on paper, and the second is in distemper on linen. In each case the figures take up so much of the image's space that the background is reduced in importance. A secondary, but significant, aspect is that both works refer to money. Will the painter be well paid or badly paid? And the misanthrope is being robbed outright.

The drawing's qualities are obvious—indeed, four copies of the work survive. It is generally considered a self-portrait made in about 1565, therefore four years before the painter's death. The artist holds a brush in his right hand and looks as if he might be looking at a model, while allowing the figure behind him to look over his shoulder at the painting he is producing. The two are clearly not looking in the same direction. However, the interpretation remains hypothetical. The second character—an art lover or connoisseur—may be a friend of the painter (the English poet John Heywood has been suggested)[220] or a symbolic figure, whose presence is a reference to the relationship between artist and audience. This much appears clear. The conclusions to be drawn from it, however, are less so because they are contradictory. Several writers see the second character in a restrictive sense: his glasses raise doubts about his appreciative faculties, and the bag he is holding emphasizes his avarice, or even that he makes money out of art. In support of the last of these, two Flemish proverbs have been quoted: "Art and science have no greater enemies than the ignorant", and "Art brings in bread, and we are headed for death."[221] The first theory we must reject is that of avarice. In fact, far from guarding his bag, the art lover is preparing to delve into it since (as René van Bastelaer already noticed as early as 1907)[222] he has already lifted its flap. As for the spectacles, do they not help to see better and, consequently, are they not proof of attentiveness? This drawing could equally well be read positively, and we could see, in the relationship between the painter and the art lover, esteem, even admiration, and the material support that may result from them. An examination of this relationship brings to mind a comparison between two great draftsmen, Bruegel in the sixteenth century and Honoré Daumier in the nineteenth (fig. 264), which could be commented on thus: In about 1565 Pieter Bruegel the Elder suggested, in *The Painter and the Art Lover*, a certain type of relationship. Curiosity lights the face of the art lover: his glance is inquiring, his lips parted. Standing behind the painter, he looks over the latter's shoulder, endeavoring to understand, humble, eager to share his feeling. The artist at his easel dominates the picture, just as he expects to reign over his work. He creates, lets others see, and they are grateful to him for it. In 1855 Honoré Daumier exhibited *M. Prudhomme Visits the Workshops*; the subject is identical to that of Bruegel's drawing, but the order of the elements and the characters' roles are profoundly different. The art lover—firmly planted in front of the work he is surveying, hands behind his back, majestically carrying his paunch as a sign of authority—is the embodiment of self-assurance. We can sense that he will make no comment, but rather give a verdict which allows no appeal. His face, seen in

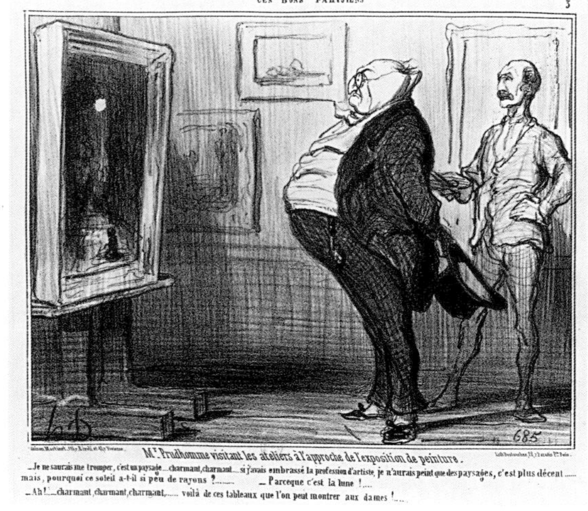

264. Honoré Daumier, *M. Prudhomme Visits the Workshops,* from the series *These Good Parisians,* 1855. Lithograph, 7¾ x 9¾ in. (19.7 x 24.8 cm). Paris, Bibliothèque nationale de France

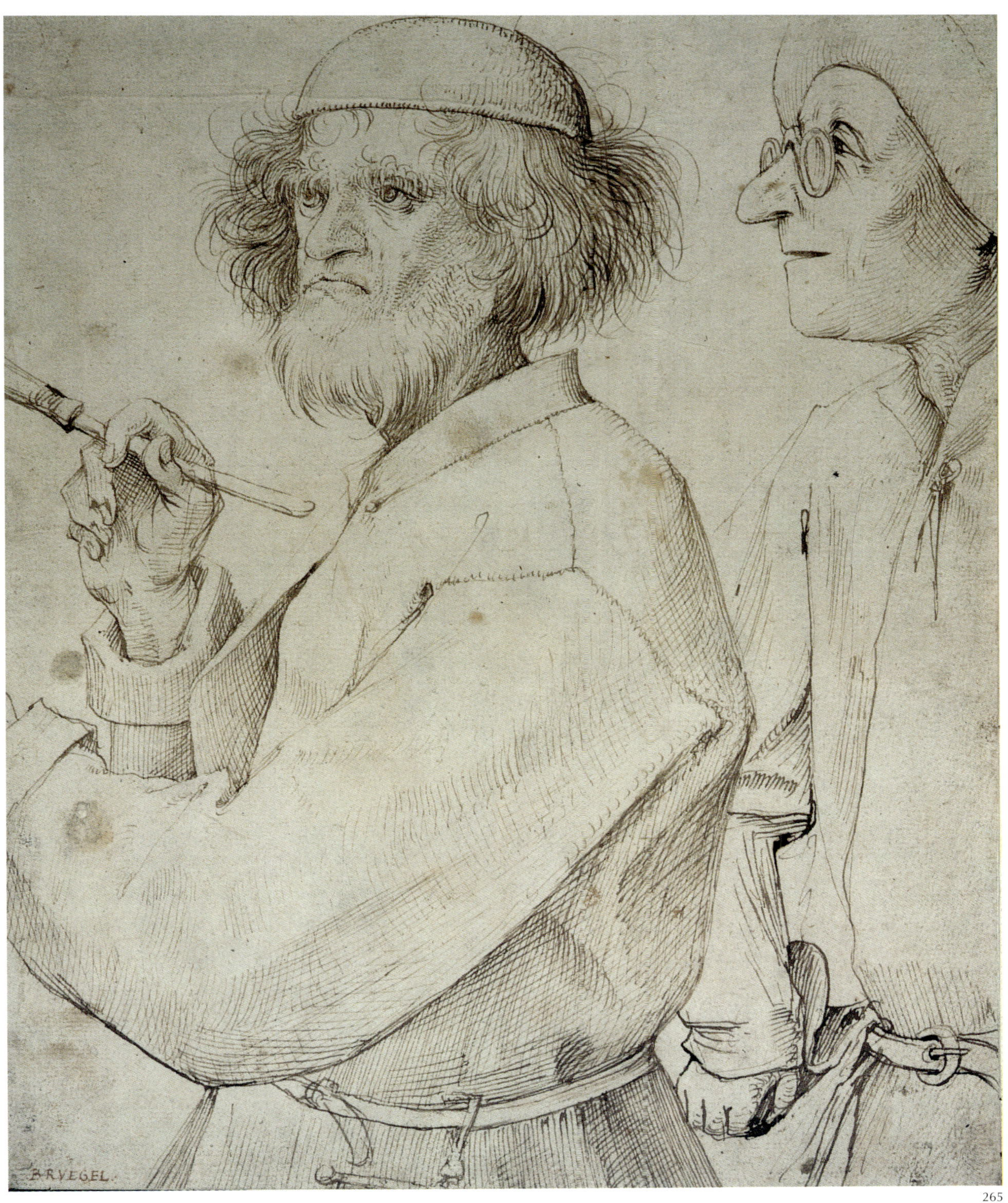

265. Pieter Bruegel, *The Painter and the Art Lover*, ca. 1565. Pen and brown ink, $9^7/_8$ x $8^1/_2$ in. (25 x 21.6 cm). Vienna, Graphische Sammlung Albertina

profile, closes in on itself by the curve of his forehead and nose, which meet his nutcracker chin, and stresses that M. Prudhomme accepts only the values of his class, the ready-made rules of a closed world, made by him and for him. The painter keeps well back, in his place, at a respectful distance. This mockery of nineteenth-century bourgeois aesthetic values marvelously illustrates that class's desire for, as André Malraux put it, "art for its personal use." The contrast between the images of Bruegel and Daumier is nevertheless revealing and, as the saying goes, "virtue lies in a middle course." And the moral suggested under the circumstances is: "While the artist's role is to show us, it is important that the viewer learn to look."[223]

To be sure, a comparison is not an argument. There is no need to look at this drawing from the point of view of critiquing of a relationship. Bruegel's humanity leads in other directions also.

A critique of the world as a whole seems best to throw light on the dark, monumental figure that towers above the legend: "Om dat de werelt is soe ongestru/ Daer om gha ic in de ru" (Because the world is so perfidious/Therefore I am in mourning). He is not so much in mourning; he personifies mourning. Even if the inscription on *The Misanthrope* of 1568 (fig. 267), a distemper on linen now in the Capodimonte Museum in Naples, is not in the painter's hand or even contemporary with him,[224] it encapsulates the spirit of this round painting, set in a gray, black-bordered square. An engraving by Jan Wierix, part of the series *Twelve Flemish Proverbs* (fig. 266), carries the same message: "I wear mourning, seeing that the world/Is so full of trickery."[225] The scenes portrayed are similar. A tall figure, dressed entirely in black, is being robbed of his bag by a smaller character who both carries and represents the globe surmounted by a cross—that is, the world. The painting's round shape takes its cue from the sphere that encloses the figure representing the world—a sphere which, in turn, defines the universe of *The Misanthrope* and gives the work its meaning and power. The engraving is more literal, for in the distance, behind the world, a wagon is being plundered in front of a torture wheel and a gallows.

While we can compare the world that is robbing the figure in *The Misanthrope* and the one in the *Proverbs* of 1559, we should note that the former is the right way up, not upside down like the inn sign in the Berlin painting, and that it is inhabited, rather than being crawled into like the one representing the proverb that advises us to "bend down if we want to make our way in the world." Here, the character's face is plump: he is doing well out of his situation. Bruegel's painting, furthermore, exists in its own right, in its clarity and complexity. The figures are both contrasting and complementary: the misanthrope is an old man with a bitter mouth, long nose, and white beard, his eyes hidden by a hood and his hands folded; the world's face is uncovered and round, with slightly open mouth and bulbous eyes, and he has the nimble hands of a thief. The bag he is stealing and about to cut free has led some to comment that the misanthrope is a hypocrite because he still possesses the very image of the world: money. The character has even been identified with heresy, a title that was attached to the painting for a time in Naples.[226] This bag is red and heart-shaped. According to Tolnay it illustrates "the proverb 'Where money is, there lies the heart.' It is no less than the heart of the hypocrite himself."[227] Perhaps, but would it not be simpler to see a heart that the world is seizing, leaving only four-pointed nails in front of the man's feet? All the more so since the bag, in the engraving, is unmistakably a purse. The ambiguity, which is not innocent, lies in Bruegel.

Behind the two figures stretches a rural landscape with copses, a windmill, and a shepherd with his flock of black and white sheep, under an evening sky with a few clouds and, on the far horizon behind the shepherd, a fire and smoke. Why see in it "the burning of the world"?[228] But—with these nails in front of the

266. Jan Wierix, *The Misanthrope*, from the series *Twelve Flemish Proverbs*, after Pieter Bruegel, ca. 1568. Engraving, diameter 7 in. (17.9 cm). Brussels, Bibliothèque royale Albert I, print room

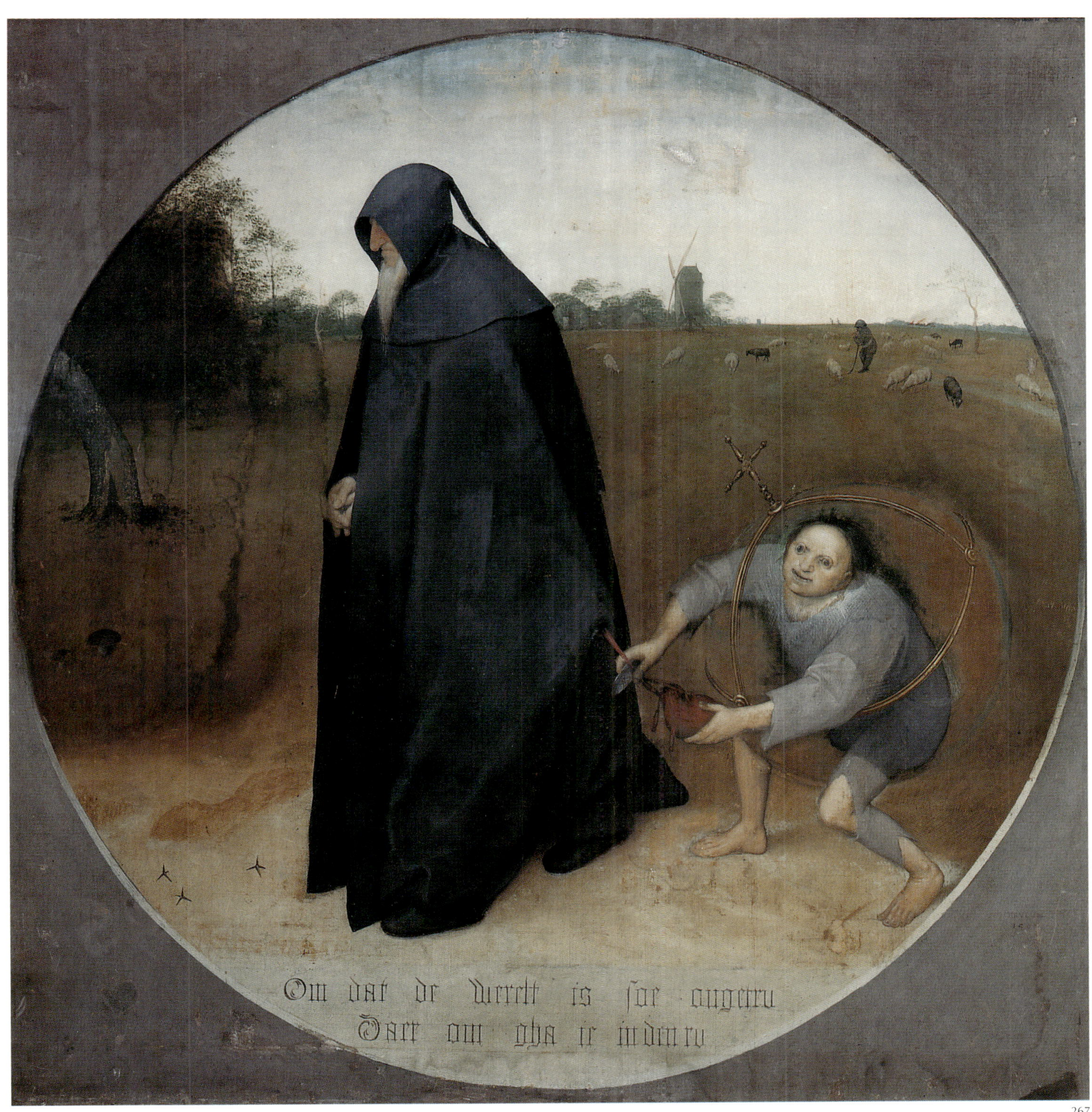

267. Pieter Bruegel, *The Misanthrope*, 1568.
Distemper on linen, 33⅞ x 33⅓ in. (86 x 85 cm).
Naples, Museo e gallerie nazionali di Capodimonte

misanthrope, these traps, these mushrooms (perhaps poisonous), and the hollow tree that awaits him—Bruegel may be, in fact, warning against misanthropy itself, which is turning its back on the shepherd and taking a wrong path, despite the thieving world. It is a disturbing image, for sure: a cruel and realistic picture of the world, a meditation, and a warning. But it is not for all that a desperate vision or one with which Bruegel identifies—but rather a rich, modulated image, a reflection on life's journey and the human condition.

SOCIETY

In *The Land of Cockaigne* (figs. 269–72), painted in 1567, proverbs proliferate once again. The roof of a shed is covered with tarts, like the one at the left in *Flemish Proverbs* (fig. 223), and an egg can be seen walking (fig. 271), like the goose egg at the center right of that picture that a woman allows to elude her in order to keep the chicken's egg, thus "letting go of a greater reward to keep a smaller one." But here the egg, stranger still, carries a knife in its shell, possibly an alchemical or sexual symbol that recalls images in the work of Bosch. An open mouth awaits the roast larks, and earthy details draw the eye: a fence made of woven sausages, a bird that settles on a pewter plate and stretches out its neck to be cut; honey is within easy reach too, and even the bushes are edible. What Bruegel is portraying here is *Luilekkerland*—the land of gluttony, known in many languages and folk traditions. To get there it is necessary to climb a mountain of pancake dough (as the small figure in the right distance is doing) that is lapped by a sea of milk. The corresponding engraving by Pieter van der Heyden (fig. 268) bears the legend: "You who are there, lazy and food-loving, peasant, soldier, or cleric, who come here and partake of everything without working…"[229] The social classes mentioned, to which can be added the knight under the shed, sum up society. In dreams or sleep, these characters are equals. Their clothing undone, their tools—spear, flail, or book—laid aside, they lose themselves in pleasant idleness.

In this work, which denounces gluttony and laziness, some have on the contrary tried to detect a reference to the troubles in the southern Netherlands and the repression by the Duke of Alva. Louis Lebeer countered such speculation by rightly pointing out that these tragic events took place in 1568, while the painting is dated 1567, and that the subject was part of folk tradition at the time.[230] A Dutch text of 1546 bears witness to this and, besides the woodcut by Erhard Schön mentioned by Tolnay,[231] Louis Lebeer reveals that there is an engraving by Pieter Baltens that depicts the scene. Bruegel and Baltens knew each other from the period when they worked together on the Mechelen triptych, before Bruegel left for Italy. In his *The Land of Cockaigne*, Pieter Baltens uses a similar composition to Bruegel's, but his is confused by a mass of detail. However, the work allows us better to appreciate the spirit of the master's synthesis, as well as the originality of his composition and the expressive power of his forms. Tolnay remarks: "The characters pivot around the central tree like the spokes of a wheel, almost as if some secret mechanism is making them revolve."[232]

The dynamism of the composition seems to emanate from the upper right quadrant of the picture, and it is produced using very few elements. The pig that is moving forward with a knife embedded in its flesh marks the start of a movement. Its slight offset from the left-right diagonal produces an impression of pivoting, which is reinforced both by the movement of the bent tree in the background and by that of the cake-bearing cactus. The curve thus produced is taken up, from left to right, by the cleric's coat, the peasant's back, and the soldier's body. Contrary to the first impression of laziness, therefore, this underlying momentum and the arrival of the little man who is just climbing down from the pancake dough illustrate the idea that Francastel senses Bruegel is trying to express in this

268. Pieter van der Heyden, *The Land of Cockaigne*, after Pieter Bruegel, ca. 1567. Engraving, 8⅛ x 10⅞ in. (20.8 x 27.6 cm). Brussels, Bibliothèque royale Albert I, print room

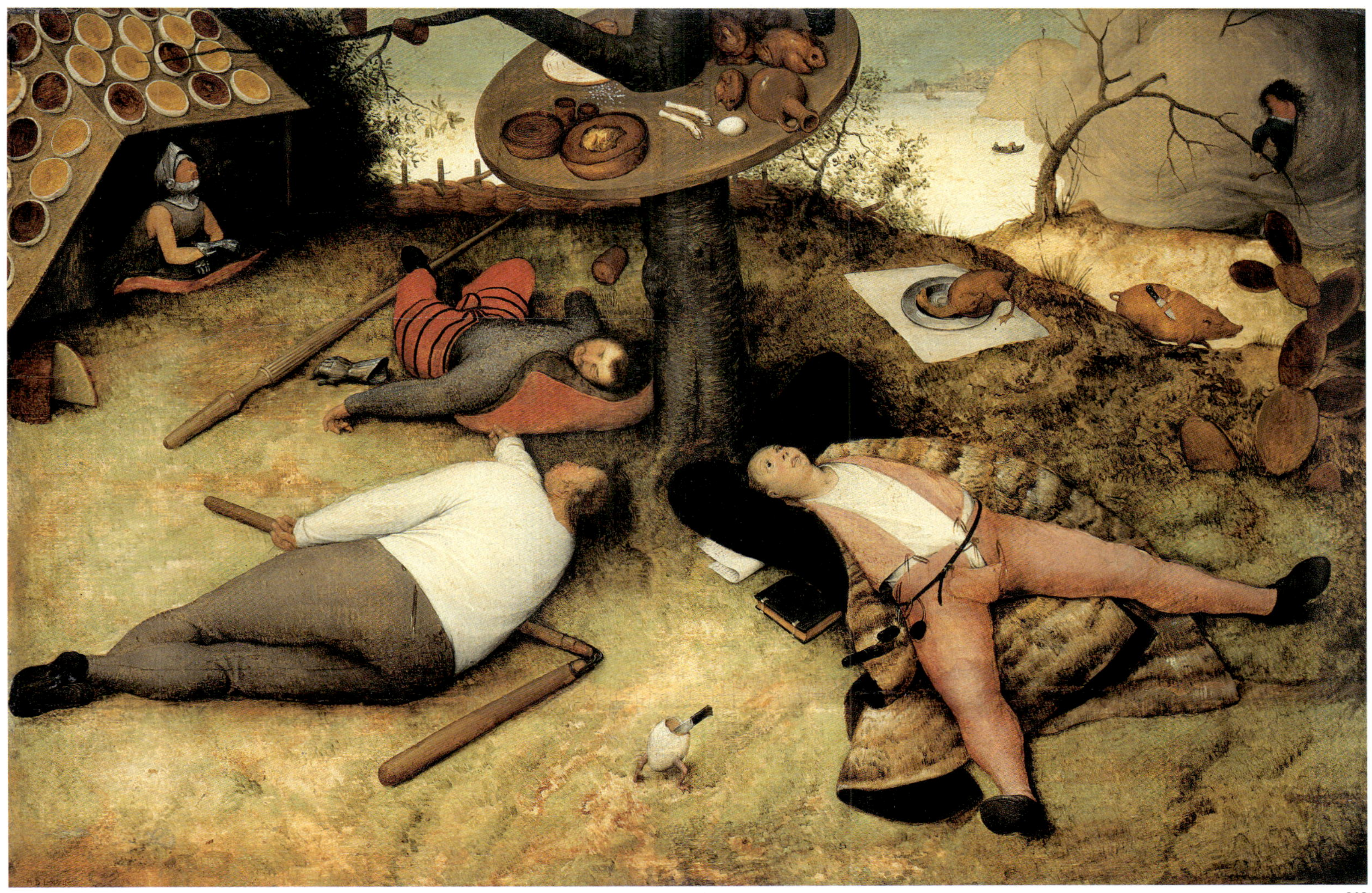

269

269–72. Pieter Bruegel, *The Land of Cockaigne,*
1567: whole work and details. Oil on panel,
20½ x 30¾ in. (52 x 78 cm.) Munich, Alte Pinakothek

painting: "He is announcing the arrival of an open society."[233] As for the pig, it
also appears in the engravings of Erhard Schön and Pieter Baltens, where its sole
function is as an illustration of the land of Cockaigne. Indeed, according to the
text of 1546, "in this land the pigs grow to the point that they run about in packs,
here and there in the fields, already deliciously well roasted, and they carry knives
on their backs so that if anyone wants to eat some they can cut a piece off with this
knife and then replace it."[234] How easily, with a small detail, a great painter can
bring a work of art to life. The image is not for all that one of happiness on earth,
however. The place is suspect, as both the text and tradition make clear, "for
being lazy and idle is never worth anything."[235]

Certainly, the human world is not a paradise in Bruegel's eyes. But this does
not mean it is a cursed, depraved, or sinister place, either. People work there, and
people relax there too. Mankind has its vices but also its virtues, and the gaze the
painter brings to bear on it is keen and balanced, but free of prior judgment.
Commentators have too often invoked the peasant world as an illustration of this.
However, leaving aside works where nature is the main subject, only five or six of
Bruegel's forty or so surviving paintings deal with peasant life itself

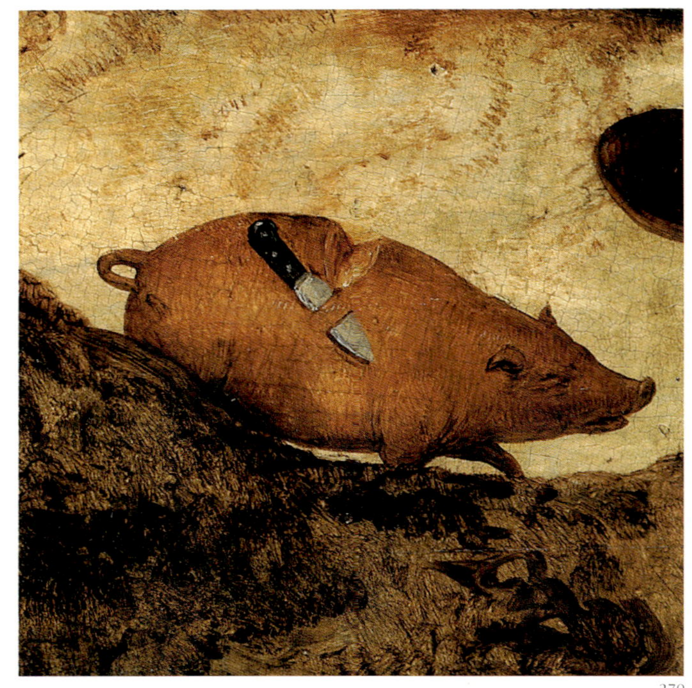

270

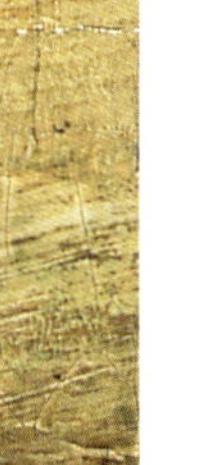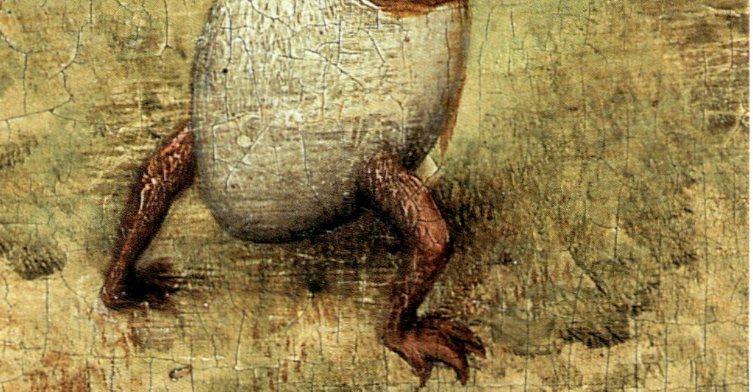

271

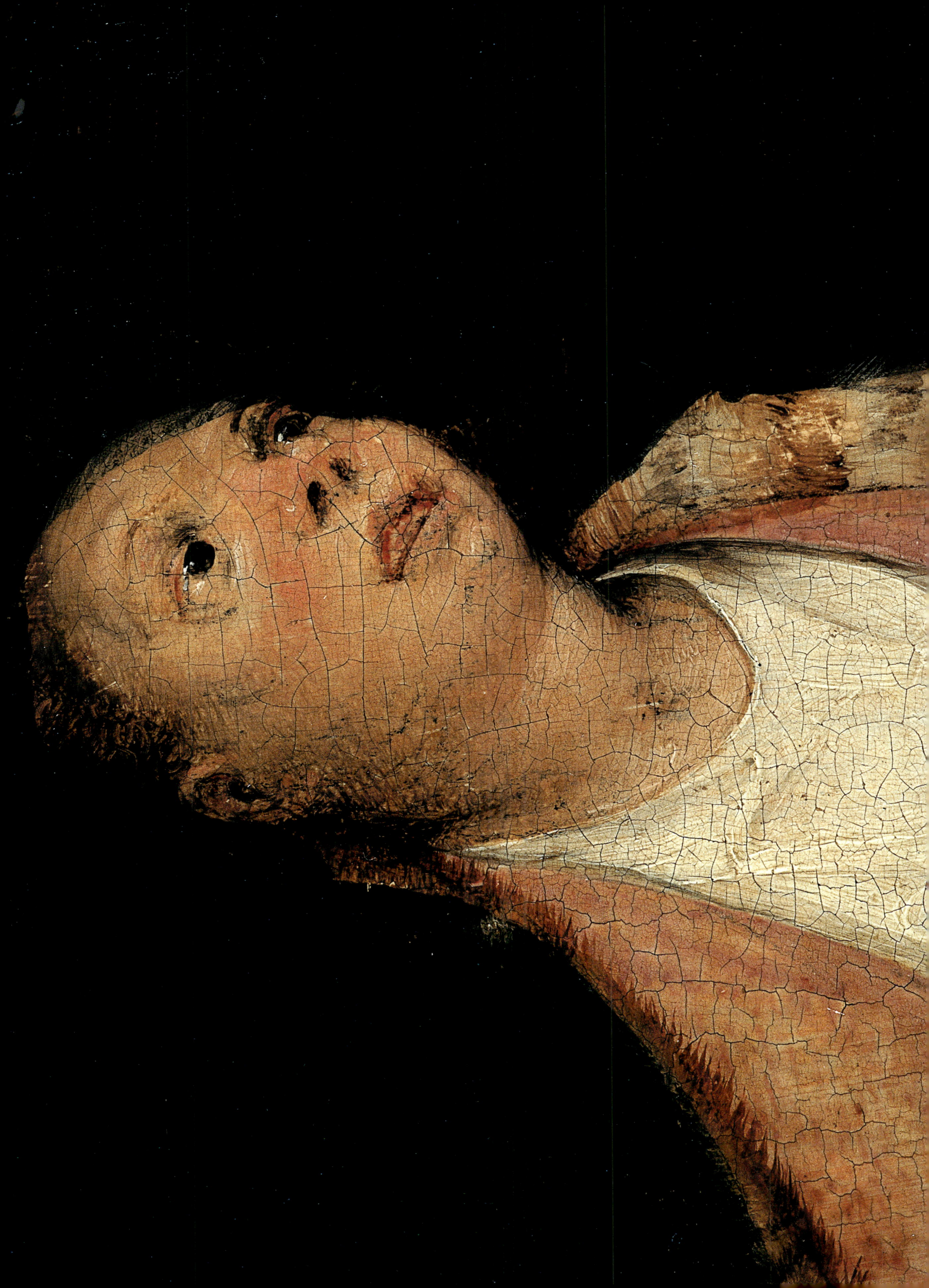

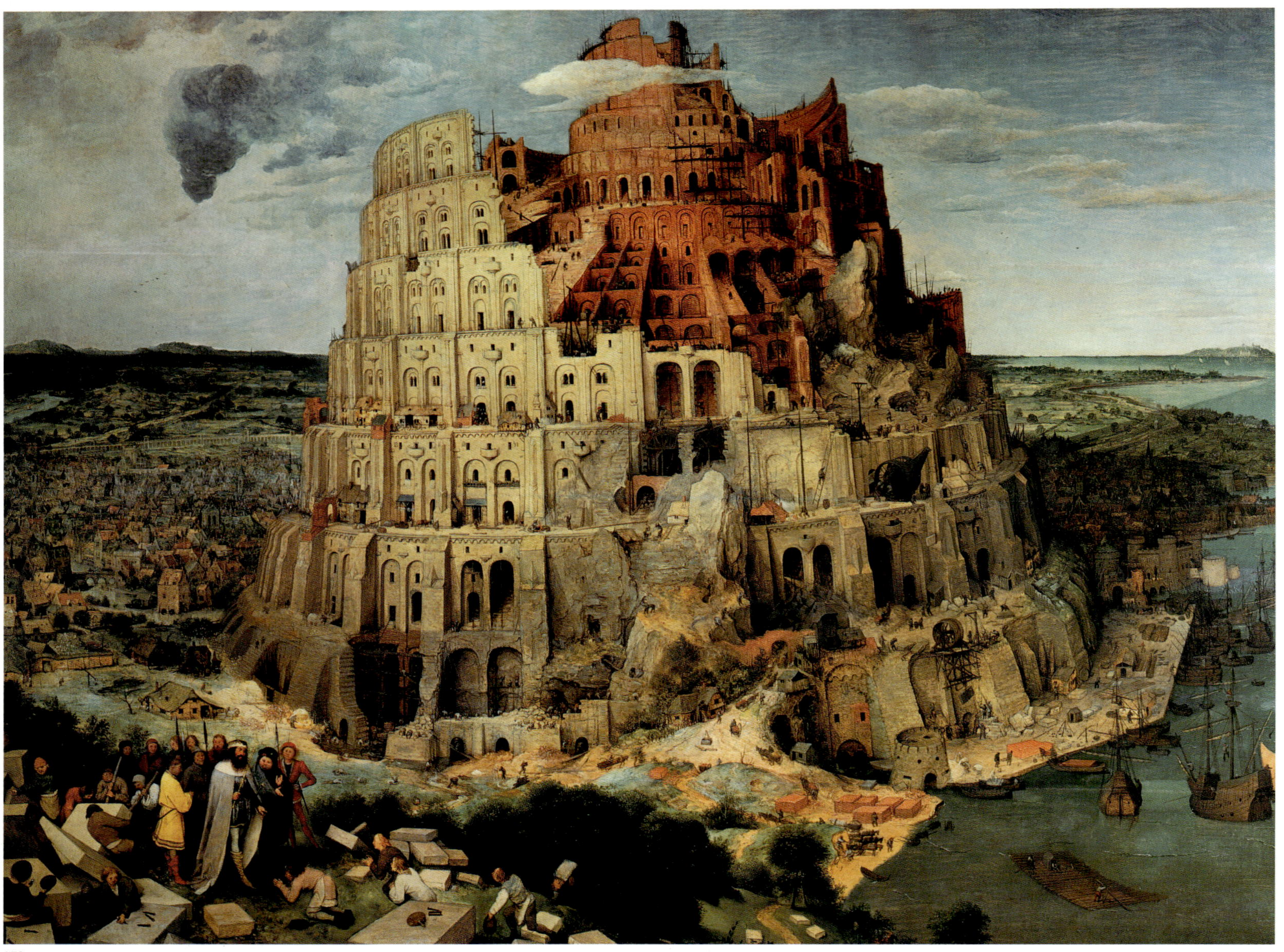

273

273 and 275–77: Pieter Bruegel, *The Tower of Babel*,
1563: whole work and details. Oil on panel, 44⅞ x 61 in.
(114 x 155 cm). Vienna, Kunsthistorisches Museum

URBAN LIFE

A painting is the creation of a space and the occupation of that space. If the plastic
arts could be summarized thus, *The Tower of Babel* (figs. 273 and 274) would
provide a conclusive illustration, for, in a physical setting with infinite nuances, the
tower's complex architectural mass rises up and cannot be ignored. We should
rather speak of towers of Babel, for Bruegel painted at least two versions of this
work known today, one now in Vienna (fig. 273), and that in Rotterdam (fig. 274),
as well as a miniature on ivory, now lost, which is mentioned in an inventory of the
possessions of the painter Giulio Clovio, whom Bruegel met during his journey
through Italy.

The theme of the tower of Babel, though biblical (Genesis XI), is equally
an image of the society that decided: Let us build a city and a tower, whose top
may reach unto heaven."[236] A double declaration, therefore: of pride aiming for

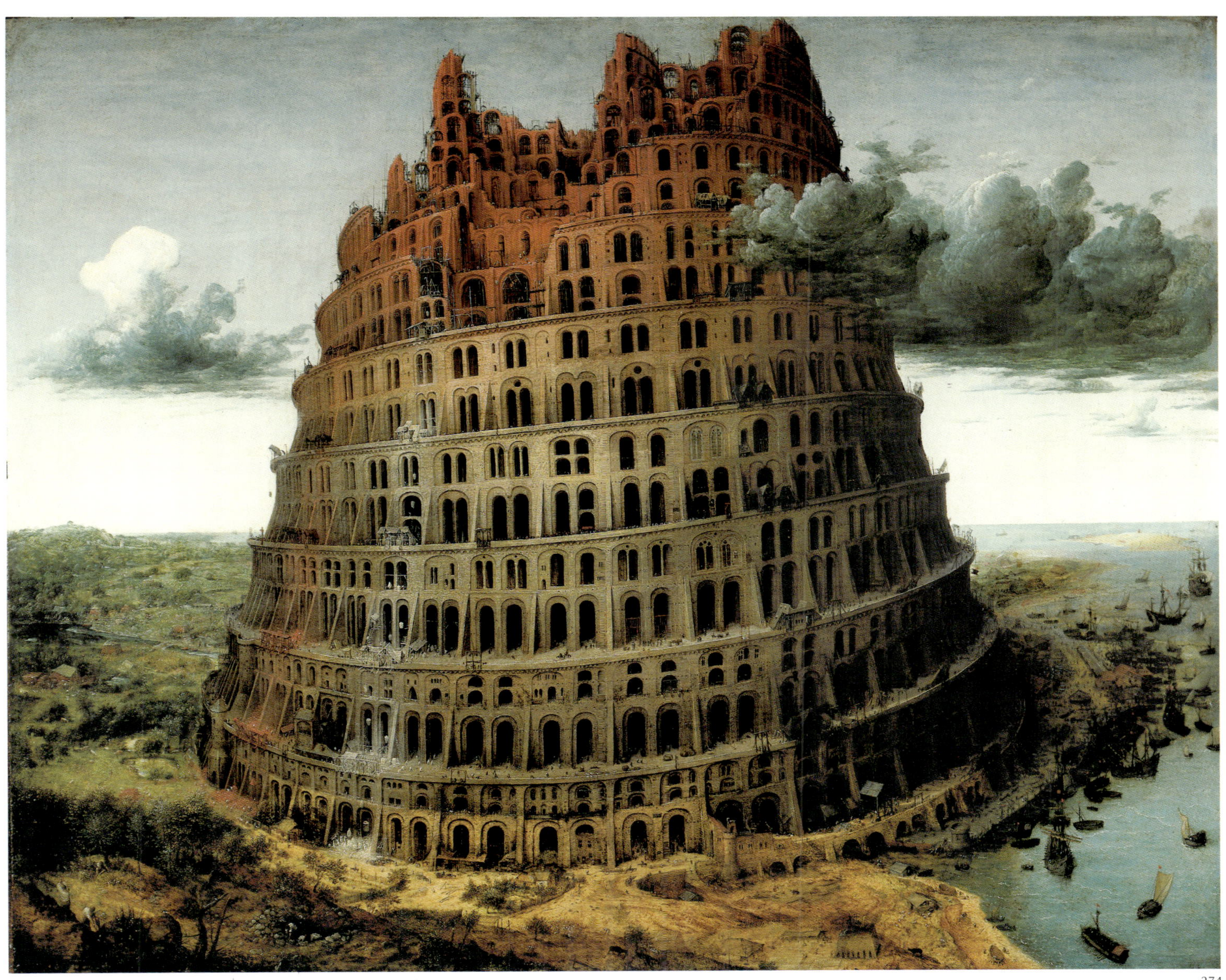

274

the sky on the one hand, and of a desire to build on the other. The defeat that
follows is not the result of ambition, but an act of God: "The people is one, and
they have all one language; and this they begin to do: and now nothing will be
restrained from them, which they have imagined to do. Go to, let us go down,
and there confound their language, that they may not understand one another's
speech."[237] Thus the enterprise got its name: "Therefore is the name of it called
Babel; because the Lord did there confound the language of all the earth."[238]
The subject therefore contains an element of ambiguity, between the desire to
build, the extravagance of the project, the scale of the defeat, and the lesson that
can be drawn from it. Was it this very complexity that led Bruegel to choose such
a subject? It cannot be ruled out. The painter loves images that do not confine
themselves to just one description. He cultivates resonances and, beneath what
appears to be obvious, loves to suggest other voices that echo the diversity of
thought and life.

274 and 278. Pieter Bruegel, *The Tower of Babel*,
ca. 1568: whole work and detail. Oil on panel,
23⅝ x 29⅜ in. (59.9 x 74.6 cm). Rotterdam,
Museum Boijmans Van Beuningen

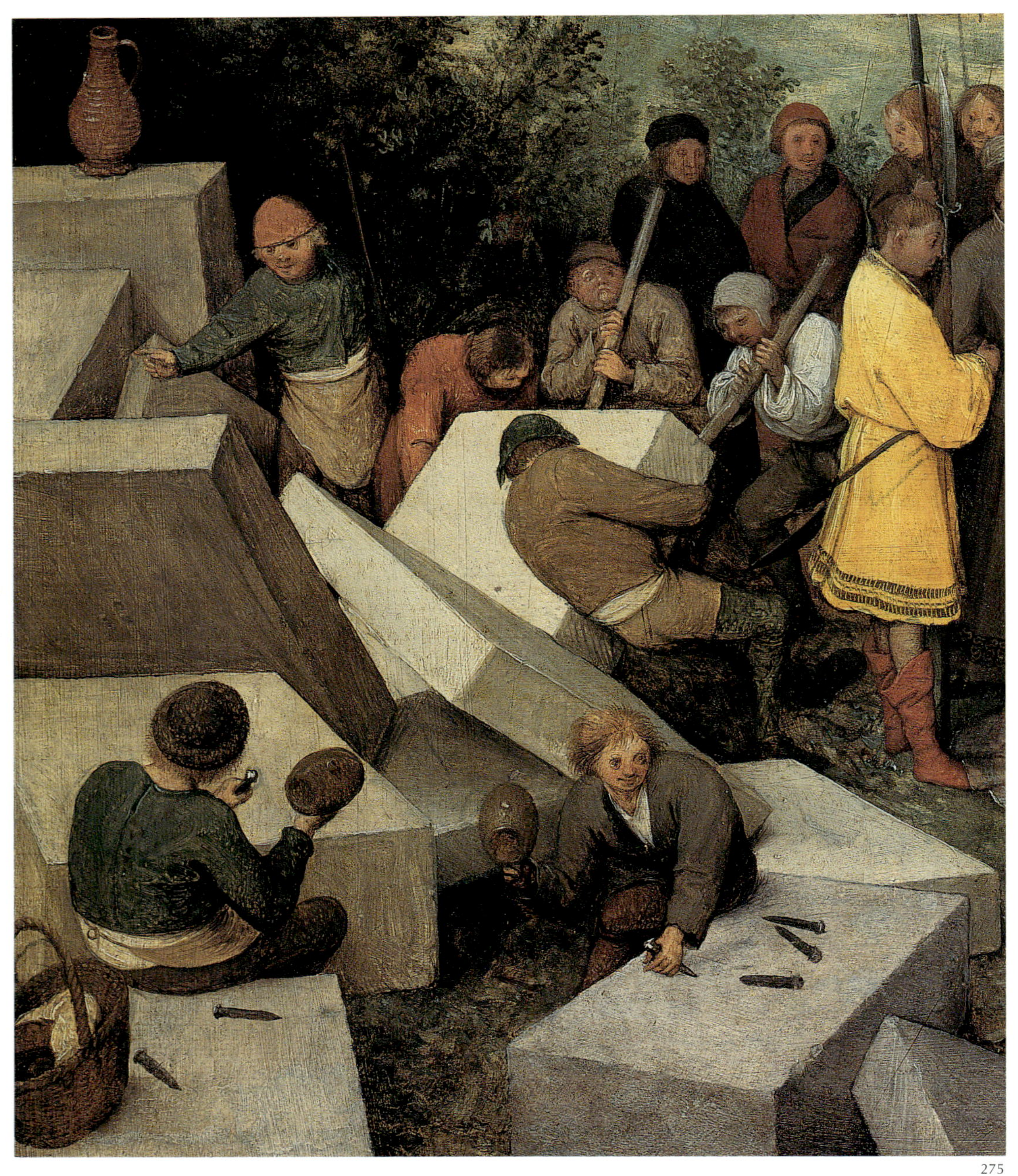

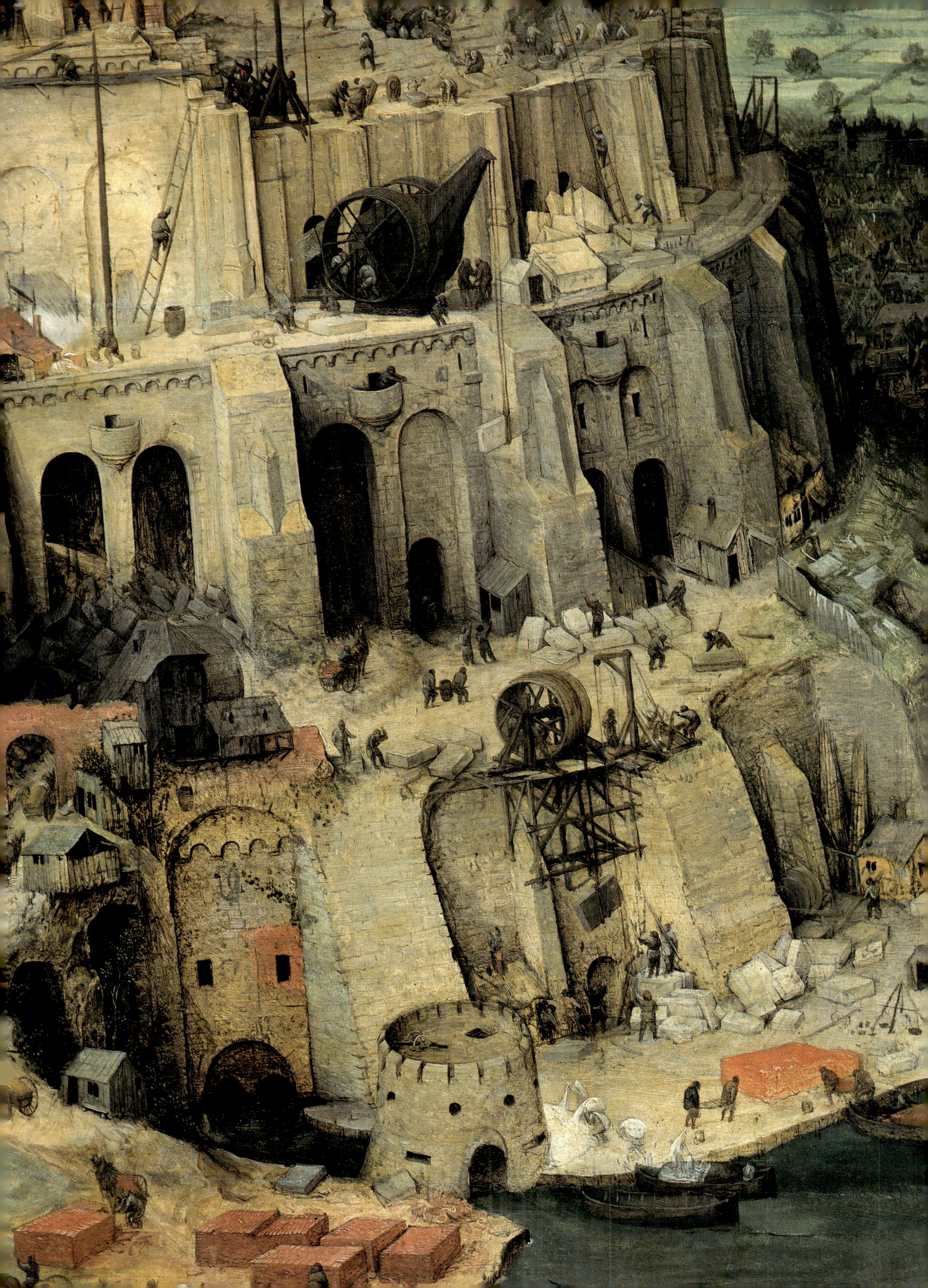

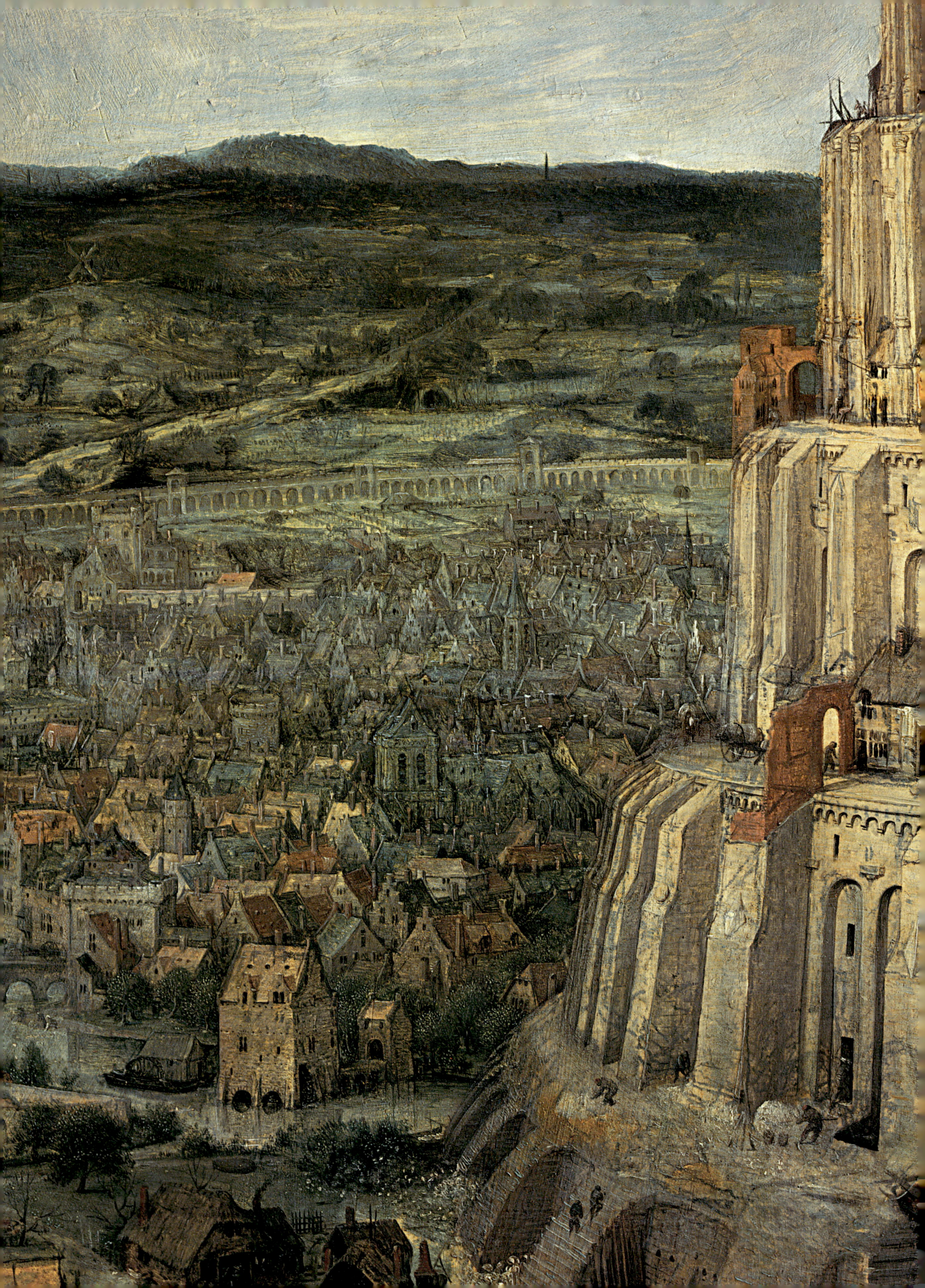

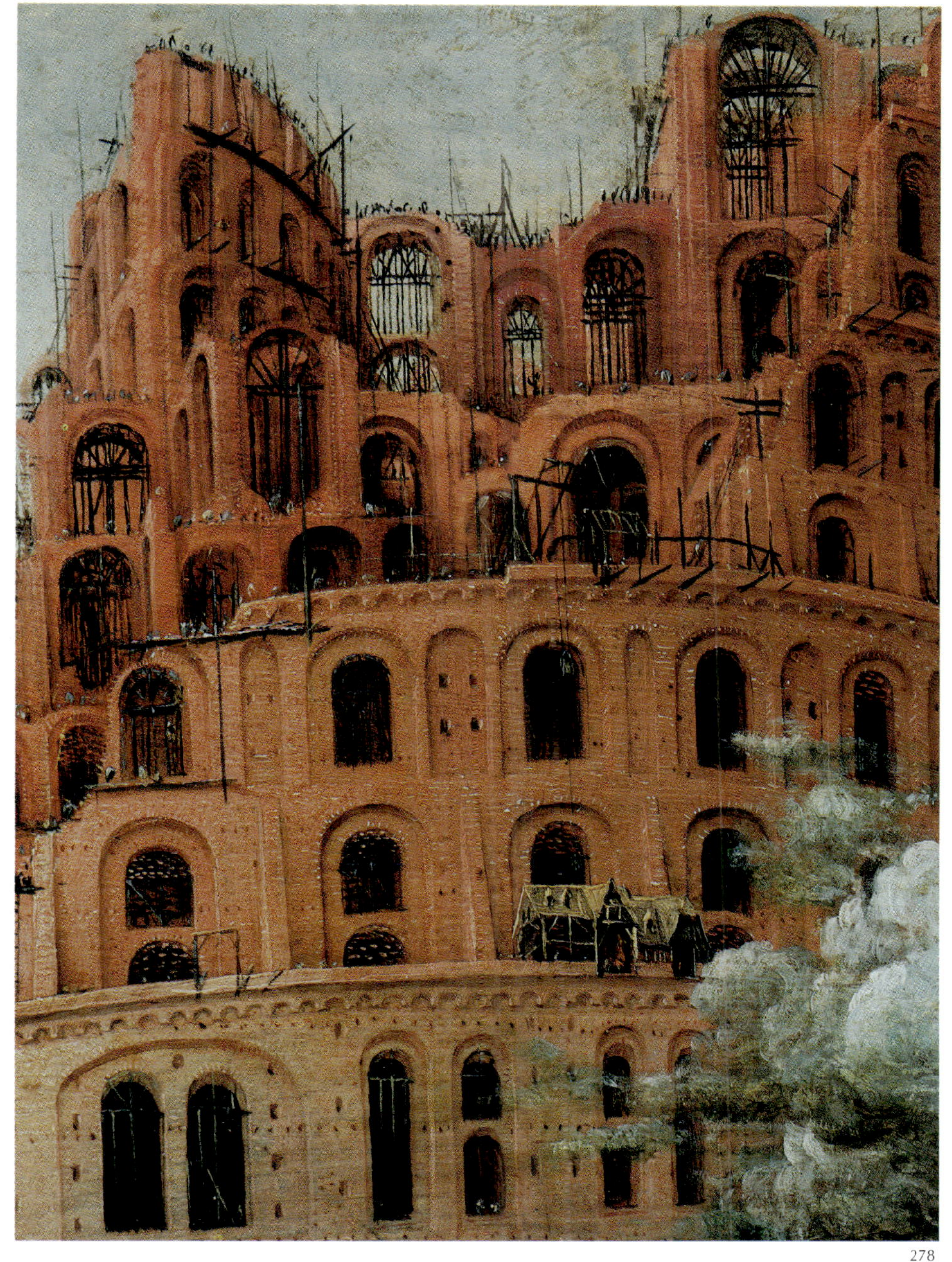

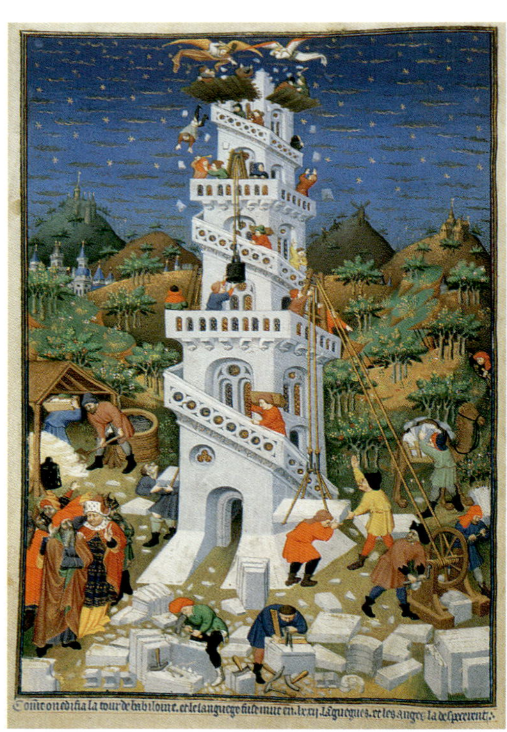

279. Bedford Master, *The Tower of Babel*,
Bedford Book of Hours, ca. 1423, fol. 17, verso.
Illumination on vellum, page dimensions:
10¼ x 9⅛ in. (26 x 18 cm). London, British Library

The iconography of *The Tower of Babel* belongs to a tradition that goes back to illuminated manuscripts such as the *Grimani Breviary* or *Bedford Book of Hours* (fig. 279) in the fifteenth century. The latter work, for example, shows a rectangular tower with an outside staircase, a Babylonian ziggurat, under construction, with its craftsmen at work, and receiving a visit from a king. The latter, who is not mentioned in Genesis, is, according to Josephus's *Jewish Antiquities*, Nimrod, builder-king and great-grandson of Noah. The theme became widespread in the sixteenth century, especially in the Netherlands, encouraged by the woodcuts of Bernard Salomon, an artist from Lyon, who illustrated numerous editions of biblical texts both in France and indeed in Flanders, from 1553.[239]

To this iconography, Bruegel contributed masterpieces. The painting now in Vienna is dated 1563. It is a large oil painting on wood, 44⅞ x 61 inches (114 x 155 centimeters), which in 1566 was part of the collection of Nicolas Jongelinck, the great art-lover who had commissioned Bruegel to paint the *Seasons* series. Van Mander mentions that later the work was in the collection of Rudolf II: "a large panel that shows the Tower of Babel seen from above with many colorful details."[240] The colossal tower, under construction, occupies the center of the painting with its broad base, and the pyramid's summit almost touches the painting's top edge. It is set in a vast landscape with a raised horizon line where, on the left, stretches a dense city huddled behind its defensive walls, beyond which the countryside rises to hills. To the right, under the long shadow of the tower, is a sheet of water with ships and behind it the sky, taking up about a quarter of the painting's height.

In the space around the building the shading of clouds counterbalances the foreground, where King Nimrod, escorted by the architect, receives homage from the stonemasons. Some prostrate themselves while others continue working the ashlars that will face the building. The difference in scale between these figures and the tower itself, where an endless multitude of human ants bustles, makes us realize its colossal size. The town on the left, with its tall houses and churches, and the sea-going ships on the right, confirm these proportions. On each floor of the tower, and in its immediate surroundings, building work is under way. The painting is an encyclopedia of the crafts employed in building at the time: supply of materials, transport, putting materials in place, choice of materials, the activities of each individual, the use of tools. It is a sort of inventory of architecture, like the inventories of sayings and diversions in *Flemish Proverbs* and *Children's Games*.

The tower itself holds our attention. At first sight it looks as if it has been broken open. Indeed, building work is continuing, with some sections close to completion and others barely started. It is clearly destined to remain unfinished, for the tower is "a paradigm of the fragmented nature of human endeavor. If it cannot be finished, this is because of hubris pushed to its utmost limits."[241] Klaus Demus also demonstrates that the architecture is unrealistic, not functional, and absurd. The outside, as far as we can see from the left-hand side, appears quite normal for this type of building. But as soon as we see the interior in pink brick, with its straight, barrel-vaulted galleries climbing toward the center, the

incompatibility of this construction becomes apparent. Hence the anxiety that
pervades the painting, unbeknown to the viewer who is at first seduced by the
stunning mastery, the richness of the subject, and the multitude of details.
Indeed, in the twentieth century, the novelist Marguerite Yourcenar would actually
denounce "The 'Tower of Babel' and its head of state, respectfully received by
the workers, who are building for him this pile of mistakes."[242] This nightmarish
architectural aberration prefigures the *Prisons* of the eighteenth-century etcher
Piranesi. The building also contains interesting references. It centers on a rocky
core which juts out to the right and in the center, where it has not yet been hewn
back to fit within the building. This rock can be compared to a painting by
Joachim Patinir, *Rest on the Flight into Egypt* (fig. 281), where the curious
formation supposedly represents the Sainte-Baume massif, near Marseille, where
Mary Magdalen is said to have gone to do her penance.[243] "Association between
the works of nature and of man" comments Francastel who, contrasting the
Babylonian building with the setting, which could be Antwerp, suggests in another
connection: "the allusion becomes more precise, less moral; it refers to works
being built by society at the time, which from then on took its architectural
framework from the rules of antiquity and the Renaissance. Taking this further,
we can wonder whether the choice of an Italian-style formula does not imply a
criticism, contrasting the creativity of ordinary towns with the mirages from
across the Alps."[244] The architecture itself in Bruegel's painting is inspired by the
Colosseum, which the artist saw when he visited Rome and whose ruins, as well
as others such as those on the Palatine hill, had struck and inspired many artists
from the Netherlands before him. Jan Gossaert drew the Colosseum in 1508,
Martin van Heemskerk painted a self-portrait showing himself in front of it in
1553, and Hieronymus Cock drew, and then published etchings of, twenty-five
views of Roman ruins (fig. 280). The last are interesting in that Bruegel may have
seen them before leaving for Italy if, as seems likely, he was then already working
at the Four Winds.

    The Tower of Babel was copied by the artist's son, Pieter Bruegel the
Younger, so faithfully that it might well have been from the original (fig. 282).
"Pieter the Younger did not omit a single one of the devices—cranes, scaffolding,
derricks, ladders, and winches—that Bruegel had depicted in such detail, despite
their microscopic scale … and also tiny huts perched on the slopes or clinging to
the walls like nests."[245] Nevertheless, the copyist modified the work noticeably.
Not only did he enlarge it (to 57 1/16 x 69 1/2 inches or 145 x 176.5 centimeters),
but he set the subject further back in the painting's field of view. Consequently,
the landscape gained in importance at the expense of the tower. While "a harmony
is established between the monstrous building and its setting"[246] the presence
and meaning of the structure lose their sharpness. It becomes a curious or strange
element in the landscape, important certainly, but no longer its essential subject.
Several other artists were to treat the subject in a similar spirit: Maarten, Lucas,
and Frederick van Valckenborch, Hendrik III van Cleve, Louis de Caullery,
Abel Grimmer, Tobias Verhaecht, Pieter Schoubroeck, and Sebastian Vranex.
The tower of Babel as an example of urban society and an inventory of hard,
daily toil was thus replaced by a decorative or amusing detail among many others.

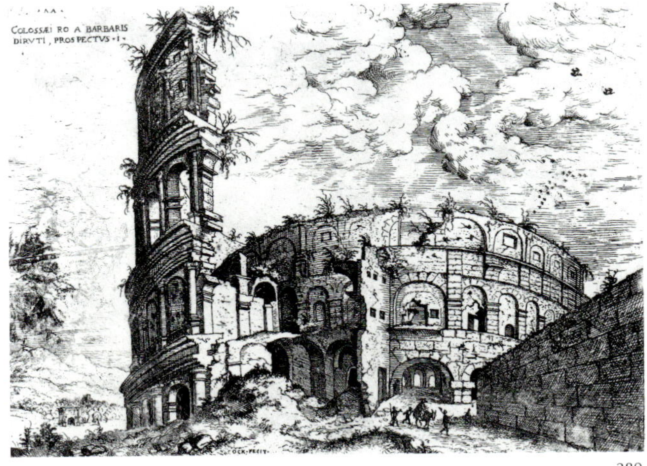

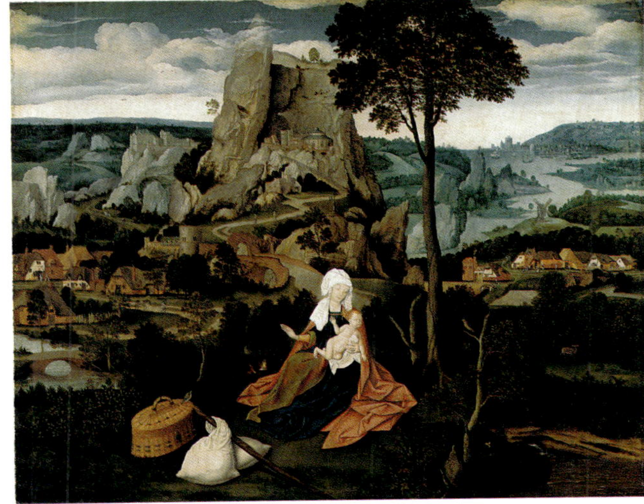

280 Hieronymus Cock, *The Colosseum* (first view), from the series
Roman Ruins, 1551. Etching, 9 1/8 x 12 5/8 in. (23.2 x 32.2 cm).
Brussels, Bibliothèque royale Albert I, print room

281. Joachim Patinir, *Rest on the Flight into Egypt*, ca. 1520.
Oil on panel, 24 3/8 x 30 3/4 in. (62 x 78 cm). Berlin, Staatliche
Museen, Gemäldegalerie

The power of Bruegel's composition, however, allows no such way out. The image certainly lends itself to discussion, for those who see in it political or religious allusions. Babel could be Rome, indicated by the reference to the Colosseum, and in that case the work might be an attack on the ostentation of Catholicism,[247] just as it could also, on the contrary, deplore religious divisions and the loss of a common faith.[248]

The power of the image in the context of social experience appears reinforced by Bruegel's other *Tower of Babel*. Van Mander mentions its existence—"another of the same subject in a smaller format"[249]—in Prague, in the possession of Rudolf II. On the back of the painting, the arms of the empress Elisabetta Farnese, second wife of Philip V of Spain, date the work's presence in his collection at about 1714, and the description of "la Torre de Bavilonia, una Pintura arig[ina]l en Tabla de mano de Brugul" corresponds closely[250] to the painting in the Rotterdam museum. Although the subject is the same as that of the Vienna painting, the way the two works are conceived, and the feeling they convey, are very different. Here, the tower's presence is more immediate, and we know that the painter had already reserved the area allocated to the subject in the white priming layer of the pigment (fig. 65).[251] The image was thus implicit in the painting even before the paint was applied. The foreground of the Vienna painting, with King Nimrod and the stonemasons, has vanished. The tower itself is more massive, its intense coloring more powerful, and the building work, which is more advanced, more complete. Its monolithic presence is dense, something like a termites' nest with what seems to be an infinity of cells seemingly growing and covering more and more territory. The town on the left has disappeared, while the port on the right, although it has retained its bustle, lies under a deeper shadow. The feeling of inaccessibility, the lowering of the horizon line, and a crown of threatening clouds all reinforce the feeling of anxiety.

The painting's date is uncertain and the subject of conflicting theories. Bruegel does not repeat himself. If he returns to a theme we ought to be able to discern a temporal logic in this such as, here, a later stage in the tower's construction, corresponding to a vision that is more synthesized but equally rich in resonances. We should therefore favor a date for the work later than 1563. The work's climate, if we can use the expression, resembles *The Magpie on the Gallows* of 1568 in many details and technical aspects.[252] While the tower is at a more advanced stage of construction and seems to have resolved the imperfections in its development, it is not completed for all that. Its summit still strains to define itself against the sky with its scaffolding and fragments of wall that cut into the space.

The bright red of the new bricks contrasts with the surfaces that have already been weathered by time. Two long trails up the building's left side show where materials are being hoisted up: One bears the white traces of chalk, the other the red of bricks—the latter the same color as the bricks that the little girl in the lower right corner of *Children's Games* (fig. 246) is making into powder to sell at her stall. These marks bear witness to the work that is everywhere, and lively activity can be observed on every level: microscopic figures among which we can discern a papal baldachin[253] and the signs of a utopian city.[254] The bustle in the port is an allusion to the maritime and commercial rise of Antwerp.

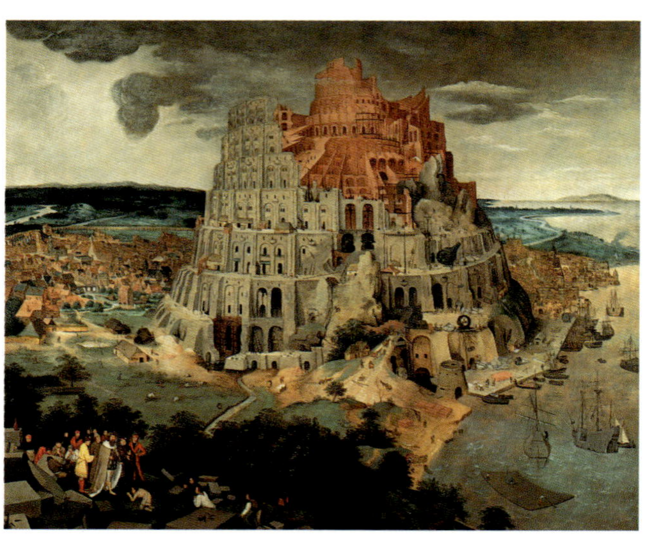

282

282. Pieter Bruegel the Younger, *The Tower of Babel*, beginning of the seventeenth century. Oil on panel, 57¹/₁₆ x 69½ in. (145 x 176.5 cm). Brussels, private collection

The painting with its immense tower is striking first and foremost by the breadth of the image in itself. Beehive or prison, seat of hubris, neither fixed nor suppressed but growing, a symbol of human folly according to Sebastian Brant, the structure is also the site of a mystery that resurfaces four centuries later in certain images by René Magritte such as *The Art of Conversation* (fig. 283) or *The Demon of Perversity*. The image remains a human one, despite its psychological force, yet it embodies a society that has put humans in second place. By contrast, *John the Baptist Preaching* seems to offer humans the choice.

JOHN THE BAPTIST PREACHING

This painting (fig. 284), signed and dated 1566, is a panel measuring approximately 37⅜ x 63½ in. (95 x 160.5 centimeters), but whose upper part has been trimmed. It belonged to the archduchess Isabella, governor of the Netherlands, and figures in her death inventory, made between 1633 and 1650, before it entered the collection of the count of Batthyany in Hungary, later going to the Budapest museum. St. John the Baptist, who is announcing the coming of Christ by pointing to him with his finger, stands on the edge of a forest, surrounded by a silent crowd. The painting's depth is achieved by the passage from the foreground, with its massive tree trunks and figures seen close up from behind, to a middle ground punctuated with ever smaller faces that display the whole range of human emotions. These figures, moreover, belong to various social classes; "all types, all ages, all temperaments meet here":[255] monks, soldiers and middle-class people, pilgrims and cooks, women and children—some have even climbed up into the trees—but also foreigners, including gypsy women. The composition is built on two diagonals: One runs from the top left corner toward the bottom right, carrying, in a sense, the crowd of listeners. This mass stops at the barrier formed by the people seen from behind, in the foreground. The other oblique springs from the figure dressed in blue, who is the apex of a triangular arrangement that guides the eye toward the luminous vista of the sky on the right, toward the water that reflects it—a river, where the baptism of Christ takes place—and toward the horizon. Two trees with thick trunks and a few standing figures reinforce this movement. The composition's angle of view has changed: it is no longer a bird's-eye view but a level one. The viewer could mingle with the crowd. This involvement in events is typical of the major works the artist made toward the end of his life. It has already appeared in *The Adoration of the Magi* of 1564, where the somewhat Mannerist movements of the Magi have some echoes in the *Sermon*.

The subject is well known: it was painted, in a similar spirit, before Bruegel by Herri met de Bles, Jan Swart van Groningen, and, some claim, by Jan van Amstel, a version of whose painting is now in the Lille museum.[256] Another link is also worth emphasizing. Pieter Coecke van Aelst, who according to Van Mander was Bruegel's teacher, made a life of St. John the Baptist in the form of six round stained glass windows, one of which depicted the sermon (fig. 285). It shows a child up in the branches of a tree, a detail that recurs in Bruegel's painting.[257]

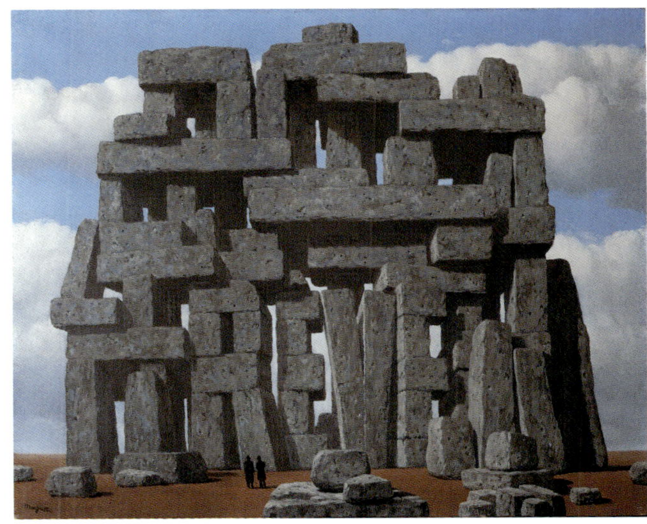

283

283. René Magritte, *The Art of Conversation*, 1950.
Oil on canvas, 25⁹⁄₁₆ x 31⅞ in. (65 x 81 cm). Private collection

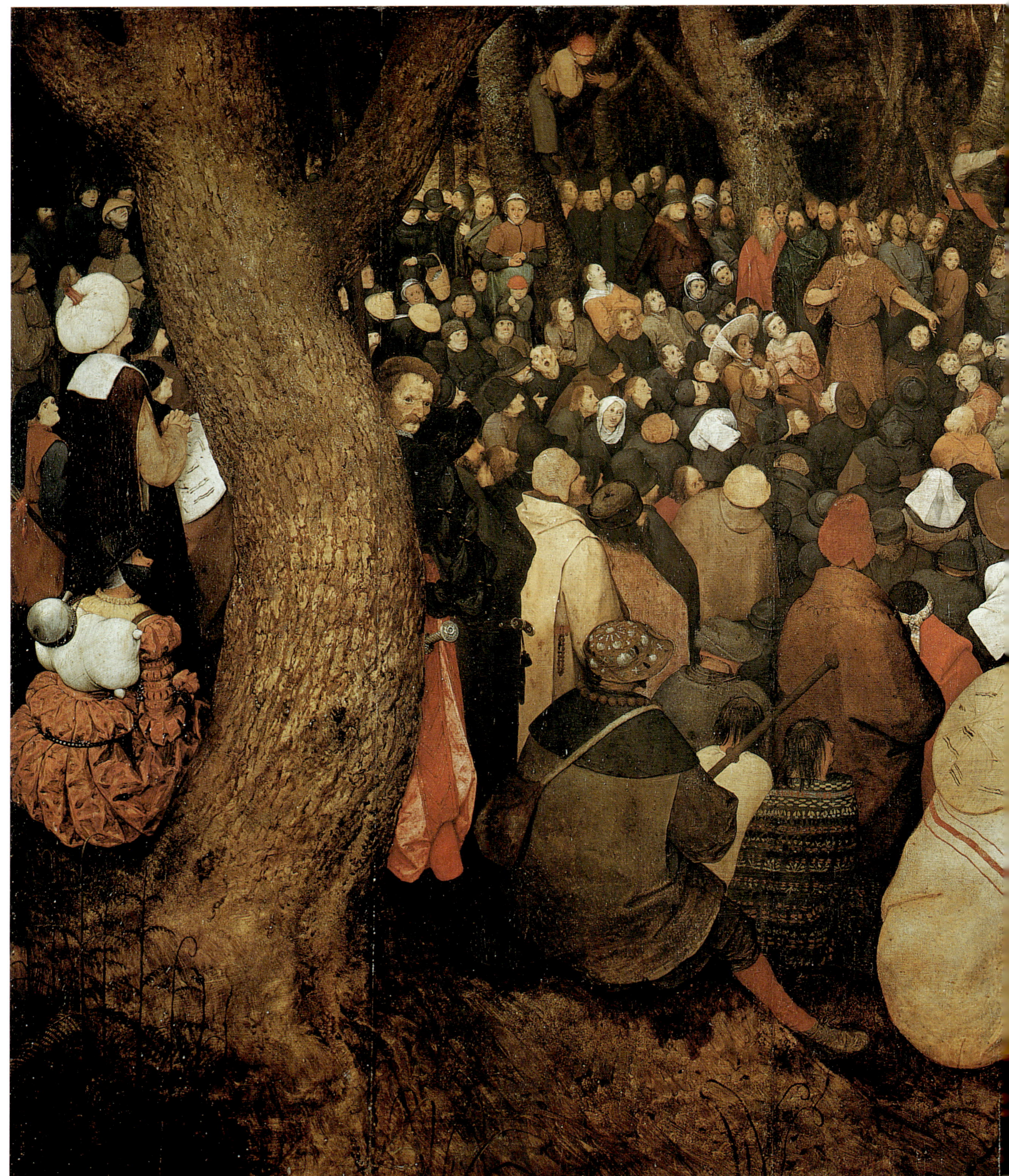

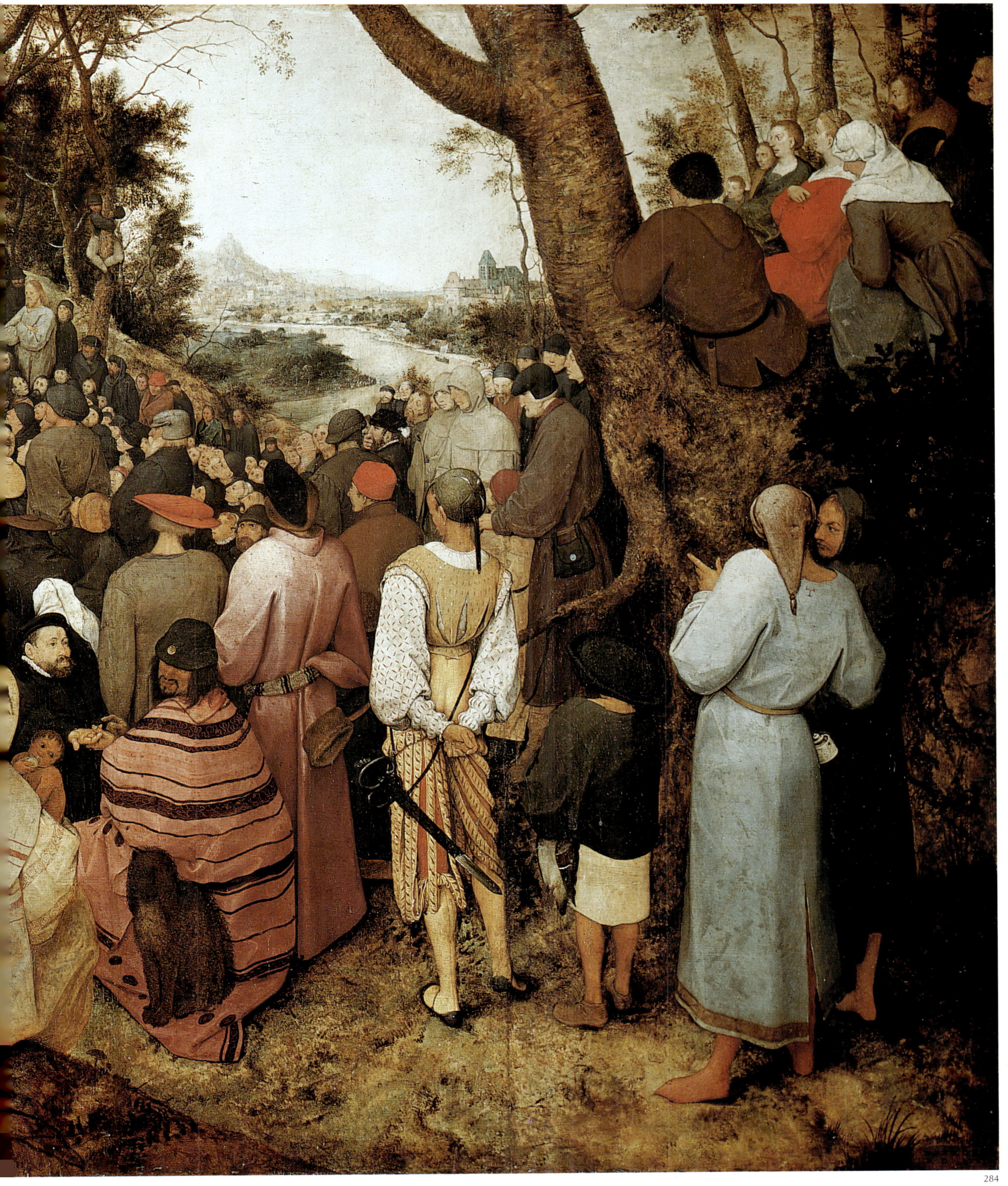

284. Pieter Bruegel, *John the Baptist Preaching*, 1566. Oil on panel,
37³⁄₈ x 63¹⁄₂ in. (95 x 160.5 cm). Budapest, Szépmüvészeti Múzeum

The latter, however, gives the theme greater breadth. In de Bles's work, for example, the sermon is often no more than an incidental scene in a landscape. Bruegel evokes a human reality, the people of his time. Indeed, the subject should be compared to the illicit open-air sermons that some Protestant preachers held at the time, discreetly, at some distance from the towns.

This is, therefore, a contemporary event, as documents from the time prove. An engraving by Frans Hogenberg depicts a Calvinist sermon held in the countryside near Antwerp in June 1566. Henri Pirenne writes: "The legend, in German, attributes the success of Calvinist ministers to the absence of Catholic sermons."[258] An account of a sermon given in June 1566, investigated by Antwerp magistrates, states that

> the minister arrived escorted by several armed men, at the place he had indicated in a previous sermon. People waited a while and, when the crowd had swelled, went toward a thicket; sentries were posted at the four corners of the area; where two trees almost touched a few pieces of turf were spread out, upon which the minister took his place … The audience consisted of both French and Walloons, among whom were women who were still breastfeeding; there were at least 4,000 to 5,000 people. Some of them climbed trees in order to follow the sermon better … This lasted from 1 o'clock to 5 o'clock … After the sermon it was announced that another would be preached in Flemish the following Saturday.[259]

That same year Bruegel transformed such an occasion into a painting which still lives. by its profound humanity and plastic genius, which go beyond the event itself. Groups, figures, and faces attract our curiosity. To the right, dominating the scene, one group appears to be attending the sermon. Some writers have identified the woman in red at the upper right with the painter's wife and the woman next to her with her mother, Mayken Verhulst, with Bruegel himself behind the two of them.[260] Tolnay, for his part, sees the painter below these: "just one head, rising above the gypsy, almost drowned in the crowd, stands out for its attentive and sad expression"; to Tolnay, the features of this man were the very ones that we see in the engravings of Lampsonius and Sadeler.[261] This is open to doubt, especially as the engravings are posthumous. Another perplexing or mysterious element is the character who, turning away from the preacher, is having his palm read by the gypsy in the foreground. Some have seen in this figure Bruegel's friend Hans Franckert,[262] others a sign of indifference or hostility to the sermon itself.[263] The presence of this group is in itself curious. Palmistry was rejected both by the Catholic church and by the reformists, and gypsies were *persona non grata* from the time of Charles V onward. Nevertheless the figures, because of their color and shape, are extremely beautiful. Are these unusual people simply there to enhance the picture and give it a strangeness that no factual or rational explanation can efface? It has also been suggested that the face may be that of the person who commissioned the painting,[264] but this would not explain his incongruous gesture. This raises— without answering it— the question of who Bruegel's clients were, information that is extremely hard to come by.

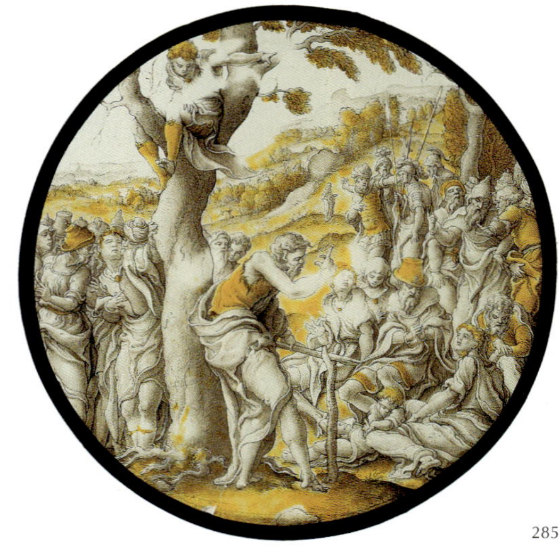

285

285. After Pieter Coecke van Aelst, *John the Baptist Preaching*, mid-sixteenth century. Stained glass. Amsterdam, Rijksmuseum

John the Baptist Preaching was a highly successful work, judging by the number of copies by the artist's sons, Pieter Bruegel the Younger and Jan Bruegel. Georges Marlier has listed twenty-three by the former, nine of them signed, and attributes three to the latter. The historian has also uncovered a *Sermon* by Pieter Baltens, mentioned by Van Mander, which owes much to Bruegel.[265] The sons' copies are inevitably not all of equal quality; interestingly, some reproduce and others omit the character having his fortune told. The best ones are such faithful copies that it seems "beyond doubt that the two brothers knew the original other than just through drawings."[266] This theory is plausible, since the work was in Brussels until the death of the archduchess Isabella in 1633. Georges Marlier adds: "The fact that *John the Baptist Preaching* was in the possession of the Governor and that so many copies were made at the height of the Counter-Reformation proves that no one saw in it any longer the slightest intention of evangelical propaganda, if indeed the depiction of the reformers' sermons had, in Pieter Bruegel's mind, any ulterior religious motive, which is very doubtful."[267] This does not change the fact that Bruegel bore witness to his age in this painting, as in all his works. The subject was common currency in the religious events of the day, and also draws on an iconographical tradition. Bruegel has given it a particular resonance, profound and drawn from experience, for society is reflected within it. Religious themes, moreover, are close to his heart, and he always treats them in an original way. It is a sermon that again dominates *Faith* (fig. 215), the drawing made in 1559 for the *Virtues* series of engravings.

Whether in the tower of Babel, or on the edge of a wood, or again in winter in *Skating Scene in front of St. George's Gate in Antwerp* (fig. 286), Bruegel involves society in his works, just as he assembles it and contrasts it in the urban setting of *The Battle of Carnival and Lent*, just as he portrays it in his depiction of proverbs, and in every picture through the importance he gives to gestures, attitudes, facial expressions, and body language. The world of the city must have been familiar to him because he lived in Antwerp and Brussels: lively cities, one a commercial metropolis that was open, with no pun intended, to the four winds, the other the administrative capital and seat of government. The human gallery could not have hoped for a keener observer.

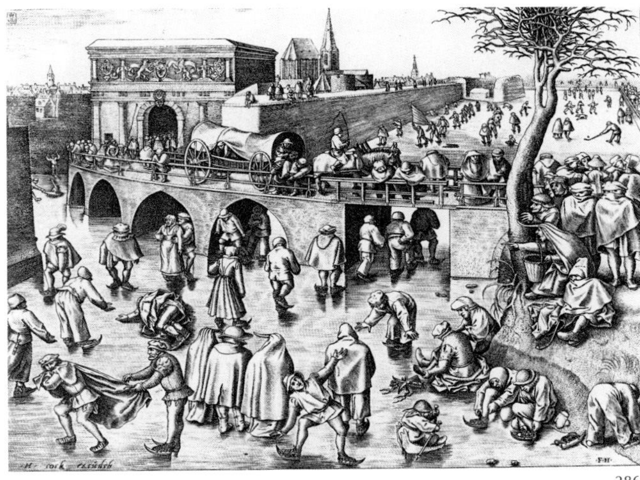

286. Frans Huys, *Skating Scene in front of St. George's Gate in Antwerp*, after Pieter Bruegel, ca. 1561. Engraving, 9¹⁄₈ x 11³⁄₄ in. (23.2 x 29.9 cm). Brussels, Bibliothèque royale Albert I, print room

PEASANT LIFE

The life of peasants was equally familiar to Bruegel. He may have been born into it; in any case, in his time town and country were adjacent, separated only by the city walls. Engravings and maps show this, and the sermons preached outside towns prove it. Bruegel loved nature, and was one of the first artists to portray it, if we think of the *Seasons* series, *The Flight into Egypt* (fig. 140), *Winter Landscape with Skaters and Bird Trap* (fig. 54), and the *Great Landscapes* (figs. 84, 165, 167), published by Hieronymus Cock in Antwerp and among Bruegel's first masterpieces.

It is not surprising, therefore, that Bruegel was interested in those who

experience the earth, the trees, and the sky in all weathers, who sow and reap, but who also relax and enjoy themselves. Van Mander is eloquent on this subject:

> Bruegel often went to the country, to village fairs and weddings; dressed as peasants they [with his friend Hans Franckert] offered gifts like everyone else, claiming to be part of the family or close relatives of the bride or groom. Here Bruegel took pleasure in watching peasants eat, drink, dance, caper about, woo, and otherwise enjoy themselves, scenes which he would then reproduce in an amusing and witty way … He knew perfectly the art of painting these peasant men and women in their traditional Kempen finery or other clothing, and of faithfully portraying the awkward, rustic movement of their dances, their running, their behaviour and mannerisms. He had an extraordinary sureness in drawing figures, and made beautiful, pure sketches in pen of landscapes drawn from life.[268]

High praise, a fine testimonial for this artist who went and captured his subjects on the spot, which must have been unusual at a time when workshops had rules clearly defined by guilds, and their work drew more on the Italian tradition than on observation of rural life. Bruegel, then, loved the country; Van Mander, his first biographer, relates this at considerable length. Why not believe him? The works are there to be seen, and the nicknames "Boeren Bruegel" (Peasant Bruegel) or Bruegel the Joker were soon attached to him and stuck, to the point, as we know, of obliterating the painter's profound character and genius to make way for a playful image. Paintings and engravings, which give such an impression at first sight, met with great success and began a tradition which lasted in Flanders until the twentieth century.

Besides drawing amusement from walking through the countryside, stopping in villages, and visiting country fairs when he lived in Brussels, the artist was no doubt seeking, through contact with the inhabitants and those who worked on the land, mankind in its pure state, laid bare, at its origins, living the seasons, exposed to the rain and the sun, as well as experiencing drama and joy. And although the work was hard, and the land often unproductive, they danced, they drank, they kissed each other hungrily. However, we should not seek a moral in any of this—whatever some may say—unless we need a pretext of our own.

Within the bounds of the peasants' world Bruegel nevertheless created a genre, of a type that would bear his name. His works, though painterly, were so in the widest sense; they fitted their subjects but were not enslaved to them. *The Wedding Dance* of 1566 (figs. 289–91), now in Detroit, illustrates this. Although the work has suffered from the passage of time—and from restoration, which has made the paint layer more transparent, to the point that some have spoken of it as a sketch[269] and others have reserved judgment on the matter[270]—the painting conveys an extraordinary vitality.

Seen from above, and encompassing a large company of peasants who are enjoying themselves at the wedding of one of their daughters, the scene captures in depth—from the foreground to the distance, along lines that guide the eye to the horizon almost on the edge of the picture—and condenses a crowd of men and women, in groups, drinking, gossiping, and dancing to the sound of bagpipes. In contrast to the feeling evoked by *John the Baptist Preaching*, here is unbridled

287

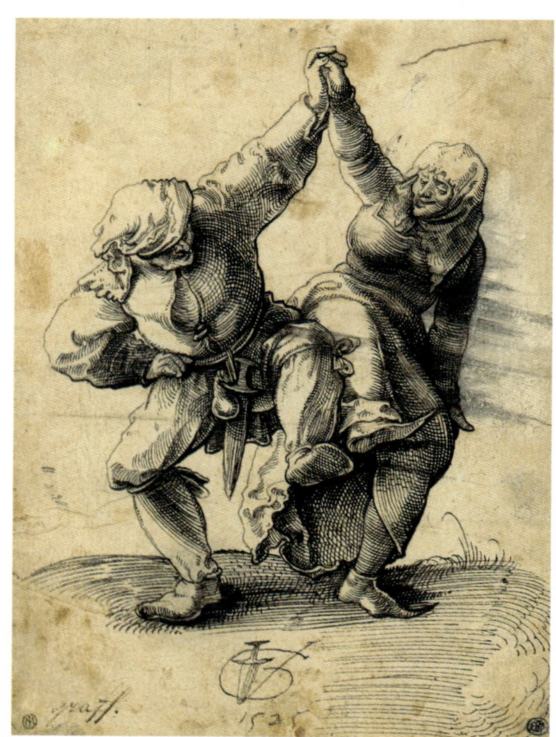

288

287. Albrecht Dürer, *The Bagpiper*, 1514. Engraving, 4⁹/₁₆ x 2⁷/₈ in. (11.6 x 7.4 cm). Paris, Bibliothèque nationale de France

288. Urs Graf, *Peasant Couple Dancing*, 1525. Pen and black ink, 8¹/₈ x 6 in. (20.6 x 15.3 cm). Paris, École nationale supérieure des beaux-arts

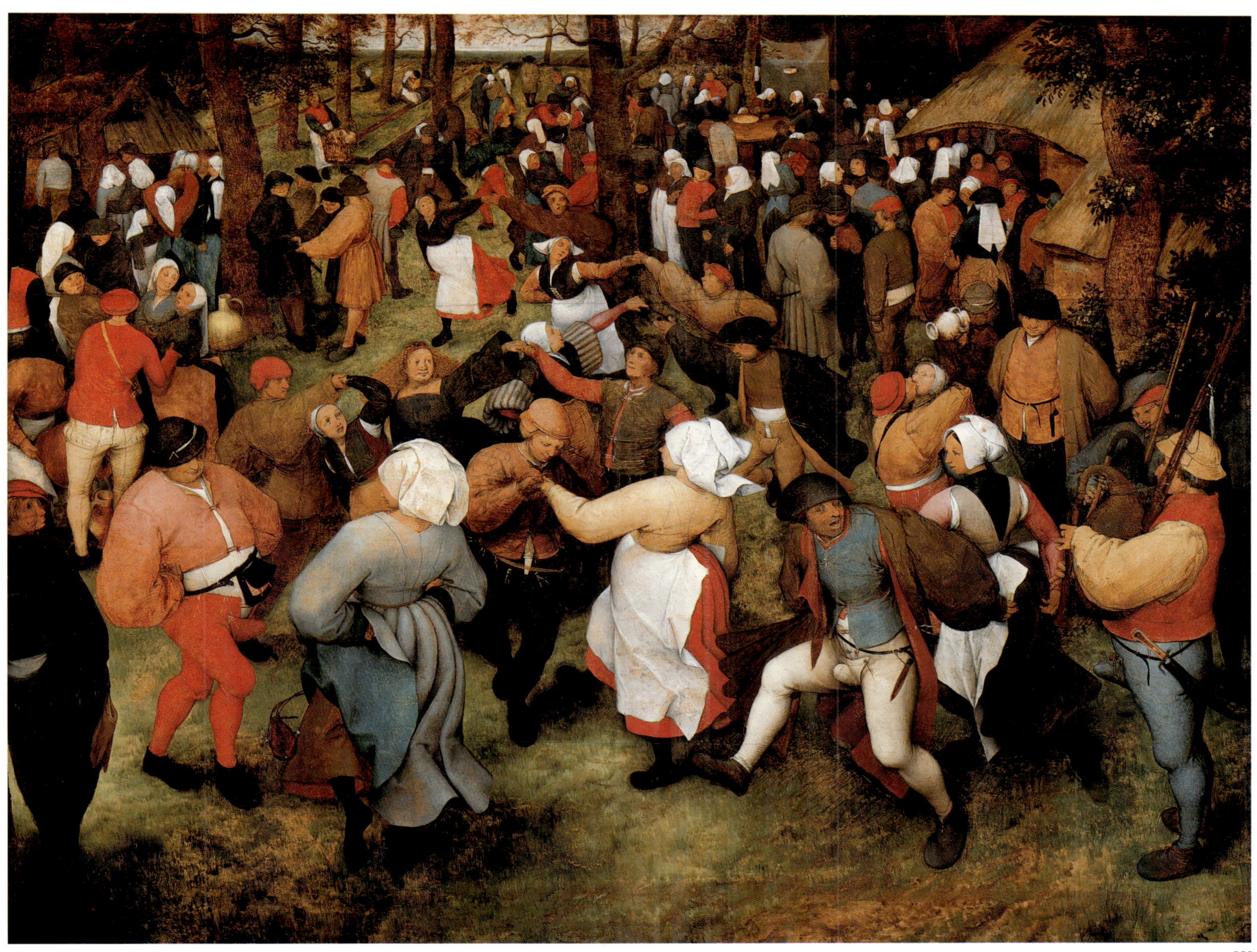

289

jollity, the life of the senses. The bride with her hair in the wind, who has joined the dancers in the center of the picture, is merely an excuse for this portrayal of merrymaking—the first such work of Bruegel's, although the subject had been dealt with in drawings and engravings by Albrecht Dürer (fig. 287), Urs Graf (fig. 288), Hans Sebald Beham, and Lucas van Leyden.

The view from above once again allows the space to be used to the full and, by the sequence of the couples, the evocation of a whole network of rhythms which, although different in form, prefigures that of Rubens's *The Kermis* (Country Fair) in the Louvre. This comparison is not only a convincing one, but it demonstrates Bruegel's fascination with movement. Its deconstruction in *The Blind Leading the Blind* (fig. 69), its use in *The Land of Cockaigne* (fig. 269), and its speeding up in *The Wedding Dance* all confirm this. The concatenation and repetition of movements here create the rhythm, which is also marked by colors—red and white—and especially by the way they punctuate the painting: white caps, red bonnets, aprons, skirts, breeches, and jerkins.

289–91. Pieter Bruegel, *The Wedding Dance*, 1566: whole work and details. Oil on panel, 47 x 62 in. (119.3 x 157.5 cm). Detroit, Institute of Arts

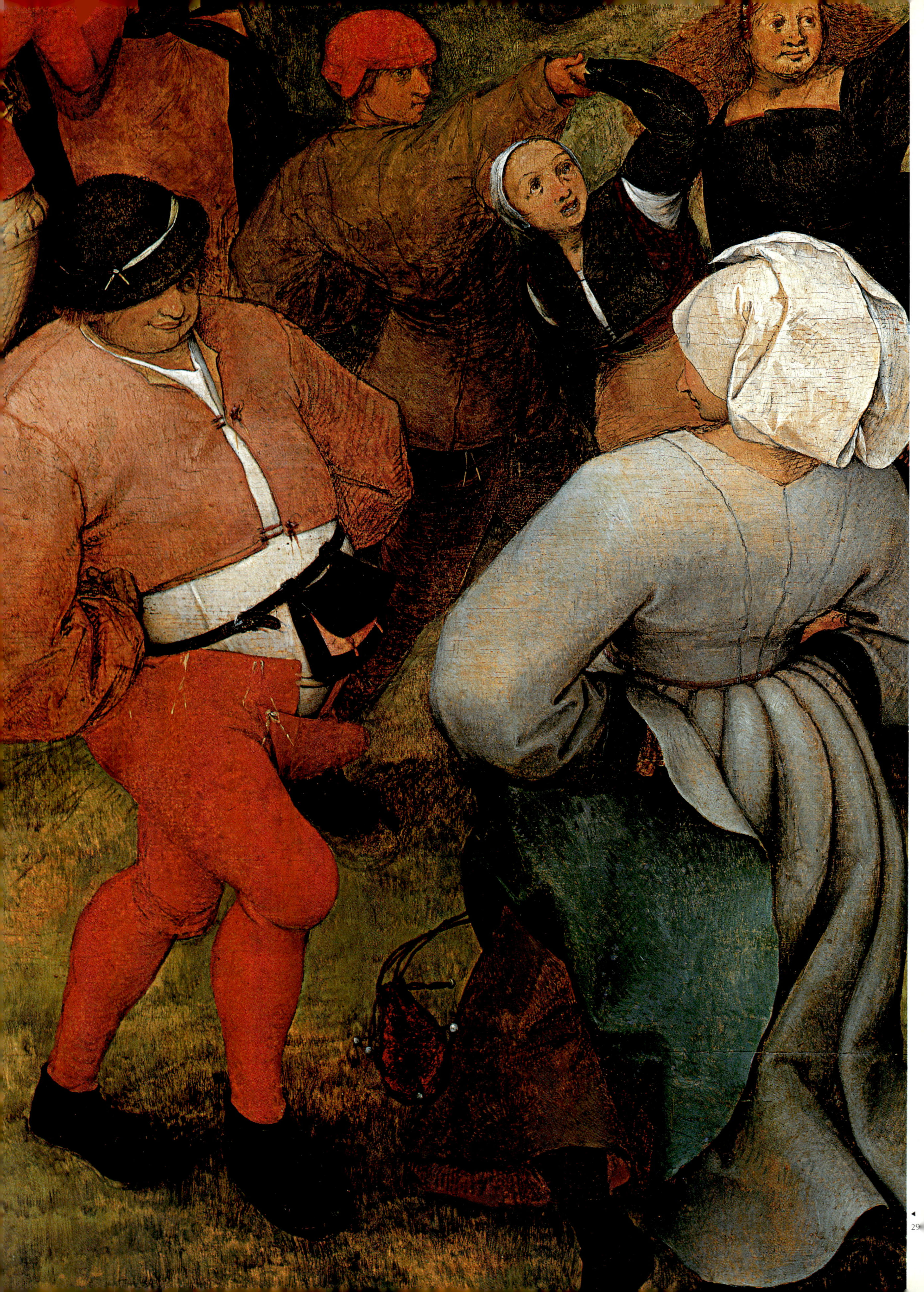

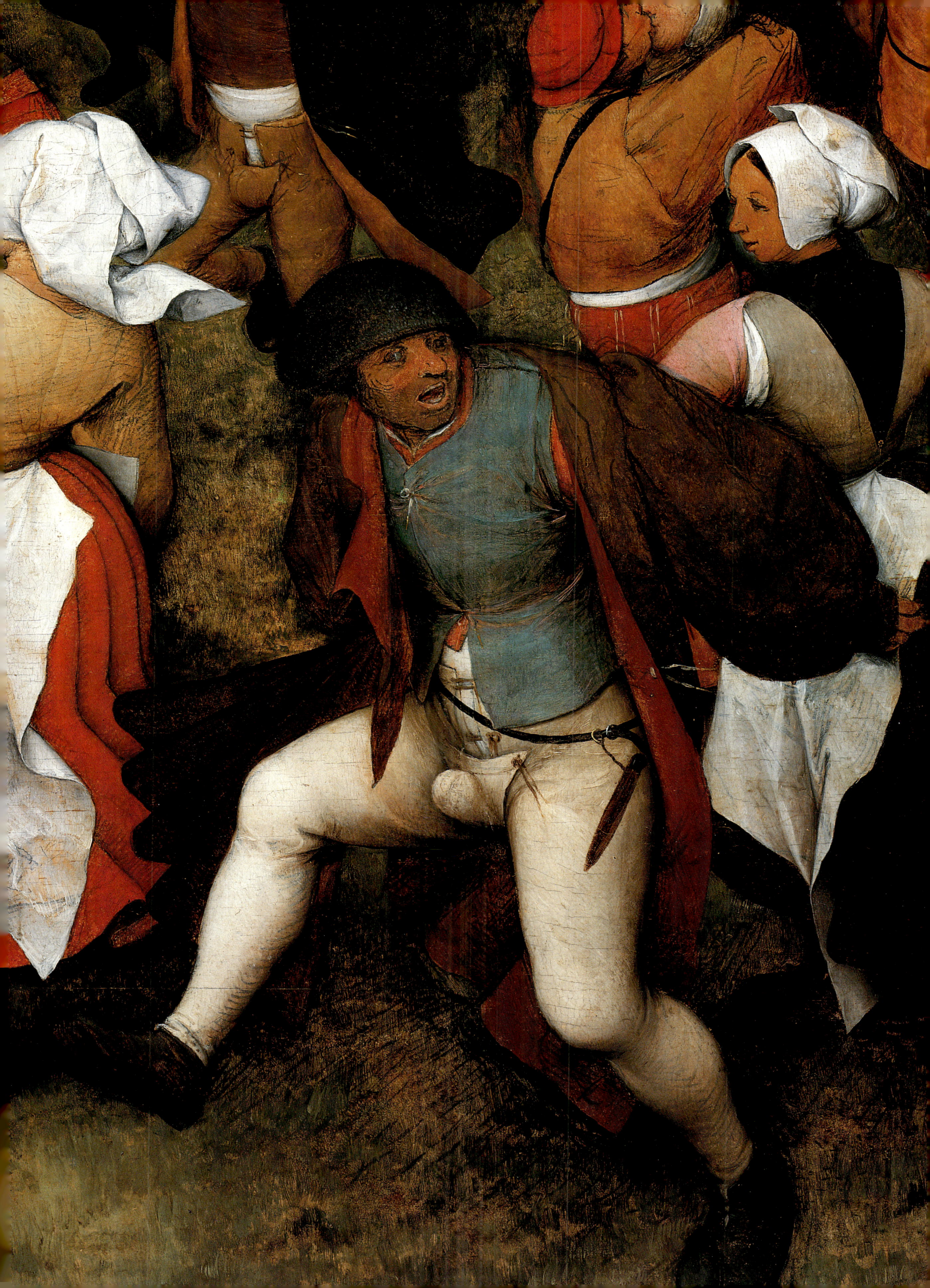

The work is not a mere entertainment for all that. To be sure, it is not a synthesis or overall view of peasant life, nor something didactic or encyclopedic, but a global view of what happens among people at a wedding that brings together a community, gives vent to their joy of living, and asserts their sexuality. On the last point the painting—where the three men in the foreground (two dancers and a bagpipe player) freed of old overpainting, openly display their virility—leaves no doubt. Should we see a moral or social judgment here, a pejorative view of the peasants' condition which runs into excess, a bourgeois judgment that condemns them?[271] Although there was such a tradition from the fourteenth century in various genres, we need not see *The Wedding Dance* as conforming with it.

Bruegel respected people too much to want to disparage them. He could view them with humor, yes; he could seek out the ridiculous, no doubt—but derision was not in his character. Perhaps the popularity of *The Wedding Dance* and pictures like it was due to certain social differences and ideas linked to them. Hans van Miegroet writes:

> By associating peasants with nature, basic drives, and freely expressed sexuality, Bruegel was in fact drawing attention to the corresponding bourgeois values: that is, culture, control of drives, and the curbing of sexuality. This negative affirmation was part of the *bourgeois offensive* of the sixteenth century, which aimed to channel, penalize, and marginalize the lower classes' different ways of behaving.[272]

The work may echo such concerns, but to say that the painter was motivated by them is to accuse him of having an intention, of being both aggressive and hypocritical, which is justified neither by contemporary or near-contemporary accounts—Van Mander's especially—nor by the works themselves. Among the latter, *The Wedding Feast* and *The Peasants' Dance* serve as excellent witnesses for the defense.

It is certain that the subject attracted attention. An engraving by Pieter van der Heyden, which states unequivocally "P. BRUEGEL. INVENT." was published by Hieronymus Cock at the Four Winds, and went into several editions.[273] *Country Wedding Dance* (fig. 292) is obviously inspired by the painting, but with significant differences. The composition is narrower rather than panoramic. The bride is not dancing, but seated in front of her *drap d'honneur* and is receiving as gifts a whole series of household objects. Although the dancers here do not display the same desires, eight lines of Flemish verse explain the scene in colorful language, encouraging the dancing and revealing that if the bride does not join in, it is because she is pregnant! The relationship between the painting and the engraving dates the latter—which carries no date—after 1566,[274] or after the death of Hieronymus Cock in 1570, as his name does not appear as publisher.[275] Some have seen in it a warning against lust and gluttony,[276] others an indication of the vitality of the people in the face of restrictions put in place by the authorities.[277] Be that as it may, it is clear that the theme of an open-air wedding dance in itself attracted interest. This very subject was endlessly copied and reproduced, in countless variations, proving that is was "one of the most popular in all early-

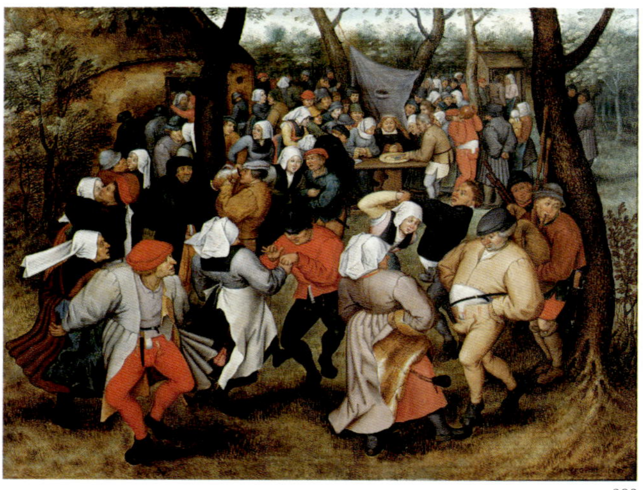

292. Pieter van der Heyden, *Country Wedding Dance*, after Pieter Bruegel, after 1566 or after 1570. Engraving, 14¾ x 16⅝ in. (37.5 x 42.3 cm). Brussels, Bibliothèque royale Albert I, print room

293. Pieter Bruegel the Younger, *Wedding Dance in the Open Air*, 1607. Oil on panel, 15⅛ x 20¼ in. (38.5 x 51.5 cm). Brussels, Musées royaux des Beaux-Arts de Belgique, Delporte-Livrauw bequest

seventeenth-century Flemish painting. Its popularity lasted throughout the century."[278] By this time it no longer contained a critical or hidden meaning—if it had ever had one in the first place.

The painting inaugurated a genre that sustained Bruegel's reputation and firmly attached it to his depictions of the country people. That the theme persisted is essentially due to Pieter Bruegel the Younger's small-format paintings These are "a sort of synthesis of the large painting in Detroit, where landscape is important, and Van der Heyden's engraving, where the lighting and background produce the effect of a night scene."[279] Georges Marlier mentions about thirty, some ten of

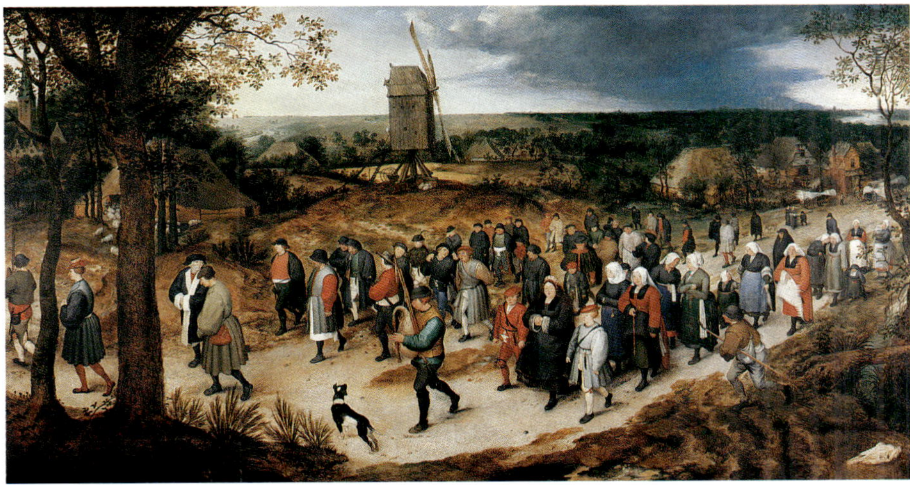

294

which are signed. One of the finest and oldest, formerly in the Delporte collection, now in the Musées royaux des Beaux-Arts in Brussels, dates from 1607 (fig. 293). In clear, bright colors, with powerful vermilion shades, its well judged composition does not have the breadth of the father's work, even though its vigor comes through strongly. In these thirty works the image of the engraving is always reversed, which raises the problem of whether the son originally transposed the work or whether Bruegel made an original drawing. The solution to the riddle, if there is one, cannot ignore the existence of half a dozen other copies where the image is not reversed. Another series sets the event in an interior; some twenty of these have been identified, in the wake of a painting in the Johnson Collection in Philadelphia, which was long considered to be by Pieter Bruegel (fig. 332).[280] Jan Bruegel and Martin van Cleve also painted this subject.

Bruegel also painted *The Wedding Procession* (fig. 294). Several copies by his son Pieter prove this, and the inventory of the possessions of Alexander Voet in 1689 even states: "A chimney painting, a wedding procession, after Bruegel the Elder."[281] The work's format is horizontal and wide, allowing space for the procession to stretch out before a broad landscape that runs from a wealthy farm on the right, where the wedding feast is being prepared, to a church whose spire can be glimpsed through the trees on the left. Led by a bagpiper, the bridegroom,

294. Attributed to Pieter Bruegel, *The Wedding Procession*, second half of the sixteenth century. Oil on panel, 24 ¼ x 45 in. (61.5 x 114.5 cm). Brussels, Musée communal

followed by two notables, walks ahead of the bride who, for her part, looks relaxed. Is the painting, which was at Northwick Park from 1830 onward, the original work? Accepted as such by Friedländer and Glück, and ruled out by Tolnay and Jedlicka, its acquisition in 1966 by the Musée communal in Brussels rallied both Genaille and Marlier to its cause. The quality of the work is not in doubt; the inventiveness and composition are Bruegelesque, as the son's versions prove (and as does the version by Jan Bruegel, which is close to it in spirit). There are many convincing details: the shepherd who is running to the scene, the notable, copied in a drawing by Rubens,[282] and the leaves of the trees on the left, which could be compared to those in *The Bird-Nester* (fig. 209) or *The Magpie on the Gallows* (fig. 360). However other aspects, such as the sheep coming out of the fold, the empty space between the figures and the windmill, and the lack of rhythm of the whole, which makes it into a sort of snapshot rather than a moment in a festive occasion, could raise doubts.

VILLAGE FAIRS

Peasant festivals such as those Bruegel witnessed were popularized in two engravings made after 1559: *Kermis at Hoboken* and *The Kermis of St. George*. The first, engraved by Frans Hogenberg and published by Bartholomaeus de Momper, has a counterpart in a drawing where the image is reversed, dated and signed 1559 BRUEGEL, which is generally considered, with few reservations, to be the original,[283] despite its poor condition. The second engraving was published at the same time by Hieronymus Cock, after an original which is now lost.[284] Both show the bustle of a festival day in a small village, with people playing and drinking, animals, archers, children frolicking, and couples kissing. In both, the inn and the church face, and contrast with, each other.

In the foreground of *Kermis at Hoboken* (fig. 297), under the banner that reads "Dit is de Gulde van Hoboken" (This is the Hoboken guild), is a cart drawn by a horse whose rider is drinking the health of the revelers gathered at the inn—while in contrast a procession carries a statue into the church. The engraving's legend emphasizes the festive character of the place, where beer is cheaper than in Antwerp, and says that the peasants, in celebrating and even in getting as drunk as beasts (another engraving of 1568 is entitled *The Drunkard Pushed into the Pigsty;* fig. 295)—will brave fasting and cold to save their kermis.[285] This seems to hint at a problem, since *The Kermis of St. George* hoists a banner that reads: "laet die boeren haer kermis houuen" (let the peasants celebrate their kermis).[286] Perhaps this was intended as a protest against the decrees of Charles V aimed at restraining excess, which the governor, Margaret of Parma, wanted to reinforce.

Consequently, as a remedy to the disorderly drinking bouts and drunkenness which are occurring in our country in various inns, taverns, and hostelries, held in secluded places away from towns, market towns, and villages, away from the high roads and other places, in fairs and kermises, and as a remedy

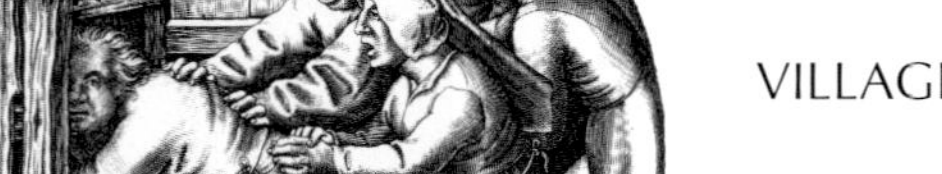

295

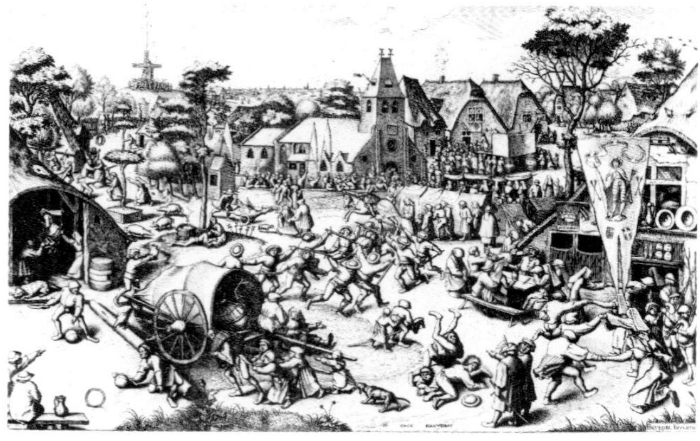

296

295. Jean Wierix, *The Drunkard Pushed into the Pigsty*, after Pieter Bruegel, 1568. Engraving, diameter 7⅛ in. (18.2 cm). Brussels, Bibliothèque royale Albert I, print room

296. Attributed to Hieronymus Cock, *The Kermis of St. George*, after Pieter Bruegel, ca. 1561. Etching and engraving, 13 x 20⅝ in. (33.2 x 52.3 cm). Brussels, Bibliothèque royale Albert I, print room

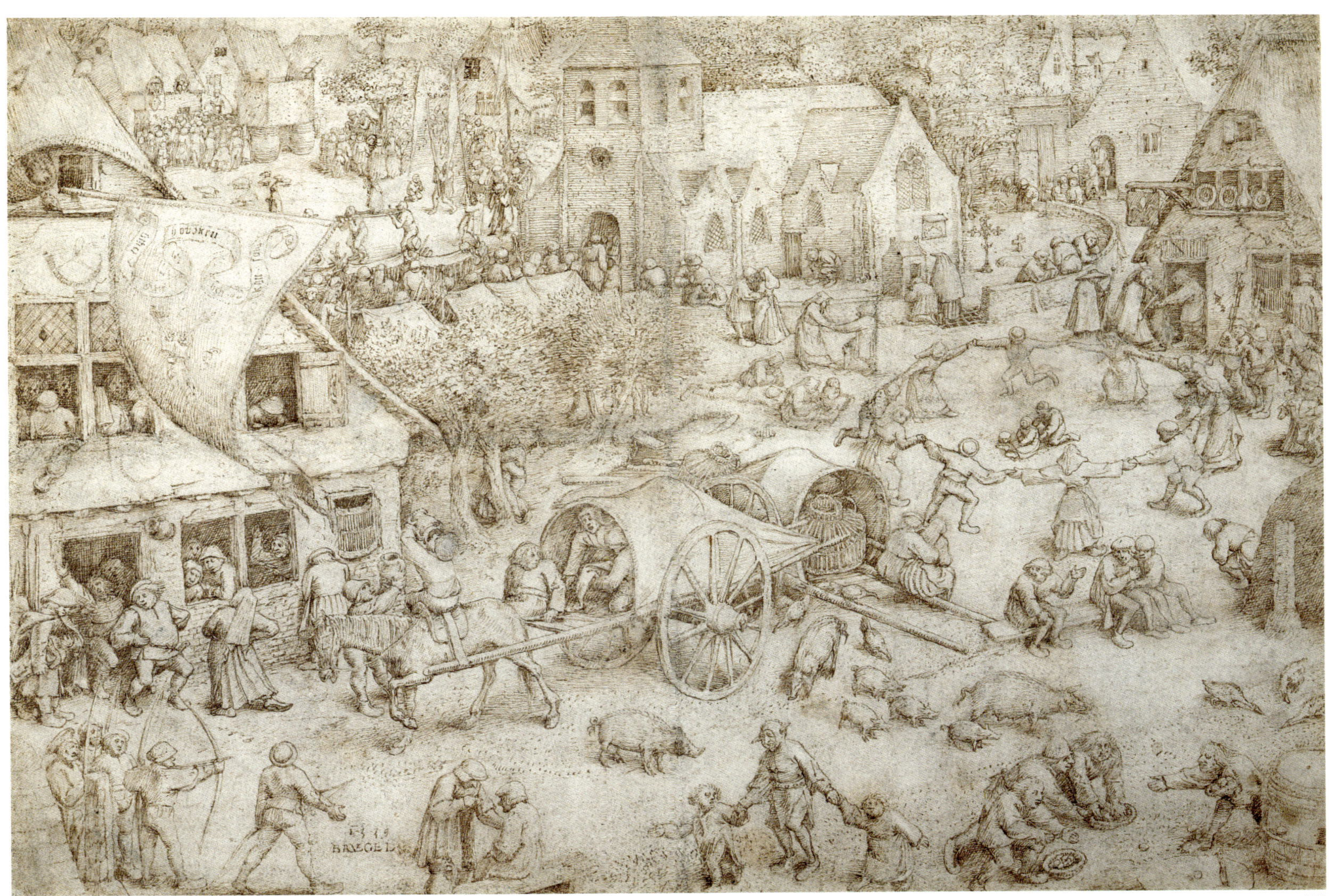

297. Pieter Bruegel, *Kermis at Hoboken*, 1559.
Pen and brown ink, 10⅜ x 15½ in. (26.5 x 39.4 cm).
London, Courtauld Institute of Art, Lee Collection

to the brawls, murders, and other problems that result, we decree and order that … the said fairs and kermises shall last but one day, on pain of a fine for each of those who hold said fairs and kermises beyond and longer than this limit of one day, as for those who attend them, and for each time that they do so, of thirty livres for each offender. Those who celebrate weddings throughout our country and its domains must not invite any more than the twenty people, and the feast of said weddings must not last beyond the day of the wedding itself and the following day until the afternoon. Those who do otherwise—both who hold the weddings and who come in larger numbers than permitted and are not close relatives—as well as those who stay longer than permitted, will each incur a fine of twenty gold caroli."[287]

Once again, the interpretation could be either a denunciation of vices, or a protection of freedoms. In both works the inn and the church, the profane and the sacred, folklore and theater, battle and pilgrimage, are neighbors in many

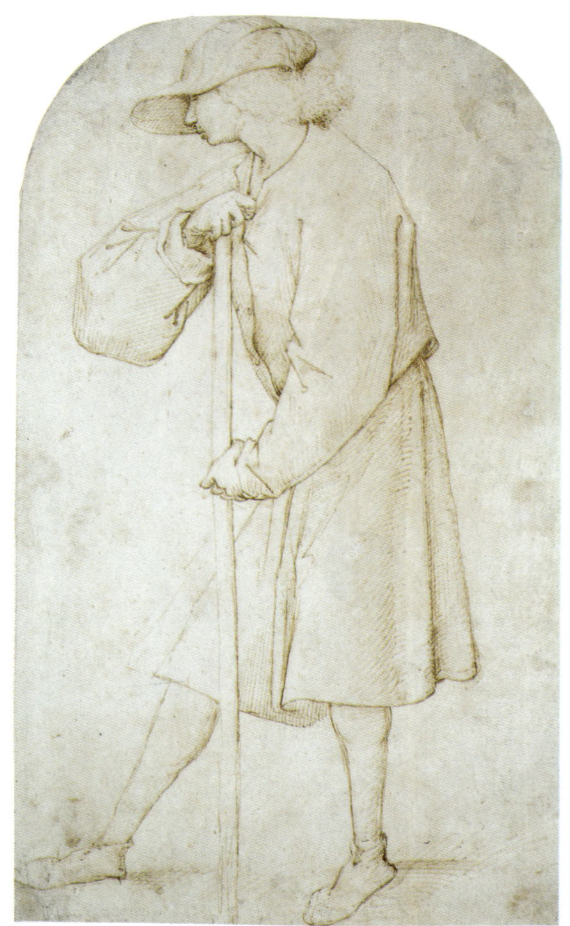

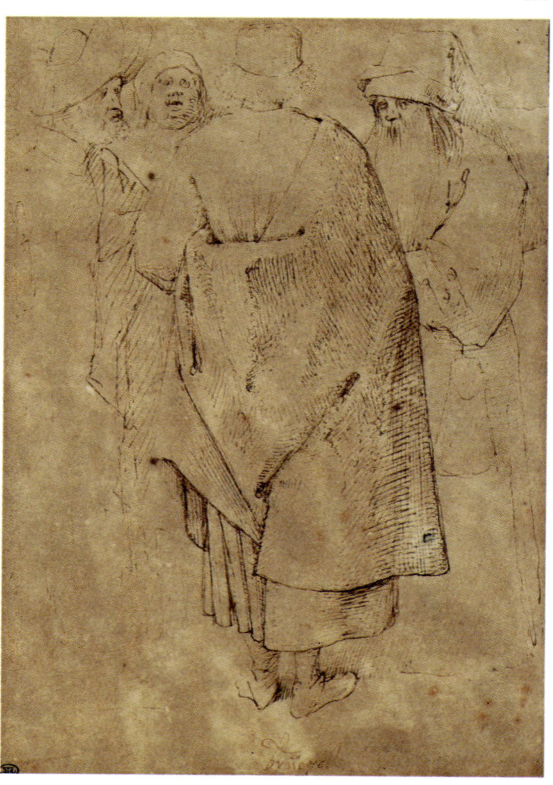

298. Pieter Bruegel, *The Goose Keeper*, ca. 1565.
Pen and brown ink, 9¾ x 5⅞ in. (24.8 x 14.9 cm).
Dresden, Staatliche Kunstsammlungen, Kupferstichkabinett

299. Pieter Bruegel, *Four Men Standing in Conversation*,
ca. 1565. Pen and brown ink, 8⅜ x 6 in. (21.2 x 15.2 cm).
Paris, Louvre, graphic arts department

varied, overlapping playlets. But this drawing was produced in the period in which Bruegel also painted *Flemish Proverbs*, *Children's Games*, and *The Battle of Carnival and Lent*. In the kermis drawings—which are inventories of different forms of enjoyment—there are many echoes of these: the fool, central character in *The Battle of Carnival and Lent*, is being guided in Hoboken by two children who are holding his hands, while in the St. George drawing several hang on to his coat tails. Here is unity of vision, of imagination, of animation, exchanges between the imaginary and the real, a portrayal of a society that lives and dreams. The spirit of the kermis clearly continued to reverberate in Bruegel's works.

Bruegel was to endow these entertaining works, which printing was to make available to a wider public, with a stature that was no longer anecdotal but monumental. By their form and painterly qualities two of his latest works—*The Wedding Feast* (fig. 300) and *The Peasants' Dance* (fig. 307)—give the peasant theme a new breadth that goes beyond the subject itself. In them he shows great attention to movement and life, a joyous realism, and an expressive power whose effects are all his own.

PEASANTS AS LARGE AS LIFE

The signs are already there in several drawings such as *The Goose Keeper* (fig. 298) and *Four Men Standing in Conversation* (fig. 299). The first figure is striking for its elegance and the gracious curve of his body, which leans on the vertical of his crook. This could be a shepherd, given the pose of the figure in the background of *The Misanthrope* (fig. 267) or in the center of *The Fall of Icarus* (fig. 325). The reference to geese is confirmed in a tondo that is part of a series of proverbs by Pieter Bruegel the Younger, which exactly reproduces the figure in a pastoral setting with this type of bird. According to Georges Marlier this is an "illustration of the saying 'who knows why geese go barefoot?'—in other words, there is a reason for everything." He adds that the same figure appears in Bruegel's *Flemish Proverbs* of 1559 "in the background on the right,"[288] therefore, facing the two bears. The second drawing, which depicts four men, is more of a sketch, although just as lifelike as the first. Are we in town or in the country? The characters appear to be well dressed, but it is their attitudes and expressions that are striking. They are captured from life, or as the Flemish would say, "*naer 't leven*" (from the life), especially when a famous group of drawings bearing that inscription was still attributed to the painter. This talking group recalls Dürer, but Bruegel has confined himself to sketching them. They are no less true to life for all that. These two drawings, to which can be added *The Painter and the Art Lover*, date from about 1565.[289]

The Wedding Feast (figs. 300–304) takes place in the interior of a barn, where friends and acquaintances sit round a table that is seen at an angle. The wall behind, of a warm, golden ocher, is formed by the harvest, whose gathering Bruegel portrays in his drawing of 1568, *Summer* (fig. 58), with a very similar composition. Large figures occupy the foreground; others decrease in size with increasing distance, following the painting's perspective. This perspective is oblique, allowing the guests to be arranged around the table while keeping a

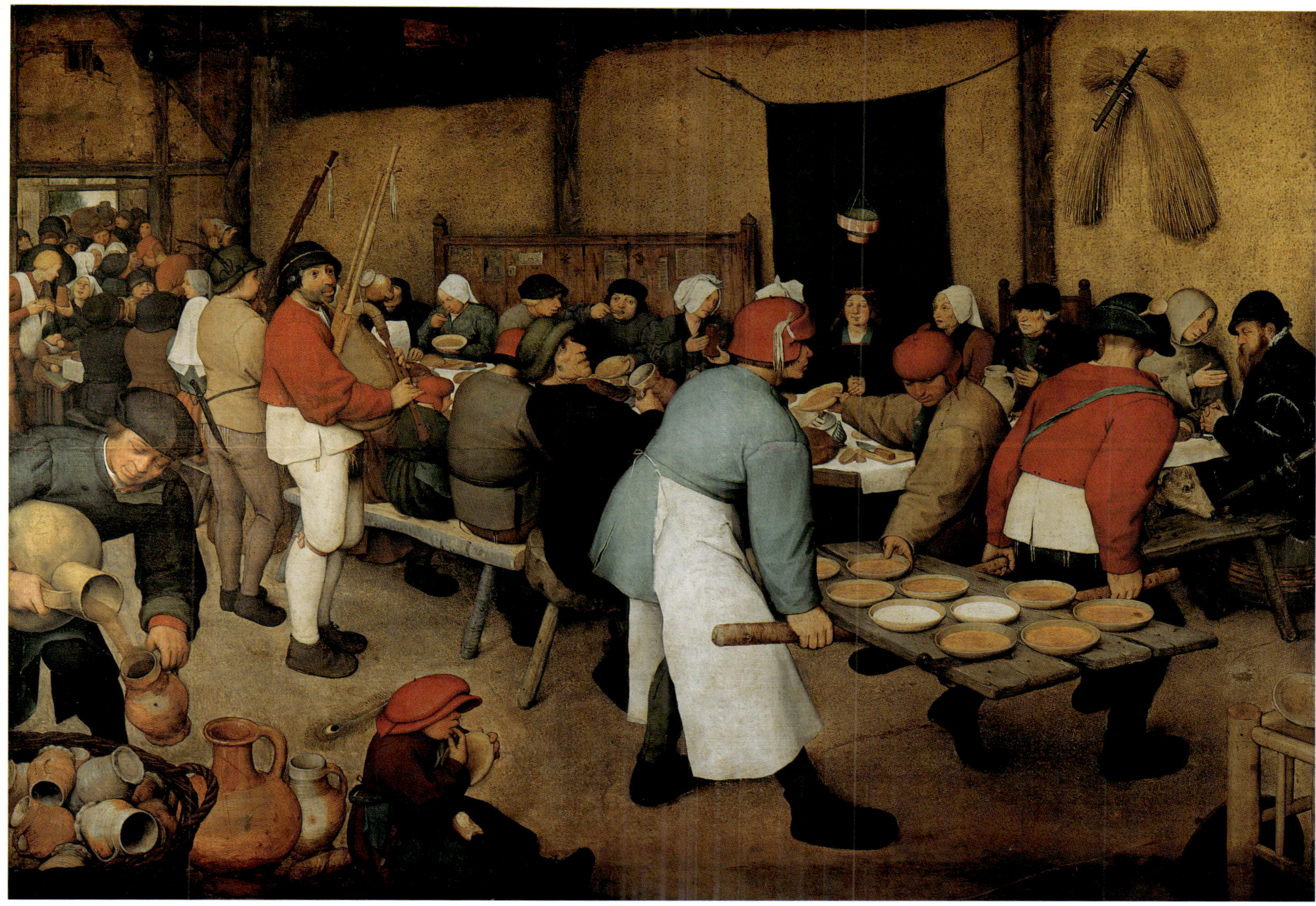

300

special place for the bride, in the right-hand third of the painting. She faces the viewer, and her presence is emphasized by a *drap d'honneur* and a paper crown. The young, round-faced woman, her hair loose and surmounted by a fine diadem, holds her hands together and lowers her eyes, as if absent or, more likely, contemplating the happy fate that awaits her. Balancing the *drap d'honneur*, two crossed wheat sheaves are held in the straw by a rake, as a sign of blessing.[290] The other guests are eating heartily or holding private conversations. Toward the left the figures bunch up, as a result of the perspective and, through the open door, more guests enter the barn. Each part of the painting is thus alive: the attitudes of the various characters, their individual gestures (which are never stereotyped), and the overall arrangement combine to re-create the event in a natural way, as if captured on the spot.

The composition, similar to that of *John the Baptist Preaching*, centers on two diagonals of different lengths. The main one begins at the door in the background and ends with the servant dressed in blue who is carrying, on a door that has been

300–304. Pieter Bruegel, *The Wedding Feast*, ca. 1568: whole work and details. Oil on panel, 44⅞ x 65½ in. (114 x 164 cm). Vienna, Kunsthistorisches Museum

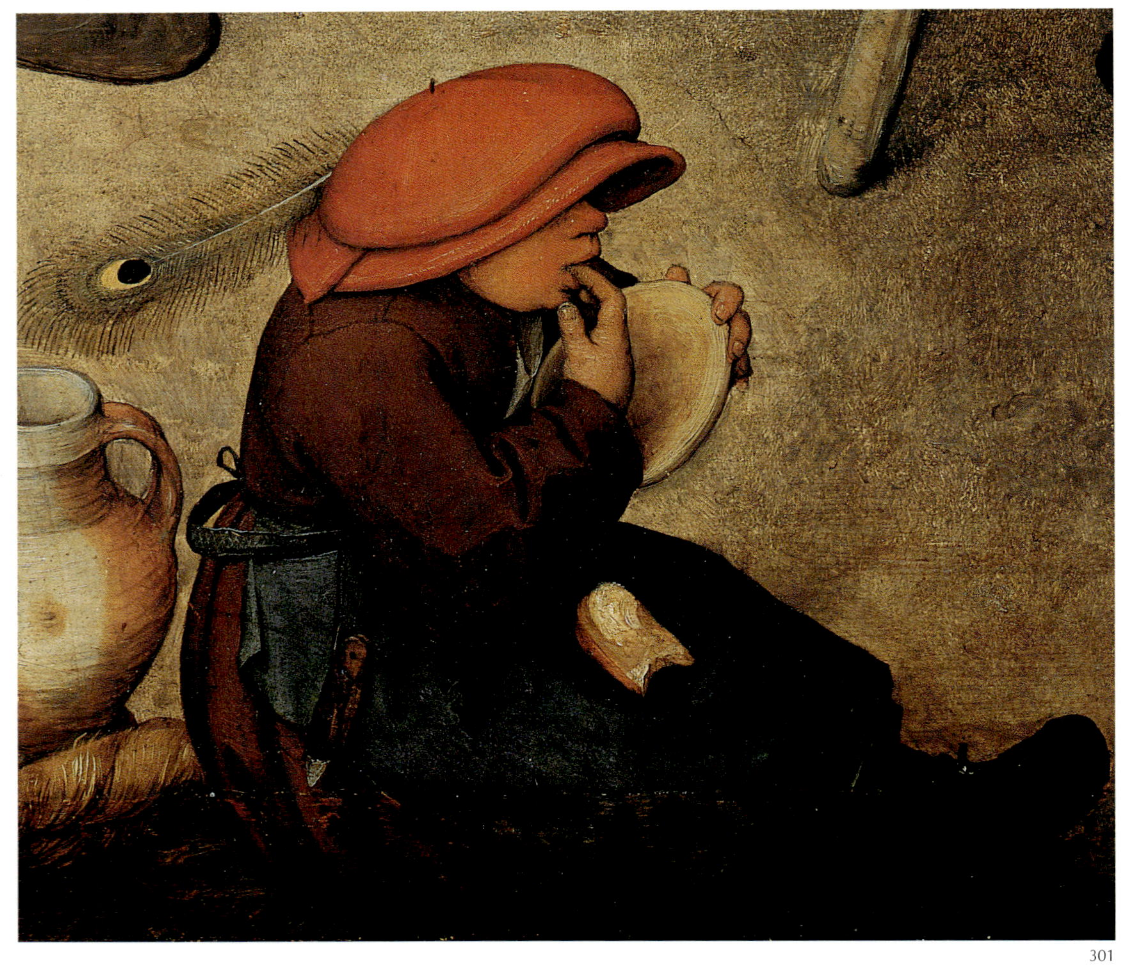

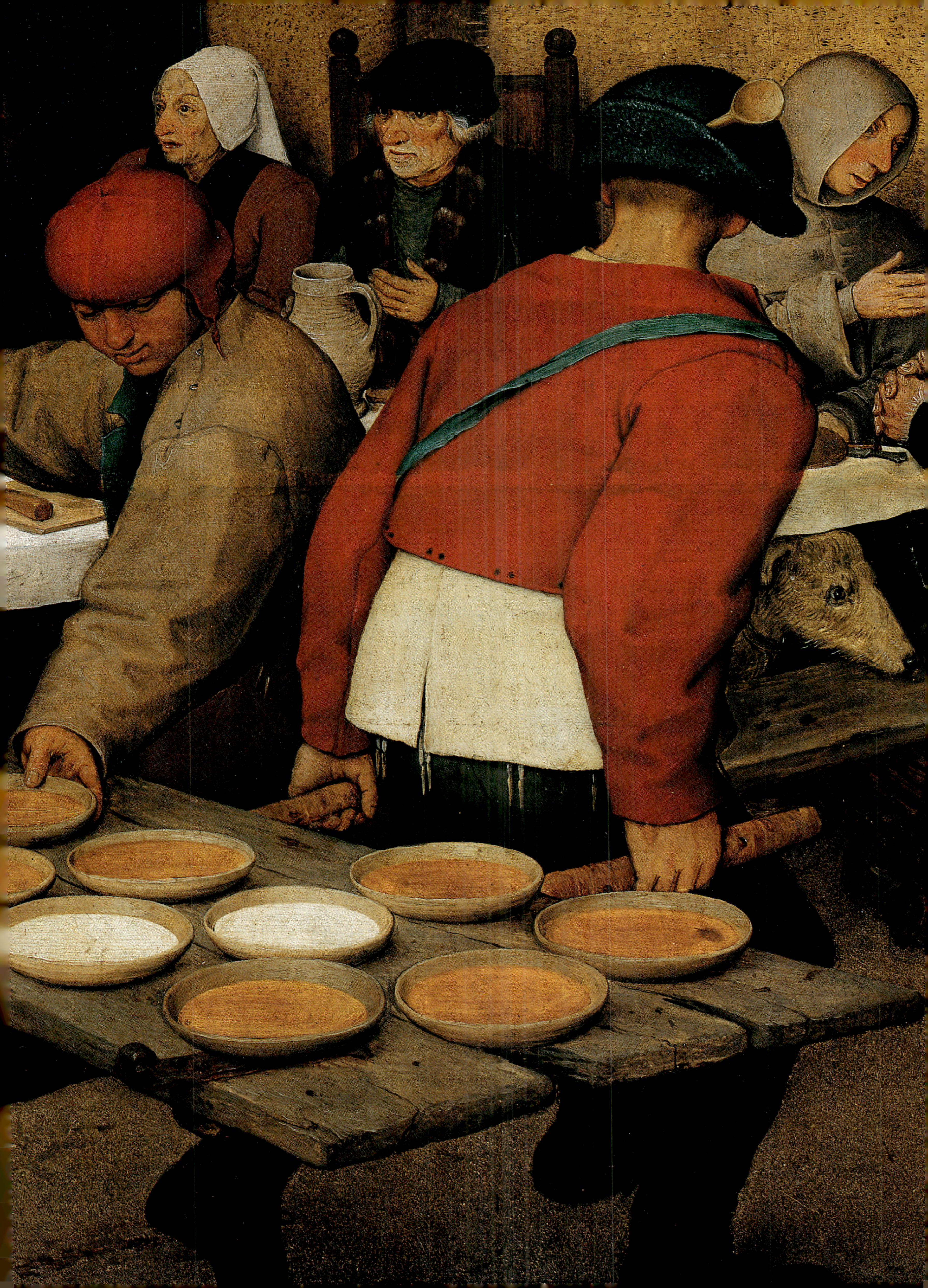

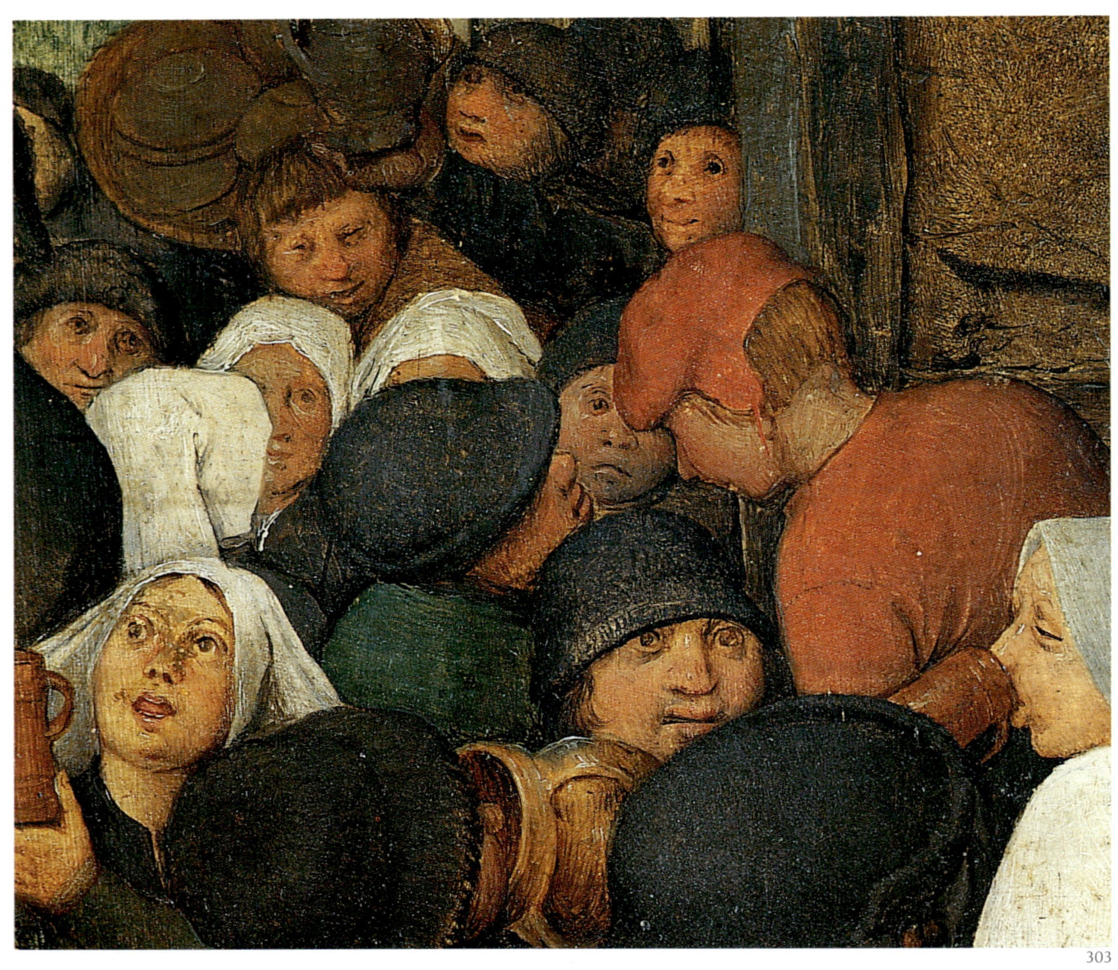

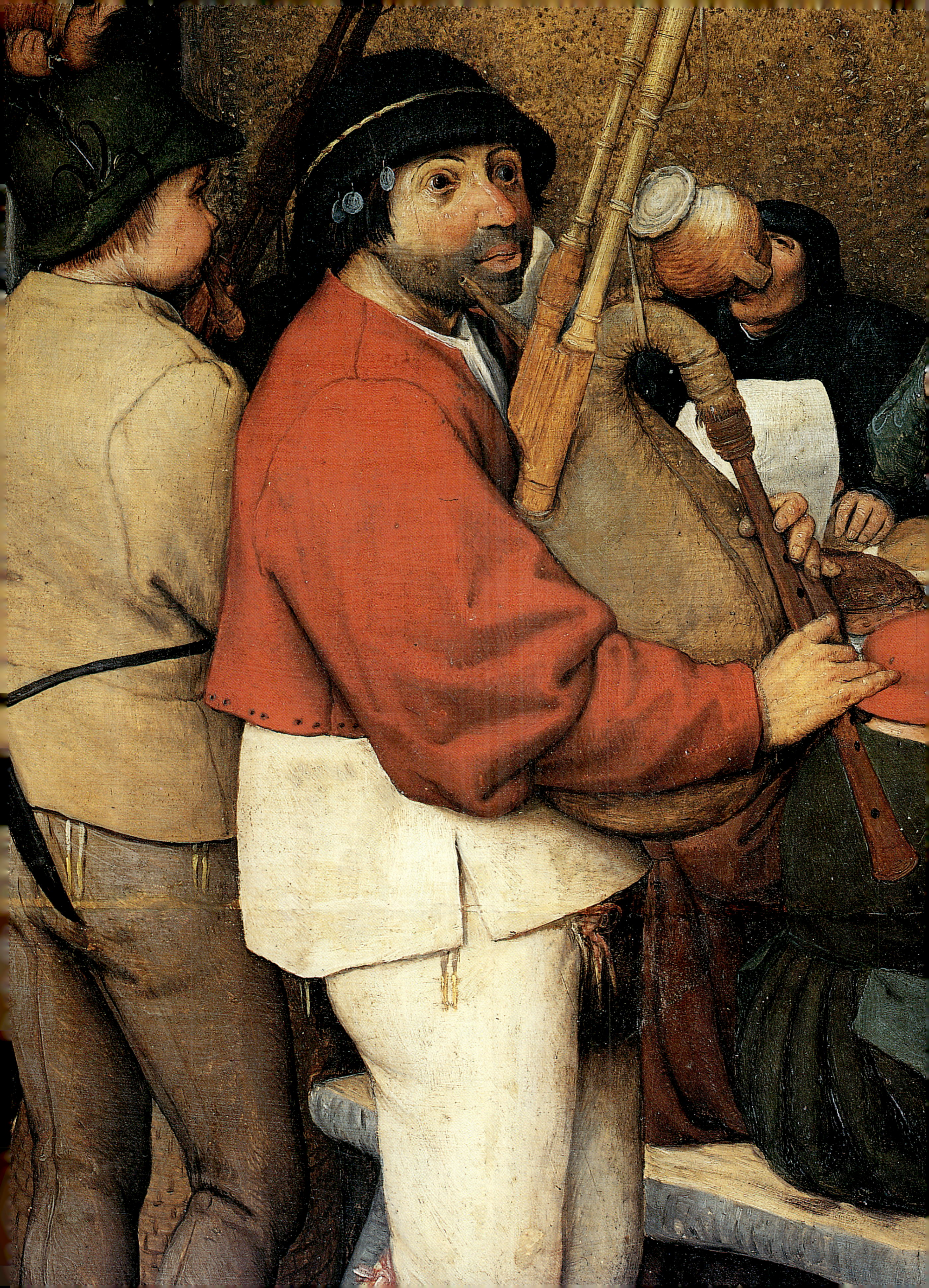

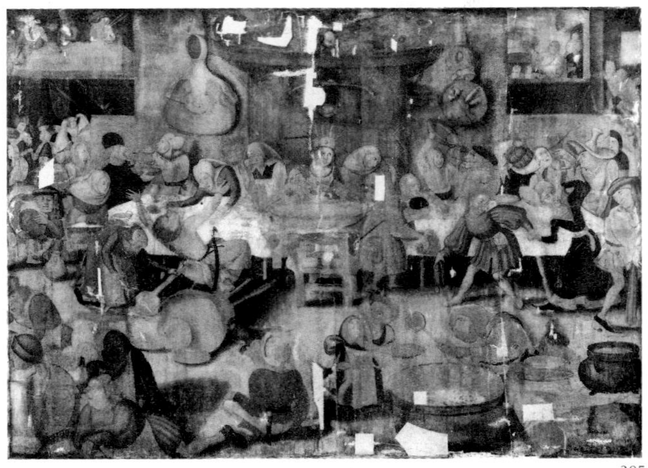

305

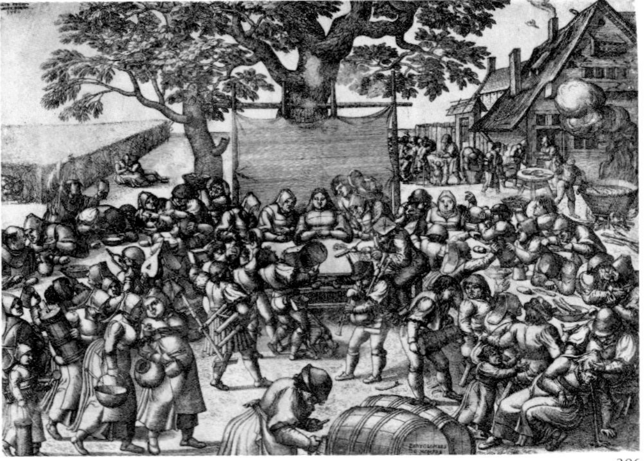

306

305. Frans or Jan Verbeeck, *Peasant Wedding*, ca. 1560 (?).
Distemper on linen, 42½ x 59⅞ in. (108 x 152 cm).
Nuremberg, Germanisches Museum

306. Pieter van der Borcht IV, *Peasant Wedding*, 1560.
Etching, 14¼ x 19¾ in. (36.2 x 50.2 cm). Brussels,
Bibliothèque royale Albert I, print room

removed from its hinges, plates of porridge. The second diagonal connects the
other servant, who is walking from left to right. These right-angled lines are
reinforced by the benches where the guests sit with their backs to the viewer, and
by the table itself. The identification of the characters, and their roles in the
wedding, raise questions. While the bride is clearly visible and framed by the
two figures in the foreground, where is her spouse? Is he the man on the first
diagonal who is handing out the dishes, or the other, on the left, who is pouring
the drink? Other suggestions have been made,[291] but do we need to find out
whether, as Klaus Demus states, "custom demands that the fiancé should not be
at the wedding festivities"?[292] The lower left corner, where the man is filling the
pitchers—with beer, no doubt—demands a look, for its fine still life of different-
sized stoneware pots and the charming figure of a little girl sitting on the floor,
wearing a bonnet that is too big for her and decorated with a peacock feather,
who is licking the finger she has used to wipe her plate. The warm ochers of the
jugs the cup-bearer is filling turn toward red as they near the child's bonnet—
red that punctuates or covers many items of clothing. Color, as always, fulfils its
function of giving rhythm to the picture, with many whites, grays, and blacks
conspicuous in the barn's monochrome tonality. Other figures also draw the eye,
such as the bagpiper in red and white, a stabilizing element in the composition
who corresponds to the bearer on the right. At the table, in front of the latter,
three characters are clearly important, because of their conspicuousness and
their clothing. The first, on the right, has a sword at his belt—does this make him
a soldier? His fine clothes may mean he is a local lord, his dog at his side. He is
talking to a Franciscan friar, which reinforces the impression that he is an
important person—perhaps a judge, like the one who had title to the painting
in a seventeenth-century inventory[293]—unless this is a self-portrait.[294] On the
other side of the friar a middle-aged man, with a fur collar, is the notary. There
are disagreements not only over these characters' identities, but also over the
meaning of the painting itself. For behind this wonderful composition some
writers have sought a desire to condemn man's baser instincts. According to
Tolnay, the wedding is no more "than an excuse to satisfy primitive urges" and—
another theory—a satirical vision of peasant life.[295] To be sure, there is good
humor, because the subject demands it. And although the painter does not hide a
certain smile, there is no intention to caricature, and a powerful naturalness asserts
itself. This last point defines the work's meaning more accurately, and perhaps
more fairly.

Weddings, be they at Cana, in more familiar settings as depicted by Pieter
Aertsen or Joachim Beuckelaer,[296] or caricatured by Frans or Jan Verbeeck
(fig. 305)[297] and Pieter van der Borcht in his engraving of 1560 (fig. 306),[298] can be
cited as immediate sources, but *The Wedding Feast* is striking above all because of
its authenticity and its form, whose "classicism" Klaus Demus rightly emphasizes.[299]
This is not an acquired classicism or one imported from Italy, but a rigor and
expressive strength that only direct experience, development, and a personal
maturing process can achieve. It is a classicism furthermore that is in no way
fixed but on the contrary rich in nuances, movement, colors, and gestures. It is
important to note that the painter no longer places himself in an elevated position

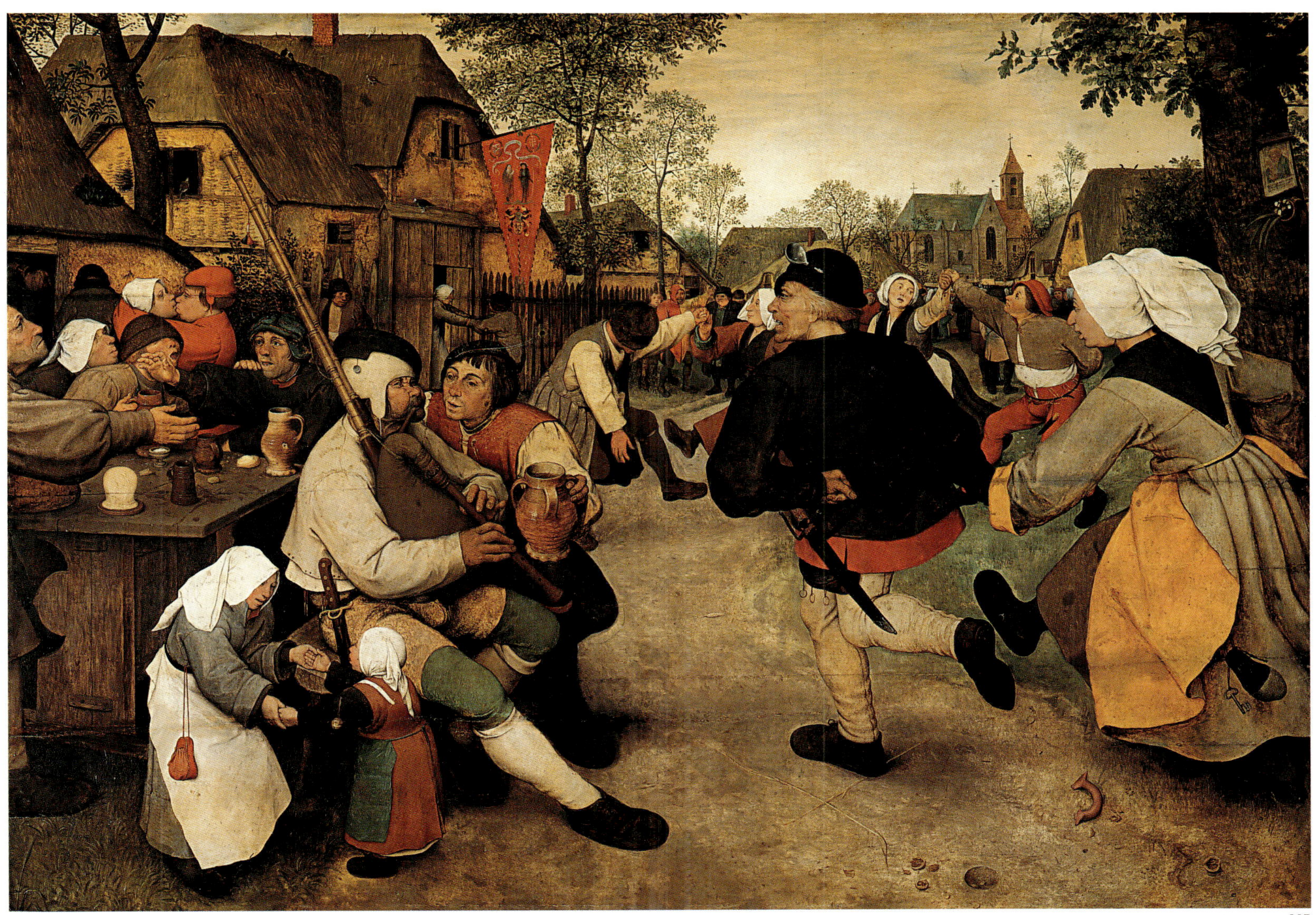

307

to capture his subject; he places himself at the same level as the scene, and the viewer thus takes part on an equal footing.

Is this a genre scene? It differs from such scenes in its monumental scale, and historically, as we know, is earlier than genre painting as such. In its originality and trueness to life, Bruegel's presence in the peasant world of the sixteenth-century southern Netherlands is comparable with that of Louis Le Nain in the context of French art in the following century. The keen vision and humanity of both cross the screen of the subject or of social customs to capture them alive. The same feeling drives *The Peasants' Dance* (figs. 307–12), where the viewer is once again on the same level as the couple who burst into the painting from the right. Here the man is dashing forward, tugging his wife along by the hand, to join those in the middle distance who are enjoying the dance. The festival has started but is not yet in full swing. The revelers are still arriving. The fool, in the middle, behind the dancers, is waiting to open the proceedings. The bagpiper on the left balances, by his size, the couple running on to the scene. Next to him is a man with a pitcher in

307–12. Pieter Bruegel, *The Peasants' Dance*, ca. 1568: whole work and details. Oil on panel, 44⅞ x 64⅝ in. (114 x 164 cm). Vienna, Kunsthistorisches Museum

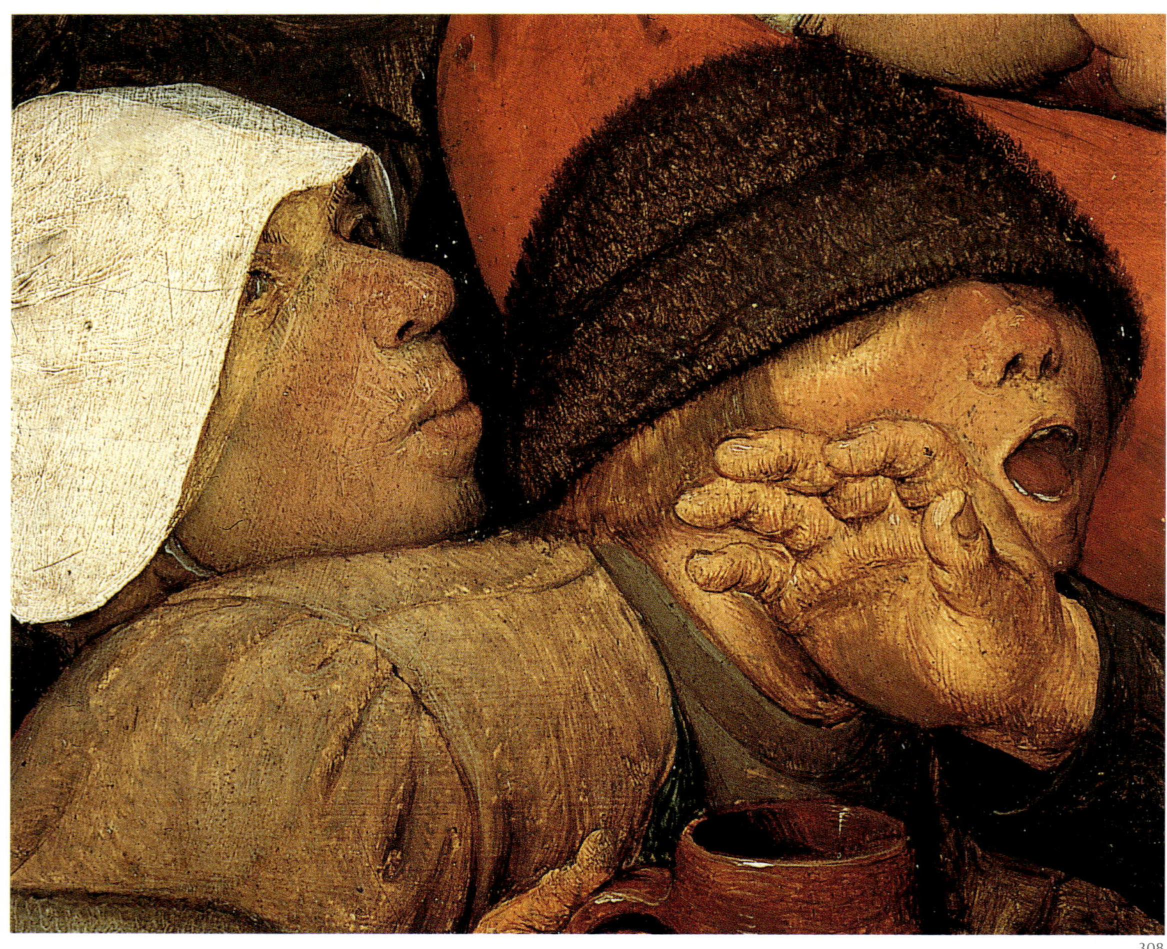

308

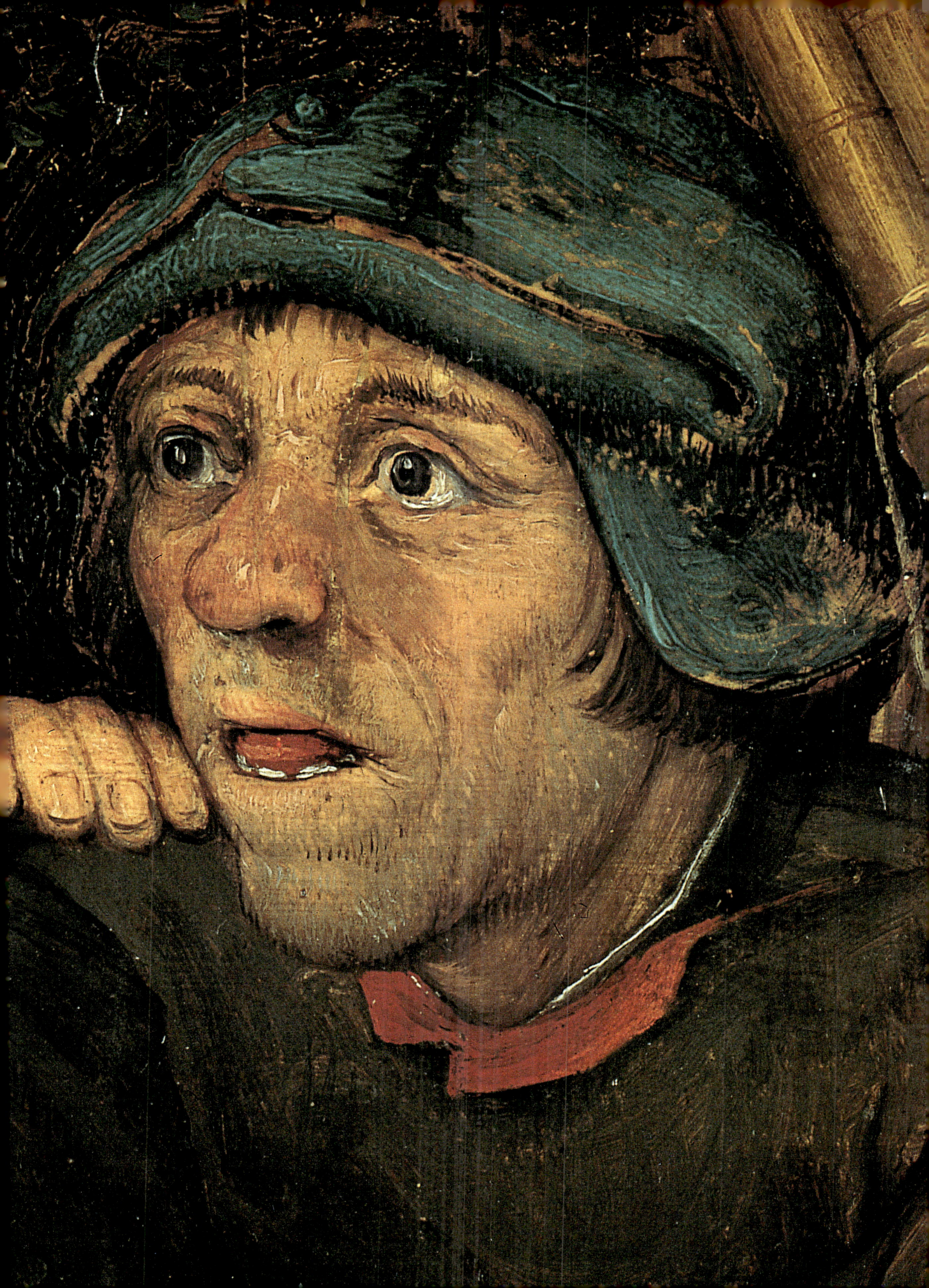

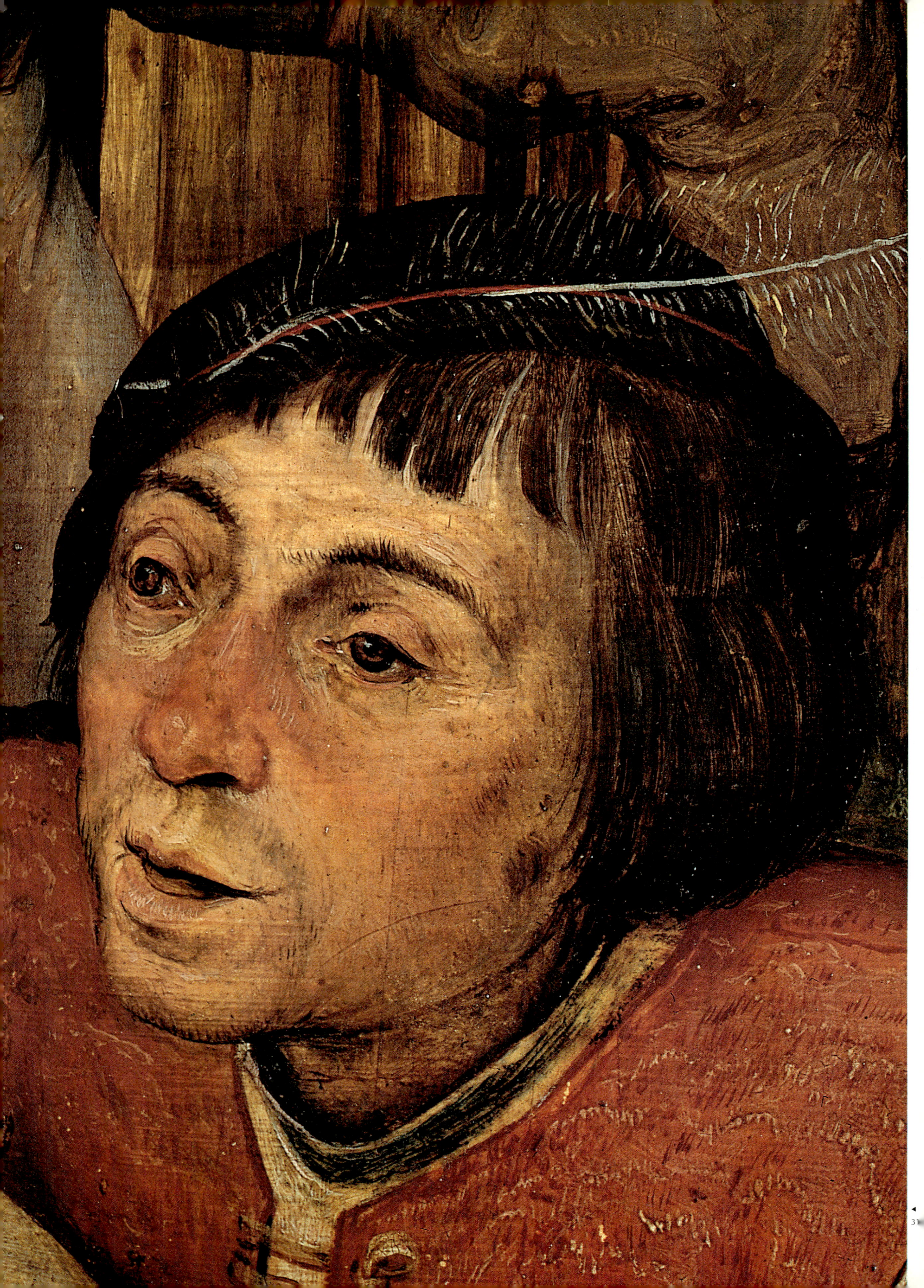

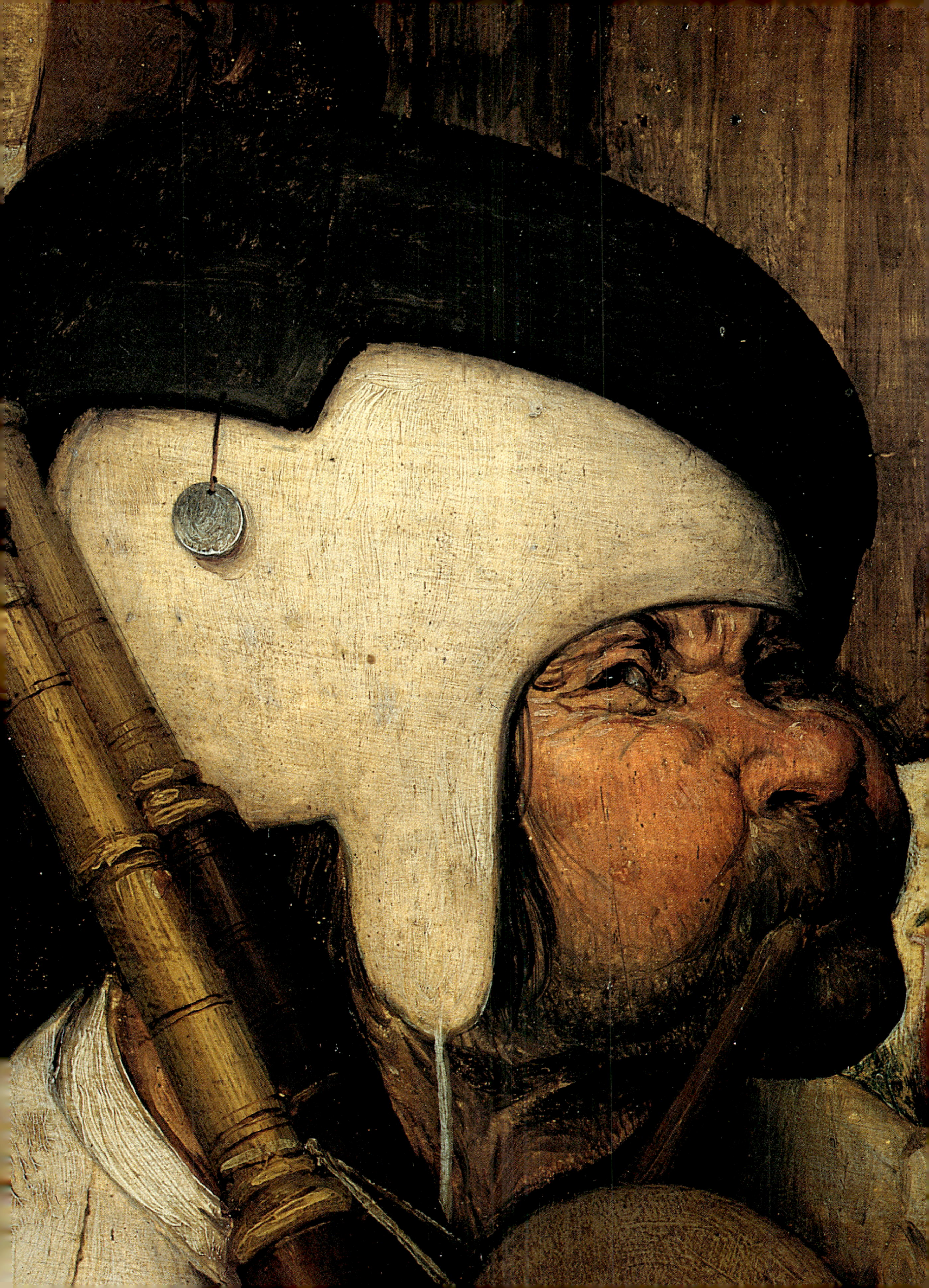

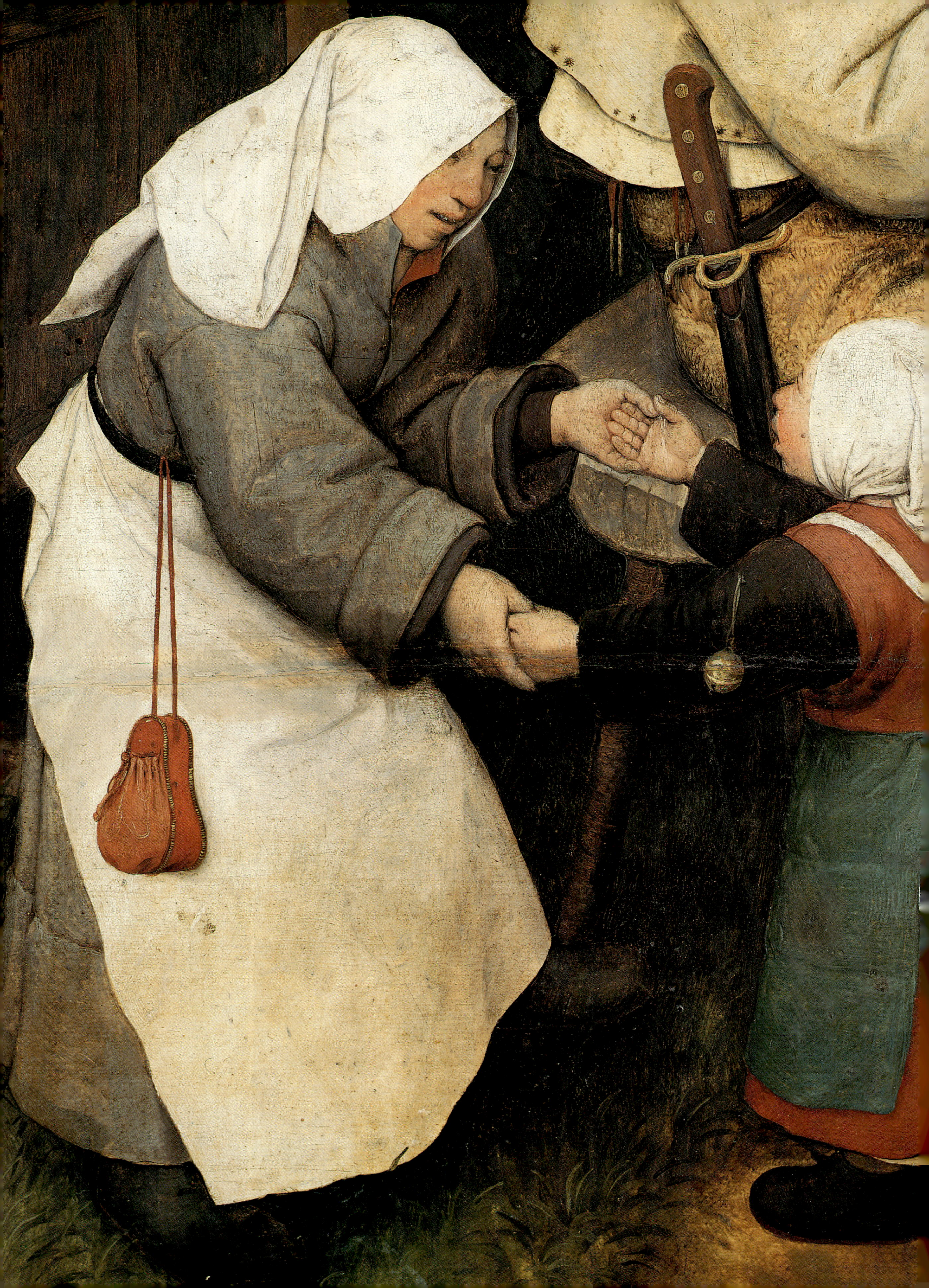

his hand who appears to have liberally quenched his own thirst, and two children who imitate the adults by miming a dance.

Behind the musician, around a table, is a lively scene—an altercation or misunderstanding—between a beggar, a woman, and two men, one of whom may be blind. There is nothing to justify a symbolic interpretation of anger here, nor anything to suggest that the couple's kiss is one of lust. Eating, drinking, and having fun in no way imply gluttony or intemperance. As for the peacock feather in the drinker's hat, it doesn't necessarily symbolize pride, as some may believe.[300]

The festivities begin and, aside from the small incidents that are part of all gatherings of people, nothing allows us to read a judgment into them. Everything begins at the door of a house that is flying a flag with crossed arrows (similar to those in the engravings *Kermis at Hoboken* and *The Kermis of St. George*) where a man is urging his companion to join the fun. The excitement is therefore just beginning, not yet unrestrained; the gestures of arms and legs create the rhythm and guide the eye, through a series of converging diagonals, from the foreground to the distance and to the church. The steeple, just like the image of the Virgin attached to the tree on the right, is in no way put into question by the excesses of the senses, or by the indulgence in vices. Spontaneity, good humor, and rejoicing are asserting their good health. The painting's movement conveys this. The impulsive entrance into the picture of the couple on the right seems to trigger the movement of the groups of people. The result is a living snapshot. This differs from other works where movement dominates: *The Wedding Dance* of 1566 is marked by a concatenation that produces a sense of duration, while *The Blind Leading the Blind* proceeds by hiccups and breaks which tumble into a fall.

Stridbeck links the painting to another engraving by Pieter van der Borcht, *The Great Flemish Kermis* of 1559, with its church in the distance (fig. 313).[301] But here the party is in full swing; the work is confused and mediocre. If comparisons must be made, we should rather think of Bruegel's own engravings. These are contemporary with Van der Borcht's, and more readable because they are better conceived. The *Peasants' Dance* in Vienna (fig. 307) is of an even higher quality, and by a long way. If we put the work in the context of the evolution of art we find, curiously, that while we seek sources that predate the work, the artist's creation always points us to later developments. Not only does its feeling of synthesis carry all before it, but its conception and inventiveness put it ahead of its time, and even out of time altogether.

The two paintings in Vienna are in the same vein, and the same format (*The Wedding Feast* has been restored along its bottom edge). For this reason some have seen them as companion works or even as parts of a series.[302] It matters little, since each is a complete work and a world in its own right artistically, formally, and in its feeling: "superb examples of painting with anthropomorphic qualities," as Aldous Huxley wrote.[303] The peasantry—this humble social class whose reactions and workings the painter knows through his love of observation—here takes on a different dimension, which retains its humor but discards superfluous detail to become a complex of themes that rivals the bacchanals of antiquity. Although they

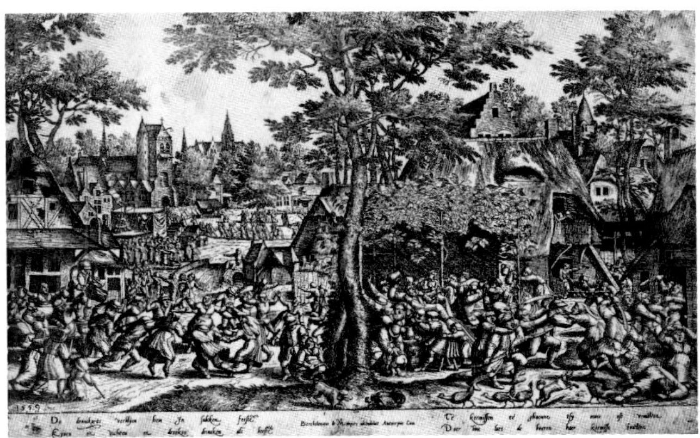

313. Pieter van der Borcht IV, *The Great Flemish Kermis*, 1559. Etching, 14¼ x 19¾ in. (36.2 x 50.2 cm). Brussels, Bibliothèque royale Albert I, print room

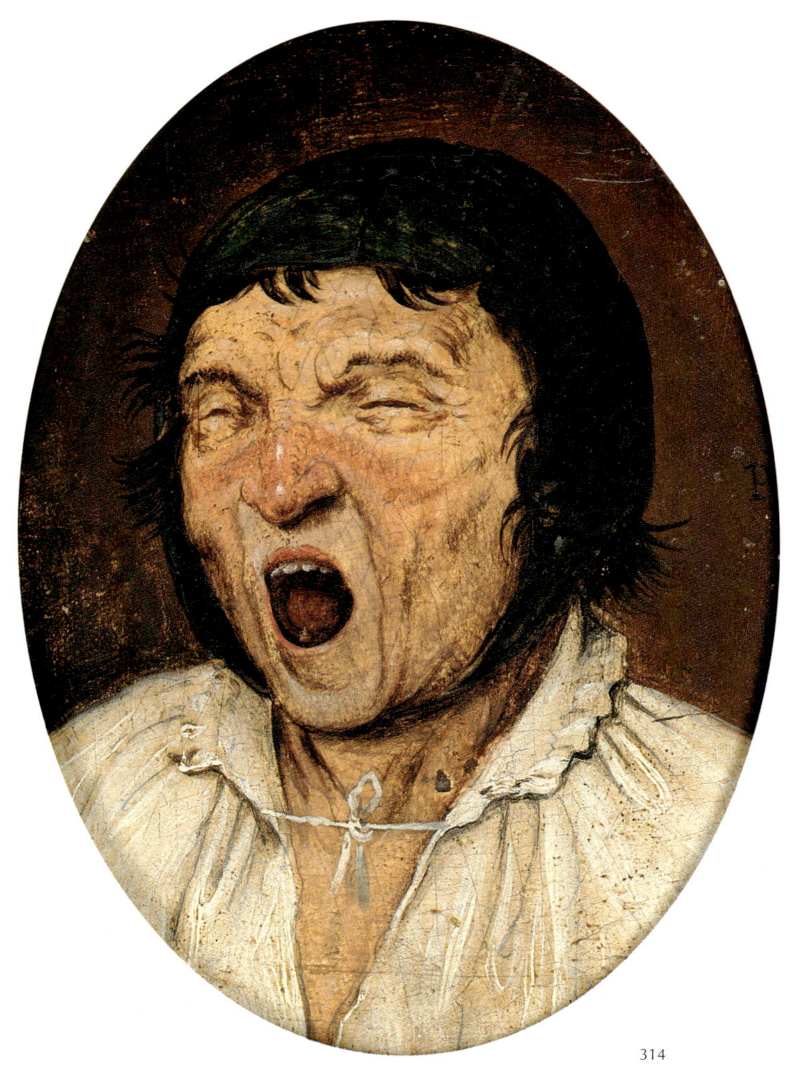

314

314. Anonymous, *The Yawner* (formerly attributed to
Pieter Bruegel). Oil on panel, 5 x 6⅝ in. (9.2 x 12.6 cm).
Brussels, Musées royaux des Beaux-Arts de Belgique

315. Attributed to Roelandt Savery, *Peasants at Table*,
1608 (?). Oil on canvas, 18⅛ x 19⅞ in. (46 x 50.5 cm).
Brussels, Musées royaux des Beaux-Arts de Belgique

316. Pieter Bruegel, *Head of an Old Peasant Woman*,
ca. 1568. Oil on panel, 8⅝ x 7 in. (22 x 18 cm).
Munich, Alte Pinakothek

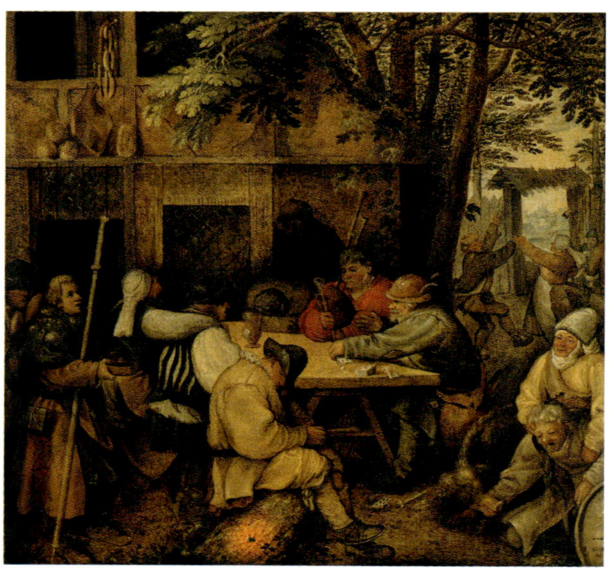

315

were later vulgarized by copies in which superficiality replaced power, during the
artist's lifetime they were extremely popular. A public sale at the mint in Antwerp
on 15 September 1572 saw the breakup of a series of paintings belonging to Jean
Noirot, master of the institution but, in the language of the day "bankrupt, a
fugitive, and at large." As well as works by Hieronymus Bosch and Frans Floris,
the collection included five by Pieter Bruegel the Elder—four of these on canvas—
probably bought during the artist's lifetime:[304] a winter landscape, two kermises, a
wedding, and "a large peasant wedding scene" probably painted on wood, which,
as the author of this recent discovery points out, was apparently the very same that
was bought "in July 1594 in Brussels by Archduke Ernest" and is now in Vienna.
In the same collection, according to the sale inventory, was a peasant wedding by
Bosch painted on canvas.

The Wedding Feast was copied, probably from the original,[305] by Pieter
Bruegel the Younger, who set the scene in the open air. The copies in this case
are few, and the subject deprived of its expressive intensity: the characters have
become puppets. As for *The Peasants' Dance*, which appears in the inventory of
Rudolf II's collection about 1612, no copy by Bruegel's son is known. However,
the work did inspire a painting by Roelandt Savery, who worked at the emperor's
court in Prague from 1603 to 1612 (fig. 315).[306]

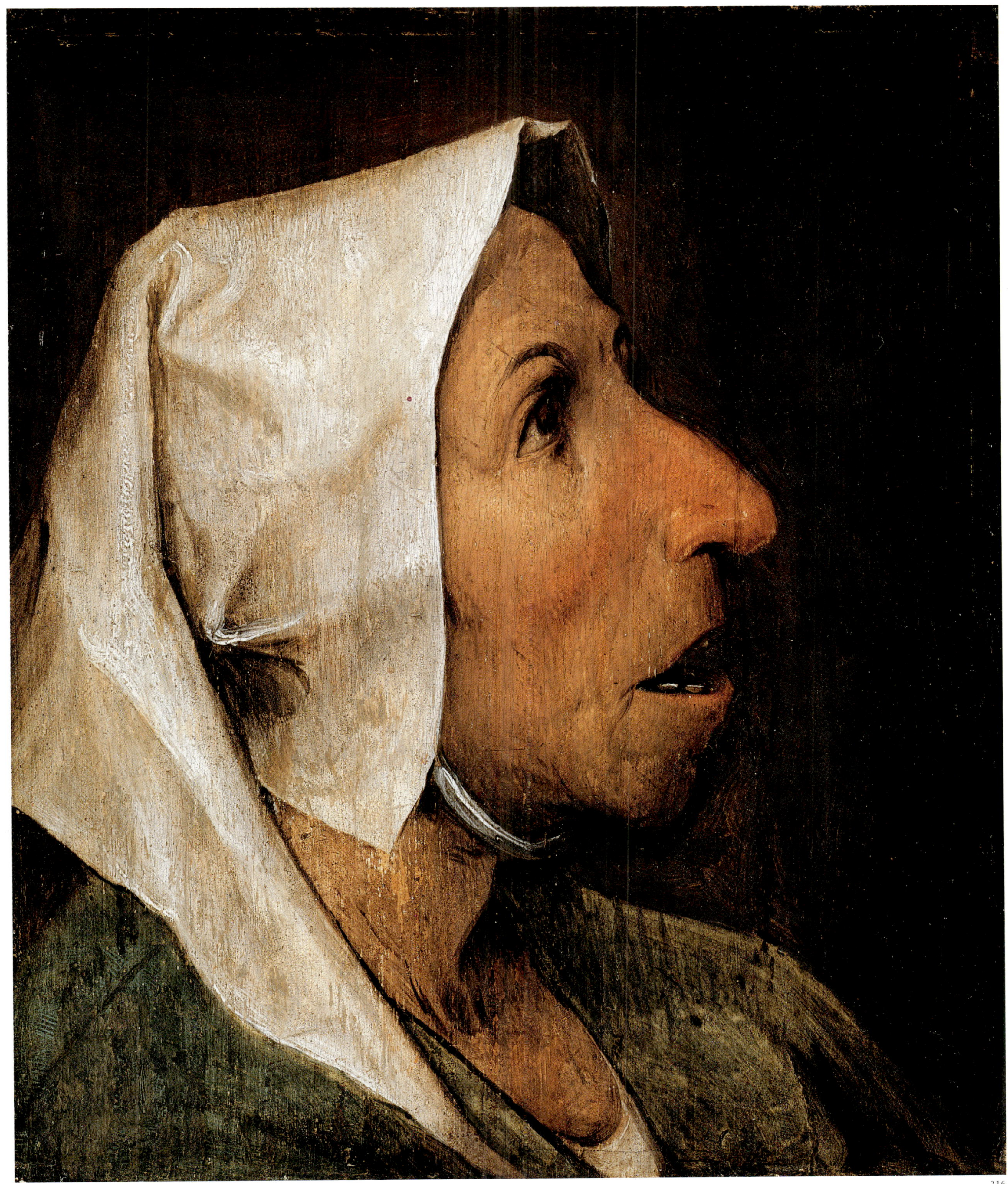

Bruegel's reputation for evoking rural life, and especially its characters, was made. In that milieu he was able to satisfy his need to observe the human face. A further demonstration of this is his *Head of an Old Peasant Woman* (fig. 316). A small panel, 8⅝ x 7 inches (22 x 18 centimeters), it demonstrates the painter's interest in individuals' facial expressions. In Bruegel's work, in fact, faces are never stereotyped if they play a role, even a secondary one, in the composition. There are no portraits as such among his surviving works. Whether Bruegel painted portraits remains an open question,[307] which makes *Head of an Old Peasant Woman* all the more interesting. Accepted as an original work by most writers, with the exception of Tolnay,[308] it belongs to the last phase of the painter's work. Probably painted from life, and depicting an expression of surprise, it reveals the painter's interest in a type more than in an individual, in synthesis more than in caricature. In this sense the image of the old woman is close, in its own context, to the image of the art lover made by Bruegel in 1565, in another context. In another connection, an image of a "yawner," by the hand of the "Old Bruegel"[309] figured in the inventory of the collection of Rubens made in 1640 after his death. Could this be the *Yawner* that is in the Musées royaux des Beaux-Arts in Brussels (fig. 314), a work whose authorship is questioned and which has a counterpart in an engraving by Lucas Vorsterman (fig. 317), who made a number of engravings for Rubens? The subject can be compared to two other medallions: *Head of a Mercenary* in the musée Fabre in Montpellier and *Study of a Head* in the musée Beaux-Arts in Bordeaux. These works, which convey idleness, anger, and envy, may have been part of a series illustrating the seven deadly sins.[310] Although the attributions are very doubtful, the Bruegelesque spirit which pervades these medallions indicates the popularity of these facial expressions such as we can observe, lifelike and vigorous, throughout the master's works, which nature and mankind alike share fully and in equilibrium, in suffering and in joy, in sunshine and in rain, in the everyday and in grisaille.

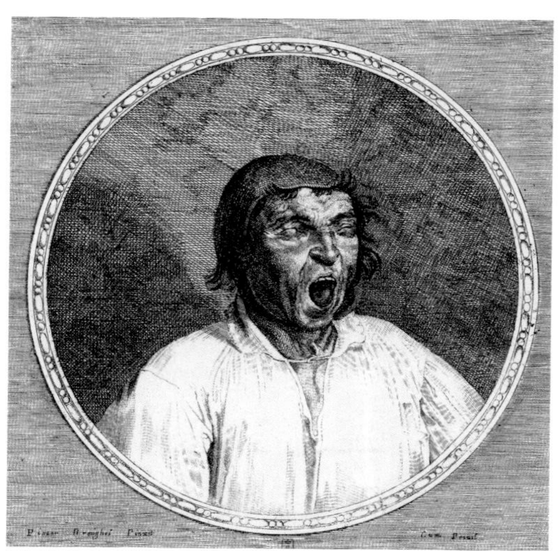

317

317. Lucas Vorsterman, *The Yawner,* after Pieter Bruegel (?), ca. 1621. Etching and Engraving, 8¼ x 8⅛ in. (20.9 x 20.7 cm). Brussels, Bibliothèque royale Albert I, print room

THE SEA

Not only did Bruegel's gaze scan the city and sweep the countryside—the sea's wide horizons were familiar to him too. Already in the two versions of *The Tower of Babel* (figs. 273 and 274) there is a port where boats arrive and leave, load and unload, as at Antwerp, where the painter's curiosity had already led him to observe and portray these activities. Ships, their equipment, and the various operations to do with sailing were familiar to him. Perhaps Antwerp, in his eyes, could even be metamorphosed into Babel. Indeed, Guicciardini wrote that with

> one glance one can take in a great sweep of river with the perpetual ebb & flow of the sea: see coming & going at all hours around the boats all manner of men of all tongues, countries, & nations, & the variety of goods and produce in which they trade: & observe so many different kinds of ships, many instruments & devices to handle & control them, so that every hour there is always something new.[311]

Each time that a question presents itself or a link is formed in the viewer's mind, the work in question can provide elements of an answer. At the time there were many foreigners in the city, where as a result many languages must have been spoken. Its ambition, and those of its merchants, was great; but while wealth may be accumulated, it can also be depleted or sometimes collapse into ruin, as shown in *The Fall of the Tower of Babel*, an engraving by Cornelis Antonisz. made in 1547.[312]

The presence of a busy port at the base of Bruegel's tower is in itself noticeable, in contrast to other artists' depictions of this theme, and betrays a particular interest in this area. The number of vessels lined up at the quayside maneuvering to dock or set sail demonstrates the artist's taste for shipping and his knowledge of the subject. Even though the painter altered the composition of the Rotterdam version of the painting (fig. 274) to give it a more dramatic, less diversified resonance than in the Vienna version (fig. 273), the port remains just as conspicuous and probably even more mysterious under the dramatic shadow. The insects appear more enslaved to their termite's nest. However, the ships remain clearly defined elements, and are part of the painting's vocabulary.

From Bruegel's earliest works, he drew and painted ships. They can be seen in estuaries, from *Landscape with the Parable of the Sower* (1557; fig. 139) to *The Return of the Herd* (1565; fig. 174); they embody moments of freedom behind the captive *Two Monkeys* (1562; fig. 213), or punctuate the distant flow of a river in *The Magpie on the Gallows* (1568; fig. 360). Although they can denote movement, travel, and exchanges between people, they also speak of discoveries and conquests at a time when the known world was expanding through exploration and cartography. Rowboats and sailing ships have a place, and play their part, in drawings and engravings too. They appear in *Flemish Proverbs* (fig. 223) to illustrate the admonition to "keep the sail in the eye of the wind"[313]; they are in *The Temptation of St. Anthony* (1556; fig. 89) and, in various strange transformations, in the portrayal of the *Vices*, in *Patience* (1557; fig. 92), and in the *Virtues* such as *Hope* (1559; fig. 214), where shipwreck and a fair wind conflict.

Ships also exist in their own right, for the beauty of their construction and the elegant movements of their sails. *Sea-Going Ships*, a series of ten engravings

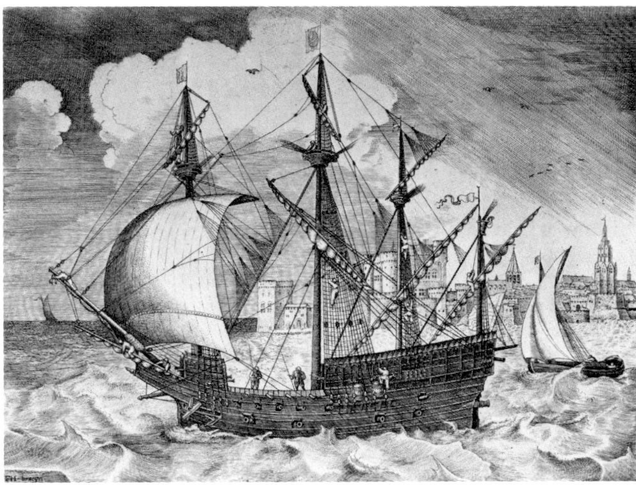

318. Frans Huys, *Four-Masted Ship*, from the series *Sea-Going Ships*, after Pieter Bruegel, 1561–62. Engraving, 8¾ x 11¼ in. (22.2 x 28.5 cm). Brussels, Bibliothèque royale Albert I, print room

319. Frans Huys, *Naval Battle in the Strait of Messina*, after Pieter Bruegel, 1561. Engraving, 16¾ x 28⅛ in. (42.5 x 71.5 cm). Brussels, Bibliothèque royale Albert I, print room

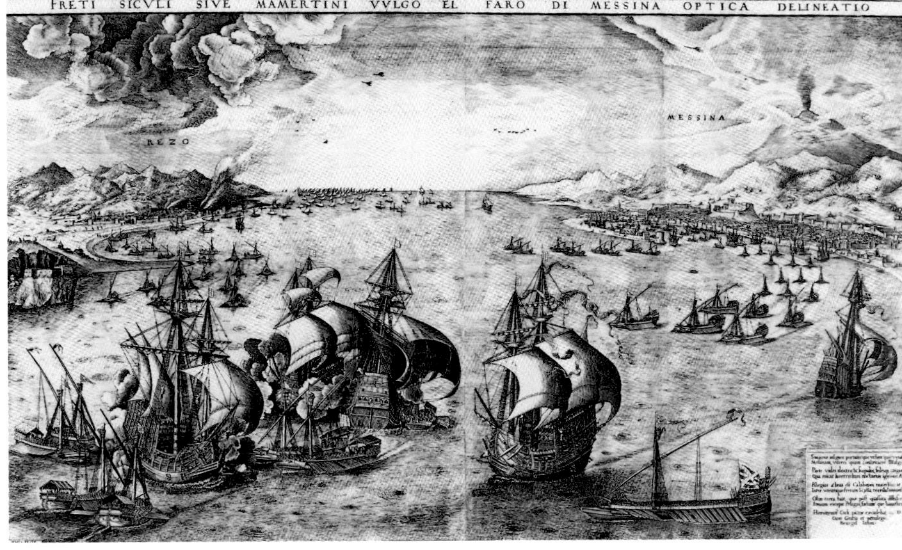

made by Frans Huys between 1561 and 1562, according to Louis Lebeer's dating, and were probably commissioned from Bruegel by Hieronymus Cock. The engravings are portraits of ships, which can be identified by their construction, equipment, and sails (fig. 318). These are also superb seascapes, combining not only ships, but light, waves, and sky, where "everything becomes complete, coalesces, and fuses into a common tension of *life.*"[314] While the series is remarkable for its quality, it also belongs to an engraving tradition that saw large numbers of works made of certain themes or ornamental subjects. The greatest artists produced such works: Lucas van Leyden made engravings of decorative subjects. Among depictions of ships, already in the fifteenth century the Master W. A., who worked at the court of Charles the Bold between 1465 and 1485, had made a series of sailing ships. Linked to Bruegel's *Sea-Going Ships* is *Naval Battle in the Strait of Messina*, a large engraving (16¾ x 28⅛ inches or 42.5 x 71.5 centimeters) made by Huys and published in 1561 by Cock, which became very popular and was printed several times. This is a "wide angle" view with a broad horizon, showing many ships orchestrated in a masterly manner (fig. 319). Apart from *View of Reggio di Calabria* (fig. 320), which might have served as a model for part of the work, no other drawing either of the place or of the ships survives. However, other comparisons can be made. Thus the *View of Naples*, or *Naval Battle in the Bay of Naples* (fig. 321), shows some similarities with the engraving of the Strait of Messina. This seascape, painted in oils on wood in a broad format that fits the subject, is embraced by the port of Naples, which is recognizable,

320. Pieter Bruegel, *View of Reggio di Calabria,* ca. 1552–60. Pen and brown ink with brown and gray wash, 6¹⁄₁₆ x 9¹⁄₂ in. (15.4 x 24.1 cm). Rotterdam, Museum Boijmans Van Beuningen

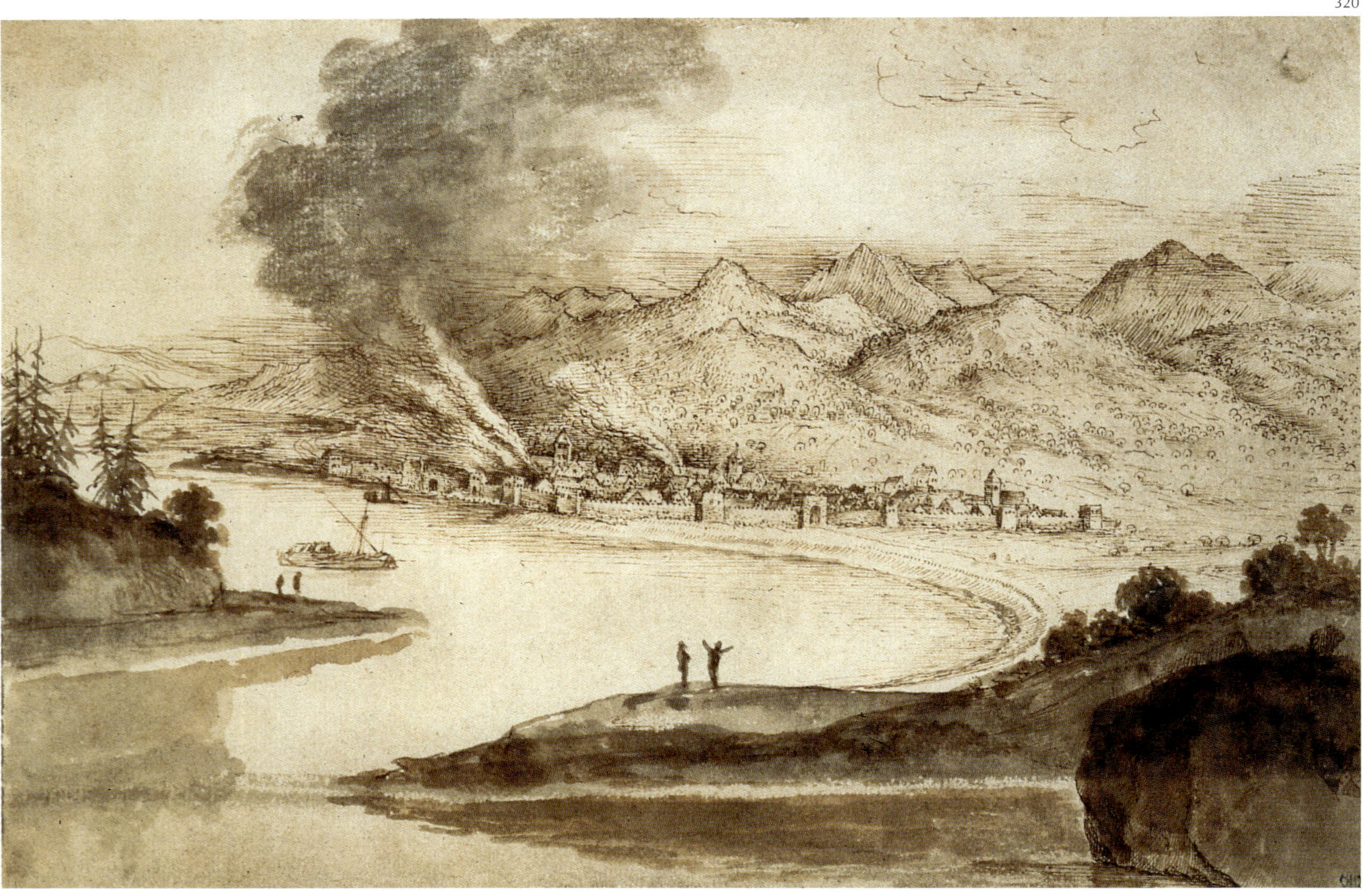

320

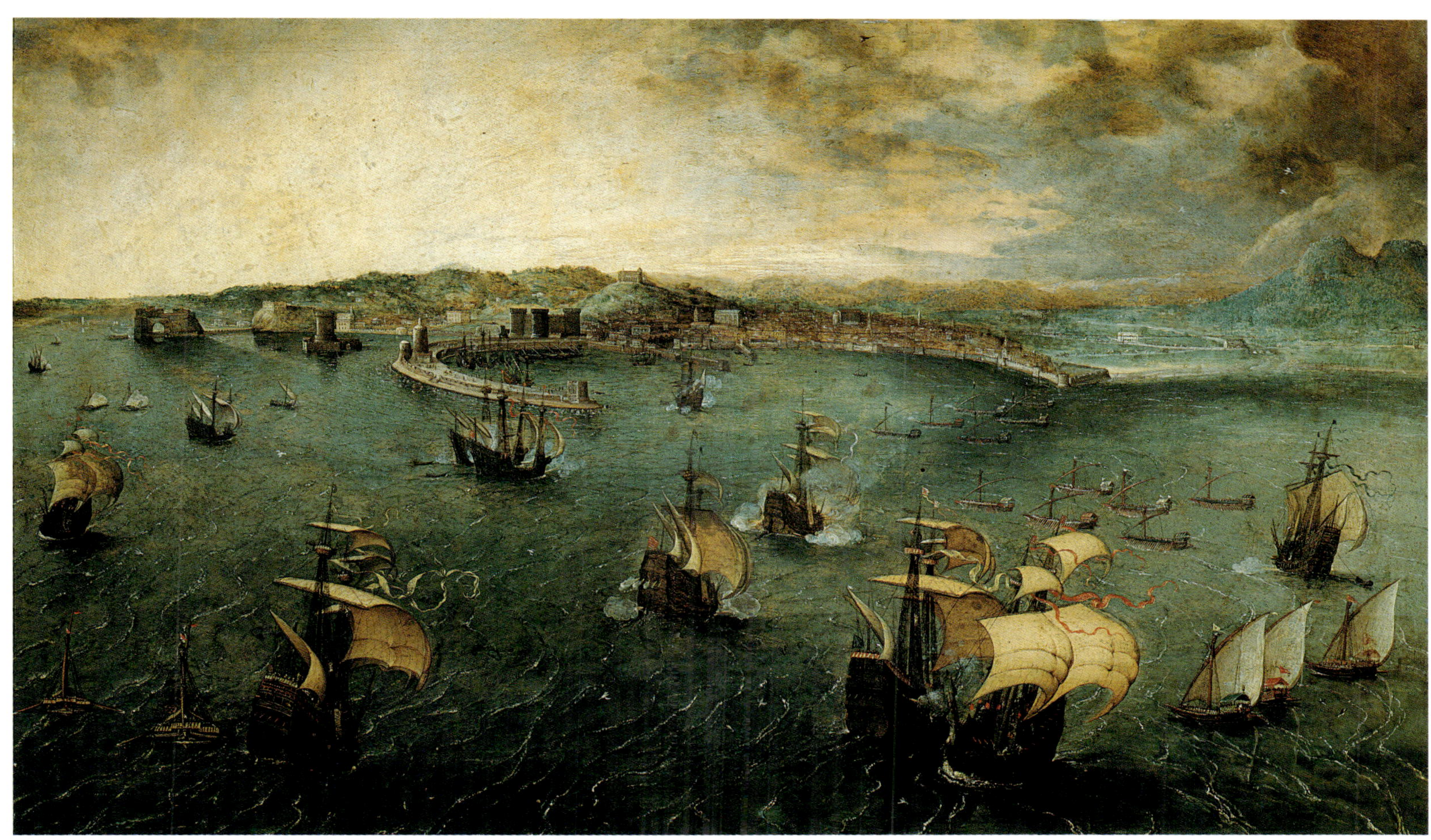

as are various monuments of the city. From left to right, we can distinguish the Castel dell'Ovo; the tower, now destroyed, of the island of San Vincenzo; the Castel Nuovo and, on the hill, the Castel Sant'Elmo. Without a date or a signature, the painting was attributed to Bruegel by Burchard in 1913[315] and has been accepted by most authorities on Bruegel's work from Tolnay to Grossmann, with the exception of Édouard Michel and Robert Genaille. The painting is either a youthful work or was made about 1562, the latter date being preferred by Marijnissen who, however, places the work among those whose authorship is questionable. The attribution is based on a comparison with the engraving of 1561 of the Strait of Messina and, from the work's subject, may be that mentioned in the inventory of the collection of Cardinal Granvelle made in 1607. Because of its medium, it cannot be the work referred to in Rubens's inventory of 1640, because that painting is described as being in distemper. Be that as it may, the painting may have been inspired by memories of Italy, transposed into a depiction where the painter has not hesitated to take liberties with the landscape by changing the pier into a curved shape. The composition, both rigorous and rhythmic, shows an undeniable sense of nature, as well as knowledge of ship construction. Only a complete scientific analysis of the painting will settle once and for all whether it is indeed by Bruegel.

In this respect a negative verdict was recently passed on another famous seascape, *The Tempest* (fig. 323), in the Kunsthistorisches Museum, Vienna, which

321. Attributed to Pieter Bruegel, *View of Naples*, or *Naval Battle in the Bay of Naples*, ca. 1562. Oil on panel, 16½ x 28 in. (42 x 71 cm). Rome, Galleria Doria Pamphilj

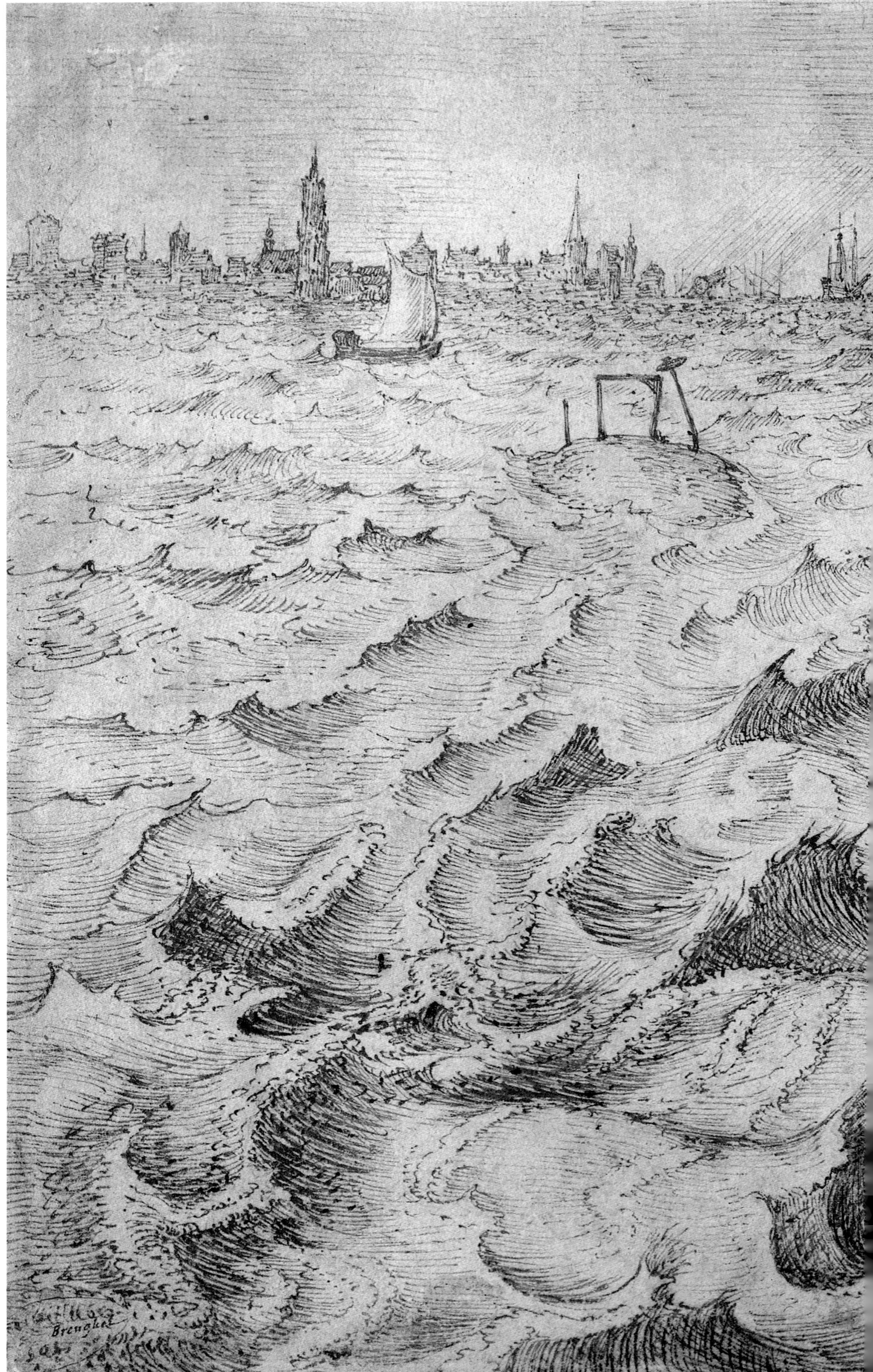

322. Pieter Bruegel, *View of Antwerp from the Scheldt*, ca. 1559. Pen and brown ink, 8 x 11¹³/₁₆ in. (20.3 x 30 cm). London, Courtauld Institute of Art, Count Antoine Seilern Collection

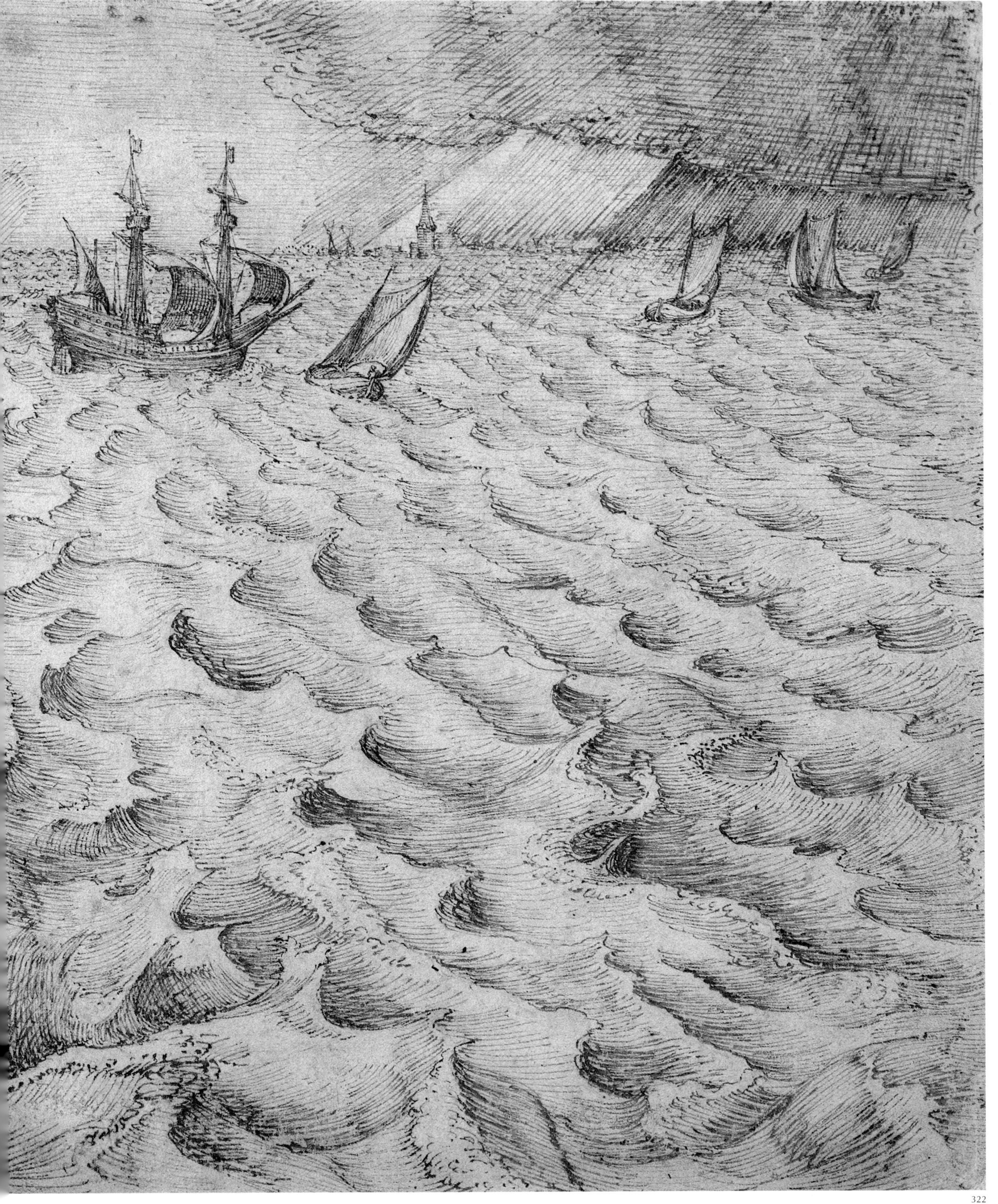

had been considered authentic since the beginning of the last century by both Alex Romdahl and Hulin de Loo, though not by Édouard Michel. Dendrochronological dating of the oak panel indicated that the tree was felled about 1580,[316] more than a decade after Bruegel's death. The tumult and tension of this work had already attracted some skepticism, as had its sketch-like paint-handling, and the fact that the outline of the ships and their sails lacks both the precision and the authority that Bruegel's careful work always shows. However, the bold manner in which the storm is portrayed could justify its attribution to a great artist. The contrast of shadows and brightness conveys a sort of climactic convulsion that causes the intrusion of a shaft of light that bounces from sail to sail and from bird to bird, as far as the horizon where, in another patch of light, rises the clearly visible spire of a church. Aside from its painterly qualities, art historians have seen a symbolic or proverbial allusion in the work, such as the whale that releases the ship in favor of the barrel, a variation on "letting go of a greater reward to keep a smaller one." The work's attribution to Joos de Momper[317] in no way reduces its quality but, strangely, has diminished its reputation. The change of attribution has caused the painting to lose some of its glamour, although, in its expressive power, it remains as worthy of admiration now as under its previous label. Certainly its style is less startling, coming after Bruegel, than it would have been during his lifetime, although it clearly follows in his footsteps—if we think, for example, of *The Gloomy Day* (fig. 187). As for the way the subject is captured and the originality of its composition, the parallel with Bruegel is equally strong—if we compare *The Tempest* with the drawing *View of Antwerp from the Scheldt* (about 1559; fig. 322).[318] The crests of waves are closer together, which is logical as this is a river and not the open sea. Nevertheless, the climactic restlessness is just as intense, and the sea monster is replaced by a reef, surmounted by a gallows, that the ship has managed to avoid in order to sail toward a church that is also, it seems, lit by a band of light. Every way is strewn with traps, like the nails on the path in *The Misanthrope*. Here, the ship has passed beyond, perhaps through will power or confidence.

The Tempest therefore belongs after Bruegel's time. Should the same be said of another ship, the one behind whose stern Icarus has fallen? The image is an exceptional and fascinating one. It refers to mythology, to Ovid's *Metamorphoses*, to the myth of Icarus who, with his father, Daedalus, took to the air with wings held together with wax. Now, disobeying the advice he was given—*Inter utrumque vola* (Fly between the sea and the sky)—the young man went too close to the sun, the fragile wax melted, and he fell. Not only was the end of this extraordinary exploit mortal, but Bruegel, in his landscape *The Fall of Icarus* (figs. 324–25),[319] emphasizes its absurdity by barely showing it at all—merely depicting two legs and a hand disappearing into the waves, and a few feathers fluttering down. The fall and its elements are reduced to a small event in comparison to the majestic sweep of the sea, bathed in light by the sun setting on the horizon. The emphasis is on the foreground: on a ploughman, a shepherd, a fisherman, and a ship returning to port, none of which pay any attention to what is happening.

Perhaps this is an expression of the world's indifference to the fate of the individual, however exceptional. This is one clear conclusion among other resonances—for this painting, like all Bruegel's creations, is pregnant with questions and possible comments. The shepherd in the composition's exact center, the

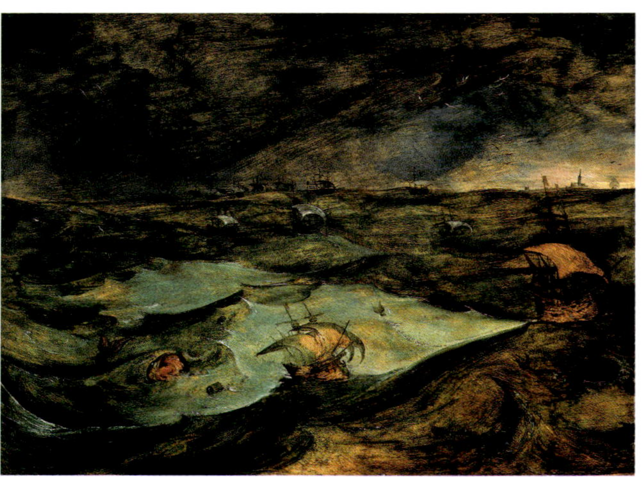

323

323. Joos de Momper the Younger, *The Tempest*, ca. 1595. Oil on panel, 28 x 38³⁄₁₆ in. (71 x 97 cm). Vienna, Kunsthistorisches Museum

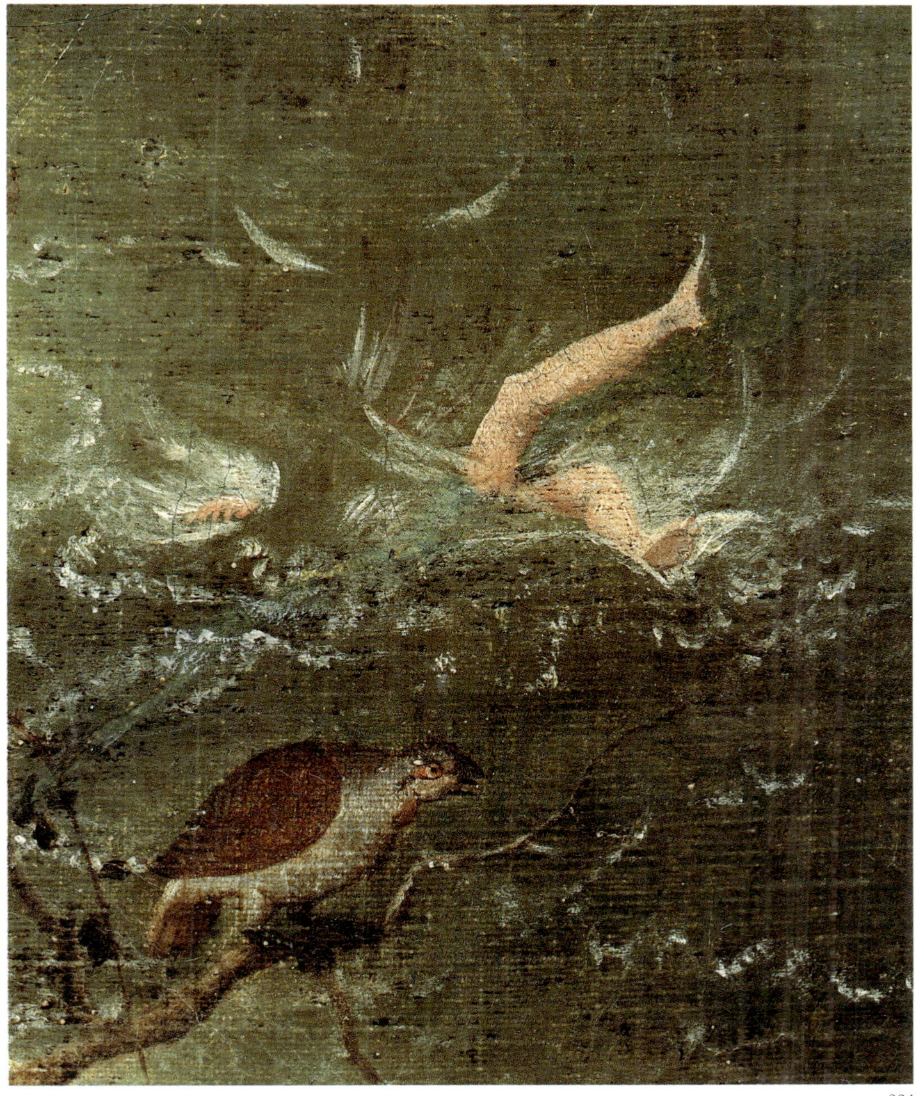

324

absence of Daedalus, the preeminence of the ploughman, are as many subjects among others, and as many questions to answer. That is not the problem, however. The work, which was unknown before 1912, when it was bought by the Musées royaux des Beaux-Arts in Brussels, has visibly suffered from the passage of time and from previous restorations. This has raised doubts in some quarters as to whether it is the work of Bruegel's brush alone. However, by its conception, vision, composition, graphic and chromatic elements, idea, and sensitivity, *The Fall of Icarus* remains no less an image of universal relevance and perfect skill such as only Bruegel could have invented.

The subject, already a common one in Roman art,[320] was in no way surprising in the sixteenth century. Indeed, humanism had made Ovid's *Metamorphoses* once again an issue of the day, not without ascribing a moralizing intent to the work. In literature as in art it became a fertile source of inspiration. In Italy, Sebastiano del Piombo used it as a source in 1511 at the Palazzo Farnesina in Rome, and from 1497, a Venetian edition of Ovid was illustrated by woodcuts, one of which showed the fall of Icarus. In Mainz, Georg Wickram illustrated the same theme

324–25. Pieter Bruegel, *The Fall of Icarus*, ca. 1555–60: detail and whole work. Oil on canvas, 28⅞ x 44 in. (73.5 x 112 cm). Brussels, Musées royaux des Beaux-Arts de Belgique

287

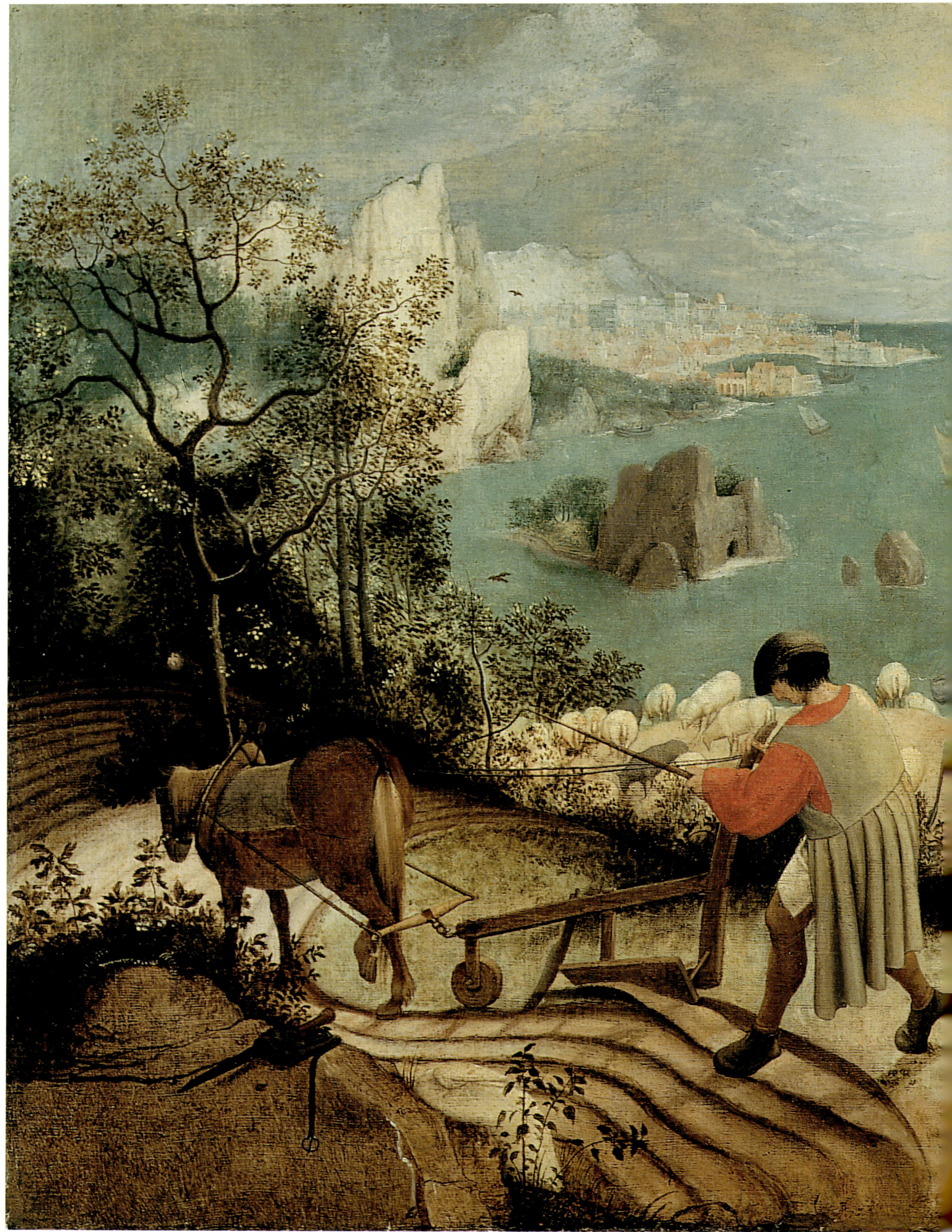

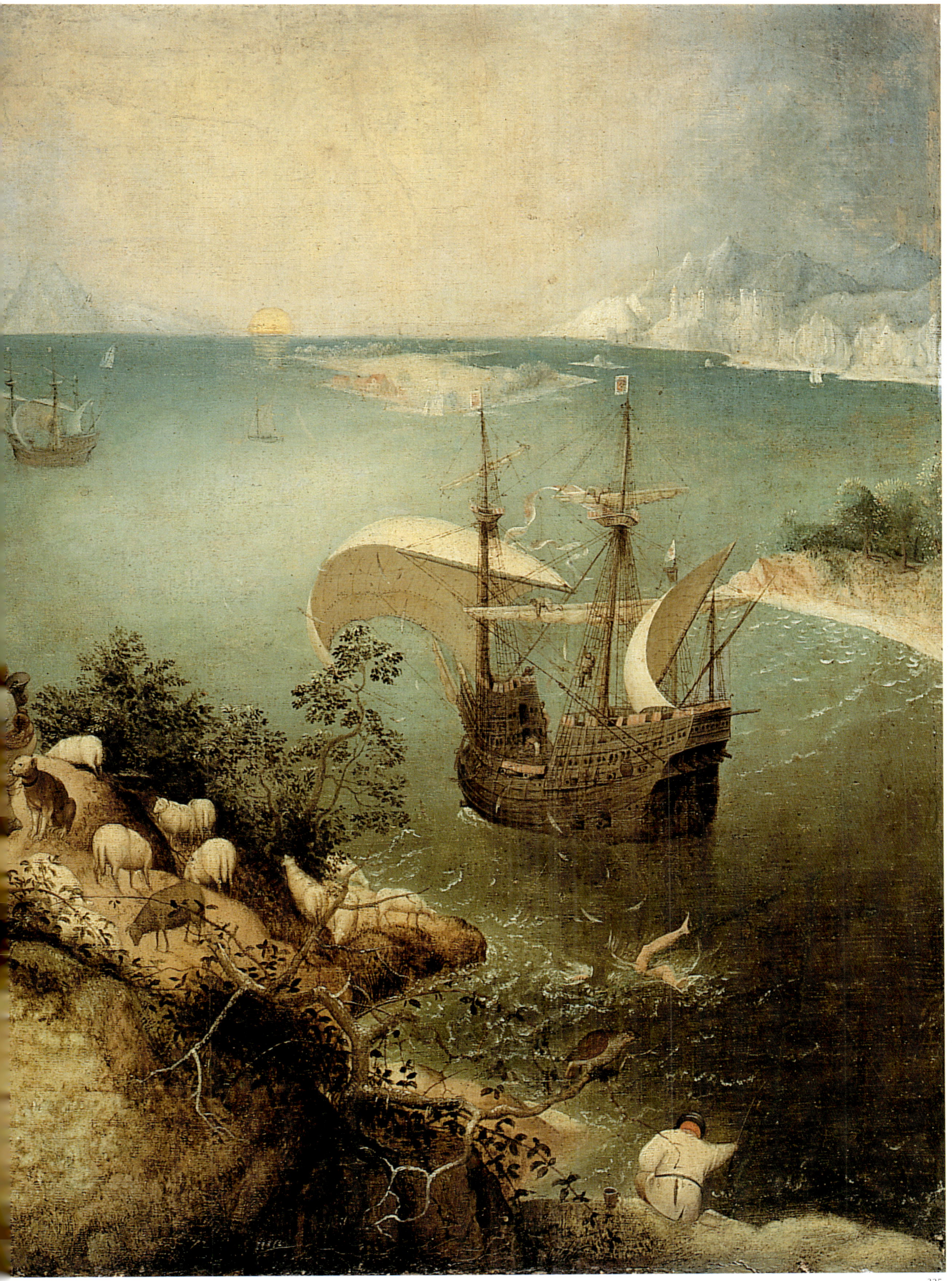

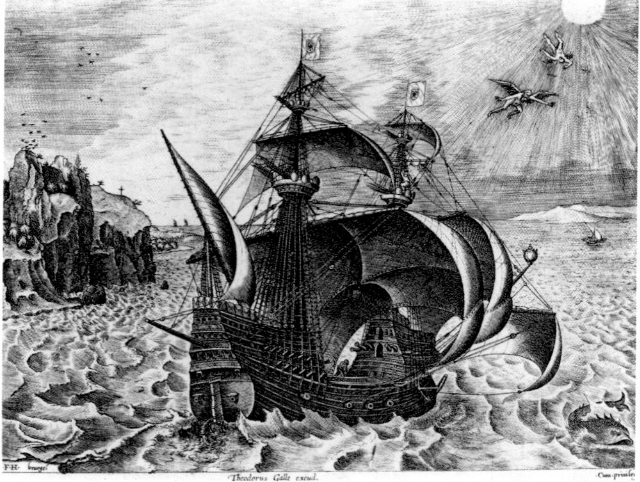

326. Attributed to Georg Hoefnagel, *Landscape Crossed by a River, with the Fall of Icarus*, after Pieter Bruegel, ca. 1595. Etching, 10⁷/₈ x 13¹/₄ in. (27.5 x 33.7 cm). Brussels, Bibliothèque royale Albert I, print room

327. Frans Huys, *Three-Masted Ship Armed with Four Crow's Nests and Two Top-Gallant Sails, with the Fall of Icarus*, from the series *Sea-Going Ships*, after Pieter Bruegel, 1561–62. Engraving, 8³/₄ x 11¹/₄ in. (22.2 x 28.7 cm). Brussels, Bibliothèque royale Albert I, print room

in a German edition of 1545. In the southern Netherlands the first edition of the *Metamorphoses*, adorned with plates, was published by the famous publisher Colard Mansion in Bruges in 1484 and, afterward, emblems and illustrated proverbs in their turn evoked the story.[321]

Bruegel's works, too, include two engravings. One is an etching attributed to Georg Hoefnagel, *Landscape Crossed by a River, with the Fall of Icarus* (fig. 326), inscribed PETRUS BREUGEL FEC.: ROMAE A° 1553, a reference to a drawing the painter presumably made there at that date during his journey in Italy; the other is an engraving by Frans Huys, part of the series *Sea-Going Ships*, showing a three-masted vessel armed with four crow's nests and two top-gallant sails and, in the sky on the right, under a blazing sun, Daedalus in flight and Icarus falling (fig. 327). In such cases it is always a good idea to ask whether the mythological scene was planned at the beginning, added by the engraver, or demanded by the publisher. It is nonetheless evident that the subject's iconography was known to Bruegel: the subject is mentioned in the inventory of the imperial collection made in Prague in 1621,[322] and the painter could simply have come to know it through his apprenticeship with Pieter Coecke; a drawing, *The Story of Daedalus*,[323] is attributed to the latter's workshop. The subject is after all undeniably there in *Pride*, made into a burin engraving by Pieter van der Heyden in 1558. Two small figures are in fact falling in the right background of the picture, one at the level of the cliff face, the other behind an oblique, next to the monster that is carrying a beehive in the shape of a tiara. This is not an addition, since the reference is there in Bruegel's original drawing of 1557 (fig. 97).

The association of the fall of Icarus with the idea of pride is thus confirmed, and links up with the notion in Sebastian Brant's *Ship of Fools*, or that formulated by the humanist Dirk Volkertsz. Coornheert in 1582. Bruegel reinforces this pessimistic and critical vision by reducing it to an allusive detail: two legs hitting the water, sole indication of a body, and an ambition, being dashed. The implacable contrast with the ship pursuing its course toward harbor, having accomplished its mission and its voyage, but especially with the huge presence of the ploughman, bent over his plough and the furrow he is cutting, endows the image with its full resonance. Should we—like those who point out, rightly, that the peasant's clothing is more symbolic of his social position than it matches the work he is doing—deduce that this painting suggests a vision of a balanced world?[324] The nobleness of work on the one hand, the aberration of pride on the other? This reading is possible, but limiting, and does not answer other questions, for the work does not limit itself to a social or moral message. Its originality and breadth go beyond a particular time and even beyond a mythological reference. The latter's importance is proved by its merely being mentioned rather than being the painting's obvious subject—like the figure of Christ in *Christ Carrying the Cross* or of St. Paul in *The Conversion of St. Paul*.

The absence of Daedalus, contrary to what we might think, gives the work a further twist. That an odd but chance event should pass unnoticed is understandable. That a double anomaly should do so would be more surprising. If we remember the moralizing message the story of Icarus embodied in the sixteenth century, denouncing recklessness and putting the right course between two

extremes, that is "flying between the two," Bruegel's image shows the terrible
result of ignoring this advice. The presence of Daedalus, flying at a reasonable
height in contrast to the other, who flew higher and burned his wings, as in the
two engravings by Bruegel, is thus no longer justified. Here the painter depicts an
episode later than that in which the fisherman, shepherd, and ploughman "see
them both pass" and "take for gods these two men capable of remaining airborne,"
as the Latin poet puts it. The insolent young man is then engulfed, as Bruegel
shows, by the Icarian Sea—so named in his memory—and his father cries: "Icarus,
Icarus, where are you? Where am I to seek you?" This astonishing sight has
therefore passed, and the onlookers have gone back to their work. The artist wants
nothing to do with a classic illustration of the myth of Icarus; he seeks a deeper
and more human representation of its moral. Recklessness, pride, prodigality of
effort lead to a fall, pictured on the right by Icarus, of whose ambition nothing but
a few feathers remain. By contrast, on the left is another symbolic element: a bag
and a sword placed on a rock. The bag represents not only wealth, but also
selfishness, and the sword that is thrust into it emphasizes its cruelty (Anger,
after all, is armed with a sword). Thus, between these two symbols, the peasant
continues on his way and, in his own way, so does Daedalus, flying, as he advised,
inter utrumque. A confirmation of this interpretation can be found in a later
illustration by Otto Vaenius for a book of *Emblems* inspired by Horace (fig. 328),
published in Antwerp in 1612 and expressing the same idea: *in medio virtus*
(virtue lies in moderation).[325] In the sky are Icarus and Daedalus in their classic
situation, under the sun at their chosen height; on the ground are three women:
Virtue in the middle holding a horn of plenty (fruit of the ploughman's work?),
with Avarice on the left clutching a bag and rummaging in a sack of coins, and on
the right Prodigality tossing money over her head. From Bruegel to Vaenius, the
depiction has passed from poetic mystery to an obviousness devoid of echoes.
The resonances set off by the first are fortunately many and varied, and the work
remains open.

It is quite another matter with the painters who, inspired by Bruegel's
composition, portrayed a true *Fall of Icarus,* such as Hans Bol (fig. 329), Lucas
van Valckenborch, Joos de Momper, and others. Their paintings, drawings,
watercolors, and engravings make the ploughman, the fisherman, or the shepherd
fully aware of what is happening in the air, in order to be faithful to the myth. By
contrast, the second version of Bruegel's painting, where Daedalus appears in
flight alone, is shocking because of this anomalous presence (fig. 330). This may be
explained by the fact that today we know this version was made after his death.[326]
The copy endeavors somehow to reconcile Bruegel's vision with the classical
depiction of the subject. Moreover, the position of the sun on the horizon in the
version that hangs in the Musées royaux in Brussels, which seems illogical in
comparison to the posthumous version, has an evocative power that the other
lacks, in its too obvious linking of cause and effect. Furthermore, the complexity
of the lighting effects and the play of shadows which reflect the direction of the
light accentuate the feeling of space and timelessness. Bruegel also makes use of
it in the engraving *The Pilgrims of Emmaus,* as the original drawing in the Musée
des Beaux-Arts in Antwerp, which has recently been rediscovered (fig. 331),

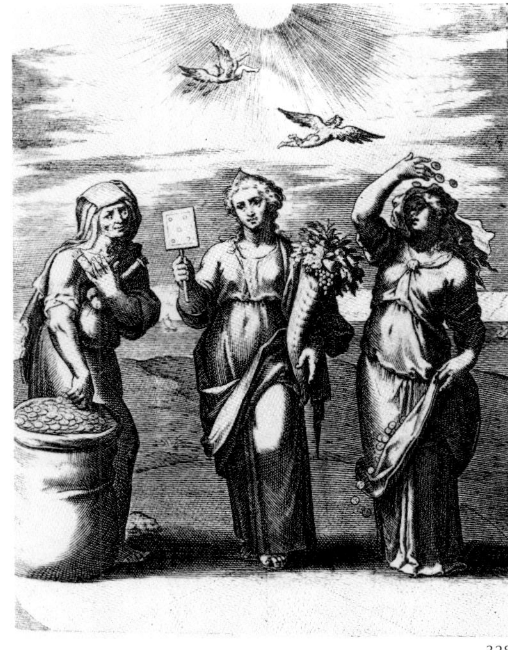

328. Otto Vaenius (Otto van Veen), *In Medio
Consistit Virtus,* illustration from *Horatii Emblemata,*
Antwerp, 1612. Paris, Bibliothèque nationale de
France, print department

confirms. But this resonance increases if we remember that *Patience*, the engraving of 1557 (fig. 92), also has a sun close to the horizon. Is not patience the opposite of recklessness? Thus Bruegel makes his images chime with each other. Now, potentially this image of the sun appeared already in the emblems of Alciat.[327] The presence of a partridge on a bush behind the fisherman—which as we know belongs to another episode in Ovid—introduces into this fall the idea of duration in time. This gray bird, whose flight is well known for following every undulation of the ground, is the only one in the painting who is looking both at Icarus and at the viewer with its laterally positioned eyes.

The subject, the scene, and the characters combine, contrast, or answer each other in discrete times and places: a Mediterranean landscape, a Brabant ploughman, a mythological figure, a sixteenth-century ship. Just as every landscape in the *Seasons* is composite, the same quality governs most of Bruegel's works, making them all the more accessible. The way this image fascinates the viewer has nothing to do with representing reality—although the plough and the boat are both perfectly reproduced and dateable—but lies instead in the unreality and timelessness it evokes. The painter has redistributed the elements of the myth and of his experience according to a new conception that gives the image its mystery. To judge the work according to its fidelity to the story is to deny the very genius of the artist.

Two accounts, dating from almost immediately after the painting was rediscovered in 1912, prove this.[328] Émile Verhaeren, a poet, wrote on 21 November 1913: "The conception is gripping … our attention is stimulated and held all the more because we must make the effort to find the poem's subject. Also, once gripped, it is not released, and this *Fall of Icarus*—which Bruegel has treated, we could say, in defiance of good sense and logic—is the one that remains most firmly etched in the viewer's memory." And here is the view of a painter on 4 November 1912—Rik Wouters, leader of the Brabant fauvists, in a letter to the painter Simon Levy: "On the subject of Museums, ours has two wonderful new Bruegels, one a distemper of the magi, but perhaps you have seen it or I told you about it in Paris. Anyway, the second one [*The Fall of Icarus*] which is recent is the most beautiful painting I knew. The comparison with Ensor is unavoidable: the whole thing is refined, first class stuff old boy, a clever drawing, qualities no modern has managed to achieve."

However some of these "qualities," and the fact that the work is neither signed nor dated, and painted on canvas, raised questions. Only paintings in oil on wood panels or in distemper on linen were known at the time. Today we know that Bruegel also painted in oil on canvas, as inventories testify.[329] The canvas support had been reinforced by being glued to two other pieces of canvas, which has made examination difficult and not very revealing. While questions are justified when comparing the painting's surface with the perfection of the paint layer in, for example, *The Fall of the Rebel Angels* (fig. 114), the innovative nature of the composition and vision in *The Fall of Icarus* is undeniable. The scene depicted recalls Bruegel's journey to Italy, the way the subject is positioned recalls *The Flight into Egypt* of 1563 (fig. 140), and the work's elements make a synthesis of the painter's art.

A painting's attribution is a major historical problem in the context of the

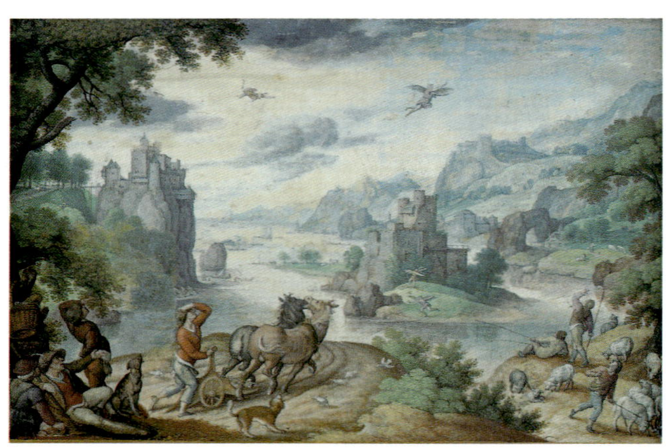

329. Hans Bol, *The Fall of Icarus*, 1590. Watercolor and distemper on paper, 5¼ x 8⅛ in. (13.3 x 20.6 cm). Antwerp, Museum Mayer van den Bergh

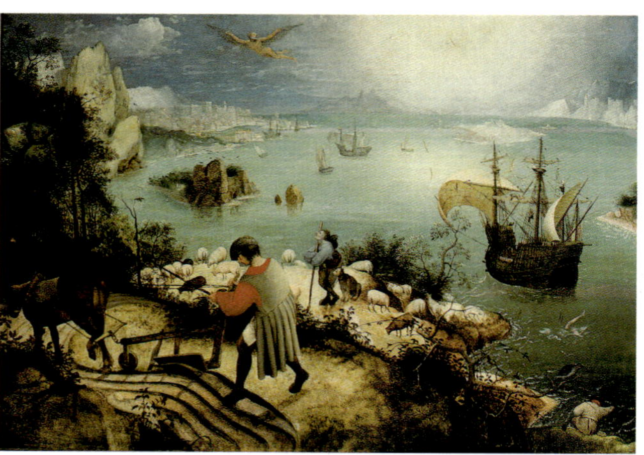

330. Anonymous, *The Fall of Icarus*, after Pieter Bruegel, end of the sixteenth century. Oil on panel, 24¹/₁₆ x 35½ in. (63 x 90 cm). Brussels, Musée David et Alice van Buuren

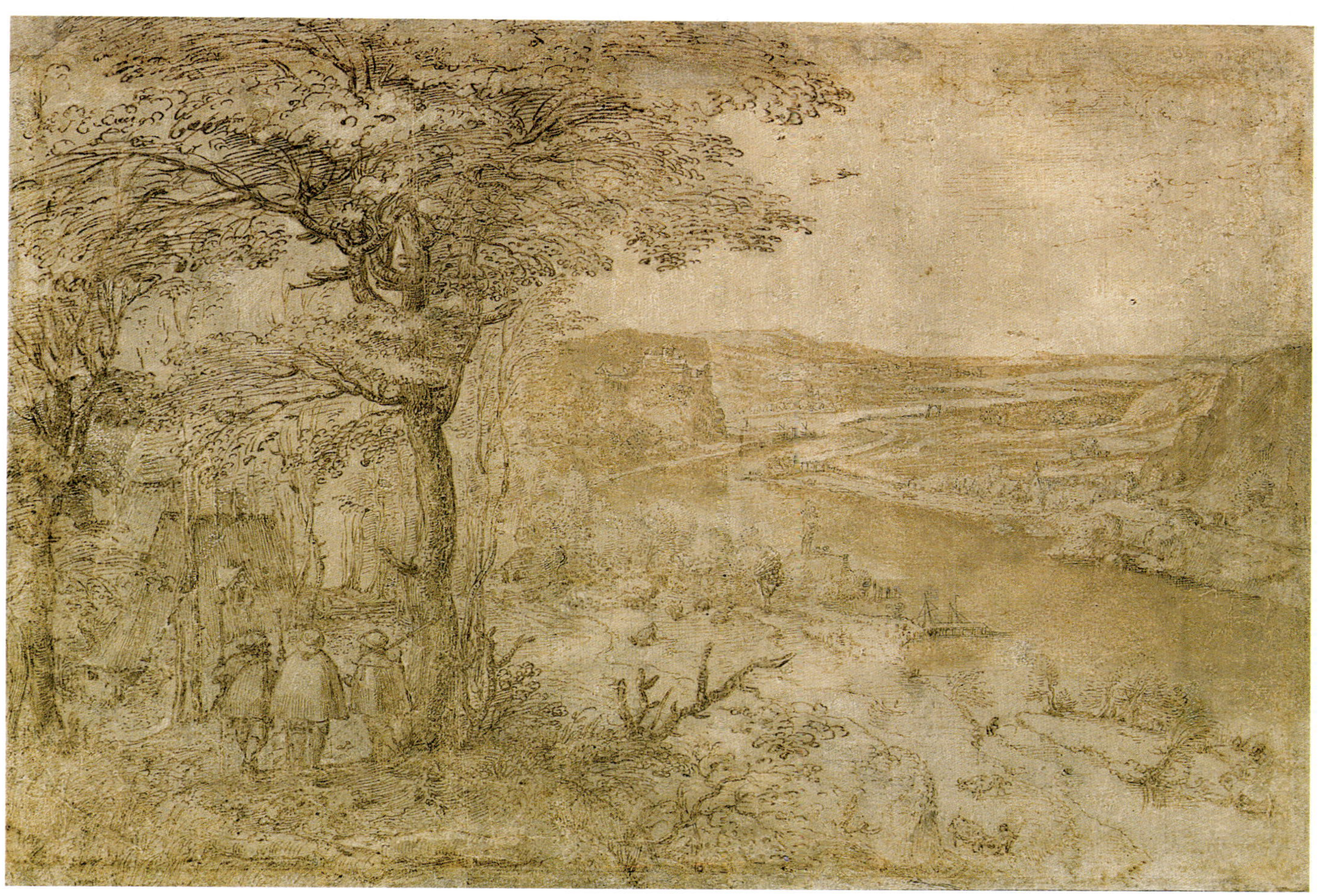

331

331. Pieter Bruegel, *The Pilgrims of Emmaus*, ca. 1553–55. Pen and brown ink with brown wash, white heightening, 10¼ x 16⅜ in. (26 x 41.5 cm). Antwerp, Koninklijk Museum voor Schone Kunsten

works of the artist to whom it is attributed. On the other hand, it is of only minor interest in the wider cultural context, whether the work in itself remains an object of admiration or curiosity, or whether it falls into obscurity because it has been deprived of its background. The rest is a matter of star quality or market value. This is not the case here, given the extraordinary number of echoes set off by *The Fall of Icarus*, in the minds of art historians from Max J. Friedländer to René Huyghe, and of writers from Marcel Brion, who hears in it "this haunting music coming from an enchanted world,"[330] to Marguerite Yourcenar, who is indignant "that a rustic, uninterested in the first air crash, continues his sowing,"[331] to the German poet Gottfried Benn to the American poet William Carlos Williams to the English poet W. H. Auden.[332]

Half a century later, for André Comte-Sponville, "the legend is quite clear here: Icarus is not burned out of our sight but right in front of us. This is why the myth is profound in its simplicity, and beautiful, and true: reality prevails over hope, which we all understand and which Bruegel, in his own way, has depicted with genius."[333]

And in all this we sense that the painting's meaning is multifarious, and always changes depending on the individual and that individual's choices. *The Fall of Icarus* is a place where the eye and the sun, the sky and the sea, the port and the sail, meet and are united. Whatever events may come to trouble it, this place belongs fully to the memory of a Bruegel for all time.

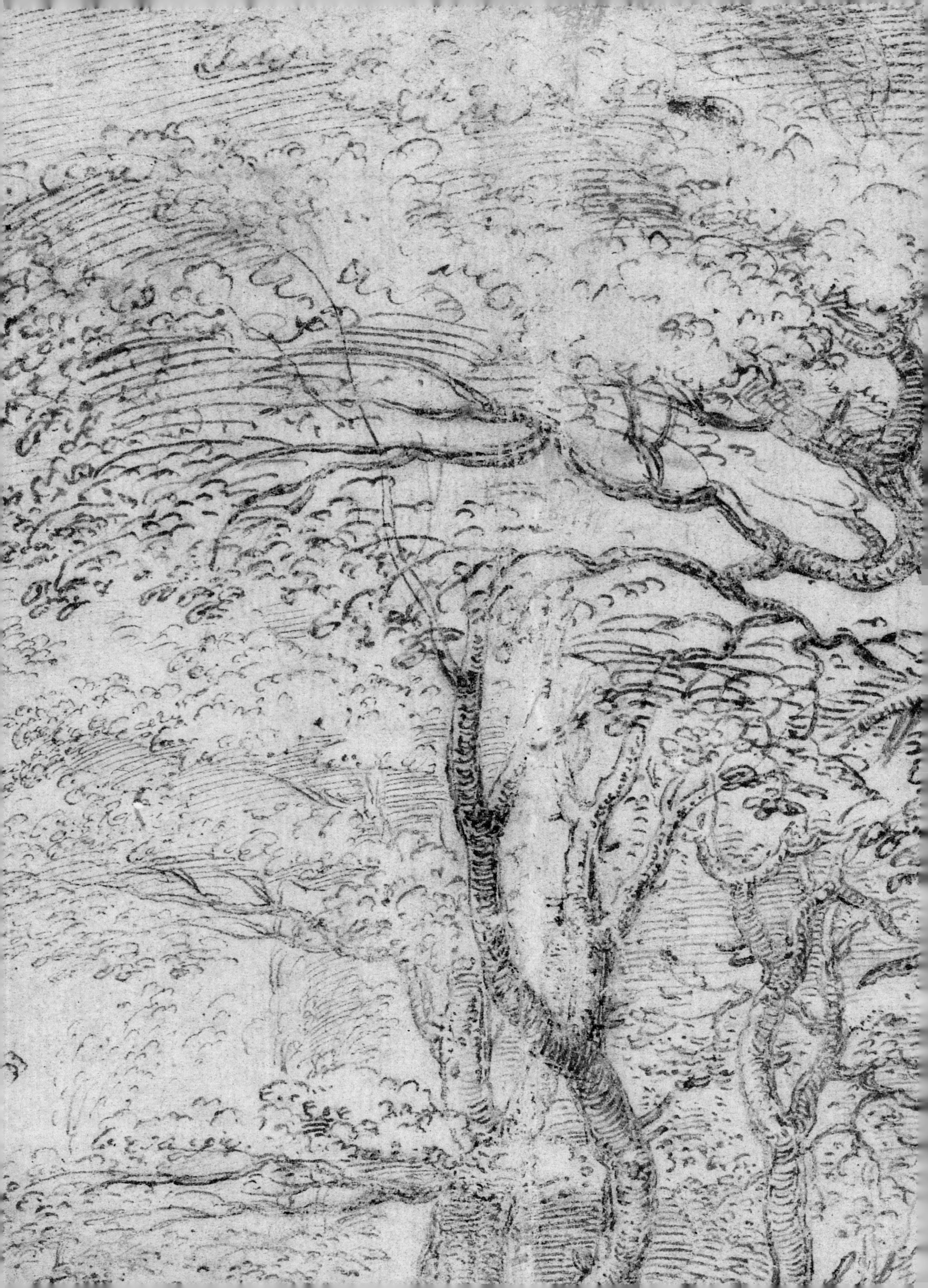

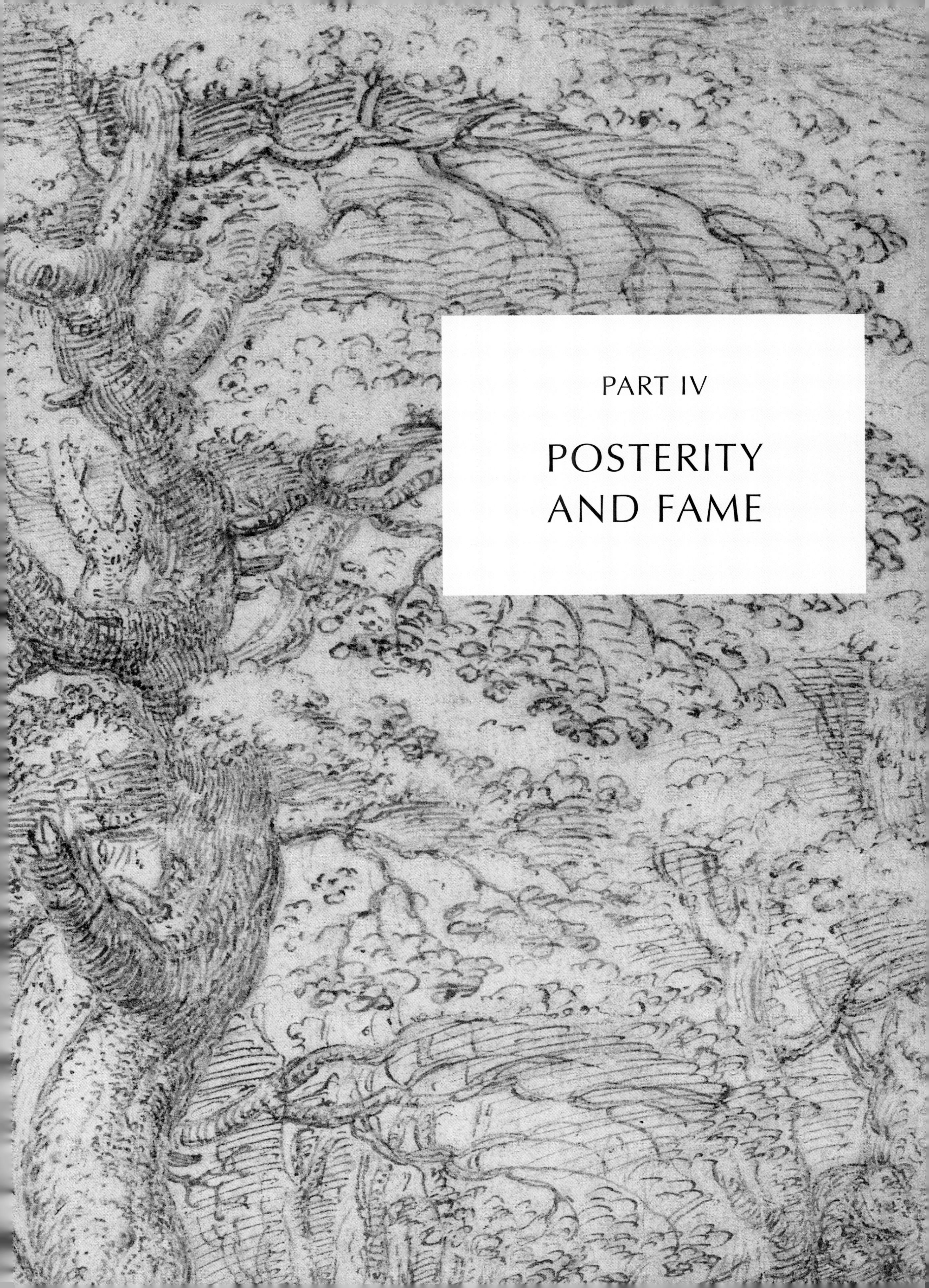

PART IV

POSTERITY AND FAME

Fame awaits the artist whose work casts a brilliant light. An artist's renown can take many forms: laudatory writings, critical acclaim, the avid collecting of his work, unsigned works attributed to him, copies after his compositions, large numbers of followers, a powerful influence on other artists and—more directly related to the works themselves—works that have been lost, but are described in other sources left to us. This last category is complex, for sources are many. Mention of now-lost paintings may surface in quotations, inventories, painted or engraved copies, or, less directly, in uncertain or controversial attributions.

LOST WORKS

We must once again turn to Van Mander to find explicit mentions of or allusions to a certain number of missing paintings. While most of the works mentioned in his biography of Bruegel are now in public collections, some—about seven, unidentified or known only through copies—must be considered lost works. The first to study these paintings was Hulin de Loo in 1907.[1] Two works have been added to Bruegel's oeuvre since he did his work: a *Tower of Babel* "in a smaller format"[2] was discovered in 1935 and is now in the Museum Boijmans van Beuningen, Rotterdam; and a second painting of Christ carrying the cross, known only through copies by Pieter Bruegel the Younger, two of which are in the Uffizi in Florence and the Fine Arts Museum in Antwerp and dated respectively 1599 and 1603.[3] This *Ascent to Calvary* has none of the breadth or power of the masterpiece in Vienna. With Christ in its center, it contrasts Jerusalem with Golgotha, the city being rich in detail, the hill threatened by dark storm clouds.

Van Mander mentions a *Temptation of Christ* "where, seen from above, as in the Alps, we plunge down onto towns and countryside that we see through masses of cloud." This may have belonged to Rubens for, in the inventory made in 1640 after that artist's death, item no. 210 is described as "The Temptation of our Lord by Bruegel." No other information is given. We can perhaps imagine it, considering the *Great Landscapes* series—*St. Jerome in the Desert* or *The Penance of Mary Magdalene*—for the Alpine setting, and from the drawing *Undergrowth with Five Bears* in the Prague museum (fig. 333), which Hieronymus Cock made into an engraving with the very title *The Temptation of Christ* (fig. 334) and where we see town and countryside not "through masses of cloud" but through the masses of trees.

The Village Wedding—an oil painting that Van Mander had seen in Amsterdam at the house of the art lover Herman Pilgrims—is described too vaguely to be identified, despite the mention of the figures' flesh being tinted "as if burned by the sun." The works that belonged to another Amsterdam collector, Willem Jakobsz, which Van Mander mentions ("two distemper paintings depicting a kermis and a village wedding and containing many amusing figures directly inspired by peasants") are cited in 1683 in the inventory of Diego Duarte, a Portuguese jeweler and merchant who had settled in Antwerp.[4] Although the kermis has since disappeared, the wedding, described in great detail by the author of the *Schilder-Boeck* —"where the bride receives her gifts [and where] we see an old peasant with a small bag hanging from his neck, counting money in the palm

332. After Pieter Bruegel, *Village Wedding in an Interior*, ca. 1575–1600. Oil on panel, 31 ¼ x 41 ⅞ in. (80.5 x 106.3 cm). Philadelphia, The Philadelphia Museum of Art, John G. Johnson Collection

PREVIOUS PAGES:

Pieter Bruegel, *Undergrowth with Five Bears* (detail), 1554. Pen and brown ink, 10 ¾ x 16 ⅛ in. (27.3 x 41 cm). Prague, Národní Galerie

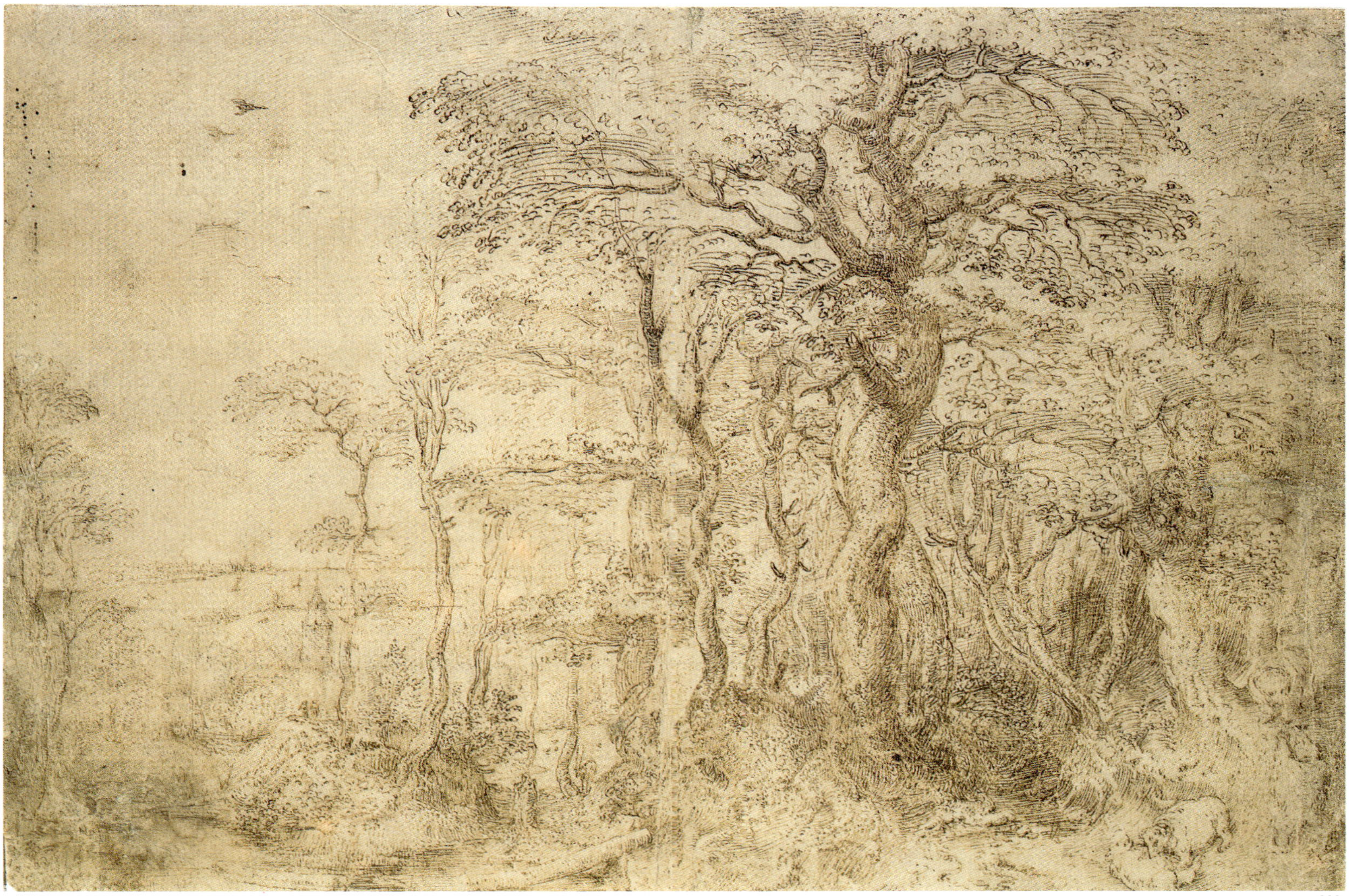

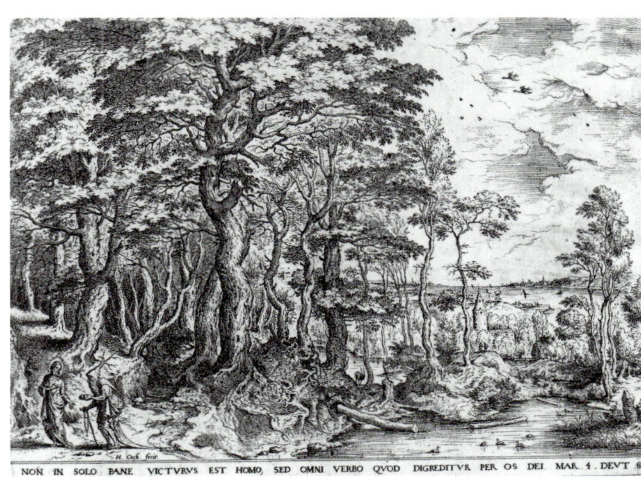

333

of his hand"—corresponds to *Village Wedding in an Interior*, now in the Johnson Collection in Philadelphia (fig. 332). Although this was painted in oils on wood panel, not in distemper, Hulin de Loo thought it was Bruegel's original; it is possible that Van Mander made a mistake about it.[5] Writers today no longer accept the attribution. Van Mander, after all, also added: "these are remarkable works." This is not the case here, but perhaps the painting in question was a version that is now lost.

There is also a puzzling phrase: "he also made a work in which truth triumphs; this was (it is said) the best of his works." Is *Daer de Waerhyt doorbreeckt* (where Truth triumphs or bursts out) the title of a painting[6] or the work's meaning? There are many theories as to which this work might be: *John the Baptist Preaching*, *The Fall of Icarus*, *The Calumny of Apelles*, the *Triumph of Death*,[7] and why not *The Triumph of Time*, with its spirit and despair, or *The Resurrection of Christ* with its light—or indeed many other subjects where the image's humanity proclaims its truth.

The Triumph of Time or of Saturn (fig. 335), an engraving published by Philipp Galle in 1574, builds up such a confused mass of allegories and symbols

333. Pieter Bruegel, *Undergrowth with Five Bears*, 1554. Pen and brown ink, 10¾ x 16⅛ in. (27.3 x 41 cm). Prague, Národní Galerie

334. Hieronymus Cock, *The Temptation of Christ*, ca. 1554. Etching, 12⅜ x 17⅛ in. (31.6 x 43.6 cm). Brussels, Bibliothèque royale Albert I, print room

that it is hard to believe that Pieter Bruegel—the print is signed "Petrus Bruegel"—could have dreamt up such a collection in order to denounce the vanity of all things. Is this attribution credible? It certainly contains, as other engravings do, echoes of other works: clearly of the series of *Twelve Flemish Proverbs*, and much more distantly of *Jesus and the Disciples on the Road to Emmaus*, an engraving made by Philipp Galle in 1571, and of *The Epileptics' Pilgrimage to Molenbeek-Saint-Jean* and *The Carnival Fools*, engraved by Hendrik Hondius in 1642.

The information Van Mander offers is not always clear. The identification of the painting "where all remedies for death are used" with *The Triumph of Death* is not convincing. The author himself admits that "it would be very hard to list all the works he made dealing with sorcery, hell, peasants, and others," let alone the "countless little allegories." Despite gaps, inaccuracies, and other problems, Van Mander remains, here too, an invaluable source.

COLLECTION INVENTORIES

The inventories of princely households and the private collections of merchants, as well as the lists drawn up of property probated in estates are always a priceless source of information, both about the reputation of artists and the tastes of their time. Thus, the inventory of the bankruptcy of Jean Noirot in 1572 allows us to establish the history of *The Wedding Feast* (fig. 300) as well as the presence of four other Bruegel works[8] in the collection of the master of the Antwerp mint. Similarly, the inventories of the Habsburg Archduke Ernest in 1595 and of the household of Cardinal Granvelle in 1607 prove that the collections of powerful people often contained major works.

The Archduke Ernest was governor of the Netherlands from 1593 to 1595. On 5 July 1594 the city of Antwerp made him a gift of the six celebrated paintings *The Twelve Months of the Year*, which it had received from Nicolas Jongelinck, who probably commissioned them from Bruegel. The inventory of these works, drawn up in Brussels on 17 July 1595,[9] also included *The Wedding Feast* that probably belonged to Noirot (fig. 300), *Children's Games* (fig. 246), *The Conversion of St. Paul* (fig. 160)—all three acquired in 1594[10]—and a *Crucifixion*, no. 16 in the inventory, which is now lost—unless it was in fact *Christ Carrying the Cross* (fig. 51), as Klaus Demus wonders, or the prototype for Bruegel the Younger's *Ascent to Calvary*.[11] After the archduke's death this collection of masterpieces went to Prague—where it became part of the collection of his brother, Rudolf II, and later to Vienna.

As for Cardinal Antoine Perrenot de Granvelle, counselor to Charles V, minister to Philip II, and *éminence grise* in the Netherlands from 1550 to 1564— he was also a connoisseur of Bruegel, whose works he kept in successive residences at Brussels, Mechelen, Besançon, and Naples. The inventory of his house in Besançon, drawn up in 1607 on the death of his nephew, mentions five paintings by the artist:[12] *The Flight into Egypt* (London, Courtauld Institute; fig. 140), *The Story of Jonah* (which may be by the artists's son, Jan Bruegel), a landscape painted

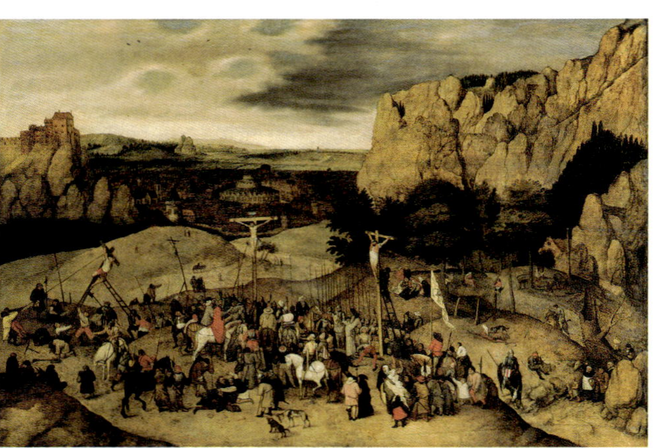

335. Philipp Galle, *The Triumph of Time or of Saturn*, after Pieter Bruegel (?), 1574, second state, signed Theodor Galle. Engraving, 8⅛ x 11⅞ in. (20.8 x 30.1 cm). Brussels, Bibliothèque royale Albert I, print room

336. Pieter Bruegel the Younger, *The Crucifixion*, 1603. Oil on panel, 45⅝ x 63¾ in. (116 x 162 cm). Antwerp, Koninklijk Museum voor Schone Kunsten

on copper (probably also by Jan), *Ships on a Calm Sea with a Distant Landscape* (which could be linked with *Naval Battle in the Strait of Messina*, engraved by Frans Huys and published by Cock in 1561 (fig. 319), or with *View of Naples* (fig. 321), and finally a painting depicting some blind people. These "blind people who held on to each other," according to the inventory, are a different version of the celebrated painting of the parable, as the document makes no mention of a fall. Of the five, only one—*The Flight into Egypt*—is specifically described as being "by the old Pieter Bruegel." The information appears to be correct and proves that the collectors distinguished between the father's and the sons' works, and that paintings in the Bruegel style were popular.

The painting of the blind men in the Granvelle collection leads us to another inventory, that of Count Cosimo Masi, secretary to Alessandro Farnese, who lived in the Netherlands from 1574 to 1594. The list, drawn up in 1602 in connection with some confiscations at the Palazzo Masi in Parma, mentions *The Blind Leading the Blind* (fig. 69) and *The Misanthrope* (fig. 267), both today in the Naples museum, as well as a copy of *Children's Games* (fig. 246).[13] These examples show that important people whose political or other duties took them to the Netherlands at the end of the sixteenth century acquired, despite the difficulties of doing so, works by Bruegel after the latter's death.

Merchants and notables did the same at the beginning of the seventeenth century. Thus the inventory of Filip I van Valckenisse, who was admitted to the guild of St. Luke in 1607 as an art dealer and art lover, and died in Antwerp on Minderbroedersstraat on 3 March 1614,[14] lists dozens of works including several cited as being by "Helschen Bruegel" (Hell Bruegel, that is, Pieter Bruegel the Younger): *Christ Carrying the Cross, Carnival and Lent, Children's Games, Peasant Wedding, The Sermon of St. John* and, according to the text, *Blauwe Huyck ende ander plaisanterije* (The Blue Cloak and other jests)—that is, a copy of *Flemish Proverbs*—but also *The Triumph of Death*, described as being by Bruegel this time and considered by most writers to be the original, which now hangs in the Prado (fig. 109). Another entry is *Een Vluchtende Schaepherder gedaen na den Oude Bruegel* (a bad shepherd after the elder Bruegel). The inventory explicitly mentions a large number of copies, one of which may be the painting now in Philadelphia, which was later attributed to the master.

Another collection, inventoried in 1621—which belonged to Nicolaes Cornelis Cheeus, who died on Venusstraat, Antwerp, on 4 July,[15] and which is considerably less important than the previous one—is nevertheless noteworthy because of the many works by Jan Bruegel, and of *Tweelf afbeeldingen op teljooren gedaen by den Ouden Bruegel* (twelve plates with figures painted by the elder Bruegel). These are the *Twelve Proverbs* now in the Mayer van den Bergh museum in Antwerp (fig. 236).[16] The work was valued at 100 guilders. This detail is interesting because the same inventory values several landscapes by Jan Bruegel at 120 guilders, proving that the son was more fashionable than the father: at the time Jan Bruegel's popularity was rising fast. The inventory also mentions *Een schilderijken Rotze* (a small painting of a rock) by Wortelmans—probably Hans, who is named lower down as the author of a landscape—after "Old Bruegel": the description therefore as for *The Bad Shepherd* in the Valckenisse collection.

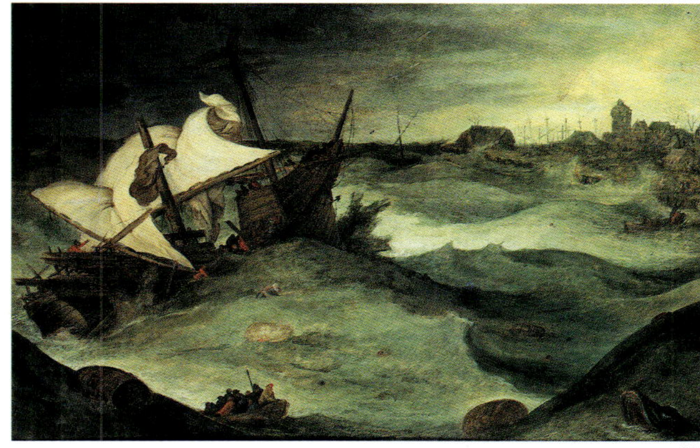

337. Jan Bruegel the Younger, *Tempest with the Sacrifice of Jonah*, ca. 1625–30. Oil on panel, 15 x 22 in. (38 x 56 cm). Vienna, Kunsthistorisches Museum

The inventory made in Prague in 1621 of the collection of the emperor Rudolf II, who had died in 1612, mentions the same Bruegel works as that of Archduke Ernest, with the addition of *Dulle Griet* (fig. 101) and the *Land of Cockaigne* (fig. 269). It also lists works that have since disappeared, such as *Village Plundered by Soldiers*, of which a copy attributed to Bruegel the Younger hangs in Douai museum (fig. 338), three *Masquerades*, *The Story of Daedalus and Icarus* (was this *The Fall of Icarus* in the Brussels museum?), a *Shepherd* painted in distemper, and *St. George*.[17] The collection, which was probably moved to Vienna under the reign of Matthias, passed into the hands of Leopold William, whose inventory of 1659 mentions also the *Bird-Nester* (fig. 209), the fragment *The Wine of St. Martin*

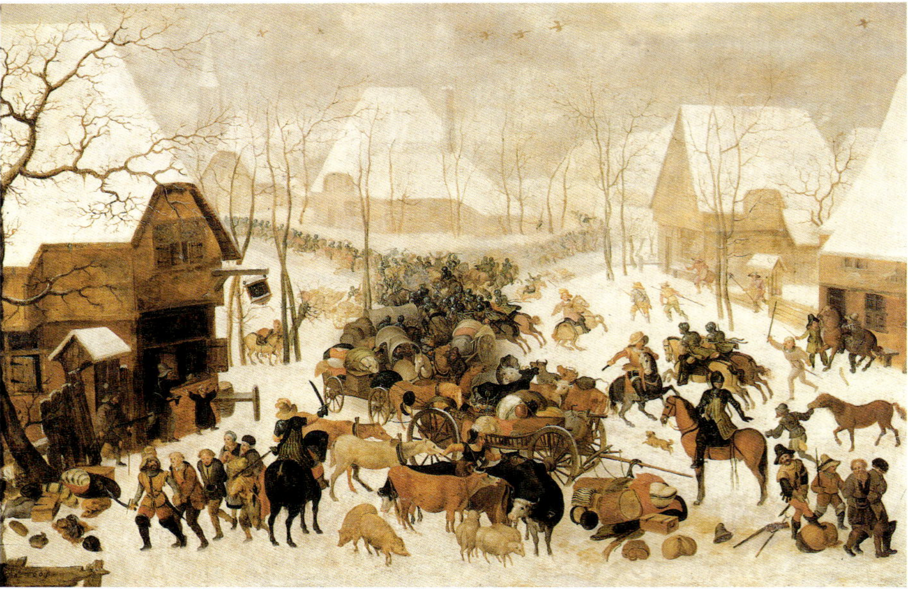

338

(now attributed to Bruegel the Younger), and two works now lost: a *Bagpiper* and a smaller-format *Massacre of the Innocents*.[18] This testifies to the enduring interest in Bruegel's works. As for Archduchess Isabella, who governed the Netherlands from 1621 to 1633, her Brussels collection included *John the Baptist Preaching* "by Old Bruegel," a *Peasant Kermis* "by Bruegel," and a *Peasant Wedding* "after Bruegel."[19]

In 1640 a list of paintings for sale in the house where Peter Paul Rubens had died was published. It was in three languages—Flemish, French, and English—and comprised 314 items, not including objects, antiques, drawings, and unfinished works.[20] In the section "pieces by old masters" are twelve works by "Old Bruegel." This is not surprising. We know that some aspects of Bruegel's technique, such as his use of a white ground layer, were taken up and amplified by the baroque artist; that Rubens and Jan Bruegel were friends and worked together on many paintings; and that a painting by Rubens, *Christ Handing the Keys to St. Peter*, would adorn Bruegel's tomb in the church of Notre-Dame-de-la-Chapelle in Brussels in 1676.

Which works appear in the inventory? A "landscape in oils with the Flight into Egypt by Old Bruegel" (no. 191), which must be the painting mentioned in

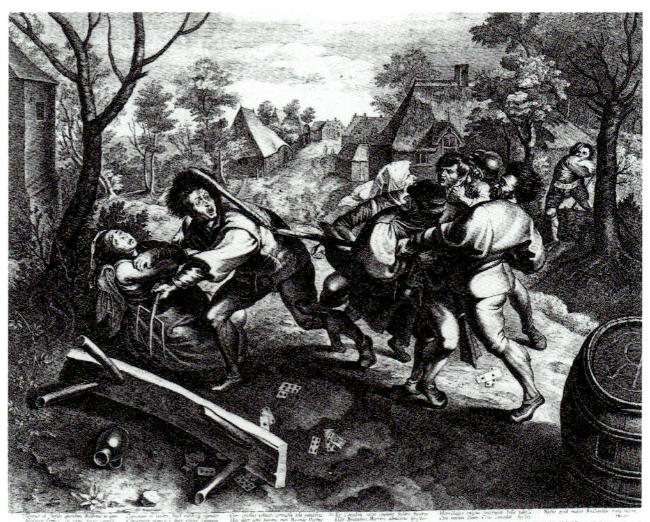

339

338. Pieter Bruegel the Younger, *Village Plundered by Soldiers*, 1605. Oil on panel, 45⅝ x 70½ in. (116 x 179 cm). Douai, Musée principal

339. Lucas Vorsterman, *Peasants' Brawl*, after Pieter Bruegel, ca. 1621. Etching and engraving, 16¾ x 30⅝ in. (42.6 x 52.5 cm). Brussels, Bibliothèque royale Albert I, print room

the Granvelle inventory of 1607; "Mont Saint-Godard by Old Bruegel" (no. 192), a lost work whose subject may be compared, according to Matthias Winner,[21] to a drawing now preserved in Dresden: *View of the Ticino Valley with the Castello Grande (Uri) and the Castello Montebello (Schwyz)*; "The Death of Our Lady in black and white by Old Bruegel" (no. 193), given by Abraham Ortelius, who had an engraving made of it by Philipp Galle in 1574; "Two small Faces in roundels by Old Bruegel" (nos. 195, 196), which Hulin de Loo believes may be compared to the *Head of a Mercenary*[22] in the Musée Fabre in Montpellier; "A Yawner by Old Bruegel" (no. 197), a subject depicted in a small panel in Brussels;[23] "A face of a Beggar in a roundel by said Bruegel" (no. 198) of which no trace remains; "A Portrait by the same" (no. 199)—no portrait by Bruegel is known today; "The Temptation of Our Lord by Old Bruegel" (no. 210), probably the work mentioned by Van Mander; "A piece showing small Boats made in distemper by the same" (no. 211), which could be linked to a work in the Granvelle collection depicting the same subject; and "A Battle between Turks and Christians by the same" (no. 212)—probably a distemper, as the English specifies "in water colors"—which has disappeared, as has "A Landscape with a fire in distemper by the same" (no. 213). Finally, among the "pieces executed by the late Mr Rubens," no. 143 is "A Battle between peasants after a drawing by Old Bruegel." What is important here is the theme of the brawl in a work made by Bruegel at the end of his life. We do not know whether this was in the form of a painting, unfinished or completed by Gillis Mostaert, but it was copied by his sons, Pieter and Jan, which showed the influence of Rubens, and made into an engraving by Lucas Vorsterman about 1621 (fig. 339) which bore the inscription PET. BRUEGEL INVENT. and a dedication to Jan Bruegel.[24]

One of the richest collections in Antwerp in the mid-seventeenth century was that belonging to Peeter Stevens, which contained, besides works by Bruegel, paintings by Van Eyck, Quentin Metsys, Hans Holbein, Rubens, and Van Dyck.[25] A wealthy cloth merchant and city benefactor who gave alms to the poor and was a patron of the arts, he appears in the center of Willem van Haecht's painting of 1628, *The Collection of Cornelis van der Geest* (Antwerp, Rubenshuis; fig. 340). Peeter Stevens also annotated a copy of Van Mander's *Schilder-Boeck* with the statement that he had seen twenty-three paintings by Bruegel, of which he possessed a dozen. The catalogue "Of the most renowned Rarities belonging to the late Mr Peeter Stevens … Which will be sold the thirteenth day of the month of August and the following days of this year 1688, in the House of the deceased" listed: "By Bruegel the elder: A very famous Heath, where peasant men and Women go to market with a cart & a swine, & others"—a lost painting which appears on the left-hand wall in *The Collection of Cornelis van der Geest,* from whom Stevens had bought it (a drawing with watercolor, in the print room in Munich, also shows the same subject);[26] "The adulterous woman, formerly a Piece belonging to the Collection of the Reverend Father Federico Borromeo, archbishop of Milan," a work in grisaille, as we know, dating from 1565; "The World turned upside down, represented in several Proverbs & Moral tales," now the *Proverbs* of 1559, in the Berlin museum; "The flight of Our Lady into Egypt, with a fine view of the Landscapes," from Granvelle's collection, later in Rubens's, now in London; "View of Mont St. Godard in Switzerland," also from

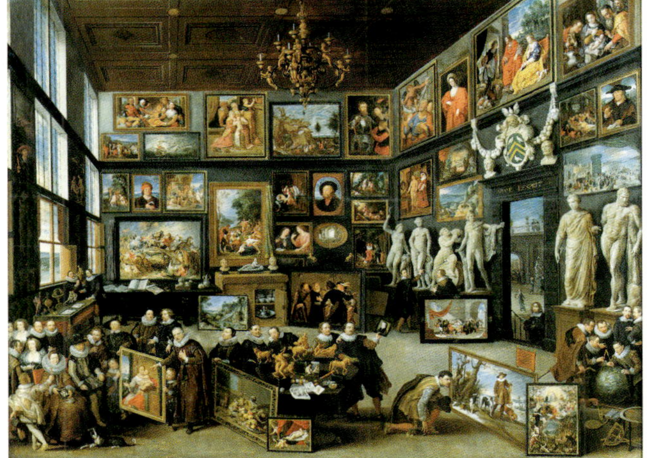

340

340. Willem van Haecht, *The Collection of Cornelis van der Geest*, 1628. Oil on panel, 39⅜ x 51⅛ in. (100 x 130 cm). Antwerp, Rubenshuis

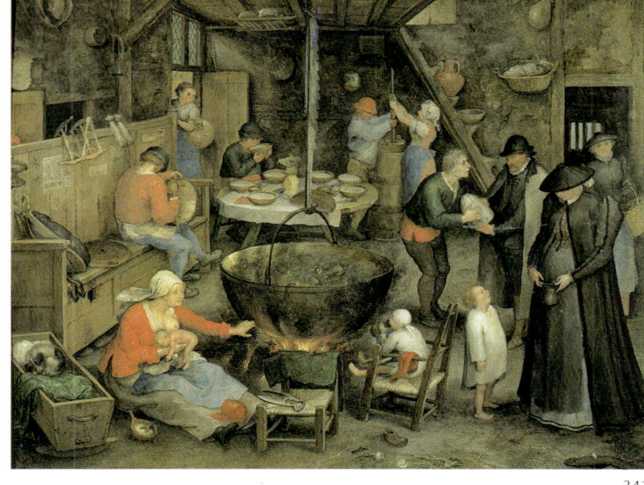

341

341. Jan Bruegel, *Visit to the Farm* or *Visit to the Wet Nurse*, ca. 1597. Oil on copper, 10⅝ x 14⅛ in. (27 x 36 cm). Vienna, Kunsthistorisches Museum

the Rubens collection, dated 1563 by Stevens on his copy of Van Mander, and now lost; "The Death of Our Lady, with the Apostles," formerly in Ortelius's collection, later in Rubens's, and now in Upton House, Banbury, England; "The Portrait of the wife of Mr Pieter Van Aelst, Painter": is this the portrait mentioned in Rubens's list of 1640? It identifies Mayken Verhulst, Pieter Coecke's wife, a painter herself and Bruegel's mother-in-law; "The Boat from which Jonah was thrown into the Sea," now lost, although the Granvelle and Rubens collections mention similar works (is it echoed in Jan Bruegel the Younger's work in Vienna's Kunsthistorisches Museum, fig. 337?); "The City of Antwerp with two Monkeys," painted in 1564 and now in Berlin (fig. 213); "Autumn," a lost work on a seasonal theme; and "a village festival," no doubt also lost.

Among the other collections of the time, that of the Antwerp painter and art dealer Herman de Neyt included, in 1642, "a small painting of cripples by Old Bruegel"—today known as *The Beggars* of 1568 (fig. 258), and in the Louvre. In 1663 the collection of Diego Duarte contained "two wonderful Bruegels" to which was added, according to the Portuguese merchant's inventory of 1682, *The Flight into Egypt* from Peeter Stevens's collection, unless this is another version of the subject.[27] *The Calumny of Apelles*, of which the drawing survives today, was sold in 1670 by the Forchoudt firm, Antwerp's biggest art dealer, and had come from the collection of a certain canon named Hilwervern.[28] Finally, the inventory of the celebrated Parisian banker, patron of the arts, and collector Everhard Jabach mentions, in 1696 "A winter scene, with many figures, in the foreground the three kings adoring Our Lord; much snow is falling and a small child is sliding about on the ice on a sledge, old Brugel"[29]—a description that identifies *The Adoration of the Magi in the Snow* of 1567 (fig. 195), now in the Reinhart collection in Winterthur.

COPIES AND IMITATORS

This sample of collections which, during the seventeenth century and chiefly in Antwerp, were enriched by the presence of Bruegel's works, reveals an infatuation with his works that was to fade as the century ended. This interest was confirmed by the large number of copies and works by imitators. The main agents of this were Bruegel's sons themselves, and their descendants. Many aspects of the output of Pieter the Younger and Jan Bruegel are therefore not just of copies of known works but reinforce the idea that there were others, now lost, to which they bear witness. This idea is based on more or less convincing, but never certain, indications. Faced with the characteristics of a work or the qualities of a composition, its spirit, and its conception, art historians have asked themselves whether there was some prototype—hence the enduring idea of lost works. Whether possible or probable, because of similarities of style or technique, this cannot be proved except in the case of works where there is a corresponding engraving. Nevertheless, because of their direct derivation, some works cannot be ignored.

Thus we must mention *Visit to the Farm*, or *Visit to the Wet Nurse* (fig. 341). In spirit these works take after the master, and several versions exist by Jan Bruegel, in color—such as that in the Kunsthistorisches Museum in Vienna—and

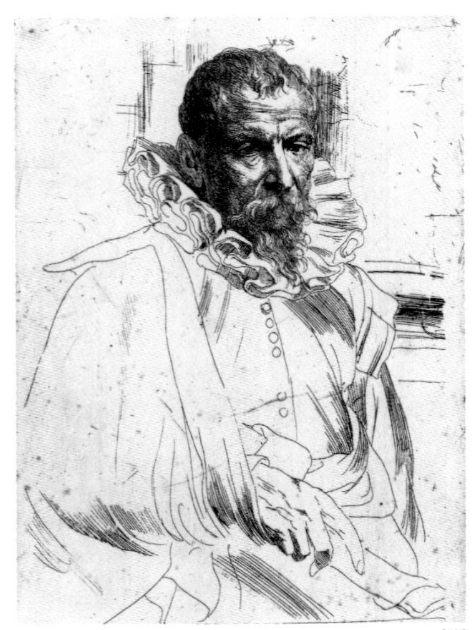

342. Anthony van Dyck, *Pieter Bruegel the Younger*, ca. 1630–31. Etching. Brussels, Bibliothèque royale Albert I, print room

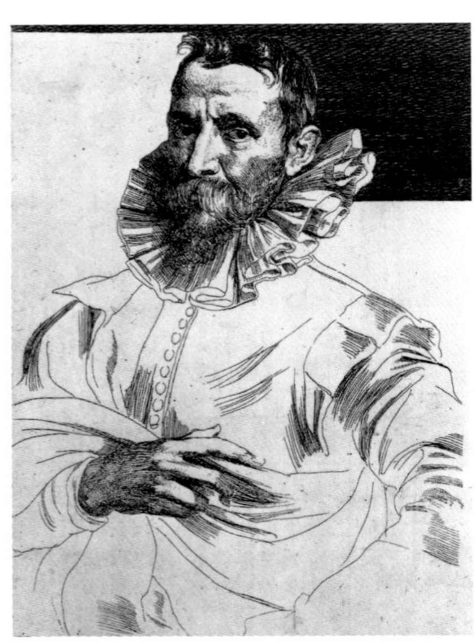

343. Anthony van Dyck, *Jan Bruegel*, ca. 1630–31. Etching. Brussels, Bibliothèque royale Albert I, print room

in grisaille, such as that in the Musée of Fine Arts in Antwerp, which suggests that there was an original work by Bruegel the Elder in the same vein and format as *The Death of the Virgin* (fig. 152) or *Christ and the Woman Taken in Adultery* (fig. 155).[30] There are also versions in color by Bruegel the Younger.

The Wine of St. Martin also warrants attention. A fragment in Vienna (fig. 344), considered to be by Bruegel the Elder in the inventory of Leopold William, is now attributed to Bruegel the Younger. It shows the popular celebration of the arrival of winter by reveling and drinking, while at the same time St. Martin shares his cloak. There are several versions of this painting, whose original may go back to the collection of Vincenzo Gonzaga I in Mantua, as it appears from an inventory dated 1627.[31] Besides the fragment in Vienna, there is a version signed by Pieter Baltens in Antwerp, and the very large and detailed one on canvas in the Brussels museum (fig. 345), which are both close, but with the image reversed, to an engraving by Guerard that mentions Jan Bruegel as the inventor and was published in the mid-seventeenth century at the request of Abraham Bruegel, grandson of Jan. This example clearly demonstrated the enduring appeal of the Bruegel style.

The Joust Between Carnival and Lent is a simplified work, reduced to just the foreground, of the celebrated painting of 1559. Pieter the Younger and Jan Bruegel made versions of it. *Kermis with Theater and Procession* is undeniably Bruegelesque in its vocabulary, and made up of elements taken from *Kermis at Hoboken* and *The Kermis of St. George*. It recalls a collage, to use a modern term. There are several copies by Bruegel the Younger—such as that in Cambridge dated 1632, that in Graz, and that in Brussels (fig. 358)—and by Pieter Baltens, in the Rijksmuseum, Amsterdam, which Georges Marlier considers may indeed be the work on which the others are based.[32] If we think of *Village Wedding*, Pieter

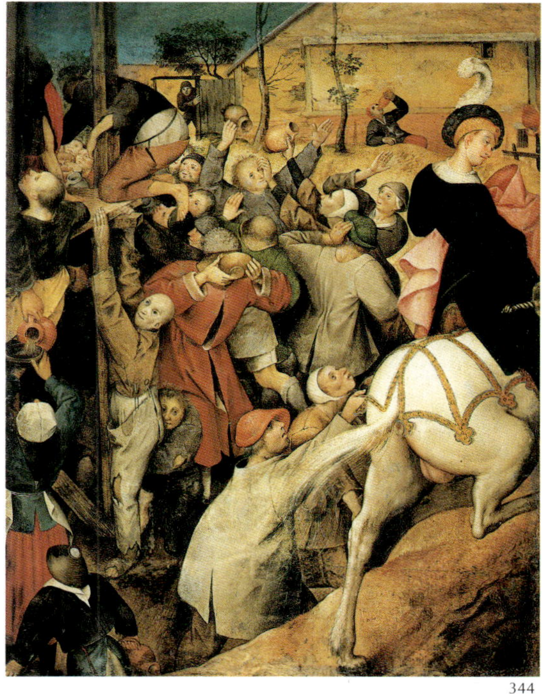

344. Pieter Bruegel the Younger (?), *The Wine of St. Martin* (fragment), end of the sixteenth century. Distemper on linen, 36¼ x 29⅞ in. (92 x 73.5 cm). Vienna, Kunsthistorisches Museum

345. Anonymous, *The Wine of St. Martin*, after Pieter Bruegel, first half of the seventeenth century (?). Oil on canvas, 57⅞ x 106⅛ in. (147 x 269.5 cm). Brussels, Musées royaux des Beaux-Arts de Belgique, Heulens-Van der Meiren gift

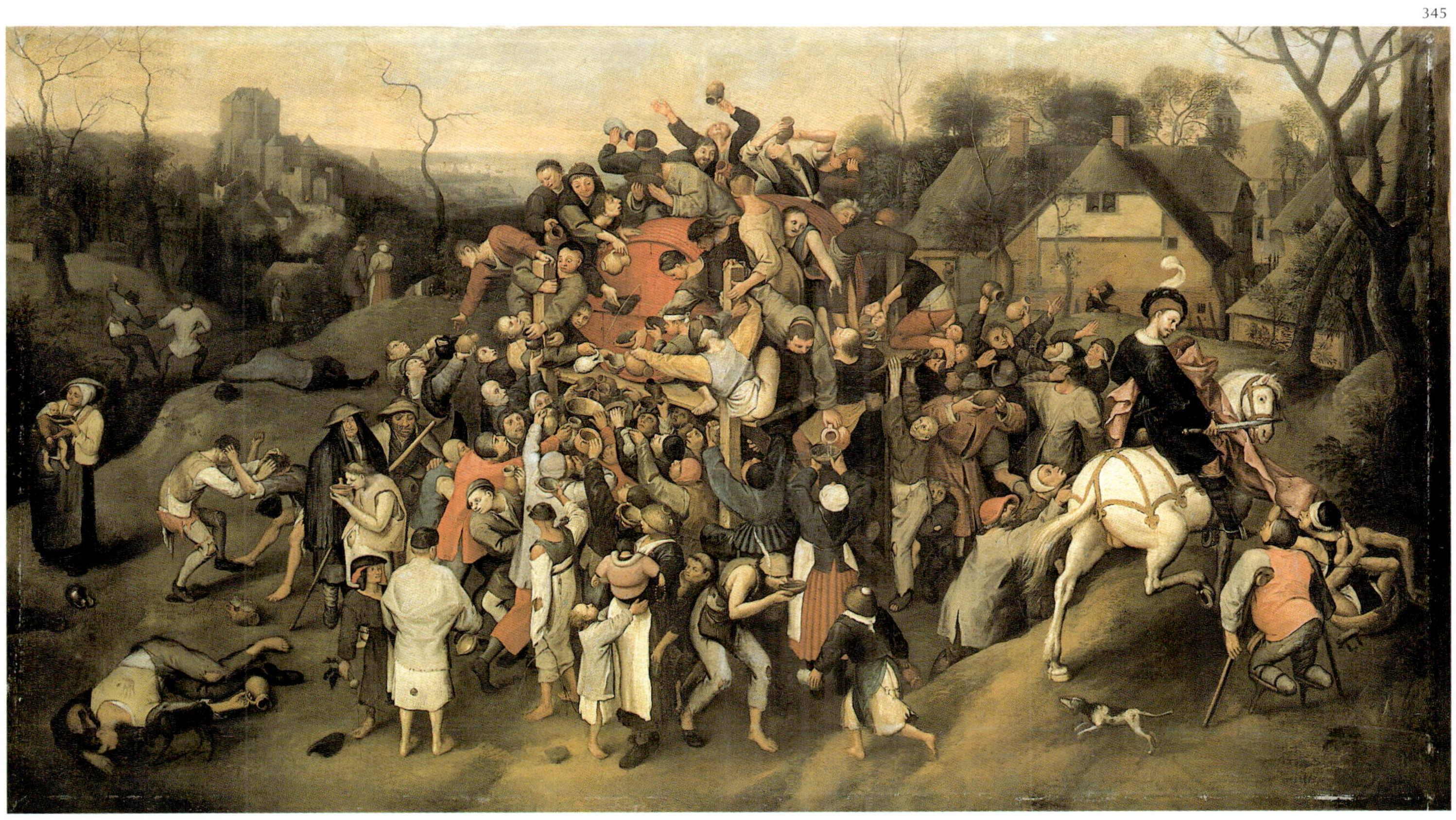

Baltens's monogrammed work in the Brussels museum, the spirit of that painting may confirm the theory.

Among religious subjects, apart from *The Ascent to Calvary* already mentioned, there is the problem of the *Crucifixion*. The subject is mentioned in Archduke Ernest's inventory at no. 16 under the title *Christi Creutzigung*. Nothing is known of this work, unless it is in fact the very beautiful, powerful, and moving painting Bruegel the Younger made in 1615, which shows a bird's-eye view and belongs to the Coppée collection in Brussels, versions of which hang in the Antwerp museum (fig. 336) and elsewhere.[33] Finally, in the same stylistic vein as the *Peasants' Brawl* in the Rubens Collection, three works stand out for their dynamism, sense of space, volumes and vacuums, their vistas to the horizon, and the facial type of the characters that are thrust into the foreground. These paintings belong to the last period and convey a pessimistic vision close to that of *The Misanthrope* or *The Blind Leading the Blind*. They are *The Bad Shepherd*, which is in Philadelphia (Johnson Collection, fig. 347) and was attributed to Bruegel by Hulin de Loo, before being attributed to Bruegel the Younger. It is an important painting of which René Huyghe, in his *Dialogue Avec le Visible* (Dialogue with the Visible) wrote that the painter "had even glimpsed the rendering of speed … in the panic of the *Shepherd Fleeing the Wolf* in Philadelphia, where the ruts project space backwards, fleeing towards the horizon along the surface of the plain which seems to turn with the curvature of the earth. We will have to wait until the twentieth century and Cassandre's poster *L'Étoile du Nord* to rediscover such a wild streaking."[34] By contrast an instant is fixed, emblematically, in the struggle depicted in *The Good Shepherd*, now in the Kronacker collection in Antwerp (fig. 346), which Fritz Grossmann considered an unfinished painting by the father, completed by Jan.[35] It is known through copies made by Bruegel the Younger, including that signed and dated 1616 which is now in Brussels (Heulens gift). The theme of the good and bad shepherds already made an appearance, as we know, in *The Parable of the Good Shepherd* engraved by Philipp Galle in 1565 (fig. 143). As for *The Attack* or *Peasants Attacked by Mercenaries*, now at the University of Stockholm (fig. 348)—a monumental and tragic work generally attributed to Pieter the son and thought to date from about 1630—cleaning revealed "the remains of an apparently authentic signature and date: M.D.L.VII with BRUEGEL written beneath" which in 1980 led Grossmann to consider attributing the work to the master.[36] Under the circumstances, an in-depth examination is essential.

Subjects depicted in engravings can also serve as starting points or reference points leading to lost works. Most notably *Rustic Wedding Dance*, engraved by Pieter van der Heyden about 1566, inspired countless paintings by Bruegel the Younger and others. *The Witch at Mallegem* of 1559 and *The Dean of Renaix* (a print of doubtful attribution, dated 1557) may have spawned depictions of the excision of the stone of madness. *Kermis at Hoboken* (about 1559) and *The Kermis of St. George* (about 1561) served as models for Bruegel the Younger among others. *Skating Scene in front of St. George's Gate in Antwerp*, of which a signed drawing dated 1558 survives,[37] was copied by Pieter the Younger and Martin van Cleve.[38]

The names of Baltens and Van Cleve demonstrate that the influence of such works was not confined to Bruegel's sons, who propagated them, but that the study of "Bruegelesque" artists is a subject in itself, all the more complex because

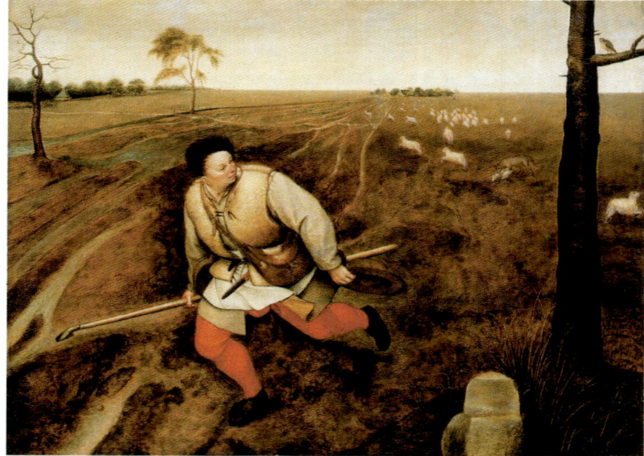

346. Attributed to Pieter Bruegel, *The Good Shepherd*, ca. 1569 (?). Oil on panel, 15¾ x 21¼ in. (40 x 54 cm). Antwerp, private collection

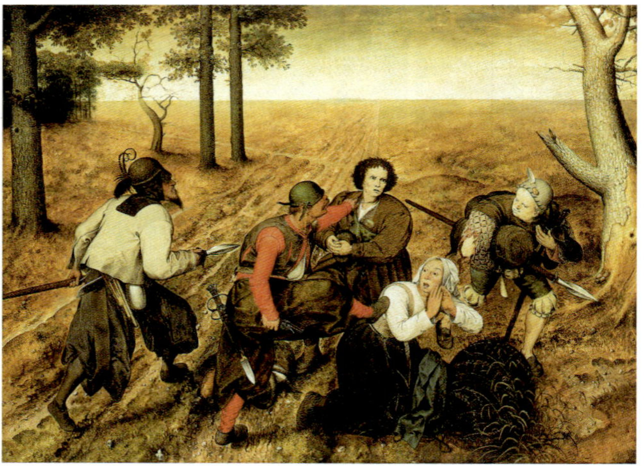

347. Pieter Bruegel the Younger, *The Bad Shepherd*, ca. 1575–1600. Oil on panel, 24¼ x 34⅛ in. (61.6 x 86.7 cm). Philadelphia, The Philadelphia Museum of Art, John G. Johnson Collection

348. Attributed to Pieter Bruegel, *The Attack* or *Peasants Attacked by Mercenaries*, ca. 1567 (?). Oil on panel, 37 x 49¼ in. (94 x 125 cm). University of Stockholm

304

it cannot be reduced to a single popular theme. Already in Bruegel's century certain names stand out through influences, parallels, and points in common. Thus Jacob Grimmer, an Antwerp landscape artist who was enrolled as a master in 1547, learned from Patenier and Bruegel. Hans Bol, miniaturist and painter of landscapes and cityscapes who made *The Fall of Icarus* (fig. 329), completed the *Four Seasons* series of engravings, begun by Bruegel in 1568 with his drawings *Spring* and *Summer*, and also made a series of paintings of the same subject. Gillis Mostaert shared with Bruegel the Bosch tradition and love of landscape. The closeness of the brothers Lucas and Martin Valckenborch is demonstrated by their kermises, seasons, and towers of Babel. Among the artists born around the middle of the century we should mention Gillis van Coninxloo, Lodewijk Toeput, the brothers Matthias and Paul Bril—who are close by their sense of nature in both painting and drawing—and also Karel van Mander, the historian himself, who made a drawing entitled *Flemish Kermis* (Paris, École nationale supérieure des beaux-arts, fig. 349). After 1560 Tobias Verhaecht was born: another landscape painter, he made several towers of Babel, and was Rubens's master.

Artists closely linked to Bruegel's drawings are also worthy of note: Jacob Savery, to whom several drawings of landscapes have been re-attributed; his younger brother Roelandt, who made the 84 drawings known as "naer het leven"; Jacques de Gheyn, who made drawings inspired by Bruegel, landscapes, and scenes of witchcraft; and Joos van Liere, to whom the *Small Landscapes* series is attributed. All these bear witness to Bruegel's influence, and to them we can add the paintings of Roelandt Savery such as *Plundered Village* of 1604, the paintings and drawings of Pieter Stevens, and the *Seasons* of Abel Grimmer—not forgetting the kermises and village or forest scenes of David Vinckboons.

In the seventeenth century—aside from Bruegel's descendants Jan Bruegel the Younger and Ambrosius, sons of Jan Bruegel, and David Teniers, Jan's son-in-law, who took up many Bruegel-inspired subjects, adapted them to the tastes of his day, and perpetuated them—we should mention Adriaen Brouwer for his landscapes and genre subjects, although these were depicted with his own genius and intensity, and Joos de Momper the Younger whose huge landscapes, both lyrical and impressionistic, include *The Tempest* in Vienna (fig. 323), attributed to him today although a few years ago it was thought to be by Bruegel. In the vast output of seascapes, landscapes, genre subjects, and biblical scenes, echoes of Bruegel can be seen in Peeters, Van Alsloot, Craesbeek, and Francken. The name of Sebastian Vrancx stands out however for his *Proverbs*, his brawls, and his battle scenes. In the great landscapes painted at the end of his life Rubens himself links up again, though in a baroque manner, with the paths Bruegel had opened through nature.

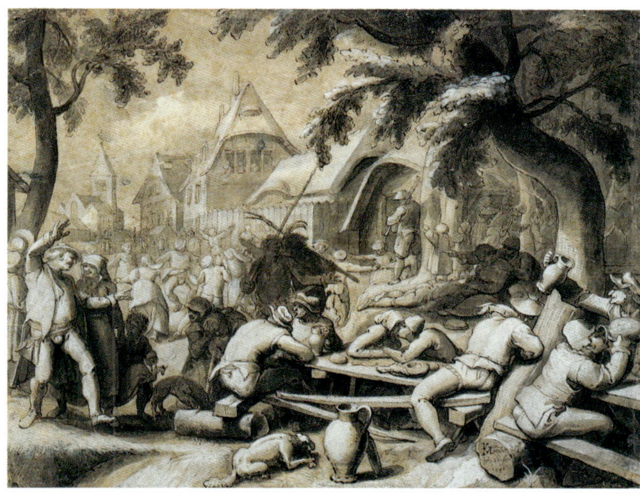

349. Karel van Mander, *Flemish Kermis*, 1591. Ink and wash, heightened with white, 13³⁄₈ x 17¹⁄₂ in. (34.1 x 44.5 cm). Paris, École nationale supérieure des beaux-arts

FROM THE WRITINGS OF THE SIXTEENTH AND SEVENTEENTH CENTURIES TO THE SILENCE OF THE EIGHTEENTH

Such is the story the images tell. As for written records, they convey the rising curve of Bruegel's fame. However, they are few. Immediately after Bruegel's death the eulogy by Dominicus Lampsonius (fig. 350) in his *Effigies of the Famous*

350

351

350. Portrait of Dominicus Lampsonius. Engraving. Paris, Bibliothèque nationale de France, print room

351. Philipp Galle, *Portrait of Abraham Ortelius*, 1595. Engraving on copper. Antwerp, Museum Plantin-Moretus

Painters of 1572, ends thus: "you deserve from all quarters and from all people praise and rewards in no way inferior to those granted to any other artist."[39] About 1600 a new edition of the engravings added a quatrain which freed Bruegel, in a sense, from the reference to a forerunner implied in Lampsonius's original question: "What is this new Hieronymus Bosch [bestowed upon the] world?" It read:[40] "This is the celebrated BRUEGEL: in life, he made the great Mother of all things fear she would be surpassed; in death, that she would herself die. Ah! If art could depict [his] character and [his] spirit, no painting on earth would be more beautiful."

This mastery of Bruegel's had already been asserted by Abraham Ortelius (fig. 351), as we know, in his *Album Amicorum*, which begins with the words: "No one will ever deny that Pieter Bruegel was the most accomplished painter of his century ... And in truth I could call him not the best of painters, but nature's painter."[41] The words of a friend, or a subjective judgment? Giovanni Lomazzo, an Italian painter and writer born in Milan in 1538, who became blind at the age of 33, published a treatise of art and painting in 1584 in which he wrote, with objectivity, of Flemish paintings: "they are admirable, and the painters who made them, Gillis Mostaert and Pieter Bruegel, deserve no little praise."[42]

At the beginning of the seventeenth century, Karel van Mander's *Schilder-Boeck* added its information and comments with which we are now familiar, while the Belgian Jesuit Carolus Scribani, in his book *Antverpia* of 1610, compared Bruegel to the celebrated Greek painter Parrhasius of Ephesus, stating: "non erit inferior Petrus Bruegelius."[43] The English poet Robert Herrick, brilliant follower of Ben Jonson and chaplain to the duke of Buckingham on the latter's expedition to the Île de Ré in 1627, encouraged his nephew, a young painter, to follow the examples of Raphael, Titian, Tintoretto, Bruegel, Coxcie, Holbein, Rubens, and Van Dyck.[44]

Cornelis de Bie, in his *Gulden Cabinet* (Golden Room) published in Antwerp in 1661, and Isaac Bullart in his *Académie des Sciences et des Arts* (Academy of Sciences and Arts) published in Paris in 1682, comment on the information given by Van Mander. The portraitist Joachim von Sandrart, a pupil of Aegidius Sadeler who engraved the allegorical effigy of Bruegel in 1606, was a tireless traveler and also a writer on art, witness his *Teutsche Academie* of 1675 and 1679. "Leaving aside Vasari, it is the most monumental book any artist has ever devoted to art," wrote Germain Bazin.[45] In it Sandrart speaks of Bruegel in eulogistic terms, describing him as "skilful and exact in the way he depicts everything with a brush, as well as his own inventions. He was regarded as outstanding in the arrangement of his figures and the attractiveness of his pen drawings.[46] Quoted by Félibien—"the old Brugle, of whom you have heard so much"—in his celebrated *Entretiens* (Conversations), published in Paris from 1666, Florent Le Comte suggests that "there were some Princes among his ancestors," speaks especially of "all the amusing and comical mannerisms with which the genius of this great man was so full," and emphasizes in his *Cabinet des Singularitez* (Room Full of Oddities) of 1699: "If Pieter Bruegel was the Callot of his time, Callot was the Pieter Bruegel of his."[47] For his part Roger de Piles, painter, writer, and diplomat, who does not weigh Bruegel in his *Balance des*

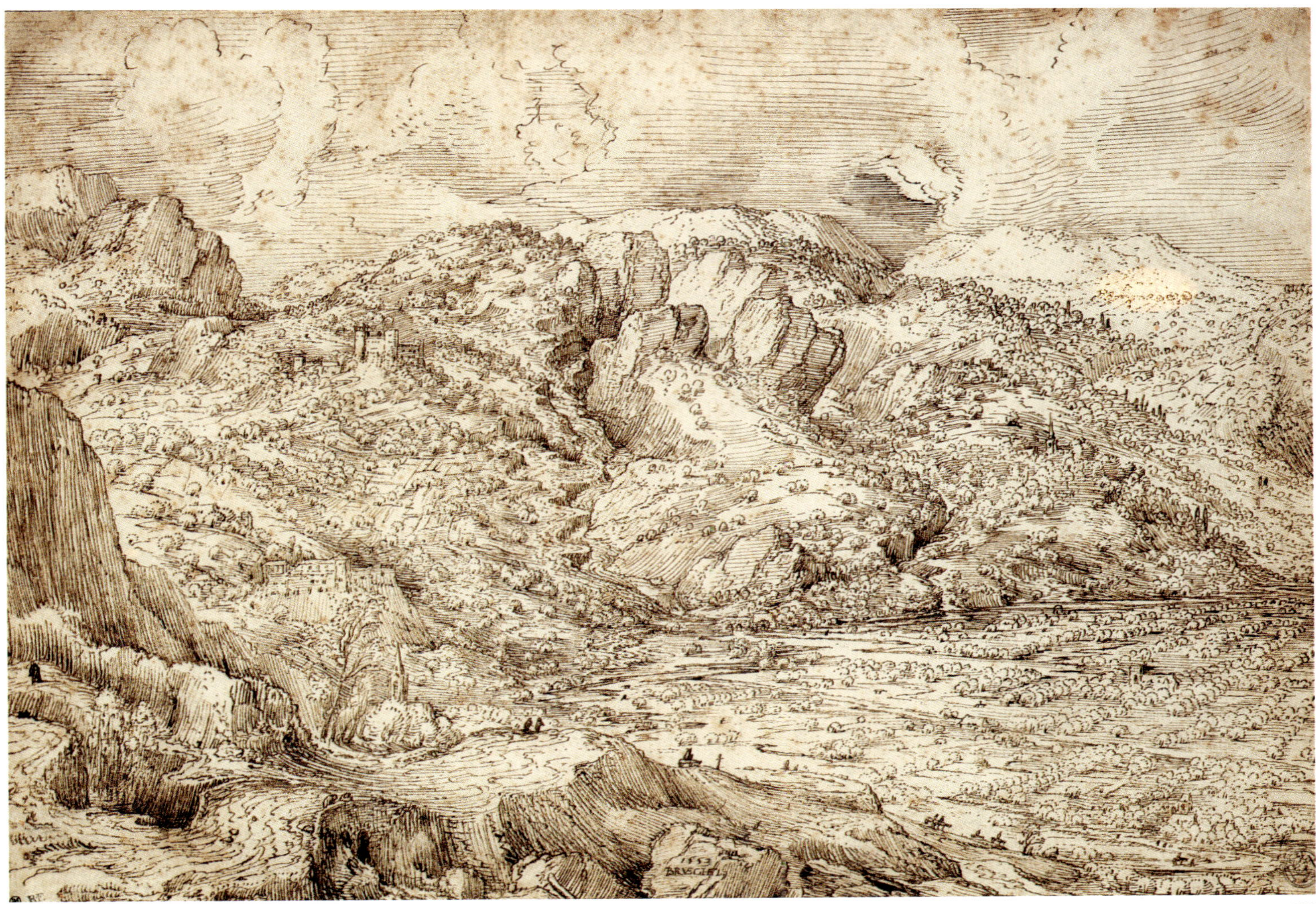

352

352. Pieter Bruegel, *Alpine Landscape*, 1553.
Pen and brown ink, 9¼ x 13½ in. (23.6 x 34.3 cm).
Paris, Louvre, graphic arts department

Peintres (Painters Weighed in the Balance), which is in his *Cours de Peinture par Principes* (Treatise on the Principles of Painting) of 1708, nevertheless calls attention to his gift for landscape and power of expression.[48]

The decline of Bruegel's reputation gathered speed in the Enlightenment! The birth of academies in Europe had already led to Bruegel being removed from the rank of artists regarded as models.[49] Consequently, writers on art such as the Dutchman Arnold Houbraken in his *Groote Schouwburg* (Great Theater) of 1718 and the Italian Pellegrino Antonio Orlandi in *Abecedario Pittorico* (Directory of Painters) of 1719 respectively refer to "buffoonery" and "burlesque and ridiculous subjects" although the latter does not ignore "color and drawing that were noble and worthy of a master."[50] And Jean-Baptiste Descamps, in his *Vie des Peintres* (Lives of the Painters) also reduces Bruegel to peasant festivities, "born to this kind of subject, he would have been its undisputed master were it not for Teniers."[51] No further comment.

Fortunately, there were also collectors of drawings. Pierre Jean Mariette wrote: "I saw at M. Crozat's two drawings by the elder Bruegel which I think were made in Italy. They are views of the Alps mountains; they bear the date 1553 and are superbly beautiful in their detail." Mariette, who at the time, in 1741, was compiling the Crozat sale catalogue, felt compelled to buy them, for to his eyes they were as beautiful as Titians (fig. 352).[52] The financier Crozat was the most famous collector in France in the eighteenth century, having bought works notably from Queen Christina of Sweden and Everhard Jabach. Mariette would not have seen eye to eye with the English painter Sir Joshua Reynolds who, while he acknowledged Bruegel's ideas, did not, apparently, think much of his technique.[53]

FROM BAUDELAIRE TO ENSOR

The nineteenth century opened under the banner of Napoleonic centralization, and the Bruegel paintings in Vienna were taken to the Louvre. In the process *The Harvest* was confiscated by a French general and thus separated from the rest of the *Seasons*, eventually going to America.[54] In 1814 Goethe recognized Bruegel's importance as a landscape painter.[55] But it is Charles Baudelaire who deserves the credit for grasping the breadth of Bruegel's genius. In 1857, not without humor, he wrote: "Everyone knows the old and unique creations of Bruegel the Joker who should not be confused, as several writers do, with Hell Bruegel. That there is a certain logic to them, a determination to be eccentric, a method in the strangeness, is not in doubt. But it is equally certain that this bizarre talent comes from something higher than some kind of artistic dare. In the fantastic paintings of Bruegel the Joker all the power of hallucination is displayed. What artist could produce such monstrously paradoxical works unless he was driven from the outset by some unknown force? In art, it is too often overlooked that what is under the control of man's will is much smaller than people believe." The reaction of a romantic, to be sure, but only initially. For Baudelaire goes on to say that Bruegel's work, "which our century—for which nothing is difficult to explain thanks to its dual quality of incredulity and ignorance—would describe simply as fantasy and caprice, contains, it seems to me, a sort of *mystery*. The latest work of certain doctors, who have at last discerned the need to explain a multitude of historic and miraculous events other than by convenient means of the Voltairian school, which saw nothing but clever deception in all things, has not yet unraveled all the mysteries of the mind. Now, I defy anyone to explain the diabolic and comical cornucopia of Bruegel the Wag other than by a sort of special, satanic grace. If you like you could say madness or hallucination rather than special grace, but the mystery would remain almost as dark. This collection of works spreads a sort of contagion; Bruegel the Joker's antics make us giddy. How can a human mind have contained so much devilry and so many marvels, created and described so many terrifying absurdities."[56]

This text, published under the title *Quelques Caricaturistes Étrangers* (Some Foreign Caricaturists)—that is, Hogarth, Cruikshank, Goya, Pinelli, and Bruegel—reveals the poet's orientation when these pages and others were republished in his *Curiosités Esthétiques* (Aesthetic Curiosities). Nevertheless, his knowledge of Bruegel was inevitably limited. In *Pauvre Belgique* (Poor Belgium), written after his unfortunate stay from 1864 to 1866, he wrote, after a visit to the

museum in Brussels: "Velvet [Jan] Bruegel/Bruegel the Elder? (see Arthur)/
Bruegel the Joker." This list of three names, which is repeated, and the mention of
Arthur (Arthur Stevens, who must have been able to provide some information),
show his confusion over the identification of works, rendered all the more
difficult—we can say in his defense—by the fact that *The Fall of the Rebel Angels*
(fig. 114) was acquired in 1846 under the name of Hell Bruegel, as was *The
Massacre of the Innocents* (fig. 353) in 1830. His judgment, which conveys how
he was challenged by the last work, is brief and to the point: "Massacre of the
innocents. A town in winter. Entry of soldiers. White ground. Persian profiles."[57]

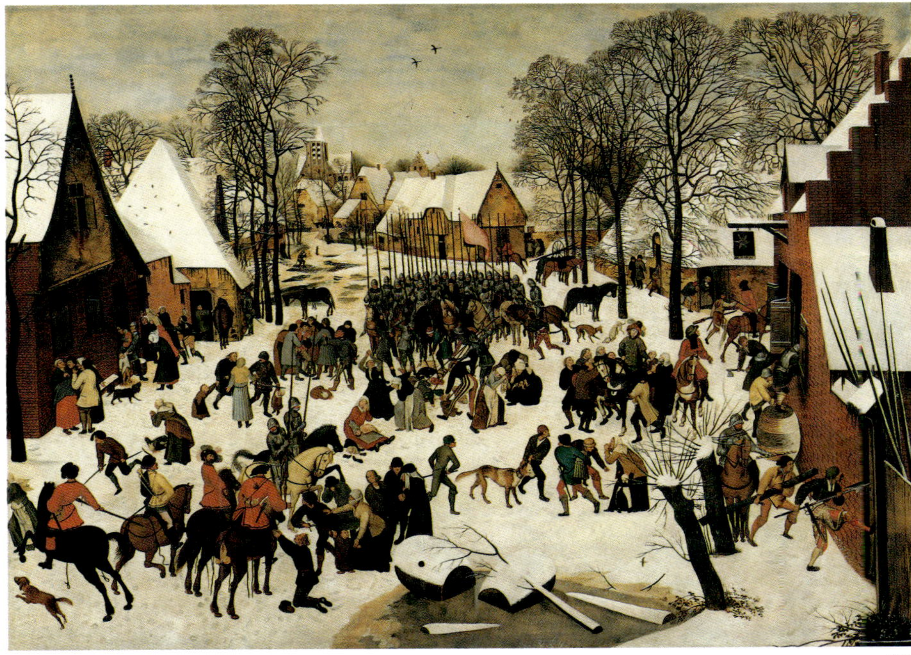

353

About ten years later, in 1875, Eugène Fromentin wrote in his journals a
detailed account of his visits to the same museum, and he barely noticed Bruegel.
Later, in his *Maîtres d'Autrefois* (Masters of the Past), he only saw him as "the
inventor of *genre*, a genius of the land."[58] The works do not even seem to have
made an impression on Hippolyte Taine. Sometimes silence or indifference are
as interesting as in-depth study. Taine—whose sense of particularism, of an art
dominated by the influence of the land and climate, cannot be doubted, and
who in 1869 made perfectly clear the failure of the Flemish school of Italian-style
painting—describes the development of sixteenth-century painting merely by
mentioning "the Bruegels" among "Jan Metsys, Van Hemessen … Vinckeboons,
the three Valkenburgs, Pieter Neefs, Paul Bril."[59] Taine, who taught at the École
nationale des beaux-arts in Paris from 1864, confirmed in *Philosophie de l'Art*
(The Philosophy of Art) some twenty years later: "It took a new flood of national
inspiration that blotted out foreign imports and restored life to the instincts of race

353. Pieter Bruegel the Younger, *The Massacre of the Innocents*,
1604 (?). Oil on panel, 47½ x 65¾ in. (120.5 x 167 cm).
Brussels, Musées royaux des Beaux-Arts de Belgique

for Flemish art to regain its vigor and achieve its goal. Only then, with Rubens and his contemporaries, did the original idea of the ensemble resurface; the elements in art, which had only been grouped together to contradict each other, combined to complement each other, and valid works took the place of dwarves."[60] Of Bruegel, there is no mention.

We must turn to a Belgian painter to reconnect with the Flemish renaissance: to Henri Leys, from Antwerp, for whom the term "pre-Rubensism" was coined.[61] This rather sentimental history painter, who met with considerable success in Brussels, Paris, and London, declared his taste in 1868 when he painted *The Workshop of Frans Floris* with extreme meticulousness. Oddly, his admiration for the Italian-inspired antithesis of Bruegel did not prevent him from appreciating Bruegel himself, or from possessing copies of his work, including *The Blind Leading the Blind*—for which the Louvre paid a hefty price at Leys's sale in Antwerp in December 1893 (fig. 263). Belgian critics deplored this loss, explaining: "It belonged, with four or five other Bruegel works—teeming, copious kermises among which was a *Wedding Feast*, a huge blow-out of stunning vigor—to the collection relinquished by Henri Leys, who loved the Bruegel works and borrowed from them, with the unique splendor of their vermilions, the freedom of their coloring and the precision of their strong expressions."[62] The sale catalogue allows us to identify these Bruegels.[63] *The Blind Leading the Blind* (no. 161) is described as "the same painting subject with a few modifications [that] is in the Naples museum, and there it has acquired great renown. That in the Leys collection, painted in oils, is more intense in color and expression." The fame of this version endures for, in the twentieth century, the French artist Ben used it in a parody (fig. 359). The note to *The Bride's Feast* (no. 182) authorizes the title to be amended to *The Wedding Feast* for it is, indeed, an open-air version of the celebrated painting in Vienna, in a similar format, probably by Pieter Bruegel the Younger.[64] *Kermis* (no. 183) can be attributed to the same artist; more precisely it can be identified as *Kermis with Theater and Procession*: the subject is perfectly described in the catalogue, and the size, 48⅜ x 61⅜ inches (123 x 156 centimeters), may allow it to be identified with a work in a collection in Zurich, which is attributed to Pieter Baltens.[65] A second *Kermis* (no. 184), signed and dated PIERRE BREUGHEL—1626, refers to the work by Bruegel the Elder that was made into an engraving, since it includes a procession into the church, and "the flag of St. George flies" at the inn. It must be *The Kermis of St. George* (fig. 354), which Marlier describes as "one of the most beautiful and most complete by Pieter the Younger, where his character asserts itself in the most brilliant manner."[66] *Skating Scene* (no. 185), signed P. BREUGHEL 1621, must have been, in fact, *Winter*, one of the *Seasons*, the series of four engravings published by Cock in 1570 of which two drawings—*Spring* and *Summer*—are by Bruegel, the two others having been commissioned from Hans Bol after his death. The painting in the Leys collection, from its description, perfectly matches the engraving, for which the drawing made by Bol appears to have been lost. The format—reversed in the note to 16⅛ x 22 inches (41 x 56 centimeters)—could be that of the Grazia version in Brussels (fig. 355).[67] The second *Bride's Feast* (no. 186), signed and dated P. BREUGHEL 1610— which is in fact *Wedding Dance in the Open Air*, its image reversed compared to

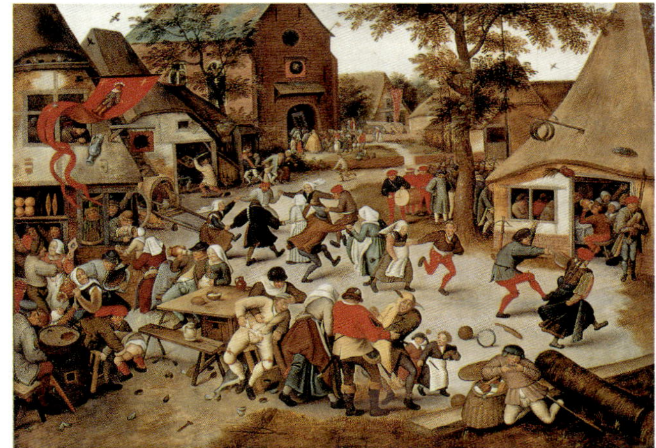

354. Pieter Bruegel the Younger, *The Kermis of St. George*, ca. 1625. Oil on panel, 28⅜ x 40½ in. (72 x 103 cm). Brussels, private collection

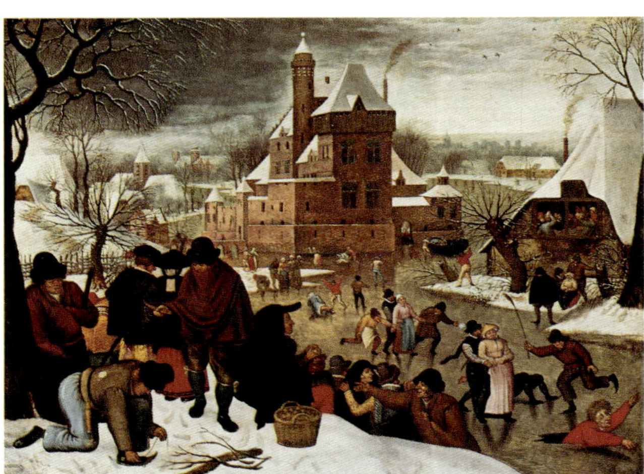

355. Pieter Bruegel the Younger, after Hans Bol, *Winter*, ca. 1620. Oil on panel, 16⅛ x 22¼ in. (41 x 56.5 cm). Brussels, private collection

that of Van der Heyden's engraving after Bruegel—can be compared to a version of the same date and similar format, exhibited in Amsterdam in 1934.[68] Finally, it should be noted that art lovers, in 1893, valued works according to the rarity of the subjects depicted, for the price paid for the six paintings was 18,100, 6,000, 1,700, 5,000, 3,500, and 1,000 francs respectively, according to a sale catalogue annotated at the time. These figures are reliable because *The Blind Leading the Blind*, now in the Louvre, fetched the price indicated.

The collection was well known, and Félicien Rops had already mocked it in his caricature *Uylenspiegel au Salon* (Uylenspiegel at the Art Exhibition) in 1857: "A Bruegel" [fake, naturally] "Mr Lies's collection," no. 695 in the catalogue.[69] The satirical drawing targets a painting by Joseph Lies entitled *The Enemy Approaches*,[70] but the allusion to the "collection" of Bruegel is aimed at the well-known and almost eponymous Henry Leys. The first was a follower of the second and Baudelaire, who knew them both, compares their names in his *Salon* (Exhibition) of 1859, and remarks: "This displaced letter resembles one of those clever games of chance, which are sometimes as sharp-witted as a man. One is the other's pupil, and they are said to be close friends."[71]

Charles Degroux, one of the first exponents of realism in Belgium, who was often considered the Belgian Millet (the French one too was an admirer of Bruegel), possessed at least four Pieter Bruegels, including one *Christ and the Adulterous Woman*[72] —works by the son, inevitably—while Alfred Stevens, fashionable artist of the Second Empire and habitué of the Parisian boulevards, reproduced on the back wall of his *The Workshop* of 1869 (fig. 356) *The Census at Bethlehem*, also by Bruegel the Younger.[73] Art in the second half of the nineteenth century felt even more the influence of Bruegel, whether in the works of Léon Frédéric, Jakob Smits, and Eugene Laermans, or in that of the members of the first Laethem-Saint-Martin school—Valerius de Saedeleer, Gustave van de Woestyne, and Albert Servaes. Neither should we forget another genius of painting, James Ensor. One example will do: his quotation of Bruegel in the painting *The Execution* of 1893 (fig. 357), where the rock pillar topped by a windmill from *Christ Carrying the Cross* is replaced by a religious building crowned in the same way.[74] These remarks above are only by way of an indication, and by no means exhaustive.

STUDIES, REFERENCES, AND POETRY

It was not until the twentieth century that Bruegel's reputation earned him a place in the history of art. He took his place on the international stage thanks to systematic studies of his works, which were often predicated upon a thesis and consequently open to question both as to their meaning and to their authenticity. In the latter department advances in scientific investigation have removed many uncertainties.

Historical and critical work began in Belgium at the end of the nineteenth century. The first articles by Henry Hymans were published in the *Gazette des Beaux-Arts* in 1890 and 1891, and his study "'Margot L'Enragée,' un Tableau Retrouvé de Pierre Breughel le Vieux" ('Dulle Griet,' a Newly-Discovered

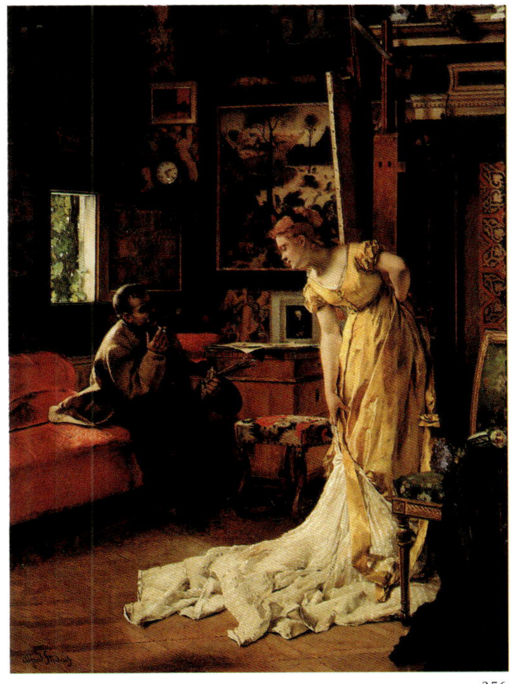

356

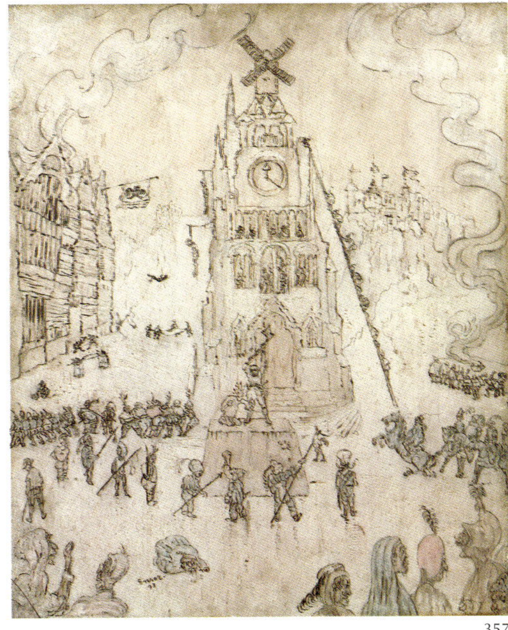

357

356. Alfred Stevens, *The Workshop*, 1869. Oil on panel, 37 x 28 in. (94 x 71 cm). Brussels, Musées royaux des Beaux-Arts de Belgique

357. James Ensor, *The Execution*, 1893. Oil, ink, and pencil on panel, 15 3/4 x 12 3/4 in. (40 x 32.5 cm). Germany, private collection

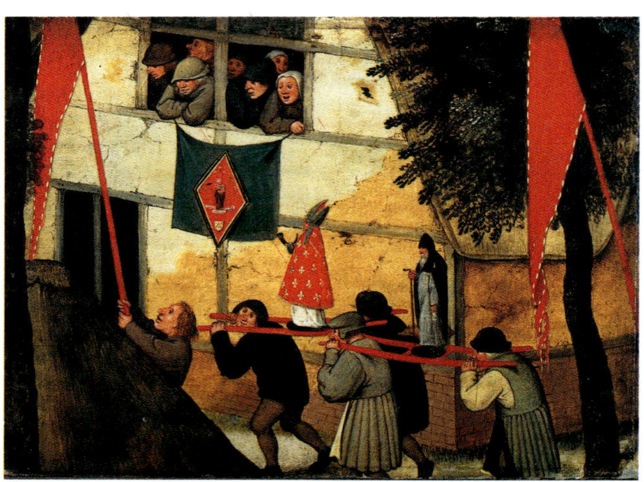

358. Pieter Bruegel the Younger, *Procession* (fragment),
ca. 1615. Oil on panel, 10⅜ x 14⅜ in. (26.5 x 36.5 cm).
Brussels, Musées royaux des Beaux-Arts de Belgique

Painting by Pieter Bruegel the Elder) dates from 1897. The exhibition of Flemish paintings held in Bruges in 1902 rehabilitated the long-neglected art of northern Europe, and allowed Georges Hulin de Loo, one of the architects of this revival, to write in *Catalogue Critique* (Critical Catalogue), in his note to *The Census at Bethlehem*: "The last of the 'gothics' and the first of the 'moderns,' Pieter Bruegel is one of the greatest figures in the history of Art."[75]

From that moment on, monographs and catalogues proliferated: René van Bastelaer and Georges Hulin de Loo in Brussels in 1907; in Vienna, a major center for Bruegel collections, Alex Romdahl in 1904–05; Max Dvorak, Gustav Glück and, later, Charles de Tolnay and Fritz Grossmann; in Berlin, Max J. Friedländer devoted a monograph to Bruegel in 1921 and, in 1937, the last volume of his monumental *Altniederländische Malerei*. The rise of Bruegel's reputation among critics in the twentieth century is reflected in the bibliography of this book.[76]

While art historians have pored feverishly over the many aspects of Bruegel, and many artists have been fascinated by his subjects and imagination, writers and poets have not remained indifferent either. Few bodies of work elicited so much comment and so many parallels in twentieth-century literature. On 21 November 1913 Émile Verhaeren—at a conference at the Université des Annales in Paris, where, according to contemporary reports "the eminent Belgian poet was applauded and recalled by the audience"—admitted that he had found in Bruegel the inspiration for his *La Bénédiction de la Mer* (The Blessing of the Sea), which he then read while projecting on to a screen *Procession* (fig. 358), a fragment of a painting now attributed to Bruegel the Younger that hangs in the Brussels museum. On the same occasion he recalled the links between the painter and Charles De Coster through the legendary character Thyl Ulenspiegel, who embodied sixteenth-century Flanders and the defense of freedom.[77] The publication in 1867 of *La Légende d'Ulenspiegel* (The Legend of Ulenspiegel) led to a revival of Belgian literature written in French; and, in 1889 Eugene Demolder, in his *Impressions d'Art* (Impressions of Art) presented Bruegel in his own way, by transposing the *Census* and the *Massacre* into prose.

It was in this spirit that James Ensor, using the ornate, earthy style of which he was so fond, took the floor at a banquet in Brussels in 1924, commemorating the four-hundredth anniversary of Bruegel's birth:

> Let us prostrate ourselves and hail the greatest of our painters. Blaze of pure art warming our hearts; volcano of Cockaigne spewing forth a thousand painterly and other delights; powerful beacon among other beacons; beacon crucified with light; lifesaving beacon; beacon of joy; beacon of comfort; stupendous beacon; beacon that never dims; beacon lighting the infinity of the seas and the earthly horizons; beacon that purifies the world full of laughter; beacon denouncing the world racked with boredom; beacon raised up in splendor; virile beacon; beacon star of gladness; wild beacon; prodigious beacon; beacon of all good *faro* lovers; beacon of smoky inns; beacon garnished with sausages; beacon garnished with lard; beacon of sterling quality; beacon of sailing ships and steamships; beacon of virgins and of woe! To you, Bruegel the Joker, Bruegel of the Marolles, Bruegel of the peasants, of the joyful serfs, of the destitute boors, the plump babies, the pale and skinny, the jabbering

brutal warriors, the large-thighed whores, the big-buttocked gossips, the
gluttonous shrews, the old troopers spitting out their teeth, the devouring
mercenaries, the screaming patients, the ignorant doctors, the learned
charlatans, the canine tooth-pullers, the bespectacled misers counting a hundred
thousand écus and the shabby notes of apothecaries with claws, the dreamy
swineherds, the gloomy fishwives, the dangerous cooks, the good-natured
devils with a sting in the tail, the clowning demons, the heroic painters, more
overheated female devils setting lewd monks afire, the damned writhing as
they are roasted, English style, coiled monkeys clad in arabesques, beauties
pawed by the burlesque kings they are tickling, cardinals with blackbirds'
beaks, puffed up lawyers, reddened with lobster, great pinched judges with
pug noses, cauldrons and pots, calves' feet and dripping-pans, proverbs in
light and shade, ironic Babels, astonishing landscapes, ultra-comical birds,
embossed weddings, thick-set brides, fat with kisses, mewing pussy-cats,
mangy dogs spraying the magi, and images, battles, brawls, and destruction....
[all this, as a salute to] ... the good God that belongs to us all, young and
old, great and small, ancient and modern, realists, constructivists, cubists,
expressionists, and Co.[78]

The speech went on and on, the inexhaustible Ensor praising his master for twice
as long again!

Ensor's fantastic paean had its theatrical counterpart in a work by Michel
Ghelderode that had a sixteenth-century Flemish canvas as its background,
brought up to date with lyrical buffoonery, slang, and an expressionist vision.
The playwright who wrote *Barabas* and *Hop Signor!*, which was a success in Paris
in 1947, wrote two works directly inspired by Bruegel: *Les Aveugles* (The Blind)
and, as we know, *La Pie sur le Gibet* (The Magpie on the Gallows). Is that
surprising? Not if we listen to Antonin Artaud in *Le Théâtre et son Double* (The
Theatre and its Double) of 1938: "the disturbing and mysterious 'Dulle Griet' by
Bruegel the Elder, where a torrential red light, though confined to certain parts of
the canvas, seems to well up on all sides, and by I know not what technical process
freezes the viewer's petrified eye a meter from the canvas. And theater is swarming
on all sides. A bustle of life held in check by a circle of white light suddenly
crashes against the nameless depths. A ghastly, grating noise rises above this
bacchanal of grubs where the bruises on human skin are all of different colors.
Real life is white and in motion; hidden life is livid and motionless; it possesses all
the possible attitudes of countless immobility. It is a dumb show, but it speaks
much more than if it had been given a language with which to express itself." And
Artaud, having already mentioned the works of Lucas van Leyden, Goya, Greco,
and Bosch, concludes: "All these paintings have a double meaning, and apart from
their purely painterly side they contain a message and reveal mysterious or terrible
aspects of nature and of the mind."[79]

The closeness of Verhaeren, Ensor, and Ghelderode, as of Felix Timmermans,
who was to transform the painter's life into a novel set in his native region, might
present a reductionist and folksy image of Bruegel. This is denounced by Artaud,
and also by the poet Paul van Ostaijen, an important figure in Flemish literature,
who wrote in 1926: "What is more, the current fad for Bruegel is too driven by a

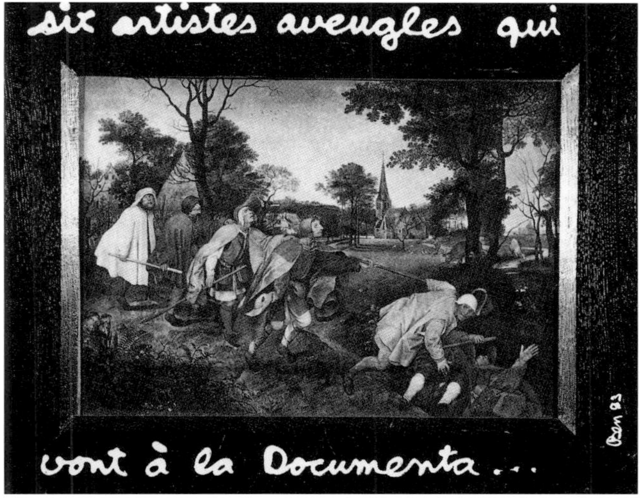

359. Ben, *Six Blind Artists on the Way to the Documenta*,
1993. Mixed media, 19⅝ x 24⅝ in. (50 x 62.5 cm).
Auction at Vuyst, Lokeren, 8 March 1997, no. 507

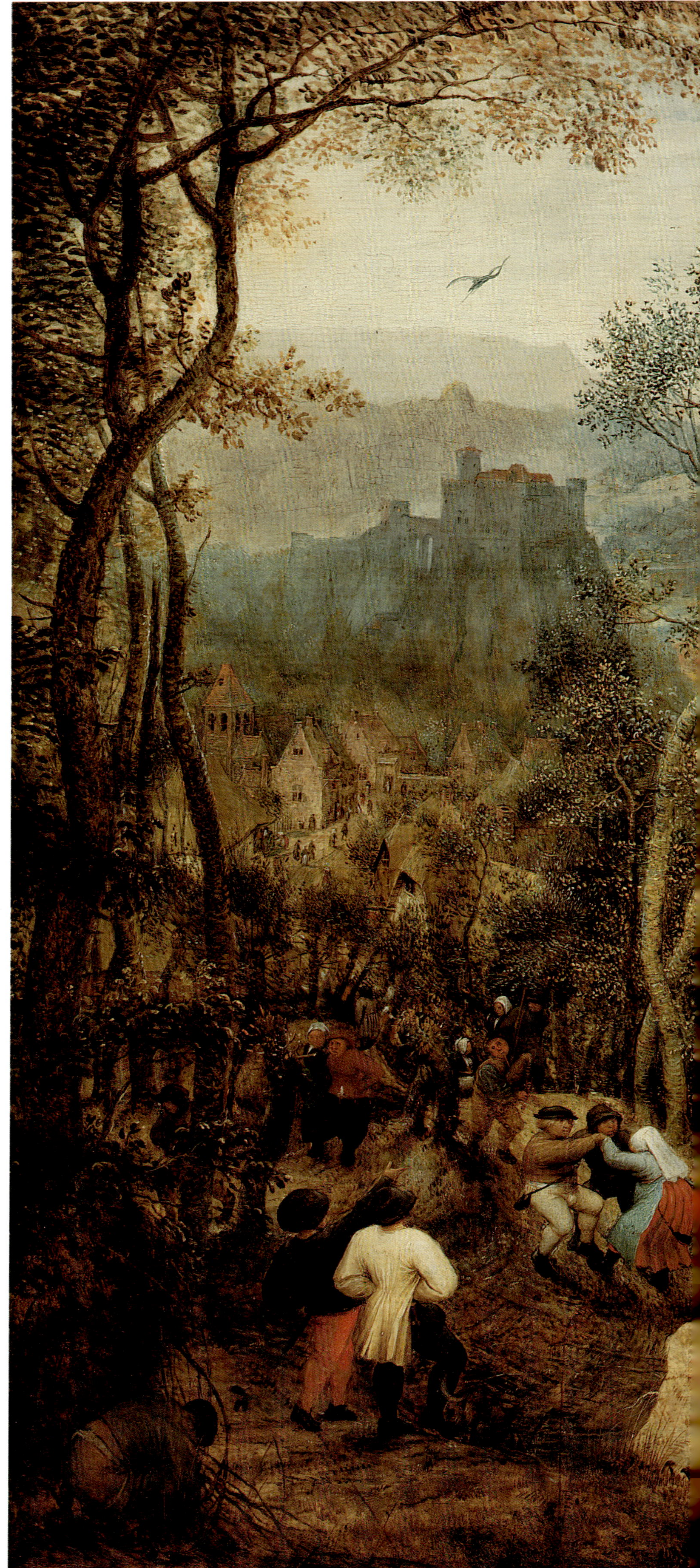

360. Pieter Bruegel, *The Magpie on the Gallows*, 1568. Oil on panel, 18 x 20 in. (45.6 x 50.8 cm). Darmstadt, Hessisches Landesmuseum. Bruegel bequeathed this work to his wife, according to Karel van Mander.

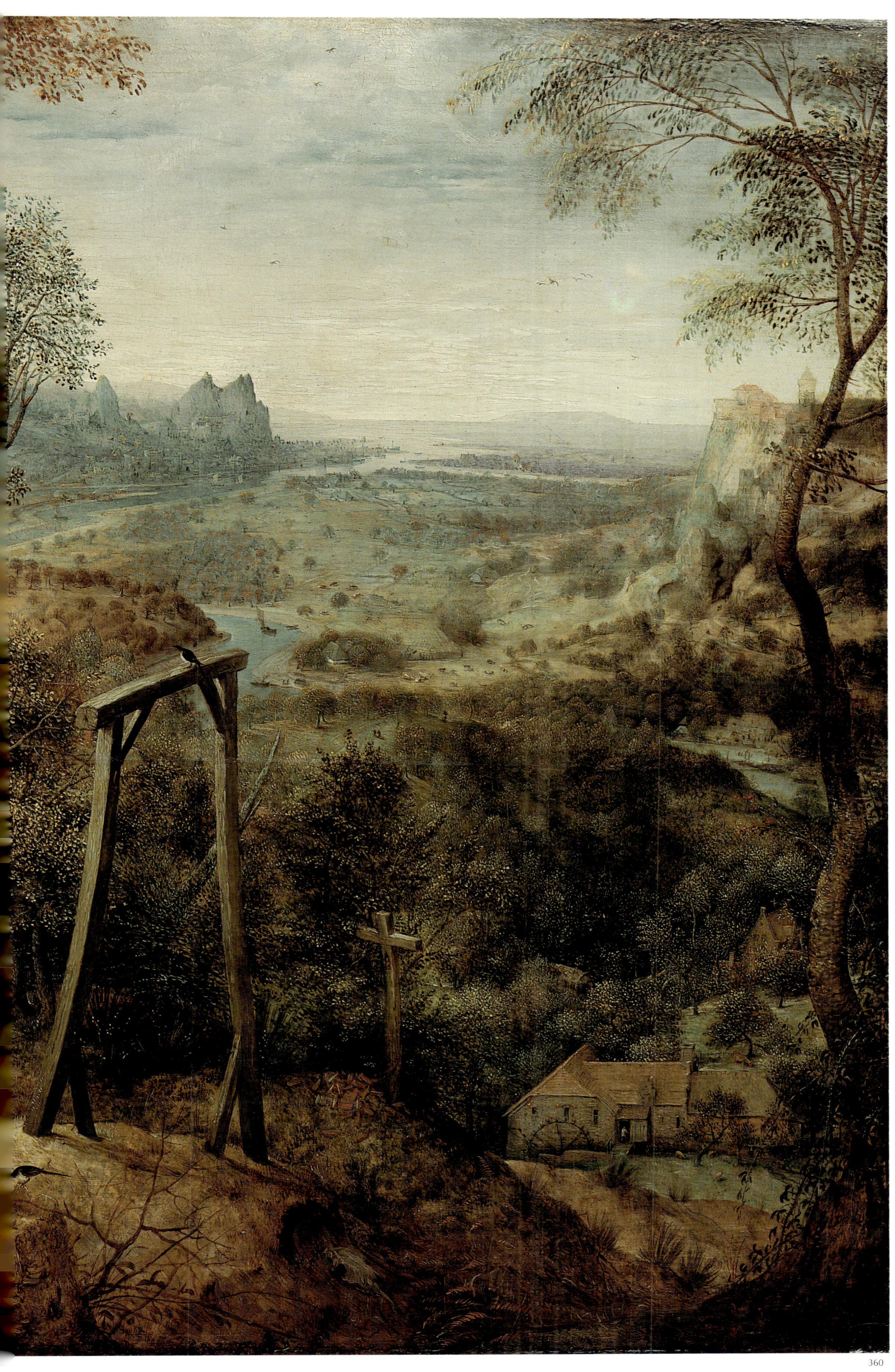

fascination with folk tradition, which leads people to consider as essential certain national elements that are purely decorative. We could almost speak of a cult of the national costume. That is not what matters. What counts is that each race aspires to universality by its own peculiar means."[80]

Would Bruegel have held the attention of Gottfried Benn, Aldous Huxley, Jean de Boschère, Aragon, Marguerite Yourcenar, or Dominique Rolin had he been otherwise? One article was entitled "Pieter Bruegel: Painter for Poets."[81] The title is well founded. An anthology could be built around the subject. Although it is unlikely for chronological reasons (despite what the author says) that Baudelaire's *Les Aveugles* (The Blind), published in 1860, was directly inspired by Bruegel—the version in the Louvre was only acquired after the poet's death, and if Baudelaire went to Leys's house in Antwerp this was not before the summer of 1864—he may have seen a reproduction or an engraving. Furthermore, the painter's vision is rural and leads to the fall, while the writer's is urban and remains horizontal, unless Baudelaire wanted to modify the spirit of the painting, for the images and echoes of Bruegel are multifarious … Examples include the America poet William Carlos Williams—whose *Pictures from Breughel and Other Poems*, a collection published in 1962, refers to a self-portrait, *Landscape with the Fall of Icarus*, *Hunters in the Snow*, *The Adoration of the Magi*, *Peasant Wedding*, *Haymaking*, *The Harvest*, *Wedding Dance in the Open Air*, *The Blind Leading the Blind*, and *Children's Games*—as well as the poems of Hugo Claus and Adonis, without forgetting W. H. Auden's famous *Musée des Beaux Arts* of 1939, where Bruegel is in the forefront from the first verse.[82]

While a certain taste for archaism, which limited emotional intensity, un-doubtedly helped Bruegel's reputation in the twentieth century, the breadth and profound truth of his work, admired in its time, have only found their true fulfillment through the resonances it has set off in later times. And these cannot be in harmony with each other or superimposed. The complexity of the ideas, the deep-seated ambiguity of every image, the personal perception of each individual multiply the appearances and reflections which can only be kept active—that is to say, alive—by the quality of their expression and the power instilled into them, by genius and its potential.

While theories can be kept to a minimum, not all lend themselves to this. The lines of force themselves are not constant. Bruegel the Joker does not inhabit every part of his works, as we know, and in any case humor ranges from witticism to caricature, and plays with mirrors. While the painter experiences the conditions of his time, contemporary events are only a stimulant for an artist, not an end in themselves, for their effect comes to an end when the cause disappears. To want to trap an artist within a given age is to kill him. A work of art glances off its time but does not stay fixed within it; from Altamira to Joan Miró and others, the dream and the reflection go on. Bruegel does not attempt to demonstrate anything using any given subject. "He starts on the outside and works inward" Aldous Huxley wrote of *Christ Carrying the Cross*. "Bruegel determinedly remains a human on-looker." Consequently, he cannot be forgotten "since he makes comments on humanity that still interest us."[83] As a result, he defies all subsequent attempts at classification.

Painting that is truly living and enriching, not only for poets or lovers who seek answers, always offers a sign that can open a way that is both welcoming and distinctive. There are many readings because of the richness of the content, which awakens the mind, begs questions, and stimulates the writer. Thus a contemporary critic, Daniel Dobbels, a thinker and writer, believes that the central mystery in *Flemish Proverbs* of 1559 was the man carrying daylight in a basket, almost in the center of the painting, slightly behind and to the left of the blue cloak (fig. 361).[84] "Hij draagt de dag met manden uit"—literally "he carries daylight outside in baskets." As for the meaning of the proverb, interpretations differ. Is it to waste time on pointless activity, or revealing that which should be hidden?[85] These interpretations do not overlap. In 1994 Danile Dobbels wrote: "There, at the heart of the *Proverbs* (at the heart of the language) is the point of daylight, as real as the point of origin of a language. Bruegel paints what comes to light between a language whose light we cannot see and the profound brightness of a daylight that cannot be described."[86] This is a new and interesting reading, and the writer refers frequently in his essay to Georges Bataille, Jacques Derrida, Gilbert Lascault, Michel Foucault, and Jacques Lacan, thus reinforcing, if that were needed, Bruegel's lasting relevance.

Curiously, however, this bearer of daylight is carrying it from indoors outside, not the opposite, as reality and logic would demand. Indeed, he is leaving a house through a rectangle of brightness—this is truly the world upside down. The exact center of the painting, in line with the blue cloak, is in fact the devil in his dark corner, taking confession (fig. 228). Might this manna of light, coming from within, be the antidote to the poison? Each of us can bring to this what he or she wants, and carries within by way of darkness or light. Bruegel is content to answer or to orientate us, and this dialogue becomes ever richer.

The inventory the painter produces—which is not repetitive, ranging from Noah's ark to contemporary elements—is doubtless drawn from a single source, human behavior, and in *Flemish Proverbs* is seen for the first time assembled in a certain order, whose complexity is happily added to by the weight of its components. If a work of art is an accident, like an individual, whatever the demands of life and the need for logic, the sole consequence of both remains a matter of chance.

This is the result, therefore: The artist—Bruegel in this case—and his work matter much more than the context in which they bloomed and out of which they arose, for without a listener there is no echo and without its specificity, no viewpoint—and no creative interchange.

Such was Bruegel, and such he remains today.

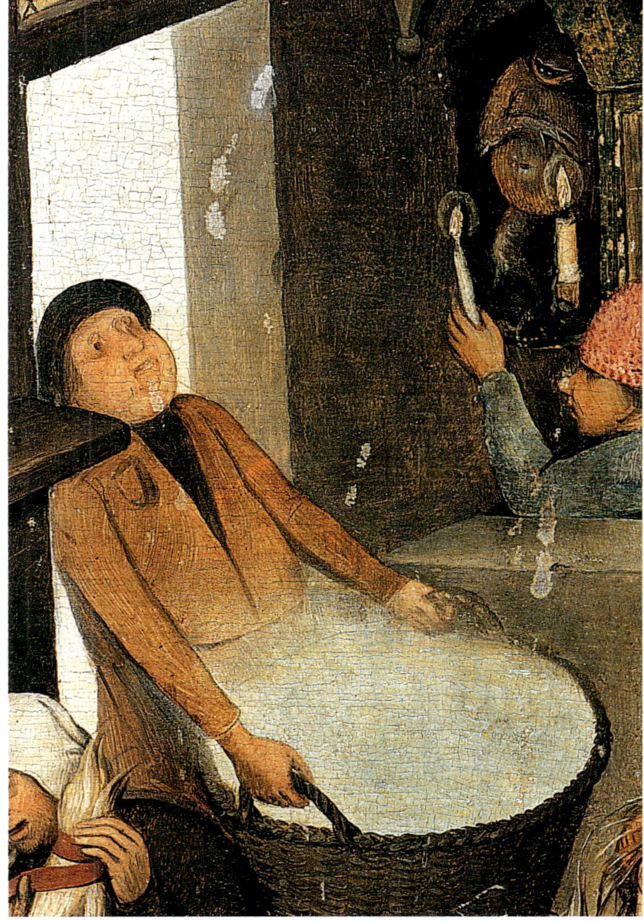

361. Pieter Bruegel, *Flemish Proverbs,* detail: *The Bearer of Daylight,* 1559. Oil on panel, 46 x 64³⁄₈ in. (117 x 163.5 cm). Berlin, Staatliche Museen, Gemäldegalerie

TIMELINE

BRUEGEL		POLITICS — RELIGION — ECONOMICS		PAINTING —
		EUROPE	*NETHERLANDS*	*EUROPE*
	1520–25	Excommunication of Luther, Edict of Worms (1520–21)	Margaret of Austria governor starting in 1508 on; resident at Mechelen	J. Clouet, *Portrait of Francis I*, Paris (ca. 1520–25)
				Birth of Antoine Caron (1521)
	1522	Adrian VI becomes Pope (1522).	Birth of Margaret of Parma (1522)	
	1523		Start of the papal Inquisition (1523)	
	1524			Death of Hans Holbein the Elder (1524)
	1525	Wars in Italy: Battle of Pavia, victory of Charles V over Francis I		
		Death of the German banker Jacob Fugger (1525)		
ca. 1525–30? Birth, place unknown	**1525–30**			
	1526			Titian, *Virgin of the Frari*, Venice (1526)
	1527	Sack of Rome by troops of Charles V (1527)	Birth of Philip II (1527)	Birth of Arcimboldo (1527)
	1528	Switzerland: Zwingli preaches the Reformation at Zurich and Basel (1528).		Death of Albrecht Dürer
				Death of Matthis Grünewald
				Birth of Veronese (1528)
	1529	Diet of Speyer forbids propagation of the Reformation in Germany. Princes and towns protest ("Protestantism").	Peace of Cambrai: Margaret of Austria and Francis I define limits of Franco-Burgundian territory. Placards threaten heretics with death (1529).	L. Cranach the Elder, *Portrait of Luther*, Florence
		Suleiman the Magnificent lays siege to Vienna (1529).		Altdorfer, *The Battle of Issus*, Munich (1529)
	1530		Death of Margaret of Austria (1530)	
	1530–35			
	1531	Switzerland: civil war between Catholic and Protestant cantons. Death of Zwingli. Peace of Kappel. Cantons granted freedom of worship (1531).	Margaret of Hungary governor. Resident in Brussels. Centralization of power. Three collateral councils	Rosso Fiorentino and Primaticcio work at Fontainebleau (ca. 1531–32).
			Antwerp: new stock exchange (1531)	
	1532			
	1533			
	1534	Act of Supremacy recognizes Henry VIII as head of the newly founded Anglican church.	Antwerp: Anabaptists banished (1534)	Death of Bellegambe (ca. 1534)
		In Münster, Anabaptists take power (1534).		Death of Correggio
				Death of Marcantonio Raimondi (1534)

GRAPHIC ARTS *NETHERLANDS*	ARCHITECTURE, SCULPTURE, DECORATIVE ARTS	LITERATURE, PHILOSOPHY, MUSIC	SCIENCE, EXPLORATION
Dürer's visit; stays in Brussels and Antwerp (1520–21) Jan Gossart, *Venus and Cupid*, Brussels (1521) Death of Gerrit David (1523) Death of Joachim J. Patinir (1524) Birth of F. Huys (1525)	Delivery in Rome of the tapestries of *The Acts of the Apostles* by Raphael, woven in Brussels (1519–21)	Death of Josquin Desprès (1521) Death of Jean Lemaire de Belges (1523)	
M. Cock dean of Antwerp guild (1526) Pieter Coecke admitted as a master to Antwerp guild Lucas van Leyden, *The Last Judgment*, Leiden (ca. 1527) Birth of Hans Vredeman de Vries (1527)	P. de Machuca, plan for Charles V's palace in Granada (1526) France: château of Azay-le-Rideau (1518–27) D. de Siloe, new plans for Granada cathedral (1528) Death of the sculptor P. Vischer (1529)	Vives, *De Subventione Pauperum* Erasmus, expanded edition of *Colloquia* Birth of Palestrina (ca. 1526) Adriaen Willaert choirmaster at San Marco, Venice Death of Machiavelli (1527) Anna Bijns, *Refreinen* Baldassare Castiglione, *Il Libro del Cortegiano* (The Courtier; 1528)	Cortez, conquest of Mexico (1519–27) Birth of the Flemish geographer Ortelius (1527) G. Budé, *Commentarii Linguae Graecae* First Portuguese expedition to Japan (1529)
Martin van Reymerswaele, *Two Tax Collectors*, London (ca. 1530) Death of Quentin Metsys (1530)	Andrea da Sangallo, first two floors of Palazzo Farnese in Rome (ca. 1530)		G. Agricola (German mineralogist), *De Re Metallica* Foundation of the Collège de France (1530)
Jan van Scorel, *Portrait of a Young Boy*, Rotterdam (1531) Bernard van Orley court painter to Mary of Hungary Death of Jan Gossart Birth of Martin de Vos (1532) Death of Cornelis Engelbrechtsz. (1533) Death of Lucas van Leyden (1533)	Netherlands: house of the guild of free boatmen in Ghent L. Blondeel, chimneypiece, hall of the Franc, Bruges (1528–31) France: church of Saint-Eustache, Paris A. Berreguete, *Altarpiece of San Benito*, Valladolid (1526–32) A. van Mulken, palace of the prince-bishops, Liège (1526–33) Michelangelo, Medici tombs, Florence (1520–34)	Rabelais, *Pantagruel* Birth of Orlande de Lassus (1532) Birth of Montaigne (1533) Rabelais, *Gargantua* (1534)	R. Estienne, *Thesaurus Linguae Latinae* (1532)

BRUEGEL		POLITICS — RELIGION — ECONOMICS		PAINTING —
		EUROPE	*NETHERLANDS*	*EUROPE*
	1535	Charles V takes Tunis Massacre of the Anabaptists of Münster and first edicts against heretics in France (1535)		Hans Holbein the Younger at the court of Henry VIII (ca. 1535)
	1535–40 **1536**		Northern Netherlands: moves towards political organization; spread of the Reformation Placards restrict the staging of plays by rhetorical societies (1536)	
	1537			
	1538			Death of Altdorfer (1538)
	1539		Ghent: socio-economic unrest; decline of the cloth industry and pressure for the city's autonomy (1539)	
	1540	Ignatius Loyola founds the Company of Jesus, which fights Protestantism England: execution of Thomas Cromwell (1540)	Ghent: intervention by Charles V and suppression of autonomist tendencies (1540)	Corneille de Lyon, *Portrait of Clément Marot*, Paris (ca. 1540) Death of Jean Clouet (ca. 1540) Death of Rosso Fiorentino Death of Parmigianino (1540)
	1540–45 **1541**	Calvin introduces Reformation to Geneva (1541).		Michelangelo, *The Last Judgment*, Vatican, Sistine Chapel (1536–41) Birth of El Greco (1541)
	1542	Franco-Habsburg war: Charles V and Henry VIII against Francis I (1542–44)	Special taxes levied for upkeep of Charles V's army (1542)	
	1543			Death of Hans Holbein the Younger (1543)
	1544		Placards announce government control of publications (1544).	
Presumed start of apprenticeship, in the workshop of Pieter Coecke in Antwerp	**1545**	Council of Trent (1545–63): organization of the Counter-Reformation France: start of persecution of Protestants (1545)	Inquisition strengthened (1545)	Death of Hans Baldung Grien (1545)
	1545–50 **1546**	Death of Luther E. Dolet, philologist and printer, burned as a heretic in Paris	University of Leuven: publication of index of forbidden books (1546)	Death of J. Romain (1546)

GRAPHIC ARTS	ARCHITECTURE, SCULPTURE, DECORATIVE ARTS	LITERATURE, PHILOSOPHY, MUSIC	SCIENCE, EXPLORATION
NETHERLANDS			
Herri met de Bles enrolled as a master (1535)		Execution of Thomas More (1535)	
Jan van Hemessen, *The Prodigal Son*, Brussels (1536)	France: château of Chambord (1526–36)	John Calvin, *Institutio Religionis Christianae* Death of Erasmus (1536)	E. Dolet, *Commentarii Linguae Latinae* (1536)
Birth of Philipp Galle L. Lombard in Rome Bernard van Orley, cartoons for stained glass windows in church of St. Gudula, Brussels (1537) Death of Joos van Cleve (ca. 1540)	H. van Pede, Audenaarde town hall (1526–37) J. Mone, recorder's house of the Franc, Bruges (1535–37) Tapestry, *Maximilian Hunting*, after Van Orley, Paris (ca. 1538) P. van Wyenhoven, chapel of the Holy Sacrament at St. Gudula, Brussels (1534–39) France: Cardinal Granvelle's palace at Besançon Benvenuto Cellini, saltcellar for Francis I, Vienna (ca. 1540)		Tartaglia (Italian mathematician), *La Nuova Scienza* (The New Science) Serlio, edition of Vitruvius's treatise on architecture (1537) Pieter Coecke: Flemish edition of Vitruvius (1539)
Death of Bernard van Orley (1541) Jan Mostaert, *An Episode in the Discovery of America*, Haarlem (ca. 1542) Lucas Gassel, *The Copper Mine*, Brussels (1544)	 Jean Goujon and Pierre Lescot, rood-screen of Saint-Germain-l'Auxerrois, Paris (ca. 1544) L. Richier, statue of the corpse of René of Châlons, Bar-le-Duc (1544) Netherlands: House of Paradise and House of the Devils, Mechelen (ca. 1540–45)	Clément Marot: French translation of the Psalms and exile in Geneva (1541) The German composer T. Susato music publisher in Antwerp Birth of the Spanish mystic St. John of the Cross (1542) Birth of the English composer William Byrd (ca. 1543) Birth of Torquato Tasso (1544)	Pizarro, Almagro, and P. de Valdivia conquer Peru (1532–41) H. de Soto, exploration west of the Mississippi (1538–41) Mercator, *Globus Terrae* Death of the Swiss physician and chemist Paracelsus (1541) F. Mendez Pinto, establishment of Portuguese warehouses in Japan (1542) Copernicus, *De Revolutionibus Orbium Caelestium* A. Vesalius, *De Humani Corporis Fabrica* (1543) S. Münster, *Cosmographia* (1544) Potosi (Peru): Spanish exploitation of silver mines A. Paré, *Manière de Traiter les Plaies* (The Method for Treating Wounds) J. Cardan, *Ars Magna* (1545)
Birth of Bartolomeus Spranger (1546)			Birth of the Danish astronomer Tycho Brahe (1546)

BRUEGEL		POLITICS — RELIGION — ECONOMICS		PAINTING —
		EUROPE	*NETHERLANDS*	*EUROPE*
Collaboration with Pieter Baltens on altarpiece of the Mechelen guild of glovemakers, 1550–51 Enrolled a master at the guild of St. Luke in Antwerp, 1551 Journey in Italy (1552–53) and first known drawing, signed and dated, 1552 Stay in Rome; name and date of 1553 appear on two engravings by Hoefnagel *Great Landscapes* series of engravings published by Hieronymus Cock in Antwerp, ca. 1555–58 Publication of *Deadly Sins* series, engraved by Pieter van der Heyden, 1558	**1547**	Accession of Edward VI in England Accession of Henri II in France; creation of the Burning Chamber court: systematic persecution of heretics Battle of Mühlberg: victory of Charles V over German Protestant princes (1547)		
	1548			Titian, *Charles V at the Battle of Mühlberg*, Madrid (1548)
	1549		The future Philip II presented to the people of Brussels	The Flemish painter H. Eworth in London (ca. 1549)
	1550		Pragmatic Sanction: regulates succession in the Seventeen Dutch Provinces as an indivisible state tied to the Spanish crown (1549) Placards forbidding secret assemblies and clandestine sermons A. Perrenot de Granvelle, bishop of Arras, counselor to Charles V Work begins on Willebroeck canal (1550)	First School of Fontainebleau (ca. 1530–50)
	1550–55 **1551**			
	1552	Franco-Habsburg war: Henri II against Charles V; French victory (1552)	Between the Sambre and the Meuse: theater of the Franco-Habsburg wars (1552)	Nicolo dell'Abbate in Fontainebleau (1552)
	1553	Accession of Mary Tudor in England (1553)		Death of Lucas Cranach the Elder (1553)
	1554	Mary Tudor marries the future Philip II of Spain: "Bloody Mary" persecutes English Protestants. (1554)		
	1555	Treaty of Augsburg: Charles V grants freedom of worship to German princes: "Cujus regio, ejus religio" (Whoever [holds] the power, his religion) Abdication of Charles V Accession of Ferdinand I, heir of the imperial title and the crown of Austria (1555)	Abdication of Charles V in Brussels Accession of Philip II, heir of the crown of Spain and the Netherlands Granvelle counselor (1555)	Jean Duvet, *The Apocalypse*. Birth of Ludovico Carracci (1555)
	1555–60 **1556**	Death of Ignatius Loyola (1556)	Charles V and Mary of Hungary leave for Spain Brussels: plague and famine, immigration forbidden (1556)	Death of Lorenzo Lotto (1556)
	1557	Bankruptcies in Spain (1557)	Antwerp: financial crisis Calvinism makes headway (1557)	
	1558	Accession of Elizabeth I in England Bankruptcies in France (1558)	Death of Charles V (1558)	

GRAPHIC ARTS *NETHERLANDS*	ARCHITECTURE, SCULPTURE, DECORATIVE ARTS	LITERATURE, PHILOSOPHY, MUSIC	SCIENCE, EXPLORATION
	Michelangelo directs building of dome of St. Peter's, Rome P. Lescot and P. Delorme, Paris, Cour Carrée, Louvre (from 1547)	Birth of Cervantes (1547)	Ortelius admitted to the Antwerp guild as a map illuminator Birth of the Flemish philologist Justus Lipsius (1547)
Hieronymous Cock opens the workshop At the Sign of the Four Winds in Antwerp (ca. 1548). Death of Pieter Coecke (1550)	Netherlands: church stalls in Hoogstraten (1531–48) J. Dubroecq, rood screen in Sainte-Waudru, Mons (1536–49) J. Goujon and P. Bontemps, Paris, Fountain of the Innocents (1548–49) Palladio, Villa Rotonda, Vicenza (ca. 1550) B. Palissy, relief pottery showing subjects from nature (ca. 1550)	Sebastian Brant's *Das Narrenschiff* (Ship of Fools) republished in Flemish in Antwerp (ca. 1548) Pléiade group of poets formed; Du Bellay's *Défense et Illustration de la Langue Française* (Defense and Glorification of the French Language) (1549) Giorgio Vasari, first edition of *Vite* (Lives of the Painters; 1550)	Birth of Karel van Mander Birth of the Flemish mathematician S. Stevin (1548) C. Plantin sets up his printing press in Antwerp (1550)
Frans Pourbus, *Portraits of Jan Fernaguut and Adriana de Buck*, Bruges (1551) Pieter Coecke, posthumous publication of *The Manners and Customs of the Turks* (1553) Frans Floris, *The Fall of the Rebel Angels*, Antwerp P. Huys, *The Last Judgment*, Brussels (1554)	P. Delorme, Château d'Anet, (1547–52) Benvenuto Cellini, *Perseus*, Florence (1553) Sansovino, Libreria della Piazzetta, Venice (1534–54) G. van Schoonbeke, Brewers' house, Antwerp (ca. 1550–55)	Birth of A. d'Aubigné Flemish composer A. Petit Coclico publishes *Musica Reservata* (1552). E. Jodelle, *Cléopâtre Captive* (Cleopatra Held Captive) Death of Rabelais (1553) T. de Bèze, *De Haereticis* (1554) Louise Labé, *Sonnets* Birth of Malherbe (1555)	Karl Gessner (Swiss zoologist and botanist), *Historiae Animalium* (1551) M. Servet (Spanish physician), *Christianismi Restitutio* (1553) Dodoneus (Flemish botanist), *Cruydeboeck* (1554) P. Pomponazzi (Italian philosopher), *De Naturalium Causis* French attempt at settlement in Brazil (1555)
Birth of Otto Vaenius (Otto van Veen; 1556) Antonis Mor, *Self-Portrait*, Florence Birth of Hendrick Goltzius (1558)	Germany: Heidelberg castle (1556–1609) Birth of Carlo Maderna (1556)	Ronsard, *Amours* (Loves; 1552–56) Birth of the Italian composer G. Gabrieli (1557) Margaret of Navarre, *Heptameron* Joachim Du Bellay, *Regrets* (1558)	Portuguese trading post established at Macao (1557) Foundation of Geneva theological academy (1558)

BRUEGEL		POLITICS — RELIGION — ECONOMICS		PAINTING —
		EUROPE	*NETHERLANDS*	*EUROPE*
First dated paintings whose attribution is unquestioned: *Flemish Proverbs* and *The Battle of Carnival and Lent,* 1559 Publication of the *Virtues* series, engraved by Philipp Galle, 1559–60	**1559** **1560**	Treaty of Cateau-Cambrésis Accession of Francis II and Mary Stuart in France Paris: first Calvinist synod Scotland: John Knox introduces Calvinism (1559) Accession of Charles IX in France. Regency of Catherine de Medici (1560)	Penalties announced in placards applied with increasing severity Philip II leaves for Spain. Margaret of Parma becomes regent. States General demands withdrawal of foreign troops (1559). Reorganization within the church: diocese of Cambrai under Mechelen once more; Granvelle made a cardinal (1560)	Birth of Annibale Carracci (1560)
Letter from Scipio Fabius to Ortelius, mentioning Bruegel, 1561 *The Fall of the Rebel Angels,* 1562	**1560–65** **1561** **1562**	Mary Stuart, now widowed, returns to Scotland (1561). France: first War of Religion and massacre at Vassy (1562)	Inauguration of Willebroeck canal Foreign troops withdrawn (1561) Brussels: clandestine sermons in the woods (1562)	F. Clouet, *Portrait of Pierre Quthe,* Paris (1562)
Marriage to Mayken Coecke in Brussels. Settles in the city, 1563 *Christ Carrying the Cross,* 1564 Birth of son, Pieter Bruegel the Younger, 1564/65 *Seasons* series Letter from Scipio Fabius to Ortelius, mentioning Bruegel, 1565	**1563** **1564** **1565** **1565–70**	France: Pacification of Amboise defines status of Protestants (1563). Accession of Maximilian II of Austria Death of John Calvin (1564)	Growing tension between Margaret of Parma and Cardinal Granvelle League of nobles against Granvelle; absenteeism from Council and withholding of payments to the king (1563) Granvelle leaves the Netherlands (1564). Nobility in control of States General (1565)	Veronese, *The Wedding at Cana*, Paris (1563) Death of Michelangelo Tintoretto, start of the cycle of the Scuola di San Rocco, Venice (1564)
Sixteen paintings belonging to Nicolaes Jongelinck deposited as security in Antwerp, 1566 Mention by Guicciardini in *Descrittione di tutti i Paesi Bassi* (Description of all the Netherlands), 1567 Birth of a second son, Jan Bruegel, sometimes known as Velvet Bruegel; mention in second edition of Vasari's *Vite,* 1568 Death in Brussels (September?) 1569	**1566** **1567** **1568** **1569** **1570**	France: Wars of Religion resume. Scotland: Calvinist uprising against Mary Stuart (1567) France: Third War of Religion Scotland: Mary Stuart flees to England (1568). England: Catholic uprising and bloody repression; plot against Elizabeth I involving Mary Stuart, who is imprisoned for life (1569)	Nobles allied to third estate sign Compromise of Breda. Revolt and brutal repression of iconoclasts (1566) Duke of Alva and his mercenaries are recalled from Lombardy to Brussels. Arrests (Van Straelen, the burgomaster of Antwerp, Egmont, and Hoorn) Margaret of Parma leaves (1567). Duke of Alva sets up the Bloedraad (Council of Blood). Confiscations, torture, hundreds executed (Egmont, Hoorn) (1568)	Jacopo Bassano, *The Adoration of the Shepherds*, Bassano (1568) Birth of Caravaggio (1570/71)

GRAPHIC ARTS	ARCHITECTURE, SCULPTURE, DECORATIVE ARTS	LITERATURE, PHILOSOPHY, MUSIC	SCIENCE, EXPLORATION
NETHERLANDS			
Pieter Aertsen, *Cook in Front of the Stove*, Brussels Jan Metsys, *Flora*, Hamburg (1559)			J. Amyot, translation of Plutarch's *Vitae* (1559)
Hieronymous Cock publishes *Scenographiae* by Hans Vredeman de Vries. Hendrick Bol enrolled as master in Mechelen (1560)	Russia: church of St. Basil, Moscow (1555–60) Germain Pilon, *The Three Graces*, Paris (ca. 1560)	Death of the German theologian Melanchthon Death of the French composer C. Janequin (1560)	
Frans Floris, *The Sea Gods' Banquet*, Stockholm (1561) Death of Jan van Scorel (1562) Death of Jan van Hemessen (ca. 1563)	L. Lombard, construction of Torrentius palace, Liège Death of A. Berruguete (1561) J. Bullant, Petit Château, Chantilly (ca. 1561) J.-B. de Toledo, plan for the Escorial Giambologna, *Neptune*, Bologna (1563)	Landjuweel (rhetorical festival) in Antwerp St. Teresa of Avila, *The Book of my Life* (1561) Ronsard, *Discours des Misères de ce Temps* (On the Miseries of our Time) Birth of Lope de la Vega M. Scève, *Microcosme* (Microcosm) Birth of the English composer John Dowland (1562)	Birth of the English philosopher Francis Bacon (1561)
Birth of Joos de Momper Jan Metsys, *The Gay Company*, Vienna (1564) Birth of Jan Savery (ca. 1565)	Michelangelo, completion of Palazzo Farnese in Rome (1564) C. de Vriendt, Antwerp town hall (1561–65)	Birth of Shakespeare (1564)	Death of Vesalius Birth of Galileo (1564)
Death of Lambert Lombard (1566) Martin de Vos, *St. Paul at Ephesus*, Brussels (1568) Death of Hieronymous Cock (1570)	Vignola, plan for church of Il Gesù, Rome (1567) Birth of the Spanish sculptor M. Montañes (1568)	Death of Nostradamus (1566) Commedia dell'arte becomes widespread D. V. Coornheert (Flemish philosopher and friend of Bruegel), *Comedie van Liet en Leedt* Birth of Monteverdi (1567) M. van Vaernewijck, *Van die beroerliçke Tijden in die Niederlanden* (1566–68) Philips Marnix van Sint-Aldegonde, *Biëncorf der Heilige Roomsche Kercke* (1569)	Guicciardini, *Descrittione di Tutti i Paesi Bassi* (Description of all the Netherlands) Destruction of French settlements in Brazil (1567) Vasari, *Le Vite* (Lives of the Painters), 2nd edition F. Goedthaels (Flemish philologist) *Les Proverbs des Anciens Flamengs et François* (Old Flemish and French Proverbs; 1568) Mercator, *Atlas* (1569) Ortelius, *Theatrum Orbis Terrarum* (1570)

CRITICAL SUMMARY OF PAINTINGS (SPECIALISTS' OPINIONS)

	Hulin de Loo 1907	Michel 1931	Tolnay 1935	Friedländer 1937	Jedlicka 1938	Glück 1951
THE ADORATION OF THE MAGI (Brussels) [fig. 74]	★ c. 1556–60	★ c. 1562	○ JB?	★ c. 1557	★ c. 1562–63	★ youthful work
LANDSCAPE WITH THE PARABLE OF THE SOWER (1557) [fig. 139]			?	★	★	★
THE FALL OF ICARUS [fig. 324]		○ imitator	★ c. 1555	★ c. 1558?	○ copy	★ c. 1554–55
FLEMISH PROVERBS (1559) [fig. 223]						
TWELVE PROVERBS [fig. 259]	★	★	○ copy PB II	★	★	○ copy PB II
THE BATTLE OF CARNIVAL AND LENT (1559) [fig. 125]	★	★	★	★	★	★
CHILDREN'S GAMES (1560) [fig. 246]	★	★	★	★	★	★
DULLE GRIET (1561) [fig. 101]	★ 1564	★ 1564	★ c. 1565–66	★ 1562?	★ c. 1562?	★ 1562
THE SUICIDE OF SAUL (1562) [fig. 253]	★	★	★	★	★	★
TWO MONKEYS (1562) [fig. 213]			★	★	★	★
THE FALL OF THE REBEL ANGELS (1562) [fig. 114]	★	★	★	★	★	★
THE TRIUMPH OF DEATH [fig. 109]	★ c. 1565–66	★ c. 1566–69	★ c. 1561–62	★ c. 1562?	★ c. 1562	★ c. 1561–62
VIEW OF NAPLES [fig. 321]		○ imitator	★ youthful work	★ c. 1558	★ c. 1555–56	★ youthful work
THE FLIGHT INTO EGYPT (1563) [fig. 140]						★
THE TOWER OF BABEL (Vienna, 1563) [fig. 273]	★	★	★	★	★	★
CHRIST CARRYING THE CROSS (1564) [fig. 51]	★	★	★	★	★	★
THE ADORATION OF THE MAGI (London, 1564) [fig. 146]	★	★	★	★	★	★
THE DEATH OF THE VIRGIN [fig. 152]		?	○ copy	★	○	★
CHRIST AND THE WOMAN TAKEN IN ADULTERY (1565) [fig. 155]						★
HAYMAKING [fig. 173]	★	★	★	★	★	★
THE HARVEST (1565)						
THE RETURN OF THE HERD (1565) [fig. 174]	★	★	★	★	★	★
HUNTERS IN THE SNOW (1565) [fig. 186]	★	★	★	★	★	★
THE GLOOMY DAY (1565) [fig. 187]	★	★	★	★	★	★
WINTER LANDSCAPE WITH SKATERS AND BIRD TRAP (1565) [fig. 54]		★	★	★	★	★
THE CENSUS AT BETHLEHEM (1566) [fig. 200]	★	★	★	★	★	★
THE MASSACRE OF THE INNOCENTS [fig. 145]	–	–	○ copy	–	–	○ copy
JOHN THE BAPTIST PREACHING (1566) [fig. 284]	–	★	★	★	★	★
THE WEDDING DANCE (1566) [fig. 289]			○ copy	★	○ copy	★
THE CONVERSION OF ST. PAUL (1567) [fig. 160]	★	★	★	★	★	★
THE ADORATION OF THE MAGI IN THE SNOW (1567) [fig. 195]			?	★	★	★
THE LAND OF COCKAIGNE (1567) [fig. 269]	★	★	★	★	★	★
THE TOWER OF BABEL (Rotterdam) [fig. 274]				★ c. 1563	★ c. 1563?	★ c. 1554–55
THE BEGGARS (1568) [fig. 258]	★	★	★	★	★	★
THE BLIND LEADING THE BLIND (1568) [fig. 69]	★					
THE MISANTHROPE (1568) [fig. 267]	★	★	★	★	★	★
THE BIRD-NESTER (1568) [fig. 209]	★	★	★	★	★	★
THE MAGPIE ON THE GALLOWS (1568) [fig. 360]	★	★	★	★	★	★
HEAD OF AN OLD PEASANT WOMAN [fig. 316]	★ before 1564	★ c. 1559	○ imitator	★ c. 1563	★ c. 1565	★ c. 1568
THE WEDDING FEAST [fig. 300]	★ c. 1566–69	★	★	★ c. 1568	★ c. 1565–66	★ 1568
THE PEASANTS' DANCE [fig. 307]	★ c. 1566–69	★	★	★ c. 1568	★ c. 1565–66	★ 1568

★ = authentic   ? = doubtful   ○ = not authentic   – = not mentioned   white = unknown   PB II = Pieter Bruegel the Younger   JB = Jan Bruegel

	Genaille 1953	Delevoy 1959	Van Puyvelde 1962	Grossmann 1973	Cibson 1977	Marijnissen 1988	Various opinions confirming authenticity
	?	★	★	★ c. 1556?	★ c. 1555	1556?	Marlier, 1963 (c. 1555–57)
	?	★	★	★	★	?	
	★ c. 1562–63	★ c. 1558	★	?	★ c. 1555–58	1555?	Baldass, 1918 (c. 1558)
	★	–	–	–	–	?	De Coo, 1965 (after 1559?)
	★	★	★	★	★	★	
	★	★	★	★	★	★	
	★ before 1564	★ 1564	★ 1561	★ 1562	★	★	
	★	★	★	★	★	★	
	★	★	★	★	★	★	
	★	★	★	★	★	★	
	★ c. 1562–63	★ c. 1568	★	★ c. 1562?	★	★	
	○	★	★	★ c. 1562–63?	★	★ c. 1562?	Burchard, 1913; Baldass, 1918; Winkler, 1924
	★	★	★	★	★	★	
	★	★	★	★	★	★	
	★	★	★	★	★	★	
	★	★	★	★	★	★	
	○	★ 1564?	★ 1556	★ c. 1564?	★	★	Glück, 1930; Popham, 1931
		★	★	★	★	★	
	★	★	★	★	★	★	
	★	★	★	★	★	★	
	★	★	★	★	★	★	
	★	★	★	★	★	★	
	★	★	★	★	★	★	
	★	★	★	★	★	★	
	–	?	–	★ c. 1565–67	★	★ c. 1565	Wied, 1980; Demus, 1981; Campbell, 1985
	★	★	★	★	★	★	
	★	–	–	★	★	★	
	★	★	★	★	★	★	
	★	★	★	★	★	★	
	★	★	★	★	★	★	
	★ c. 1566–67	★	★	★ c. 1563	★ c. 1568	★	
	★	★	★	★	★	★	
	★	★	★	★	★	★	
	★	★	★	★	★	★	
	★	★	★	★	★	★	
	★	–	★	★	★ c. 1564	★ c. 1568	
	★ c. 1566	★ c. 1568	★	★ c. 1567	★ c. 1567–68	★ c. 1567	
	★ c. 1566	★ c. 1568	★	★ c. 1567	★ c. 1567–68	★ c. 1567	

PAINTINGS (CONTINUED)

FORMER OR RECENT ATTRIBUTIONS

The following are works certain writers believe may have been, or could now be, attributed to Bruegel. The writers' names appear in brackets.

The Archangel Michael. Eindhoven, private collection
(Friedländer, Glück, Denis)

The Attack. University of Stockholm
(Karling, Grossmann)

The Yawner. Brussels, Musées royaux des Beaux-Arts de Belgique
(Hulin de Loo, Michel, Van Camp, Gibson)

The Good Shepherd. Antwerp, private collection
(Grossmann)

The Fall of Icarus. Brussels, Musée David et Alice van Buuren
(Glück, Delevoy, Van Puyvelde, Grossmann)

The Wedding Procession. Brussels, Musée communal
(Friedländer, Glück, Genaille, Marlier)

The Wedding Dance. Antwerp, Koninklijk Museum voor Schone Kunsten.
(Hulin de Loo, Michel)

Peasant Dance in front of an Inn. Paris, former Bentick-Thyssen collection
(Friedländer, Van Puyvelde)

Study for a Battle between the Thin and the Fat. Copenhagen, Statens Museum for Kunst
(Hulin de Loo, Friedländer)

Study of a Head. Bordeaux, Musée des Beaux-Arts
(Van Camp)

Jesus Driving the Money-Changers from the Temple. Copenhagen, Statens Museum for Kunst.
(Friedländer, Glück)

The Battle of Carnival and Lent. Boston, Museum of Fine Arts
(Swarzenski)

The Massacre of the Innocents. Brussels, former Descamps collection
(Van Puyvelde)

The Massacre of the Innocents. Vienna, Kunsthistorisches Museum
(Hulin de Loo, Glück, Genaille, Van Puyvelde)

The Bad Shepherd. Philadelphia, The Philadelphia Museum of Art, John G. Johnson Collection
(Hulin de Loo, Glück)

Still Life with Herrings. Rotterdam, Museum Boijmans Van Beuningen
(Friedländer)

Village Wedding in an Interior. Philadelphia, The Philadelphia Museum of Art, John G. Johnson Collection
(Hulin de Loo, Valentiner)

Landscape with an Artist Drawing. London, National Gallery
(Glück)

Landscape with Christ Appearing to the Apostles. Private collection
(Tolnay, Grossmann, Friedländer, Gibson)

Landscape with an Episode in the Life of St. Catherine. Washington, National Gallery of Art, Samuel H. Kress Collection
(Glück)

Landscape with a Hermit. London, Courtauld Institute of Art, Count Antoine Seilern Collection
(Grossmann)

Winter Landscape with Skaters and Bird Trap. London, private collection
(Shipp, Van Puyvelde)

Landscape with Ships and a City in Flames. Dortmund, private collection
(Grossmann)

Night Landscape with a Hermit. Indianapolis, Clowes Fund
(Glück)

Landscape with St. Christopher. Switzerland (?), private collection
(Van Puyvelde)

Peasants Making Bundles of Firewood. Birmingham, Barber Institute
(Friedländer, Van Puyvelde)

John the Baptist Preaching. Milan, Duca collection
(Van Puyvelde)

The Tempest. Vienna, Kunsthistorisches Museum
(From Hulin de Loo, 1907, to Grossmann, 1966, with the exception of Michel)

The Temptation of St. Anthony. Washington, National Gallery of Art, Samuel H. Kress Collection
(Van Puyvelde, Friedländer, Glück, Delevoy)

Head of a Mercenary. Montpellier, Musée Fabre
(Hulin de Loo, Van Camp)

Three Soldiers. New York, Frick Collection
(Munhall, Gibson)

The Wine of St. Martin. Vienna, Kunsthistorisches Museum
(Hulin de Loo, Friedländer, Van Puyvelde)

DRAWINGS

Given the disagreements between specialists following the publication of Hans Mielke's catalogue in 1997, drawings whose attribution to Bruegel is questioned by this writer are in parentheses. The author also reinstates works whose attribution to Bruegel has been dismissed, and lists others that have been recently discovered.

River Landscape, 1552. Paris, Louvre, graphic arts department (fig. 80)

Mountain Landscape with Italian Cloister, 1552. Berlin, Staatliche Museen, Kupferstichkabinett (fig. 10)

Wooded Landscape with Three Windmills. 1552. Milan, Biblioteca Ambrosiana (fig. 164)

(*View of a Valley*, ca. 1552. Pen and brown ink, 5⅜ x 12¾ in. [13.7 x 32.4 cm]. Dresden, Kupferstichkabinett)

View of Reggio di Calabria, ca. 1552–60. Rotterdam, Museum Boijmans Van Beuningen (fig. 320)

View of the Ripa Grande, ca. 1552–53. Chatsworth, The Duke of Devonshire and the Chatsworth Settlement Trustees (fig. 9)

Mountain Landscape with Fortified Town, or *Heroic Town*, 1553. London, British Museum, Department of Prints and Drawings (fig. 163)

Mountain Landscape with River and People Walking, 1553. Pen and red-brown ink, 9 x 13 in. (22.8 x 33.8 cm). London, British Museum, Department of Prints and Drawings

Alpine Landscape, 1553. Paris, Louvre, graphic arts department (fig. 352)

Landscape with St. Jerome, 1553. Washington, National Gallery of Art (fig. 171)

Italian River Landscape with the Holy Family and a Cloister, or *The Rest on the Flight into Egypt,* ca. 1553–54. Berlin, Staatliche Museen, Kupferstichkabinett (fig. 141)

(*Mountain Landscape with River, Village, and Castle*, ca. 1552–53. Pen and brown ink, 14 x 17⅜ in. [35.7 x 44.3 cm]. New York, The Pierpont Morgan Library)

Undergrowth with Five Bears, 1554. Prague, Národní Galerie (fig. 333)

(*Mountain Landscape: the Martinswand near Zirl*, ca. 1554–55. Berlin, Staatliche Museen, Kupferstichkabinett) [fig. 8]

("*Waltersspurg*" *Mountainous Landscape*, ca. 1554–55, Brunswick [Maine], Bowdoin College Museum of Art) [fig. 11]

(*Alpine Landscape*, ca. 1555. Cambridge, Mass., Harvard University, Fogg Art Museum) [fig. 78]

(*View of a Valley*, or *View of the Ticino Valley*, ca. 1554–55. Pen and brown ink on black chalk, 5⅜ x 12¾ in. [13.7 x 32.4 cm]. Dresden, Staatliche Kunstsammlungen, Kupferstichkabinett)

Alpine Landscape Crossed by a Deep Valley, 1555. Paris, Louvre, graphic arts department (fig. 13)

The Pilgrims of Emmaus, ca. 1553–55, preliminary sketch for the *Great Landscapes* series. Antwerp, Koninklijk Museum voor Schone Kunsten (fig. 331)

Solicitudo Rustica, 1555, preliminary sketch for the *Great Landscapes* series. London, British Museum (fig. 142)

The Temptation of St. Anthony, 1556. Oxford, Ashmolean Museum (fig. 89)

The Big Fish Eat The Little Fish, 1556. Vienna, Graphische Sammlung Albertina (fig. 16)

The Ass at School, 1556. Berlin, Staatliche Museen, Kupferstichkabinett (fig. 81)

Avarice, from the *Deadly Sins* series, 1665. London, British Museum, Department of Prints and Drawings (fig. 96)

Anger, from the *Deadly Sins* series, 1557. Florence, Uffizi (fig. 93)

Sloth, from the *Deadly Sins* series, 1557. Vienna, Graphische Sammlung Albertina (fig. 94)

Pride, from the *Deadly Sins* series, 1557. Paris, Institut néerlandais, Fondation Custodia, F. Lugt collection (fig. 97)

Gluttony, from the *Deadly Sins* series, 1557. Paris, Institut néerlandais, Fondation Custodia, F. Lugt collection (fig. 95)

Envy, from the *Deadly Sins* series, 1557. Switzerland, private collection (fig. 98)

Lust, from the *Deadly Sins* series, 1557. Brussels, Bibliothèque royale Albert I, print room (fig. 100)

The Last Judgment, 1558. Vienna, Graphische Sammlung Albertina (fig. 106)

Elck, 1558. London, British Museum, Department of Prints and Drawings (fig 238)

The Alchemist, 1558. Berlin, Staatliche Museen, Kupferstichkabinett (fig. 45)

Skating Scene in front of St. George's Gate in Antwerp, 1558 or 1559. Pen and brown ink, 8⅜ x 11¾ in. (21.3 x 29.8 cm). United States, private collection

Kermis at Hoboken, 1559. London, Courtauld Institute of Art, Lee Collection (fig. 297)

Faith, from the *Virtues* series, 1559. Amsterdam, Rijksmuseum, Rijksprentenkabinet (fig. 215)

Hope, from the *Virtues* series, 1559. Berlin, Staatliche Museen, Kupferstichkabinett (fig. 214)

Charity, from the *Virtues* series, 1559. Rotterdam, Museum Boijmans Van Beuningen (fig. 216)

Justice, from the *Virtues* series, 1559. Brussels, Bibliothèque royale Albert I, print room (fig. 217)

Prudence, from the *Virtues* series, 1559. Brussels, Musées royaux des Beaux-Arts de Belgique (fig. 219)

Fortitude, from the *Virtues* series, 1560. Rotterdam, Museum Boijmans Van Beuningen (fig. 220)

Temperance, from the *Virtues* series, 1560. Rotterdam, Museum Boijmans Van Beuningen (fig. 221)

View of Antwerp from the Scheldt, ca. 1559. London, Courtauld Institute of Art, Count Antoine Seilern Collection (fig. 322)

Christ in Limbo, 1561 (?). Vienna, Graphische Sammlung Albertina (fig. 138)

The Resurrection of Christ, ca. 1562. Rotterdam, Museum Boijmans Van Beuningen (fig. 157)

The Magician's Fall, 1564. Amsterdam, Rijksmuseum, Rijksprentenkabinet (fig. 134)

Spring, 1565. Vienna, Graphische Sammlung Albertina (fig. 193)

The Calumny of Apelles, 1565. London, British Museum, Department of Prints and Drawings (fig. 153)

The Goose Keeper, ca. 1565. Dresden, Staatliche Kunstsammlungen, Kupferstichkabinett (fig. 298)

The Painter and the Art Lover, ca. 1565. Vienna, Graphische Sammlung Albertina (fig. 265)

Four Men Standing in Conversation, ca. 1565. Paris, Louvre, graphic arts department (fig. 299)

The Wedding of Mopsus and Nisa, ca. 1566. New York, Metropolitan Museum of Art, Department of Prints (fig. 88)

Summer, 1568. Hamburg, Hamburger Kunsthalle, Kupferstichkabinett (fig. 58)

The Beekeepers, 1568. Berlin, Staatliche Museen, Kupferstichkabinett (fig. 85)

REINSTATED WORKS
Village Street, ca. 1552. Leiden, Prentenkabinett der Rijksuniversiteit
Mule Caravan on a Mountainside, ca. 1552 (?). Rotterdam, Museum Boijmans Van Beuningen
Hills and a Broad Valley, ca. 1552. Brunswick, Herzog Anton Ulrich-Museum
Pastorale,1552. Oslo, Nasjonalgelleriet
Wooded Landscape with View over the Sea, ca. 1553. Cambridge (Mass.) private collection
Herd of Cows in front of a Farm, ca. 1553. Washington, National Gallery of Art
Wooded Landscape with Muleteer, ca. 1553. London, private collection
Bear in the Forest, ca. 1554. London, British Museum
Marsh with Fisherman, 1554. Brussels, Bibliothèque royale Albert I
Landscape after Campagnola, 1554. Berlin, Staatliche Museen
Basrode River Landscape, ca. 1556. Berlin, Staatliche Museen
River Landscape with Village, ca. 1556. Paris, Louvre
River Landscape with Fisherman, ca. 1556. Paris, Louvre
Hunting Wild Rabbits, 1560. Paris, Institut néerlandais, Fondation Custodia
Bagpiper, ca. 1565. New York, private collection

ENGRAVINGS

First on this list are engravings made from an original drawing by Bruegel. Under the heading "Interpretative Engravings" come those made from original Bruegel works which were not necessarily intended for engravings, from a drawing believed to be by Bruegel, or from one in the manner of Bruegel. Aside from a few minor changes, the classification made by Louis Lebeer (1969) remains the most reliable.

Johannes or Lucas van Duetecum (?), series of 12 *Great Landscapes*, ca. 1555–58. Etchings and engravings:
Prospectus Tyburtinus, 12⅝ x 16¾ in. (32.2 x 42.7 cm)
S. Hieronymus in Deserto, 12⅝ x 16¾ in. (32.2 x 42.2 cm)
Magdalena Poenitens, 12⅝ x 16⅝ in. (32.2 x 42.2 cm)
Alpine Landscape Crossed by a Deep Valley, 12⅝ x 16⅝ in. (32 x 42.2 cm)
Insidiosus Auceps, 12⅝ x 16¾ in. (32 x 42.4 cm)
Plaustrum Belgicum, 12⅝ x 16¾ in. (32.1 x 42.6 cm) (fig. 84)
Solicitudo Rustica, 12⅝ x 16½ in. (32.2 x 42.1 cm)
Nundinae rusticorum, 12½ x 16½ in. (31.7 x 42.1 cm)
Euntes in Emaus, 12¾ x 16⅝ in. (32.3 x 42.3 cm)
Fuga Deiparae in Aegyptum, 12⅜ x 15½ in. (31.5 x 42 cm)
Pagus Nemorosus, 12⅝ x 16¾ in. (32.2 x 42.7 cm) (fig. 165)
Milites Requiescentes, 12⅝ x 16¾ in. (32.1 x 42.4 cm) (fig. 167)

Johannes or Lucas van Duetecum (?), *Great Alpine Landscape*, ca. 1558–59. Etching and engraving, 14½ x 18⅜ in. (36.8 x 46.8 cm) (fig. 166)

Pieter van der Heyden (attributed), *The Temptation of St. Anthony*, 1556. Engraving, 9⅝ x 12½ in. (24.5 x 32 cm)

Pieter van der Heyden, *Patience*, 1557. Engraving, 13⅜ x 17¼ in. (34 x 44 cm) (fig. 92)

Pieter van der Heyden, *The Big Fish Eat The Little Fish*, 1557. Engraving, 9 x 11⅝ in. (22.9 x 29.6 cm) (fig. 17)

Pieter van der Heyden, *The Ass at School*, 1557. Engraving, 9¼ x 11⅞ in. (23.4 x 30.3 cm) (fig. 82)

Pieter van der Heyden, *Deadly Sins* series, 1558. Engravings:
Anger, 8¾ x 11½ in. (22.3 x 29.3 cm)
Sloth, 8⅞ x 11½ in. (22.5 x 29.2 cm)
Pride, 22.5 x 29.2 cm (8.86 x 11.50 in.).
Covetousness, 8¾ x 11½ in. (22.4 x 29.3 cm)
Gluttony, 8¾ x 11½ in. (22.3 x 29.3 cm)
Envy, 8⅞ x 11⅝ in. (22.7 x 29.5 cm)
Lust, 8⅞ x 11⅝ in. (22.5 x 29.5 cm) (fig. 99)

Pieter van der Heyden, *The Last Judgment*, 1558. Engraving, 8⅞ x 11⅝ in. (22.5 x 29.5 cm)

Pieter van der Heyden, (attributed), *Elck*, ca. 1558. Engraving, 9 x 11½ in. (22.8 x 29.4 cm) (fig. 237)

Philipp Galle, *The Alchemist*, ca. 1558. Engraving, 12 x 17¼ in. (32 x 44 cm) (fig. 47)

Pieter van der Heyden, *The Witch at Mallegem*, 1559 (?). Engraving, 14 x 18⅞ in. (35.5 x 48 cm) (fig. 243)

Pieter van der Heyden, *The Madmen's Festivities*, ca. 1559. Engraving, 12¾ x 17¼ in. (32.5 x 43.7 cm) (fig. 241)

Frans Hogenberg (?), *Kermis at Hoboken*, ca. 1559. Engraving, 11¾ x 16 in. (29.8 x 40.8 cm) (fig. 34)

Philipp Galle (attributed), series of seven *Virtues*, 1559–60. Engravings:
Faith, 8⅞ x 11⅓ in. (22.3 x 28.7 cm)
Hope, 8⅞ x 11¼ in. (22.3 x 28.8 cm)
Charity, 8¾ x 11⅗ in. (22.2 x 28.9 cm)
Justice, 8⅞ x 11¼ in. (22.3 x 28.7 cm)
Prudence, 8⅞ x 11½ in. (22.5 x 29.3 cm)
Fortitude, 8⅞ x 11 in. (22.3 x 28.7 cm)
Temperance, 8⅞ x 11 in. (22.3 x 28.7 cm)

Hunting Wild Rabbits, 1560 (?). Original etching, 8⅞ x 11½ in. (22.3 x 29.1 cm) (fig. 86)

Pieter van der Heyden, *Christ in Limbo*, ca. 1561 (?). Engraving, 9⅛ x 11½ in. (23.2 x 29.1 cm) (Fig. 135)

Philipp Galle (attributed), *The Parable of the Wise and Foolish Virgins*, ca. 1560–61 (?). Engraving, 8¾ x 11¼ in. (22.1 x 28.6 cm) (fig. 136)

Frans Huys, *Naval Battle in the Strait of Messina*, 1561. Engraving, 16¾ x 18⅛ in. (42.5 x 71.5 cm) (fig. 318)

Frans Huys, *Sea-Going Ships* series, 1561–2. Engravings:
Dutch Three-Masted Merchant Vessel, 9¼ x 7⅝ in. (24 x 19.4 cm)
Four-Masted Vessel with Cannon, Sailing towards a Port, 11⅜ x 8½ in. (28.9 x 21.7 cm)
Three-Masted Ship with Cannon in the Open Sea, Accompanied by a Brigantine, 12⅜ x 9⅝ in. (31.4 x 24.5 cm) (fig. 83)
Three-Masted Ship with Cannon, Four Crow's Nests, and Two Top-Gallant Sails, 8¾ x 11¼ in. (22.2 x 28.7 cm) (fig. 327)
Four-Masted Ship, Putting out to Sea, 8¾ x 11¼ in. (22.2 x 28.5 cm). (fig. 318)
Three-Masted Vessel with Cannon, at Anchor near a Town, 9 x 11¼ in. (23 x 28.7 cm)
Four-Masted Vessel and Two Three-Masted Vessels with Cannon, at Anchor by a Fortified Island with Lighthouse, 8¾ x 11⅜ in. (22.2 x 28.9 cm)
Two Four-Masted Galleases in a Rising Squall, 8⅝ x 11¼ in. (22 x 28.6 cm)
Two Galleys Following a Three-Masted Vessel with Cannon, 8¾ x 10⅞ in. (22.3 x 27.8 cm)
Fleet of Galleys Accompanied by a Ship with Cannon, 8¾ x 11⅜ in. (22.3 x 29 cm)

Frans Huys, *Skating Scene in front of St. George's Gate in Antwerp*, ca. 1561. Engraving, 9⅛ x 11¾ in. (23.2 x 29.9 cm) (fig. 286)

Hieronymus Cock (attributed), *The Kermis of St. George*, ca. 1561. Etching and Engraving, 13 x 20⅝ in. (33.2 x 52.3 cm) (fig. 296)

Pieter van der Heyden, *The Haberdasher Robbed by Monkeys*, 1562. Engraving, 8⅞ x 11⅜ in. (22.5 x 29 cm) (fig. 242)

Pieter van der Heyden, *The Battle of the Money-Boxes and the Safes*, ca. 1563. Engraving, 9¼ x 12 in. (23.6 x 30.4 cm) (fig. 239)

Pieter van der Heyden, *The Thin Kitchen*, 1563. Engraving, 8⅜ x 1⅜ in. (22 x 29 cm) (fig. 131)

Pieter van der Heyden, *The Fat Kitchen*, 1563. Engraving, 8⅜ x 11½ in. (22 x 29.2 cm) (fig. 132)

Pieter van der Heyden, *St. James and The Magician Hermogenes*, 1565. Engraving, 8¾ x 11⅜ in. (22.2 x 29 cm) (fig. 133)

Pieter van der Heyden, *The Magician's Fall*, 1565. Engraving, 8¾ x 11⅜ in. (22 2 x 28.8 cm) (fig. 134)

Philipp Galle, *The Parable of the Good Shepherd*, 1565. Engraving, 8⅞ x 11⅝ in. (22.5 x 29.5 cm)

Anonymous, *The Masquerade of Bear Cub and Valentine*, 1566. Wood engraving, 10¾ x 16⅛ in. (27.5 x 41 cm) (fig. 87)

Pieter van der Heyden, *Country Wedding Dance*, after 1566 or after 1570. Engraving, 14¾ x 16⅝ in. (37.5 x 42.3 cm) (fig. 292)

Pieter van der Heyden, *The Land of Cockaigne*, ca. 1567. Engraving, 8⅛ x 10⅞ in. (20.8 x 27.6 cm) (fig. 268)

Jean Wierix, *The Drunkard Pushed into the Pigsty*, 1568. Engraving, diameter 7⅛ in. (18.2 cm) (fig. 295)

Pieter van der Heyden, *Spring*, 1570 (published posthumously). Engraving, 9 x 11¼ in. (22.8 x 28.7 cm)

Pieter van der Heyden (attributed), *Summer*, 1570 (published posthumously). Engraving, 8⅞ x 11⅛ in. (22.5 x 28.3 cm) (fig. 59)

Pieter van der Heyden, *The Wedding of Mopsus and Nisa*, 1570 (published posthumously). Engraving, 8¾ x 11⅜ in. (22.2 x 29 cm) (fig. 124)

INTERPRETATIVE ENGRAVINGS

Anonymous, *The Dean of Renaix*, after Pieter Bruegel the Elder (?), 1557 (?). Engraving, 11⅛ x 16 in. (28.3 x 40.6 cm) (fig. 240)

Philipp Galle (attributed), *The Resurrection of Christ*, after 1562. Engraving, 18¼ x 12⅞ in. (46.5 x 32.8 cm) (fig. 156)

Jan Wierix and Pieter van der Heyden (?), *Series of Twelve Flemish Proverbs*, ca. 1568. Tondo Engravings, diameter ca. 7 in. (17.7 cm) (figs. 259 and 266)

Philipp Galle, *Jesus and his Disciples on the Road to Emmaus*, 1571. Engraving, 9¾ x 7½ in. (24.8 x 19.2 cm)

Philipp Galle, *The Assumption of the Virgin*, 1574. Engraving, 12 x 16⅜ in. (31 x 41.7 cm) (fig. 151)

Philipp Galle, *The Triumph of Time or of Saturn*, 1574. Engraving, 8⅛ x 11⅞ in. (20.8 x 30.1 cm) (fig. 335)

Pieter Perret, *Christ and the Adulterous Woman*, 1579. Engraving, 10⅜ x 13⅜ in. (26.5 x 34.1 cm)

Attributed to Georg Hoefnagel, *Landscape Crossed by a River, with Mercury Kidnapping Psyche*, ca. 1595. Etching, 10⅝ x 13½ in. (27 x 34.2 cm)

Attributed to Georg Hoefnagel, *Landscape Crossed by a River, with the Fall of Icarus*, ca. 1595. Etching, 10¾ x 13¼ in. (27.5 x 33.7 cm) (fig. 326)

Lucas Vorsterman, *Peasants' Brawl*, ca. 1621. Etching and Engraving, 16¾ x 20⅝ in. (42.6 x 52.5 cm) (fig. 339)

Lucas Vorsterman, *The Yawner*, ca. 1621. Etching and Engraving, 8¼ x 8⅛ in. (20.9 x 20.7 cm) (fig. 316)

Hendrik Hondius, *The Epileptics' Pilgrimage to Molenbeek-Saint-Jean* (three engravings) and *The Carnival Fools* (two), 1642. Engravings

1

DOMINICUS LAMPSONIUS
Pictorum aliquot celebrium Germaniae inferioris effigies,
Antwerp 1572

To Pieter Bruegel, painter.
Who is this new Hieronymus Bosch [offered to the] world, who can imitate, with brush or crayon, the inspired dreams of his master with such skill that sometimes he even surpasses him? You deserve praise, Pieter, both for your humor and for your art. For, in the manner of your former master, and thanks to the jokes and wit with which you abound, you deserve from all quarters and from all people praise and rewards in no way inferior to those granted to any other artist.

2

ABRAHAM ORTELIUS
Album Amicorum, MS about 1573,
Cambridge, Pembroke College

To the *Manes:*
No one will ever deny that Pieter Bruegel was the most accomplished painter of his century—unless they are jealous, a competitor, or ignorant of his art. As for the fact that he has left us in his prime, should I blame Death—which, having observed this man's artistic mastery, thought him older than he was—or, rather, Nature, which, skillfully and ingeniously imitated, feared it would be held in contempt? I cannot easily say.

Dedicated to the memory of his friend
by Abraham Ortelius, filled with sorrow.

It is said that the painter Eupompus, when asked which of his predecessors he imitated, gestured towards the great multitude of men and said that it was necessary to imitate nature herself, not a particular artist. This thought is a fitting one for our Bruegel, of whom I always say that his paintings speak not of artifice, but of nature. And, in truth, I could call him not the best of painters, but "nature's painter." This is why I feel he is worthy of being imitated by all.

Bruegel painted many things that are impossible to paint—as Pliny said of Apelles. In all his works there is always something to understand beyond what is depicted; Eunapius, in Jamblicus, says the same of Timanthus. Artists who paint beautiful young people in the flush of youth and wish to add to their paintings a certain seductiveness and grace of their own invention completely ruin their work and depart both from their models and from true beauty. Our Bruegel is free of such a flaw.

3

KAREL VAN MANDER
Het Schilder-Boek […], Haarlem, 1604,
Pages 233 rº, 233 vº, and 234 rº
Translated from the Dutch by Elaine M. Stainton.
Original spellings of names have been retained.

The Life of Pieter Brueghel, Eminent Painter of [the town of] Brueghel

Nature was wise to recognize and to seize upon a man who has been shown by time to be excellent, in choosing the gifted and spirited Pieter Brueghel from among the country folk of an obscure village of Brabant and, finding in him a man to represent her magnificently with his brush—and those country folk, as well— raising him among us to enduring fame in the art of painting. He was born near Breda in the village of Brueghel, from which his own name and that of his descendants is derived. He learned his art from Pieter Koeck van Aelst, whose daughter he later married, and whom he often carried about in his arms when she was little.

After this, he went to work for Jeroon Kock, and after that traveled in France and Italy. He studied the style of Jeroon van den Bosch well, and he himself also made many similar weird and comical scenes, for which he became known as "Pieter the Joker." Few pieces by his hand can be looked at earnestly without laughing; in fact, however serious and grim one might be, one cannot help laughing, or at least smiling. On his travels he painted many pictures after nature, so that it was said that while he was journeying through the Alps, he had swallowed the mountains and cliffs whole and when he returned home spat them out on canvas and panel, so truthfully was he able to record these and other works of nature.

He settled down in Antwerp, entering the guild of painters there in the year of our lord 1551. He did a lot of work for a merchant named Hans Franckert, a fine and noble man, who liked to chat with Brueghel and spent time with him every day. With this Franckert he would go—both men dressed as farmers—on excursions among the country people, to their fairs and weddings, bringing gifts like everyone else and acting as if they were friends of the bride or groom. Brueghel delighted in observing the farmers' manner of eating and drinking, dancing and leaping, courting, and of the other ways they had of enjoying themselves, which he then set down with great skill in watercolor or oils, as he was highly accomplished in both media. He knew well the characteristic dress and bearing of the men and women of Kempen and other rural districts, and their coarse manner of dancing, walking, standing or moving about. He was remarkably sure of the way he set down his figures and made clear and beautiful pen sketches of landscapes after nature.

As long as he remained in Antwerp he lived with a servant woman, whom he would have married had she not so often lied to him, which was repugnant to his love of truth. He made an agreement with her that he would cut a mark on a stick for every lie she told, and for this purpose he chose a long stick, saying that if the stick became full of notches within a certain time, the wedding would not take place. The stick was full within a short time. Finally, the widow of Pieter Koeck moved to Brussels, and he fell in love with her daughter, the very one whom he had once carried about in his arms, and he married her. But the mother requested that Brueghel move from Antwerp to Brussels so that he would leave his former lover behind and forget her. And so this was done. He was a quiet and pleasant man who spoke little, but in company he was something of a jokester, and he enjoyed startling people, even his own students, with ghostly noises and pranks that he played.

Some of Brueghel's most important works are now in the Emperor's collection, to wit: a large picture of the Tower of Babel, seen from above, with many colorful details; there is also a smaller version of the same subject; there are also two paintings of Christ Carrying the Cross, executed in a very natural manner, but containing various comic incidents; then there is a Massacre of the Innocents, in which, as I have said elsewhere, there is much to see, all very true to life, for example, there is a whole family pleading for the life of a peasant child whom a soldier intent on murder has seized in order to kill it; the despair of the swooning mother, and other events as well, are very realistically done. Finally, there is a Conversion of St. Paul, with a very beautiful mountain landscape.

It would be very hard to list everything that Brueghel did. He painted scenes of sorcery, of country life, of hell, and many other subjects. He painted a Temptation of Christ, seen from above, as if from the Alps, looking down on cities and countryside through breaks in the clouds; he painted a picture of "Dulle Griet" pillaging a town before the mouth of hell, with a crazed expression on her face and bizarrely dressed. I believe that this and other pictures are also in the Emperor's collection. Another gentleman, the art-lover Herman Pilgrims of Amsterdam, owns a very beautiful Peasant Wedding in oil, in which the faces and the bare limbs of the country people are yellow and brown as if burned by the sun, their skin ugly and very different from that of city-dwellers. He also painted a picture in which Lent and Carnival are fighting. In another, all sorts of medicines are being used against death, and another depicting all sorts of children's games; and innumerable pictures of little allegorical scenes. Another art-loving gentleman, Willem Jacobsz., who lives near the Nieuwe Kerk in Amsterdam, owns two paintings, one a country fair, the other a peasant wedding, both full of comic figures and incidents directly inspired by country people. Among those giving presents to the bride is an old farmer with a little money bag hanging around his neck, who is busy counting the money into his hand. These are remarkable paintings. Shortly before he died, the town council of Brussels commissioned Brueghel to paint several pictures of the digging of a canal from Brussels to Antwerp, but because of his death these were never completed.

Many of Brueghel's strange compositions and comical scenes can be in his engravings, but he made skillful and beautiful drawings, accompanied by inscriptions that for their time were often very biting and derisory. On his deathbed, he asked that his wife burn these, either because he regretted having done them, or because he feared that she might fall into some difficulty because of them or have to make explanations regarding them. In his will he left his wife a painting of a Magpie on the Gallows. By this magpie he meant to signify the babbling of tongues, which he thus delivered to execution. Moreover, he painted a picture of the Triumph of Truth, which according to his own statement was his best work.

He left behind two sons who were also good painters. The first, called Pieter, studied with Gillis van Conincxloo and painted portraits from life. Jan, who learned to paint in watercolor with his grandmother, the widow of Pieter van Aelst, learned to paint in oil from a certain Pieter Goekindt, who had many beautiful things in his house. After this, he traveled to Cologne and later to Italy. He made a name for himself with his landscapes with little figures in them which are very beautifully painted.

Lampsonius addressed Brueghel with these words:

[here follows the quotation from Lampsonius, given here as source no. 1]

NOTES

CHAPTER I

1. Most writers give 5 September, taking their cue from Wauters (1887–88). Others, including Hand in Washington/New York catalogue (1986, 91) and Gibson (1991[1], 18), give 9 September. Marlier (1969, 4) gives 13 December.

2. Derived from an unpublished translation by Professor René Hoven, eminent Latinist at the University of Liège, to whom we are grateful. The spelling "Bruegel" is that used today.

3. The painting, sold in 1765 by the church council, has been kept since 1936 by the Staatliche Museen in Berlin (H. Van Nuffel, in *Notre-Dame-de-la-Chapelle à Bruxelles 1134–1984*, Brussels, 1984, 29–30); D. Freedberg, *Rubens. The Life of Christ after the Passion*, London, Harvey Miller/Oxford University Press, 1984, 91–94.

4. Until 1771, according to Wauters (1883, 321–22).

5. Guicciardini (1582, 96).

6. Bazin (1963, 26).

7. Martiny (1964, 9).

8. Van Mander (1604, fol. 233 recto). See "Biographical Sources," 3, 332.

9. Guicciardini (1582, 153).

10. Vasari (1981–9, 10, 180).

11. Rombouts and Van Lerius (1961, 174–78).

12. Thus Bedaux and Van Gool (1974), on the basis of an analysis of an engraved portrait of Bruegel and its accompanying text, by Aegidius Sadeler after B. Spranger (1606), date Bruegel's birth as 1527 or 1528; Verougstraete and Van Schoute (1993), following the study of Pieter Bruegel the Younger's *The Triumph of Death* of 1626, which they believe commemorated both the father's death and that of Jan Bruegel, suggest 1525. Others give more recent dates (see Marijnissen, 1988, 15).

13. Among others Grossmann (1973[1], 12–13) and Lebeer (1969, 5–6).

14. Van Mander (1604). See "Biographical Sources," 3, 332.

15. Marlier (1966, 30).

16. Friedländer (1976, 13–14); Tolnay (1935, I, 60).

17. Sweertius in Marlier (1966, 31).

18. Van Mander (1604). See "Biographical Sources," 3, 332.

19. Monballieu (1964, 92–110). According to this writer Bruegel's time at Dorisi's workshop was between September 1550 and October 1551.

20. Van Mander (1604). See "Biographical Sources," 3, 332.

21. Guicciardini (1582, 152).

22. Lebeer, (1969, 8).

23. Lebeer, (1969, 9); Allart, in Brussels/Rome catalog (1995, 115).

24. Lebeer, *ibid.*, 9. The drawings showing Martinswand and Waltersspurg have since 1991 been attributed to R. Savery by Mielke (1997, 77–78) who, on the first drawing, agrees with Münz (1961, 232–33).

25. Tolnay (1978, 394; 1980, *passim*) attributes a series of miniatures to Bruegel.

26. Denucé (1932, 256).

27. Duverger (1984–89, IV, 306).

28. Guicciardini (1582, 193).

29. S. Fabius, cited in Popham (1931, 188).

30. Van Mander (1604). See "Biographical Sources," 3, 333.

31. Onclincx (1985, 728–29) mentions the presence of Bruegel in Brussels "in about 1561," a date which could be explained, we feel, by the inauguration that year of the Antwerp–Brussels canal for which, according to Van Mander, the artist received several commissions for paintings later and not only during the "time necessary for him to be married".

32. Popham (1931, 188).

33. Denucé, (1932, II, 5); Marijnissen (1988, 12); Buchanan (1990, 541).

34. Van Den Branden (1883, 444) mentions this in connection with Jan (Velvet) Bruegel's journey to Italy; also mentioned by Wauters (1887–88, 29).

35. Lampsonius (1572). See "Biographical Sources," 1, 332.

36. A. Ortelius (about 1573). See "Biographical Sources," 2, 332; Popham (1931, 187).

37. Piot (1884, IV, 524); Wauters (1914, 87–90).

38. Van Mander (1604). See "Biographical Sources," 3, 333.

39. Wauters (1887–88, 19); Lebeer (1969, 5).

40. Pirenne (1949, II, 162).

41. Dumont (1977, 183–84).

42. R. Wangermée, *La Musique Flamande dans la Société des XVe et XVIe Siècles*, Brussels, Arcade, 1965, 139.

43. Pirenne, (1949, II, 187).

44. Letter of 3 December 1576 in M. Gachard, *Correspondance de Philippe II*, V, Brussels/Ghent/Leipzig, C. Muquardt, 1879, 595.

45. Gibson (1981, *passim*).

46. For the whole of this chapter see below, "Chronological Table," 318–19.

CHAPTER II

1. Van Mander (1604). See "Biographical Sources," 3, 333.

2. Guicciardini (1582, 153).

3. Lampsonius (1572). See "Biographical Sources," 1, 332.

4. Van Lennep (1966, 230–232).

5. Paris/Hamburg catalogue (1985–86, no. 83).

6. Verhaeren (1913, 53).

7. Lhote (1939–41, 95).

8. Marijnissen (1988, 224).

9. The two-headed eagle also appears in Bruegel's painting, though less accurately reproduced. On a technical level the comparison with Van Amstel is confirmed here; Van Mander (1604) said of this artist that backgrounds contributed to his painting's overall effect, and that Bruegel followed him in this.

10. James Ensor, *Christ Entering Brussels* (1888, Malibu, Getty Museum).

11. Genaille (1979, 185).

12. Auner (1956, 105).

13. Demus (1981, 83) sums up this question.

14. The technical comments in this chapter are the fruit of long conversations, starting in 1963, with Albert Philippot, who took on the restoration of the Bruegel works at the Brussels museum (see Roberts-Jones *et al.*, 1969, 9–41). Technical data were established at our request by the Institut royal du patrimoine artistique in Brussels, under the direction of René Sneyers and later Liliane Masschelein, assisted by Albert Philippot, Jacqueline Folie, Régine Guislain–Wittermann, and Daniel Soumeryn.

15. Van Mander (1604). See "Biographical Sources," 3, 333.

16. Vasari (1981–9, 3, 385).

17. Lammertse (1994, 400–403).

18. Wolfthal (1989, *passim*).

19. Philippot *et al.* (1969, 5–32).

20. Grossmann (1973[1], 14).

21. Philippot *et al.* (1969, 6).

22. Smolderen (1995, 38).

23. Van Leeuwen (1970, 25–39).

24. Oberhuber (1980, 62–63).

25. *Ibid.*

26. Meij (1980, 73). The drawing cited, which is in Cambridge, is accepted as Bruegel's by most writers, but Mielke (1997, 77) suggests it is by R. Savery.

27. Robinson, in Washington/New York catalog (1986, 154–57).

28. Lebeer (1969, 29); K. Oberhuber, cited by Freedberg (1989, 104).

29. Marijnissen (1988, 159). Mielke (1997, 61) believes that the drawing at the Fondation Custodia in Paris, whose image is reversed and is generally referred to as a copy, may in fact be a preparatory sketch.

30. Lebeer (1969, 150).

31. Butts and Koerner in the Saint Louis/Cambridge catalog (1995, 93).

CHAPTER III

1. Lampsonius (1572). See "Biographical Sources," 1, 332.

2. Combe (1948, 439).

3. Tolnay (1952, no. 46); Lebeer (1969, 54).

4. Hand, in *Early Netherlandish Painting* catalog, Washington, National Gallery, 1986, 32.

5. Lebeer (1969, 56).

6. Meij (1980, 90).

7. Combe (1948, 439).

8. Barnouw (1947, 20).

9. Oberhuber (1980, 68).

10. Meij (1980, 87).

11. Marijnissen (1988, 98).

12. Van Mander (1604). See "Biographical Sources," 3, 333.

13. Van Schoute *et al.* (1995, 7).

14. Van Mander (1604). See "Biographical Sources," 3, 333.

15. Hymans (1987, *passim*); De Coo (1978, 33).

16. Fierens (1949, 35); Jedlicka (1938, 92).

17. Marijnissen (1988, 192).

18. *Ibid.*

19. Panse and Schmidt (1967, 10). Antifeminism is discussed by Marijnissen (1988, 187–92) and Gibson (1991[1], 102–108).

20. Nieuwdorp (1985, n.p.).

21. Tolnay (1935, 31).

22. Verougstraete and Van Schoute (1993, 43).

23. Van Mander (1604). See "Biographical Sources," 3, 333. The link is made notably by Romdahl (1905, 121) and Hulin de Loo in Van Bastelaer and Hulin de Loo (1907, 300) and Marijnissen (1988, 16).

24. Jedlicka (1938, 103).

25. Gibson (1991[1], 72).

26. Friedländer (1921, 102).

27. Moxey (1973, 49).

28. Van Mander (1604). See "Biographical Sources," 3, 333.

29. Verougstraete and Van Schoute (1993, 36, 43).

30. Marijnissen (1988, 16, n. 17).

31. Sneyers (1969, 18).

32. Van Bastelaer and Hulin de Loo (1907, 118); Grossmann (1973[1], 92).

33. Demus (1981, 62).

34. Gaignebet and Ricoux (1988, 12–21).

35. *Ibid.*, 20.

36. Folie, in Marlier (1969, 118).

37. Marijnissen (1988, 148).

38. Gibson (1980, 39); Stridbeck (1956[2], 198).

39. S. Franck (1544), cited by Demus in Balis *et al.* (1987, 67).

40. Gaignebet and Ricoux (1988, 21).

41. Lebeer (1969, 136–41).

42. *Ibid.*, 144.

43. Marijnissen (1988, 165).

44. Stechow, cited by Gibson (1991[1], 42).

45. Letter from F. Stuyck del Bruyère to the chief curator L. van Puyvelde, Antwerp, 8 February 1930. Archive of the Musées royaux des Beaux-Arts de Belgique, no. 5870/129.

46. Tolnay (1935, 36).

47. *The Princes Gate Collection* catalog, London, Courtauld Institute Galleries, 1981, no. 8.

48. Glück (1948, 449).

49. For example, Dvorak (1928, 239), Vanbeselaere (1944, 63).

50. Davies (1968, 21).

51. Van Mander (1604). See "Biographical Sources," 3, 333.

52. Demus (1981, 119).

53. Campbell (1985, 14).

54. *Ibid.*, 17.

55. *Ibid.*, 16.

56. Lebeer (1969, 146); Freedberg (1989, 165).

57. Popelier (1969, *passim*).

58. Urbach (1978, 252).

59. Duverger (1984–89, IV, 306).

60. Popham (1931, 187).

61. Grossmann (1973[1], 196).

62. Urbach (1978, 250).

63. Marlier (1969, 93–95).

64. Urbach (1978, 145–51).

65. Grossmann (1973[1], 196).

66. Genaille (1976, 107).

67. For more on the calumny of Apelles, see I. Aghion *et al.*, *Héros et Dieux de l'Antiquité*, Paris, Flammarion, 1994, 40–43, and Cast (1981).

68. Vasari (1981–99, 4, 263).

69. Van Mander (1604). See "Biographical Sources," 3, 333.

70. Tolnay (1952, no. A21) Münz (1961, 239).

71. Grossmann (1954[1], 54–63); Mielke (1997, 62–63).

72. Grossmann (1952, 222); Freedberg (1989, 185).

73. Van Lennep (1966, 233).

74. Gibson (1991, 132–33); Lebeer (1969, 184); Marijnissen (1988, 170).

75. Whitlow, in Saint Louis/Cambridge catalog (1995, 55).

76. Wood panel, 53¾ x 10 in. (136.5 x 25.5 cm). Brussels, Musées royaux des Beaux-Arts de Belgique, inv. 726.

77. Van Mander (1604). See "Biographical Sources," 3, 333.

78. Demus in Balis *et al.* (1987, 92).

79. Ortelius (about 1573). See "Biographical Sources," 2, 332.

80. *Ibid.*

81. Cf. *supra* ("The Italian Journey," "The Art of Drawing").

82. Van Mander (1604). See "Biographical Sources," 3, 332.

83. Meij (1980, 75).

84. We might also have mentioned *Mountainous Landscape with River, Village, and Castle*, now in the Pierpont Morgan Library, New York (see Robinson in Washington/New York catalogue [1986, 93–94]) and ruled out by Mielke (1997, 74–75) on account of the watermark.

85. Dürer in Marlier and Goris (1970, 94).

86. Genaille (1987, 146).

87. Vasari, letter of 12 February 1547, cited by W. S. Gibson in Tokyo/Kyoto catalog (1990, 17).

88. Brussels, Musées royaux des Beaux-Arts de Belgique, inv. 4630.

89. Mariette, *Abecedario*, V, 391–92, cited in Paris catalog (1967, 120).

90. Allart in Brussels/Rome catalog (1995, 112).

91. Gibson in Tokyo/Kyoto catalog (1990, 12).

92. See Chapter I, "Landmarks in a Life," n. 33.

93. Demus (1981, 87).

94. *Ibid.*, 86–94.

95. Genaille (1953, 93).

96. Marijnissen (1988, 253). Professor Émile Biemont, of the University of Liège, points out that "the practice of beginning the calendar year on 1 January dates from 1 January 1576, in accordance with the reform instituted by the king of Spain, Philip II. Before this reform two dating systems were used, according to which the year began either at Christmas or at Easter The use of Easter became widespread during the 13th century."

97. W. C. Williams, *Pictures from Brueghel and Other Poems*, Norfolk, J. Laughlin, 1962, 8.

98. Tolnay and Bianconi (1981, 103). On the other hand, some writers point to local elements such as the church, in this case comparable to that at Itterbeek (Van Linthoudt, 1990, 34). These topographical theories underline the composite nature of Bruegel's landscapes.

99. Demus, in Balis *et al.* (1987, 88).

100. *Ibid.*, 88.

101. For half a century, the work was a companion to the work and life of Dr Franz Delporte, an enlightened art lover who left his collection to the Brussels museum in 1974.

102. Such as Glück, Menzel, Grossmann, and Marijnissen.

103. Marlier (1969, 242–50).

104. Friedländer (1976, 27).

105. Van Mander (1604). See "Biographical Sources," 3, 333.

106. Genaille (1980[2], 143–52).

107. Tolnay (1935, 41).

108. Grossmann (1973[1], 203).

109. Gibson in Tokyo/Kyoto catalogue (1990, 20).

110. M. de Ghelderode, *La Pie sur le Gibet*, in *Théâtre*, III, Paris, Gallimard, 1953, 35.

111. Marijnissen and Seidel (1969, 99).

112. Marlier (1969, 62–64).

113. Hulin de Loo in Van Bastelaer and Hulin de Loo (1907, 290).

114. Bye (1923, 24–5) points out other parallels in the illuminations of *The Very Rich Hours of the Duke of Berry*, the *Turin-Milan Hours* and, especially relevant to this painting, the *Grimani Breviary*.

115. Marlier, in Brussels catalogue (1963, 72).

116. Tokyo/Kyoto catalogue, 1990, 136.

117. Marlier, in Brussels catalogue (1963, 72).

118. Hulin de Loo, in Van Bastelaer and Hulin de Loo (1907, 291).

119. Tolnay (1935, 36).

120. For example, in the 15th century, the book of hours now in the national library in Madrid, no. Vit. 25–3, fol. 57.

121. Cf. *supra* ("Drawings for Prints").

122. Vinken (1957) cited by Marijnissen (1988, 348).

123. This text by Colijn van Rijssele, republished in Haarlem about 1561, is cited by Marijnissen, *ibid.*

124. Glück (1963, 86).

125. Francastel (1995, 52).

126. Demus (1981, 107).

127. Janson (1952, 4).

128. Tolnay (1935, 45).

129. Delevoy (1959, 69).

130. Janson (1952, 154).

131. Panofsky (1939, 195).

132. Glück (1963, 59).

133. Terlinden (1942, 249).

134. Monballieu (1983, *passim*); Genaille (1983[2], 237–38).

135. Stridbeck (1956[2], 210), derived from a French translation by Marijnissen (1988, 202).

136. Meij (1980, 92).

137. *Ibid.*, 94.

138. Freedberg (1989, 19).

139. Stridbeck, cited by Klein (1963, 243).

140. Lebeer (1969, 104).

141. Romdahl, cited by Klein (1963, 244).

142. Meij (1980, 97).

143. Drawings now in the Fondation Custodia in Paris (*Temperance*) and the Städelsches Kunstinstitut, Franfurt (*Justice* and *Faith*).

144. Marijnissen (1988) and Mori (1992) list 85 proverbs, Tolnay and Bianconi 118; see the latter work.

145. Gibson (1991[1], 65). Van Gils (1940–41, I, 1–52).

146. Van Mander (1604). See "Biographical Sources,"
3, 333.
147. Gibson (1991[1], 66).
148. Ella S. Siple, "A 'Flemish Proverb,' Tapestry in
Boston," *The Burlington Magazine*, LXIII, 1933, 29–35.
The episodes mentioned occur in Bruegel's painting;
the cloak is a sort of hooded cape with a peak; the blue
color symbolizes cuckolded husbands.
149. Demus in Balis *et al.* (1987, 66).
150. Tolnay (1935, 23).
151. Tolnay and Bianconi (1981, 94).
152. Lebeer (1939–40, *passim*).
153. Cf. *supra* ("From Carnival to Lent").
154. Tolnay (1935, 18).
155. Erasmus, *The Praise of Folly*, Paris, Garnier-
Flammarion, 1964, 14).
156. Grauls (1957, 116).
157. F. Rabelais, *Oeuvres Complètes*, La Nouvelle
Revue française, "La Pléiade," 1938, 59.
158. Briels (1980, 224).
159. Gessler (1933, 103).
160. Folie, in Marlier (1969, 125–26).
161. Lebeer (1939–40, *passim*).
162. Grauls (1960, 107–64).
163. Marlier (1969, 121–22).
164. Rabelais, *op. cit.* (n. 57), 832.
165. Marijnissen (1988, 137); Mori (1992, 257).
166. De Coo (1965, *passim*).
167. Nieuwdorp (1992, 40).
168. Marijnissen (1988, 384).
169. De Coo (1965, 90).
170. Lebeer (1969, 155).
171. *Ibid.*, 156.
172. *Ibid.*, 76.
173. For the mark of Hieronymus Cock, see Rotterdam
catalog (1988, 82).
174. Lebeer (1969, 78).
175. *Ibid.*, 79; Gibson (1991[1], 54).
176. Freedberg (1989, 131).
177. Cf. *supra* ("The Lessons of 'The Alchemist'").
178. Würtenberger (1957, 78).
179. Freedberg (1989, 160–61).
180. Lebeer (1969, 134).
181. *Ibid.*, 86.
182. Van Lennep (1965, 109).
183. Lebeer (1969, 84).
184. *Ibid.*, 180.
185. Würtenberger (1957, 119–20, 138).
186. Lebeer (1969, 87).
187. Janson (1952, 221, fig. 13 and plates XLI–XLII).
188. Van Mander (1604[4], 108).
189. Mori (1988[2] *passim*); Vanden Branden (1981,
31–40).
190. Demus (1981, 68).
191. Van Mander (1604). See "Biographical Sources,"
3, 333.
192. Rabelais, *op. cit.* (note 157), 86–89.
193. Demus (1981, 68).
194. Delevoy (1959, 58).
195. Hindman (1981, 454).
196. Tolnay (1935, 26).
197. Hindman (1981, 469).
198. S. Brant, *Das Narren Schiff*, Basel, Bergmann
d'Olpe, 1494; French edition *La Nef Des Fous*,
Brussels, Seghers/Strasbourg, Nuée-bleue, 1979, 129.

199. Demus (1981, 71).
200. Hindman (1981, 461–63).
201. Catalogs cited in Hindman (1981, 466).
202. Demus (1981, 71).
203. Philippot (1994, 192).
204. Laffont-Bompiani, *Dictionnaire des Personnages*,
Paris, Société d'édition de dictionnaires et encyclopédies,
1960, 564.
205. Michel (1953, 42).
206. Glück (1963, 88).
207. Delevoy (1959, 76).
208. Tolnay (1935, 48).
209. Marquet (1977, 11–13).
210. Maeterlinck (1907, 310–11) sees a satire on heretical beggars, and Sudeck (1931, 28–29) a satire on the
clergy.
211. Matthew, XV, 14.
212. Claudel, *Journal*, II, 412. We are grateful to the
rector Gérald Antoine for drawing our attention to this
quotation.
213. Marijnissen (1988, 365–68).
214. Claessens and Rousseau (1969, plate 53a) regarding
the proposition of Dr. Tony Michel Torrilhon.
215. Marlier (1969, 113).
216. Glück (1963, 89); Marlier (1969, 111–16 and
360–62).
217. Freedberg (1989, 174).
218. Marijnissen (1988, 365–66).
219. Williams, *op. cit.* note 97.
220. Van Gils (1940–41, II, 48).
221. Anzelewsky, in Berlin catalogue (1975, 80–82).
222. Van Bastelaer and Hulin de Loo (1907, II, 201).
223. Roberts-Jones (1989, 11–13).
224. Vervliet, cited by Marijnissen (1988, 360).
225. Lebeer (1969, 158).
226. Tolnay and Bianconi (1981, 110).
227. Tolnay (1935, I, 47).
228. *Ibid.*
229. Lebeer (1955, 208).
230. *Ibid.*, *passim*.
231. Tolnay (1935, I, 66, note 57; II, fig. 123).
232. *Ibid.* I, 27.
233. Francastel (1995, 204).
234. Lebeer (1955, 204).
235. *Ibid.* 214.
236. Genesis XI, 4.
237. Genesis XI, 6–7.
238. Genesis XI, 9.
239. Roberts-Jones-Popelier (1989–91, 266–73).
240. Van Mander (1604). See "Biographical Sources,"
3, 333.
241. Demus in Balis *et al.*, 1987, 76.
242. M. Yourcenar, *Souvenirs Pieux*, Paris, Gallimard,
1974, 55.
243. Demus (1981, 79).
244. Francastel (1995, 134).
245. Marlier (1969, 96).
246. *Ibid.*
247. Elliston Weiner, cited by Marijnissen (1988,
210–11).
248. Gibson (1991[1], 97).
249. Van Mander (1604). See "Biographical Sources,"
3, 333.
250. Lammertse (1994, 402).
251. Cf. *supra* ("The Layers of a Painting").

252. Tolnay (1938, 119–20); Genaille (1953, 88);
Lammertse (1994, 402–03).
253. Klamt (1979, 46–49).
254. Mansbach (1982, 49).
255. Marlier (1969, 47).
256. Tolnay (1935, 86); Gibson (1989, 33) attributes it
to the Master of the Sermon of Lille.
257. Marlier (1966, 373–74).
258. Pirenne (1949, II, 254).
259. Marlier (1969, 49).
260. Auner (1956, 114–15); Menzel (1966, 78). A
similar composition can be found in Rembrandt, for
example in the engraving *The Triumph of Mardochée*.
261. Tolnay (1935, 43).
262. Glück (1963, 84).
263. Grossmann (1973[1], 200).
264. Marijnissen (1988, 305).
265. Marlier (1969, 47–59).
266. *Ibid.*, 52.
267. *Ibid.*
268. Van Mander (1604). See "Biographical Sources,"
3, 332–33.
269. Scheyer (1965, 168–69).
270. Tolnay (1935) and Jedlicka (1938) for example.
271. Van Miegroet (1992, 140).
272. *Ibid.*
273. Lebeer (1969, 148).
274. *Ibid.*
275. Freedberg (1989, 166).
276. *Ibid.*, 167.
277. M. Carroll, cited by Huvane in Freedberg (1989,
167). K. Moxey (in Freedberg, *ibid.*, 49) gives a
summary of the various theories.
278. Marlier (1969, 188).
279. *Ibid.*, 87.
280. *Ibid.*, 186–211.
281. *Ibid.*, 169–70.
282. Jaffé (1979, 39–40).
283. Hand, in Washington/New York catalogue (1986,
99–100); Lebeer (1969, 90–92). Mielke (1997, 55–56)
considers it an original.
284. Lebeer, *ibid.*, 129; Freedberg (1989, 158).
285. Marijnissen (1988, 115).
286. Lebeer (1969, 129); Freedberg (1989, 134–35).
287. Decree of Charles V of 7 October 1531, in
Lameere (1902, 270–71).
288. Marlier (1969, 159).
289. Hand, in Washington/New York catalog (1986,
104). For *The Painter and the Art Lover* cf. *supra*
("Creator or Misanthrope?"). Mielke (1977, 63–64)
also mentions a *Bagpiper*.
290. Demus in Balis *et al.* (1987, 96).
291. Marijnissen (1988, 317).
292. Demus in Balis *et al.* (1987, 96).
293. Marijnissen (1988, 316–17). The imperial
inventory of 1659 mentions "a peasant wedding where
a Franciscan friar is seated next to the magistrate".
294. Jedlicka (1938, 263–64).
295. Tolnay (1935, I, 53).
296. Gibson (1991[1], 166).
297. Hulin de Loo in Van Bastelaer and Hulin de Loo
(1907, 305). For Verbeeck's peasant weddings, see
Vandenbroeck (1984, 79–124).
298. Hollstein (1949, III, 103).
299. Demus in Balis *et al.* (1987, 97).

300. Stridbeck (1956², 220); Grossmann (1973¹, 201).

301. Stridbeck (1956², 216).

302. Tolnay (1935, I, 62–64).

303. A. Huxley, *Breughel*, in *Collected Essays*, New York, Harper & Brothers, 1958, 142.

304. Smolderen (1995, 33–39).

305. Marlier (1969, 177).

306. Demus (1981, 116).

307. Cf. *infra*, ("Collection Inventories," n. 25).

308. Tolnay (1935, I, 98).

309. Hulin de Loo in Van Bastelaer and Hulin de Loo (1907, 331–32). See Chapter IV, n. 23.

310. Van Camp (1950, 389–91 and 1954, 217–23).

311. Guicciardini (1582, 107).

312. Elliston Weiner in Amsterdam catalog (1986, II, 281).

313. *The Flemish Proverbs* (1559), Berlin.

314. Lebeer (1969, 110–13).

315. Burchard, cited by Glück (1963, 37).

316. Demus (1981, 135); Klein (1983, 71).

317. Demus (1981, 128–38).

318. Marijnissen (1988, 158). *The Princes Gate Collection* catalogue, London, Courtauld Institute Galleries, 1981, no.127, considers the drawing a mature work, about 1559.

319. All references, not spelt out here, can be found in *The Fall of Icarus*, which is devoted to this work, See Roberts-Jones (1974, *passim*).

320. E. Nyenhuis, in *Lexicon Iconographicum Mythologiae Classicae*, III, 1, Zurich/Munich, Artemis Verlag, 1986, 313–21.

321. For editions of Ovid also see G. Duplessis, *Essai Bibliographique sur les Différentes Éditions des Oeuvres d'Ovide*, Paris, Vve Léon Techener, 1889, *passim*, and, for the emblems, Weisstein (1982, 67).

322. Hulin de Loo in Van Bastelaer and Hulin de Loo (1907, 340).

323. Marlier (1966, 300–301).

324. Kavaler (1986, 98); Baldwin (1986, 104).

325. Tervarent (1958, I, 222–23).

326. Brussels, Musée Van Buuren. A recent dendrochronological analysis (1996) provides proof.

327. Roberts-Jones (1974, 40).

328. Verhaeren (1913, 55); R. Wouters in N. Wouters, *La Vie de Rik Wouters à Reavers son Oeuvre*, Brussels, Lumière, 1944, 58.

329. Smolderen (1955, 38). As for the painting in question, neither recent reflectographic analysis nor radiocarbon dating has been decisive.

330. Brion (1936, 40).

331. M. Yourcenar, *op. cit.* n. 242 to this chapter, 55.

332. W. H. Auden, *Musée des Beaux-Arts*, in *The Collected Poetry of W. H. Auden*, New York, 1945, 3.

333. A. Comte-Sponville, *Vivre*, Paris, PUF, 1988, 239. We are grateful to the poet Fernand Verhesen for bringing this text to our attention.

CHAPTER IV

1. Hulin de Loo in Van Bastelaer and Hulin de Loo (1907, 323–65).

2. Van Mander (1604). See "Biographical Sources," 3, 333.

3. Marlier (1969, 280–82).

4. Dogaer (1971, 210).

5. Hulin de Loo in Van Bastelaer and Hulin de Loo (1907, 310).

6. *Ibid.*, 326; Van Mander (1604). See "Biographical Sources," 3, 333.

7. Auner, Van Gils, Marijnissen, in Marijnissen (1988, 16, note 17); Verougstraete et Van Shoute (1993, 36).

8. Smolderen (1995, 38–39).

9. De Maeyer (1955, 259).

10. Coremans (1847, 102, 109).

11. Demus (1981, 81); Marlier (1969, 287).

12. Hulin de Loo in Van Bastelaer and Hulin de Loo (1907, 327–30).

13. Meijer (1988, 183).

14. Filipczak (1987, 215).

15. Duverger (1984–89, 172–77).

16. De Coo (1965, 90–97).

17. Hulin de Loo in Van Bastelaer and Hulin de Loo (1907, 336–41).

18. *Ibid.*, 242–45.

19. De Maeyer (1955, 422–23).

20. Duverger (1984–89, 301–09).

21. Winner, in Berlin catalogue (1975, 5–6). This drawing is questioned by Mielke (1997, no. A3, 75–76), who suggests it may be by R. Savery.

22. Hulin de Loo in Van Bastelaer and Hulin de Loo (1907, 331).

23. Hulin de Loo considers it original (*ibid.*, 332). See fig. 314.

24. *Ibid.*, 333–36; Marlier (1969, 264–74).

25. Briels (1980, *passim*).

26. Tolnay (1935, I, fig. 92).

27. Briels (1980, 195) See also note 4 to this chapter and Glück (1963, 62).

28. Marijnissen (1988, 244).

29. Glück (1963, 79–80).

30. Marlier (1969, 256).

31. Mattioli (1976, 32); Bedoni (1983, 173–75).

32. Marlier (1969, 304).

33. *Ibid.*, 285–94, where the author, like Glück (1963, 115), mentions a Latin text by Arnoldus Buchelius in his *Res Pictoriae*, claiming to have seen a "crucifix van Bruegel" of 1559 at the house of Bartholomeus Ferreris of Leiden.

34. Huyghe (1955, 150).

35. Grossmann, cited by P. and F. Roberts-Jones in Brussels catalogue (1980, 58).

36. Grossmann, in Brussels catalogue (1980, 59); Karling (1976, 1–18).

37. Lebeer (1969, 126). The drawing is mentioned by Mielke (1997, 55 and 166).

38. Marlier (1969, 356–57).

39. Lampsonius (1572). See "Biographical Sources," 1, 332.

40. Briels, (1980, 193–94). Derived from a translation from the Latin by Professor René Hoven, who believes this quatrain "does not seem to be by Lampsonius himself, but by a rather clumsy imitator" (letter of 18/4/1996).

41. Ortelius (about 1573). Lampsonius (1572). See "Biographical Sources," 2, 332.

42. Tolnay and Bianconi (1981, 11).

43. Briels (1980, 195).

44. R. Herrick, *To his Nephew, to be Prosperous in His Art of Painting*, in *Hesperides* (*Poems*, London, 1936, 170). We are grateful to Professor Jean Weisgerber for providing this reference.

45. Bazin (1986, 62).

46. Sandrart, cited in Von Löhneysen (1956, 148, derived from the authors' translation to French).

47. Félibien (1705, II, 272); Le Comte (1702, 217–18).

48. Von Löhneysen (1956, 148).

49. Winner, in Berlin catalogue (1975, 3).

50. Houbraken, cited in Marijnissen (1988, 43); Orlandi, cited in Tolnay and Bianconi (1981, 11).

51. Descamps (1840, 60).

52. Mariette, cited in Paris catalogue 1967, 108.

53. Tolnay and Bianconi (1981, 11).

54. Glück (1963, 74).

55. Von Löhneysen (1956, 150).

56. Baudelaire (1961, 1022–24).

57. *Ibid.*, 1434.

58. Fromentin (1984, 580).

59. Taine (1909, II, 38).

60. *Ibid.*, 340.

61. Fierens (1948, 487).

62. E. Verlant, in *La Jeune Belgique*, Brussels, 1894, 96.

63. *L'Atelier Leys*, sale, Antwerp, 19–23 December 1893, 30–34 (annotated copy, library of the Musées royaux des Beaux-Arts de Belgique, Brussels).

64. Marlier (1969, 180) mentions rural versions but does not appear to have known the Leys collection. The work reproduced on 181 is very similar but signed and dated 1626.

65. Marlier (1969, 302–05).

66. *Ibid.*, 381.

67. *Ibid.*, 238.

68. *Ibid.*, 188.

69. Caricature by F. Rops, in *Uylenspiegel au Salon*, Brussels, 157.

70. Exposition *Générale des Beaux-Arts. 1857*, Brussels, 1857, 84. Today this painting is in the Musée des Beaux-Arts, Antwerp (inv. 1099).

71. Baudelaire (1961, 1068).

72. Catalogue of the sale of the estate of Charles De Groux, Brussels, 6–7 June 1870.

73. Roberts-Jones-Popelier (1996, *passim*).

74. X. Tricot, *James Ensor. Catalogue Raisonné des Peintures*, I, Antwerp, 1992, no. 351.

75. Hulin de Loo, in Bruges sale catalogue (1902, 100).

76. See also Michel (1938), Grossmann (1973¹), Tolnay and Bianconi (1981), Marijnissen (1988).

77. Verhaeren (1913, 50–60).

78. *Le Soir*, 31 May 1924; reproduced in *Les Écrits de James Ensor*, Brussels, 1944, 126–27.

79. A. Artaud, *Le Théâtre et son Double*, Paris, Gallimard, 1938, 129.

80. Hadermann, *Het Vuur in de Verte. Paul van Ostaijens Kunstoppvattingen in het Licht van de Europese Avant-Garde*, Antwerp, Ontwitkkeling, 1970, 117 (derived from a translation by Hadermann, to whom we are grateful for drawing attention to this text).

81. Burness (1972–73, 157–62).

82. W. H. Auden, *The Collected Poetry*, New York, 1945, 3.

83. Huxley, 1958, 139–43, *op. cit.*, n. 303, Chapter III.

84. Dobbels (1994, 65).

85. Grauls (1957, 91–92); Tolnay and Bianconi (1981, 94).

86. Dobbels (1994, 66).

BIBLIOGRAPHY

The bibliography has been written with the assistance of Bénédicte Schifflers. Without aiming to be exhaustive, this bibliography covers Bruegel's works, their artistic and historic context, and the painter's influence on others. It lists the reference works used, alphabetically by author with their date of publication, and brings together general studies, monographs, and the main articles published in journals and catalogues. Exhibition catalogues are ordered alphabetically by place, with their dates.

BOOKS AND ARTICLES

ALLART, 1993
Dominique Allart, "Approche de la Technique Picturale de Pieter Bruegel l'Ancien," *ICOM Committee for Conservation*, I, 1993, 65–69.

ALPERS, 1972–73
Svetlana Alpers, "Bruegel's Festive Peasants," *Simiolus*, 6, 3/4, 1972–73, 163–76.

ALPERS, 1975–76
Svetlana Alpers, "Realism as a Comic Mode: Low-Life Painting seen Through Bredero's Eyes," *Simiolus*, 8, 3, 1975–76, 115–44.

ARGAN, 1984
Giulio C. Argan, "Cultura e Realismo di Pieter Bruegel," *Classico, Anticlassico. Il Rinascimento da Brunelleschi a Bruegel*, Milan, Feltrinelli, 1984, 399–410.

ARNDT, 1967
Karl Arndt, "Frühe Landschaftszeichnungen von Pieter Bruegel d. Ä.," *Pantheon*, XXV, 1967, 97–104.

ARNDT, 1972
Karl Arndt, "Pieter Bruegel d. Ä. und die Geschichte der 'Waldlandschaft'," *Jahrbuch der Berliner Museen*, XIV, 1972, 69–121.

AUNER, 1956
Michael Auner, "Pieter Bruegel. Umrisse eines Lebensbildes," *Jahrbuch der kunsthistorischen Sammlungen in Wien*, 52, 1956, 5 –122.

BAIE, 1938
Eugène Baie, *Le Siècle des Gueux (Histoire de la Sensibilité Flamande sous la Renaissance*, III, *Le Rameau en Fleurs)*, Bruxelles, Nouvelle Société d'éditions, 1938, 285–450.

BAKHTIN, 1970
Mikhaïl Bakhtin, *L'Oeuvre de François Rabelais et la Culture Populaire au Moyen Âge et sous la Renaissance*, translated from the Russian by Andrée Robel, Paris, Gallimard, 1970.

BALDASS, 1918
Ludwig von Baldass, "Die niederländische Landschaftsmalerei von Patinir bis Bruegel," *Jahrbuch der kunsthistorischen Sammlungen des allerhöchsten Kaiserhauses*, 34, 1918, 111–57.

BALDASS, 1948
Ludwig von Baldass, "Les paysanneries de Pierre Bruegel," *Les Arts Plastiques*, 11–12, 1948, 471–84.

BALDASS, 1960
Ludwig von Baldass, *Hieronymus Bosch*, London, Thames & Hudson, 1960 (1st edition in German: Vienna, Anton Schroll & Co., 1943).

BALDWIN, 1986
Robert Baldwin, "Peasant Imagery and Bruegel's 'Fall of Icarus'," *Konsthistorisk Tidskrift*, LV, 1986, 101–14.

BALIS et al., 1987
Arnout Balis *et al.*, *La Peinture Flamande au Kunsthistorisches Museum de Vienne*, Antwerp, Fonds Mercator/Zurich, Verlag Hans, "Flandria Extra Muros," 1987.

BARNOUW, 1947
Adriaan J . Barnouw, *The Fantasy of Pieter Brueghel*, New York, Lear, 1947.

BARNOUW, 1949
Adriaan J. Barnouw, "Bruegels Verzoeking van den Heiligen Antonius," *Miscellanea Leo van Puyvelde*, Brussels, Éditions de la connaissance, 1949, 104–06.

BAUDELAIRE, 1961
Charles Baudelaire, *Oeuvres complètes*, Paris, Gallimard, "La Pléiade," 1961.

BAUER, 1984
Linda and George Bauer, "The Winter Landscape with Skaters and Bird Trap by Pieter Bruegel the Elder," *The Art Bulletin*, LXVI, 1, March 1984, 145–50.

BAZIN, 1963
Germain Bazin, "L'École Flamande aux Prises avec la Renaissance," *Le Siècle de Bruegel. La peinture en Belgique au XVIᵉ siècle*, see Brussels catalogue, 1963, 23–28.

BAZIN, 1986
Germain Bazin, *Histoire de l'Histoire de l'Art de Vasari à nos Jours*, Paris, Albin Michel, 1986.

BEDAUX, VAN GOOL, 1974
J. B. Bedaux and A. van Gool, "Bruegel's Birthyear, Motive of an Ars/Natura Transmutation," *Simiolus*, 7, 3, 1974, 133–56.

BEDONI, 1983
Stefania Bedoni, *Jan Brueghel in Italia e il Collezionismo del Seicento,* Florence/Milan, 1983.

BENESCH, 1965
Otto Benesch, *The Art of the Renaissance in Northern Europe. Its Relation to the Contemporary Spiritual and Intellectual Movements*, London, Phaidon, 1965.

BERNARD, 1908
Charles Bernard, *Pierre Bruegel l'Ancien*, Brussels, G. Van Oost & Cⁱᵉ, 1908.

BEVERS, 1995
Holm Bevers, "Pieter Bruegel as a Draughtsman," *The World of Bruegel. The Coppée Collection and Eleven International Museums*, see Tobu catalogue, 1995.

BIJNS, 1875
Anna Bijns, *Refereynen, naar de nalatenschap van Mr A. Bogaers uitgegeven door W. L. van Helten*, Rotterdam, 1875.

BIJNS, 1975
Anna Bijns, *Meer zuurs dan zoets*, introduction by Lode Roose, Hasselt, Heideland, "Poëtisch Erfdeel der Nederlanden," 1975 (1st edition: 1968).

BONICATTI, 1969
Maurizio Bonicatti, "Pieter Brueghel il Vecchio. La Riforma e l'Inquisizione nei Paesi Bassi. Secoli XIV–XVI," *Studi sull'Umanesimo*, V, Florence, La Nuova Italia Editrice, 1969, 177–254.

BOUCQUEY, 1991
Thierry Boucquey, "Mirages de la Farce. Fête des Fous, Bruegel et Molière," *Purdue University Monographs in Romance Languages*, 33, Amsterdam/Philadelphia, John Benjamin, 1991.

BOYEN, 1969
Yves Boyen, "Sur les Traces de Pierre Bruegel," *Brabant*, 4, 1969, 53–67.

BRECHT, 1957
Bertolt Brecht, "Verfremdungseffekt in erzählenden Bildern des älteren Brueghel," *Bildende Kunst*, 4, 1957, 229–33.

BRIELS, 1980
Jan Briels, "Amator Pictoriae Artis. De Antwerpse kunstverzamelaar Peeter Stevens (1590–1668) en zijn Constkamer," *Jaarboek van het Koninklijk Museum voor Schone Kunsten Antwerpen*, 1980, 137–226.

BRION, 1936
Marcel Brion, *Breughel*, Paris, Plon, 1936.

BRUMBLE, 1979
H. David Brumble III, "Peter Brueghel the Elder: the Allegory of Landscape," *The Art Quarterly*, New Series, II, 2, 1979, 125–39.

BUCHANAN, 1990
Iain Buchanan, "The collection of Niclaes Jongelinck, II: The 'Months' by Pieter Brueghel the Elder," *The Burlington Magazine*, CXXXII, 1049, August 1990, 541–50.

BURNESS, 1972–73
Donald B. Burness, "Pieter Brueghel: Painter for Poets," *Art Journal*, XXXII/2, winter 1972–73, 157–62.

BUYSSENS, 1954
O. Buyssens, "De Schepen bij Pieter Bruegel de Oude. Proeve van identificatiën," *Mededelingen van de Academie van Marine van België*, VIII, 1954, 159–91.

BYE, 1923
Arthur Edwin Bye, "Pieter Brueghel's 'Fall of Icarus' in the Brussels Museum," *Art Studies* 1, 1923, 22–27.

CALMANN, 1960
Gerta Calmann, "The Picture of Nobody. An Iconographical Study," *Journal of the Warburg and*

Courtauld Institutes, XXIII, 1–2, January–June 1960, 60–104.

CAMPBELL, 1985
Lorne Campbell, *The Early Flemish Pictures in the Collection of her Majesty The Queen,* Cambridge, Cambridge University Press, 1985.

CARROLL, 1987
Margaret D. Carroll, "Peasant Festivity and Political Identity in the Sixteenth Century," *Art History,* X, 3, September 1987, 289–314.

CAST, 1981
David Cast, *The Calumny of Apelles. A Study in the Humanist Tradition,* New Haven/London, Yale University Press, 1981.

CHASTEL, 1968
André Chastel, *La Crise de la Renaissance, 1520–1600,* Geneva, Skira, "Art, Idées, Histoire," 1968.

CLAESSENS, DASNOY, 1968
Bob Claessens and Albert Dasnoy, "Deux paysages marins. I. Combat Naval dans la Baie de Naples. II. La Chute d'Icare," *Peinture vivante,* 5. (RTB-Cultura), 19–20, 5th year, 1967–1968, Brussels, Cultura, 1968.

CLAESSENS, ROUSSEAU, 1969
Bob Claessens and Jeanne Rousseau, *Notre Bruegel,* Antwerp, Fonds Mercator, 1969.

COHEN, 1911
Walter Cohen, "Bruegel, Pieter d. Ä.," *Thieme Becker Allgemeines Lexikon der bildenden Künstler von der Antike bis zur Gegenwart,* edited by Ulrich Thieme and Felix Becker, V, Leipzig, Seemann, 1911, 100–102.

COLIN, 1936
Paul Colin, *Bruegel le Vieux,* Paris, Librairie Floury, "Anciens et Modernes," 9, 1936.

COLLOBI RAGGHIANTI, 1990
Licia Collobi Ragghianti, *Dipinti Fiamminghi in Italia 1420–1570. Catalogo,* Bologna, Calderini, 1990.

COMBE, 1948.
Jacques Combe, "Jérôme Bosch dans l'art de Pierre Bruegel," *Les Arts Plastiques,* 11–12, 1948, 435–46.

COORNHERT, 1585
D. V. Coornhert, *Recht ghebruyck ende misbruyck van tydlycke have. Van Rijckdom/Nodruft en ghebreck ick beluyck t'onzaligh misbruyck/mettet zaligh ghebruyck* (translated from Latin: *De rerum usu et abusu*), Leiden, Christophe Plantin, 1585.

COREMANS, 1847
A. Coremans, "L'Archiduc Ernest, sa Cour, ses Dépenses, 1593–1595. D'après les Comptes de Blaise Hütter, son Secrétaire Intime et Premier Valet de Chambre," *Comptes Rendus des Séances de la Commission Royale d'Histoire,* XIII, 1847, 85–147.

COX, 1951
Trenchard Cox, *Pieter Bruegel (c. 1527–1569),* London, Faber & Faber, 1951.

CRUCY, 1928
François Crucy, *Les Bruegel,* Paris, Rieder, "Maîtres de l'Art Ancien," 1928.

CUTTLER, 1968
Charles D. Cuttler, *Northern Painting. From Pucelle to Bruegel. Fourteenth, Fifteenth and Sixteenth Centuries,* New York, Holt, Rinehart and Winston, 1968, 469–85.

DAVIES, 1968
Martin Davies, *Early Netherlandish School, National Gallery Catalogues,* London, The National Gallery, 1968 (3rd edition, revised).

DE BIE, 1662
Cornelis De Bie, *Het guldea cabinet vande edele vry schilder–const inhoudende den lof vande Schilders, Architecten, Beldt–houwers ende Plaedt–snijders van deze eeuw,* Antwerp, Juliaen van Montfort, 1662.

DEBLAERE, 1969
Albert Deblaere S. J., "Erasmus, Bruegel en de humanistische Visie," *Vlaanderen,* 103, January–February 1969, 12–20.

DEBLAERE, 1977
Albert Deblaere S. J., "Bruegel and the Religious Problems of his Time," *Apollo,* CV, 181, March 1977, 176–80.

DE COO, 1965
Jozef De Coo, "Twaalf spreuken op borden van Pieter Bruegel de Oude," *Bulletin des Musées royaux des Beaux-Arts de Belgique,* XIV, 1965, 83–104.

DE COO, 1975
Jozef De Coo, "Die bemahlten Holzteller bekannte und neuentdeckte. Ihr Schmuck und seine Herkunft," *Wallraf-Richartz Jahrbuch,* XXXVII, 1975, 85–118.

DE COO, 1978
Jozef De Coo, "Bruegel," *Museum Mayer Van den Bergh. Catalogus,* I, Antwerp, 1978, 32–46.

DEINHARD, 1967
Hanna Deinhard, *Bedeutung und Ausdruck. Zur Soziologie der Malerei,* Berlin, Neuwied, "Soziologische Essays," 1967, 44–60.

DELEN, 1935
A. J. J. Delen, *Histoire de la Gravure dans les Anciens Pays-Bas & dans les Provinces Belges des Origines Jusqu'à la Fin du XVIIIe siècle,* II.2, Le XVIe Siècle. Les Graveurs d'Estampes, Paris/Brussels, Van Oest, 1935.

DELEVOY, 1959
Robert L. Delevoy, *Bruegel,* Geneva, Skira, 1959 (2nd edition 1990).

DELUMEAU, 1967
Jean Delumeau, *La Civilisation de la Renaissance,* Paris, Arthaud, "Les Grandes Civilisations,' 1967.

DE MAEYER, 1955
Marcel De Maeyer, "Albrecht en Isabella en de schilderkunst. Bijdrage tot de Geschiedenis van de XVIIe eeuwse schilderkunst in de zuidelijke Nederlanden," *Verhandelingen van de Koninklijke Vlaamse Academie voor Wetenschappen, Letteren en Schone Kunsten van België, Klasse der Schone Kunsten,* 9, Brussels, 1955.

DE MEYERE, 1941
Victor De Meyere, *De Kinderspelen van Pieter Bruegel den Oude (Å 1527–1569), verklaard door Victor De Meyere,* Antwerp, Gevaert, no date (1941).

DEMUS, 1981
Klaus Demus, "Bruegel, Pieter d. Ältere," *Flämische Malerei von Jan van Eyck bis Pieter Bruegel d. Ä. Katalog der Gemäldegalerie der Kunsthistorischen Museum Wien,* Vienna, Herold, 1981, 61–136.

DENIS (ed.), 1961
Valentin Denis (editor), *All the Paintings of Pieter Bruegel,* translated from the Italian by Paul Colacicchi, London, Oldbourne, "The Complete Library of World Art," 1, 1961 (1st edition: *Tutta la Pittura di Pieter Bruegel,* Milan, Rizzoli, 1952).

DENUCÉ, 1931
Jean Denucé, *Kunstuitvoer in de 17e eeuw te Antwerpen. De Firma Forchoudt,* Antwerp De Sikkel, "Bronnen voor de geschiedenis van de Vlaamse kunst," I, 1931.

DENUCÉ, 1932
Jean Denucé, *De Antwerpsche "Konstamers". Inventarissen van kunstverzamelingen te Antwerpen in de 16e en 17e eeuwen,* Antwerp, De Sikkel, "Bronnen voor de geschiedenis van deVlaamse kunst," II, 1932.

DE PAUW–DE VEEN, 1970
Lydia De Pauw-De Veen, *Jérôme Cock: Éditeur d'Estampes et Graveur, 1507(?)–1570,* see Brussels catalogue, 1970.

DE PAUW–DE VEEN, 1979
Lydia De Pauw-De Veen, "Das Brüsseler Blatt mit Bettlern und Krüppeln: Bosch oder Bruegel?," *Pieter Bruegel und seine Welt. Ein Colloquium veranstaltet vom Kunsthistorischen Institut der Freien Universität Berlin und dem Kupferstichkabinett der staatlichen Museen Stiftung preußischer Kulturbesitz, 13–14 November 1975,* Berlin, Gebr. Mann, 1979, 149–57.

DESCAMPS, 1840
Jean-Baptiste Descamps, *Vie des Peintres Flamands et Hollandais, par Descamps, Réunie à celle des Peintres Italiens et Français, par d'Argenville,* I, Marseille, Jules Barile, 1840.

DEZALLIER D'ARGENVILLE, 1745
Antoine-Joseph Dezallier d'Argenville, *Abrégé de la Vie des Plus Fameux Peintres, avec Leurs Portraits Gravés en Taille–Douce [...],* II, Paris, De Bure, 1745.

DOBBELS, 1994
Daniel Dobbels, *Brueghel,* Paris, Maeght Éditeur, "Chroniques anachroniques," 1994.

DOGAER, 1971
G. Dogaer, "De inventaris der schilderijen van Diego Duarte," *Jaarboek van het Koninklijk Museum voor Schone Kunsten Antwerpen,* 1971, 195–221.

DREYER, 1977
Peter Dreyer, "Bruegels Alchimist von 1558. Versuch einer Deutung ad sensum mysticum," *Jahrbuch der Berliner Museen,* XIX, 1977, 69–113.

DUMONT, 1977
Georges-Henri Dumont, *Histoire de la Belgique,* no place, Hachette, 1977.

DUNDES, STIBBE, 1981
Alan Dundes and Claudia A. Stibbe, *The Art of Mixing Metaphors. A Folkloristic Interpretation of the "Netherlandish Proverbs" by Pieter Bruegel the Elder,* Helsinki, "Suomalainen Tiedeakatemia/Academia Scientiarum Fennica, FF Communications, 230," 1981.

DUVERGER, 1984–89
Erik Duverger, *Antwerpse Kunstinventarissen uit de zeventiende eeuw (Fontes Historiae Artis Neerlandicae. Bronnen voor de Kunstgeschiedenis van de Nederlanden,* I), I–IV, Brussels, Koninklijke Academie voor Wetenschappen, Letteren en Schone Kunsten van België, 1984–89.

DVORAK, 1928
Max Dvorak, "Pieter Bruegel der Ältere," *Kunstgeschichte als Geistesgeschichte. Studien zur abendländischen Kunstentwicklung (Gesammelte Werke,* I), Munich, R. Piper & Co, 1928, 219–57.

DVORAK, 1992
Max Dvorak, *Pierre Bruegel l'Ancien*, translated by
Ernest Klaruill, Brionne, Gérard Monfort, 1992.
EGNER, 1978
Claus Peter Egner, "Pieter Breughel d. Ä.
Boschnachahmer oder Boschnachfolger?," *Alte und
Moderne Kunst*, 23rd year, 159, 1978, 5–10.
ELLISTON WEINER, 1985
Sarah Elliston Weiner, *The Tower of Babel in
Netherlandish Painting*, doctorate thesis, New York,
Columbia University, 1985.
ERTZ, 1979
Klaus Ertz, *Jan Brueghel der Ältere (1568–1625). Die
Gemälde mit kritischem Oeuvrekatalog*, Cologne,
DuMont, 1979.
FAGGIN, 1968
Giorgio T. Faggin, *La Pittura ad Anversa nel
Cinquecento*, Florence, Marchi & Bertolli, 1968.
FAGGIN, 1969
Giorgio T. Faggin, "Tra Bosch e Bruegel: Jan
Verbeeck," *Critica d'Arte*, 16th year, XXXIV, 108,
December 1969, 53–65.
FAGGIN, 1953
Giuseppe Faggin, *Brueghel*, Verona, Mondadori, 1953.
FALKENBURG, 1988
Reindert Leonard Falkenburg, *Joachim Patinir.
Landscape as an Image of the Pilgrimage of Life*,
Amsterdam/Philadelphia, John Benjamins Publishing
Company, "Oculi. Studies in the Arts of the Low
Countries," 1988.
FALKENBURG, 1990
Reindert Leonard Falkenburg, "Antithetical
Iconography in Early Netherlandish Landscape
Painting," *Bruegel and Netherlandish Landscape
Painting from the National Gallery Prague*, see
Tokyo/Kyoto catalogue, 1990.
FALKENBURG, 1993
Reindert Leonard Falkenburg, "Pieter Bruegels
'Kruisdraging': een proeve van 'close–reading'," *Oud
Holland*, 107, 1, 1993, 17–33.
FÉLIBIEN, 1705
André Félibien, *Entretiens sur les Vies et les Ouvrages
des plus Excellens Peintres, Anciens et Modernes*, II,
London, David Mortier, 1705 (original edition: Paris,
P. Le Petit, 1666–88).
FERBER, 1966
S. Ferber, "Pieter Bruegel and the Duke of Alba,"
Renaissance News, XIX, 3, 1966, 205–19.
FIERENS, 1947
Paul Fierens, *Le Fantastique dans l'Art Flamand*,
Brussels, Editions du Cercle d'art, 1947, 62–67.
FIERENS, 1948
Paul Fierens, "Postérité de Bruegel aux XIXe et XXe
siècles," *Les Arts Plastiques*, 11–12, 1948, 485–94.
FIERENS, 1949
Paul Fierens, *Peter Brueqel. Sa Vie, son Oeuvre, son
Temps*, Paris, Richard–Masse, 1949.
FILIPCZAK, 1987
Zirka Zaremba Filipczak, *Picturing Art in Antwerp
1550–1700*, Princeton (N.J.), Princeton University
Press, 1987.
FRAENGER, 1923
Wilhelm Fraenger, *Der Bauern–Bruegel und das
Deutsche Sprichwort*, Erlenbach/Zürich, Eugen
Rentsch, "Die Romische Bibliothek," 1923.

FRANCASTEL, 1995
Pierre Francastel, *Bruegel*, Paris, Hazan, 1995 (posthu-
mous edition).
FRANZ, 1969
Heinrich Gerhard Franz, *Niederländische
Landschaftsmalerei im Zeitalter des Manierismus*, 2 vols.,
Graz, "Forschungen und Berichte des Kunsthistorischen
Institutes der Universität Graz," II, 1969.
FREEDBERG, 1989
David Freedberg (editor), *The Prints of Pieter Bruegel
the Elder,* see Tokyo catalogue, 1989.
FRIEDLÄNDER, 1921
Max I. Friedländer, *Pieter Bruegel*, Berlin, Im
Propyläen Verlag, 1921.
FRIEDLÄNDER, 1976
Max J. Friedländer, *Pieter Bruegel*, commentary and
notes by Henri Pauwels, Leiden, A. W. Sijthoff/
Brussels, Editions de la Connaissance, "Early
Netherlandish Painting," XIV, 1976 (1st edition in
German: *Pieter Bruegel und Nachträge zu den früheren
Bänden*, Leiden, A. W. Sijthoff, "Die
Altniederländische Malerei," XIV, 1937).
FROMENTIN, 1984
Eugène Fromentin, *Oeuvres Complètes*, Paris,
Gallimard, "La Pléiade," 1984.
GAIGNEBET, 1972
Cl. Gaignebet, "Le Combat de Carnaval et de Carême
de P. Bruegel (1559)," *Annales: Économies, Sociétés,
Civilisations*, XXVII, 1972, 313–45.
GAIGNEBET, RICOUX, 1988
Cl. Gaignebet and O. Ricoux, "Le Combat de Carnaval
et Carême," *Carnavals et Mascarades*, edited by Pier
Giovanni d'Ayala and Martine Boiteux, Paris, Bordas,
1988, 12–21.
GENAILLE, 1953
Robert Genaille, *Bruegel l'Ancien*, Paris, Pierre Tisné,
1953.
GENAILLE, 1976
Robert Genaille, *Pierre Bruegel l'Ancien*, Bruxelles, La
Renaissance du Livre, 1976.
GENAILLE, 1979
Robert Genaille, "La 'Montée au Calvaire' de Bruegel
l'Ancien," *Jaarboek van het Koninklijk Museum voor
Schone Kunsten Antwerpen*, 1979, 143–96.
GENAILLE, 1980[1]
Robert Genaille, "'Naer den ouden Bruegel'. La Rixe
des Paysans," *Jaarboek van het Koninklijk Museum voor
Schone Kunsten Antwerpen*, 1980, 61–97.
GENAILLE, 1980[2]
Robert Genaille, "La Pie sur le Gibet," *Relations
Artistiques entre les Pays–Bas et l'Italie à la Renaissance.
Études Dédiées à Suzanne Sulzberger*, Brussels/Rome,
"Études d'Histoire de l'Art Publiées par l'Institut
Historique Belge de Rome," IV, 1980, 143–52.
GENAILLE, 1981
Robert Genaille, "Le 'Dénombrement de Bethléem' et
la Persistance des Goûts Anversois chez Bruegel
l'Ancien," *Jaarboek van het Koninklijk Museum voor
Schone Kunsten Antwerpen*, 1981, 61–95.
GENAILLE, 1982
Robert Genaille, "Carel van Mander et la Jeunesse de
Bruegel l'Ancien," *Jaarboek van het Koninklijk Museum
voor Schone Kunsten Antwerpen*, 1982, 119–51.
GENAILLE, 1983[1]
Robert Genaille, "De Breugel à G. van Coninxloo.

Remarques sur le Paysage Maniériste à la Fin du XVIe
siècle," *Jaarboek van het Koninklijk Museum voor
Schone Kunsten Antwerpen*, 1983, 129–67.
GENAILLE, 1983[2]
Robert Genaille, "Sur les 'Deux Singes' de P. Bruegel,"
Gazette des Beaux-Arts, CII, December 1983, 237–38.
GENAILLE, 1987
Robert Genaille, "Le Paysage dans la Peinture des
Anciens Pays–Bas de Patinier à Bruegel," *Jaarboek van
het Koninklijk Museum voor Schone Kunsten
Anttwerpen*, 1987, 143–83.
GENAILLE, 1988
Robert Genaille, "Le Paysage dans la Peinture des
Anciens Pays–Bas au Temps de Bruegel," *Jaarboek van
het Koninklijk Museum voor Schone Kunsten
Antwerpen*, 1988, 137–87.
GÉRARD, 1978
Jo Gérard, *Bruegel et son Époque*, Brussels, Paul
Legrain, 1978.
GERSZI, 1976
Teréz Gerszi, "Bruegels Nachwirkung auf die
niederländischen Landschaftsmaler um 1600.
Herausgestaltung der Waldlandschaftsdarstellung,"
Oud Holland, 90, 4, 1976, 201–29.
GERSZI, 1982
Teréz Gerszi, "Pieter Bruegels Einfluß auf die
Herausbildung der niederlandischen See- und
Küstenlandschaftsdarstellung," *Jahrbuch der Berliner
Museen*, XXIV, 1982, 143–87.
GESSLER, 1933
Jean Gessler, "Le 'Journaal' de C. Huygens, le Jeune,"
Revue Belge d'Archéologie et d'Histoire de l'Art, III, 2,
April 1933, 97–135.
GIBSON, 1980
Michael Gibson, *Bruegel*, Paris, Nouvelles Editions
Françaises, "Grands Peintres classiques," 1980.
GIBSON, 1965
Walter S. Gibson, "Some Notes on Pieter Bruegel the
Elder's 'Peasant Wedding Feast'," *The Art Quarterly*,
XXVIII, 3, 1965, 194–208.
GIBSON, 1973
Walter S. Gibson, *Hieronymus Bosch*, London, Thames
and Hudson, "World of Art" (French edition: *Jérôme
Bosch*, Paris, Thames and Hudson, "L'Univers de
l'Art," 1995).
GIBSON, 1978
Walter S. Gibson, "Some Flemish Popular Prints from
Hieronymus Cock and His Contemporaries," *The Art
Bulletin*, LX, 4, December 1978, 678–81.
GIBSON, 1979
Walter S. Gibson, "Bruegel's 'Dulle Griet' and Sexist
Politics in the Sixteenth Century," *Pieter Bruegel und
seine Welt. Ein Colloquium veranstaltet vom
Kunsthistorischen Institut der Freien Universität Berlin
und dem Kupferstichkabinett der staatlichen Museen
Stiftung preußischer Kulturbesitz, 13–14 November
1975*, Berlin, Gebr. Mann, 1979, 9–15.
GIBSON, 1981
Walter S. Gibson, "Artists and Rederijkers in the Age
of Bruegel," *The Art Bulletin*, LXIII, 3, September
1981, 426–46.
GIBSON, 1989
Walter S. Gibson, "Mirror of the Earth." *The World
Landscape in Sixteenth-Century Flemish Painting*,
Princeton (N.J.), Princeton University Press, 1989.

GIBSON, 1990
Walter S. Gibson, "Pieter Bruegel the Elder and the Flemish World Landscape of the Sixteenth Century," *Bruegel and Netherlandish Landscape Painting from the National Gallery Prague*, see Tokyo/Kyoto catalog, 1990, 11–23.

GIBSON, 1991[1]
Walter S. Gibson, *Bruegel*, London, Thames and Hudson, "World of Art," 1991 (1st edition 1977).

GIBSON, 1991[2]
Walter S. Gibson, *Pieter Bruegel the Elder: Two Studies*, Spencer Museum of Art, The University of Kansas, "The Franklin D. Murphy Lectures," XI, 1991.

GLÜCK, 1930
Gustav Glück, "A Newly Discovered Painting by Brueghel the Elder," *The Burlington Magazine*, LVI, June 1930, 284–86.

GLÜCK, 1935
Gustav Glück, "Uber einige Landschaftsgemälde Peter Bruegels des Älteren," *Jahrbuch der kunsthistorischen Sammlungen in Wien,* new series, IX, 1935, 151–65.

GLÜCK, 1937
Gustav Glück, *Pieter Brueghel le Vieux*, translated by Jean Petithughenin, Paris, Hypérion, 1937.

GLÜCK, 1943
Gustav Glück, "Peter Brueghel the Elder and Classical Antiquity," *The Art Quarterly,* VI, 1943, 167–87.

GLÜCK, 1948
Gustav Glück, "Le 'Paysage avec la Fuite en Egypte' de Pierre Bruegel le Vieux," *Les Arts Plastiques*, 11–12, 1948, 447–54.

GLÜCK, 1963
Gustav Glück, *Das große Bruegel–Werk*, Vienna/Munich, Anton Schroll & Co., 1963 (1st edition: Vienna, Anton Schroll & Co, 1951; also in English edition: *Peter Brueghel the Elder*, London, Thames & Hudson, 1958).

GOEDTHALS, 1568
François Goedthals, *Proverbes Anciens Flamengs et François,* Antwerp, Christophe Plantin, 1568.

GOMBRICH, 1973
Ernst H. Gombrich, "Dürer, Vives and Bruegel," *Album Amicorum J. G. van Gelder,* The Hague, Nijhoff, 1973, 132–34.

GRAULS, 1938
Jan Grauls, *De spreekwoorden van Pieter Bruegel den Oude (Â 1527–1569), verklaard door Jan Grauls,* Antwerp, Gevaert, no date (1938).

GRAULS, 1939
Jan Grauls, "Uit Bruegels Spreekwoorden," *Annuaire des Musées royaux des Beaux-Arts de Belgique,* II, 1939, 91–107.

GRAULS, 1939–40
Jan Grauls, "Ter verklaring van Bosch en Bruegel," *Gentsche Bijdragen tot de Kunstgeschiedenis,* 6, 1939–40, 139–60.

GRAULS, 1957
Jan Grauls, *Volkstaal en volksleven in het werk van Pieter Bruegel*, Antwerp/Amsterdam, Standaard, 1957.

GRAULS, 1960
Jan Grauls, "Het spreekwoordenschilderij van Sebastiaan Vrancx," *Bulletin der Musées royaux des Beaux-Arts de Belgique*, 3–4, 1960, 107–64.

GRAZIANI, 1973
René Graziani, "Pieter Bruegel's 'Dulle Griet' and Dante," *The Burlington Magazine*, CXV, 841, April 1973, 209–19.

GRIETEN, 1988
Stefaan Grieten, "De iconografie van de Toren van Babel bij Pieter Bruegel: traditie, vernieuwing en navolging," *Jaarboek van het Koninklijk Museum voor Schone Kunsten Antwerpen*, 1988, 97–136.

GRIMME, 1973
Ernst Günther Grimme, *Pieter Bruegel d. Ä. Leben und Werk,* Cologne, DuMont Schauberg, 1973.

GROSSMANN, 1952
Fritz Grossmann, "Bruegel s 'Woman Taken in Adultery' and Other Grisailles," *The Burlington Magazine,* XCIV, August 1952, 218–29.

GROSSMANN, 1954[1]
Fritz Grossmann, "The Drawings of Pieter Bruegel the Elder in the Museum Boymans and Some Problems of Attribution," *Bulletin Museum Boymans Rotterdam*, V, 2, July 1954, 41–63.

GROSSMANN, 1954[2]
Fritz Grossmann, "The Drawings of Pieter Bruegel the Elder in the Museum Boymans. Postscript: Notes on the Landscape Drawings of Bruegel,' *Bulletin Museum Boymans Rotterdam*, V, 3, November 1954, 76–85.

GROSSMANN, 1959
Fritz Grossmann, "New Light on Bruegel. I: Documents and Additions to the Oeuvre; Problems of Form," *The Burlington Magazine*, CI, 678–69, September–October 1959, 341–46.

GROSSMANN, 1960
Fritz Grossmann, "Bruegel, Pieter the Elder," *Encyclopedia of World Art*, New York, 1960, columns 632–51.

GROSSMANN, 1973[1]
Fritz Grossmann, *Pieter Bruegel. Complete Edition of the Paintings*, London, Phaidon, 1973, 3rd edition, revised (1st edition 1955).

GROSSMANN, 1973[2]
Fritz Grossmann, "Notes on some Sources of Bruegel's Art," *Album Amicorum J. G van Gelder*, The Hague, Nijhoff, 1973, 147–54.

GUICCIARDINI, 1582
Lodovico Guicciardini, *Description de touts les Pais–Bas [...], reveue, & augmentée plus que de la moitié par le mesme autheur [...]*, translated from the Italian by François de Belle Forest, Antwerp, Christophe Plantin, 1582. (original edition: Lodovico Guicciardini, *Descrittione [...] di tutti i Paesi Bassi,* Antwerp, Guglielmo Silvio, 1567).

HAGEN, 1994
Rose-Marie and Rainer Hagen, *Pierre Bruegel l'Ancien. Vers 1525–1569: Paysans, Fous et Démons*, translated from the German by Thérèse Chatelain-Südkamp, Cologne, Taschen, 1994.

HAND, 1986
John Oliver Hand, "The Sixteenth Century," *The Age of Bruegel: Netherlandish Drawings in the Sixteenth Century*, see Washington/New York catalog, 1986, 1–11.

HAUSENSTEIN, 1916
Wilhelm Hausenstein, *Der Bauern–Bruegel. Mit einem Vorwort zur neuen Ausgabe über Bruegel den Belgier,* Munich, R. Piper & Co., 1916 (1st edition: Munich, R. Piper & Co., 1910).

HAUSER, 1963
Henri Hauser, *La Modernité du XVIe siècle (Cahier des Annales*, 21), preface by Fernand Braudel, Paris, A. Colin, 1963 (1st edition: Paris, Alcan, "Bibliothèque de la Revue Historique," 1930).

HAVERKAMP BEGEMANN, 1979
Egbert Haverkamp Begemann, "Joos van Liere," *Pieter Bruegel und seine Welt. Ein Colloquium veranstaltet vom Kunsthistorischen Institut der Freien Universität Berlin und dem Kupferstichkabinett der staatlichen Museen Stiftung preußischer Kulturbesitz, 13–14 November 1975*, Berlin, Gebr. Mann, 1979, 17–28.

HILLS, 1957
Jeanette Hills, *Das Kinderspielbild von Pieter Bruegel d. Ä. (1560). Eine volkskundliche Untersuchung*, X, Vienna, "Veröffentlichungen des Osterreichischen Museums fur Volkskunde," 1957.

HINDMAN, 1981
Sandra Hindman, "Pieter Bruegel's 'Children's Games', Folly and Chance," *The Art Bulletin*, LXIII, 3, September 1981, 447–75.

HOCKE, 1967
Gustav René Hocke, *Labyrinthe de l'Art Fantastique. Le Maniérisme dans l'Art Européen*, translated from the German by Cornelius Heim, Paris, Editions Gonthier, 1967 (original edition: *Die Welt als Labyrinth. Manier und Manie in der europäischen Kunst. Von 1520 bis 1650 und in der Gegenwart*, Hamburg, Rowohlt, 1957; revised and expanded German edition: 1991).

HOLLSTEIN, s.d. (1949)
F. W. H. Hollstein, *Dutch and Flemish Etchings, Engravings and Woodcuts, ca. 1450–1700*, III: *Boeckhorst–Brueghel*, Amsterdam, Menno Hertzberger, no date (I: 1949).

HOLM, 1964
Edith Holm, *Pieter Bruegel und Bernart van Orley. Die Jagd als Motiv in der niederländischen Kunst um 1550*, Hamburg/Berlin, Paul Parey, "Die Jagd in der Kunst," 1964.

HOOGEWERFF, 1954
Godefridus Joannes Hoogewerff, *Het landschap van Bosch tot Rubens*, Antwerp, De Nederlandsche Boekhandel, 1954.

HULIN DE LOO, 1907
See VAN BASTELAER, HULIN DE LOO

HÜTT, 1957
Wolfgang Hütt, "Brecht sieht Brueghel," *Bildende Kunst*, 4, 1957, 227–28.

HUXLEY, 1939
Aldous Huxley, *Breughel*, in *Collected Esays*, New York, Harper & Brothers, 1958.

HUYGHE, 1955
René Huyghe, *Dialogue avec le Visible*, Paris, Flammarion, 1955.

HUYGHE, 1965
René Huyghe, *Les Puissances de l'Image. Bilan d'une Psychologie de l'Art*, Paris, Flammarion, 1965.

HYMANS, 1890[1]
Henri Hymans, "Pierre Breughel le Vieux. Premier article," *Gazette des Beaux-Arts*, III, part 5, 1 May 1890, 361–75.

HYMANS, 1890[2]
Henri Hymans, "Pierre Breughel le Vieux. Deuxième article," *Gazette des Beaux-Arts*, IV, part 5, 1 November 1890, 361–73.

HYMANS, 1891
Henri Hymans, "Pierre Breughel le Vieux. Troisième et Dernier Article," *Gazette des Beaux-Arts*, V, part 1, 1 January 1891, 20–40.

HYMANS, 1897
Henri Hymans, "Margot l'Enragée. Un tableau Retrouvé de Pierre Breughel le Vieux," *Gazette des Beaux-Arts*, XVIII, 1897, 500 and *sqq.*

JAFFÉ, 1979
Michael Jaffé, "Rubens and Bruegel," *Pieter Bruegel und seine Welt. Ein Colloquium veranstaltet vom Kunsthistorischen Institut der Freien Universität Berlin und dem Kupferstichkabinett der staatlichen Museen Stiftung preußischer Kulturbesitz, 13–14 November 1975*, Berlin, Gebr. Mann, 1979, 37–42.

JANSON, 1952
Horst W. Janson, *Apes and Ape Lore in the Middle Ages and the Renaissance (Studies of the Warburg Institute*, XX), London, The Warburg Institute, University of London, 1952.

JEDLICKA, 1938
Gotthard Jedlicka, *Pieter Bruegel. Der Maler in seiner Zeit,* Erlenbach/Zürich, Eugen Rentsch, 1938 (republished Erlenbach/Zürich, 1947).

KARLING, 1976
Sten Karling, "The Attack by Pieter Bruegel the Elder in the Collection of the Stockholm University," *Konsthistorisk Tidskrift*, VL, 1976, 1–18.

KATONA, 1963
Emeric Katona, "La Prédication de Saint Jean-Baptiste de Bruegel," *Bulletin du Musée Hongrois des Beaux-Arts*, 22. 1963, 41–69.

KAVALER, 1986
Ethan Matt Kavaler, "Pieter Bruegel's Fall of Icarus and the Noble Peasant," *Jaarboek van het Koninklijk Museum voor Schone Kunsten Antwerpen*, 1986, 83–98.

KLAMT, 1979
Johann-Christian Klamt, "Anmerkungen zu Pieter Bruegels Babel-Darstellungen," *Pieter Bruegel und seine Welt. Ein Colloquium veranstaltet vom Kunsthistorischen Institut der Freien Universität Berlin und dem Kupferstichkabinett der staatlichen Museen Stiftung preußischer Kulturbesitz, 13–14 November 1975*, Berlin, Gebr. Mann, 1979, 43–49.

KLEIN, 1963
H. Arthur Klein, *Graphic Worlds of Peter Bruegel the Elder*, New York, Dover Publications, 1963.

KLEIN, 1968
H. Arthur and Mina C. Klein, *Peter Bruegel the Elder. Artist of Abundance,* New York, The Macmillan Company, 1968.

KLEIN, 1983
Peter Klein, "L'Examen Dendrochronologique des Panneaux Peints," *Revue de l'Art*, 60, 1983, 71–72.

KLEIN, 1995
Peter Klein, "Dendrochronology on Paintings of Pieter Bruegel the Elder and Jan Brueghel," *Le Dessin Sous-Jacent dans la Peinture*, colloque X, Louvain-la-Neuve, Université catholique de Louvain, Institut supérieur d'archéologie et d'histoire de l'art, 5–7 September 1993, Louvain-la-Neuve, Collège Erasme, 1995, 13–20.

KOSTYSHYN, 1990
Stephen J. Kostyshyn. *An Important Landscape by Peeter Baltens*, Vienna, Lucas, 1990.

KOSTYSHYN, 1994
Stephen J. Kostyshyn, *"Door tsoecken men vindt": A Reintroduction to the Life and Work of Peeter Baltens alias Custodis of Antwerp (1527–1584)*, 3 vols., doctorate thesis, Case Western Reserve University, Ann Arbor (Michigan), 1994.

KUNZLE, 1977
David Kunzle, "Brüegel's Proverb Painting and the World Upside Down," *The Art Bulletin*, LIX, 2, June 1977, 197–202.

LAMEERE, 1902
M. Lameere, *Recueil des Ordonnances des Pays-Bas. Deuxième Série 1506–1700, III, 8 Janvier 1529–11 Décembre 1536*, Brussels, 1902, 265–73.

LAMMERTSE, 1994
Friso Lammertse, "Pieter Bruegel the Elder. The Tower of Babel," *1400–1550. Van Eyck to Bruegel. Dutch and Flemish Painting in the Collection of the Museum Boymans–Van Beuningen, Rotterdam*, 1994, 400–403.

LAMPSONIUS, 1956
Dominicus Lampsonius, *Les Effigies des Peintres Célèbres des Pays–Bas*, critical edition by Jean Puraye, no place. (Paris/Bruges), Desclée de Brouwer, 1956 (original edition: Dominicus Lampsonius, *Pictorum Aliquot Celebrium Germaniae Inferioris Effigies*, Antwerp, 1572).

LAVALLEYE, 1966
Jacques Lavalleye, *Lucas van Leyden. Peter Bruegel l'Ancien. Gravures. Oeuvre complet,* Paris, Arts et Métiers Graphiques, 1966.

LEBEER, 1939–40
Louis Lebeer, "De Blauwe Huyck," *Gentsche Bijdragen tot de Kunstgeschiedenis*, 6, 1939–40, 161–229.

LEBEER, 1949
Louis Lebeer, "La Kermesse d'Hoboken," *Miscellanea Leo van Puyvelde*, Brussels, Editions de la Connaissance, 1949, 99–103.

LEBEER, 1955
Louis Lebeer, "Le Pays de Cocagne (Het Luilekkerland)," *Miscellanea Erwin Panofsky. Bulletin des Musées royaux des Beaux-Arts de Belgique*, IV, 1955, 199–214.

LEBEER, 1969
Louis Lebeer, *Catalogue Raisonné des Estampes de Bruegel l'Ancien*, Brussels, Bibliothèque royale Albert I[er.] 1969 (republished as: Louis Lebeer, *Bruegel. Les Estampes. Catalogue Raisonné*, Brussels, Lebeer Hossmann, 1991).

LEBEER, 1970
Louis Lebeer. "Pierre Bruegel l'Ancien. L'oiseleur perfide," *Peinture Vivante, 7. (RTB- Cultura)*, 4, 7th year, 1969–70, Brussels, Cultura, 1970.

LE COMTE, 1702
Florent Le Comte, *Cabinet des Singularitez d'Architecture, Peinture, Sculpture et Graveure* [...], II, Brussels, Lambert Marchant, 1702.

LEDERER, 1961
Jean Lederer, "Les Mendiants de Bruegel. Un Document pour l'Histoire des Flandres sous l'Occupation Espagnole," *Scrinium Lovaniense, Mélanges Historiques Etienne Van Cauwenbergh,*

Leuven, Publications universitaires de Louvain, 1961, 452–65.

LE FANU HUGHES, 1989
Penelope Le Fanu Hughes, *Bruegel,* London, Tiger Books International, "The History and Techniques of the Great Masters," 1989.

LE ROY LADURIE (editor), 1994
Emmanuel Le Roy Ladurie (editor), *Paysages, Paysans. L'Art et la Terre en Europe du Moyen Age au XXe Siècle*, Paris, RMN, 1994.

LEWIS, 1973
Anthony J. Lewis, "Man in Nature: Peter Brueghel and Shakespeare," *Art Journal*, XXXII, 4, summer 1973, 405–13.

LHOTE, 1939–41
André Lhote, *Traité du Paysage*, Paris, Librairie Floury, 1939–41.

LIESS, 1979–80
Reinhard Liess, "Die kleinen Landschaften Pieter Bruegels d. Ä im Lichte seines Gesamtwerkes (1. Teil)," *Kunsthistorisches Jahrbuch Graz*, 15/16, 1979–80, 1–116.

LIESS, 1981
Reinhard Liess, "Die kleinen Landschaften Pieter Bruegels d. Ä. im Lichte seines Gesamtwerkes (2. Teil)," *Kunsthistorisches Jahrbuch Graz*, 17, 1981, 35–150.

LIESS, 1982
Reinhard Liess, "Die kleinen Landschaften Pieter Bruegels d. Ä. im Lichte seines Gesamtwerkes (3. Teil)," *Kunsthistorisches Jahrbuch Graz*, 18, 1982, 79–164.

LOMAZZO, 1584
Giovanni Paolo Lomazzo, *Trattato dell'Arte della Pittura, Diviso in Sette Libri,* Milan, Paolo Gottardo Pontio, 1584.

LUGT, 1927
Frits Lugt, "Pieter Bruegel und Italien," *Festschrift für Max J. Friedländer zum 60. Geburtstag,* Leipzig, Seeman, 1927, 111–29.

MAETERLINCK, 1903[1]
Louis Maeterlinck, "Nederlandsche spreekwoorden handelend voorgesteld door Pieter Breughel den Oude," *Verslagen en Mededelingen der Koninklijke Vlaamsche Academie voor taal– en letterkunde*, Ghent, January–June 1903, 109–29.

MAETERLINCK, 1903[2]
Louis Maeterlinck, "Pieter Breughel de Oude en de prenten van zijnen tijd," *Verslagen en Mededelingen der Koninklijke Vlaamsche Academie voor taal– en letterkunde*, Ghent, July–December 1903, 59–76.

MAETERLINCK, 1907
Louis Maeterlinck, *Le Genre Satirique dans la Peinture Flamand*e, Antwerp–Ghent, Académie royale de Belgique/Brussels, G. van Oest & Cie, 1907 (1st edition 1903).

MANSBACH, 1982
S. A. Mansbach, "Pieter Bruegel's Tower of Babel," *Zeitschrift für Kunstgeschichte*, XLV, 1, 1982, 43–56.

MARCQ-VEROUGSTRAETE, VAN SCHOUTE, 1976
Hélène Marcq–Verougstraete and Roger Van Schoute, "Le Dessin de Peintre (Dessin Sous-Jacent) chez Pierre Bruegel: l'Adoration des Mages de la National Gallery à Londres," *Nederlands Kunsthistorisch Jaarboek,*

XXVI. *Scientific Examination of Early Netherlandish Painting*, 1975, Bussum, Fibula–Van Dishoeck, 1976, 259–67.

MARIETTE, 1741
Pierre–Jean Mariette, *Description Sommaire des Desseins des Grands Maistres d'Italie, des Pays–Bas et de France du Cabinet de Feu M. Crozat, avec des Réflexions sur la Manière de Dessiner des Principaux Peintres*, Paris, Pierre–Jean Mariette, 1741, 105–7.

MARIETTE, 1851–1853
Pierre–Jean Mariette, *Abecedario et Autres Notes Inédites de cet Amateur sur les Arts et les Artistes*, published by P. de Chennevières and A. de Montaiglon, I, Paris, J. B. Dumoulin, 1851–53, 188 (6 vols.: 1851–60).

MARIJNISSEN, 1969
Roger H. Marijnissen, "Het wetenschappeljjk onderzoek van Bruegels oeuvre," *Vlaanderen*, 103, January–February 1969, 4–11.

MARIJNISSEN, 1976
Roger H. Marijnissen, "Bosch and Bruegel on human folly," *Travaux de l'Institut pour l'Etude de la Renaissance et de l'Humanisme*, V: *Folie et Déraison à la Renaissance*, Brussels, Editions de l'Université de Bruxelles, 1976, 41–52.

MARIJNISSEN, 1979
Roger H. Marijnissen, "De Eed van Meester Oom. Een Voorbeeld van Brabantse Jokkernij uit Bruegels Tijd," *Pieter Bruegel und seine Welt. Ein Colloquium veranstaltet vom Kunsthistorischen Institut der Freien Universität Berlin und dem Kupferstichkabinett der staatlichen Museen Stiftung preußischer Kulturbesitz, 13–14 November 1975*, Berlin, Gebr. Mann, 1979, 51–61.

MARIJNISSEN, 1988
Roger H. Marijnissen, *Bruegel. Tout l'Oeuvre Peint et Dessiné*, with the collaboration of P. Ruyfelaere, P. van Calster and A. W. F. M. Meij, Antwerp, Fonds Mercator/Paris, Albin Michel, 1988.

MARIJNISSEN, SEIDEL, 1969
Roger H. Marijnissen and Max Seidel, *Bruegel le Vieux*, Brussels, Arcade, 1969.

MARLIER, 1954
Georges Marlier, *Erasme et la Peinture Flamande de son Temps*, Damme, Editions du musée van Maerlant, 1954.

MARLIER, 1965
Georges Marlier, "Peeter Balten, Copiste ou Créateur?", *Bulletin des Musées royaux des Beaux-Arts de Belgique*, XIV, 1965, 127–42.

MARLIER, 1966
Georges Marlier, *La Renaissance Flamande. Pierre Coeck d'Alost*, Brussels, Robert Finck, 1966.

MARLIER, 1969
Georges Marlier, *Pierre Brueghel le Jeune*, posthumous edition completed and annotated by Jacqueline Folie, Brussels, Robert Finck, 1969.

MARLIER, GORIS 1970
Georges Marlier and J. A. Goris, *Le Journal de Voyage d'Albert Dürer dans les Anciens Pays-Bas, 1520–1521*, translated with commentary by J. A. Goris and Georges Marlier, Brussels, Editions de la Connaissance, 1970.

MARQUET, 1977
Léon Marquet, *Origine d'un Type Carnavalesque: le VÊHÛU de Malmédy*, Brussels, Commission royale belge du Folklore, "Folklore et Art populaire de Wallonie," 1977.

MARTINY, 1964
Victor G. Martiny, "A Propos de la Maison Dite de Breughel, rue Haute à Bruxelles," *Bulletin de la Commission royale des monuments et des sites*, XV, 1964, 9–45.

MATTIOLI, 1976
Donatella Mattioli, "Nuove Ipotesi sui Quadri di 'Bruol Vecchio' Appartenuti ai Gonzaga," *Civiltà Mantovana*, 10th year, 55–56, 1976, 32–43.

MEIJ, 1980
A. W. F. M. Meij, "Dessins de Pierre Bruegel," *Bruegel. Une Dynastie de Peintres, Europalia 80 Belgique*, see Brussels catalogue, 1980, 73–101.

MEIJER, 1988
Bert W. Meijer, *Parma e Bruxelles. Committenza e Collezionismo Farnesiani alle due Corti*, Milan, Silvana, 1988.

MENZEL, 1966
Gerhard W. Menzel, *Pieter Bruegel der Ältere*, Leipzig, Seeman, 1966.

METTRA, 1976
Claude Mettra, *Brueghel*, Paris, Scréel, "Le Peintre et l'Homme," 1976.

MICHEL, 1931[1]
Édouard Michel, "Pierre Bruegel le Vieux et Pieter Coecke d'Alost," *Mélanges Hulin de Loo*, Brussels–Paris, Librairie nationale d'art et d'histoire, 1931, 266–71.

MICHEL, 1931[2]
Édouard Michel, *Bruegel*, Paris, G. Grès et Cie, "Maîtres d'Autrefois," 1931.

MICHEL, 1938
Édouard Michel, "Bruegel et la Critique Moderne," *Gazette des Beaux-Arts*, 6th series, XIX, January 1938, 27–46.

MICHEL, 1948
Édouard Michel, "Bruegel ou non Bruegel," *Les Arts Plastiques*, 11–12, 1948, 460–70.

MICHEL, 1953
Édouard Michel, *Catalogue Raisonné des Peintures. Musée National du Louvre*, Paris, 1953, 38–43.

MICHEL, 1892
Émile Michel, *Les Brueghel*. Paris, Librairie de l'art, "Les Artistes Célèbres," 1892.

MIEDEMA, 1977
Hessel Miedema, "Realism and Comic Mode: the Peasant," *Simiolus*, 9, 4, 1977, 205–19.

MIEDEMA, 1981
Hessel Miedema, "Feestence boeren – lachende dorpers. Bij twee recente aanwinsten van het Rijksprentenkabinet," *Bulletin van het Rijksmuseum*, 29th year, 4, 1981, 191–213.

MIELKE, 1979
Hans Mielke, "Radierer um Bruegel," *Pieter Bruegel und seine Welt. Ein Colloquium veranstaltet vom Kunsthistorischen Institut der Freien Universität Berlin und dem Kupferstichkabinett der staatlichen Museen Stiftung preußischer Kulturbesitz, 13–14 November 1975*, Berlin, Gebr. Mann, 1979, 63–71.

MIELKE, 1991
Hans Mielke, "Noch einmal zum Problem von Pieter Bruegels Landschaftszeichnungen. Eigene Studien oder Ableitungen?," *Münchner Jahrbuch der bildenen Kunst*, XLII, 1991, 137–47.

MIELKE, 1994
Hans Mielke, "La Question des Paysages Forestiers dans l'Oeuvre de Pieter Bruegel," *Le Paysage en Europe du XVIe au XVIIe siècle*. Transactions of the conference held at the Louvre, 25–27 January 1990, Paris, RMN, 1994, 15–23.

MIELKE, 1997
Hans Mielke, *Pieter Bruegel. Die Zeichnungen*, Turnhout, Brepols, 1997 (posthumous edition).

MILNE, 1990
Louise Shona Milne, *Dreams and Popular Beliefs in the Imagery of Pieter Bruegel the Elder, c. 1528–1569*, doctorate thesis, Boston University, 1990, Ann Arbor (Michigan), 3 vols.

MONBALLIEU, 1964
A. Monballieu, "P. Bruegel en het altaar van de Mechelse Handschoenmakers (1551)," *Handelingen van de Koninklijke Kring voor Oudheidkunde, Letteren en Kunst van Mechelen*, LXVIII, 1964, 92–110.

MONBALLIEU, 1969
A. Monballieu, "Een werk van P. Bruegel en H. Vredeman de Vries voor de tresorier Aert Molckeman," *Jaarboek van het Koninklijk Museum voor Schone Kunsten Antwerpen*, 1969, 113–35.

MONBALLIEU, 1974[1]
A. Monballieu, "De 'Kermis van Hoboken' bij P. Bruegel, J. Grimmer en C. Mostaert," *Jaarboek van het Koninklijk Museum voor Schone Kunsten Antwerpen*, 1974, 139–68.

MONBALLIEU, 1974[2]
A. Monballieu, "De kunstenaarsfamilie Verhulst Bessemeers," *Handelingen van de Koninklijke Kring voor Oudheidkunde, Letteren en Kunst van Mechelen*, LXXVIII, 1974, 104–21.

MONBALLIEU, 1979
A. Monballieu, "De 'Hand als teken op het kleed' bij Bruegel en Baltens," *Jaarboek van het Koninklijk Museum voor Schone Kunsten Antwerpen*, 1979, 197–209.

MONBALLIEU, 1981
A. Monballieu, "P. Bruegels 'Schaatsenrijden de St.–Jorispoort te Antwerpen', de betekenis van het jaartal 1553 en een archiefstuk," *Jaarboek van het Koninklijk Museum voor Schone Kunsten Antwerpen*, 1981, 17–29.

MONBALLIEU, 1983
A. Monballieu, "De 'Twee Apjes' van P. Bruegel of de Singerie (seignerie) over de Schelde te Antwerpen in 1562," *Jaarboek van het Koninklijk Museum voor Schone Kunsten Antwerpen*, 1983, 191–210.

MORI, 1976
Yoko Mori, "The Influence of German and Flemish Prints on the Works of Pieter Bruegel," *Bulletin of Tama Art School*, II, 1976, 17–60.

MORI, 1988[1]
Yoko Mori, *The Complete Paintings of Peter Bruegel*, Tokyo, Chuokoron-Sha, 1988 (in Japanese).

MORI, 1988[2]
Yoko Mori, *Flemish Children's Games in the Sixteenth Century: Iconographical Studies of Bruegel's "Children's Games,"* doctorate thesis, Division of Comparative Culture, Graduate School of International Christian University, Tokyo, 1988 (in Japanese).

MORI, 1992
Yoko Mori, *Pieter Bruegel. Spreekwoorden en volksleven*, Tokyo, Hakuosha, 1992 (in Japanese).

MORI, 1995
Yoko Mori, "A Proposal for Reconsidering Bruegel: an Integrated View of his Historical and Cultural Milieu," *The World of Bruegel. The Coppée Collection and Eleven International Museum*, see Tobu catalog, 1995, 41–60.
MOXEY, 1973
Keith P. F. Moxey, "The Fates and Pieter Bruegel's Triumph of Death," *Oud Holland*, 87, 2–3, 1973, 49–51.
MOXEY, 1982
Keith P. F. Moxey, "Pieter Bruegel and The 'Feast of Fools'," *The Art Bulletin*, LXIV, 4, December 1982, 640–46.
MOXEY, 1989
Keith P. F. Moxey, *Peasants, Warriors and Wives. Popular Imagery in the Reformation*, Chicago/London, The University of Chicago Press, 1989.
MÜLLER, 1996
Jürgen Müller, "Bruegel, Pieter, d. Ä.," *Saur Allgemeines Künstler-Lexikon. Die bildende Künstler aller Zeiten und Völker*, XIV, Münich–Leipzig, Saur, 1996, 474–78.
MÜLLER HOFSTEDE, 1979
Justus Müller Hofstede, "Zur Interpretation von Bruegels Landschaft. Asthetischer Landschaftsbegriff und Stoische Weltbetrachtung," *Pieter Bruegel und seine Welt. Ein Colloquium veranstaltet von Kunsthistorischen Institut der Freien Universität Berlin und dem Kupferstichkabinett der staatlichen Museen Stiftung preußischer Kulturbesitz, 13–14 November 1975*, Berlin, Gebr. Mann, 1979, 73–142.
MÜNZ, 1961
Ludwig Münz, *Bruegel. The Drawings. Complete Edition*, translated from the German manuscript by Luke Herrmann, London, Phaidon Press, 1961.
MUNHALL, 1966
F. Munhall, "The Frick's Brueghel," *Apollo*, LXXXIII, 1966, p. 393.
MUYLLE, 1981
Jan Muylle, "Pieter Bruegel en Abraham Ortelius. Bijdrage tot de literaire receptie van Pieter Bruegels werk," *Archivum Artis Lovaniense. Bijdragen tot de Geschiedenis van de Kunst der Nederlanden*, Leuven, Peeters, 1981, 319–37.
MUYLLE, 1984[1]
Jan Muylle, "'Pier den Drol' — Karel van Mander en Pieter Bruegel. Bijdrage tot de literaire receptie van Pieter Bruegels werk ca. 1600," *Wort und Bild in der niederländischen Kunst und Literatur des 16. und 17. Jahrhunderts*, introduction by Herman Vekeman, Justus Müller Hofstede, Erftstadt, Lukassen, 1984, 137–44.
MUYLLE, 1984[2]
Jan Muylle. "Pieter Bruegel en de kunsttheorie. Een interpretatie van de tekeningen 'De Schilder voor zijn Ezel': ideëel zelfportret en artistiek credo," *Jaarboek van het Kominklijk Museum voor schone Kunsten Antwerpen*, 1984, 189–202.
NEEFS, 1876
Emmanuel Neefs, *Histoire de la Peinture et de la Sculpture à Malines*, I: *La Gilde de Saint-Luc, l'Académie des Beaux-Arts. Les Peintres Malinois*, Ghent, E. Vanderhaeghen, 1876.
NIEUWDORP, 1985
Hans J. Nieuwdorp, "Over de interpretatie van Pieter Bruegel's Dulle Griet," *Pierre van Soest, Dulle Griet*, Venlo, 1985.
NIEUWDORP, 1992
Hans J. Nieuwdorp, with contributions from Iris Kockelbergh, *Musée Mayer van der Bergh Anvers*, Brussels, Crédit communal, "Musea Nostra," 1992.
NOVOTNY, 1948
Fritz Novotny, *Die Monatsbilder Pieter Bruegels d. Ä.*, Vienna, F. Deuticke, "Kunstdenkmäler," 1948.
OBERHUBER, 1979
Konrad Oberhuber, "Pieter Bruegel und die Radierungsserie der Bauernköpfe," *Pieter Bruegel und seine Welt. Ein Colloquium veranstaltet vom Kunsthistorischen Inistitut der Freien Universität Berlin und dem Kupferstichkabinett der staatlichen Museen Stiftumig preußischer Kulturbesitz, 13–14 November 1975*, Berlin, Gebr. Mann, 1979, 143–47.
OBERHUBER, 1980
Konrad Oberhuber, "Des dessins de Pierre Bruegel l'Ancien," *Bruegel. Une dynastie de peintres, Europalia 80 Belgique*, see Brussels catalogue, 1980, 60–72.
OBERHUBER, 1981
Konrad Oberhuber, "Bruegel's Early Landscape Drawings," *Master Drawings*, XIX, 2, summer 1981, 146–56.
ONCLINCX, 1985
Georges Onclincx, "Note sur une biographie manuscrite (XVIIIe s.) de Pierre Bruegel l'Ancien mentionnant son décès et son inhumation," *Revue Belge de Philologie et d'Histoire*, LXIII, 4, 1985, 726–30.
ORTELIUS, 1968
Abraham Ortelius, *Album Amicorum*, facsimile edition translated and annotated by Jean Puraye in *De Gulden Passer*, 45th year, 1967 and 46th year, 1–3, 1968.
OSTEN, VEY, 1969
G. von der Osten and H. Vey, *Painting and Sculpture in Germany and the Netherlands 1500–1600*, Harmondsworth, Penguin, "Pelican History of Art," 1969.
PANOFSKY, 1939
Erwin Panofsky, *Studies in Iconology. Humanistic Themes in the Art of the Renaissance*, New York, Oxford University Press, 1939.
PANSE, SCHMIDT, 1967
F. Panse and Heinrich J. Schmidt, *Pieter Bruegels Dulle Griet. Bildnis einer psychisch Kranken*, Leverkusen, Bayer, 1967.
PHILIPPOT, 1994
Paul Philippot, *La Peinture dans les Anciens Pays-Bas. XVe–XVIe Siècle*, Paris, Flammarion, "Idées et Recherches," 1994.
PHILIPPOT *et al.*, 1969
Albert Philippot, Nicole Goetghebeur, and Régine Guislain–Wittermann, "L'Adoration des Mages de Bruegel au musee des Beaux-Arts de Bruxelles. Traitement d'un 'Tuechlein'," *Bulletin de l'Institut Royal du Patrimoine Artistique*, XI, 1969, 5–33.
PILES, 1699
Roger de Piles, *Abrégé de la Vie des Peintres, Avec des Réflexions sur leurs Ouvrages, Et un Traité du Peintre Parfait, & de la Connoissance des Desseins, & de l'Utilité des Estampes*, Paris, François Muguet, 1699 (reprinted Hildesheim, Georg Holms, 1969).
PIOT (editor), 1884
Charles Piot (editor), *Correspondance du Cardinal de Granvelle 1565–1583*, IV, Brussels, Hayez, 1884.
PIRENNE, 1949
Henri Pirenne, *Histoire de Belgique des Origines à Nos Jours*, II, Brussels, La Renaissance du livre, 1949.
PIRON, 1965
André Piron, "Nouvelles recherches concernant les peintres Joachim le Patinier et Henri Blès," *La Nouvelle Revue Wallonne*, XIV, 2, January 1965, 101–12; XIV, 3, April 1965, 157–71; XIV, 4, July–September 1965, 215–28.
PLARD, 1958
H. Plard, "Sur le 'Repas de Noces' de Bruegel l'Ancien," *Revue Belge de Philologie et d'Histoire*, XXXVI, 2, 1958, 467–75.
PLUIS, 1979
Jan Pluis, *Kinderspelen op tegels*, Assen, Van Gorcum, 1979.
POLI, BACCHESCHI, 1976
Franco de Poli and Edi Baccheschi, *Bruegel*, Milan, Mondadori, "I Geni dell'Arte," 1976.
POPELIER, 1969
Françoise Popelier, "Image des Luttes Religieuses dans la Peinture des Anciens Pays-Bas," *Bulletin des Musées royaux des Beaux-Arts de Belgique*, 3–4, 1969, 121–39.
POPELIER, 1970
Françoise Popelier, "Pierre Bruegel l'Ancien. La Chute des Anges rebelles," *Peinture Vivante*, 7, 3, 7th year, 1969–70, Brussels, Cultura, "RTB-Cultura," 1970.
POPHAM, 1931
A. E. Popham, "Pieter Bruegel and Abraham Ortelius," *The Burlington Magazine*, LIX, October 1931, 184–88.
POPPER, 1971
L. Popper, "Peter Brueghel der Ältere 1520 (?)–1569," *Acta Historiae Artium Academiae Scientiarum Hungaricae*, XVII, 1–2, 1971, 6–10.
PORTMAN, HEINEN–TARDENT, 1962
Paul Portman and A. M. Heinen-Tardent, *Brueghel, Jeux d'Enfants*, Lausanne, Payot, 1962.
PRATER, 1977
Andreas Prater (editor), *Pieter Bruegel der Ältere, um 1525–1569*, Munich, Bruckmann, 1977.
RAUPP, 1986
Hans–Joachim Raupp, *Bauernsatiren. Entstehung und Entwicklung des bäuerlichen Genres in der deutschen und niederländischen Kunst ca 1470–1570*, Niederzier, Lukassen, 1986.
REZNICEK, 1979
E. K. J. Reznicek, "Bruegels Bedeutung für das 17. jahrhundert," *Pieter Bruegel und seine Welt. Ein Colloquium veranstaltet vom Kunsthistorischen Institut der Freien Universität Berlin und dem Kupferstichkabinett der staatlichen Museen Stiftung preußischer Kulturbesitz, 13–14 November 1975*, Berlin, Gebr. Mann, 1979, 159–164.
RIGGS, 1977
Timothy A. Riggs, *Hieronymnus Cock. Printmaker and Publisher* (doctorate thesis, Yale University, 1971), New York and London, Garland Publishing, 1977.
RIGGS, 1979
Timothy A. Riggs, "Bruegel and his Publisher," *Pieter Bruegel und seine Welt. Ein Colloquium veranstaltet vom Kunsthistorischen Institut der Freien Universität Berlin und dem Kupferstichkabinett der staatlichen*

Museen Stiftung preußischer Kulturbesitz, 13–14 November 1975, Berlin, Gebr. Mann, 1979, 65–173.
ROBERTS, 1993
Keith Roberts, *Bruegel*, translated from the English by Laurent Gonzalez, Paris, Editions Cercle d'art "Points cardinaux," 1993 (2nd French edition; English original: London, Phaidon, 1971).
ROBERTS-JONES, 1969
Philippe Roberts-Jones, "Pour un vrai Bruegel," *Brabant*, 4, 1969, 4–13.
ROBERTS-JONES, 1970
Philippe Roberts-Jones, "Pierre Bruegel l'Ancien. Le Dénombrement de Bethléem," *Peinture Vivante*, 7, 7th year, 1969–70, Brussels, Cultura, "RTB-Cultura," 1970.
ROBERTS-JONES, 1974
Philippe Roberts-Jones, *Bruegel. La Chute d'Icare (Musée de Bruxelles)*, Fribourg, Office du livre "Les chefs-d'oeuvre absolus de la peinture," 1974.
ROBERTS-JONES, 1989
Philippe Roberts-Jones, "Image donnée. Image reçue," *Mémoires de la Classe des Beaux-Arts*, 2nd series, XVI, 1, Brussels, Académie royale Belgique, 1989, 11–13 and *passim*.
ROBERTS-JONES *et al.*, 1969
Philippe Roberts-Jones *et al.*, *Bruegel. Le Peintre et son Monde*, Brussels, Laconti, 1969.
ROBERTS-JONES-POPELIER, 1989–1991
Françoise Roberts-Jones-Popelier, "Quelques sources iconographiques d'Abel Grimmer," *Bulletin des Musées royaux des Beaux-Arts de Belgique*, 1–3, 1989–91, 265–82.
ROBERTS-JONES-POPELIER, 1996
Françoise Roberts-Jones-Popelier, "Brueghel le Jeune dans 'L'Atelier' d'Alfred Stevens," *Mélanges Pierre Colman, Revue des Historiens de l'Art, des Archéologues, des Musicologues et des Orientalistes de l'Université de Liège*, 15, 1996, 194–96.
ROBINSON, WOLFF, 1986
William W. Robinson and Martha Wolff, "The Function of Drawings in the Netherlands in the Sixteenth Century," *The Age of Bruegel: Netherlandish Drawings in the Sixteenth Century*, see Washington/New York catalogue, 1986, 25–40.
ROMBOUTS, VAN LERIUS 1862–1876
Philippe-Félix Rombouts and Théodore-François Xavier Van Lerius (transcribed and annotated by), *Les Liggeren et Autres Archives Historiques de la Gilde Anversoise de Saint-Luc, sous la Devise: "wt ionsten versaemt,"* with an introduction by Horst Gerson, I, Amsterdam, N. Israel, 1961 (Antwerp/The Hague edition reprinted 1862–76).
ROMDAHL, 1905
Axel L. Romdahl, "Pieter Brueghel der Ältere und sein Kunstschaffen," *Jahrbuch der kunsthistorischen Sammlungen des allerhöchsten Kaiserhauses*, 25, 3, 1905, 85–169.
ROMDAHL, 1947
Axel L. Romdahl, *Pieter Bruegel den Äldre*, Stockholm, P.A. Norstedt & Söner, 1947 (in Swedish).
ROMDAHL, 1949
Axel L. Romdahl, "Le style figuré de Pierre Brueghel," *Miscellanea Leo van Puyvelde*, Brussels, Éditions de la Connaissance, 1949, 107–10.
ROOSES, 1880.
Max Rooses, *Geschiedenis der Antwerpsche Schilderschool*, I, Antwerp, Louis Legros, 1880.

SAMUEL, 1976
Edgar R. Samuel, "The Disposal of Diego Duarte's Stock of Paintings," *Jaarboek van het Koninklijk Museum voor Schone Kunsten Antwerpen*, 1976, 309–24.
SAUR, *Allgemeines Künstler-Lexikon* (see MÜLLER, 1996)
SCHEYER, 1965
Ernst Scheyer, "'The Wedding Dance' by Pieter Bruegel the Elder in the Detroit Institute of Arts: Its Relations and Derivations," *The Art Quarterly*, XXVIII, 3, 1965, 167–93.
SCHUBERT, 1970
Dietrich Schubert, *Die Gemälde des Braunschweiger Monogrammisten. Ein Beitrag zur Geschichte der Niederländischen Malerei des 16. Jahrhunderts*, Cologne, Dumont Schauberg, 1970.
SCHULT-KEHM, 1983
Elke M. Schult-Kehm, *Pieter Bruegels der Ältere "Kampf des Karnevals gegen die Fasten" als Quelle volkskundlicher Forschung*, Frankfurt am Main–Berne–New York, Verlag Peter Lang, "Artes Populares. Studia ethnographica et folkloristica," 1983.
SEDLMAYR, 1959[1]
Hans Sedlmayr, "Die 'Macchia' Bruegels," *Epochen und Werke. Gesammelte Schriften zur Kunstgeschichte*, 1, Vienna/Munich, Herold, 1959, 274–318.
SEDLMAYR, 1959[2]
Hans Sedlmayr, "Pieter Bruegel: der Sturz der Blinden. Paradigma einer Strukturanalyse," *Epochen und Werke. Gesammelte Schriften zur Kunstgeschichte*, I, Vienna/Munich, Herold, 1959, 319–56.
SHIPP, 1954
H. Shipp, "The Original 'Winter Landscape with a Bird Trap' by Pieter Bruegel," *Apollo*, LIX, 1954, 1.
SIP, 1960
Jaromir Sip, *Pierre Brueghel l'Aîné. La Fenaison*, translated by Claude Ancehot, Prague, Artia, "Les détails," 1960.
SMOLDEREN, 1973–74
Luc Smolderen, "Nicolas Jonghelinck," *Biographie Nationale de Belgique (supplément.)*, 10, Brussels, Académie royale des Sciences, des Lettres et des Beaux-Arts de Belgique, 1973–74, 390–91.
SMOLDEREN, 1995
Luc Smolderen, "Tableaux de Jérôme Bosch, de Pierre Bruegel l'Ancien et de Frans Floris Dispersés en Vente Publique a la Monnaie d'Anvers en 1572," *Revue Belge d'Archéologie et d'Histoire de l'Art*, LXIV, 1995, 33–41.
SNEYERS, 1969
René Sneyers, "La restauration des Bruegel des Musées royaux des Beaux–Arts de Belgique," *Brabant*, 4, 1969, 14–27.
SPICER, 1970
Joaneath Ann Spicer, "The 'Naer het leven' Drawings: by Pieter Bruegel or Roelandt Savery?," *Master Drawings*, VIII, 1, spring 1970, 3–30.
STECHOW, 1954
Wolfgang Stechow, *Pierre Brueghel le Vieux (vers 1525–1569)*, Paris, Flammarion, 1954 (1st edition in English: New York, Harry N. Abrams Inc., 1954).
STECHOW, 1990
Wolfgang Stechow, *Pieter Bruegel the Elder*, New York, Harry N. Abrams Inc., 1990 (1st edition 1954).

STEIN-SCHNEIDER, 1986
H. Stein-Schneider, "Pieter Bruegel, Peintre Hérétique, Illustrateur du Message Familiste," *Gazette des Beaux-Arts*, VI series, 128th year, CVII, February 1986, 71–74.
STERCK, 1969
Jef Sterck, "Bruegel en de volkstaal," *Vlaanderen*, 103, January–February 1969, 39–40.
STRIDBECK, 1956[1]
Carl Gustaf Stridbeck, "'Combat between Carnival and Lent' by Pieter Bruegel the Elder. An Allegorical Picture of the Sixteenth Century," *Journal of the Warburg and Courtauld Institutes*, XIX, 1–2, January–June 1956, 96–109.
STRIDBECK, 1956[2]
Carl Gustaf Stridbeck, *Bruegelstudien. Untersuchungen zu den ikonologischen Problemen bei Pieter Bruegel d. Ä. sowie dessen Beziehungen zum niederländischen Romanismus*, Stockholm, Almqvist & Wiksell, "Acta Universitatis Stockholmiensis, Stockholm Studies in History of Art," 1956.
STUBBE, 1964
Dr. Achilles Stubbe, *Bruegel en de Renaissance. Het probleem van het Maniërisme*, Hasselt, Heideland, "Vlaamse Pockets," 1964.
SUDECK, 1931
Elisabeth Sudeck, *Bettlerdarstellungen vom Ende des XV. Jahrhunderts bis zu Rembrandt*, Strasbourg, J. H. Ed. Heitz, "Studien zur Deutschen Kunstgeschichte," 1931.
SULLIVAN, 1977
Margaret A. Sullivan, "Madness and Folly: Peter Bruegel the Elder's Dulle Griet," *The Art Bulletin*, LIX, 1, March 1977, 55–66.
SULLIVAN, 1981
Margaret A. Sullivan, "Peter Bruegel the Elder's Two Monkeys: A New Interpretation," *The Art Bulletin*, LXIII, 1, March 1981, 114–26.
SULLIVAN, 1991
Margaret A. Sullivan, "Bruegel's Proverbs: Art and Audience in the Northern Renaissance," *The Art Bulletin*, LXXIII, 3, September 1991, 431–66.
SULLIVAN, 1992
Margaret A. Sullivan, "Bruegel's 'Misanthrope': Renaissance Art for a Humanist Audience," *Artibus et historiae*, 26, 1992, 143–62.
SULLIVAN, 1994
Margaret A. Sullivan, *Bruegel's Peasants. Art and Audience in the Northern Renaissance*, Cambridge, Cambridge University Press, 1994.
SWARZENSKY, 1951
H. Swarzensky, "The Battle between Carnival and Lent," *Bulletin of the Museum of Fine Arts*, Boston, XLIX, 2, 1951, 2–11.
SYBESMA, 1991
Jetske Sybesma, "The Reception of Bruegel's 'Beekeepers': A Matter of Choice," *The Art Bulletin*, LXXIII, 3, September 1991, 467–78.
TAINE, 1909
Hippolyte Taine, *Philosophie de l'art*, II, Hachette, 1909.
TERLINDEN, 1942
C. Terlinden, "Pierre Bruegel le Vieux et l'Histoire," *Revue Belge d'Archéologie et d'Histoire de l'Art*, XII, 4, 1942, 229–57.
TERVARENT, 1958
Chevalier Guy de Schoutheete de Tervarent, *Attributs et Symboles dans l'Art Profane, 1450–1600; Dictionnaire*

d'un Langage Perdu, I, Genève, Droz, "Travaux d'Humanisme et Renaissance," XXIX, 1958.
THEUWISSEN, 1979
Jan Theuwissen, "Volkskundliche Aspekte im Werke Pieter Bruegels," *Pieter Bruegel und seine Welt. Ein Colloquium veranstaltet vom Kunsthistorischen Institut der Freien Universität Berlin und dem Kupferstichkabinett der staatlichen Museen Stiftung preußischer Kulturbesitz, 13–14 November 1975,* Berlin, Gebr. Mann, 1979, 175–85.
THIEME-BECKER, *Allgemeines Lexikon* (see COHEN, 1911).
TOLNAY, 1925
Karl Tolnai [Charles de Tolnay], *Die Zeichnungen Pieter Bruegels,* Munich, R. Piper & Co., 1925.
TOLNAY, 1935
Charles de Tolnay, *Pierre Bruegel l'Ancien, 2* vols., Brussels, Nouvelle Société d'éditions, "Bibliothèque du XVIᵉ Siècle," 1935.
TOLNAY, 1938
Charles de Tolnay, "La seconde 'Tour de Babel' de Pierre Bruegel l'Ancien," *Annuaire des Musées royaux des Beaux-Arts de Belgique,* I, 1938, 113–21.
TOLNAY, 1948
Charles de Tolnay, "'Le Peintre et l'Amateur' de Pierre Bruegel le Vieux," *Les Arts Plastiques,* 11–12, 1948, 455–59.
TOLNAY, 1951
Charles de Tolnay, "Bruegel et l'Italie," *Les Arts Plastiques,* 2, 1951, 121–30.
TOLNAY, 1952
Charles de Tolnay, *The Drawings of Pieter Bruegel the Elder,* London, A. Zwemmer, 1952.
TOLNAY, 1965
Charles de Tolnay, *Hieronymus Bosch,* 2 vols., Baden-Baden, Holle, 1965 (in German) [1ˢᵗ edition Basel, Holbein, 1937].
TOLNAY, 1972
Charles de Tolnay, "Pierre Bruegel l'Ancien. À l'occasion du quatre-centième anniversaire de sa mort," *Evolution Générale et Développements Régionaux en Histoire de l'Art,* I, Transactions of the 22ⁿᵈ international history of art conference, Budapest, 1969, Budapest, Akamémiai Kiadó, 1972, 31–44.
TOLNAY, 1978
Charles de Tolnay, "A New Miniature by Pieter Bruegel the Elder," *The Burlington Magazine,* CXX, 903, June 1978, 393–97.
TOLNAY, 1980
Charles de Tolnay, "Further Miniatures by Pieter Bruegel the Elder," *The Burlington Magazine,* CXXII, 930, September 1980, 616–23.
TOLNAY, BIANCONI, 1981
Charles de Tolnay and Piero Bianconi, *Tout l'Oeuvre Peint de Bruegel l'Ancien,* new edition revised and updated by Robert Fohr, Paris, Flammarion, 1981 (1ˢᵗ edition: Milan, Rizzoli, 1967).
URBACH, 1978
Zsuzsa Urbach, "Notes on Bruegel's Archaism. His Relation to Early Netherlandish Painting and other Sources," *Acta Historiae Artium Academiae Scientiarum Hungaricae,* XXIV, 1–4, 1978, 237–56.
URBACH, 1990
Zsuzsa Urbach, "Die Bedeutung der Alten Niedenlander für Bruegels 'Kreuztragung' in Wien," *Sitzungsberichte*

der kunstgeschichtliche Gesellschaft zu Berlin, n.f. (new series), 38, October 1989–July 1990, 9–12.
VALENTINER, 1930
W. R. Valentiner, "A Rediscovered Painting by Pieter Bruegel the Elder," *Apollo,* XII, 72, December 1930, 395–99.
VAN BASTELAER, 1908
René van Bastelaer, *Les Estampes de Peter Bruegel l'Ancien,* Brussels, G. van Oest & Cⁱᵉ, 1908; new edition translated and revised by Susan Fargo Gilchrist, *The Prints of Peter Bruegel the Elder,* San Francisco, Alan Wofsy Fine Arts, 1992.
VAN BASTELAER, HULIN DE LOO, 1907
René van Bastelaer and Georges Hulin de Loo, *Peter Bruegel l'Ancien, son Oeuvre et son Temps. Étude Historique Suivie des Catalogues Raisonnés […],* 2 vols., Brussels, G. van Oest & Cⁱᵉ, 1907.
VANBESELAERE, 1944
Walther Vanbeselaere, *Peter Bruegel en het nederlandsche Maniërisme,* Tielt, Lannoo, 1944.
VANBESELAERE *et al.,* 1969
Walther Vanbeselaere *et al.,* "Pieter Bruegel de Oude," *Vlaanderen* (special issue), 103, January–February 1969.
VAN BEYLEN, 1961
J. van Beylen, "De Uitbeelding en de dokumentaire waarde van schepen bij enkele oude meesters," *Bulletin des Musées royaux des Beaux-Arts de Belgique,* 10th year, 3–4, September–December 1961, 123–50.
VAN DEN BRANDEN, 1883
F. Jos. Van den Branden, *Geschiedenis der Antwerpsche schilderschool,* Antwerp, J.-E. Buschmann, Rijnpoortvest, 1883.
VANDEN BRANDEN, 1981
Jean-Pierre Vanden Branden, "Les Jeux d'Enfants de Pierre Bruegel," *Mister VIP,* 1, September–October 1981, 31–40.
VANDENBROECK, 1984
Paul Vandenbroeck, "Verbeeck's peasant weddings: a study of iconography and social function," *Simiolus,* 14, 2, 1984, 79–124.
VAN CAMP, 1950
Gaston van Camp, "Nouvelles Acquisitions aux Musées royaux des Beaux-Arts de Belgique," *Les Arts Plastiques,* 5–6, November–December 1950, 389–91.
VAN CAMP, 1954
Gaston van Camp, "Pierre Bruegel a-t-il peint une série des sept pechés capitaux?," *Revue Belge d'Archéologie et d'Histoire de l'Art,* XXIII, 3–4, 1954, 217–23.
VAN GELDER, 1960
J. G. van Gelder, "Pieter Bruegel: 'Na(e)rt het leven' of naar 'het leven'", *Bulletin des Musées royaux des Beaux-Arts de Belgique,* IX, 1–2, March–June 1960, 29–36.
VAN GILS, 1940–41
J. B. F. van Gils, *Een andere kijk op Pieter Bruegel den Ouden,* The Hague, "Humanitas," 1940–41, 2 vols.
VAN HOUTTE, 1979
J. A. van Houtte, "Die niederländische Umwelt Pieter Bruegels," *Pieter Bruegel und seine Welt. Ein Colloquium verantaltet vom Kunsthistorischen Institut der Freien Universität Berlin und dem Kupferstichkabinett der staatlichen Museen Stiftung preußischer Kulturbesitz, 13–14 November 1975,* Berlin, Gebr. Mann, 1979, 29–35.

VAN LEEUWEN, 1970
Frans M. van Leeuwen, "Iets over het handschrift van de 'naar het leven' tekenaar," *Oud Holland,* 85, 1, 1970, 25–32.
VAN LEEUWEN, 1971
Frans M. van Leeuwen, "Figuurstudies van 'P. Bruegel'," *Simiolus,* 5, 3/4, 1971, 139–49.
VAN LENNEP, 1965
Jacques van Lennep, "L'Alchimie et Pierre Bruegel l'Ancien," *Bulletin des Musées royaux Beaux-Arts de Belgique,* XIV, 1965, 105–26.
VAN LENNEP, 1966
Jacques van Lennep, *Art et Alchimie. Étude de l'Iconographie Hermétique et de ses Influences,* Brussels, Éditions Meddens, "Art et savoir," 1966.
VAN LENNEP, 1984
Jacques van Lennep, *Alchimie. Contribution à l'Histoire de l'Art Alchimique,* Brussels, Crédit communal, 1984.
VAN LINTHOUDT, 1990
Joseph van Linthoudt. "Bruegel et le Payottenland," *Brabant Tourisme,* June 1990, 21–44.
VAN MANDER, 1604¹
Karel van Mander, *Het Schilder-boeck waerin voor eerst de leerlustighe jueght den grondt der edel vry schilderconst in verscheyden deelen wort voorghedraghen. Daer nae in dry deelen t'leven der vermaerde doorluchtighe schilders des ouden, en nieuwen tyds; […] Alcmaer, Jacob de Meester voor Passchier van Westbusch tot Haerlem, 1604,* Haarlem, 1604.
VAN MANDER, 1604²
Karel van Mander, *Le Livre des Peintres. Vie des Peintres Flamands, Hollandais et Allemands (1604),* translation, notes, and commentary by Henri Hymans, I, Paris, J. Rouam, 1884.
VAN MANDER, 1604³
Karel van Mander, *The Lives of the Illustrious Netherlandish and German Painters, from the First Edition of the Schilder-boeck (1603–1604),* facsimile edition with translation and annotation by Hessel Miedema, III: *Lives,* Doornspijk, Davaco, 1996.
VAN MANDER, 1604⁴
Karel van Mander, *Le Livre de Peinture,* introduction and annotation by Robert Genaille, Paris, Hermann, "Miroirs de l'art," 1965.
VAN MANDER, 1604⁵
Karel van Mander, *Uvtbeeldinge der figueren … Alles seer nut den vernuftighen Schilders/en oock Dichters/ hun Personnagien in vertooninghen/oft anders/toe te maken. By een ghebracht en gheraemt/door C. van Mander, Schilder,* Alkmaar 1604.
VAN MANDER, 1643
Karel van Mander, *Uitbeelding der figuren vertoonde hoe de heydenen hun goden hebben afgebeeldt en onderscheyden; hoe d'Egyptenaren hun verburgen meyningen met dieren en andre dingen, te kennen geven. Alles voor de rijm-schrijvers en schilders zeer nut. Eertijdts door C. van Mander geraamt en geraapt; mare nu door J. Zoet in goet Duytsch gebrogt,* Amstelderam, Jan Barentsz. Smient, 1643.
VAN MIEGROET, 1986
Hans J. van Miegroet, "The twelve months reconsidered: how a drawing by Pieter Stevens clarifies a Bruegel enigma," *Simiolus,* 16, 1, 1986, 29–35.
VAN MIEGROET, 1992
Hans J. van Miegroet, "Pierre Bruegel l'Ancien, la

'Danse des paysans'," *La Peinture Flamande dans les Musées d'Amérique du Nord*, Antwerp, Fonds Mercator, "Flandria extra muros," 1992, 138–40.

VAN PUYVELDE, 1945
Leo van Puyvelde, *Pieter Bruegel. The Dulle Griet in the Mayer van den Bergh Museum Antwerp*, London, Percy Lund Humphries & Co., "The Gallery Books," 10, no date (1945).

VAN PUYVELDE, 1962
Leo van Puyvelde, *La Peinture Flamande au Siècle de Bosch et Breughel*, Paris/Brussels, Elsevier, 1962.

VAN SCHOUTE *et al.*, 1995
Roger van Schoute, Hélène Verougstraete, and M. C. Garrido, "La 'Dulle Griet' et le 'Triomphe de la Mort' de Pierre Bruegel. Observations technologiques," *Le Dessin Sous-Jacent dans la Peinture*, conference X, Louvain-la-Neuve, Université catholique de Louvain, Institut superieur d'archéologie et d'histoire de l'art, 5–7 September 1993, Louvain-la-Neuve, Collège Érasme, 1995, 7–12.

VASARI, 1981–89
Giorgio Vasari, *Les Vies des Meilleurs Peintres, Sculpteurs et Architectes*, translation and edition with commentary supervised by André Chastel, Paris, Berger-Levrault, 1981–89, 12 vols. (republication of Giorgio Vasari, *Le Vite dei Più Eccellenti Pittori, Scultori e Archiettori*, 2nd edition, Florence, J. Giunti, 1568).

VELDMAN, 1977
Ilja M. Veldman, *Maarten van Heemskerck and Dutch Humanism in the Sixteenth Century*, Maarsen, Gary Schwartz, 1977.

VERHAEREN, 1913
Émile Verhaeren, "La Vie Flamande," *Journal de l'Université des Annales*, I, 1, 15, December 1913, 50–60.

VERMEYLEN, 1928
August Vermeylen, "Bruegel et l'Art Italien," *Cahiers de Belgique*, 1, February 1928, 1–8.

VERMEYLEN, 1953[1]
August Vermeylen, "Pieter Brueghel de Oude als schilder van landschappen," *Verzameld Werk*, III: *De vlaamse letteren van Gezelle tot heden, Verspreid Proza*, Brussels, A. Manteau, 1953, 427–44.

VERMEYLEN, 1953[2]
August Vermeylen, "Van Bosch tot Bruegel en zijn kring," *Verzameld Werk*, III: *De vlaamse letteren van Gezelle tot heden, Verspreid Proza*, Brussels, A. Manteau, 1953, 445–79.

VEROUGSTRAETE, VAN SCHOUTE, 1993
Hélène Verougstraete and Roger van Schoute, "'The Triumph of Death' by Pieter Bruegel the Elder and Pieter Brueghel the Younger. Intellegetur plus semper quam pingitur," *Le Dessin Sous-Jacent dans la Peinture*, conference IX, Louvain-la-Neuve, Université catholique de Louvain, Institut supérieur d'archéologie et d'histoire de l'art, 12–14 September 1991, Louvain-la-Neuve, Collège Érasme, 1993, 213–40.

VISSER, no date
M. J. C. Visser, *Pieter Bruegel. Een nieuwe interpretatie*, Zutphen, De Walburg Pers, no date.

VLIEGHE, 1977[1]
Hans Vlieghe, "Overname van motieven uit het werk van Mantegna in schilderijen van Pieter Bruegel de Oude," *Bulletin des Musées royaux des Beaux-Arts de Belgique*, 3/4, July/December 1962, 277–84.

VLIEGHE, 1977[2]
Hans Vlieghe, "Une grande collection anversoise du dix-septième siècle: le cabinet d'Arnold Lunden, beau-frère de Rubens," *Jahrbuch der Berliner Museen*, XIX, 1977, 172–204.

VOET, 1976
Léon Voet, *L'Age d'Or d'Anvers. Essor et Gloire de la Métropole au Seizième siècle*, Antwerp, Mercator, 1976.

VON LÖHNEYSEN, 1956
Hans-Wolfgang von Löhneysen, *Die Ältere Niederländische Malerei. Künstler und Kritiker*, Eisenach/Kassel, Erich Röth, 1956, 141–52.

VON SANDRART, 1675
Joachim Von Sandrart, *Der Teutschen Academie. Zweyter Theil. Von der alt-und neu-berühmten Egyptischen, Griechischen, Römischen, Italienischen, hoch- und NiederTeutschen Bau-, Bild-und Mahlerey Künstlere Lob und Leben*, I, Nuremberg, Johann-Philipp Miltenberger, 1675, 259 (chapter IX: Anton Morus und andere vier künstlere. LXXVIII : Peter Breugel, Mahler aus Breugel).

WAUTERS, 1883
A.-J. Wauters, *La Peinture Flamande*, Paris, Librairie-Imprimeries réunies, 1883.

WAUTERS, 1887–88
A.-J. Wauters, "La famille Breughel," *Annales de la Société d'Archéologie de Bruxelles*, 1, 1887–88, 7–79.

WAUTERS, 1914
A.-J. Wauters, "Pierre Bruegel et le Cardinal Granvelle," *Bulletins de la Classe des Lettres et des Sciences Morales et Politiques et de la Classe des Beaux-Arts, Academic Royale de Belgique*, 1914, 87–90.

WEGENER, 1995
Ulrike B. Wegener, *Die Faszinatiom: des Maßlosen. Der Turmbau zu Babel von Pieter Bruegel bis Athanasius Kircher* (Studien zur Kunstgeschichte, 93), Hildesheim/Zurich/New York, Georg Olms Verlag, 1995.

WEISSTEIN, 1982
Ulrich Weisstein, "The Partridge Without a Pear Tree: Pieter Bruegel the Elder as an illustrator of Ovid," E. S. Shaffer (editor), *Comparative Criticism. A Yearbook*, 4, Cambridge, Cambridge University Press, 1982, 55–83.

WEYNS, 1969[1]
Jozef Weyns, "Bruegel en het stoffelijke kultuurgoed van zijn tijd," *Vlaanderen*, 103, January–February 1969, 24–29.

WEYNS, 1969[2]
Jozef Weyns, "Bij Bruegel in de leer voor honderd-en-een dagelijkse dingen," (Boknijkse berichten, IX), *Ons Heem. Tijdschrift van net verbond voor Heemkunde*, XXIII, 3, 1969, 97–131.

WHITE, 1979
Christopher White, "'The Rabbit Hunters' by Pieter Bruegel the Elder" *Pieter Bruegel und seine Welt. Ein Colloquium veranstaltet vom Kunsthistorischen Institut der Freien Universität Berlin und dem Kupferstichkabinett der staatlichen Museen Stiftung preußischer Kulturbesitz, 13–14 November 1975*, Berlin, Gebr. Mann, 1979, 187–91.

WIED, 1980
Alexander Wied, *Bruegel*, London, Studio Vista, 1980 (1st edition in Italian: Milan, Mondadori, 1979).

WIED, 1996
Alexander Wied, "Pieter Bruegel [the Elder]," *The Dictionary of Art*, 4, London, Macmillan/New York, Grove, 1996, 894–910.

WILLIAMS, 1962
William Carlos Williams, *Pictures from Brueghel and Other Poems*, Norfolk, J. Laughlin, 1962.

WILLIAMS, JACQUOT, 1960
Sheila Williams and Jean Jacquot, "Ommegangs anversois du temps de Bruegel et de van Heemskerck," *Les Fêtes de la Renaissance*, II, *Fêtes et Cérémonies au Temps de Charles Quint*, IIe Congrès de l'Association internationale des historiens de la Renaissance, Brussels/Antwerp/Ghent/Liège, 2–7 September 1957, Paris, Éditions du CNRS, 1960, 359–88.

WINKLER, 1924
Friedrich Winkler, *Die Altniederländische Malerei. Die Malerei in Belgien und Holland von 1400–1600*, Berlin, Im Propyläen Verlag, 1924, 330–57.

WINNER, 1979
Matthias Winner, "Zu Bruegels 'Alchimist'," *Pieter Bruegel und seine Welt. Ein Colloquium veranstaltet vom Kunsthistorischen Institut der Freien Universität Berlin und dem Kupferstichkabinett der staatlichen Museen Stiftung preußischer Kulturbesitz, 13–14 November 1975*, Berlin, Gebr. Mann, 1979, 193–202.

WINNER, 1985
Matthias Winner, "Vedute in Flemish landscape drawings of the 16th century" *Netherlandish Mannerism. Papers given at a symposium in Nationalmuseum Stockholm, 21–22 September 1984*, edited by Görel Cavalli-Björkman, Stockholm, Nationalmuseum, 1985, 85–96.

WOLFTHAL, 1989
Diane Wolfthal, *The Beginnings of Netherlandish Canvas Painting: 1400–1530*, Cambridge/New York/Melbourne/Sydney, Cambridge University Press, 1989.

WÜRTENBERGER, 1957
Franzsepp Würtenberger, *Pieter Bruegel d. Ä. und die deutsche Kunst*, Wiesbaden, Franz Steiner, 1957.

WYSS, 1988
Beat Wyss, "Der Dolch am linken Bildrand. Zur Interpretation von Pieter Bruegels Landschaft mit dem Sturz des Ikarus," *Zeitschrift Für Kunstgeschichte*, LI, 2, 1988, 222–42.

WYSS, 1990
Beat Wyss, *Pieter Bruegel. Landschaft mit Ikarussturz. Ein Vexierbild des humanistischen Pessismismus*, Frankfurt am Main, Fischer Taschenbuch, 1990.

ZUPNICK, 1964
Irving L. Zupnick, "Bruegel and the Revolt of the Netherlands," *Art Journal*, XXIII, 4, 1964, 283–89.

ZUPNICK, 1966
Irving L. Zupnick, "The Meaning of Bruegel's 'Nobody' and 'Everyman'," *Gazette des Beaux-Arts*, LXVIII, 6th series, May–June 1966, 157–70.

ZWOLLO, 1979
An Zwollo, "Jacob Savery, Nachfolger von Peter Bruegel und Hans Bol," *Pieter Bruegel und seine Welt. Ein Colloquium veranstaltet vom Kunsthistorischen Institut der Freien Universität Berlin und dem Kupferstichkabinett der staatlichen Museen Stiftung preußischer Kulturbesitz, 13–14 November 1975*, Berlin, Gebr. Mann, 1979, 203–13.

EXHIBITION CATALOGUES

AMSTERDAM, 1934
De Helsche en de Fluweelen Brueghel en hun invloed op de kunst in de Nederlananden, Amsterdam, N. V. Kunsthandel P. de Boer, 10 February–26 March 1934.

AMSTERDAM, 1986
Kunst voor de beeldenstorm. Noordnederlandsche kunst 1525–1580, Amsterdam, Rijksmuseum, 13 September–23 November 1986, 2 vols.

BERLIN, 1975
Pieter Bruegel d. Ä. als Zeichner. Herkunft und Nachfolge, Berlin, Staathiche Museen Preußischer Kulturbesitz, Kupferstichkabinett, 19 September–16 November 1975 (introduction by Matti Winner).

BRUGES, 1902
Exposition de tableaux flamands des XIVe, XVe et XVIe siècles. Catalogue critique, Ghent, A. Siffer, 1902.

BRUSSELS, 1963
Le Siècle de Bruegel. La peinture en Belgique au XVIe siècle, Brussels, Musées royaux des Beaux-Arts de Belgique, 27 September–24 November 1963.

BRUSSELS, 1969[1]
Pierre Bruegel et son temps, Brussels, Banque de Bruxelles, 15–21 September 1969.

BRUSSELS, 1969[2]
See ROBERTS–JONES *et al.*, 1969

BRUSSELS, 1970
Jérôme Cock: éditeur d'estampes et graveur, 1507(?)–1570, Brussels, Bibliothèque royale Albert I, 21 November–24 December 1970 (catalogued by Lydia De Pauw-De Veen).

BRUSSELS, 1980
Bruegel. Une dynastie de peintres, Europalia 80 Belgique, Brussels, palais des Beaux-Arts, 18 September–18 November 1980.

BRUSSELS, 1985
Splendeurs d'Espagne et les villes belges 1500–1700, Europalia 85 España, 2 vols., Brussels, palais des Beaux-Arts, 25 September–22 December 1985.

BRUSSELS/ROME, 1995
Fiamminghi a Roma 1508/1608. Artistes des Pays-Bas et de la principauté de Liège à Rome à la Renaissance, Brussels, palais des Beaux-Arts, 24 February–21 May 1995/Rome, Palazzo delle Esposizioni, 7 June–4 September 1995.

COLOGNE/ANTWERP/VIENNA, 1992–93
Von Bruegel bis Rubens. Das goldene Jahrhundert der flämischen Malerei, Cologne, Wallraf-Richartz-Museum, 4 September–22 November 1992/Antwerp, Koninklijk Museum voor Schone Kunsten, 12 December 1992–8 March 1993/Vienna, Kunsthistorisches Museum, 2 April–20 June 1993.

FLORENCE/PARIS, 1980–81
L'Époque de Lucas de Leyde et Pierre Bruegel, Dessins des anciens Pays-Bas. Collection Frits Lugt, Florence, Istituto Universitario Olandese di Storia dell'Arte, 25 October–30 November 1980/Paris, Institut néerlandais, 26 February–12 April 1981, Fondation Custodia.

GENEVA, 1991
L'Oeuvre gravé de Breughel, Geneva, Salon international du livre et de la presse (Palexpo), 27 April–26 May 1991 (Lausanne/Paris, Bibliothèque des arts, 1991).

GHENT, 1976
Eenheid en Scheiding in de Nederlanden 1555–1585, Ghent, Centrum voor Kunst en Cultuur, 9 September–8 November 1976 (directed by J. Decavele).

KAMAKURA, 1972
Exposition des estampes de Peter Bruegel l'Ancien, Kamakura, Museum of Modern Art, 18 March–16 April 1972.

PARIS, 1965
Le XVIe siècle européen. Peintures et dessins dans les collections publiques françaises, Paris, Petit Palais, October 1965–January 1966.

PARIS, 1967
Le Cabinet d'un grand amateur, P.-J. Mariette (1694–1774). Dessins du XVe au XVIIIe siècle, Paris, Louvre, galerie Mollien, 1967.

PARIS, 1994
Paysages, paysans. L'art et la terre en Europe du Moyen Age au XXe siècle, Paris, 1994 (directed by Emmanuel Le Roy Ladurie).

PARIS/HAMBURG, 1985–86
Renaissance et maniérisme dans les écoles du Nord. Dessins des collections de l'école des Beaux-Arts, Paris. École nationale supérieure des beaux–arts, 16 October–16 December 1985/Hamburg, Hamburger Kunsthalle, 16 May–29 June 1986 (Paris, Presses de l'Ensb-a, 1985).

ROTTERDAM, 1988
In de Vier Winden. De prentuitgeveridj van Hieronymus Cock 1507/10–1570 te Antwerpen, Rotterdam, Museum Boymans–van Beuningen, 1988.

ST. LOUIS/CAMBRIDGE, 1995
The Printed World of Pieter Bruegel the Elder, St. Louis (Mo.), The St. Louis Art Museum, 4 April–23 June 1995/Cambridge (Mass.), Arthur M. Sackler Museum, Harvard University, 2 September–12 November 1995 (edited by Barbara Butts and Joseph Leo Korner, with a commentary by Betha Whitlow).

TOKYO, 1989
The Prints of Pieter Bruegel the Elder, Tokyo, Bridgestone Museum of Art, 7 January–26 February 1989 (edited by David Freedberg).

TOKYO, 1995
The World of Bruegel. The Coppée Collection and Eleven International Museums, Tokyo, Tokyo Museum of Art, 28 March–25 June 1995.

TOKYO/KYOTO, 1990
Bruegel and Netherlandish Landscape Painting from the National Gallery Prague, Tokyo, The National Museum of Western Art, 20 March–27 May 1990/Kyoto, The National Museum of Modern Art, 10 July–16 September 1990 (Tokyo, The National Museum of Western Art, 1990).

VIENNA, 1967–68
Zwischen Renaissance und Barok. Das Zeitalter von Bruegel und Bellange. Werke aus dem Besitz der Albertina, Vienna, Albertina, 9 November 1967–18 February 1968 (*Die Kunst der Graphik*, IV, Vienna, Albertina, 1967).

WASHINGTON/NEW YORK, 1986
The Age of Bruegel: Netherlandish Drawings in the Sixteenth Century, Washington, National Gallery of Art, 7 November 1986–18 January 1987/New York, The Pierpont Morgan Library, 30 January 1987–5 April 1987 (Cambridge University Press, 1986).

INDEX

Figures in italic refer to pages with illustrations.

TITLES OF WORKS BY PIETER BRUEGEL